FAMILY LAW
AND THE HUMAN RIGHTS ACT 1998

FAMILY LAW
AND THE HUMAN RIGHTS ACT 1998

Heather Swindells QC, MA(OXON)
Andrew Neaves
Martine Kushner
St Philip's Chambers, Birmingham

Rupert Skilbeck, Barrister
36 Bedford Row, London

Family Law

1999

Published by Family Law
a publishing imprint of
Jordan Publishing Limited
21 St Thomas Street
Bristol BS1 6JS

British Library Cataloguing-in-Publication Data
A catalogue record for this book is available from the British Library.

ISBN 0 85308 573 0

Typeset by Mendip Communications Ltd, Frome, Somerset
Printed by MPG Books Ltd, Bodmin, Cornwall

FOREWORD

By The Rt Hon Lord Justice Ward

How well I remember *In re K D (A Minor) (Ward: Termination of Access)* [1988] 1 AC 806 when I invited the House of Lords to consider the importance of my client's fundamental human right that there should be no interference by the public authority with the exercise of her right to respect for her family life. This was, I believe, the first time that the Convention for the Protection of Human Rights and Fundamental Freedoms was raised in their Lordships' house in a family matter. It will now not be the last. The Human Rights Act 1998 is bound to have a tremendous impact on the development of child and family law, as it will in other areas of our domestic law.

As everyone conversant with the Convention case-law will quickly appreciate, family life has already presented the Strasbourg Court with several controversial and difficult problems and, following implementation of the Act in October 2000, the rights contained in the Convention will be directly enforceable at all levels of the UK courts.

This timely and admirably clear book provides family law practitioners with everything they require to familiarise themselves both with these important new rights, and the substantial body of cases which interpret them. The implications will so stretch the ingenuity of practitioners and strain the imagination of the judges that this book, written with care but with common sense, will become the *vade mecum* not only for the family lawyer seeking to master the practical significance of this momentous development in our law but also for the judges and justices who will shape it.

SIR ALAN WARD
November 1999

PREFACE

Upon the implementation of the Human Rights Act 1998 in October 2000, the Convention for the Protection of Human Rights and Fundamental Freedoms (the Convention) will emerge from the wings to take centre stage in our domestic law. Its impact upon family law will be substantial and far-reaching. This book is intended to provide a practical 'one-stop' guide for family law practitioners.

Part A is a short survey of the Human Rights Act 1998 and the Convention. It aims to provide:

(i)   an introduction to the general principles and approach adopted by the European Court to the human rights guaranteed by the Convention and the principal Articles affecting family law; and

(ii) a summary of how the Human Rights Act 1998 will translate those rights into our domestic family law.

Part B looks in more detail at the Convention case-law and explores the likely impact of the Convention and its jurisprudence on the key areas of our domestic family law.

Part C sets out summaries of:

(i)   the seminal Convention cases which have established the general principles applied by the European Court; and

(ii) the leading Convention cases on family law.

Part D includes the Human Rights Act 1998, the Convention and the Rules of the European Court for easy reference.

We are very grateful to the Right Honourable Lord Justice Ward for his Foreword. We also thank Annabel Walker QC and David Hershman who undertook the task of checking the text. The book is a joint enterprise and we dedicate it to our respective families for their patience and support.

HEATHER SWINDELLS QC
ANDREW NEAVES
MARTINE KUSHNER
St Philip's Chambers, Birmingham

RUPERT SKILBECK
36 Bedford Row, London

November 1999

CONTENTS

PART D   APPENDICES

TABLE OF CASES

References are to paragraph numbers. References in *italics* are to page numbers. **Bold italics** show where case summaries are set out.

TABLE OF STATUTES

References are to paragraph numbers. References in *italics* are to page numbers. ***Bold italics*** show where material is set out.

TABLE OF STATUTORY INSTRUMENTS

References are to paragraph numbers. References in *italics* are to page numbers.

TABLE OF MATERIAL FROM OTHER JURISDICTIONS

References are to paragraph numbers. References in *italics* are to page numbers.

TABLE OF INTERNATIONAL LEGISLATION

References are to paragraph numbers. References in *italics* are to page numbers. ***Bold italics*** show where material is set out.

Table of International Legislation

TABLE OF ABBREVIATIONS

the Convention	Convention for the Protection of Human Rights and Fundamental Freedoms
the Court or the European Court	European Court of Human Rights
HFE Act 1990	Human Fertilisation and Embryology Act 1990
HRA 1998	Human Rights Act 1998
the Rules	Rules of the European Court of Human Rights

STOP PRESS

On Thursday 29 October 1999, the Lords of Appeal in Ordinary handed down their judgments in the House of Lords on three important cases affecting human rights issues, thus providing a graphic demonstration of how the Convention for the Protection of Human Rights and Fundamental Freedoms will play a leading role in our legal system as from 2 October 2000.

We examine each of the three cases below and, as a reflection of the importance of these cases during the interim period between the enactment of the HRA 1998 and the bringing into force of its main provisions, in greater detail than one would normally expect in a 'Stop Press'.

R v DPP, ex parte Kebilene and Others

In *R v DPP, ex parte Kebilene and Others*[1] the majority of the House of Lords overturned the Divisional Court's ruling[2] that the DPP's decision to proceed with a prosecution under s 16A of the Prevention of Terrorism (Temporary Provisions) Act 1989 was amenable to judicial review and unlawful.

Incompatibility

In the Divisional Court the Lord Chief Justice took the view that s 16A of the 1989 Act undermined the presumption of innocence[3] and Laws LJ went further by observing that the DPP was in law obliged to consider whether s 16A was compatible with Art 6(2) of the Convention.

Lord Steyn, in the leading judgment in the House of Lords, disageed with Laws LJ that the DPP is at this stage legally bound to form a view on the issue of compatibility and ruled that, absent dishonesty or *mala fides* or an exceptional circumstance, the decision of the DPP to consent to the prosecution is not amenable to judicial review. He emphasised that:

> 'While the passing of the Human Rights Act 1998 marked a great advance for our criminal justice system it is in my view vitally important that, so far as the courts are concerned, its application in our law should take place in an orderly manner which recognises the desirability of all challenges taking place in the criminal trial or on appeal. The effect of the Divisional Court was to open the door too widely to delay in the conduct of criminal proceedings. Such satellite litigation should rarely be permitted in our criminal justice system.'

Although the case was dealing specifically with the criminal justice system, it is likely to have a more general application and will be a lesson which the higher courts in the Family Division will not be slow to heed, especially as delay is a central issue in all children cases.

---

1   http://www.parliament.the-stationery-office.co.uk/pa/ld199899/ldjugmt/jd99. . ./kabel-2ht 30/10/99.
2   [1999] 3 WLR 175; the Court of Appeal decision is referred to in Part A at **2.27** and **2.28**.
3   Ibid at 190F, per Lord Bingham of Cornhill.

Parliamentary sovereignty

Lord Steyn, however, rejected the argument of the DPP that the judgment of the Divisional Court had been in conflict with the principle of parliamentary sovereignty in the context of unambiguous primary legislation viz s 16 of the 1989 Act. In considering the interpretative obligation under s 3(1) of HRA 1998 in the context of the whole HRA 1998, he highlighted that:

> 'It is crystal clear that the carefully and subtly drafted Human Rights Act 1998 preserves the principle of Parliamentary sovereignty. In a case of incompatibility, which cannot be avoided by interpretation under section 3(1), the courts may not disapply the legislation. The court may merely issue a declaration of incompatibility which then gives rise to a power to take remedial action: see section 10.'

Margin of appreciation

Lord Hope of Craighead went on to tackle the controversy relating to whether and, if so, how 'the margin of appreciation' should be transported into our domestic jurisprudence[1]. He said:

> 'This brings me to another matter ... which, I believe, needs now to be judicially recognised. The doctrine of the "margin of appreciation" is a familiar part of the jurisprudence of the European Court of Human Rights ... This doctrine is an integral part of the supervisory jurisdiction which is exercised over state conduct by the international court. By conceding a margin of appreciation to each national system, the court has recognised that the Convention, as a living system, does not need to be applied uniformly by all states but may vary in its application according to local needs and conditions. This technique is not available to the national courts when they are considering Convention issues arising within their own countries. But in the hands of the national courts also the Convention should be seen as an expression of fundamental principles rather than a set of mere rules. The questions which the courts will have to decide in the application of these principles will involve questions of balance between competing interests and issues of proportionality.'

Although he, therefore, came down in favour of the view that the doctrine of the margin of appreciation does not apply when a national court is considering the Human Rights Act 1998, he went on to say:

> 'In this area difficult choices may have to be made by the executive or the legislature between the rights of the individual and the needs of society. In some circumstances it will be appropriate for the courts to recognise that there is an area of judgment within which the judiciary will defer, on democratic grounds, to the considered opinion of the elected body or person whose act or decision is said to be incompatible with the Convention. This point is well made at p. 74, para 3.21 of *Human Rights Law and Practice*[2] ... where the area in which these choices may arise is conveniently and appropriately described as the "discretionary even of judgment". It will be easier for such an area of judgment to be recognised where the Convention itself requires a balance to be struck[3], much less so where the right is stated in terms which are unqualified. It will be easier for it to be recognised where the issues involve questions of social or economic policy, much less so where the rights are of high constitutional importance or are of a kind where the court are especially well placed to assess the need for protection ...'

---

1   The differing views are set out in Part A at **1.17**.
2   (Butterworths, 1999) of which Lord Lester of Herne Hill QC and Mr David Pannick QC are the General Editors.
3   For example, Articles 8–11.

Thus he was recognising that there may well be a place in our national law for an analogous 'domestic' doctrine of margin of appreciation.

Reynolds v Times Newspapers Limited and Others[1]

In libel proceedings where the issues included qualified privilege at common law the majority of the House of Lords (3 to 2) upheld the Court of Appeal's decision that the publication concerned was a publication which should not in the public interest be protected by privilege in the absence of proof of malice.

Taking as his starting point 'freedom of expression', Lord Nicholls of Birkenhead highlighted that:

> 'freedom of expression will shortly be buttressed by statutory requirements. Under section 12 of the Human Rights Act . . . the Court is required, in relevant cases, to have particular regard to the importance of the freedom of expression. The common law is to be developed and applied in a manner consistent with Art 10 of the European Convention . . .'

His subsequent review of the jurisprudence of the Strasbourg Court showed no trace of endorsement of a generic privilege in the political context.

Lord Cooke of Thorndon and Lord Steyn agreed with Lord Nicholls that the court's approach in considering the development of the common law should be to act now upon the reality that the HRA 1998 will soon be in force.

The interim period

It appears, therefore, that the House of Lords has expressed differing approaches as to how to apply the Convention in the interim period before the HRA 1998 comes into force. When the Court is interpreting primary legislation, the *Kebilene* case supports the argument that it is premature at this stage to argue points of incompatibility with Convention rights. On the other hand, where the Court is considering the application of our common law, the *Reynolds* case supports the argument that it is legitimate at this stage to argue that regard should be had to the Act and that the common law should be applied and developed in a manner consistent with Convention rights.

Fitzpatrick v Sterling Housing Association Ltd[2]

The House of Lords allowed the appeal against the majority decision of the Court of Appeal[3] and held that as a matter of law a same-sex partner of a deceased tenant can establish the necessary familial link for the purposes of succession under the provisions of the Rent Act 1977 (as amended).

Although they rejected Ward LJ's dissenting view in the Court of Appeal insofar as he concluded that Mr Fitzpatrick succeeded as a 'spouse' under the succession provisions, they upheld his judgment that Mr Fitzpatrick was entitled to succeed to the tenancy as 'a member of the family'.

---

1   http://www.parliament.the-stationery-office.co.uk/pa/ld199899/ldjudgmt/jd991. . ./rey01.ht 30/10/99.
2   http://www.parliament.the-stationery-office.co.uk/pa/ld199899/ldjudgmt/jd991 . . . /fitz02.ht 30/10/99.
3   Referred to at Part B at **12.38**.

Lord Clyde went on to consider whether his decision was in conflict with the jurisprudence of the European Court of Human rights. Whilst he noted that the European Court had confined the application of Art 12 to traditional marriage between persons of opposite biological sex and the Commission had held that a stable homosexual relationship did not fall within the scope of the right to respect for family life, he took into account the developing nature of the jurisprudence, the recognition that family life may encompass other de facto relationships such as in *X, Y and Z v UK*[1] and the recent admissibility decision in *Salgueiro da Silva Mouta v Portugal*[2]. He concluded:

> 'That the relationship in the present case may not, as the law currently stands, constitute "family life" for the purposes of Art 8 of the Convention does not require a restrictive meaning to be given to the reference to the tenant's family in the legislation before us.'

---

1   24 EHRR 143.
2   Application No 33290/96 (1 December 1998).

PART A

OVERVIEW OF THE HUMAN RIGHTS ACT 1998 AND THE CONVENTION

Chapter 1

THE EUROPEAN CONVENTION

INTRODUCTION

1.1 In 1950, the Convention for the Protection of Human Rights and Fundamental Freedoms (commonly known as the European Convention on Human Rights) ('the Convention') established the first international complaints procedure which enabled an individual to have access to an international court against the State.

1.2 The Human Rights Act 1998 ('HRA 1998') incorporates the Convention into our domestic law by providing a scheme whereby our domestic law is enacted, interpreted and amended so that it is compatible with the Convention. Its principal effect is that individuals can enforce the Convention rights against the State in our domestic courts.

1.3 Until recently, there were two international bodies which were responsible for applying the Convention: the European Commission of Human Rights ('the Commission'), and the European Court of Human Rights ('the Court'). As from 1 November 1998 the Commission and the Court have been replaced by a new single full-time European Court of Human Rights.

1.4 In the field of family law, the Convention has already had an influence on our domestic law. Family legislation such as the Children Act 1989 and the Family Law Act 1996 has been drafted in order to comply with the Convention. The Convention has been used:

(i) to resolve legislative ambiguity, recognising a presumption that Parliament does not intentionally legislate in breach of the international obligations under the Convention[1];
(ii) as an aid to developing our common law[2]; and
(iii) as a guide to public policy.

IMPLEMENTATION

1.5 Upon the implementation of the HRA 1998, the Convention will move into the very core of our legal system. Under the HRA 1998, so far as it is possible to do so, our domestic legislation must be read and given effect so as to be compatible with the Convention rights. The courts must act in a way which is compatible with the Convention rights and must take into account Convention case-law. Potentially, its impact upon family law is, therefore, highly significant.

1.6 As an essential backdrop to the later, more detailed, discussion on the likely impact of the Convention on family law, Part A of this book aims to provide a

---

1   *Re M and H (Minors)* [1990] 1 AC 721, per Lord Brandon.
2   *DPP v Jones* [1999] 2 WLR 625 at 634: held that where the common law was uncertain and developing, regard should be had to the Convention in resolving uncertainty and in determining how it should develop.

practical short guide for the family law practitioner which sets out in general summary form:

- the Articles which primarily concern family law (in brief);
- the Convention principles and approach;
- the framework of the HRA 1998 relevant to family law;
- the principal Articles affecting family law (in more detail);
- the seminal Convention case-law;
- the structure and practice of the new European Court of Human Rights.

THE PRINCIPAL CONVENTION RIGHTS AFFFECTING FAMILY LAW

1.7   The principal rights guaranteed by the Convention which concern family law and are included in the HRA 1998 are:

- the right to life **(Art 2)**;
- the protection from torture and inhuman degrading treatment or punishment **(Art 3)**;
- the right to liberty and security of the person **(Art 5)**;
- the right to a fair trial **(Art 6)**;
- the protection of private and family life, home and correspondence **(Art 8)**;
- the right to freedom of expression **(Art 10)**;
- the right to marry and found a family **(Art 12)**;
- freedom from discrimination in the delivery of Convention rights **(Art 14)**;
- the right to education **(Art 2 of the First Protocol)**.

Articles 6 and 8 will be of primary importance in the field of family law.

Article 9 (freedom of thought, conscience and religion) is closely related to Art 8 and Art 2 of the First Protocol and may also have an impact upon family law. Article 1 of the First Protocol (protection of property) may be relevant to the fields of matrimonial finance and domestic violence.

1.8   It should be noted that the following Articles of the Convention have been omitted from the HRA 1998: Art 1 (obligation to respect human rights); Article 13 (right to an effective domestic remedy); Arts 15–59 (operational provisions for the European Court) and the remaining Protocols (including the Seventh Protocol, Art 5 (equality between spouses)). Although Art 5 of the Seventh Protocol is not implemented by the HRA 1998, it is likely that it will be included in other legislation[1].

1.9   Also excluded are any designated derogations or reservations[2]. Currently, there is a derogation registered in respect of Art 5(3) (which relates to the detention of terrorist suspects) and a reservation entered in respect of Art 2 of the First Protocol (which relates to the right of education)[3].

---

1   White Paper: *Rights Brought Home: The Human Rights Bill* (Cm 3782), paras 4.15 and 4.16.
2   HRA 1998, s 1(2) and ss 14 to 17.
3   Ibid, Sch 3, Parts I and II.

GENERAL PRINCIPLES OF INTERPRETATION

1.10   In interpreting the Convention, the Convention organs have developed a broad purposive approach[1]. The Court has emphasised that its provisions should be interpreted and applied so as to make its safeguards practical and effective[2].

1.11   The Convention has been given a dynamic or evolutive interpretation. It is a 'living instrument' which must be interpreted in the light of present-day conditions[3]. It is, therefore, the Court's task to gauge when a new social standard has reached a sufficiently wide acceptance to have determinative effect upon the meaning of the Convention. An example is *Marckx v Belgium*[4] where the Court applied to the status of illegitimate children a new approach which had been adopted by the 'great majority' of the contracting States. In the interpretation of the Convention, crucial roles are played by:

(i)   the doctrine of the margin of appreciation; and
(ii) the principle of proportionality.

The margin of appreciation

1.12   Broadly, the margin of appreciation means that a State, when making a decision which involves a Convention right, has a measure of discretion, which is subject to the ultimate supervision of the Convention organs[5].

1.13   In *Handyside v UK*[6], the Court stated the doctrine as follows:

'By reason of their direct and continuous contact with the vital forces of their countries, state authorities are in principle in a better position than the international judge to give an opinion on the exact content of those requirements (of morals) as well as the 'necessity' of a 'restriction' or 'penalty' intended to meet them ... it is for the national authorities to make the initial assessment of the reality of the pressing social need implied by the notion of 'necessity' in this context. Consequently (this) leaves the contracting state a margin of appreciation. This margin is given both to the domestic legislator ('prescribed by law') and to the bodies, judicial amongst others, that are called upon to interpret and apply the laws in force. Nevertheless (this) does not give the contracting state an unlimited power of appreciation. The Court, which, with the Commission, is responsible for ensuring the observance of those states' engagements, is empowered to give the final ruling on whether a 'restriction' or 'penalty' is reconcilable (with the freedom protected by the particular Article). The domestic margin of appreciation thus goes hand in hand with a European supervision.'

1.14   The basis of the doctrine is, therefore, that the Convention organs are subsidiary to the national systems safeguarding human rights and that the national courts are better placed than the international judge to balance legitimate public purposes in their own country.

---

1   *Golder v UK* 1 EHRR 524 (see **p 329**). (Cases which are discussed in Part C: Case Summaries are cross-referred at first instance in bold type.)
2   *Loizidou v Turkey* 20 EHRR 99, para 72.
3   *Tyrer v UK* 2 EHRR 1, para 31 (see **p 358**).
4   2 EHRR 330, para 41 (see **p 342**).
5   *Handyside v UK* 1 EHRR 737, para 48 (see **p 331**).
6   Ibid.

1.15   Thus the Convention organs' task, in exercising their supervisory function, is not to take the place of the competent national authorities but rather to review the decisions they deliver pursuant to their power of appreciation. This does not mean that the supervision is limited to whether the respondent State exercised its discretion reasonably, carefully and in good faith; what the Convention organs have to do is to look at the interference complained of in the light of the case as a whole and determine whether it was proportionate to the legitimate aim pursued and whether the reasons adduced by the national authorities to justify it were relevant and sufficient[1].

1.16   The level of scrutiny under the margin of appreciation in the Convention cases is, consequently, more rigorous than that under the concept of *Wednesbury* unreasonableness as traditionally applied by the domestic courts. The domestic courts have already stated that greater scrutiny is required where fundamental rights are involved[2].

> 'For incorporation to be effective, as Parliament intends, British courts will have to engage in an effective control of the reasons given for interference and their sufficiency . . . and will have to go beyond a heightened *Wednesbury* review, whilst still respecting the decision making discretion of the primary decision maker.'[3]

1.17   There are two differing views as to how this doctrine will be transported into our domestic law.

(1) The first view is that the doctrine is for use only by the European Court in its supervisory role as defining the relationship between a supernational court and national authorities.

(2) The second view is that there should be a place in our national law for an analogous 'domestic' margin of appreciation. On this view, it will be for the domestic courts, when assessing the sufficiency of the reasons given for an interference with a Convention right, to judge whether the decision-maker has exceeded the margin of appreciation[4].

1.18   If the second view prevails, as the judiciary will hold a pivotal role in the national machinery for safeguarding human rights, they may feel less circumscribed by the restraint which the Strasbourg Court has sometimes shown when considering the margin of appreciation claimed by the executive and, therefore, go on to apply a narrower margin.

1.19   The scope of the margin of appreciation is not static but varies from Article to Article and according to the context of the individual case. By way of an example in the field of family law, in *Johansen v Norway*[5], the European Court has said:

---

1   *Handyside v UK* 1 EHRR 737, para 50; *The Observer and the Guardian v UK* 14 EHRR 153 and *Jersild v Denmark* 19 EHRR 1, para 30 which represent the predominant view of the Court as to the scope of its function of review.

2   *R v Ministry of Defence ex parte Smith* [1996] QB 517 at 558E–559A, 564A–F and 565C. There are increasing references to 'margin of appreciation' in domestic judicial review law: eg *R v Radio Authority ex parte Bull* [1998] QB 294 at 309E.

3   Bratza and Duffy, *Practitioner's Handbook of EC Law* Ch 32, paras 32.2.13 and 32.2.16.

4   *R v Ministry of Defence ex parte Smith* [1996] QB 517 at 554E–F, per Sir Thomas Bingham MR (as he then was).

5   23 EHRR 33, para 64 (see **p 337**).

'... perceptions as to the appropriateness of intervention by public authorities in the care of children vary from one Contracting State to another, depending on such factors as traditions relating to the role of the family and to State intervention in family affairs and the availability of resources for public measures in this particular area ... The margin of appreciation so to be accorded to the competent national authorities will vary in the light of the nature of the issues and the seriousness of the interests at stake. Thus the Court recognises that the authorities enjoy a wide margin of appreciation in assessing the necessity of taking a child into care ...'

Proportionality

1.20 The principle of proportionality underlies the whole of the Convention. It has a particular importance where the Convention expressly permits restrictions upon a Convention right such as in Arts 8–11 as it is a crucial element of the requirement of 'necessity'. Any such interference with a right must 'correspond to a pressing social need and be proportionate to the legitimate aim pursued by the State'[1].

1.21 Proportionality requires a reasonable relationship between the means employed and the aim sought to be realised[2]. In *Soering v UK*[3] the Court stated:

'Inherent in the whole Convention is a search for a fair balance between the demands of the general interest of the community and the requirements of the protection of the individual's fundamental human rights.'

Considerations of proportionality, therefore, arise in achieving this 'fair balance'.

1.22 It has also been imported into other Articles such as Art 6 in respect of restrictions on access to the court and the non-discrimination rule in Art 14[4]. Finally, it is central to the determination as to whether or not positive obligations exist in respect of the rights and freedoms guaranteed by the Articles[5].

Principles justifying an interference

1.23 There are four underlying principles which have become settled in the Convention case-law as justifying an interference with a Convention right. The interference must:

(1) be in accordance with the law;
(2) serve a legitimate aim;
(3) be necessary in a democratic society;
(4) not be discriminatory.

As to 'lawfulness', it is not enough for the State merely to point to a rule of law, whether domestic or international, which permits interference with the right. The law relied upon must:

– not grant an unfettered discretion[6];

---

1   *Silver v UK* 5 EHRR 344, para 97.
2   *Ashingdane v UK* 7 EHRR 528, para 57 (see **p 309**); *James v UK* 8 EHRR 123, para 50 (see **p 336**).
3   11 EHRR 439, para 89.
4   *Belgian Linguistic Case (No 2)* 1 EHRR 252 (see **p 311**).
5   *Rees v UK* 9 EHRR 56, para 37 (see **p 350**).
6   *Malone v UK* 7 EHRR 14, para 68.

- be formulated with sufficient precision to enable the citizen to regulate his conduct and for him to foresee, to a degree that is reasonable in the circumstances, the consequences which a given action may entail[1];
- be adequately accessible[2].

As to 'legitimate aims', the State must identify the objective of its interference with an individual's right and show that the reason for the interference is a proper one.

As to 'necessity', the State must clearly demonstrate:

- the need for the interference;
- that the interference is fair;
- that the interference is in proportion to that need.

As to 'non-discrimination', discrimination occurs where 'the distinction has no objective or reasonable justification'[3] and for the prohibition on discrimination to be infringed there must be 'no reasonable relationship of proportionality between the means employed and the aim sought to be pursued'[4].

Generally, the court is more likely to be concerned with the conditions of 'necessity' and 'non-discrimination'.

In practice

1.24   The Strasbourg Court generally applies a structured approach in determining whether there has been a violation of the Convention by considering the following questions, which particularly arise under Arts 8–11.

- Does the complaint fall within the ambit of the right claimed?
- Has there been an interference with the right?
- Is the interference lawful?
- What are the aims of the interference?
- Are those aims legitimate?
- Has the State demonstrated relevant and sufficient reasons for the interference?
- Taking into account the margin of appreciation, are those reasons proportionate to the restriction being placed upon the enjoyment of the right?

After incorporation, it will be incumbent upon the domestic courts in family cases to carry out a similar exercise.

---

1   *Sunday Times v UK (No 1)* 2 EHRR 245, para 49 (see **p 357**).
2   Ibid, para 49; *Malone v UK* 7 EHRR 14, para 68.
3   *Belgian Linguistic Case (No 2)* 1 EHRR 252, para 10.
4   Ibid, para 10.

Chapter 2

THE FRAMEWORK OF THE HRA 1998 RELEVANT TO FAMILY LAW

COMPATIBILITY

2.1   The new key requirement in our domestic law will be that public authorities, including the courts, must exercise their powers in a way which is *compatible* with the Convention.

Interpretation of legislation

2.2   Section 3 provides that primary and subordinate legislation (whenever enacted) must, so far as it is possible, be read and given effect in a way which is *compatible* with the Convention rights. This powerful interpretative section is the lynch-pin of the Act.

2.3   The courts will be required to interpret legislation so as to uphold the Convention rights unless the legislation itself is so clearly incompatible with the Convention that it is impossible to do so[1]. This goes far beyond the present rule which enables the courts to take the Convention into account in resolving legislative ambiguity[2]. This 'rule of construction' is to apply to past as well as future legislation[3].

2.4   To the extent that it affects the meaning of a legislative provision, the courts will not be bound by previous interpretations and will be able to build up a new body of case-law, which takes into account the Convention rights[4]. This is likely to have an important impact upon our domestic law of precedent, as a court may well find that in interpreting legislation so as to uphold the Convention rights it has to disregard previous Court of Appeal authority. Some guidance as to how far the courts may go in interpreting legislative provisions so as to conform with the Convention may be gained by looking at EC law where a similar exercise is carried out.

2.5   In *Webb v Emo Air Cargo (UK) Ltd*[5], it was held that where national law is open to more than one interpretation, it is the one which is consistent with EC law which must be adopted. The House of Lords has further established that domestic courts are under a duty to give a purposive construction to the interpretation of domestic legislation so as to accord with EC law[6]. This may be done by implying the words necessary to achieve this result[7] or by using the power to discard individual words, where necessary[8].

---

1   White Paper: *Rights Brought Home: The Human Rights Bill* (Cm 3782) ('White Paper'), para 2.7.
2   Ibid, para 2.7.
3   Ibid, para 2.8.
4   Ibid, para 2.8.
5   [1993] 1 WLR 49; see *Practitioners' Handbook of EC Law* (Bar European Court), para 5.5.
6   *Pickstone v Freemans Plc* [1989] 1 AC 66; *Litster v Forth Dry Dock Co Ltd* [1990] 1 AC 546 at 554G–H and 559D–F.
7   *Pickstone v Freemans Plc* (above).
8   *O Brien v Sim-Chem Ltd* [1980] ICR 573 at 580F.

Declaration of incompatibility

2.6   **Section 4** provides that the higher courts may make a '*declaration of incompatibility*' where they are satisfied that a provision of primary or subordinate legislation is incompatible with the Convention. As such a declaration will be a matter of importance, the power to make it has been reserved to the higher courts (House of Lords, the Judicial Committee of the Privy Council, the Court of Appeal and the High Court[1]). They will be able to make a declaration in any proceedings before them in the High Court, on judicial review or in considering an appeal from a lower court. The decision by the higher court will itself be appealable[2].

2.7   The Government has the right to intervene in any of the proceedings where such a declaration is a possible outcome. Section 5 gives the Crown the right to have notice that a court is considering whether or not to make a declaration, together with a right to be joined as a party.

2.8   A declaration of incompatibility is not binding on the parties to the proceedings in which it is made nor does it change the law, which continues to apply[3]. This is to preserve parliamentary sovereignty. The courts, therefore, do not have the power to set aside primary legislation, either past or future, on the ground of incompatibility[4]. They may, however, strike down or set aside secondary legislation which is incompatible with the Convention, unless the terms of the parent statute make this impossible[5]. Such a declaration will, however, 'almost certainly'[6] prompt the Government and Parliament to change the law. Section 10 of and Sch 2 to the Act provide a fast-track procedure for remedial action to amend the legislation.

Public authority

2.9   **Section 6** makes it unlawful for a public authority to act in a way which is *incompatible* with the Convention rights, save insofar: (a) that it could not have acted differently as a result of primary legislation; or (b) where the relevant primary legislation or subordinate legislation cannot be read or given effect to so as to be compatible with Convention rights and the authority was acting so as to give effect to or to enforce those provisions.

2.10   An act includes 'a failure to act'[7]. 'Public authority' includes: (a) a court or any tribunal in which legal proceedings may be brought[8]; and (b) 'any person certain of whose functions are functions of a public nature'[9]. It includes, therefore, central government and local authorities. In the family law field, the definition of 'public authority' will include a local authority exercising a care jurisdiction and acting as an adoption agency. An adoption agency (other than a local authority) is also likely to qualify as a public authority.

---

1   HRA 1998, s 4(5).
2   White Paper, para 2.9.
3   HRA 1998, s 4(6).
4   White Paper, para 2.13.
5   Ibid, para 2.15.
6   Ibid, para 2.10.
7   HRA 1998, s 6(6).
8   Ibid, s 21.
9   Ibid, s 6(3). Parliament is excluded but not the House of Lords in its judicial capacity.

2.11   However, in relation to a particular act, a person is not 'a public authority' if the nature of the act is private[1]. A person may, therefore, be a public body in respect of some his functions, but not in respect of others. Thus the Official Solicitor is likely to be a public body when acting as an *amicus curiae* but not when acting as a litigation friend on behalf of a child in care proceedings.

2.12   Section 6(2) provides the public authority with a defence that its act is not unlawful under s 6(1) if, under primary legislation, it could not have acted differently, or if the primary legislation under which it acted cannot be read or given effect in a way which is compatible with Convention rights.

2.13   It must follow from s 6(1), which provides that it will be unlawful for a public authority, including a court, to act in a way which is incompatible with a Convention right, that Convention rights will have precedence over our current domestic common law and equity. In the field of family law, the domestic courts, and therefore all family practitioners, will have to apply lateral thinking to our present precedent and practice to test whether or not they are compatible with the relevant Convention right, and if not, they must yield to the Convention right[2].

BREACHES AND REMEDIES

Bringing proceedings for a breach of the Convention

2.14   **Section 7** provides that a person who claims that a public authority has acted or proposes to act in a way, which is unlawful because *incompatible* with the Convention rights, may:

(a) bring proceedings against that authority under the Act in the appropriate court or tribunal; or
(b) rely on the Convention rights in any legal proceedings but only if he is or would be a victim of the unlawful act.

2.15   Individuals will, therefore, be able to argue violation of their Convention rights in the domestic courts at all levels from the outset. Normally, Convention points will be taken under s 7(1)(b) in the context of ordinary proceedings. 'Legal proceedings' in s 7(1)(b) are defined as including proceedings brought by or at the instigation of a public authority and an appeal against the decision of the court or tribunal. If no such proceedings are available, under s 7(1)(a) it is still possible for individuals to bring a case under the Act on a Convention ground alone[3]. The proviso in each case is that the applicant must be 'a victim' or prospective victim of the unlawful act alleged. Only in those circumstances will an applicant in judicial review proceedings be taken as having a sufficient interest for *locus standi*[4].

2.16   The appropriate court or tribunal for an application under s 7(1)(a) has not yet been defined by rules made by the Lord Chancellor or the Secretary of State. A claim under section 7(1)(a) has to be brought within one year or an

---

1   HRA 1998, s 6(5).
2   On 'lateral thinking', see Emmerson, editor of the *Human Rights Law Review*, *Archbold News*, 13 March 1998.
3   White Paper, para 2.3.
4   HRA 1998, s 7(3).

extended equitable period of time, subject to a stricter timetable being imposed by the rules[1]. Proceedings under s 7(1)(a) in respect of a judicial act may be brought only by exercising a right of appeal, on an application for judicial review or in such other forum as may be prescribed by the rules[2]. Damages may not be awarded in respect of a judicial act in good faith[3] nor against the Crown unless the appropriate person is joined to the proceedings[4].

Amending legislation

2.17   **Section 10 and Sch 2** provide for the amendment of legislation by remedial order so as to remove incompatibility either in response to a declaration of incompatibility or to a finding of a violation of the Convention by the European Court.

2.18   **Section 19** requires a written statement of compatibility for future primary legislation. Although not binding on the courts, this may be used for guidance in cases of uncertainty.

Remedies

2.19   **Section 8** provides that a court or tribunal, where it finds an authority to have acted unlawfully, may grant such relief or remedy or make such order within its powers as it considers appropriate. The court is, therefore, able to enforce Convention rights by granting any appropriate remedies within its powers.

2.20   A damages award can be made only by a court with jurisdiction to do so[5]. As it is doubtful that family courts have such jurisdiction, if damages are sought the claim will have to be made in the civil courts. No award of damages can be made unless the court is satisfied in all the circumstances that the award is necessary to afford just satisfaction to the person in whose favour it is made[6]. In determining whether to award damages or the amount of an award, the court has to take account of awards by the European Court under Art 41[7]. These tend to be modest[8]. This will not, however, prejudice an appropriate damages award which would be available otherwise than under the HRA 1998[9]. In practice, in the field of family law it is likely that the Convention point will be taken in ordinary proceedings under s 7(1)(b) and will there be employed to reinforce the party's legal argument rather than for the purpose of seeking a specific remedy for violation of a Convention right. However, where a specific remedy for a violation is called for, the family court will be restricted to its statutory powers and, in the case of the High Court, its inherent jurisdiction. It has been suggested that an alternative remedy may be by way of declaratory relief[10].

1   HRA 1998, s 7(5).
2   Ibid, s 9(1).
3   Ibid, s 9(3): the only exception is compensation under Art 5(5) of the Convention.
4   Ibid, s 9(4).
5   Ibid, s 8(2).
6   Ibid, s 8(3).
7   Ibid, s 8(4).
8   In *A v UK* 27 EHRR 611 (see **p 305**) and *Osman v UK* [1999] 1 FLR 193 (see **p 348**) where the UK was found to be in breach, the applicants were each awarded £10,000.
9   HRA 1998, s 11.
10   *Rayden and Jackson on Divorce and Family Matters: The Human Rights Act 1998 – A Special Bulletin for Family Lawyers* (Butterworth Law), para 2.32.

CONVENTION CASE-LAW

Strasbourg law in the UK courts

2.21 **Section 2** provides that domestic courts and tribunals must take into account Convention case-law. The case-law should be used as guidance and not as binding precedent. In assessing the weight to be given to Convention case-law, the following matters should be borne in mind.

– The Convention is a 'living instrument' which evolves to meet changing social circumstances and, therefore, Convention case-law places less reliance upon established precedent than domestic law. In general, this means that older decisions are less reliable as a guide.

– Decisions of the Court have greater weight than admissibility decisions of the Commission.

– Decisions generally turn upon whether an individual's rights have been infringed in the particular circumstances, although some general principles may be discerned from them

– The European Court allows 'a margin of appreciation' to national authorities which varies according to the particular point in issue. By way of example, a wide margin of appreciation has been permitted to national authorities in assessing the necessity of taking children into care, whereas a stricter scrutiny has been applied to the restrictions placed by those authorities on parental rights and access to children[1].

Sources of Convention case-law

2.22 The European Human Rights Reports ('EHRR')[2] contain most of the judgments of the European Court, together with headnotes, and certain of the Commission's reports and decisions. The official series for the Court judgments is Series A Nos 1–338[3] until 1996 and Reports of Judgments and Decisions ('RJD') in annual volumes from 1996. The principal source for Commission cases is Decisions and Reports ('DR'), published by the Commission. Consolidated index volumes, which list cases by name, number and subject matter, are also produced. Supplementary sources include: Collections of Decisions of the European Commission ('CD') for 1955–1974; Yearbook of the European Convention of Human Rights ('YB'), published annually, which contains selected Commission decisions as to admissibility; Digest of Strasbourg case-law ('Digest')[4] which contains extracts from the case-law of both the Court and the Commission, including some Commission cases not reported elsewhere; International Human Rights Reports ('IHRR')[5] which contains decisions of other major human rights monitoring bodies. On the internet: http://www.dhcour.coe.fr (for the Court) and http://www.dhcommhr.coe.fr (for the Commission).

---

1   *Johansen v Norway* 23 EHRR 33, para 64.
2   Sweet & Maxwell.
3   Carl Haymanns Verlag.
4   Ibid.
5   Human Rights Law Centre, University of Nottingham.

SAFEGUARDS

No restriction of claim

2.23   **Section 11** provides that a person's reliance on a Convention right does not restrict the application of any other right or freedom in domestic law or the right to bring any claim or proceedings which he could make or bring apart from ss 7 to 9.

Freedom of expression

2.24   **Sections 12 and 13** introduce safeguards in respect of the exercise of the rights to freedom of expression and the freedom of thought, conscience and religion.

KEY DEFINITIONS

2.25   'Public authority' is defined in wide terms to include central and local government; s 6(3)(a) making it clear that courts and tribunals at all levels are within the definition. 'Victim' is defined as 'any person, non-governmental organisation or group of individuals claiming to be the victim of a violation by one of the High contracting parties of the rights set forth in the Convention or the protocols thereto'[1]. Where children are concerned, parents may act unless there is a conflict of interest.

RETROSPECTIVITY

2.26   **Section 22(4)** provides that where proceedings are brought by or at the instigation of a public authority, a person who claims that he is a victim of an unlawful act committed by a public authority under s 6(1) may rely on Convention rights in any legal proceedings under s 7(1)(b), whenever the act occurred; but otherwise s 7(1)(b) does not apply to an act taking place before the coming into force of that section.

2.27   It follows that a party to proceedings brought by or instigated by a public authority (including appeals in proceedings which were brought by a public authority) may take a Convention point or argue that the authority has acted unlawfully under s 6(1) even where the act occurred prior to the HRA 1998 coming into force. This, therefore, should be borne in mind by local authorities when deciding to bring proceedings which are likely to continue after the HRA 1998 is brought into force.

2.28   In the recent Court of Appeal decision of *Regina v DPP, ex parte Kebilene*[2], the role and jurisdiction of the domestic courts during the interim period between enactment and the bringing into force of the main provisions of the HRA 1998 were considered in the context of the Divisional Court's review of the DPP's

---

1   Art 34 of the Convention.
2   (1999) *The Times*, 31 March.

discretion to prosecute under the Prevention of Terrorism (Temporary Provisions) Act 1989.

2.29 Lord Bingham of Cornhill said that 'the Convention, despite its recent advance towards incorporation, had not crossed the Rubicon separating prospective from binding law'. He agreed with the argument that unless and until the provisions of the HRA 1998 were brought into force, so becoming part of domestic law, they had no binding effect and the Convention could not be relied upon to counter the plain and unambiguous effect of primary domestic legislation. Nevertheless, he went on to say that it was appropriate for the DPP to take account of the probable consequences of any incompatibility between primary domestic legislation and the articles of the Convention when exercising his discretion under the 1989 Act, including the prospect of a successful appeal to the European Court of Human Rights.

HORIZONTALITY

2.30 The object of the Convention is essentially that of protecting the individual against arbitrary interferences by State and, therefore, it establishes 'vertical' duties between the State and the individual. However, the European Court has stated, for example in respect of Art 8, that 'it does not merely compel the State to abstain from such interference: in addition to this primarily negative undertaking, there may be positive obligations inherent in an effective "respect" for family life'[1], and these may also include an obligation upon the State to protect a private individual's Convention rights against infringement by other private individuals[2].

2.31 In *Hokkanen v Finland*[3], where the grandparents refused to comply with court orders granting the father custody, the European Court held that 'the principle' that Art 8 includes a right for the parent to have measures taken to facilitate his re-union with his child and an obligation for the national authorities to take such action (a principle which had been established in public care cases) 'must be taken as also applying to cases such as the present where the origin of the provisional transfer of care is a private arrangement'.

2.32 Thus the Convention has a measure of 'horizontal' effect by placing positive obligations upon the State to protect the Convention rights of private individuals from interference by other private individuals giving the State a part in regulating disputes between private individuals which involve a Convention right. This is reinforced by s 6 of the HRA 1998 which provides that it is unlawful for a court, as a public authority, to act in a way which is incompatible with a Convention right. The likely effect of this is that the courts will not only have the duty of acting compatibly with the Convention in cases involving other public authorities but also in developing the common law in deciding cases between individuals[4].

---

1   *Marckx v Belgium* 2 EHRR 330, para 31; *X and Y v The Netherlands* 8 EHRR 235 (see **p 360**).
2   *Hokkanen v Finland* 19 EHRR 139 (see **p 333**).
3   Ibid, paras 55–56, 58.
4   HL Official Report (5th series) col 783, 24 November 1997.

2.33   In practice, under the HRA 1998, private individuals, such as the parents in a residence application, are not under any express duty as between themselves to comply with the Convention. However, once the court, as a public authority, is seized of the application under s 8 of the Children Act 1989, it is under a duty under s 3 of the HRA 1998 to read and give effect to s 8 in a way which is compatible with Convention rights which will include deciding whether there is any interference with Art 8 and, if so, whether the interference is justifiable according to Art 8(2). It must take into account any relevant Convention case-law under s 2 of the HRA 1998. Under s 6 of the HRA 1998, it must act and not fail to act in a way which is incompatible with a Convention right. In this way, the HRA 1998 gives the Convention a horizontal effect in private disputes between individuals.

Chapter 3

THE PRINCIPAL ARTICLES WHICH CONCERN FAMILY LAW

3.1   The principal Articles of the Convention which concern family law fall into four broad categories:

(1)   the rights relating to life and liberty;
(2)   the right to a fair trial;
(3)   the rights relating to privacy;
(4)   the right to education.

ARTICLE 2: RIGHT TO LIFE

3.2   Article 2(1) reads:

> 'Everyone's right to life shall be protected by law. No one shall be deprived of his life intentionally save in the execution of a sentence of the court following his conviction of a crime for which this penalty is provided by law.'

Article 2 guarantees the most basic human right, the right to life, and is one of the fundamental rights of the Convention, from which no derogation is possible and whose provisions must be strictly construed[1]. The only exceptions are listed in Art 2(2). The protection of the right to life imposes a broader obligation on the State than merely requiring it to refrain from taking life intentionally. The State is enjoined to take appropriate steps to safeguard life[2].

3.3   In *X v UK*[3], a case where a public vaccination scheme caused the death of some children, the Commission held that the State's obligation to take adequate steps to protect life might give rise to medical care issues, but on the facts came to the conclusion that there had been no violation of Art 2. Save for a Commission decision that Art 2 does not cover national health policy in general[4], the nature and extent of the State's obligation has since remained largely untested.

3.4   Issues in the area of medical care which might possibly arise in the future include those suffering from a permanent vegetative state (PVS) or anorexia nervosa where there is a rejection of treatment or a mother who rejects a Caesarean section where there is an immediate risk to the lives of the baby and herself or who proposes to take drugs which may be harmful to the foetus. In *Airedale National Health Service Trust v Bland*, a case concerning a PVS patient[5], Lord Goff, in considering the applicable principles of law, highlighted that:

> '... the fundamental principle is the principle of the sanctity of human life – a principle long recognised not only in our own society but also in most, if not all,

---

1   *McCann v UK* 21 EHRR 97, para 147.
2   *X v UK* Application No 7154/75 (Rep), (12 October 1978) 14 DR 31 at 32.
3   Ibid.
4   *Taylor Family and Others v UK* Application No 23412/94, (30 August 1994) 79-A DR 127; a case brought by the parents of the children killed by the nurse, Beverly Allitt.
5   [1993] AC 789 at 863H.

civilised societies throughout the modern world, as indeed evidenced by its recognition ... in article 2 of the European Convention for the Protection of Human Rights and Fundamental Freedoms (1953).'

3.5   In the field of family law, Art 2 has also been invoked on questions concerning abortion, which has proved controversial. There has been an apparent reluctance to recognise an absolute right to life for an unborn child[1] and, to date, all the cases involving the question whether abortion violates the right to life have failed to cross the admissibility threshold; in each case the right to respect for the right of the private life of the pregnant mother has prevailed.

3.6   Other right to life issues concerning the unborn child include those relating to human fertilisation and embryology in the context of artificial human reproduction techniques. The extent to which an infertile couple may derive a right of access to new medical technologies is largely unexplored in the Convention case-law. Forms of birth control and sterilisation are also likely to raise issues under Art 2, as well as under Art 12 of the Convention. These issues have not yet been ventilated in either the Court or the Commission, though the Commission, in an unpublished decision, has stated that an operation for sterilisation might, in certain circumstances, involve a breach of Art 2[2].

A key case under Art 2 is *Paton v UK*[3].

ARTICLE 3: FREEDOM FROM TORTURE OR INHUMAN OR DEGRADING TREATMENT OR PUNISHMENT

3.7   Article 3 provides:

'No-one may be subjected to torture or to inhuman or degrading treatment or punishment.'

It is expressed in unqualified terms, from which there may be no derogation. It is, therefore, an absolute guarantee of the freedom it protects[4]. 'Torture' has been defined as 'deliberate inhuman treatment causing very serious and cruel suffering'[5]. 'Ill treatment' must attain a minimum level of severity if it is to fall within the scope of Art 3[6]. The assessment of this minimum is relative: 'it depends on the circumstances of the case, such as the nature and context of the treatment, its duration, its physical and mental effects and, in some circumstances, the sex, the age and state of health of the victim'[7]. 'Degrading treatment' is treatment which grossly humiliates[8] or degrades or which rouses in the victim feelings of fear, anguish and inferiority capable of humiliating and debasing him and possibly breaking his physical or moral resistance[9]. 'Degrading' has the same meaning in

---

1   *Paton v UK* 3 EHRR 408 paras 9, 17–23; *Bruggeman and Scheuten v FRG* 3 EHRR 244, para 60 (see **p 316**).
2   Application No 1287/61 (unpublished).
3   3 EHRR 409.
4   *Ireland v UK* 2 EHRR 25, para 163 (see **p 335**).
5   *Ireland v UK* (above).
6   *Costello-Roberts v UK* 19 EHRR 112, para 30 (see **p 319**); *A v UK* [1998] 2 FLR 959.
7   *A v UK* (above).
8   *The Greek Case* (1969) 12 YB (the Greek case) at 186.
9   *Ireland v UK* (above).

respect of punishment as it does in respect of treatment[1]. The minimum level which must satisfy Art 3 in the context of 'degrading treatment' depends, in particular, on the nature and context of the punishment itself and the method of its execution[2].

3.8   Article 3 has been invoked in cases concerning corporal punishment in the school and in the home. In *Costello-Roberts v UK*[3], the Court, by five votes to four, held that a disciplinary measure, by which a boy was given three 'whacks' on the bottom with a gym shoe over his trousers by the headmaster with no-one else present, but which left no visible bruising, was not of the level of severity to fall within the scope of 'degrading punishment'. In contrast, in *Y v UK*[4], where a boy was caned four times through his trousers by the headmaster which caused four weals across his buttocks with heavy bruising and swelling, the Commission held that this did constitute degrading treatment and punishment. Further, in *Warwick v UK*[5], where a 16-year-old girl caught smoking was given one stroke of the cane on her hand by the headmaster in the presence of the deputy headmaster which caused two large bruises on the palm of her hand, the Commission found a violation of Art 3, attaching particular importance to the fact that the punishment consisted of a physical injury, which was not trivial, inflicted by a man in the presence of another man on a 16-year-old girl, who was of marriageable age.

3.9   *A v UK*[6] is a landmark case concerning corporal punishment in the home. A boy aged 9 was beaten with a garden cane by his step-father on more than one occasion with considerable force. The step-father was subsequently acquitted of assault occasioning actual bodily harm, having argued the defence of reasonable chastisement. The nine judges of the European Court found unanimously that the treatment of the kind which occurred in this case reached the level of severity prohibited by Art 3 and concluded that the State should be held responsible for the beating of the applicant by his step-father. What is of particular significance is the Court's statement that States are:

> 'required to take measures designed to ensure that individuals within their jurisdiction are not subjected to torture or inhuman or degrading treatment or punishment, including such ill treatment administered by private individuals. Children and other vulnerable individuals, in particular, are entitled to state protection, in the form of effective deterrence against such serious breaches of personal integrity'.

3.10   The decision in *A v UK* is likely to have particular resonance in public law cases, especially the relationship between the inhuman treatment prohibited by Art 3 and the significant harm threshold in s 31 of the Children Act 1989 where the State has failed to protect over a prolonged period of time.

3.11   *KL v UK*[7], a recent Commission decision, has further pointed the way. The applicants were five children who had been ill-treated by their parents over five years before they were finally placed in care. They complained that the local

---

1   *Ireland v UK* (above).
2   *Tyrer v UK* 2 EHRR 1 (see **p 347**).
3   19 EHRR 112.
4   17 EHRR 233 (see **p 361**).
5   Application No 9471/81 (Rep), (18 July 1986) 60 DR 5, paras 86 and 87.
6   27 EHRR 611.
7   26 EHRR CD 113.

authority had failed to take appropriate steps to protect them from abuse and that this constituted a violation of Art 3. The Commission found the complaint admissible and the case is pending in the European Court[1].

3.12   Compulsory sterilisation is also likely to be a breach of Art 3. However, it is likely that compulsory medical treatment, such as force-feeding and compulsory administration of drugs, where it is in accordance with the established principles of medical science and is necessary to prevent death or serious injury, would not be treated as inhuman or degrading simply by reason of lack of consent[2]. In *Herczegfalvy v Austria*[3], the Court held that '... as a general rule, a measure which is a therapeutic necessity cannot be regarded as inhuman or degrading. The Court must nevertheless satisfy itself that the medical necessity has been convincingly shown to exist'. The Commission has further held that, although force feeding 'does involve degrading elements which in certain circumstances may be regarded as prohibited by Art 3', the State's obligation under Art 2 prevails over Art 3; the former obligation calling 'for positive action on the part of the Contracting parties, in particular an active measure to save lives ...'[4]. It is unlikely, therefore, that Art 3 will have any realistic impact upon the approach taken by the domestic court in respect of the anorexia nervosa cases[5].

Key cases under Art 3 include: *Tyrer v UK, Costello-Roberts v UK, Warwick v UK, Y v UK, A v UK* and *Herczegfalvy v Austria*[6].

ARTICLE 5: THE RIGHT TO LIBERTY AND SECURITY OF THE PERSON

3.13   Under Art 5, everyone has the right to liberty and security of the person.

'Liberty' means the physical liberty of the person[7] and 'security of the person' is interpreted in the context of physical liberty[8]. The main objective is to prevent arbitrary interference by a public authority with an individual's personal 'liberty'[9].

The right to liberty is not absolute and is subject to the exceptions set out in Art 5(1)(a)–(f), which are exhaustive and are given a narrow interpretation[10].

3.14   Permitted exceptions, particularly affecting family law, are as follows.

'The lawful arrest or detention of a person for non-compliance with the lawful order of a court' (Art 5(1)(b)).

This permits the detention of a person who has failed to comply with a court order, such as in cases of civil contempt, and has included:

---

1   See also: *TP and KM v UK* 26 EHRR CD 85.
2   *Herczegfalvy v Austria* 15 EHRR 437.
3   Ibid, paras 79–83.
4   *X v FRG* 7 EHRR 152.
5   *Re W (A Minor) (Medical Treatment: Court's Jurisdiction)* [1993] Fam 64; *Re C (Detention: Medical Treatment)* [1997] 2 FLR 180.
6   All above.
7   *Engel v Netherlands* 1 EHRR 647, para 58.
8   *East Africa Asians v UK* 3 EHRR 76 at 89, para 220 (see **p 321**).
9   Ibid, para 222.
10   *Engel v Netherlands* (above), para 57; *Winterwerp v Netherlands* 2 EHRR 387, para 37.

–   detention in a mental hospital for a refusal to undergo a psychiatric examination ordered by the court[1];
–   a failure to undergo a blood test in a paternity suit[2]. Although the Commission was of the opinion that enforcing a blood test on a person was a deprivation of liberty even if the deprivation was of very short duration, it went on to hold that it fell within Art 5(1)(b);
–   a failure to make a declaration of assets[3].

The detention must aim at securing the fulfilment of 'a specific and concrete obligation which he has until then failed to satisfy', and must 'not tend to punish past behaviour'[4]. The exception is primarily intended where there has been a wilful or negligent breach of an obligation[5].

> 'The detention of a minor by lawful order (i) for the purpose of educational supervision or (ii) his lawful detention for the purpose of bringing him before the competent legal authority.'[6]

3.15   In *Bouamar v Belgium*[7], an adolescent boy with psychological problems and a history of aggressive behaviour was provisionally detained by nine court orders for periods which eventually amounted to 119 days in 10 months. He was placed in a remand prison with no education facilities without being charged with any criminal offence or provided with legal advice. None of the open remand centres which did have educational facilities would take him because of his difficult behaviour. During the 10 months, he was shuttled to and fro between the remand prison and his family.

3.16   The Court rejected the Government's argument that it had acted within the scope of Art 5(1)(d) and found that the detention was too long. The Court said:

> '. . . sub-paragraph (d) does not preclude an interim custody measure being used as a preliminary to a regime of supervised education, without itself involving any supervised education. In such circumstances, however, the imprisonment must be speedily followed by actual application of such a regime in a setting (open or closed) designed and with sufficient resources for the purpose.'[8]

3.17   The second of the two permitted grounds under Art 5(1)(d) is intended to cover the situation where a minor is detained so as to secure his removal from harmful surroundings[9]. *Abbott v UK*[10] is an example of a Convention case which had a direct impact upon delegated legislation arising from the Children Act 1989. It was concerned with a ward who in 1987 was placed in secure accommodation in proceedings in respect of which he was not a party, nor was there anyone, even a guardian ad litem, to represent him. The case before the Commission settled on the Government's proposals to amend the then draft

---

1   *X v FRG* Application No 6659/74, (1975) 3 DR 92.
2   *X v Austria* Application No 8278/78, (1979) 18 DR 154.
3   *X v FRG* Application No 9546/81, (1983) 1 Digest Supp, para 5.1.4.2.
4   *Johansen v Norway* Application No 10600/83, (1985) 44 DR 155 at 162.
5   *McVeigh v UK* Application No 8022/7, (1981) 25 DR 15.
6   Art 5(1)(d).
7   11 EHRR 1 (see **p 314**).
8   Ibid, para 50.
9   *Abbott v UK* Application No 15006/89, (1990) 67 DR 290.
10   Ibid.

Children (Secure Accommodation) Regulations 1991[1], to include measures for the ward to be joined as a party[2].

3.18   Other permitted exceptions include: (i) the lawful detention of a person after conviction by a competent court; and (ii) the lawful arrest or detention of a person for the purpose of bringing him before the competent court on reasonable suspicion of having committed an offence.

3.19   The guaranteed rights include:

–   being informed promptly of the reasons for arrest and of any charge (Art 5(2)). Any person arrested must be told, in simple, non-technical language that he can understand, the essential legal factual grounds for his arrest, so as to be able, if he sees fit, to apply to a court to challenge its lawfulness in accordance with para 5(4)[3];
–   being brought promptly before a judge and being entitled to a trial within a reasonable time or to release pending trial (ie a right to bail) (Art 5(3));
–   being entitled to take proceedings by which the lawfulness of his detention shall be decided speedily by the Court (Art 5(4));
–   an enforceable right of compensation for the victim of arrest or detention in contravention of Art 5 (Art 5(5)).

3.20   Issues have arisen over the relationship between Art 5 and Art 8, where parental restrictions have led to a deprivation of liberty of a child. In *Nielsen v Denmark*[4], at the request of the mother who had sole parental rights, a 12-year-old boy was placed in a closed psychiatric ward for treatment. The boy, acting through his father, complained that his hospitalisation was a deprivation of liberty contrary to Art 5 on the grounds that the ward was a closed ward, he was unable to receive visitors except with the agreement of the staff, special permission was required in respect of telephone calls and he was under almost under constant surveillance. He further alleged that his mother's sole intention was to prevent him from joining his father.

3.21   The Court treated the mother's request as an exercise of parental rights and responsibilities and, as such, a fundamental element of family life under Art 8 in the sense that it was within her parental competence:

'to decide where the child must live and also impose, or authorise others to impose, various restrictions on the child's liberty. Thus the children in school or other recreational institution must abide by certain rules which limit their freedom of movement and their liberty in other respects. Likewise a child may have to be hospitalised for medical treatment.'[5]

The Court accepted that the mother had consented to the child's hospitalisation for the protection of his health and in those circumstances the parental restriction fell outside Art 5[6]. It found that the restrictions to which the applicant was subject

---

1   SI 1991/1505.
2   This was achieved by Family Proceedings Rules 1991, r 5.5, inserted by the Family Proceedings (Amendment) Rules 1991, r 14. See also *Re AS (Secure Accommodation Order)* [1999] 1 FLR 103.
3   *Fox, Campbell and Hartley v UK* 13 EHRR 157, para 40.
4   11 EHRR 175 (see **p 345**).
5   Ibid, para 61.
6   Ibid, para 69.

were no more than the normal requirements for the care of a child of 12 years of age receiving treatment in hospital[1].

3.22 In the field of family law, Art 5 is most likely to arise, therefore, in contempt cases, cases concerning powers of arrest, judgment summonses, secure accommodation orders[2], and the inherent jurisdiction of the Court to detain children[3].

Key cases under Art 5 include *Nielsen v Denmark*[4] and *Bouamar v Belgium*[5].

ARTICLE 6: RIGHT TO A FAIR TRIAL

3.23 In the determination of his civil rights and obligations or of any criminal charge against him, everyone is entitled to a fair and public hearing within a reasonable time by an independent and impartial tribunal established by law.

Generally

3.24 Article 6 holds a paramount position in the Convention; its key principle being fairness. As such, it will have a pre-eminent place in our domestic law. It applies to both civil and criminal proceedings, although the contracting States have a greater latitude when dealing with civil cases[6].

3.25 Although paras 2 and 3 are expressed as applying to criminal proceedings, the Court has also held them to be implicit requirements in respect of fairness in proceedings generally[7]. They include: (i) a presumption of innocence; (ii) the right to be informed of the accusation; (iii) the right to adequate time and facilities for the preparation of the defence; (iv) the right to defend or to have legal assistance; (v) the right to examine witnesses; (vi) the right to an interpreter; and will apply to contempt and committal proceedings arising out of civil proceedings.

These requirements under Art 6(2) and (3) will be relevant in contempt and committal proceedings in family cases, especially in those cases where unrepresented parties are brought before the court on a power of arrest. Article 6 has also been applied to proceedings involving administrative decisions on an individual's rights and obligations.

3.26 For Art 6 to apply:

– the rights and obligations claimed must be private 'civil rights and obligations';

---

1 11 EHRR 175.
2 See *Re AS (Secure Accommodation Order)* [1999] 1 FLR 103, where Bracewell J emphasised the importance of procedural fairness and, therefore, post-implementation of the HRA 1998 the procedural requirements under Art 6 are likely to demand strict compliance.
3 *Re C (Detention: Medical Treatment)* [1997] 2 FLR 180.
4 11 EHRR 175.
5 11 EHRR 1; see also *Abbott v UK* Application No 15006/89, (1990) 67 DR 290 (secure accommodation).
6 *Dombo Beheer v Netherlands* 18 EHRR 213, para 32 (see **p 320**).
7 *Albert and Le Compte v Belgium* 5 EHRR 533, para 30 (see **p 307**).

– there must be an arguable claim in domestic law, the decision on which will be determinative of the civil rights and obligations;
– there must be a 'contestation' or dispute about those rights and obligations of a genuine and of a serious nature.

Civil rights and obligations

3.27   'Civil rights and obligations' refer to rights and obligations in private law[1] and have been interpreted widely.

Article 6 applies to:

– family private law cases[2];
– public law decisions such as placing children in care[3], involving parental contact to children[4], fostering[5], and adoption[6], where State action is directly determinative of the right;
– child abduction;
– domestic violence cases and secure accommodation applications;
– ancillary relief applications.

3.28   A right to property is also recognised as a civil right for the purposes of Art 6. Decisions as to bankruptcy[7] and the capacity to administer property[8] have been held to be subject to Art 6.

3.29   Certain rights involving an individual and the State have, however, been classified as public law rights and, therefore, as being outside the scope of Art 6. These include rights concerning immigration and nationality[9], State education[10], the right to medical treatment[11], legal aid in civil cases[12], although some of these cases may well be re-examined in the future. Issues such as welfare benefits, for example, which were initially held to be outside the ambit of Art 6, have subsequently been held to fall within its scope.

In certain circumstances, it may not apply to assessments imposed by the Child Support Agency[13].

Basis in domestic law
3.30   In *H v Belgium*[14], the Court held:

---

1   *Ringeisen v Austria* 1 EHRR 455, para 94 (see **p 351**); *H v Belgium* 10 EHRR 339, paras 44–47 (see **p 329**).
2   *Airey v Ireland* 2 EHRR 305, para 21 (judicial separation) (see **p 306**); *Rasmussen v Denmark* 7 EHRR 371, para 32 (paternity) (see **p 349**).
3   *Olsson v Sweden (No 1)* 11 EHRR 259 (see **p 347**).
4   *W v UK* 10 EHRR 29 (see **p 358**); *Eriksson v Sweden* 12 EHRR 183 (see **p 323**).
5   *Eriksson v Sweden* (above).
6   *Keegan v Ireland* 18 EHRR 342, para 57 (see **p 340**).
7   *Anca v Belgium* Application No 10259/83, (1994) 40 DR 170.
8   *Winterwerp v Netherlands* 2 EHRR 387 (followed from a decision to detain a mentally disordered person).
9   *Agee v UK* Application No 7729/76, (1976) 7 DR 164 (deportation); *X, Y, Z, V and W v UK* Application No 3325/67, 10 YB 528 (1967) (entry); *S v Switzerland* Application No 13325/27, (1988) 59 DR 256 (nationality).
10 *Simpson v UK* (1989) 64 DR 188 (elementary education) and *X v FRG* Application No 10192/83, (1984) 7 EHRR 141 (university).
11 *L v Sweden* (1989) 61 DR 62.
12 *X v FRG* (1970) 32 CD 56.
13 *Logan v UK* 22 EHRR CD 181.
14 10 EHRR 339, para 40.

'Article 6(1) extends only to "contestations" (disputes) over (civil) "rights and obligations" which can be said, at least on arguable grounds, to be recognised under domestic law; it does not in itself guarantee any particular content for (civil) "rights and obligations" in the substantive law of the Contracting States.'

The applicant must, therefore, have an arguable claim arising under domestic law, though the argument need only be tenable[1].

Dispute

3.31 The principles which emerge from the Convention case-law include[2]:

– Conformity with the spirit of the Convention requires that the word 'contestation' should not be construed too technically and should be given a substantive rather than formal meaning[3].

– The dispute may relate not only to the actual existence of a right but also its scope or the manner in which it may be exercised[4]. It may concern both questions of fact and questions of law[5].

– The dispute must also be 'genuine and of a serious nature'[6]. In *Logan v UK*[7], for example, which concerned a complaint about the amount of child maintenance imposed by the Child Support Agency, the Commission concluded that there was no dispute of a genuine or serious nature about any civil right or obligation where the applicant accepted that the maintenance imposed by the CSA was calculated correctly under domestic legislation and it was uncontested that there was no scope under the applicable provisions for the costs of access visits to be taken account of in the assessment, which was the basis of the applicant's claims.

– Private civil rights or obligations have to be the object of the dispute and the result of the proceedings must be directly decisive for such a right. Mere tenuous connections or remote consequences do not suffice for Art 6[8]. The character of the legislation which governs the matter to be determined (civil, commercial, administrative law etc) and that of the authority which is invested with jurisdiction in the matter (ordinary court, administrative body etc) are of little consequence[9]; what matters is whether the outcome of the proceedings is decisive for private rights and obligations.

Administrative decisions

3.32 Article 6 applies to administrative decisions, where they are directly decisive of an individual's civil rights and obligations, and it requires that the State provide a right to challenge the decision before a tribunal with the Art 6 guarantees[10].

---

1   *Neves e Silva v Portugal* (1989) Series A, No 153–A, para 37.
2   *Benthem v Netherlands* 8 EHRR 1, para 32 (see **p 312**).
3   *Le Compte, Van Leuven and De Meyere v Belgium* 4 EHRR 1, para 45.
4   Ibid, para 49.
5   Ibid, para 51.
6   *Benthem v Netherlands* 8 EHRR 1, para 32.
7   22 EHRR CD 181.
8   *Ringeisen v Austria* 1 EHRR 455, para 94; *Le Compte, Van Leuven and De Meyre v Belgium* (above), para 47.
9   *Ringeisen v Austria* (above), para 94.
10   *Le Compte, Van Leuven and De Meyre v Belgium* (above), para 51.

3.33 One of the central questions which has arisen is whether in these circumstances the tribunal should have full jurisdiction to examine the merits of an administrative decision or simply a power of judicial review. The European Court has clearly favoured the full jurisdiction, particularly in child care cases.

3.34 In the seminal (pre-Children Act 1989) family law case of *W v UK*[1], the applicant father complained to the European Court about decisions taken by the local authority restricting and finally terminating his access to his child in care, the absence of remedies against those decisions during the currency of a parental rights resolution affecting him and of the length of the related wardship proceedings. The Court rejected the Government's argument that no 'right' within the ambit of Art 6 was in issue. The Government had contended that the notion of parental 'rights' over children was outmoded; the right being that of the child, not the parent, and, in any event, any parental right ceased to have a separate existence on the making of a care order or the passing of a parental rights resolution.

3.35 The Court held that although under English law access to children in care was a matter for the local authority's discretion, the effect of a care order or a parental rights resolution was not to extinguish the rights and responsibilities of the natural parent in respect of the child. It further emphasised that 'the extinction of all parental rights in regard to access would scarcely be compatible with fundamental notions of family life which Art 8 of the Convention is designed to protect'[2]. The Court went on to hold that although it was open to the father to challenge the parental rights resolution by applying for judicial review, as, on such an application, the courts would not review the merits of the decision, but would confine themselves to ensuring that the authority did not act illegally, unreasonably or unfairly, the availability of judicial review was insufficient to fulfil the rights guaranteed under Art 6. The Court stated that: 'in a case of the present kind' what Art 6 required was that the tribunal have 'jurisdiction to examine the merits' of the local authority decision[3].

3.36 This strong approach of the European Court paves the way for future challenges to local authority decisions in child care cases, particularly in respect of care plans in those cases where currently the domestic court would be left with the stark choice of either accepting an unsatisfactory care plan or refusing to make a much needed care order[4]. Since in child-care cases the children's future rights, in particular, in respect of their relationship with their natural family depend upon the care plan, it is arguable that it cannot be compatible with the Convention for a care judge to be unable to look behind the plan when determining Art 8 rights. Article 6, together with Art 8, may, therefore, provide an effective mechanism for keeping the implementation and progress of the care plan under a measure of judicial control and review after a final care order.

Key cases in respect of the general principles under Art 6 include: *Ringeisen v Austria, Le Compte, Van Leuven and De Meyere v Belgium, Benthem v Netherlands*[5].

---

1   10 EHRR 29.
2   Ibid, para 77.
3   Ibid, para 82.
4   See *Re J (Minors) (Care: Care Plan)* [1994] 1 FLR 253; *Re L (Sexual Abuse: Standard of Proof)* [1996] 1 FLR 116; *Re T (A Minor) (Care Order: Conditions)* [1994] 2 FLR 423; generally *Manchester City Council v F* [1993] 1 FLR 419.
5   All above.

A key family law case in respect of administrative decisions is *W v UK*[1].

The Article 6 guarantees

3.37   Article 6 guarantees the following rights:

–   the right of access to a court;
–   the right to a fair hearing;
–   the right to a hearing within a reasonable time;
–   the right to an independent and impartial tribunal established by law;
–   the right to a public hearing and the public pronouncement of judgment.

Right of access to a court

3.38   One of the most significant steps which the European Court has taken has been to interpret Art 6 as conferring an effective right of access to a court in the determination of civil rights and obligations.

3.39   In *Golder v UK*[2], where a prisoner was refused permission to contact a solicitor with a view to bringing libel proceedings against a prison officer, the Court held that this refusal, by hindering his right of access to the courts, constituted a breach of Art 6. It said:

> 'It would be inconceivable, in the opinion of the Court, that Art 6(1) should describe in detail the procedural guarantees afforded to parties in a pending lawsuit and should not first protect that which alone makes it in fact possible to benefit from such guarantees, that is, access to a court. The fair, public and expeditious characteristics of judicial proceedings are of no value at all if there are no judicial proceedings ... it follows that the right of access constitutes an element which is inherent in the right stated by Art 6(1). The Court thus reaches the conclusion ... that Article 6(1) secures to everyone the right to have any claim relating to his civil rights and obligations brought before a court or tribunal.'[3]

3.40   In the landmark case of *Osman v UK*[4], where the applicant's claim in negligence against the police in the domestic court had been struck out on the ground of public policy, the European Court held that there had been a violation of Art 6 in that the rule excluding action against the police for negligence in the investigation and suppression of crime 'constituted a disproportionate restriction on the Applicant's right of access to a court'. This case is likely to have far-reaching consequences in the context of the tortious liability of local authorities in the exercise of their child protection duties where, to date, public policy considerations have prevailed in the domestic court[5].

3.41   Other potential areas in family law where the right of access under Art 6 may have an impact include: (i) providing for a wider representation of children so as to give them a greater voice in private law proceedings than they presently enjoy under s 10(8) of the Children Act 1989; (ii) challenging orders which may

---

1   Above.
2   1 EHRR 524.
3   Ibid, paras 35 and 36.
4   [1999] 1 FLR 193.
5   *X (Minors) v Bedfordshire County Council* [1995] 2 AC 663. See also *Barrett v Enfield London Borough Council* [1999] 2 FLR 426.

make mediation a prerequisite or alternative to litigation; and (iii) challenging orders under s 91(14) of the Children Act 1989. However, in the latter case, given the margin of appreciation, it is doubtful that the section will be held to be incompatible with Art 6, as access is not denied but is a threshold to cross.

EFFECTIVE ACCESS: LEGAL AID

3.42   The right is a right of *effective* access to a court. This was made clear in *Airey v Ireland*[1], where legal aid was denied to a wife who wished to bring High Court proceedings for a decree of judicial separation but lacked the means to employ a lawyer. The Court emphasised the complexity of the procedure, the complicated points of law, the need to call and examine expert witnesses and the emotional involvement of the parties[2]. It held that in these circumstances the possibility of appearing in person before the High Court did not provide the wife with an effective right of access to the court. For the access to be effective, she required legal representation, which for a person in her financial circumstances meant legal aid.

3.43   The Court said:

> '... Article 6(1) may sometimes compel the State to provide for the assistance of a lawyer when such assistance proves indispensable for an effective access to court either because legal representation is rendered compulsory, as is done by the domestic law of certain Contracting States for various types of litigation, or by reason of the complexity of the procedure or of the case.'

The *Airey* principle is, therefore, potentially of considerable significance in those family cases where legal aid is generally refused such as to defendants in divorce proceedings or in non-molestation injunction proceedings where they can be settled on the basis of undertakings or in the future may be withheld, for example, from litigants until they have attempted mediation under the Family Law Act 1996.

3.44   However, it should be noted that the Commission has attempted to keep the *Airey* principles within narrow confines[3]. In a case concerning a refusal of legal aid for an appeal to the Crown Court in affiliation proceedings, where it was argued that it involved complicated points of law, expert witnesses and emotional involvement, the Commission found no complex point of law and no violation, noting that the applicant fully understood the nature of the proceedings, was able to obtain blood test evidence on his behalf and was able to present his evidence and submissions afresh. Nor did the fact that the child's mother was legally aided constitute the refusal of legal aid for him a breach of Art 6. The Commission has recognised that, given the limited resources available, a system of legal aid can operate effectively only by establishing a machinery to select those cases which should be legally aided by imposing limitations, such as requiring a financial contribution or that the proposed litigation has a reasonable prospect of success, provided the decision whether or not to grant legal aid is not taken arbitrarily[4].

---

1   2 EHRR 305, para 24 (see p 306).
2   Ibid.
3   *AW Webb v UK* Application No 9353/81, (11 May 1983) 33 DR 133; *W v FRG* Application No 11564/85 (Dec), (4 December 1985) 45 DR 291.
4   *X v UK* Application No 8158/78, (10 July 1980) 21 DR 95.

3.45 Further, it has been established that, to be effective, the right of access under Art 6 requires that a person be given personal and reasonable notice of any administrative decision which interferes with his civil rights and obligations, so that he has adequate time to challenge it in court[1].

THE *ASHINGDANE* PRINCIPLES

3.46 The right of access to the courts is, however, not absolute but may be subject to limitations which are permitted by implication, since the right of access 'by its very nature calls for regulation by the State, regulation which may vary in time and place according to the needs and resources of the community and of individuals'[2].

3.47 This has given rise to the following '*Ashingdane* principles':

– In laying down such regulations the State enjoys a certain 'margin of appreciation' but the limitations applied must not restrict or reduce the access left to the individual in such a way or to such an extent that 'the very essence of the right' is impaired[3].

– Furthermore, a limitation will not be compatible with Art 6(1) if it does not pursue a legitimate aim and if there is not a reasonable relationship of proportionality between the means employed and the aim sought to be achieved[4].

3.48 In accordance with these Ashingdane principles, limitation periods for bringing claims are permitted, insofar as they serve the legitimate aims of ensuring legal certainty and finality, protect potential defendants from stale claims and evidential unreliability because of the passage of time[5].

3.49 In *Stubbings v UK*[6], the applicants were sexual abuse victims who claimed that the psychological after-effects of abuse prevented them from realising they had a cause of action against the abusers until after the expiry of the limitation period of six years from the age of majority. The Court held that the limitation period did not impair the very essence of the right of access to the court and there was no violation. However, it did say:

> 'There has been developing awareness in recent years of the range of problems caused by child abuse and its psychological effects on victims, and it is possible that the rules on limitation of actions applying in member States ... may have to be amended to make special provision for this group of claimants in the future.'[7]

PUBLIC POLICY IMMUNITIES

3.50 Further difficulties arise where there is an immunity which prevents a claim being brought. *Ashingdane v UK*[8] itself concerned a statutory immunity which barred civil actions by mental patients against staff or health authorities.

---

1   *De La Pradelle v France* (1992) Series A, No 253-B.
2   *Golder v UK* (above), para 38.
3   *Ashingdane v UK* 7 EHRR 528, para 57.
4   Ibid.
5   *Stubbings v UK* 23 EHRR 213, para 49 (see **p 356**).
6   Ibid; see also *X v Sweden* Application No 9707/82 (Rep), (6 October 1982) 31 DR 223 (a paternity case).
7   *Stubbings v UK* 23 EHRR 213, para 54.
8   Above; also *Fayed v UK* 18 EHRR 393 (see **p 325**).

The Court found that the legislative restrictions on recourse to court by mental patients were intended to reduce the risk of unfair harassment of those responsible for their case and that this was a legitimate aim. In those circumstances, the restrictions limiting the liability of the responsible authorities to acts done negligently or in bad faith did not impair the essence of the applicant's right to a court or transgress the principle of proportionality[1].

3.51   However, the issue of public policy immunity was considered by the European Court in the recent case of *Osman v UK*[2]. The applicants' negligence claim against the police had been struck out on the ground that public policy required police immunity from suit in relation to the investigation and suppression of crime. The applicants argued in the European Court that although they had established all the constituent elements of the duty of care[3], the domestic court had been constrained by precedent to apply the doctrine of police immunity developed by the House of Lords in *Hill v Chief Constable of West Yorkshire*[4]. The European Court held that the applicants must be taken to have a right to seek an adjudication on the admissibility and merits of an arguable claim and that, therefore, Art 6(1) was applicable. The Court went on to hold that the application of the exclusionary rule constituted a disproportionate restriction on the applicants' right of access to the court and was a breach of Art 6(1). It observed that:

> 'the application of the rule in this manner without further inquiry into the existence of competing public interest considerations only serves to confer a blanket immunity on the police ... and amounts to an unjustifiable restriction on an applicant's right to have a determination on the merits of his or her claim against the police in deserving cases.'[5]

3.52   *Osman v UK* is likely to have a fundamental impact upon cases concerning breaches of the local authorities' statutory duty and common law duty of care in safeguarding the welfare of children. In *X (Minors) v Bedfordshire County Council*[6], the House of Lords took into account public policy considerations and held that: (i) the statutes concerned did not create a private law remedy; and that (ii) in child abuse cases there was no direct duty of care, as such a duty would cut across the statutory system for the protection of children and might, in a delicate situation, make local authorities adopt a more cautious approach to the prejudice of children. Whether such an approach will be maintained in the future in the face of Art 6(1) is now open to doubt, particularly as these doubts have recently been reinforced by the House of Lords' decision in *Barrett v Enfield London Borough Council*[7].

Key cases in respect of the right of access under Art 6 include: *Golder v UK, Osman v UK, Airey v Ireland, Ashingdane v UK* and *Stubbings v UK*[8].

---

1   *Ashingdane v UK* (above), paras 56–59.
2   [1999] 1 FLR 193.
3   Ie (i) the proximity of the parties; (ii) the foreseeability of harm; (iii) the fairness, justice and reasonableness of imposing a duty of care.
4   [1989] AC 53.
5   [1999] 1 FLR 193 at 232 B–C.
6   [1995] 2 AC 633.
7   [1999] 2 FLR 426 at 430H–433A, per Lord Browne-Wilkinson.
8   All above.

Right to a fair hearing

3.53 The 'fair hearing guarantee' includes:

- the principle of 'equality of arms';
- freedom from self-incrimination;
- access to evidence;
- presence in court;
- adversarial argument;
- reasons for the judgment.

THE PRINCIPLE OF 'EQUALITY OF ARMS'

3.54 In *Dombo Beheer v The Netherlands*[1], the Court held:

> 'It is clear that the requirement of "equality of arms", in the sense of a "fair balance" between the parties, applies in principle to "cases concerning civil rights and obligations" as well as to criminal cases. The Court agrees with the Commission that as regards litigation involving opposing private interests, "equality of arms" implies that each party must be afforded a reasonable opportunity to present his case – including his evidence – under conditions that do not place him at a substantial disadvantage vis-à-vis his opponent.'

3.55 The European Court has emphasised that the concept of a fair trial, of which the principle of the equality of arms is a principal feature, 'has undergone a considerable evolution in the Court's case-law, notably in respect of the importance attached to appearances and to the increased sensitivity of the public to the fair administration of justice'[2]. It is arguable, therefore, that the applicant does not have to demonstrate an actual absence of equality but need only show a potential lack of procedural equality.

3.56 The principle of 'equality of arms' has been held to require: (i) equal treatment between the court-appointed expert and the expert witness for the defence[3]; and (ii) parties to civil proceedings to be allowed to cross-examine witnesses[4] and be informed of the detailed reasons for an administrative decision so as to enable the applicant to mount a reasoned challenge to it[5].

3.57 In family law, the principle of 'equality of arms' has the potential for making a considerable impact upon the current practice relating to expert reports in child care cases where complex medical issues are involved.

FREEDOM FROM SELF-INCRIMINATION

3.58 In *Saunders v UK*[6], a criminal case concerning the use at a trial of statements by the accused previously obtained by DTI inspectors, the European Court recalled that:

> 'Although not specifically mentioned in Art 6 of the Convention, the right to silence and the right not to incriminate oneself are generally recognised international standards, which lie at the heart of the notion of a fair procedure under Art 6.'

---

1   18 EHRR 213, paras 32–33; also *Stran Greek Refineries and Stratis Andeadis v Greece* (1994) Series A, No 301-B, paras 46 and 49; *Feldbrugge v The Netherlands* 8 EHRR 425, para 44 (see **p 327**); *Van de Hurk v The Netherlands* 18 EHRR 481, para 57.
2   *Borgers v Belgium* 15 EHRR 92, para 24 (see **p 313**).
3   *Bonisch v Austria* 9 EHRR 191, paras 32 and 33–34.
4   *X v Austria* Application No 5362/72, (1972) 42 CD 145.
5   *Hentrich v France* 18 EHRR 440, para 56.
6   23 EHRR 313, para 68 (see **p 353**); also *Funke v France* 16 EHRR 297 para 44.

3.59   The Court rejected the argument that only statements which are self-incriminating could fall within the privilege against self-incrimination and held that 'bearing in mind the concept of fairness in Art 6, the right not to incriminate oneself cannot reasonably be confined to statements of admission of wrongdoing or to remarks which are directly incriminating'. However, it went on to say that whether a particular applicant has been subject to compulsion to incriminate himself so as to render the proceedings unfair and thus a breach of Art 6 will 'depend upon an assessment of the circumstances of each case as a whole'[1].

3.60   In family law, the privilege against self-incrimination was considered by the House of Lords in *Re L (A Minor) (Police Investigation: Privilege)*[2] in the context of the disclosure of an unfavourable expert report. As on the particular facts privilege had been waived, it was found unnecessary to decide whether in law the report was protected from disclosure by the privilege against self-incrimination. Although the Convention case-law has to date considered the privilege against self-incrimination in the field of criminal proceedings, there is clearly scope in the future to review the whole area of privilege in the light of Art 6.

3.61   Furthermore, Arts 6 and 8 are likely to have a significant impact: (i) upon the High Court's current view[3] that, in all cases where the welfare of the child is the court's paramount consideration, there is a positive duty upon parties and their legal advisers to make full and frank disclosure of all matters material to welfare whether favourable or adverse to their own case; and (ii) generally upon the whole issue of litigation privilege in the context of the Children Act 1989[4].

3.62   A further problematic area concerns the confidentiality of parents' evidence in care proceedings where criminal proceedings are pending. In a recent first instance decision, *Re L (Care: Confidentiality)*[5], the limited protection provided by s 98(2) of the Children Act 1989 which concerns the non-admissibility of statements or admissions made in care proceedings in proceedings for an offence other than perjury, was highlighted. It was argued that s 98 did not preclude a parent being cross-examined as to such statements or admissions in the criminal proceedings. Johnson J said[6]:

> 'Initially, I had thought that it would be possible to achieve absolute protection for the parents by making an injunction the effect of which would be to preclude any party or person present at the hearing of the care proceedings from divulging anything said whether in writing or orally by the parents except for the purpose of arriving at decisions about the future upbringing of the children. . . . On reflection it seems to me that no injunction . . . could afford absolute protection . . . Indeed such an injunction, and possibly s 98(2) itself, might fall foul of Art 6 of the European Convention on Human Rights.'

---

1   *Saunders* (above), para 73.
2   [1997] AC 16. At the time of writing, the case of *Re L* is pending in the European Court.
3   *Oxfordshire County Council v P* [1995] Fam 161; also *Essex County Council v R (Note)* [1994] Fam 167 and *In Re DH (A Minor) (Child Abuse)* [1994] 1 FLR 679; see also dissenting judgment of Lord Nicholls of Birkenhead in *In Re L (A Minor) (Police Investigation: Privilege)* [1997] AC 16 at 35D–36D.
4   *In Re L (A Minor)* (above), in particular the dissenting judgment of Lord Nicholls at 30–35; *Vernon v Bosely (No 2)* [1998] 1 FLR 804. NOTE: *Niemitz v Germany* 16 EHRR 19 where the Court recognised legal professional privilege (see **p 346**).
5   [1999] 1 FLR 165.
6   Ibid, at 168 E–G.

ACCESS TO EVIDENCE

3.63 It is not inherent in the right to a fair hearing under Art 6 that any particular evidential rules must be followed in the domestic courts. Evidential rules are, therefore, a matter for each contracting State[1]. By way of example, in *G v France*[2] it was held that rules as to the burden of proof in civil proceedings were for the domestic courts to determine.

3.64 Nevertheless, boundaries have been established. For example, Art 6 has been held to require that a party be allowed to consult the relevant evidence which is available to the authorities[3] and to obtain the attendance and examination of witnesses on his behalf under the same conditions as witnesses against him (as under Art 6(3)(d) in criminal cases). Further, in *Hendriks v The Netherlands*[4], where the applicant father in a contact case was allowed to read a report of the Council for the Protection of Children but not to keep a copy, the Commission did not exclude that such circumstances may prejudice an applicant's position before the Court, so as to constitute a breach of Art 6[5].

3.65 In *H v France*[6], which concerned a clinical negligence claim against a hospital, the applicant submitted that a failure to appoint an expert to determine the causal link between the hospital's negligence and his disability, despite his express requests, contravened Art 6(1). The Government contended that it was for the court to judge whether the measure requested would serve any useful purpose. The European Court agreed with the Government, but added that the Court 'must, however, ascertain whether the proceedings as a whole were fair as required by Article 6(1)'. This leaves open the possibility that, on the particular facts of a case, the refusal of a court to order an expert report at the request of a party may cause the hearing to be unfair and, consequently, a violation of Art 6.

PRESENCE IN COURT

3.66 In civil cases, a right to appear in person may be implied in the right to a fair hearing in certain particular circumstances; for example, where an assessment of a party's conduct is involved[7] or where 'the personal character and manner of life' of a party is directly relevant[8]. The right will, therefore, generally apply to family cases.

3.67 The right to be present at an appeal, however, depends upon the special features of the proceedings involved, the role of the appellate court and the particular facts of the case[9]. This is an area where the national authorities have a margin of appreciation.

3.68 The right to be present at an oral hearing may be waived, but for the waiver to be effective it must be established in an unequivocal manner and be attended by minimum safeguards commensurate to its importance[10].

---

1   *Schenk v Switzerland* 13 EHRR 242, para 46.
2   Application No 11941/86, (1988) 57 DR 100.
3   *Feldbrugge v The Netherlands* 8 EHRR 425.
4   5 EHRR 223.
5   Ibid, para 142; see also *McMichael v UK* 20 EHRR 205, para 80 (below) (see **p 344**).
6   12 EHRR 74, paras 60 and 61.
7   *Muyldermans v Belgium* 15 EHRR 204, paras 62–64.
8   *X v Sweden* Application No 434/58, (1959) 2 YB 354 at 372.
9   *Ekbatani v Sweden* 13 EHRR 504, para 27.
10 *Poitrimol v France* 18 EHRR 130, para 31.

3.69   In the field of family law, the right to give oral evidence implied in the right to fair trial under Art 6 is likely to be relevant in those cases where currently there is no oral evidence, for example, in child abduction cases[1] or in ex parte applications such as the making of emergency protection orders. There may also be an argument under Art 6 for more fully contested interim care proceedings in which at present orders are frequently made without oral evidence, and where 'issue estoppel' is argued.

ADVERSARIAL ARGUMENT
3.70   It has been held to be a requirement of a fair trial that the proceedings are 'adversarial' which broadly means that 'all evidence must in principle be produced in the presence of the party with a view to adversarial argument'[2].

3.71   In *McMichael v UK*[3], the applicants had been unable to see confidential reports and documents submitted before and during care proceedings concerning their children. The Court held that whilst in the sensitive domain of family law involving children there may be good reasons for opting for an adjudicatory body (of specially trained persons with substantial experience of children) that does not have the composition or procedure of a court of law of the classic kind (in that it follows a procedure which is less formal and confrontational than that of ordinary courts), nevertheless,

> 'as a matter of general principle the right to a fair – adversarial – trial means the opportunity to have the knowledge of and comment on the observations filed or evidence adduced.'[4]

It concluded that the lack of disclosure of such vital documents as social reports was a breach of Art 6, as it was capable of affecting the ability of participating parents not only to influence the outcome of the children hearing but also to assess their prospects on appeal. It further found that the requirement of an adversarial trial had not been fulfilled.

3.72   Article 6 therefore creates a general requirement of fairness and openness in adversarial litigation. This is particularly important in litigation between the State and parents in respect of children, but also applies to private law cases. The domestic court's present approach is that 'care proceedings are essentially non-adversarial'[5]. This is an approach which, upon incorporation, is potentially incompatible with the rights guaranteed under Art 6 which require adversarial argument and, therefore, may require re-consideration.

REASONS FOR THE JUDGMENT
3.73   A fair hearing requires that national courts must give reasons for their judgments, which 'indicate with sufficient clarity the grounds on which they based the decision', so as to make it 'possible for a party to exercise usefully the right of

---

1   See the argument in *Re K (Abduction: Psychological Harm)* [1995] 2 FLR 550 in respect of Art 20 of the Hague Convention on Child Abduction at 556C–557E, per Leggatt LJ.
2   *Barbera, Messegue and Jabardo v Spain* 11 EHRR 360, para 78.
3   20 EHRR 205.
4   Ibid, para 80; also *Lobo Machado v Portugal* 23 EHRR 79, para 31.
5   *In Re L (A Minor) (Police Investigation: Privilege)* [1997] AC 16 at 26H, per Lord Jauncey of Tullichettle; also *Oxfordshire County Council v M* [1994] Fam 151.

appeal available to him'[1]. However, although Art 6(1) obliges the courts to give reasons for their judgments, it does not require a detailed answer to every argument. The extent to which this duty applies may vary according to the nature of the decision[2], but should include final decisions and any ruling which is decisive of the outcome.

Key cases in respect of the right to a fair hearing under Art 6 include: *Dombo Beheer v The Netherlands, Borgers v Belgium, Saunders v UK, Barbera Messegue and Jabardo v Spain* and *Hadjianastassiou v Greece*[3].

A right to a hearing within a reasonable time

3.74   Article 6(1) requires that cases be heard within a reasonable time and 'underlines the importance of rendering justice without delays which might jeopardise its effectiveness and credibility'[4].

3.75   In family cases, time runs from the initiation of the court proceedings and continues until the case is finally determined including any appeal[5]. The reasonableness of the length of the proceedings depends on the particular circumstances of the case, the relevant factors being:

– the complexity of the case;
– the conduct of the parties;
– the manner in which the matter was dealt with by the administrative and judicial authorities[6];
– the importance of what is at stake for the applicant[7].

3.76   Special emphasis has been placed on this last factor in cases concerning children. In *H v UK*[8], where a mother complained of the 'deplorable delay' of almost 2 years in court proceedings concerning contact to her child in care (by which time she had not seen her child for 3½ years and the child had become settled with prospective adopters), the Court stressed that:

> 'not only were the proceedings decisive for her future relations with her own child, but they had a particular quality of irreversibility, involving as they did what the (domestic) High Court graphically described as the "statutory guillotine" of adoption. In cases of this kind the authorities are under a duty to exercise exceptional diligence since . . . there is always the danger that any procedural delay will result in the de facto determination of the issue submitted to the court before it has held the hearing. And, indeed, this was what happened here.'[9]

In addition, only delays attributable to the State may justify a finding of a failure to comply with the 'reasonable time' requirement[10]. Examples include delays in the conduct of the hearing by the court[11] and in issuing judgment[12].

---

1   *Hadjianastassiou v Greece* 16 EHRR 219, para 33 (see **p 330**); *H v Belgium* 10 EHRR 339, para 53.
2   *Hiro Balani v Spain* 19 EHRR 566, para 27.
3   All above.
4   *H v France* 12 EHRR 74, para 58.
5   *H v UK* 10 EHRR 95, para 70.
6   *König v FRG* 2 EHRR 170, para 99.
7   *H v UK* (above) paras 71 and 85.
8   Ibid.
9   Ibid, para 85.
10   Ibid, para 71.
11   *König v FRG* (above).
12   *Reilly v Ireland* Application No 21624/93 (Rep), 22 February 1995.

3.77 Although the State is not responsible for delays which are attributable to the applicant, this does not 'absolve the courts from ensuring compliance with the requirements of Art 6 concerning reasonable time'[1]. It is, therefore, the State's obligation to take appropriate steps to ensure that proceedings are prosecuted expeditiously and 'to organise their legal systems so as to allow the courts to comply with the requirements of Art 6(1)'[2]. Excuses that a large number of cases are pending, therefore, are unacceptable. If, however, the authorities move expeditiously to remedy an exceptional situation, a temporary backlog will not constitute a breach[3].

3.78 Delay in children's cases in future, therefore, will not only be prejudicial to the welfare of the child under s 1(2) of the Children Act 1989 but also be a breach of Art 6 of the Convention.

Right to an independent and impartial tribunal
3.79 Article 6(1) guarantees the right to a hearing before an independent and impartial tribunal established by law.

3.80 'Tribunal' is categorised by its judicial function and must satisfy the requirements of independence, impartiality, duration of its members' terms of office and procedural guarantees[4]. 'Independent' means 'independent of the executive and also of the parties'[5]. In determining independence, regard may be had to 'the manner of appointment of the members and the duration of their term of office, the existence of guarantees against outside pressures and the question whether the body presents an appearance of independence'[6]. 'Impartiality' normally denotes absence of prejudice or bias[7]. The existence of impartiality for the purpose of Art 6(1) must be determined '(1) according to a subjective test, that is on the basis of the personal conviction of a particular judge in a given case and also (2) according to an objective test, that is ascertaining whether the judge offered guarantees sufficient to exclude any legitimate doubt in this respect'[8].

Right to a public hearing and public pronouncement
3.81 Article 6(1) provides that everyone is entitled to a public hearing and to a judgment pronounced publicly. This right to a public hearing is, however, subject to express restrictions in Art 6(1), namely that 'the press and public may be excluded from all or part of the trial in the interests of morals ... where the interests of juveniles or the private lives of the parties so require or to the extent strictly necessary in the opinion of the court in special circumstances where publicity would prejudice the interests of justice'. The court may apply a proportionality test in deciding whether a restriction is justified.

3.82 In family proceedings, the exclusion of the public from divorce proceedings has been justified as being for the protection of the private lives of the

1   *Union Alimentaria Sanders SA v Spain* (1989) Series A, No 157, para 35.
2   *Buchholz v FRG* 3 EHRR 597, para 51.
3   Ibid, para 51; *Zimmermann and Steiner v Switzerland* 6 EHRR 17, para 29.
4   *Belilos v Switzerland* 10 EHRR 466, para 64.
5   *Ringeisen v Austria* 1 EHRR 455, para 95; *Le Compte, Van Leuven and De Meyere v Belgium* 4 EHRR 1, para 55.
6   *Campbell and Fell v UK* 7 EHRR 165, para 78.
7   *Piersack v Belgium* 5 EHRR 169, para 30.
8   *Hauschildt v Denmark* 12 EHRR 266, para 46.

parties[1]. Equally, the exclusion of the press and the public from cases concerning children is justifiable as being in the interests of juveniles or for the protection of their private lives.

3.83 The current practice of hearing children cases in private has already been considered by the Court of Appeal in the light of Art 6 in *Re PB (Hearings in Open Court)*[2]. The father's application for the hearing of the parties' residence applications to be in open court had been refused at first instance and, on appeal, the long-established practice in the High Court and county court of hearing children cases in private was upheld. In considering Art 6, Butler-Sloss LJ said[3]: 'It would seem to me that the present procedures in family proceedings are in accordance with the spirit of the Convention'.

3.84 Peter Gibson LJ, in agreement with Butler-Sloss LJ, did not regard the present practice as inconsistent with Art 6 and noted that the Article itself recognises that the right to a public trial is qualified where the interests of juveniles or the protection of private life of the parties so require.

3.85 A question which may arise in the future under Art 6 is whether the hearing of ancillary relief cases in chambers can be justified as being for the protection of private lives. In Scotland, for example, ancillary relief applications are heard in open court.

3.86 The right to a public hearing, however, is not automatic in respect of appeal proceedings. The Court has held on a number of occasions that:

> 'provided that there has been a public hearing at first instance, the absence of public hearings before a second and third instance may be justified by the special features of the proceedings at issue. Thus, leave to appeal proceedings and proceedings involving only questions of law, as opposed to questions of fact, may comply with the requirements of Art 6, although the appellant was not given an opportunity of being heard in person by the appeal court.'[4]

A party may also waive the right to a public hearing, provided the waiver is unequivocal and does not run counter to any important public interest consideration[5].

3.87 Although the right to public pronouncement is expressed in absolute terms and is not subject to any exceptions, the Court has rejected a literal interpretation and held that the form of the 'publicity' to be given to the judgment in domestic law must be assessed in the light of the special features of the proceedings and by reference to the object and purpose of Art 6(1)[6]. It was recognised that 'many member States ... have a longstanding tradition of recourse to other means, besides reading out aloud, for making public the decisions of all or some of their courts ... for example, deposit in a registry accessible to the public'[7].

---

1   *X v UK* Application No 7366/76, (1977) 2 Digest 452.
2   [1996] 2 FLR 765.
3   Ibid, at 768C–E.
4   *Ekbatani v Sweden* 13 EHRR 504, para 31; *Monnell and Morris v UK* 10 EHRR 205, para 58 (leave to appeal).
5   *Hakansson v Sweden* 13 EHRR 1, para 66.
6   *Pretto v Italy* 6 EHRR 182, para 26; *Axen v Germany* 6 EHRR 195, para 31; *Sutter v Switzerland* 6 EHRR 272, paras 32–34.
7   *Axen v Germany* 6 EHRR 195, para 31.

3.88   In the context of this right of public pronouncement under Art 6, it is interesting to note Peter Gibson's observation in the *Re PB* case: 'It is a future question whether judgment should be given in open court'[1]. He went on to say:

> 'Under English law it need not be so given. But the Court has power to give judgment publicly and in exercising its discretion it can take into account the provision of Art 6(1) that judgment should be pronounced publicly, though if so pronounced, it should be done in such a way as to avoid detriment to the child.'[2]

The public pronouncement of judgments is, therefore, an area which may well have to be re-examined upon incorporation of the Convention[3].

ARTICLE 8: THE RIGHT TO RESPECT FOR PRIVATE AND FAMILY LIFE

3.89   Article 8 directly concerns family law and will have an important influence upon its future development. Article 8(1) provides that everyone has the right to respect for his private and family life, his home and his correspondence. Article 8(2) sets out the conditions upon which the State may interfere with the enjoyment of the right, namely that there shall be no interference by a public authority with the exercise of the right except such as: (a) is in accordance with the law; and (b) is necessary in a democratic society (i) in the interests of national security, public safety or the economic well-being of the country, (ii) for the prevention of disorder or crime, (iii) for the protection of health or morals, or (iv) for the protection of the rights and freedoms of others.

3.90   In Convention cases, the European Court has adopted the practice of considering each of the following stages in turn:
–   scope of the right;
–   nature of the interference which is alleged to restrict the enjoyment of the right;
–   lawfulness of the interference;
–   legitimate aims of the interference;
–   necessity for the interference in democratic society, ie whether there are relevant and sufficient reasons for the interference which are proportionate to the restriction on the enjoyment of the right when taking into account the margin of appreciation.

The scope of the Article 8 right

3.91   In *Kroon v The Netherlands*[4], the European Court stated that the essential object of Art 8 is 'to protect the individual against arbitrary action by the public authorities'.

3.92   Article 8(1) protects the right to *respect* for private and family life. In *X and Y v The Netherlands*[5], the European Court stated the underlying principle as follows:

---

1   *Re PB (Hearings in Open Court)* [1996] 2 FLR 765 at 770F.
2   Ibid, at 770F–G; see Family Proceedings Rules 1991, r 4.16(7).
3   See also *Hodgson v Imperial Tobacco* [1998] 1 WLR 1056.
4   19 EHRR 263, para 31 (see **p 342**).
5   8 EHRR 235, para 23; also the earlier case of *Marckx v Belgium* 2 EHRR 330, para 31.

'(Art 8) does not merely compel the State to abstain from ... interference: in addition to this primarily negative undertaking, there may be positive obligations inherent in an effective respect for private and family life ... These obligations may involve the adoption of measures designed to secure respect for private life even in the sphere of the relations of individuals beween themselves.'

The 'positive obligations' inherent in Art 8, therefore, include those which oblige the State to take action:

– to ensure that the right is secured for the individual; and
– to ensure that the individual's right is protected against infringements by other individuals[1].

3.93 However, the boundaries between the State's positive and negative obligations under Art 8 do not lend themselves to precise definition. The applicable principles are, therefore, that 'in both contexts regard must be had to the fair balance that has to be struck between the competing interests of the individual and the community as a whole; and in both contexts the State enjoys a certain margin of appreciation'[2].

Private life
3.94 The concept of private life is not limited to a right to privacy but also includes the right to establish and develop relationships with other human beings. In *Niemitz v Germany*[3], the Court said:

'... it would be too restrictive to limit the notion (of private life) to an 'inner circle' in which the individual may live his own personal life as he chooses and to exclude therefrom entirely the outside world not encompassed within that circle. Respect for private life must also comprise to a certain degree the right to establish and develop relationships with other human beings.'[4]

THE CATEGORIES OF PRIVATE LIFE
3.95 The categories of 'private life' have been interpreted widely to include the following aspects of family law.

Gender
3.96 In three post-operative transsexual cases, *Rees v UK*[5], *Cossey v UK*[6] and *Sheffield and Horsham v UK*[7], the Court has held that there was no obligation on the State to change the birth certificates of transsexuals to reflect their new identities. In the *Sheffield* case, the Court found that in view of absence of any noteworthy scientific development in the area of transsexualism since the *Rees* judgment and the lack of a sufficiently broad consensus among the contracting States on how to deal with the range of the complex issues raised by transsexualism, individual States remained entitled to rely on the margin of appreciation to defend a refusal to recognise in law a transsexual's post-operative gender[8]. The Court was not

---

1   *Airey v Ireland* 2 EHRR 305, para 32.
2   *Kroon v The Netherlands* 19 EHRR 263, para 31.
3   16 EHRR 97.
4   Ibid, para 29.
5   9 EHRR 56.
6   13 EHRR 622 (see **p 319**).
7   [1998] 2 FLR 928 (see **p 354**).
8   Ibid, paras 55 at 940F–G and 58 at 941D–F.

persuaded on the facts that the detriment suffered was sufficiently serious as to override the State's margin of appreciation as was the case in *B v France*[1] where a transsexual suffered humiliating aggravation through being unable to obtain a change of name and papers to reflect the change of gender. In *B v France*, the detriment (which included the refusal to change her birth certificate and forename which were permissible under French law and the difficulties she experienced in the area of social and professional integration) was held to be sufficiently serious and the Court found a breach of Art 8.

Sexual life

3.97   In *Dudgeon v UK*[2], a case concerning the private activities of adult homosexuals, the Court described sexual life as being 'the most intimate aspect' of private life[3]. The applicant had complained that under the law in force he was liable to criminal prosecution on account of his homosexual conduct whether the act took place in public or private and irrespective of the age or consent of the participants and that the very existence of the law caused him fear of harassment and blackmail. The Court said:

> 'the maintenance in force of the impugned legislation constitutes a continuing interference with the applicant's right to respect for his private life (which includes his sexual life) within the meaning of Art 8, paragraph (1).'[4]

Physical and moral integrity of the person

3.98   In the important case of *X and Y v The Netherlands*[5], where a 16-year-old mentally handicapped girl was sexually assaulted but had no legal capacity to appeal against the prosecution's decision not to pursue criminal charges, the Court found that the absence of a practical and effective criminal remedy amounted to a failure on the part of the State to secure respect for her private life. The Court stated that 'the concept of private life covers the physical and moral integrity of the person, including his or her sexual life' and, in considering the positive obligations inherent in an effective respect for family life, emphasised that 'these obligations may involve the adoption of measures designed to secure respect for private life even in the sphere of the relations of individuals between themselves'[6]. Positive obligations further arise in respect of the protection to be afforded to children who have been subjected to physical chastisement in the home and at school[7].

3.99   Private life also encompasses protection against compulsory medical intervention such as compulsory blood tests in paternity actions[8]. In *X v Austria*[9], the applicant complained that the obligation upon him to submit to a blood test in affiliation proceedings was a violation of Art 8. The Commission held that although a compulsory medical intervention, even if it is of minor importance,

---

1   16 EHRR 1 (see **p 310**).
2   4 EHRR 149; also *Norris v Ireland* 13 EHRR 186 and *Modinos v Cyprus* 16 EHRR 485 ('the homosexual cases'); in contrast, *Laskey, Jaggard and Brown v UK* 24 EHRR 39.
3   4 EHRR 149, para 52.
4   Ibid, para 41.
5   8 EHRR 235.
6   Ibid, paras 22 and 23.
7   *Costello-Roberts v UK* 19 EHRR 112; also *A v UK* 27 EHRR 611.
8   *X v Austria* Application No 8278/78, (1979) 18 DR 154.
9   Ibid.

must be considered as an interference with this right, the intervention on the facts was justifiable.

3.100 Generally, intervention, such as compulsory vaccination tests, has been justified on the grounds of health under Art 8(2)[1]. Directions with regard to the medical and psychiatric examination or other assessment of a child under section 38(6) of the Children Act 1989, where the court makes an interim care or supervision order, may nonetheless have to be considered in the light of Art 8.

Personal information

3.101 Access to and protection of personal information falls within the ambit of private life. A seminal case is *Gaskin v UK*[2]. The applicant had been taken into the care of Liverpool City Council and remained in its care for 18 years, during the major part of which he was placed with various foster-parents. The local authority kept certain confidential documents concerning him and his care. The applicant contended that he was ill-treated in care and had attempted to obtain details of the information on these records. Liverpool City Council resolved that the information should be made available subject to the consent of the contributors to the file. A number of the contributors refused their consent and the applicant complained that the refusal of access to all his case records was a breach of Art 8.

3.102 The Court agreed with the Commission that the file provided a substitute record for the memories and experience of the parents of the child who is not in care: 'It no doubt contained information concerning highly personal aspects of the applicant's childhood, development and history and could thus constitute his principal source of information about his past and formative years[3]. The question of his access, therefore, fell within the ambit of Art 8.

3.103 In considering the balance to be struck between the general interest of the community and the interests of the individual, the Court had regard to the fact that confidentiality of public records was of importance for receiving objective and reliable information and that such confidentiality can also be necessary for the protection of third persons. They held that a system, like the British one which makes access to records dependent on the consent of the contributor, can in principle be considered to be compatible with the obligations under Art 8. On the other hand:

> 'persons in the situation of the applicant have a vital interest, protected by the Convention, in receiving information necessary to know and to understand their childhood and early development ... under the (British system), the interests of the individual seeking access to records relating to his private and family life must be secured when a contributor to the records either is not available or improperly refuses consent. Such a system is only in conformity with the principle of proportionality if it provides that an independent authority finally decides whether access has to be granted in cases where the contributor fails to answer or withholds his consent. No such procedure was available to the applicant in the present case.'[4]

3.104 However, their conclusion that there was a breach of Art 8 was reached without expressing any opinion on whether general rights of access to personal

1   *Acmanne v Belgium* Application No 10435/83 (Dec), (10 December 1984) 40 DR 251.
2   12 EHRR 36 (see **p 328**).
3   Ibid, paras 36–37.
4   Ibid, para 49.

data and information may be derived from Art 8. Upon incorporation, this is a field where the domestic court may well find itself called upon to decide such questions of general principle.

3.105   The other important area of personal information is the gathering of medical data and the maintenance of medical records, although this is generally justified under Art 8(2)[1]. The principle of confidentiality has been recently emphasised in *Z v Finland*[2] which concerned the disclosure of sensitive medical information about a person's HIV infection during a criminal trial. The Court said:

> 'the protection of personal data, not least medical data, is of fundamental importance to a person's enjoyment of his or her right to respect for private and family life. Respecting the confidentiality of health data is a vital principle in all the legal systems of all the Contracting Parties . . . It is crucial not only to respect the sense of privacy of a patient but also to preserve his or her confidence in the medical profession and in the health services in general.'[3]

Paternity

3.106   Private life also been held to include issues such as whether a putative parent is the parent of a child. In *Rasmussen v Denmark*[4], the applicant, having divorced his wife, was ordered to pay maintenance for her and her two children and sought to bring proceedings to dispute the paternity of one child out of time, which the national court refused. The Court found that the facts fell within the ambit of Art 8:

> 'Article 8, for its part, protects not only "family" but also "private" life. Even though the paternity proceedings which the applicant wished to institute were aimed at the dissolution of existing family ties, the determination of his legal relations (with the child) undoubtedly concerned his private life.'[5]

It went on to hold that there had been no violation of Art 8.

Name

3.107   Although Art 8 does not contain any explicit reference to names, names have been held to constitute a means of personal identification, a link to a family and to involve the right to establish and develop relationships with others and thus fall within the concept of private life in Art 8[6]. The Court has, however, afforded a wide margin of appreciation as to the restrictions on permissible changes of name.

3.108   In *Stjerna v Finland*[7], where the Finnish applicant claimed that his Swedish surname gave rise to practical difficulties and a pejorative nickname, the Court found that there had been no interference under Art 8 because the sources of inconvenience complained of by the applicant were insufficient to raise an issue of failure to respect his private life. It stated:

---

1   *Yvonne Chave nee Jullien v France* Application No 14461/88 (Dec), (9 July 1991) 71 DR 141.
2   25 EHRR 371.
3   Ibid, para 95.
4   7 EHRR 371; see also *Nyland v Finland* Application No 27110/95 (Dec), (29 June 1999).
5   Ibid, para 33.
6   *Burghartz v Switzerland* 18 EHRR 101, para 24; *Stjerna v Finland* 24 EHRR 195, para 37. See also *Guillot v France* (1996) V No 19 p 1593, paras 21–22 (forenames).
7   24 EHRR 195.

'Despite the increased use of personal identity numbers in Finland and in other Contracting States, names retain a crucial role in the identification of people. Whilst recognising that there may exist genuine reasons prompting an individual to wish to change his or her name, the Court accepts that legal restrictions on such a possibility may be justified in the public interest; for example in order to ensure accurate population registration or to safeguard the means of personal identification and of linking the bearers of a given name to a family.'[1]

Article 8 will, therefore, be relevant consideration in the future in applications to cause a child to be known by a new surname under ss 8 and 13 of the Children Act 1989[2].

RESPECT FOR PRIVATE LIFE

3.109   A good illustration of the positive obligations which arise from the right to respect for private life is provided by *Gaskin v UK*[3]. In argument before the European Court the Government stressed the importance of confidentiality in keeping records for an effective operation of the child care system (which the Court acknowledged[4]) and that any positive obligation had been discharged by the steps taken to obtain the waivers of confidentiality. This was rejected by the majority of the Court who concluded that the positive obligation on the State required an independent adjudication on the question of the confidentiality of the documents. This led to the implementation in our domestic law of the Access to Social Services Records Act 1990, Access to Personal Files Act 1987 and the Access to Health Records Act 1990.

Family life
3.110   Article 8(1) guarantees the right to respect for family life.

THE EXISTENCE OF FAMILY LIFE

3.111   Although there is no definition of 'family life' in the Convention, 'family' has been interpreted widely by the European Court. In *Keegan v Ireland*[5], the Court held that:

'the notion of "the family" ... is not confined solely to marriage-based relationships and may encompass other de facto "family" where the parties are living together outside of marriage. A child born out of such a relationship is *ipso iure* part of that 'family' unit from the moment of his birth and by the very fact of it. There thus exists between the child and his parents a bond amounting to family life even if at the time of his or her birth the parents are no longer cohabiting or if their relationship has then ended.'

3.112   In *X, Y and Z v UK*[6], it was held that in determining whether a relationship can amount to 'family life' a number of factors may be relevant, 'including whether the couple live together, the length of their relationship and whether they have demonstrated their commitment to each other by having

---

1   24 EHRR 195, para 39.
2   *Re B (Change of Surname)* [1996] 1 FLR 791; *Dawson v Wearmouth* [1997] 2 FLR 629; *P v N (Child Surname)* [1997] 2 FCR 65; *Re C (Change of Surname)* [1998] 1 FLR 549.
3   12 EHRR 36.
4   *Gaskin v UK* (above), para 43.
5   18 EHRR 342, para 44.
6   [1997] 2 FLR 892 at 900, para 36 (see **p 360**); *Marckx v Belgium* (above), para 31; *Keegan v Ireland* 18 EHRR 342, para 44 and *Kroon v The Netherlands* (above), para 30.

children together or by any other means …'. The existence of a 'family life' is, therefore, a question of fact.

3.113   Once the existence of a family tie with a child has been established, 'the State must act in a manner calculated to enable that tie be developed and legal safeguards must be established that render possible as from the moment of birth or as soon as practicable thereafter the child's integration in his family'[1].

FAMILY RELATIONSHIPS

Husband and wife
3.114   The central relationships of family life are those of husband and wife and parent and child. Family life always exists within marriage. 'Family life' does not cease upon the separation or divorce of the parents[2] and a parent's right to a family life is not terminated by a residence order made in favour of the other parent. In *Berrehab v The Netherlands*[3], where a Morrocan citizen was refused a residence permit after a divorce from his Dutch wife, thus inhibiting his contact with his daughter, the Court stated that 'cohabitation was not a sine qua non of family life between parents and minor children' and that a bond amounting to family life existed, even if the parents were not living together. However, it recognised that subsequent events may break that tie and for 'family life' to continue, it was necessary to maintain the relationship between parent and child[4].

The natural parent
3.115   Parent includes a natural parent where there has been a cohabitation or other factors which show a relationship of sufficient constancy as to create de facto family ties[5]. Examples where a 'family life' has been found include: *Kroon v The Netherlands*[6], where the parties had a longstanding relationship in the course of which they had four children, though in fact never lived together; and *Söderbäck v Sweden*[7], where the unmarried father had never had a stable relationship with the mother but had shown some commitment to contact, albeit that the contact was limited because of the mother's resistance.

3.116   A natural parent who donates sperm or an egg for the purpose of artificial insemination does not have a right to respect for family life solely by that fact [8]. The blood tie per se may not, therefore, be sufficient to establish a family life[9]. A natural father has also been held by the Commission to have no right to joint custody as against the mother[10].

The illegitimate family
3.117   The members of the 'illegitimate' family enjoy the Art 8 guarantees on an equal footing with members of a 'traditional' family[11]. The landmark case on

1   *Kroon v The Netherlands* 19 EHRR 263, para 32.
2   *Keegan v Ireland* 18 EHRR 342.
3   *Berrehab v The Netherlands* 11 EHRR 322 (see **p 313**).
4   Ibid, para 21.
5   *Kroon v The Netherlands* 19 EHRR 263, para 30; *Keegan* (above), para 44.
6   19 EHRR 263.
7   [1999] 1 FLR 250 (see **p 355**).
8   *G v The Netherlands* Application No 16944/90, 16 EHRR CD 38.
9   *MB v UK* 22920/93 (Dec), (6 April 1994) 77–A DR 108.
10   *N v Denmark* Application No 13557/88, (1989) 63 DR 167 at 170.
11   *Marckx v Belgium* 2 EHRR 330, para 40.

the illegitimate family is *Marckx v Belgium*[1], where the applicant mother and her infant daughter complained that aspects of the illegitimacy laws in Belgium (including the requirement that maternal affiliation could be established only by a formal act of recognition and the limitations on the mother's capacity to give or bequeath and the child's capacity to take or inherit property) infringed Art 8 taken alone and in conjunction with Art 14.

3.118 The Court held that the legislation failed to respect the applicant's family life and constituted discrimination in violation of Art 14 by virtue of the lack of any objective and reasonable justification for the differences in treatment between the legitimate and illegitimate family. It stated that Art 8 makes no distinction between the 'legitimate' and 'illegitimate' family and that the positive obligations inherent in an effective 'respect' for family life mean that 'when the State determines in its legal system the regime applicable to certain family ties such as between an unmarried mother and her child it must act in a manner calculated to allow those concerned to lead a normal family life' which implied that there should be legal safeguards for the child's integration into the family[2].

Unmarried fathers
3.119 Unmarried fathers, however, are not in the same position as married fathers or unmarried mothers[3]. In English law, the Children Act 1989 does not automatically give unmarried fathers parental responsibility for their children. What it does is provide a vehicle whereby an unmarried father may acquire parental responsibility either by agreement with the child's mother or a court order under s 4 or the making of a residence order where the court would have also granted a s 4 parental responsibility order.

3.120 Although it is probable that these provisions will enable English law to comply with the Convention, there are potential areas of disadvantage to unmarried fathers who have not acquired parental responsibility where in the future breaches of Arts 8 and 14 may be arguable; for example where:

– the court has power to revoke a parental responsibility order in the case of unmarried fathers[4];
– the consent of an unmarried father is not required before the court makes an adoption or freeing for adoption order[5];
– an unmarried father need not be informed of an adoption application unless he is maintaining the child, nor consulted by adoption agencies as to his wishes and feelings, where this is not practicable[6];
– the unmarried father may not be able to establish a breach of a right of custody within the meaning of the Hague Convention on child abduction[7];
– a child may not be removed from the jurisdiction without either the consent of everyone with parental responsibility or the leave of the court[8].

1   *Marckx v Belgium* 2 EHRR 330.
2   Ibid, para 31.
3   *Keegan v Ireland* (above); in contrast *McMichael v UK* 20 EHRR 205 (both adoption cases).
4   Children Act 1989, s 4(3); *Re P (Terminating Parental Responsibility)* [1995] 1 FLR 1048.
5   Adoption Act 1976, s 72(1) as amended.
6   *Re L (A Minor) (Adoption: Procedure)* [1991] 1 FLR 171.
7   *Re J (A Minor) (Abduction: Custody Rights)* [1990] 2 AC 562.
8   Children Act 1989, s 13.

The approach of the European Court has been to take such issues on an individual case basis.

3.121   In *Keegan v Ireland*[1], which concerned the placement of a child for adoption by the mother without the unmarried father's knowledge or consent, the Court held that the relationship between the applicant and the mother had the hallmark of family life and, consequently, the placement in those circumstances amounted to an interference with his right to respect for family life, as it 'not only jeopardised the proper development of the father's ties with the child but also set in motion a process which was likely to prove irreversible, thereby putting the applicant at a significant disadvantage in his contest with the prospective adopters for the custody of the child'[2].

3.122   In contrast, in *McMichael v UK*[3], the unmarried father complained, inter alia, that he had been discriminated against contrary to Art 14 in conjunction with Art 8 when his child was placed in care and freed for adoption, as under Scots law, unlike the mother, he had no parental rights from the child's birth, no legal right to custody and no right to participate in the proceedings. In rejecting his complaint, the Court held that the aim of the relevant legislation which was to provide a mechanism for identifying 'meritorious' fathers who might be accorded parental rights thereby protecting the interests of the child and the mother, was legitimate and the conditions imposed on natural fathers for obtaining recognition of their parental role respected the principles of proportionality. It found, therefore, that there was an objective and reasonable justification for the difference of treatment.

3.123   As the English law relating to parental responsibility in respect of unmarried fathers is very similar to that of Scots law, it follows from the *McMichael* case that it would be highly likely that our domestic law currently would be held to comply with Arts 8 and 14. This was the view of Hale J in *Re W; Re B (Child Abduction: Unmarried Father)*[4]. However, Hale J went on to say:

> 'There may come a time when the Parliament of this country, having considered the policy matters further, decides to eliminate those differences. Or there may come a time when so many of the Contracting States to the Convention decide to do so that the currently wide margin of appreciation allowed in this area narrows so far as to oblige us to do so.'[5]

Paternity
3.124   Paternity issues have caused the European Court some difficulty. A presumption of paternity in favour of married fathers does not contravene the Convention. However, in *Kroon v The Netherlands*[6], the Court said that 'respect for family life requires that biological and social reality should prevail over legal presumption which flies in the face of both established fact and the wishes of those concerned'.

---

1   18 EHRR 342.
2   Ibid, para 55.
3   20 EHRR 205.
4   [1998] 2 FLR 146 at 163D–168G.
5   Ibid, at 168F–G.
6   19 EHRR 263, para 40.

3.125   In the *Kroon* case, the child concerned had been born of a stable relationship between the mother and the natural father but at a time when they were not living together, as the mother was still married to another man. Under Dutch law, it was impossible to obtain recognition of the biological father's paternity unless the husband denied paternity. The Court found that the relationship between father and child qualified as 'family life' and that there was a positive obligation on the part of the competent authorities to allow complete family ties to be formed between them as expeditiously as possible. Futhermore, it held that a solution which only allowed a father to create a legal tie if he married the child's mother could not be regarded as compatible with the notion of the respect for family life.

3.126   In contrast, in *MB v UK*[1], the Commission did not find that the domestic court's refusal to order blood tests on the child of a married woman, in respect of whom the applicant claimed to be the father (but was making no application for custody), constituted a breach of Art 8, as this would have disrupted the security of the family unit in which the child was being brought up. It stated:

> '… there are sound reasons of legal certainty and security of family relationships for States to apply a general presumption according to which a married man is regarded as the father of his wife's children and to require good cause before allowing the presumption to be disturbed. On the same basis, it is justifiable for domestic courts to give the greater weight to the interests of the child and the family in which it lives than the interest of an applicant in obtaining verification or otherwise of a biological fact'.

Grandparents and other family relationships
3.127   In *Marckx v Belgium*[2], the Court expressed the opinion that:

> '"family life" within the meaning of Art 8 includes at least the ties between near relatives, for instance, those between grandparents and grandchildren, since such relatives may play a considerable part in family life. "Respect" for a family life so understood implies an obligation for the State to act in a manner calculated to allow these ties to develop normally.'

In cases involving grandparents[3], the Commission has examined each case on its facts to determine whether there are sufficient links to amount to family life. Where a grandparent is denied contact to a grandchild in care, the Commission has further taken the view that, unlike most parental contact, this does not automatically amount to an interference with the right to respect for family life but may do so if it diminishes what in all the circumstances would be regarded as necessary to preserve a normal grandparent–grandchild relationship.

3.128   The Convention has also been held to cover relationships between siblings[4] and uncle and nephew[5]. *In Boyle v UK*[6], the applicant uncle had had

---

1   Application No 22920/93 (Dec), (6 April 1994) 77–A DR 108.
2   2 EHRR 330, para 45.
3   *Branton v UK* Application No 12399/85 (Dec) (9 March 1988); *Price v UK* Application No 12402/86, (14 July 1988) 55 DR 224; *Lawlor v UK* (Dec), Application No 12763/87, (14 July 1988) 57 DR 216. See also *Hokkanen v Finland* 19 EHRR 139, paras 63–64 and *Bronda v Italy* [1998] EHRLR 756.
4   *Moustaquim v Belgium* 13 EHRR 802, para 36.
5   *Boyle v UK* 19 EHRR 179, paras 41–46 (see **p 315**).
6   19 EHRR 179.

frequent contact with the child from birth and, as they lived in close proximity, he had spent considerable time with him. The guardian ad litem in the care proceedings described him as a 'good father figure' to the child. The Commission held that there was a significant bond between uncle and nephew and that the relationship fell within the scope of the concept of 'family life'[1]. However, it went on to draw a distinction between a denial of parental contact and that of a relative in respect of a child in care:

> 'Where a parent is denied access to a minor child taken into care, there is in general an interference with the parent's right to respect for family life ... This is not necessarily the case where other close relatives are concerned. Access by relatives to a child is normally at the discretion of the child's parents and, where a care order has been made in respect of the child, this control of access passes to the local authority. A restriction of access which does not deny a recoverable opportunity to maintain the relationship will not of itself show a lack of respect for family life.'[2]

Adoption

3.129   Adoption has been held to create a family life between the adopted child and adoptive parents[3]. 'Family life' has also been held to include the relationship between a foster-parent and a foster-child, although the Court noted that the content of family life may depend on the nature of the fostering arrangements[4].

Homosexuals

3.130   Homosexual unions do not currently fall within the scope of the right to respect for family life under Art 8[5]. In *Kerkhoven v Netherlands*[6], which concerned a lesbian relationship, the Commission held that the partner of the mother could not rely on either the family life provisions or the private life provisions of Art 8 to claim parental authority over the child born to the mother by artificial insemination.

3.131   However, attitudes to homosexuality are evolving and a pointer to the future is to be found in the recent Commission case, *Salgueiro da Silva Mouta*[7], where the applicant father who was living in a homosexual relationship, alleged that the domestic court had awarded custody to the mother on the basis of his homosexuality in violation of his right to respect for family life in conjunction with Art 14 and a violation of his right to respect for private life in that the court had specified that he must hide his homosexuality in his meetings with his daughter. The Commission held that his complaints were admissible.

3.132   Although the Court recognised that a transsexual's relationship with his partner and child may constitute a de facto family life, it did not find that Art 8

---

1   19 EHRR 179, paras 44–45.
2   Ibid, para 46.
3   *X v France* Application No 9993/82, (1982) 31 DR 241.
4   *Gaskin v UK* 12 EHRR 36, para 49; also *X v Switzerland* Application No 8257/78 (Dec), (10 July 1978) 13 DR 248; see also *Rieme v Sweden* 16 EHRR 155.
5   *S v UK* Application No 11716/85, (1986) 47 DR 272; *B v UK* Application No 16106/90, (1990) 64 DR 278.
6   Application No 15666/89 (19 May 1992).
7   Application No 33290/96 (Dec), (1 December 1998) [Section IV]. See also *Frette v France* Application No 36515/97 [Section III]; *Lustig-Praen and Becket v UK and Smith and Grady v UK* (1999) *The Times*, 11 October.

imposed a positive obligation to recognise in law the parental role of the transsexual father[1]. This issue is also likely to be re-visited in the future.

RESPECT FOR FAMILY LIFE

3.133   The European Court has interpreted 'respect' for family life widely. In the key case of *Marckx v Belgium*[2], it held that there had been a violation of the right to respect for family life, where the State failed to provide a system of domestic law which safeguarded an illegitimate child's integration into its family.

3.134   In *W v UK*[3], an important and influential case concerning public law, the Court established the fundamental principle that the decision-making process in child care cases must provide sufficient procedural protection of the parents' interests. The applicant had complained about the procedures followed by the local authority in their decision to terminate his contact to his child in care, the absence of remedies against that decision and the length of the proceedings. The Court held that:

> 'The mutual enjoyment by parent and child of each other's company constitutes a fundamental element of family life. Furthermore, the natural family relationship is not terminated by reason of the fact that the child is taken into public care. It follows ... that the Authority's decisions resulting from the procedure at issue amounted to interferences with the applicant's right to respect for family life.'[4]

The debate centred, therefore, on the question of whether the procedures followed had respected the applicant's family life. The Court recognised that, in reaching decisions in so sensitive an area, local authorities were faced with an extremely difficult task and that they must, therefore, be allowed a measure of discretion[5]. The Court went on to say:

> 'On the other hand, predominant in any consideration of this aspect of the present case must be the fact that the decisions may well prove to be irreversible: thus, where a child has been taken away from his parents and placed with alternative carers, he may in the course of time establish with them new bonds which it might not be in his interests to disturb or interrupt by reversing a previous decision to restrict or terminate parental access to him. This is accordingly a domain in which there is an even greater call than usual for protection against arbitrary interferences[6] ... The relevant considerations to be weighed by a local authority in reaching decisions on children in its care must perforce include the views and interests of the natural parents. The decision-making process must, therefore, ... be such as to secure that their views and interests are made known to and duly taken into account by the local authority and that they are able to exercise in due time any remedies available to them.'[7]

3.135   It should, therefore, be noted that Art 8 does import a notion of a 'fair procedure' into those administrative decisions, which necessarily interfere with family relationships such as taking children into care or adoption. This is particularly demonstrated in *McMichael v UK*[8], where the parents were denied a

---

1   *X, Y and Z v UK* 24 EHRR 143.
2   2 EHRR 330.
3   10 EHRR 29.
4   Ibid, para 59.
5   Ibid, para 62.
6   Ibid.
7   Ibid, para 63.
8   20 EHRR 205, para 91.

right of access to confidential social work reports and documents on their children in care either before or during proceedings, the Court said that there is:

> '... (a) difference in the nature of the interests protected by Articles 6(1) and 8. Thus, Article 6(1) affords a procedural safeguard, namely "the right to a court" in the determination of one's "civil right and obligations"; whereas not only does the procedural requirement inherent in Article 8 cover administrative procedures as well as judicial proceedings, but it is ancillary to the wider purpose of ensuring proper respect for, inter alia, family life. The difference between the purpose pursued by the respective safeguards afforded by Articles 6(1) and 8 may, in the light of the particular circumstances, justify the examination of the same set of facts under both Articles. As regards the instant case, the facts complained of had repercussions not only on the conduct of judicial proceedings ... but also on "a fundamental element of the family life of the two applicants".'

The Court judged it appropriate, therefore, to examine the facts also under Art 8 and found that there had been a breach[1].

3.136　　The State's positive obligation does not cover support for the substance of family life. For example, there is no obligation upon the State to admit alien spouses of the applicants to join them[2], although deportation of a member of a family where the family is already established may result in a breach of the right to respect for family life[3].

3.137　　The right to respect for family life was recently considered in *Re C (A Child) (HIV Test)*[4], a first instance decision, where a local authority applied for an order that a baby be subjected to an HIV test notwithstanding the vehement opposition of her parents. Wilson J held that 'it was possible to discern in the law a rebuttable presumption that the united appraisal of both parents was correct in identifying where the welfare of the child lay'. He found support for such a presumption in s 1(5) of the Children Act 1989, which prohibited the court from making any order under the Act unless it is considered that to do so would be better for the child than to make no order and from Art 8 under which the parents and the baby had the right to have their family life respected. He concluded, however, on the facts of the particular case that the overwhelming advantages of testing overrode the wishes of the parents.

Home

3.138　　Article 8 guarantees the right to respect for the home. 'Home' has been widely interpreted. Generally, it is where one lives on a settled basis, although it can include a place where one intends to live[5] and where one has been absent for a period of time, provided sufficient continuing links are retained[6].

3.139　　In *Niemitz v Germany*[7], where the applicant lawyer's offices were searched pursuant to a warrant in order to obtain information about the identity

---

1　　See also *Boyle v UK* 19 EHRR 179, para 57 (case conference); UK 17071/90 (Dec), (13 February 1990) (child abuse register); 14114/88 (Dec), (12 December 1988), 15993/90 (Dec), (15 January 1990) and 16184/90 (Dec), (7 May 1990) (provision of legal representation).
2　　*Agee v UK* (1976) 7 DR 164; *Abdulaziz, Calabas and Balkandali v UK* 7 EHRR 471.
3　　*Berrehab v Netherlands* 11 EHRR 322; *Moustaquim v Belgium* 13 EHRR 802.
4　　(1999) *The Times*, 14 September.
5　　*Gillow v UK* 11 EHRR 335, para 46; also *Buckley v UK* 23 EHRR 101, para 54.
6　　Ibid, para 46.
7　　16 EHRR 97.

and whereabouts of a third party, the Court interpreted 'home' as including professional or business premises[1] and found that there had been a violation of Art 8. The search had not been accompanied by any special procedural safeguards such as an independent observer and, more importantly, it impinged upon professional secrecy (or legal professional privilege) of a lawyer to an extent which was disproportionate[2].

3.140 The right is not a positive right to a home but a right to occupy and not be expelled or evicted[3]. It includes the right to peaceful enjoyment of the home[4]. The other principal element of the right is the protection it affords against entry by the authorities to arrest, search and seize. Although the burden is on the authorities to justify such interference, where the entry is pursuant to a court order such as a search order (formerly known as *Anton Piller* order), this is likely to be a sufficient safeguard[5].

3.141 However, in *McLeod v UK*[6], where in contempt of court the wife had failed to deliver up certain property to the husband and the husband went to her home accompanied at his solicitor's request by police officers to collect his property, the Court found that the entry into her home was disproportionate to the legitimate aim of preventing breach of the peace, as the police had failed to look at the court order which did not entitle the husband to collect and, in any event, they should not have entered her home, once it was clear that she was not present.

Correspondence

3.142 Article 8 guarantees the right to respect for correspondence. Correspondence has been interpreted to include written and telephone communications. In the *Niemitz* case[7], the search carried out at the lawyer's offices also included an examination of four cabinets with data concerning clients as well as six individual files. These documents were held to be 'correspondence' for the purposes of Art 8, notwithstanding that they were of a professional nature. The Court further noted that the word 'correspondence' was not qualified in any way in the Article and thus followed an earlier decision relating to correspondence in the form of telephone calls[8].

3.143 In *Klass v FRG*[9], telephone-tapping was held to constitute a violation of Art 8. This provision may, therefore, in future be relevant in those cases where taped telephone conversations are sought to be adduced in evidence, for example, in private law cases and ancillary relief applications.

3.144 The right to respect for correspondence is also relevant in the public law context. In *Andersson v Sweden*[10], the social welfare authorities had prohibited all contact between the applicant mother and son, when he was taken into care to protect his health and development, including all correspondence and telephone

---

1   16 EHRR 97, para 31.
2   Ibid, para 37.
3   *Wiggins v UK* Application No 7456/76, (1978) 13 DR 40; *Cyprus v Turkey* 4 EHRR 282.
4   *Arrondelle v UK* Application No 7889/77, (1982) 26 DR 5.
5   *Chappell v UK* 12 EHRR 1 (*Anton Piller* order); but see also the *Niemitz* case (above).
6   [1998] 2 FLR 1048.
7   16 EHRR 97.
8   *Niemitz v Germany* (above), para 32; *Huvig v France* 12 EHRR 528, paras 8 and 25.
9   2 EHRR 214; also *Kopp v Switzerland* 27 EHRR 91.
10 14 EHRR 615 (see **p 308**).

conversations so as to avoid harm to him. The Commission found that 'telephone conversations between family members are covered by the notions of "family life" and "correspondence" within the meaning of Art 8'[1] and that there had been a breach of Art 8.

Justifiable interference

3.145 Once the applicant has established the fact of interference, it is for the State to show that the interference may be justified under Art 8(2), namely that it is 'in accordance with the law' and 'necessary in a democratic society' for the protection of one of the aims in subparagraph (2). The European Court's approach is to consider in order: 'lawfulness', 'aim' and 'necessity'.

Lawfulness

3.146 The expressions 'prescribed by law' and 'in accordance with the law' were considered in the *Sunday Times* case[2] and *Malone v UK*[3] and *Olsson v Sweden*[4], from which the following general principles emerge: First, the interference in question must have some basis in domestic law. This includes not only statute but also common law, equity, international law and Community law[5]. Secondly, the law must be adequately accessible; the citizen must be able to have an indication that it is adequate in circumstances of the legal rules applicable to a given case, 'the accessibility requirement'. Thirdly, a norm cannot be regarded as a 'law' unless it is formulated with sufficient precision to enable the citizen to regulate his conduct: he must be able – if need be with appropriate advice – to foresee, to a degree that is reasonable in the circumstances, the consequences which a given action may entail: 'the foreseeability requirement'. Fourthly, the phrase does not merely refer back to domestic law but also relates to the quality of law, requiring it to be compatible with the rule of law; it thus implies that there must be a measure of protection in domestic law against arbitrary interferences by public authorities with the rights safeguarded by, inter alia, Art 8(1). Fifthly, a law which confers a discretion is not in itself inconsistent with the requirement of foreseeability, provided that the scope of the discretion and the manner of its exercise are indicated with sufficient clarity, having regard to the legitimate aim of the measure in question, to give the individual adequate protection against arbitrary interference.

3.147 Lawfulness was a key issue in three child-care cases. In *Olsson v Sweden (No 2)*[6] and *Eriksson v Sweden*[7], the Court found that restrictions imposed by the local authority on parental contact to children in care were not 'in accordance with the law' as there was a lacuna in Swedish domestic law permitting such restrictions. In contrast, in *Olsson v Sweden (No 1)*[8], where Swedish law permitted the taking of children into care in 'rather general' terms, the Court nevertheless accepted that this satisfied the concept of 'law'.

---

1   14 EHRR 615, para 72.
2   *Sunday Times v UK (No 1)* 2 EHRR 245, paras 47–50; also *Silver v UK* 5 EHRR 347, paras 86–88.
3   7 EHRR 14, paras 67.1 and 51.
4   11 EHRR 259, para 61.
5   *Groppera Radio AG v Switzerland* 12 EHRR 321.
6   (1992) Series A, No 250, para 76.
7   12 EHRR 183, para 67.
8   11 EHRR 259.

Aim

3.148　It is for the State to identify the aim of its interference and to show that it falls within the list of broad purposes in Art 8(2). As the purposes are widely drawn, States have generally been able to satisfy the 'legitimate aim' test. Examples in the family law context include separating children from their parents in the interests of the rights of the children[1] or for the protection of their health or morals[2].

Necessity

3.149　The State must show that the interference is 'necessary in a democratic society'. It is this criterion which has claimed the greatest attention of the Court in the family law field. 'Necessary' in this context does not have the flexibility of such expressions as 'useful', 'reasonable' or 'desirable', but implies the existence of a 'pressing social need' for the interference in question[3]. Although it is for the national authorities to make the initial assessment of the pressing need in each case, their decision remains subject to the review of the Court; in particular, the Court must be satisfied that the interference is proportionate to the legitimate aim pursued.

3.150　In considering 'democratic values', particularly in those cases which concern fundamental moral issues, the Court has relied upon a consensus 'European standard' among the laws of the contracting States. Examples include *Marckx v Belgium*[4] (illegitimacy), *Dudgeon v UK* and *Norris v Ireland*[5] (adult homosexual relationships) and *Tyrer v UK*[6] (judicial corporal punishment).

3.151　The dominant element of the requirement of necessity is the principle of proportionality, which is used to find a balance between the applicant's interests and the community's interests[7] and requires a reasonable relationship between the aim and the means used to achieve it[8]. In assessing whether an interference is 'proportionate to the legitimate aim', a wide 'margin of appreciation' is generally taken into account by the Court. The 'necessity requirement' has played a crucial part in child-care cases, which is most clearly demonstrated by a triology of Scandanavian cases.

3.152　In *Olsson v Sweden (No 1)*[9], the children in care were placed in separate foster-homes a long distance from the parental home. In assessing whether this interference with the parents' rights was 'necessary' in the children's interests, the Court set out the following approach: that in exercising its supervisory jurisdiction, it 'cannot confine itself to considering the impugned decisions in isolation, but must look at them in the light of the case as a whole; it must determine whether the reasons adduced to justify the interference at issue are "relevant and sufficient"'[10]. It concluded that the authority, notwithstanding its margin of

---

1　　11 EHRR 259.
2　　*Andersson v Sweden* 14 EHRR 615.
3　　*Dudgeon v UK* 4 EHRR 149, paras 51 and 52.
4　　2 EHRR 330.
5　　*Dudgeon v UK* (above), para 60; *Norris v Ireland* 13 EHRR 186, para 46.
6　　2 EHRR 1, paras 31 and 38.
7　　*Sporrong and Llonroth v Sweden* 5 EHRR 35, para 69.
8　　*James v UK* 8 EHRR 123.
9　　11 EHRR 259, paras 74 and 77.
10　　Ibid, para 68.

tion, did not have relevant or sufficient reasons for the implementation of the care decision, as this was inconsistent with the ultimate aim of reuniting the natural family[1].

3.153   In *Eriksson v Sweden*[2], the applicant complained about the local authority's decision to prohibit her for an indefinite period from removing her daughter from a foster-home, the restrictions imposed on her access to the child and the failure to re-unite them. The Court again emphasised that a mother's right to respect for family life includes a right to take measures with a view to her being united with her child[3] and concluded that the severe and lasting restrictions on access combined with the long duration of the prohibition on removal are not proportionate to the legitimate aims pursued[4].

3.154   In *Johansen v Norway*[5], which also concerned a mother's deprivation of parental rights and of contact with her daughter, the Court held that:

> '... taking of a child into care should normally be regarded as a temporary measure to be discontinued as soon as circumstances permit and any measures of implementation of temporary care should be consistent with the ultimate aim of reuniting the natural parent and child. In this regard a fair balance has to be struck between the interests of the child in remaining in public care and those of the parents in being united with the child. In carrying out this balancing exercise, the Court will attach particular importance to the best interests of the child, which depending upon their nature and seriousness may override those of the parent. In particular ... the parent cannot be entitled under Art 8 of the Convention to have such measures taken as would harm the child's health and development.'[6]

It concluded that the national authority had overstepped their margin of appreciation.

3.155   The approach under the Convention is therefore different from that adopted by English law. The starting point under Art 8 is that the parent does have a right to family life which must be given effective respect and must not be interfered with unless the interference is justified under Art 8(2). The welfare of the child becomes relevant at the point when the Court is considering whether the interference with the parents' right is justified as 'necessary'. This difference of approach was recently confirmed by the Court of Appeal in *R v Secretary of State for the Home Department, ex parte Gangadeen and Khan*[7], where Hirst LJ said that the Convention organs interpret Art 8 on the basis that the scales start even with no preferences being given to the interests of the child[8].

Impact

3.156   The following fundamental issues, therefore, emerge from the Convention organs' interpretation of Art 8, which will have a substantial impact upon domestic private law (s 8 contact orders) and public law (s 34 contact orders, especially s 34(4)):

---

1   11 EHRR 259, paras 81 and 83.
2   12 EHRR 183.
3   Ibid, para 71.
4   Ibid.
5   23 EHRR 33.
6   Ibid, para 78.
7   [1998] 1 FLR 762.
8   Ibid, at 773H–774B.

– Article 8 does not support the notion that paramountcy is to be given to the interests of the child[1].

– Although neither parent may claim a right to a residence order[2], parents do have a 'right' to contact[3]. This challenges the domestic law approach that parents do not have a right of contact[4]. In the seminal (pre-Children Act 1989) case of *W v UK*[5], the Government had contended that the notion of parental 'rights' over children was outmoded and that the right was that of the child and not that of the parent. The European Court rejected this contention.

– Public authorities (which will include the court) are obliged to take measures to facilitate the reunification between parents and children. The cases in the public law context include *Olsson v Sweden*[6], *Eriksson v Sweden*[7] and *Andersson v Sweden*[8] and in the private law context *Hokkanen v Finland*[9] where the maternal grandparents persistently refused to comply with court orders for access and the non-enforcement of the father's right of access was held to constitute a breach.

– The obligation upon public authorities is, however, not absolute and, whilst they must do their utmost to facilitate the understanding and co-operation of all concerned, any obligation to apply coercion is limited since the rights of all concerned have to be taken into account, and more particularly the best interests of the child[10].

3.157 Other areas of potential tension between domestic law and Convention law include:

– Leave to remove a child permanently from the jurisdiction. The domestic court's current approach is that the application is to be considered on the premise that the welfare of the child is paramount and that leave should not be withheld unless the interests of the child and the custodial parent are shown to be incompatible[11]. It is arguable that this approach does not give sufficient weight to respect for the family life of the parent remaining under Art 8.

– Adoption. It is at least open to question whether the 'guillotine' effect of adoption in domestic law would withstand the challenge of the Convention. However, it should be noted that in *Söderbäck v Sweden*[12], an adoption case, the

---

1   In *Johansen v Norway* 23 EHRR 33 the Court did emphasise that it would attach particular importance to the best interests of the child which, depending on their nature and seriousness, may override the interests of the parent: para 78.
2   *X v Sweden* Application No 172/56, 1 YB 211.
3   *Hendriks v Netherlands* 5 EHRR 233, paras 94–95; *B v UK* 10 EHRR 87, para 60 (see **p 358**); *Peter Whitear v UK* 1997 3 EHRLR 291.
4   *Re KD (A Minor) (Access: Principles)* [1988] 2 FLR 139 at 155.
5   10 EHRR 29.
6   17 EHRR 134, para 90.
7   12 EHRR 183, para 71.
8   14 EHRR 615, para 91.
9   19 EHRR 139, paras 55–58.
10 Ibid, para 58.
11 *Re K (A Minor) (Removal from Jurisdiction)* [1994] 2 FCR 98; *Re B (Minors)(Removal from Jurisdiction)* [1994] 2 FCR 309; *Re H (Application to Remove from Jurisdiction)* [1998] 1 FLR 848.
12 [1999] 1 FLR 250.

European Court found that there had been no violation of Art 8. Although the Court accepted that an adoption order amounted to an interference with the father's respect for family life, it held that, in view of the infrequent and limited nature of the contact between the father and the daughter, the decision fell within the State's margin of appreciation. Given the aim of the adoption, which was to consolidate and formalise the child's family ties, the adverse effects of the adoption on the father's relationship with the child had not been disproportionate.

ARTICLE 10: RIGHT TO FREEDOM OF EXPRESSION

3.158   Under Art 10(1), everyone has the right to freedom of expression, including freedom to hold opinions and to receive and impart information and ideas without interference by public authority and regardless of frontiers. The right is not absolute, as it is subject, in Art 10(2), to a number of permitted exceptions. These must be narrowly interpreted and the necessity for any restriction must be convincingly established[1].

3.159   In *Handyside v UK*[2], the Court said:

> 'Freedom of expression constitutes one of the essential foundations of a (democratic) society, one of the basic conditions for its progress and for the development of every man. Subject to Art 10(2), it is applicable not only to "information" or "ideas" that are favourably received or regarded as inoffensive or as a matter of indifference, but also to those that offend, shock or disturb the state or any sector of the population. Such are the demands of that pluralism, tolerance and broadmindedness without which there is no "democratic society".'

'Freedom of expression' has been interpreted widely and includes the negative freedom of not to speak. It may therefore be relevant to issues relating to the privilege against self-incrimination[3]. Section 12 of the HRA 1998, which specifically deals with freedom of expression, reinforces the protection for the media.

Injunctions to prevent media publicity

3.160   The freedom to hold opinions and to receive and impart information and ideas without interference by public authority under Art 10 has previously been taken into account by the domestic courts in injunction cases to prevent the exposure of children to media publicity[4].

3.161   In *Re Z (A Minor) (Identification: Restrictions on Publication)*[5], following extensive media attention, the child's parents had obtained an injunction restraining publication of her identity and a second injunction was granted against the mother restraining her from communicating any matter relating to the child's education. Subsequently, a television company wished to make a film

1   *Thorgierson v Iceland* 14 EHRR 843, para 63.
2   1 EHRR 737.
3   *K v Austria* (1993) Series A, No 255–B Com Rep, paras 45, 49.
4   *Re H (Minors) (Injunction: Public Interest)* [1994] 1 FLR 519, per Ward LJ at 526D–G.
5   [1997] Fam 1.

about the child and the treatment she was receiving at a specialised institution. The mother applied for a discharge or variation of the injunctions to enable both her daughter and herself to participate in the programme.

3.162   The Court of Appeal held that where the court was not exercising a supervisory role over an aspect of a child's care and upbringing, it should not restrain publications which were not directed at the child, his carers or his upbringing and which only peripherally related to him, but where the court was required to determine any question with respect to the upbringing of the child, the welfare of the child was its paramount consideration, to which the public interest in freedom of publication was subordinated. At first instance, Cazalet J had said:

> 'Furthermore, in regard to article 10 of (the Convention), I bear in mind the importance of the freedom of publication, not least the media, but I am satisfied that the exception to article 10 (2) is clearly established ...'

3.163   Subsequently, in *A and Byrne and Twenty-Twenty Television v UK*[1], the mother complained to the Strasbourg Court, invoking Art 8 and Art 10. The Commission held that, in the context of Art 10 it:

> 'must take into account that the right and freedom of expression is one of the essential foundations of a democratic society and that prior restraints call for the "most careful scrutiny" (*Observer and Guardian v UK* 14 EHRR 153, paras 59–60). In addition, in considering the 'duties and responsibilities' of the applicants as persons exercising their freedom of expression through the making and production of a television programme, the potential impact of the programme on the public and, consequently, on (the child) must be considered to be an important factor (*Jersild v Denmark* 19 EHRR 1, para 31).'

3.164   The Commission found that the refusal to vary or discharge the injunctions constituted a justifiable interference with the applicants' rights within the meaning of Art 10(2) of the Convention and dismissed the complaint as manifestly ill-founded. It added that:

> '... the (domestic) High Court considered that if it had to carry out a balancing exercise (for the purposes of Art 10 or otherwise) between the welfare of (the child) and the public interest in the programme, it would firmly see the scales as coming down in favour of there being an order against the programme being made. The High Court, accordingly, considered that the exceptions contained in Article 10(2) of the Convention had been established, although it emphasised that it was cognisant of the importance to be accorded to freedom of publication and of the media ... While the Commission accepts that the high profile nature of (the child's) parents, and, consequently, of (the child) herself could increase public interest in, and the impact of, the programme, the Commission considers it to be justifiable to favour (the child's) welfare over the greater public impact of the proposed programme consequent of (the child's) notoriety'.

3.165   Generally, therefore, where a judge exercises a discretion in favour of restraining publication of information relating to children, there is unlikely to be future conflict between domestic law and the Convention, as in the majority of cases the interests of the children will require the restrictions on publication.

---

1   25 EHRR CD 159: for the approach of the European Court generally, see *Goodwin v UK* 22 EHRR 123; *Prager and Oberschlick v Austria* 21 EHRR 1 and *De Haes v Belgium* 25 EHRR 1; also the earlier case of *Sunday Times v UK (No 1)* 2 EHRR 245.

However, in the light of ss 12(2) and (3) of the HRA 1998 there may be difficulty in the future in obtaining an ex parte injunction[1].

Access to information

3.166   The freedom to receive information was touched upon in *Gaskin v UK*[2], where the applicant was seeking access to records held by a local authority from the time when he was in foster-care. The Court decided the case on its facts under Art 8 rather than Art 10 and stated that: 'in the circumstances of the present case, Art 10 does not embody an obligation on the state concerned to impart the information in question to the individual'[3].

3.167   For the present, therefore, one cannot derive from Art 10 a general right of access to information. However, in *Open Door and Dublin Well Woman v Ireland*[4], the Court did find that there was a breach of Art 10 where an injunction prevented the provision of information services concerning abortion and so there are some signs that the Court is moving slowly in the direction of a general right of access.

ARTICLE 12: RIGHT TO MARRY AND FOUND A FAMILY

3.168   Article 12 provides:

> 'Men and women of a marriageable age have the right to marry and to found a family, according to the national laws governing the exercise of this right.'

Article 12 lays down that the exercise of the right is subject to the national laws of the contracting States and such matters as the formalities of marriage, questions of capacity, minimum age and consanguinity and the founding of a family by adoption are for the national law[5]. The national laws must not, however, interfere with the right so as to restrict or reduce it in such a way or to such an extent that the very essence of the right is impaired[6].

Key cases include *Rees v UK, Cossey v UK, F v Switzerland*[7] and *Johnston v Ireland*[8].

Right to marry

3.169   In *Rees v UK*[9], where a transsexual applicant had had his application to alter his birth certificate refused, it was held that:

> '... the right to marry guaranteed by Art 12 refers to the traditional marriage between persons of the opposite biological sex. This appears also from the wording of the

---

1   See the Access to Justice Bill which extends s 97(2) of the Children Act 1989 to the High Courts and county courts and may, therefore, lessen the necessity in the future for applying for an injunction to prevent the publication of the identity of children in Children Act proceedings.
2   12 EHRR 36.
3   Ibid, para 52.
4   15 EHRR 244.
5   *F v Switzerland* 10 EHRR 411 para 32 (see **p 324**); *Khan v UK* Application No 11579/85, (1986) 48 DR 253.
6   *Rees v UK* 9 EHRR 56, para 50; *Van Oosterwijk v Belgium* (1980) Series A, No 40 Com Rep, para 56.
7   All above.
8   9 EHRR 203 (see **p 338**).
9   9 EHRR 56.

Article which makes it clear that Article 12 is mainly concerned to protect marriage as the basis of the family.'[1]

Article 12 does not, therefore, give a right to marry to a transsexual under his or her new gender[2] or to homosexuals to marry one another[3].

3.170 The imposition of delay in the exercise of the right to marry has been found to affect the very essence of the right to marry. In *F v Switzerland*[4], following his third divorce, a temporary prohibition on remarriage was imposed on the applicant. The Court found that although the stability of marriage was a legitimate aim which was in the public interest, the time restriction was unreasonable and disproportionate[5].

Right to found a family

3.171 The right to found a family is absolute in the sense that the State has no right to interfere with it[6]. However, it does not mean that a person must at all times be given the actual possibility 'to procreate his descendants' and consequently the State is not required to provide opportunities for a couple to found a family by allowing for the consummation of the marriage[7].

3.172 Founding a family can include founding a family by adoption[8]. It does not, however, guarantee a right to adopt or otherwise integrate into a family a child who is not the natural child of the couple concerned. It is left to national law to determine whether, or subject to what conditions, the exercise of the right in such a way may be permitted. Conditions imposed upon adoptions can, however, be scrutinised under the Convention[9].

3.173 There is no indication that a State has an obligation to provide a system of adoption, nor any particular form of adoption and in *X and Y v UK*[10] the Commission said that a State was not obliged to recognise a foreign adoption. Unmarried persons cannot claim a right to adopt[11].

3.174 As to non-married persons, in *Marckx v Belgium*[12] the mother of an illegitimate child claimed that 'a right not to marry' was inherent in the guarantee embodied under Art 12 and that in order to confer upon her daughter the status of a 'legitimate' child, she would have to contract a marriage. The Court noted that there was no legal obstacle confronting the mother 'in the exercise of the freedom to marry or remain single' and declined to decide whether there was a right not to marry. It held that the issue fell outside the scope of Art 12[13].

---

1   9 EHRR 56, para 49.
2   Ibid; also *Cossey v UK* 13 EHRR 622.
3   *S v UK* Application No 11716/85, (1986) 47 DR 274.
4   10 EHRR 411; also *Hamer v UK* Application No 7114/75 (Rep), (13 December 1979) 24 DR 5;
    Draper v UK 8186/78 (Rep), 24 DR 72 (10 July 1980) (refusing serving prisoners the right to marry an infringement).
5   10 EHRR 411, paras 36 and 40.
6   *X v UK* Application No 6564/74, 2 DR 105.
7   Ibid.
8   *X and Y v UK* Application No 7229/75, (1977) 12 DR 32.
9   Ibid.
10 Ibid.
11 *X v Belgium and The Netherlands* Application No 6482/147, (1975) 7 DR 75.
12 2 EHRR 330.
13 Ibid, para 67.

3.175   Artificial reproduction is another relevant issue under Art 12. Currently, Art 12 does not apply where a single woman wishes to resort to artificial reproductive techniques. The unmarried and the single person, therefore, have no remedy where the right to found a family is dependent upon adoption or artificial reproduction. These are issues which may be reviewed in the future. Other examples of interferences with a right to found a family would include programmes of compulsory sterilisation or abortion.

ARTICLE 14: PROHIBITION OF DISCRIMINATION

3.176   Article 14 provides:

> 'The enjoyment of the rights and freedoms set forth in this Convention shall be secured without discrimination on any ground such as sex, race, colour, language, religion, political or other opinion, national or social origin, association with a national minority, property, birth or other status.'

Although the list of prohibitive grounds set out in the Article is not exhaustive[1], Art 14 is concerned only with discriminatory treatment which has as its basis a 'personal characteristic (status)' by which persons or groups of persons are distinguishable from each other[2].

3.177   As to the meaning of 'discrimination', the *Belgian Linguistic Case (No 2)*[3], in which a number of French-speaking parents in Belgium complained that certain provisions of the Belgian linguistic legislation relating to education infringed, inter alia, Art 14, established the following test:

> 'It is important . . . to look for the criteria which enable a determination to be made as to whether or not a given difference in treatment, concerning of course the exercise of one of the rights and freedoms set forth, contravenes Article 14. On this question the Court, following the principles which may be extracted from the legal practice of a large number of democratic states, holds that the principle of equality of treatment is violated if the distinction has no objective and reasonable justification. The existence of such a justification must be assessed in relation to the aim and effects of the measure under consideration, regard being had to the principles which normally prevail in democratic societies. A difference of treatment in the exercise of a right laid down in the Convention must not only pursue a legitimate aim: Article 14 is likewise violated when it is established that there is no reasonable relationship of proportionality between the means employed and the aim sought to be realised.'

For Art 14 to apply, the applicant must, therefore, show that he is: (i) subject to a difference in treatment from others in a similar situation[4]; (ii) in the enjoyment of one of the rights protected by the Convention[5]; (iii) which difference cannot be objectively and reasonably justified, having regard to the concepts of legitimate aim, proportionality and margin of appreciation[6].

---

1   *James v UK* 8 EHRR 123, para 74.
2   *Kjeldsen, Busk Madsen and Pedersen v Denmark* 1 EHRR 711, para 56 (see **p 339**).
3   1 EHRR 252, para 10 at p 284.
4   *Marckx* (above), para 32.
5   *Rasmussen v Denmark* 7 EHRR 371, para 29; *Van der Mussele v Belgium* 6 EHRR 163, para 43.
6   *Marckx* (above), para 33.

Difference in treatment

3.178   The difference in treatment which is relevant for the purposes of Art 14 is where the applicant can demonstrate that his position is analogous to or 'relevantly similar'[1] to the position of those in the group he has identified as enjoying the more favourable treatment.

3.179   The following family situations have been held *not* to be analogous: married couples with unmarried couples[2], a natural father with a natural mother concerning procedural rights relating to children[3], a natural father and a married father concerning rights in respect of their children[4], and a stable lesbian union with family life[5]. It is, however, likely that in the future, differences in treatment between married men and unmarried men in respect of their children will not be justifiable.

The relationship between Article 14 and the other Convention rights

3.180   Article 14 complements the other substantive provisions of the Convention and the Protocols. It has no independent existence since it has effect solely in relation to 'the enjoyment of the rights and freedoms' safeguarded by those provisions. Although the application of Art 14 does not necessarily presuppose a breach of those provisions (as to this extent it has an autonomous meaning), there can be no room for its application unless the facts fall within the ambit of one or more of the substantive Articles[6].

3.181   In *Inze v Austria*[7], in which the legitimate child was given precedence under the Austrian law of intestacy over the illegitimate applicant in respect of their deceased mother's farm, the applicant did not claim a violation of Art 1 of the First Protocol taken alone but argued that the priority given to legitimate heirs was a violation of Art 14. The Court found that his Art 14 complaint could be brought because it fell within the ambit of Art 1 of the First Protocol.

3.182   In *Hoffman v Austria*[8], the applicant mother, a Jehovah's Witness, complained that she had been denied custody of her children on the ground of her religious convictions contrary, inter alia, to Arts 8 and 14. Since the interference with her family life was based upon discrimination on religious grounds, the Court found a breach of Art 14 taken in conjunction with Art 8 and

---

1   *Marckx* (above), para 32; *Van der Mussele v Belgium* 6 EHRR 163, para 46; *Sunday Times v UK (No 2)* 14 EHRR 229, para 58; also *Stubbings v UK* 23 EHRR 213, paras 66–73.

2   *Lindsay v UK* Application No 11089/84 (Dec), (11 November 1986) 49 DR 181; also *Saucedo Gomez v Spain* Application No 37784/97 (Dec), (19 January 1998) (complaint that a refusal to grant the family home to the applicant on her separation from her partner was discriminatory as the right she claimed could arise only where the couple were married was held inadmissible).

3   *MB v UK* Application No 22920/93 (Dec), (6 April 1994) 77–A DR 108; *Rasmussen* (above), paras 34–42.

4   *McMichael v UK* 20 EHRR 205, para 98.

5   *S v UK* Application No 11716/85, (1986) 47 DR 274.

6   *Rasmussen v Denmark* 7 EHRR 377, para 29; *Belgian Linguistic Case (No 2)* (above), para 9.

7   10 EHRR 394, paras 36 and 40 (see **p 334**).

8   17 EHRR 293, paras 36 and 37 (see **p 332**).

took the view that it was unnecessary to consider Art 8 taken alone. Generally, however, where a breach of a substantive Article is found, the European Court finds it unnecessary to consider Art 14 as a separate issue.

Justification

3.183   A difference in treatment is justified, if it pursues a legitimate aim, and, if there is a reasonable relationship of proportionality between the means employed and the aim sought to be realised[1]. Whether there is a reasonable justification will depend upon the facts of each case and the width of the margin of appreciation will vary according to the grounds upon which persons are differently treated.

3.184   For example, exceptional grounds would be necessary in order for the State to justify discrimination against illegitimate children. In *Marckx v Belgium*[2], the Court rejected the State's argument that the aim of certain illegitimacy rules was to support and encourage the traditional family and went on to find that there was no objective or reasonable justification under Art 14 for applying different inheritance rules to illegitimate children.

Key cases include the *Belgian Linguistic Case (No 2), Markx v Belgium, Rasmussen v Denmark, Inze v Austria, Hoffman v Austria and McMichael v UK*[3].

FIRST PROTOCOL, ARTICLE 2: THE RIGHT TO EDUCATION

3.185   Article 2 of the First Protocol reads:

> 'No person shall be denied the right to education. In the exercise of any functions which it assumes in relation to education and to teaching, the state shall respect the rights of parents to ensure such education and teaching are in conformity with their own religious and philosophical convictions.'

The UK made a reservation in respect of the principle in the second sentence to the effect that the principle is accepted only so far as it is compatible with the provision of efficient instruction and training and the avoidance of unreasonable public expenditure[4].

Generally

3.186   The right to education in Art 2 of the First Protocol has been framed in negative terms rather than in positive terms. In the *Belgian Linguistic Case (No 2)*[5], it was established that the rights guaranteed by the first sentence are:

– a right of access to existing educational institutions;
– a right to be educated in the national language or in one of the national languages. From this, a right to an effective education has been inferred;

---

1   *Belgian Linguistic Case (No 2)* (above), para 10 at p 284.
2   2 EHRR 330.
3   All above.
4   Part II of Sch 3 to the HRA 1998.
5   1 EHRR 252.

– a right to official recognition of the studies a student has successfully completed.

3.187 It is for the State to regulate the right to education, and whilst it may have regard to 'the needs and resources of the community and of individuals', such regulation must 'never injure the substance of the right to education nor conflict with other rights enshrined in the Convention'[1]. The right to an effective education does not require the State to establish at its own expense, or to subsidise, education of any particular type or at any particular level[2]. Nor is there a right of access to a particular State school of choice[3]. The right to education has been held to be concerned primarily with elementary education and not necessarily to more advanced studies such as technology[4]. However, this approach may well be reviewed in the future.

State schools/private schools/home education
3.188 The State is responsible for both state schools and private schools[5]. Although there is a right to start and run a private school, it is always subject to regulation by the State in order to ensure in particular the quality of the education[6]. The Commission has made it clear that Art 2 of the First Protocol implies a right for the State to establish compulsory schooling, be it in State schools or private tuition, of a satisfactory standard, and that verification and enforcement of educational standards is an integral part of that right[7].

3.189 The issue of special educational needs has been raised in a number of Commission cases. Although parental views have been acknowledged, on the facts to date the Commission has given the greater weight to the educational authorities' assessment as to the child's needs and as to the efficient use of educational resources[8].

Religious and philosophical convictions
3.190 The parents' right is to have their religious and philosophical convictions respected. It applies to all systems of education and to administrative matters such as school discipline[9] as well as academic matters.

3.191 'Respect' means more than 'acknowledge' or 'take into account'; it implies a positive obligation on the part of the State[10]. 'Convictions' have been defined as denoting views that attain a certain level of cogency, seriousness, cohesion and importance[11]. 'Philosophical convictions' have been defined as

---

1   *Belgian Linguistic Case (No 2)* 1 EHRR 252, para 5 at pp 281–282.
2   Ibid, para 13 at p 299.
3   *X v UK* Application No 11644/85 (Dec), (1 December 1986).
4   *X v UK* Application No 5962/72, (1975) 2 DR 50; *15 Foreign Students v UK* Application No 7671/76, (1977) 9 DR 185.
5   *Kjedsen, Busk Madsen and Pedersen v Denmark* 1 EHRR 711.
6   *Ingrid Jordebo Foundation of Christian Schools and Ingrid Jordebo v Sweden* Application No 11533/85, (1987) 51 DR 125.
7   *Family H v UK* Application No 10233/83 (Dec), (6 March 1984) 37 DR 105.
8   *Graeme v UK* Application No 13387/88 (Dec), (5 February 1990) 64 DR 158; *Klerks v The Netherlands* Application No 25212/94, (4 July 1995) 82 DR 129.
9   *Campbell and Cosans v UK* 4 EHRR 293, para 35; also *Warwick v UK* Application No 9471/81, (1986) 60 DR 5; *B and D v UK* Application No 9303/81, (1986) 49 DR 44.
10   *Campbell and Cosans v UK* 4 EHRR 293, para 37(a) (see **p 317**).
11   Ibid, para 36.

'such convictions as are worthy of respect in a democratic society ... and are not incompatible with human dignity; in addition they must not conflict with the fundamental right of the child to education ... '[1]. In respect of 'education' and 'teaching', the Court has said that 'the education of children is the whole process whereby in any society, adults endeavour to transmit their beliefs, culture and other values to the young, whereas teaching or instruction refers in particular to the transmission of knowledge and to intellectual development'[2].

3.192   The right provides protection against indoctrination by the state in schools[3]. However, school curricula are a matter for the State, and in *Kjeldsen, Busk Madsen and Pedersen v Denmark*[4] where the applicant parents objected to sex education, the Court held that parents cannot object to the integration of religious or philosophical teaching into the curriculum, as such objection would have disruptive consequences for the organisation of teaching. What the parent is entitled to is that this information be conveyed 'in an objective, critical and pluralistic manner'.

Relationship with other Articles

3.193   In those cases where discrimination can be demonstrated in respect of access to education, a breach under Art 14 of the Convention may also arise[5]. Corporal punishment as a disciplinary measure in school has exercised the Court both under Art 2 of the First Protocol and under Art 3 of the Convention[6]. Article 2 of the First Protocol has a close relationship with Arts 8, 9 and 10. In the *Kjeldsen* case[7] the Court stated:

> 'The provisions of the Convention and Protocol must be read as a whole ... Accordingly, the two sentences of Article 2 must be read not only in the light of each other but also in particular of Articles 8, 9 and 10 of the Convention which proclaim the right of everyone including the parents and children "to respect for his private and family life", to "freedom of thought, conscience and religion" and to "freedom ... to receive and impart information and ideas".'

The Article also has a direct relationship with Art 5(1)(d) which deals with deprivation of liberty for the purpose of educational supervision[8].

OTHER ARTICLES WHICH MAY IMPACT ON FAMILY LAW

Article 9: Freedom of thought, conscience and religion

3.194   Under Art 9, everyone has the right to freedom of thought, conscience and religion including the right to change his religion or belief. This is an absolute right. It also includes the freedom to manifest his religion or belief in worship,

---

1   *Campbell and Cosans v UK* 4 EHRR 293, para 36.
2   Ibid, para 33.
3   *Kjeldsen, Busk Madsen and Pederson v Denmark* 1 EHRR 711, para 56.
4   Ibid, para 53; also *Valsamis v Greece* 24 EHRR 294.
5   *Belgian Linguistic Case (No 2)* 1 EHRR 252.
6   *Campbell and Cosans v UK* (above); *Tyrer v UK* 2 EHRR 1; *Costello-Roberts v UK* 19 EHRR 112; *A v UK* (above).
7   Above, para 52.
8   *Bouamar v Belgium* 11 EHRR 1.

teaching, practice and observance. This is subject to the limitations of 'lawfulness' and 'necessity in a democratic society'.

3.195 As enshrined in Art 9, freedom of thought, conscience and religion is one of the foundations of a 'democratic society' within the Convention. 'It is, in its religious dimension, one of the most vital elements that go to make up the identity of believers and of their conception of life, but it is also a precious asset for atheists, agnostics, sceptics and the unconcerned'[1]. It therefore protects the non-religious as well as the religious and includes such issues as pacifism or vegetarianism and veganism.

3.196 The rights protected by Art 9 often overlap with other Convention rights such as those under Art 8 and Art 2 of the First Protocol and the Court has tended to deal with Art 9 issues under these other Articles. In *Hoffmann v Austria*[2], for example, the Court treated the question of custody, where one of the parents was a Jehovah's Witness, as falling within Art 8 rather than Art 9. It is, therefore, unlikely that Art 9 by itself will have any real impact upon the approach currently taken by the domestic court in the blood transfusion cases involving Jehovah's Witnesses.

3.197 In a recent case, *Re J (Specific Issue Orders: Muslim Upbringing and Circumcision)*[3], Wall J made a prohibited steps order to prevent the circumcision of a 5-year-old boy without the permission of the court. In the course of his judgment he considered Art 9. He accepted that the father's right to manifest his religion included the right to arrange for the circumcision of his child, and went on to consider whether, if a restriction on that freedom were imposed by the court, such an interference was justifiable. He concluded that where two parents have equal rights under Art 9, limitations on the right of one parent to manifest his religion could be imposed if the exercise of that right infringed or conflicted with the rights and freedoms of the other parent or child and was not in the best interests of the child. He further found that prohibiting circumcision in those circumstances was not discriminatory under Art 14.

Article 1 of the First Protocol: right to property

3.198 Article 1 of the First Protocol provides that:

'every natural person or legal person is entitled to the peaceful enjoyment of his possessions. No one shall be deprived of his possessions except in the public interest and subject to the conditions provided for by law and by the general principles of international law. The preceding provisions shall not, however, in any way impair the right of a state to enforce such laws as it deems necessary, to control the use of property in accordance with the general interest or to secure the payment of taxes or other contributions or penalties.'

Article 1 in substance guarantees the right of property[4] and includes all interests in land and matrimonial assets.

3.199 Ancillary relief applications and occupation orders, which deprive a person of their possessions, fall within Art 1 of the First Protocol. There are, however, no reported Convention cases which deal with ancillary relief appli-

---

1   *Kokkinakis v Greece* 17 EHRR 397.
2   17 EHRR 293.
3   [1999] 2 FLR 678.
4   *Marckx v Belgium* 2 EHRR 330, para 63.

cations and, therefore, there is no guidance as to how Art 1 will impact upon matrimonial finance cases.

3.200   Article 1 of the First Protocol also becomes relevant to family law in the context of: (i) pensions and, potentially, pension sharing orders; and (ii) inheritance when it is combined with Art 14, although in both cases its impact is likely to be of limited effect.

Article 5 of the Seventh Protocol: equality of rights of spouses

3.201   Article 5 of the Seventh Protocol reads:

> 'Spouses shall enjoy equality of rights and responsibilities of a private law character between them, and in their relations with their children, as to marriage, during marriage, and in the event of its dissolution. This Art shall not prevent states from taking such measures as are necessary in the interests of children.'

The Article relates to the rights and responsibilities of spouses under private law. Only spouses are protected.

3.202   The Explanatory Memorandum states that Art 5 'should not be understood as preventing the national authorities from taking due account of all relevant factors when reaching decisions with regard to the division of property in the event of the dissolution of marriage'[1]. Further, Art 5 does not prevent the State from taking measures which may result in the spouses not having equal private law rights and responsibilities in their relations with their children where this is necessary in the interests of the children.

3.203   This provision has the potential for giving rise in future ancillary relief applications to the critical questions: (i) whether or not the right to equality enshrined in Art 5 of the Seventh Protocol requires an equal division of the spouses' assets on divorce; and (ii) if yes, whether and to what extent s 25 of the Matrimonial Causes Act 1973 is incompatible with the Convention and requires amendment.

3.204   This may be one of the reasons why Art 5 of the Seventh Protocol has not yet been included in the HRA 1998, as the Government foresaw the potential incompatibility between our domestic law in relation to the property rights of spouses and the Seventh Protocol[2]. The Government has, however, laid down a marker that it intends 'to legislate to remove these inconsistencies when a suitable opportunity occurs, and then to sign and ratify the Protocol'[3].

---

1   Explanatory Memorandum, para 38.
2   White Paper: *Rights Brought Home: The Human Rights Bill* (Cm 3782), paras 4.15 and 4.16.
3   White Paper: para 4.15.

Chapter 4

THE NEW EUROPEAN COURT: A BRIEF SUMMARY

4.1   On 1 November 1998, a new permanent, full time, single European Court of Human Rights was established in accordance with the Eleventh Protocol to the Convention. The procedural rules which now apply are the Rules of the European Court of Human Rights (4 November 1998) ('the Rules').

STRUCTURE AND PROCEDURE OF THE NEW COURT

4.2   To consider the cases brought before it, the new European Court sits in:

–   A Committee comprising three judges which may, by unanimous vote, declare individual applications[1] inadmissible or strike them off the list[2]. The decision is final. If the Committee makes no such decision, the application is forwarded to the Chamber.

–   A Chamber consisting of seven judges which decides upon: (i) the admissibility; and (ii) the merits of the case[3]. The decision on admissibility is taken separately unless the Court in exceptional circumstances decides otherwise. The Chamber may at once declare the application inadmissible or strike it out of the Court's list of cases[4]. Alternatively, it may decide to: (i) request the parties to submit further relevant material; (ii) give notice to the respondent contracting party and invite that party to submit written observations on the application; and (iii) invite the parties to submit further observations in writing[5]. At the request of the parties or of its own motion, it may decide to hold a hearing at which the parties will be also invited to address the issues on the merits[6]. If admissible, the Chamber, acting through the Registrar, enters into contact with the parties with a view to securing a friendly settlement[7]. The friendly settlement negotiations are confidential and without prejudice to the parties' arguments in the contentious proceedings. If a friendly settlement is effected, the Court strikes the case out of its list by means of a decision which is confined to a brief statement of the facts and of the solution[8]. If no agreement is reached, the case proceeds. The Chamber may invite the parties to submit further evidence and written observations[9] and a hearing on the merits is held, if the Chamber decides of its own motion, or if one of the parties requests it, provided there has been no hearing addressing the merits at the admissibility stage[10]. The conduct of the hearing is governed by Rules 63–70. If the Chamber considers that the case raises a serious

---

1   Eleventh Protocol, Art 34.
2   Ibid, Arts 27(10) and 28.
3   Ibid, Art 29.
4   Rules of Court of the ECHR ('the Rules'): r 54(1).
5   Ibid, r 54(3).
6   Ibid, r 54(4).
7   Ibid, r 62.
8   Eleventh Protocol, Art 39.
9   The Rules, r 59 (1).
10   Ibid, r 59(2).

question affecting the interpretation of the Convention or the protocols or where the resolution of a question before it might have a result inconsistent with a judgment previously delivered, the Chamber may relinquish jurisdiction in favour of the Grand Chamber, unless one of the parties in the case objects[1]. The judgment of the Chamber becomes final: (i) when the parties declare that they will not request that the case be referred to the Grand Court; or (ii) three months after the date of judgment, if a reference to the Grand Chamber has not been requested; or (iii) when the Grand Chamber rejects the request to refer[2]. Where the Chamber finds that there has been a violation of the Convention, it generally gives in the same judgment a ruling on just satisfaction[3].

– A Grand Chamber comprising of 17 judges which deals with the cases where the Chambers has relinquished jurisdiction[4]. In exceptional cases, the Grand Chamber may re-hear a case. This is conditional on at least five of the judges of the Grand Chamber accepting that the case raises a serious question affecting the interpretation or application of the Convention and the Protocols or ' a serious issue of general importance'[5]. It must be at the request of any party within a period of 3 months from the date of judgment.

The Plenary Court does not hear cases. It is responsible for appointing the President of the Chambers, constituting Chambers, adopting rules of procedure and for the election of Presidents and Vice-Presidents of the Court.

PRACTICE

4.3   Under Art 34 of the Eleventh Protocol the Court may receive applications from any person, non-governmental organisation or group of individuals claiming to be the victim of a violation by one of the contracting parties of the rights set forth in the Convention or the protocols.

4.4   An application has to be made on the application form provided by the registry[6], signed by the applicant or by the applicant's representative[7] and must set out[8]:

– the name, date of birth, nationality, sex, occupation and address of the applicant;
– the name, occupation and address of the representative, if any;
– the name of the contracting party or parties against which the application is made;
– a succinct statement of facts;
– a succinct statement of the alleged violations of the Convention and the relevant arguments;

---

1   Eleventh Protocol, Art 30.
2   Ibid, Art 44; also r 74 of the Rules.
3   The Rules, r 75(1).
4   Eleventh Protocol, Art 31; also r 72 of the Rules.
5   Ibid, Art 43; also r 73 of the Rules.
6   The Rules, r 47.
7   Ibid, r 45.
8   Ibid, r 47.

- a succinct statement on the applicant's compliance with the admissibility criteria;
- the object of the application as well as a general indication of any claims for just satisfaction which the applicant may wish to make under Art 41 of the Convention;
- copies of any relevant documents and, in particular, the decisions, whether judicial or not, relating to the object of the application.

4.5   Once the case is registered, a judge is designated as a Judge Rapporteur who examines the application, decides whether the application is to be considered by a Committee or by a Chamber and in either case prepares a written report[1] which is then taken into account in their respective deliberations[2].

4.6   Any plea of inadmissibility must be raised by the respondent contracting party in its written or oral submissions on the admissibility of the application submitted[3].

4.7   Any claim which the applicant may wish to make for just satisfaction under Art 41 of the Convention must be set out in the written observations on the merits, or if no such written observations are filed, in a special document filed no later than 2 months after the decision declaring the application admissible[4]. Itemised particulars of all claims made, together with supporting documents are required; otherwise the Chamber may reject the claim in whole or in part[5].

4.8   A contracting party may intervene as a third party in all cases before the Chamber or the Grand Chamber where one of its nationals is an applicant. It has the right to submit written comments and to take part in the proceedings[6].

4.9   As to the admissibility criteria, the Court may only deal with the matter after all domestic remedies have been exhausted; generally, in civil cases, this is the Court of Appeal. It may, however, be necessary to go to the House of Lords where, for example, there are conflicting decisions of the Court of Appeal. In child-care cases, it may not be necessary even to apply to the Court of Appeal, which rarely intervenes on issues of fact. The Court can only deal with the matter within a period of 6 months from the date on which the final decision was taken. It must not deal with any individual application which is anonymous, or substantially the same as a matter which has already been examined by the Court.

4.10   The Court shall declare inadmissible any individual application which it considers:

(a) incompatible with the provisions of the Convention:
  (i)   *ratione personae:* where the complaint is against a State which has not signed the Convention or Protocol or against an individual for whom the State is not responsible or where the applicant is not a victim;
  (ii) *ratione materiae:* where the complaint falls outside the ambit of the Article relied upon or concerns a right which is not included in the Convention;

---

1   The Rules, r 49.
2   Ibid, rr 53 and 54.
3   Ibid, r 55.
4   Ibid, r 60(1).
5   Ibid, r 60(2).
6   Eleventh Protocol, Art 36; also r 6.

(iii) *ratione temporis:* where the complaint concerns events which occurred before a contracting State's acceptance of the right of individual petition under Art 25;

(iv) *ratione loci:* where the complaint concerns events in a territory outside the contracting State;

(b) manifestly ill-founded:

(i) where the complaint is not supported by the evidence adduced or otherwise is not substantiated;

(ii) where the facts do not in fact disclose an interference with the right invoked;

(iii) where there is an interference but it is one which is justified on the grounds contained in the Article;

(iv) where the applicant ceases to be a victim;

(c) an abuse of the right of application:

(i) where there is fraud or deliberate misrepresentation;

(ii) where the application is vexatious;

(iii) where the claim is based on matters for which the applicant is in fact responsible;

(iv) where there has been a breach of the rules of confidentiality.

PART B

THE LIKELY IMPACT OF THE CONVENTION ON FAMILY LAW

Chapter 5

THE UNBORN CHILD

ABORTION

Key Articles

5.1   Article 2 (right to life), Art 3 (inhuman treatment), Art 8 (right to respect for private and family life), Art 10 (freedom of expression).

The right to life: Article 2

5.2   Issues relating to abortion have proved controversial in both domestic and Convention law and the Commission has tended to avoid a definition of 'life' under Art 2 in the context of the unborn child.

5.3   Under domestic criminal law, an unborn child has a right to be born alive but this is subject to the overriding principles that the mother's physical and mental health and safety have precedence and that she has a right to terminate a pregnancy where the child will be born with serious handicap[1].

Case-law

5.4   Cases involving abortion have been brought by potential fathers seeking to prevent an abortion. In *Paton v British Pregnancy Advisory Service Trustees*[2], in an injunction application brought by a father, the domestic court held that a foetus did not have a legal right to obtain an injunction until it was born and had a separate existence from its mother. In *Paton v UK*[3], the father later made a complaint to the Commission that there had been a violation of the foetus' right to life under Art 2 by the State in allowing his wife to terminate a 10-week pregnancy on health grounds. The Commission, in ruling that there was no breach, stated:

> 'both the general usage of the term "everyone" in the Convention . . . and the context in which this term is employed in Article 2 . . . tend to support the view that it does not include the unborn.'[4]

The Commission further held that there was no 'absolute' right to life of the foetus on the following grounds:

> 'The "life" of the foetus is intimately connected with, and cannot be regarded in isolation from, the life of the pregnant woman. If Article 2 were held to cover the

---

1   Abortion Act 1967, s 1(1) as amended; see also the offences under s 1 of the Infant Life (Preservation) Act 1929 (child destruction); ss 58 and 59 of the Offences Against the Person Act 1861 (procuring a miscarriage) and s 60 (endeavouring to conceal the birth); and s 1 of the Infanticide Act 1938 (infanticide). See also *Re SG (Adult Mental Patient: Abortion)* [1991] 2 FLR 329.

2   [1979] 1 QB 276 at 279 C–D per Sir George Baker P; affirmed by Court of Appeal in *C v S* [1988] QB 135; see also *Burton v Islington HA* [1993] QB 204 where it was held that although the foetus did not enjoy an independent legal identity, a child who suffered pre-natal injuries due to negligence during the mother's pregnancy, had a cause of action at birth.

3   3 EHRR 408.

4   Ibid, para 9.

foetus and its protection under Article 2 were, in the absence of any express limitation, seen as absolute, an abortion would have to be considered as prohibited even where the continuance of the pregnancy would involve serious risk to the life of the pregnant woman. This would mean that the unborn life of the foetus would be regarded as of higher value than the life of the pregnant woman. The "right to life" of a person already born would thus be considered as subject not only to the express limitations mentioned in (Article 2 (2)), but also to a further implied limitation.'[1]

It, however, declined to consider whether Art 2 does not cover the foetus at all or whether it recognises a 'right to life' of the foetus with implied limitations[2].

5.5 In *H v Norway*[3], a 14-week-old foetus was lawfully terminated under Norwegian law on the statutory ground that 'the pregnancy, birth or care for the child may place the woman in a difficult situation in life', ie on social rather than medical grounds. Although the father's complaint that the lack of protection for the life of the unborn child in these circumstances was a violation of Art 2 failed, the Commission did 'not exclude that in certain circumstances' the foetus could enjoy protection under Art 2. It did not, however, go on to specify the nature of those circumstances and, given the width of the statutory ground which was approved in *H v Norway*, they must be regarded as being limited in scope.

5.6 It is the wide divergence in the national laws of the contracting States relating to abortion that has led to the Commission's cautious approach in respect of Art 2 'in such a delicate area'[4] to be that the contracting States must have a broad discretion and, as a result, to date, all the abortion cases have failed to cross the admissibility threshold.

Impact

5.7 Under both domestic and Convention case-law, potential fathers have been refused injunctive relief to prevent the mother from having a lawful abortion on health grounds, and under Convention case-law on social hardship grounds. The rights of the mother have in each case prevailed over the rights of the father. It is, therefore, unlikely that the incorporation of the Convention into domestic law will have the effect of re-opening the door closed to potential fathers by the *Paton* case and *C v S*. However, the present reluctance to recognise the absolute right to life of the unborn child may in the future change as medical techniques advance and moral values evolve and there may be future challenges to the Abortion Act 1967 on the grounds that its provisions are incompatible with Art 2.

Inhuman treatment: Article 3

Case-law

5.8 The issue of pain caused to the foetus in the course of an abortion was raised in *H v Norway*[5]. The Commission found this complaint under Art 8 to be manifestly unfounded upon the material before it.

---

1   3 EHRR 408, paras 18 and 19.
2   Ibid, para 23.
3   Application No 17004/90 (Dec), (19 May 1992) (unpublished).
4   Ibid.
5   Ibid.

Impact

5.9   As the decision in *H v Norway* turned upon the evidence adduced before the Commission, there is a possibility that as medical technology develops evidence may become available in the future to substantiate such complaint. However, for the present, it is unlikely that Art 3 will have an impact upon the abortion issue.

Respect for private life: Article 8

Case-law

5.10   A Convention point involving abortion may arise where a pregnant woman claims a wider right to abortion than that provided for under the domestic law as part of her right to respect for private life under Art 8.

5.11   In *Bruggeman and Scheuten v FRG*[1], the Commission considered whether a State's refusal to allow a woman to have an abortion where the pregnancy was unwanted violated her right to a private life. Under German law, lawful abortion had been restricted to certain specified grounds and the applicants complained that as a result they would either have to renounce sexual intercourse or to apply methods of contraception or to carry out a pregnancy against their will. The Commission refused to decide whether the unborn child is to be considered a 'life' in the sense of Art 2 of the Convention or whether it could 'be regarded as an entity which under Art 8(2) could justify an interference "for the protection of others" '[2] and went on to find that:

> 'Not every regulation of the termination of unwanted pregnancies constitutes an interference with the right to respect for private life of the mother. Article 8(1) cannot be interpreted as meaning that pregnancy and its termination are, as a principle, solely a matter of the private life of the mother.'[3]

Impact

5.12   It remains possible that the European Court may in a future Convention case find a violation where the national law imposes restrictions, which in the social context then prevailing, are considered to be an interference with the mother's right to privacy. However, in the light of the Commission's approach in *H v Norway*, the restrictions under our current domestic law relating to abortion are, for the present and immediate future, likely to be acceptable to both the European Court and the domestic court.

Freedom of expression: Article 10

Case-law

5.13   The leading Convention case is *Open Door Counselling and Dublin Well Woman v Ireland*[4], where the applicants who provided counselling to pregnant women in and about Dublin complained under Art 10 of an injunction imposed

PART B
IMPACT OF THE CONVENTION

---

1   3 EHRR 244.
2   Ibid, para 60.
3   Ibid, para 61.
4   15 EHRR 244.

by the Irish courts which effectively restrained the imparting of information to pregnant women concerning abortion facilities outside Ireland.

5.14   The Court found that there had been a violation of Art 10. It was not disputed that the injunction interfered with the applicants' freedom to impart information. The issues which arose were whether the restriction had a legitimate aim under Art 10(2), was necessary in a democratic society and satisfied the proportionality test.

5.15   In respect of the first issue, the Court took into account that the basis for the protection afforded under Irish law to the right to life of the unborn child was the profound moral values concerning the nature of life reflected in the stance of the majority of the Irish people against abortion reflected in a referendum and held that 'the restriction pursued the legitimate aim of the protection of morals of which the protection in Ireland of the right to the life of the unborn child is one aspect'[1]. The Court made clear, however, that it was not called upon to examine whether a right to abortion is guaranteed under the Convention or whether the foetus is encompassed by the right to life as contained in Art 2[2].

5.16   In respect of the second and third issues, the Court's view was that, although national authorities 'enjoy a wide margin of appreciation in respect of morals, particularly in an area such as the present which touches on matters of belief concerning the nature of human life, ... this power of appreciation is not unlimited'[3], and it went on to hold that the injunction, which imposed a perpetual restraint on the provision of information to pregnant women concerning abortion facilities abroad, regardless of age, state of health or their reasons for seeking counselling on the termination of pregnancy was too sweeping and, therefore, disproportionate to the aims pursued. The Court observed that 'limitations on information concerning activities which, notwithstanding their moral implications, have been and continue to be tolerated by national authorities, call for careful scrutiny by the Convention institutions as to their conformity with the tenets of democratic society'.

Impact
5.17   It follows from the *Open Door* case that even where abortion is unlawful in a contracting State, women may claim a right of access to information relating to abortions performed lawfully in another contracting State. The case has, however, a wider significance in that it shows the European Court taking its first tentative steps towards deriving from Art 10 a general right of access to information.

OTHER MEANS OF PROTECTION FOR THE UNBORN CHILD

Key Articles

5.18   Article 2 (right to life), Art 3 (inhuman treatment) and Art 8 (right to respect for private and family life).

---

1   15 EHRR 244, para 63.
2   Ibid, para 66.
3   Ibid, para 68.

Domestic law

5.19   Under domestic civil law, there is no power by which any person or authority can take steps to make a mother care for herself (eg where she proposes to take harmful drugs), and therefore her unborn child, other than where the mother suffers from mental disorder and the provisions of the Mental Health Act 1983 apply.

5.20   Although in two first instance decisions the court gave authority in the first for an emergency Caesarean section to be performed and, in the second, for the termination of labour either by forceps delivery or by Caesarean section where the mothers were not suffering from mental disorder and had not given consent[1], the Court of Appeal in *Re MB (Medical Treatment)*[2] in establishing the principles which were to apply in such cases held, inter alia, that:

> 'a competent woman who has the capacity to decide may, for religious reasons, other reasons, for rational or irrational reasons or for no reason at all, choose not to have medical intervention, even though the consequence may be the death or serious handicap of the child she bears, or her own death. In that event the courts do not have the jurisdiction to declare medical intervention lawful and the question of her own best interests objectively considered, does not arise.'[3]

Impact of the Convention

5.21   The Convention organs have not directly considered whether the State must provide adequate protection under Arts 2, 3 and 8 in these circumstances. However, if in the future recognition were to be given to the absolute right to life of the foetus in the light of evolving moral values and scientific advances, then this would open up the way for challenging the current lack of measures to protect the unborn child from harmful acts of pregnant mothers.

Sterilisation

5.22   Forms of birth control and sterilisation have been unexplored by the Convention organs, save for an unpublished decision which stated that an operation for sterilisation might in certain circumstances involve a breach of Art 2. However, there is clearly a future potential in this area for issues to arise where Arts 2, 3, 8 and 12 may become relevant.

HUMAN FERTILISATION AND EMBRYOLOGY

Key Articles

5.23   Article 2 (right to life), Art 3 (inhuman treatment), Art 8 (right to respect for private and family life) and Art 12 (right to found a family).

---

1   *Re S (Adult: Refusal of Medical Treatment)* [1993] Fam 123; *Norfolk and Norwich Healthcare (NHS) Trust v W* [1996] 2 FLR 613.

2   [1997] 2 FLR 426; see also *St George's Healthcare NHS Trust v S; R v Collins and others, ex parte S* [1998] 3 All ER 673.

3   Ibid, at 436H–437A per Butler-Sloss LJ.

Domestic law: a summary

5.24   In domestic law, the creation, use and storage of human embryos outside the body is regulated under the Human Fertilisation and Embryology Act 1990 ('HFE Act 1990') by the Human Fertilisation and Embryology Authority. The regulatory framework encompasses, among other things, in vitro fertilisation ('IVF'), donor insemination and research involving the creation or use of human embryos. Anyone undertaking an activity governed by the HFE Act 1990, without an HFEA licence, may be guilty of a criminal offence.

Assisted reproduction

5.25   Assisted reproduction by artificial insemination is the placing in a woman of sperm, eggs or an embryo. Conception can be procured either by mixing sperms and eggs (conventional IVF) or by injecting a single sperm directly into the egg (ICSI: intracytoplasmic sperm injection).

5.26   The sperm may be given by the woman's husband (AIH) or by another man (AID). Where a married woman gives birth to a child born as a result of either AIH or AID, her husband is treated in law as the father of the child[1]. Where an unmarried couple together seek licensed treatment services[2] and the woman gives birth as a result of AID, it is again her male partner, rather than the donor of the sperm, who is treated for legal purposes as the father of the child[3]. Where a child is born as a result of assisted reproduction without the consent of the husband/partner, the child is treated in law as having no father.

5.27   IVF can also involve the donation of an egg or eggs by one woman (the donor) to another (the donee). Section 27(1) of the HFE Act 1990 provides that where there is a donation of eggs and semen or embryo (ie where the fertilised egg is implanted in a woman), the donee who gives birth is to be treated as the child's mother. Although the section does not deal with the position where only the eggs are donated, the assumption is that the donee who gives birth should be treated as the child's mother.

5.28   The HFE Act 1990 prohibits the storage of eggs or sperm without the consent of the donor[4]. In *R v Human Fertilisation and Embryology Authority, ex parte Blood*[5], where the sperm was taken whilst the donor was in a coma and where no consent had previously been given by him for storage, the Authority was held to be correct in refusing a licence for treatment involving the use of his sperm.

Surrogacy

5.29   Where a woman is unable to carry a child full term, surrogacy provides a method whereby she can have her own child. Although the Surrogacy Arrange-

---

1   HFE Act 1990, ss 28(2), s 49(3), 7(4).
2   Ibid, Sch 2.
3   Ibid, ss 28(3) and 29(1); also *U v W (Attorney General Intervening)* [1997] 2 FLR 282.
4   Ibid, Sch 3, para 8.
5   [1997] 2 FLR 742. However, the Court of Appeal went on to hold that the authority had a wide discretion to allow the export of sperm and, on refusing Mrs Blood's request to export the sperm to Belgium, the authority had failed to consider the effect of the EC Treaty whereby a citizen was entitled to receive services in another Member State. No precedent was being created as in the future no sperm would be stored without written consent. Therefore, in the exceptional circumstances of the present case, the authority was given an opportunity to reconsider its decision in the light of the judgment.

ments Act 1985 makes those who make surrogacy arrangements on a commercial basis criminally liable, the Act does not forbid all surrogacy arrangements.

5.30 Partial surrogacy is where the surrogate mother (ie the mother who gives birth to the child) is the genetic mother in the sense that it is her egg which is fertilised by the semen of the commissioning father. The surrogate mother is the child's mother for all purposes and has parental responsibility. If she is married, the child is treated as the child of the surrogate mother and her husband, unless it is shown that he did not consent to the insemination. If she is not married, the commissioning and donating father is the genetic father and is entitled to seek a parental responsibility order.

5.31 Total surrogacy is either where the surrogate mother receives an egg from another woman, the commissioning mother, which has been fertilised by the commissioning father's semen or she receives an unfertilised egg which is then fertilised with the semen of the commissioning father. Although the genetic parents are the commissioning parents, under the HFE Act 1990 it will be the surrogate mother who is to be treated as the mother[1] and her husband who is to be treated as the father unless it is shown that he did not consent[2].

5.32 Section 30 of the HFE Act 1990 provides for a married couple as commissioning parents to apply for an order that they be treated in law as the parents of a child born to a woman by partial or total surrogacy. They may seek care and control under the inherent jurisdiction of the High Court[3] and thereafter apply for an adoption order or they may apply for a residence or contact order under the Children Act 1989 if they have the consent of the surrogate mother[4] or have looked after the child for at least 3 years[5] or with leave of the court[6]. If the surrogate mother places the child with the commissioning parents for adoption, the placement is illegal unless pursuant to an order of the High Court or with 'a relative'[7] which would only include a commissioning father where the surrogate mother is unmarried or, if married, her husband did not consent to the insemination.

Cloning[8]

5.33 In 1997, Dolly the sheep, the first vertebrate cloned from the cell of an adult animal, claimed world-wide attention and raised international concern about the future evolution of cloning technology, particularly in the context of 'human reproductive cloning' which involves the creation of a human being who is genetically identical to another.

PART B
IMPACT OF THE CONVENTION

---

1   HFE Act 1990, s 27(2).
2   Ibid, s 28.
3   *Re C (A Minor) (Wardship: Surrogacy)* [1985] FLR 846; but see *Re P(Minors)(Wardship: Surrogacy)* [1987] 2 FLR 421 which demonstrates the difficulties facing commissioning parents where the surrogate mother has appropriate parenting skills.
4   Children Act 1989, s 10(5)(c)(iii).
5   Ibid, s 10(5)(b).
6   Ibid, s 10(2)(b).
7   Adoption Act 1976, s 11.
8   For a detailed discussion, see the Joint Paper by the Human Genetics Advisory Commission and the Human Fertilisation and Embryology Authority 'Cloning Issues in Reproduction, Science and Medicine' (issued December 1998) and a paper 'Medical Legal Issues Arising From Extra Corporeal Fertilisation' given by Simon Fishel, PhD to the FLBA Annual Conference, 9 May 1998.

'Reproductive cloning' is where an entire animal is produced from a single cell by asexual reproduction. It is to be distinguished from 'therapeutic cloning' which involves the medical and scientific application of cloning technology (such as research which might lead to the replacement of damaged or diseased tissues or organs without the risk of rejection reactions) which does not result in the production of genetically identical foetuses or babies.

5.34   Two distinct methods have been used to clone animals and thus, in theory, human beings:

(1) 'Embryo splitting': the artificial division of a single embryo which replicates the natural process giving rise to identical twins. In this case, both the nuclear genes and the small number of mitrochondrial genes are identical.

(2) 'Nuclear replacement': a process which involves the introduction of genetic material (in the form of an individual cell nucleus removed from either an embryonic, foetal or an adult cell) into an unfertilised egg or embryo whose own genetic material (nucleus) has been removed. In this case, the nuclear genes of the clones would be identical, but the mitrochondrial DNA of such clones would be different.

The HFE Act 1990 expressly prohibits the nuclear substitution of an embryo or any cell whilst it forms part of an embryo. Embryo splitting and the nuclear replacement of eggs, although not expressly prohibited by the Act, both involve the use or creation of embryos outside the body and therefore fall within the Act. The Act permits research involving human embryos under licence and within strict limits which must not exceed the fourteenth day of their development. The research must appear to the Authority to be necessary or desirable:

– to promote advances in the treatment of infertility;
– to increase knowledge about the causes of congenital disease or about the causes of miscarriages;
– to develop more effective techniques of contraception or methods for detecting the presence of gene or chromosome abnormalities in embryos before implantation.

This list is not exhaustive and may be extended by the Secretary of State for Health.

5.35   The Authority's current policy is that it will not licence any research which has reproductive cloning as its aim. It will consider other types of research involving embryo splitting or nuclear replacement in eggs, provided it falls within one of the purposes described above or any future regulations.

Convention case-law

5.36   The European Court has only recently taken some hesitant steps towards exploring the implications for family life under Art 8 where a child is born as a result of assisted reproduction and, consequently, lags behind the more innovative approach adopted by the Commission and in our domestic law under the HFE Act 1990.

5.37   The tentative approach of the European Court is demonstrated in the recent case of *X, Y and Z v UK*[1]. X, a female-to-male transsexual, had formed a permanent and stable relationship with Y, a woman, in 1979. That year, he underwent gender reassignment surgery. In 1990, X and Y applied through their general practitioner for AID and in 1991 the hospital ethics committee agreed to provide treatment and asked X to acknowledge himself to be the father of the child within the meaning of the HFE Act 1990. On 30 January 1992, Y was impregnated through AID treatment with sperm from an anonymous donor and Z was born on 13 October 1992. X was not permitted to be registered as Z's father and X, Y and Z complained of a violation of Art 8. The Court held that, although Art 8 was applicable in the present case, there had been no violation of Art 8.

5.38   The Commission acknowledged that it had yet to find in any case that 'family life' exists where there is no blood link or legal nexus of marriage or adoption[2]. However, in this case it did adopt a more robust approach and found that the relationships enjoyed by the applicants fulfilled both the appearance and substance of 'family life' and observed that the only element which detracted from this was the fact that X was registered at birth as being of the female sex with the consequences that he was under a legal incapacity to marry the child's mother or register on the child's birth certificate as father: 'this element, whether seen as biological or historical, cannot outweigh the reality of the applicants' situation which is otherwise indistinguishable from the traditional notion of family life'. It further noted that the UK, in the context of children born by artificial insemination by donor, has itself for the purposes of the HFE Act 1990 accepted that there are circumstances where a 'father' need not be linked to a child either by blood or by marriage to its mother. The Commission went on to find that the applicants enjoyed 'family life' within the meaning of Art 8(1) of the Convention. It considered that although there was the possibility of X obtaining a residence order in respect of Y, this could not be regarded as providing X with legal recognition of his role as father and parent[3]. It concluded that 'having regard in particular to the welfare of Z and her security within her family unit . . . the absence of an appropriate legal regime reflecting the applicants' family ties discloses a failure to respect their family life'[4].

5.39   Whilst the Court likewise considered in the circumstances of the case that de facto family ties linked the three applicants and that Art 8 was, therefore, applicable, it shied away from the more progressive view of the Commission. In considering the margin of appreciation, the Court said:

> 'It is true that the Court has held in the past that where the existence of a family tie with a child has been established, the State must act in a manner calculated to enable that tie to be developed and legal safeguards must be established that render possible, from the moment of birth or as soon as practicable thereafter, the child's integration in his family[5]. However, hitherto in this context it has been called upon to consider

1   20 EHRR 143.
2   See eg *X v France* Application No 9993/82, (5 October 1982) 31 DR 241; *S and S v UK* Application No 10375/83 (Dec), (10 October 1984) 40 DR 196; *Price v UK* Application No 12402/86 (Dec), (14 July 1988) 55 DR 224; *Boyle v UK* 19 EHRR 179.
3   *Boyle v UK* 19 EHRR 179, para 65.
4   Ibid, para 69.
5   See eg *Marckx v Belgium* 2 EHRR 330; *Johnston v Ireland* 9 EHRR 203, para 72; *Keegan v Ireland* 18 EHRR 342, para 18.

only family ties existing between biological parents and their offspring. The present case raises different issues, since Z was conceived by AID and is not related, in the biological sense, to X, who is a transsexual ... it has not been established before the Court that there exists any generally shared approach among the High Contracting Parties with regard to the manner in which social relationships between a child conceived by AID and the person who performs the role of father should be reflected in law. Indeed, according to the information available to the Court, although the technology of medically assisted procreation has been available in Europe for several decades, many of the issues to which it gives rise, particularly with regard to the question of filiation, remain the subject of debate. For example, there is no consensus amongst the Member States of the Council of Europe on the question whether the interests of the child conceived in such a way are best served by preserving the anonymity of the donor of the sperm or whether the child should have the right to know the donor's identity. Since the issues in the case, therefore, touch on areas where there is little common ground amongst the Member States ... and generally speaking, the law appears to be in a transitional stage, the respondent state must be afforded a wide margin of appreciation.'

5.40   In an earlier Commission case, *G v The Netherlands*[1], the applicant agreed to donate sperm to a lesbian couple who wanted to have a child by a known donor. On her birth the child's mother was her legal guardian and a court order later appointed the other partner as joint guardian. The applicant visited the couple regularly during the pregnancy and after the birth, even baby-sitting. The applicant wanted to establish a regular pattern of access, including staying access; whereupon the couple broke off all contact with him. Before the Commission, he complained under Art 8 that the State had unjustly considered that there was no family life between him and his child.

5.41   The Commission held that 'family life' in the sense of Art 8 implies 'close personal ties in addition to parenthood' and that the situation in which a person donates sperm only to enable a woman to become pregnant through artificial insemination does not of itself give the donor a right to respect for family life with the child. It went on to hold that the applicant's contact with the child, both in itself and together with his donorship, formed an insufficient basis for the conclusion that as a result such a close personal tie has developed between them that their relationship fell within the scope of 'family life'. The complaint was therefore rejected.

5.42   In two other Commission cases[2], prisoners complained under Art 12 that they had been refused artificial insemination by AID of their wives who due to age or health were not able to wait for their release. Each case was struck off when permission was granted and given the circumstances it is difficult to see how the Government could have argued that the interference was justified.

5.43   To date, surrogacy issues have not been considered either by the Commission or the Court.

---

1   16 EHRR CD 39 and *Kroon v The Netherlands*, 19 EHRR 263, para 32.
2   Application No 10822/84 (Dec), (7 May 1987) and 17142/90 (Dec), (10 July 1991); also Application No 20004/92 (Dec), (7 May 1993).

Impact

5.44 The field of human fertilisation and embryology will confront the European Court and the domestic courts with difficult and novel questions relating to, for example, the treatment of children born by artificial reproduction techniques and their relationships with their non-biological 'parents'. The domestic court, as a human rights' court, will have an important role to play in providing a dynamic interpretation of the rights guaranteed under Articles 2, 3, 8 and 12 of the Convention to meet these new challenges and in developing the human rights' jurisprudence to deal with the complex legal issues arising from the future evolution of reproductive technology.

5.45 *Assisted reproduction technology* has already generated a number of controversial issues which have caused general disquiet and are likely to become amongst the major legal, social and ethical problems of the future.

5.46 *Posthumous conception,* as already witnessed in the *Blood* case

5.47 *Older mothers,* who wish to use the technology to have children beyond the conventional age for child-bearing. If they were denied access to the new technology simply on the grounds of age, it may be arguable that there has been a violation of Arts 8 and 12 in conjunction with Art 14.

5.48 *Genetic diagnosis.* The technology is now available to undertake genetic/ chromosome analysis for pre-conception diagnosis, for example, of such diseases as the onset of a future cancer and can also be used for gender selection. Questions which may arise would be whether the rights guaranteed under Arts 8 and 12 include a parental right of 'embryo veto' where embryos free from disease or of the desired sex may be selected and compromised embryos aborted. In the future, it may also be scientifically possible to choose the characteristics of a child. Such questions, however, will inevitably create a tension between the Art 8 and Art 12 rights and the right to life under Art 2.

5.49 *Cloning by asexual reproduction.* This has the potential for raising a number of difficult issues of which the following examples are no more than a cross-section:

Example 1: whether the right to life for an individual under Art 2 should be interpreted to include a right to their own genetic identity and, if so, whether the existence of a clone, stripped of its uniqueness, would be regarded as degrading under Art 3. Would, therefore, a distinction have to be made between different artificial technologies depending on whether they have natural counterparts or not? IVF, for example, has a natural counterpart whereas cloning by nuclear replacement does not.What would all this mean for genetically identical twins produced by natural process? If clones were perceived to be and in consequence treated as less than human, would this constitute an infringement of their Convention rights in conjunction with Art 14?

Example 2: the implications of single or multiple 'copies' of a living or dead foetus, baby, child or adult. For example, parents may wish to 'replace' a child killed in an accident. Another example may be where a child is terminally ill and requires an organ transplant and there are no compatible donors. The parents may wish to have a further child, produced by cloning, to be a compatible organ donor. For the cloned child, would this constitute a violation of Art 3 as being 'inhuman or degrading treatment' in the sense that human dignity requires that human beings ought to be treated as an 'end' in their own right and not merely as a 'means'? As there are likely to be serious psychological consequences for the child of a dead foetus, should the child be denied access to his genetic history and, if so, would this constitute a violation of Arts 8 and 10?

Example 3: the implications of the use of cloning to resolve a couple's infertility problems. Where both individuals of a couple are infertile or where the prospective father has non-functional sperm, they may see one of the advantages of cloning as producing a child as closely related to oneself as possible without having to resort to the donated eggs and sperm of others. Another example would be where a lesbian couple wish to have a child. A cell nucleus from one woman could be inserted into the egg of the other and the resulting embryo implanted into the uterus of the woman who donated the egg. In the light of the *X, Y and Z* case, it will clearly take a considerable length of time and significant future development in attitudes before such controversial situations are likely to be regarded as falling within Arts 8 and 12.

5.50   Under s 28 of the HFE Act 1990, where a child is carried by a woman as a result of placing in her an embryo or sperm and eggs or by artificial insemination, the husband is treated as the father of the child unless it is shown that he did not consent. Were this interpreted as a presumption, given the Court's view in *Kroon v The Netherlands*[1] that respect for family life requires that biological and social reality prevail over legal presumption, it may be arguable that this constitutes a breach of Art 8.

5.51   As to surrogacy, Arts 8 and 12 could be employed in the future to strengthen the position of the genetic commissioning parents in those cases where they are currently disadvantaged as against the surrogate mother.

---

1   19 EHRR 263, para 40.

Chapter 6

THE CHILD – PUBLIC LAW AND ADOPTION

INTRODUCTION

6.1   The majority of Convention cases involving family law have concerned children cases and most of those have involved public law. Although the family lawyer may not automatically think of public law cases as inevitably involving issues of fundamental human rights and freedoms, they invariably do.

6.2   Within the delicate balance to be struck in all such cases, both in principle and in practice, between the rights of the parents or carers on the one hand, and the rights of their children on the other, with the possibilities of disposal enlarged by the duties, powers and responsibilities of the local authority, lie fundamental issues of human rights. The most obvious examples of 'interference' by a 'public authority' with an individual's 'right to respect for his family life' are the removal of children from their natural families together with subsequent decisions relating to contact, placement and adoption. Prima facie, all such interferences are in breach of Convention rights established by Art 8 unless authorised by the exceptions thereto. Convention cases in relation to Art 8 have therefore tended to focus upon the exceptions to Art 8, particularly upon the varieties of interference which are considered 'necessary in a democratic society'.

6.3   Convention cases involving public law have emphasised the importance of procedural safeguards, including parental access to information so as to permit them to make informed decisions and to have access to the decision-making process. Thus the organs of the Convention have asserted a degree of judicial control over the exercise of administrative discretion in public law cases which may have ramifications in relation to care planning and the means of control of that process both before and after the making of a care order.

6.4   Recent developments in the jurisprudence of the Convention organs, particularly that affecting Arts 3 and 6, has emphasised that the State has positive obligations to adopt measures to give effective support to human rights rather than merely to refrain from actions which are injurious to them. This development arises, in part, from the willingness of the Court to read those aforementioned Articles conjunctively with Art 1. These developments may have a significant impact on the duties of local authorities to children in their care and 'at risk' within their areas of responsibility and may have ramifications in relation to their current immunity from suit in children cases. At present, it is far from clear where the boundaries to these developments will be drawn.

Key Articles

6.5   Article 6 (fair hearing); Art 8 (right to respect for family life); Art 14 (prohibition of discrimination).

THE RIGHTS OF THE CHILD

6.6 Article 8(1) provides that everyone has the right to respect for his private and family life, his home and his correspondence.

6.7 Article 8(2) sets out the circumstances, in general terms, in which the State may interfere with the enjoyment of the right. It also provides that there shall be no interference by a public authority with the exercise of the right except such as is in accordance with the law and is necessary in a democratic society in the interests of national security, public safety or the economic well-being of the country for the prevention of disorder or crime, for the protection of health or morals, or for the protection of the rights and freedoms of others.

6.8 The Court has developed a practice when dealing with an issue under Art 8 of considering each of the following matters in turn:

- the scope of the right;
- the nature of the interference which is alleged to restrict the enjoyment of the right;
- the lawfulness of the interference;
- the legitimate aims of the interference;
- the necessity for the interference in a democratic society (ie whether there are relevant and sufficient reasons for the interference which are proportionate to the restriction on the enjoyment of the right when taking into account the margin of appreciation).

The scope of the rights created by Article 8

6.9 The primary objective of Art 8 is to protect individuals against arbitrary action by public authorities. In *Kroon v The Netherlands*[1], the Court stated:

'The Court reiterates that the essential object of Article 8 is to protect the individual against arbitrary action by the public authorities. There may in addition be positive obligations inherent in effective "respect" for family life. However, the boundaries between the State's positive and negative obligations under this provision do not lend themselves to precise definition. The applicable principles are nonetheless similar. In both contexts regard must be had to the fair balance that has to be struck between the competing interests of the individual and of the community as a whole; and in both contexts the State enjoys a certain margin of appreciation.'

'Public authorities' not only include local authorities whose interventions in private and family lives falls within the ambit of Art 8 but also includes the courts.

The existence of family life

6.10 In the first stage in any inquiry to determine whether there has been any interference with the right to respect for 'family life', the Convention organs determine whether 'family life' is in existence. The Convention does not define the concept of 'family life' and nor has the Court or the Commission attempted to make good the deficiency. 'Family' has been interpreted widely by the European Court and the evolutive nature of the case-law continues to expand the recognised

---

1   19 EHRR 263.

scope of 'family life', taking into account the nature of rapidly developing European attitudes.

6.11   In *Keegan v Ireland*[1], the Court held that:

> 'the notion of "the family" is not confined solely to marriage-based relationships and may encompass other de facto "family ties" where the parties are living together outside of marriage. A child born out of such a relationship is *ipso jure* part of that "family" unit from the moment of his birth and by the very fact of it. There thus exists between the child and his parents a bond amounting to family life even if at the time of his or her birth the parents are no longer cohabiting or if their relationship has then ended.'

The facts of the case were that an unmarried father who had no parental rights sought custody of his child who had been placed for adoption by the mother without his knowledge. He had enjoyed a relationship of approximately 2 years' duration with the mother. They had at one time planned to marry but they parted before the child was born. He had seen the baby on only one occasion. The Court held that the nature of the parental relationship meant that the father had a 'family life' with his child 'from the moment of the birth'.

6.12   Whether 'family life' is found to exist in the circumstances of a particular case is a question of fact. In *X, Y and Z v UK*[2], it was held that in determining whether a relationship can amount to 'family life' a number of factors may be relevant, 'including whether the couple live together, the length of their relationship and whether they have demonstrated their commitment to each other by having children together or by any other means . . .'.

The rights of the child

Respect for 'family life'
6.13   Where family life is found to exist the children of the family will be entitled, in their own right, to respect for their 'family life'. Because the majority of children cases are initiated by adult applicants, 'family life' has tended to be defined in terms of the adult relationships around the children, rather than upon the children and the means by which their needs are met.

6.14   However, there is a growing recognition that child applicants may be able to succeed in making a rather stronger case than an adult arguing a similar case on the basis of co-extensive rights of his own to respect for his 'family life'. In the case of *Berrehab v The Netherlands*[3], the Court held that although the Convention does not guarantee a right to aliens to reside in a particular country, because of B's continuing ties with his daughter, which continued after he was divorced from his Dutch wife, the Netherlands was in breach of Art 8 of the Convention by refusing to grant him a residence permit and subsequently expelling him. Although complaints by both B and his daughter succeeded before the Court, it is clear from the reasoning of the Court that it was the child's entitlement to respect for her family life and need for continuing contact with her father which was especially influential in the outcome. The Court observed:

---

1   18 EHRR 342.
2   20 EHRR 143.
3   11 EHRR 322.

'As to the extent of the interference (in relation to the applicants' right to respect for their family life), it is to be noted that there had been very close ties between Mr. Berrehab and his daughter for several years and that the refusal of an independent residence permit and the ensuing expulsion threatened to break those ties. That effect of the interferences in issue was the more serious as Rebecca needed to remain in contact with her father, seeing especially that she was very young.

Having regard to these particular circumstances, the Court considers that a proper balance was not achieved between the interests involved and that there was therefore a disproportion between the means employed and the legitimate aim pursued. That being so, the Court cannot consider the disputed measures as being necessary in a democratic society. It thus concludes that there was a violation of Article 8.'

6.15   The rights of children under Art 8 extend to their relationships with their siblings[1], their parents and their extended families. In public law cases, their rights extend to issues concerning contact and to family rehabilitation.

6.16   Children in care may themselves complain that their rights under the Convention have been infringed by measures taken by local authorities ostensibly for their protection. There have on occasions been issues about who may be an appropriate representative for a child in making such a complaint[2]. The organs of the Convention have not shown an entirely consistent approach to this question. In *Eriksson v Sweden*, the Court found a violation of the mother and the child's rights under Arts 6 and 8 as a result of severe restrictions upon contact over a long period. No issue was raised as to the mother's standing to make a complaint on behalf of the child. The Commission has, however, in a number of other cases, been influenced by the standing of the parent in domestic law to represent the child's interests. In *Hokkanen v Finland*[3], the father was not permitted to represent the child's interests before the Commission since he had no right by Finnish law to represent the child. There is, however, some authority to suggest that in the absence of an actual or potential conflict of interest between the representative of the child and the interests of the child the organs of the Convention may be less restrictive.

Respect for 'private life'
6.17   Children also enjoy protection of their private lives under Art 8. Private life has been interpreted broadly and it includes the moral and physical integrity of the child concerned. Article 8 may involve the imposition of positive obligations upon the State including, 'the adoption of measures designed to secure a respect for private life even in the sphere of relations of individuals between themselves'. In *X and Y v The Netherlands*[4], X and Y were father and daughter. Dutch criminal law required any female complainant in rape proceedings to personally file a complaint. Y was 16 years of age and mentally incompetent. When she was raped in a private home for mentally disabled children there proved to be no means by which prosecution of her attacker could legitimately be initiated. The Court held that the State had a responsibility under Art 8 to provide criminal as well as civil remedies against such attacks within the private sphere. Both the Court and the Commission have observed that 'private life' includes not only moral integrity

---

1   *Moustaquim v Belgium* 13 EHRR 802.
2   See *Eriksson v Sweden* 12 EHRR 183 and *Hokkanen v Finland* 19 EHRR 139.
3   19 EHRR 139.
4   *X and Y v The Netherlands* 8 EHRR 235.

but also the physical integrity of the person. In *Costello-Roberts v UK*[1], the Court accepted that the protection for individual physical integrity may well be wider than the protection afforded by Art 3. Therefore, Art 8 may well afford children and others greater protection from domestic violence than does Art 3. In that case, the complaint was not established, not least because the context of the complaint was a punishment inflicted at a boarding preparatory school and in the view of the Court the very fact of placing the child at such a school necessarily involved some interference with his private life, nor were the effects of the punishment on his physical or moral integrity considered sufficiently serious to bring it within Art 8.

6.18   The protection afforded by Art 8 to 'private life' extends to protection from compulsory physical intervention such as blood tests in paternity actions. Private life has also been held to include the right of access to personal records and information relating to a childhood in care[2] and the confidentiality of medical records[3].

6.19   Names have been held to fall within the scope of Art 8 as a means of identification and a link with family[4]. However, the margin of appreciation the Court has allowed in relation to restrictions upon permissible changes of name has been considerable[5].

The rights of the illegitimate child

6.20   The leading case on the illegitimate family is *Marckx v Belgium*[6]. The members of the 'illegitimate family' are equally entitled to enjoy the rights and freedoms guaranteed by Art 8 as members of a 'traditional' family. The applicants, a mother and her illegitimate infant daughter, complained that limitations upon the mother's capacity to give or bequeath property to her daughter violated Art 8 and Art 14. The Court held that Belgian law violated both Articles by virtue of the lack of any objective and reasonable justification for the differences in treatment between the legitimate and illegitimate family.

6.21   The Court has adopted a similar approach to that adopted in *Berrehab's* case[7] in the case of *Johnston v Ireland*[8]. In that case, a joint application by the daughter and her biological parents, the biological parents unsuccessfully argued that Art 8 protection of family life extended to the right to a formal termination of marriage. Although the parents' claim failed, the daughter's claim succeeded, based upon the disadvantageous situation in which her illegitimate status placed her, and her parents succeeded on the same ground on the basis of her success. The Court noted:

'As it (the Court) observed in its *Marckx*[9] judgment, "respect" for family life, understood as including the ties between near relatives, implies an obligation for the

1   19 EHRR 112.
2   *Gaskin v UK* 12 EHRR 36.
3   *Z v Finland* 25 EHRR 371.
4   *Burghartz v Switzerland* 18 EHRR 101, para 24.
5   *Stjerna v Finland* 24 EHRR 195.
6   2 EHRR 330.
7   See above.
8   9 EHRR 203.
9   See above.

State to act in a manner calculated to allow these ties to develop normally. And in the present case the normal development of the natural family ties between the first and second applicants and their daughter requires, in the Court's opinion, that she should be placed, legally and socially, in a position akin to that of a legitimate child.

Examination of the third applicant's present legal situation, seen as a whole, reveals, however, that it differs considerably from that of a legitimate child; in addition, it has not been shown that there are any means available to her or her parents to eliminate or reduce the differences. Having regard to the particular circumstances of this case and notwithstanding the wide margin of appreciation enjoyed by Ireland in this area, the absence of an appropriate legal regime reflecting the third applicant's natural family ties amounts to a failure to respect her family life.'

Paramountcy principle

Domestic law

6.22   By s 1(1) of the Children Act 1989, in determining any question relating to a child's upbringing and the administration of his property a court must have regard to which course will best serve the interets of the child's welfare, the court's 'paramount consideration'. When doing so, the court must take into account the general principle that delay is likely to be prejudicial to the welfare of the child[1], the matters set out in s 1(3), and all the circumstances of the case relevant to that child. However, ultimately, the answer to a single question will be determinative, 'what is best for the welfare of the child?'.

6.23   It is important to recognise that the 'balancing exercise' that the court must undertake in any children case concerning the upbringing of a child is one in which the various circumstances of the case must be weighed only to the extent that they are relevant to the welfare of the chid. Parents, for example, do not have the right to insist that their interests should have an independent existence in the court's deliberations beyond the determination of what is conducive to the welfare of their child.

6.24   The domestic courts have sometimes appeared to struggle to find an acceptable formulation of the correct approach for a court seized of an issue between a parent and a non-parent as to which of them should be allowed to care for a child. In *Re K (A Minor) (Custody)*[2], Waite J said:

'... the judge proceeded however, in the remainder of his judgment, as though the question before him had been, "Which claimant will provide the better home?" The question he ought, of course, to have been asking was, "Are there any compelling factors which require me to override the prima facie right of this child to an upbringing by its surviving natural parent?"'

However, in *Re H (A Minor) (Custody: Interim Care and Control)*[3], Lord Donaldson MR interpreted *Re K* as follows:

'So it is not a case of parental right opposed to the interests of the child, with an assumption that parental right prevails unless there are strong reasons in terms of the interests of the child. It is the same test which is being applied, the welfare of the child. And all that Re K is saying, as I understand it, is that of course there is a strong

---

1   Children Act 1989, s 1(2).
2   [1990] 2 FLR 674, CA.
3   [1991] 2 FLR 109.

supposition that, other things being equal, it is in the interests of the child that it shall remain with its natural parents. But that has to give way to particular needs in particular situations.'

6.25 Nonetheless, the approach adopted in *Re K* has been confirmed by the Court of Appeal more recently in *Re D (Care: Natural Parent Presumption)*[1], in which the court found that the presumption in favour of the natural parent outweighed, on the particular facts of the case, the value of placing the child in the same home as his half siblings. It was held that the question for the court was whether there were any compelling factors which overrode the prima facie right of a child to an upbringing by its surviving natural parent.

The impact of the Convention

6.26 Wherever family life is found to be in existence, each of the family members will, independently, be entitled to respect for their family life. The Convention does not provide that the rights of children are paramount.

6.27 The court will proceed by giving the right of each family member to respect for his private life and famly life equal weight and then determining to what extent, if at all, the rights of family members are in conflict. The welfare of the child becomes relevant only when the Court comes to consider whether interference with the rights of family members is justified as 'necessary', under the second limb of Art 8(2) (the foregoing sentence assumes that the child is not the applicant).

6.28 The Convention organs have adopted an anroach to the principles upon which children cases should be decided which is fundamentally different from the approach demanded by the Children Act 1989. This fundamental difference was recently confirmed and summarised by Hirst LJ in the case of *R v Secretary of State for Home Department, ex parte Gangadeen and Khan*[2] on the basis that the Convention organs interpret Art 8 with no preferences being given to the interests of the child. The Court of Appeal had before it two appeals against the refusal, in each of the cases, of judicial review of the Secretary of State's decision to remove the appellant from the UK. The cases were listed together because they both raised an important question of principle, namely, where such a decision affected the interest of a child of the prospective deportee, whether the Secretary of State was obliged to give preference to the interest of the child as the paramount consideration in the process having regard to the principles of Art 8 of the Convention. A large number of Convention cases were cited in argument and reviewed in the course of judgment but, of those, Hirst LJ regarded only one as of significant assistance, *Berrehab v The Netherlands*[3], since it was the only one which bore directly on the question of the balance between immigration policy and the rights of children. Hirst LJ stated that:

'In my judgment these three cases demonstrate quite clearly that, in their interpret-ation of Article 8 in the present context, the Human Rights Court and the Commission approach the problem as a straightforward balancing exercise, in which the scales start even, and where the weight to be given to the considerations on each side of the balance is to be assessed according to the individual circumstances of the

---

1   [1999] 1 FLR 134.
2   [1998] 1 FLR 762, CA.
3   (1988) 11 EHRR 322.

case; thus they do not support the notion that paramountcy should be given to the interests of the child.'

6.29   However, this interpretation of Art 8 by the organs of the Convention does not mean that, in practice, parents are able to successfully assert a right that their own interests should necessarily prevail and override those of their chldren in the balancing exercise. In the case of *Johansen v Norway*[1], a public law case, the Court held:

> '... A fair balance has to be struck between the interests of the child in remaining in public care and those of the parents in being united with the child. In carrying out this balancing exercise, the court will attach particular importance to the best interests of the child, which depending upon their nature and seriousness may override those of the parent. In particular ... the parent cannot be entitled under article 8 of the Convention to have such measures taken as would harm the child's health and development.'

6.30   In the private law case of *Hokkanen v Finland*[2], the persistent failure of the authorities to enforce the father's right of contact in the face of the maternal grandparents' persistent refusal to comply with court orders providing for it, was held to amount to a breach of the father's respect for family life. The test propounded by the Court was whether the authorities had 'taken all necessary steps to facilitate reunion as can reasonably be expected in the circumstances'. The right to contact in such circumstances was said not to be an absolute one and the Court was careful to state that extensive recourse to coercion would not be justified. The Court did not make clear in specific terms precisely what it was that the authorities should have done which they had failed to do but were clear that 'organising a few meetings' was insufficient.

6.31   In the seminal public law case, *W v UK*[3], argument before the court brought into sharp focus the difference of approach between the Convention and that of the courts of the UK. The case concerned a complaint about restriction and ultimate denial of parental contact to a child following a parental rights resolution (the case was heard prior to the coming into force of the Children Act 1989). The Government argued the following.

– The complaint (under Art 6) could have no substance unless domestic law recognised a legal right to access in such circumstances. It was argued that domestic law recognised no 'civil right' in the parents in such circumstances.

– The notion of 'parental rights' over children was outmoded; furthermore, according to English judges, the so-called 'right' of access by a parent to his child was preferably described as a right in the child.

– The right was, in any event, a rhetorical one and not a legal right.

– Even if there had been a legal right, it ceased to be upon the making of the care order or the passing of the parental rights resolution.

The Court was not prepared to accept any one of those submissions and found that the parents did retain rights even following a parental rights resolution and their Convention rights under both Art 6 and Art 8 had been violated.

---

1   23 EHRR 33.
2   19 EHRR 139.
3   10 EHRR 29.

6.32 In domestic private law cases, the Convention organs' interpretation of Art 8 is likely to have a substantial impact, as follows.

– A means will no doubt be sought to reconcile the principle of paramountcy of the welfare of the child under domestic law with the notion that the starting point under Art 8 is that all family members have a right to respect for their private and family life.

– Under Art 8, parents and, arguably, other family members, have a 'right' to contact in contrast to the attitude of the domestic courts that contact is a right of the child and not of parents[1].

– Public authorities, including the courts, will have a responsibility to adopt reasonable measures to facilitate contact between parents and their children[2].

– Applications for leave to permanently remove a child from the jurisdiction may in future reveal incompatibility between domestic law and Art 8. The present approach of the domestic courts is to determine such an issue on the basis of the paramountcy principle with the gloss that leave should not be withheld unless the interests of the child and the residential parent are shown to be incompatible[3]. This approach may fail to give sufficient respect to the family life of the contract parent.

Parental rights

6.33 Family life always exists within marriage. The concept of 'family life' embraces husband and wife and their children. 'Family life' does not automatically cease upon the separation or divorce of the parents[4] and a parent's right to a family life is not terminated by a residence order made in favour of the other parent. However, in order for family life to be maintained as the child grows older, a continuing relationship between parent and child is necessary[5].

6.34 No distinction between the rights of married parents is made by the Convention organs in respect of private law. In a case where the husband and wife sought to register the wife's name as their family name and use the husband's name before the family name, the Court has held that sexual equality was a major aim of the contracting States and that therefore very strong reasons had to be given for different treatment on the ground of sex[6].

6.35 Presumptions of paternity in favour of married fathers have been held to pursue legitimate aims of certainty and security in family relationships.

6.36 Neither parent may claim a 'right' to a residence order[7]. However, parents do have a conditional 'right' to contact under the provisions of Art 8 in contrast to the conventional approach under domestic law that contact is a right of the child and not the parent.

1   *Re KD (A Minor) (Access: Principles)* [1988] 2 FLR 139 at 155.
2   *Hokkanen v Finland* 19 EHRR 139.
3   *Re K (A Minor) (Removal from Jurisdiction)* [1992] 2 FLR 98.
4   *Keegan v Ireland* 18 EHRR 342.
5   *Berrehab v Netherlands* (1988) 11 EHRR 322; *Singh v UK* (1967) 10 YB 478.
6   *Burghartz v Switzerland* (1994) 18 EHRR 101.
7   *X v Sweden* Application No 172/56, 1 YB 211.

The natural father

6.37   Parents include natural fathers where there has been cohabitation or such other demonstration of commitment to a continuing relationship with the child so as to constitute de facto family life. A child born to parents who had a relationship which included cohabitation is part of the 'family unit' for the purposes of Art 8 even where, by the time of the birth the parents are no longer cohabiting[1]. Equally, a long-standing relationship between parents of four children gave rise to 'family life' within the meaning of Art 8 even though the relationship did not extend to marriage or even to cohabitation[2]. However, in the case of *MB v UK*[3], where an applicant claimed to be the father of a child born to a married woman and sought to establish paternity by means of a blood test, the Commission did not find that 'family life' was established. The Commission distinguished the *Keegan* case on the basis that paternity was in issue in the instant case and there had been no cohabitation nor planning of the conception. A planned conception will not, of itself, suffice to establish 'family life'. A natural parent who donates sperm or an egg for the purpose of artificial insemination does not have a right to respect for family life solely by virtue of that fact[4]. It therefore follows that the blood tie per se may not be sufficient to establish a family life. In *MB v UK*[5], the applicant claimed to be the father of a child born during the course of a marriage between the mother and another man. The domestic courts' refusal to order a blood test on the child to allow the applicant to pursue his claim did not give rise to a violation of Art 8, nor to violation of Arts 6 and 14. The Commission attached particular importance to the disruption of the stability and security of the home where the child would be brought up. A natural father has been held by the Commission to have no right to joint custody as against the mother[6].

6.38   The 'illegitimate' family enjoys the Art 8 guarantees on the same footing as a 'traditional' family[7]. This does not, however, place unmarried fathers in the same position as married fathers or unmarried mothers[8]. The Children Act 1989 does not automatically give unmarried fathers parental responsibility for their children. However, the Act does provide the means by which an unmarried father may acquire parental responsibility:

–   by agreement with the child's mother;
–   by court order under s 4 of the Children Act 1989;
–   by the making of a residence order in his favour for so long as such order remains in force.

6.39   The domestic courts have repeatedly stressed that the granting of a parental responsibility order is designed to do no more than confer the status of fatherhood, which the father would have had had the parents been married, and

---

1   *Keegan v Ireland* (1994) Series A, No 290.
2   *Kroon v The Netherlands* 19 EHRR 263.
3   Application No 22920/93 (Dec), (1994) 77-A DR 108.
4   *G v The Netherlands* Application No 16944/90, (1993) 16 EHRR CD 38.
5   Application No 22920/93 (Dec), (1994) 77-A DR 108.
6   *N v Denmark* Application No 13557/88, (1989) 63 DR 167 at 170.
7   *Marckx v Belgium* (above), para 40.
8   *Keegan v Ireland* (above); in contrast *McMichael v UK* (1995) 20 EHRR 205 (both adoption cases).

the law should, wherever possible, give its stamp of approval to a father who had shown the necessary level of commitment[1]. However, considerations of the paramountcy of the welfare of the child determine whether such an application should be granted, so that even where a father can show the requisite commitment, attachment and appropriate and genuine reasons for making an application for parental responsibility it may not be appropriate to grant it in the light of the father's cruelty to the child[2]. Under the Children Act 1989, a natural father may therefore be unable to acquire parental responsibility. Additionally, a natural father may, having acquired parental responsibility, lose it as the result of revocation by the court[3].

6.40   In the public law case *McMichael v UK*[4], the male applicant complained that as a result of his status as an unmarried father in Scottish law he had no parental rights from the moment of his child's birth, unlike the mother, and he had no right to participate in the 'freeing' proceedings which followed the child being placed in care. The Court rejected his complaint that the difference in treatment amounted to a violation of Art 14 or of Art 14 in conjunction with Art 8. The Court recalled that:

> 'According to the Court's well established case-law, a difference of treatment is discriminatory if it has no reasonable and objective justification, that is, if it does not pursue a legitimate aim or if there is not a reasonable relationship of proportionality between the means employed and the aim sought to be realised.'[5]

In addition, the Court, dealing specifically with the father's complaints, said this:

> 'As the Commission remarked, "it is axiomatic that the nature of the relationships of natural fathers with the children will inevitably vary, from ignorance and indifference at one end of the spectrum to a close stable relationship indistinguishable from the conventional matrimonial-based family unit at the other". As explained by the Government, the aim of the relevant legislation, which was enacted in 1986, is to provide a mechanism for identifying "meritorious" fathers who might be accorded parental rights, thereby protecting the interests of the child and the mother. In the Court's view, this aim is legitimate and the conditions imposed on natural fathers for obtaining recognition of their parental role respect the principle of proportionality. The Court therefore agrees with the Commission that there was an objective and reasonable justification for the difference of treatment complained of.'[6]

6.41   Because of the close similarity of Scots law relating to parental responsibility to that of English law, the reasoning employed by the Court in the *McMichael* case[7] would seem to be equally applicable to validating the provisions of English law relating to the acquisition and termination of parental responsibility. It is highly likely that for the time being domestic law would be regarded by the Court as compatible with the Convention. The Government has proposed changes to domestic law which would give parental responsibility to all unmarried fathers who register the birth of their children. This would simultaneously

PART B
IMPACT OF THE CONVENTION

---

1   *Re C and V (Contact and Parental Responsibility)* [1998] 1 FLR 392.
2   *Re H (A Minor) (Parental Responsibility)* [1998] 1 FLR 855.
3   *Re P (Terminating Parental Responsibility)* [1995] 1 FLR 1048, and see s 4(3) of the Children Act 1989.
4   20 EHRR 205.
5   Ibid, para 97.
6   Ibid, para 99.
7   20 EHRR 205.

significantly expand the number of natural fathers who acquire parental responsibility while maintaining a system within which it is readily ascertainable who has, and who does not have, parental responsibility. The *McMichael* case was decided on 25 January 1995. This is a sphere where attitudes have been changing at a significant pace and it is far from clear that our law will remain compatible with the Convention unless kept under review.

6.42　　　In the case of *Re W; Re B (Child Abduction: Unmarried Father)*[1], Hale J expressed the view that domestic law relating to parental responsibility was consistent with our obligations under the Convention, but added:

> 'There may come a time when the Parliament of this country, having considered the policy matters further, decides to eliminate those differences. Or there may come a time when so many of the Contracting States to the Convention decide to do so that the current wide margin of appreciation allowed in this area moves so far as to oblige us to do so.'

6.43　　　A natural father who does not have parental responsibility will be potentially disadvantaged in a number of respects in domestic private law:

- his consent is not required before his child may be removed from the jurisdiction[2];
- he may not be able to establish a breach of a 'right of custody' within the meaning of the Hague Convention on the Civil Aspects of International Child Abduction[3].

These differences of treatment may in future be the basis of successful claims that the right to respect for his family life has been violated under Art 8 or that of discrimination under Art 14.

6.44　　　A presumption of paternity in favour of married fathers does not of itself contravene the Convention. However, in *Kroon v The Netherlands*[4], the European Court said that biological and social reality should prevail over legal presumptions and the quest for legal certainty of relations and, consequently, any presumption of paternity must be rebuttable. In contrast, in *MB v UK*[5] the Commission did not find that the domestic court's refusal to order blood tests on the child of a married woman, in respect of whom the applicant claimed to be the father, constituted a breach of Art 8, since this would have disrupted the stability and security of the home where the child was being brought up[6].

Homosexual unions

6.45　　　Homosexual unions do not fall within the 'family life' provision of Art 8. In *Kerkhoven v Netherlands*[7], which concerned a lesbian relationship, the Commission held that the partner of the mother could not rely on either the family life provisions or the private life provisions of Art 8 to claim parental authority over the child born to the mother by artificial insemination. However,

1　　　[1998] 2 FLR 146 at 163D–168G.
2　　　Children Act 1989, s 13.
3　　　*Re J (A Minor) (Abduction: Custody Rights)* [1990] 2 AC 562.
4　　　19 EHRR 263.
5　　　Application No 22920/93 (Dec), (6 April 1994) 77-A DR 108.
6　　　*S v UK* Application No 11716/85, (1986) 47 DR 272; *B v UK* Application No 16106/90, (1990) 64 DR 278.
7　　　Application No 15666/89 (19 May 1992).

attitudes to homosexuality are evolving and this may be reconsidered in the future. There are signs that our own judges may be prepared to be more liberal and progressive than the judges of the European Court in dealing with these issues[1].

Transsexual unions

6.46   In *X, Y and Z v UK*, X, the first applicant, was a female-to-male transsexual who lived in a stable relationship of long-standing with a woman, Y, the second applicant, who gave birth to a child, Z, the third applicant, as a result of artificial insemination by donor. The procedure (AID) had been applied for by X and Y with the support of their general practitioner and was eventually carried out in X's presence after a successful appeal against the hospital ethics committee's initial rejection of their application. Following the birth, X and Y were not able to register X as Z's father although Z was given X's surname in the register. X and Y complained they were denied respect for their family and private life as a result of the lack of recognition of X's role as a father to Z and that the resulting situation in which they were placed was discriminatory. The Commission declared the complaints under Arts 8 and 14 admissible. The Commission gave weight to the family's emotional and psychological need for recognition against which it found no overriding reason against recognition.

6.47   However, the Court's approach was almost the reverse of that of the Commission. The Court recognised that a transsexual's relationship with his partner could, and on the facts of this case did, amount to 'de facto' family life, within the meaning of Art 8. The Court distinguished the present case from three previous cases involving transsexuals which had been brought before the Court which had involved an absence of recognition under domestic law of the right to recognition of the transsexual's own change of identity (gender)[2]. The Court also distinguished the approach it had adopted in a number of previous cases[3], where once the existence of a family tie with a child was found to have been established the Court had ruled that the State must act in a manner calculated to allow that tie to be developed and legal safeguards must be established to enable the child's integration in his family, on the basis that in those cases the Court was considering family ties between biological parents and their children.

6.48   The feature of the reasoning of the Court which was ultimately decisive was that there was no common European standard with regard to the granting of parental rights to transsexuals and that although it had not been suggested that the change in the law sought by the applicants would be harmful to such children as Z, neither did the Court accept that it would necessarily be of advantage to them.

6.49   In the *Rees*[4] case, the Court recognised the need for appropriate legal measures affecting transsexual to be kept under review having regard in particular

PART B
IMPACT OF THE CONVENTION

---

1   See the judgment of Singer J in *Re W (Adoption: Homosexual Adopter)* [1997] 2 FLR 406, and the judgment of Waite LJ in *Fitzpatrick v Sterling Housing Association* [1998] 1 FLR 6, at 20F.

2   *B v France* (1992) Series A, No 232-C; *Rees v UK* (1986) Series A, No 106; *Cossey v UK* (27 September 1990) Series A, No 184.

3   *Marckx v Belgium* (1979) Series A, No 31; *Johnston v Ireland* (1986) Series A, No 112: *Keegan v Ireland* 18 EHRR 342; *Kroon v The Netherlands* (1994) Series A, No 297-C.

4   9 EHRR 56.

to scientific and societal developments. In the most recent such case, *Sheffield and Horsham v UK*[1], evidence was adduced to demonstrate that of 37 countries, only four, of which the UK was one, refused to allow a change to be made to a person's birth certificate to reflect re-assigned sex. The Court followed its earlier decisions in the *Rees* and *Cossey*[2] cases but again noted that this is an area that needs to be kept under review and 'it would appear that the respondent State has not taken any steps to do so'. The decision was that of a majority (11:9). This is an area where attitudes continue to evolve and should this issue be revisited in the future, particularly if the facts disclose some more pressing reason for positive recognition of the parenting role of a transsexual, a different judgment may be reached.

The rights of the extended family

6.50   In cases involving grandparents[3], the Commission has held that links between grandparents and grandchildren will vary from family to family and, therefore, each case has to be examined on its facts to determine whether there are sufficient links to amount to family life. The Commission has taken the view that different standards apply to grandparental contact than those concerning parental contact. In the *Price* case, the Commission found that a decision by the local authority to end all contact between grandparents and their grandchild constituted an interference with their right to respect for family life but appropriate procedures while their grandchild was in care were such as to provide them with meaningful consultation, the facility to make representations at case conferences and to seek a review of the case.

In the context of private law, if grandparental contact were to be reduced below the level considered necessary to sustain the normal grandparent/grandchild relationship, a violation of Art 8 may be found.

6.51   In the case of *Boyle v UK*[4], the Commission found that an uncle had a relationship with a child of such a nature, he had acted as a 'father figure' and had known the child from birth, although he did not live with the child, that a denial of contact by social services when the child was taken into care in the absence of any meaningful consultation with him amounted to an interference with his right to respect for his family life. The Commission emphasised that although, in general, where a parent is denied contact to a child taken into care there is an interference with the parent's right to respect for family life, the same does not necessarily apply where other close relatives are concerned. The commission noted that contact by close relatives to children is normally at the discretion of the child's parents and, when a child has been taken into care, the exercise of that discretion passes to the local authority. A restriction of contact in those circumstances which does deny 'a recoverable opportunity' to maintain the relationship will not of itself violate Art 8.

6.52   In determining whether relationships within the extended family are such as to attract the protection of Art 8, it is likely that the Court will have regard

---

1   [1998] 2 FLR 928.
2   13 EHRR 622.
3   *Branton v UK* Application No 12399/85 (Dec), (9 March 1988); *Price v UK* Application No 12402/86, (14 July 1988) 55 DR 224; *Lawlor v UK* Application No 12763/87 (Dec), (14 July 1988) 57 DR 216; also *Marckx v Belgium* 2 EHRR 330.
4   19 EHRR 179.

to the quality of the relationship and its importance to the relative and, in particular, to the child rather than to the nominal relationship alone.

Relationships beyond the natural and extended family

6.53   The Convention has also been held to apply to the relationship between the adopted child and adoptive parents[1]. 'Family life' has also been held to include the relationship between a foster-parent and foster-child, although the Court noted that the content of family life may depend on the nature of the fostering arrangements[2].

The balancing exercise

6.54   Article 8(2) establishes the criteria, in principle, by which interference with an applicant's right to respect for his private or family life may be justified. The basic criteria are that the interference should be 'in accordance with the law' (lawful) and 'necessary in a democratic society' (necessary) in order to achieve one of the aims set out in subparagraph 2 (legitimate aims).

Lawful
6.55   Because domestic private law is dominated by the provisions of the Children Act 1989 which clearly identifies 'the welfare of the child' as the 'paramount consideration' for the court in determining any matter concerned with the upbringing of a child or the administration of his property, it is likely to prove to be extremely difficult for an applicant to argue successfully that an interference is not in accordance with the law. This difficulty is made the greater because 'the law' has been interpreted broadly by the Court to include not only domestic law but also international or community law.

Legitimate aim
6.56   This is the context in which the court must consider whether the interference is justified, inter alia, 'for the protection of the rights and freedoms of others', or 'for the protection of health or morals'. Although these aims are further subject to the requirement that they must be 'necessary in a democratic society', it is in this way that the interests of children and other family members are protected in the context of children cases. It is for the State to identify the aim of its interference and demonstrate that it falls within the list of approved aims set out in Art 8(2). It should be noted that the Article does not expressly mention the rights of children, and nor are they or the rights of other family members given any special status by the words of the Article.

Necessity
6.57   Necessity in this context requires that there should be a 'pressing social need' for the interference in question[3]. The assessment of the national authorities that such a 'pressing social need' exists is subject to the review of the court which must be satisfied that the interference is proportionate to the legitimate aim

PART B
IMPACT OF THE CONVENTION

---

1   *X v France* Application No 9993/82, (1982) 31 DR 241.
2   *Gaskin v UK* (1989) 12 EHRR 36, para 49; also *X v Switzerland* Application No 8257/78 (Dec), (10 July 1978) 13 DR 248.
3   *Dudgeon v UK* 4 EHRR 149.

pursued. It is the principle of proportionality which is central to the concept of necessity in a democratic society. Inherent in the principle of proportionality is the need for there to be a fair balance between, on the one hand, a legitimate aim sought to be achieved by the interference, and on the other, the means chosen to pursue its realisation. Although the State is usually allowed a wide margin of appreciation the decision is usually informed by a consensus found in the laws of contracting States, particularly in cases involving fundamental moral issues. The 'necessity requirement' has played an important part in child-care cases.

6.58   In *W v UK*[1], the European Court established the fundamental principle that the decision-making process in child-care cases must provide sufficient procedural protection of the parents' interests. The local authority had made a number of decisions including placement in long-term foster-care with a view to adoption and the termination of contact without informing the parents. This was compounded by substantial delays in the proceedings. The Court found that, notwithstanding the wide margin of appreciation as to how such cases should be managed, the exclusion and delay which had occurred in the case were not necessary for the protection of the rights of the child and that in breach of Art 8 the parents had not been afforded the requisite protection of their interests.

6.59   In children cases the Court has, on occasion, demonstrated a willingness to begin to approach a review of the merits of a decision of the court of a contracting State. In *Olsson v Sweden (No 1)*[2], the children in care were placed in separate foster-homes a long distance from the parental home. In assessing whether this interference with the parents' rights was 'necessary' in the children's interests, the test which the Court applied was whether the authority had 'relevant and sufficient reasons' for acting as it did. It concluded that the authority did not have relevant or sufficient reasons for its decision, which was inconsistent with the goal of rehabilitation to the natural family. It is by means of reviewing the decisions of the courts of the contracting States in such a way that the Court makes its closest approach to reviewing decisions upon the merits.

Religion
6.60   Article 14 of the Convention states:

> 'The enjoyment of the rights and freedoms set forth in this Convention shall be secured without discrimination on any ground such as sex, race, colour, language, religion, political or other opinion, national or social origin, association with a national minority, property, birth or other status.'

Discrimination on the ground of, inter alia, religous belief is prohibited by Art 14 insofar as enjoyment of the rights and freedoms of the Convention are concerned. Article 14 does not create a free-standing prohibition on all forms of discrimination. In *Belgian Linguistic Case (No 2)*[3], the Court recognised that its provisions 'had no independent existence'. In terms of its practical effect, it is as if the provisions of Art 14 were an integral part of each of the other substantive Articles.

6.61   Although Art 14 does not, within its own provisions, expressly create any exceptions to its application, in practice the organs of the Convention have

---

1   10 EHRR 29.
2   11 EHRR 259.
3   1 EHRR 252.

accepted that not every difference in treatment in the enjoyment of convention rights and freedoms is necessarily prohibited. The accepted test is whether differences in treatment have objective and reasonable justification. The court will have regard to the intended purpose of the discriminatory measure, its actual effect and the normal principles which regulate democratic societies. In addition, the difference in treatment must be proportionate to the objective sought to be realised by it.

6.62 The leading case on discrimination on religious grounds, *Hoffman v Austria*[1], arose in the context of private law. The Court found by a narrow majority (5:4) that a decision of the Austrian Supreme Court by which the applicant lost the custody of her children to her former husband and which was influenced to a significant extent by the mother's adopted beliefs as a Jehovah's Witness was a violation of Art 14. The mother had complained of violations of her Convention rights under Arts 8 and 14 but the Court found that the interference with her family life was based upon discrimination on religious grounds and took the view that it was unnecessary to give independent consideration to her Art 8 complaint. The more usual practice of the Court is to express its decision in terms of a breach of the substantive Article and then to decline to consider Art 14 on the basis that no separate issue arises. The fact that in this case the Court chose to express its decision in terms of Art 14 seems to illustrate that the Court was concerned to emphasise that its decision was based upon discrimination on the grounds of religion. The decision, atlhough arrived at by a narrow majority, is a strong one, not least because the religious beliefs with which it was concerned have long been associated with significant issues involving health and the social and emotional development of children. Despite the fact that the express concerns of the Austrian Supreme Court were accepted by the Court as legitimate, the protection of the health and rights of the children (matters such as blood transfusions and social isolation were raised), a violation of Art 14 was found because it was not reasonably proportionate to base the decision essentially upon religious belief.

6.63 In general, the Court has been robust in applying the prohibition upon discrimination on the grounds of religion. The Court found no objective and a reasonable justification for the difference in status of the applicant church in *Canea Catholic Church v Greece*[2] compared with that of the Orthodox Church, which produced a situation in which the church could not take legal proceedings to protect its property rights.

6.64 There are, however, limits to the Court's willingness to protect religious freedoms. In *Valsamis v Greece*[3], a child Jehovah's Witness was suspended from school when she failed to participate with her school in a procession on Greek national day. The child's parents complained that her participation offended their religious and pacifist beliefs. The Court found that of the requirement that she should participate in the school procession was not such as to amount to an interference with her right to freedom of religion. It seems from this decision that, in order to found a violation, a particular measure must, viewed objectively, conflict with religious beliefs in some significant particular.

---

1   (1992) Series A, No 222.
2   27 EHRR 521.
3   24 EHRR 294.

Remedies

6.65   While recognising the diversity of the contracting States and their legal systems, the Convention and its organs seek to establish minimum international standards and to identify the minimum standards of human rights which the legal system of a contracting State should attain.

6.66   Each of the contracting States is itself primarily responsible for the protection of human rights of its own citizens and those present within its jurisdiction, as each have acknowledged by the terms of Art 1. The Convention organs' function is not to act as a court of appeal from domestic courts' decisions on the basis that the judgment of the domestic court was wrong but rather to ensure compliance with the Convention. The Court and the Commission have seen their proper function primarily as bodies exercising a supervisory jurisdiction which is subsidiary to systems for safeguarding human rights within the national systems of each of the contracting States. This is the proper context in which the remedies available under the Convention for breach of the terms of its Articles should be seen.

6.67   The provision of awards of damages to those who have suffered violations of their Convention rights is not the primary objective of the European Convention. Article 13 establishes that each of the contracting States are obliged to provide a remedy to all those who have an arguable claim that their rights under the Convention have been violated. Article 26 requires the exhaustion of domestic remedies available to the applicant as a precondition of seeking such a remedy from the organs of the Convention. The effect of those two Articles taken together illustrates that a complaint to the European Court is intended to be the remedy of last resort.

6.68   Awards of damages made to applicants by the European Court in respect of violations of Convention rights tend to be extremely low by the standards of the domestic courts of the UK.

6.69   The principle value of the Convention and its incorporation for the family lawyer will be to provide an additional basis of argument in support of a client's rights before the domestic court. It may provide an additional and possibly indispensable means of justifying the order a client hopes to achieve as a result of proceedings. In a children case, damages will never have been the client's original objective within the proceedings, may not in any event be awarded by the domestic family courts, and are highly unlikely, in the event of any award by the Court, to be regarded by a client as 'real' compensation. Such feelings are only likely to be exacerbated by the typical scale of the awards of damages by the Court. One further relevant consideration is that a complaint typically takes approximately 5 years to reach a final resolution in the Court and thus cannot be seen as an expeditious practical remedy.

6.70   Article 41 of the Convention states:

> 'If the Court finds that there has been a violation of the Convention or the protocols thereto, and if the internal law of the High Contracting Party concerned allows only partial reparation to be made, the Court shall, if necessary, afford just satisfaction to the injured party.'

An analysis of the level of awards of damages in child-care cases is beyond the scope of this book. However, by way of example:

In *W v UK*[1], where there was a lack of any effective consultation with the parents by the local authority concerned and a violation of Art 6 as a result of lack of access to court, an award of £12,000 for anguish and distress was made.

In *Keegan v Ireland*[2], where breaches of Arts 6 and 8 were found as a result of a lack of procedural rights for the father, an award of 10,000 Irish Punts was made for trauma and feelings of injustice.

In *McMichael v UK*[3], where breaches of Arts 6 and 8 arose from defects in procedural safeguards for parents' interests, £8,000 was awarded for trauma and feelings of injustice.

The family courts do not in any event have any power to make awards of damages even were they to be persuaded that Convention rights had been violated and damage suffered as a result.

6.71 The Human Rights Act 1998 provides, by s 4, that the higher courts may make a 'declaration of incompatibility' where they are satisfied that a provision of primary or subordinate legislation is incompatible with the Convention. Such a declaration does not have the effect of changing the law nor is it binding upon the parties. It is not a remedy but rather an admission of defeat. Moreover, in such circumstances no entitlement to any other form of remedy arises which, prima facie, is inconsistent with the obligations imposed by Art 13.

Article 13 of the Convention states:

> 'Everyone whose rights and freedoms as set forth in this Convention are violated shall have an effective remedy before a national authority notwithstanding that the violation has been committed by persons acting in an official capacity.'

6.72 In a case of incompatibility between the Convention and primary legislation, the courts do not have the power to set aside legislation on the ground of incompatibility. However, such a declaration would probably ('almost certainly' in the words of the White Paper[4]) lead to a change in the law. Section 10 provides a fast-track procedure for remedial action.

6.73 As a system for providing compensation to those whose rights have been violated, the Convention and its organs leave a good deal to be desired. It should be remembered, however, that providing a system of compensation is not the major purpose of the Convention. Incorporation will not further the purpose of providing compensation to those who have suffered violations of their Convention rights.

---

1   10 EHRR 29.
2   18 EHRR 342.
3   20 EHRR 205.
4   White Paper: *Rights Brought Home* (Cm 3782), para 2.7.

THE RIGHT TO A FAIR HEARING

Article 6(1)

6.74   Article 6(1) of the Convention states:

'In the determination of his civil rights and obligations or of any criminal charge against him, everyone is entitled to a fair and public hearing within a reasonable time by an independent and impartial tribunal established by law. Judgment shall be pronounced publicly but the press and public may be excluded from all or part of the trial in the interest of morals, public order or national security in a democratic society, where the interests of juveniles or the protection of the private life of the parties so require, or to the extent strictly necessary in the opinion of the court in special circumstances where publicity would prejudice the interests of justice.'

6.75   The guarantee of 'a fair and public hearing within a reasonable time' has the potential to make considerable impact on current law and practice in the field of public law. The 'fair hearing' guarantee includes the following elements:

–   the principle of 'equality of arms';
–   freedom from self-incrimination;
–   access to evidence;
–   presence in court;
–   adversarial argument;
–   reasons for the judgment.

Equality of arms

6.76   The principle *equality of arms* may have considerable effect upon expert evidence in public law children cases. In particular, the present practice of requiring the parties jointly to instruct a single expert, together with the restriction upon disclosing the case papers without leave frequently leaves one of the parties at a substantial disadvantage in the proceedings, confronted with an expert whose evidence is inimical to their case and without the ability to commission expert guidance from another expert to direct the cross-examination of that witness.

Privilege against self-incrimination

6.77   The *privilege against self-incrimination* has been considered only recently in the field of public law by the House of Lords[1]. The court held that there was a clear distinction between legal professional privilege and the privilege attaching to the reports of third parties prepared for the purposes of litigation. The court held that litigation privilege is 'a creature of adversarial procedure', and that, since care proceedings were non-adversarial in character and 'far removed' from normal actions, and that in care proceedings considerations of the welfare of the child were determinative, litigation privilege had no place. Although on the particular facts of the case it was found that privilege in an unfavourable expert report had been waived and that the mother could not therefore claim privilege against self-incrimination, the decision that litigation privilege had no place in care proceedings would be open to challenge on the basis of Art 6(1). Indeed, in his dissenting judgment Lord Nicholls asserted that Art 6 read in conjunction with Art 8 required that parties to care proceedings should have the right to obtain

---

1   *Re L (Police Investigation: Privilege)* [1996] 1 FLR 731.

legal advice in confidence as part of their right to a 'fair hearing' and were accordingly as entitled to litigation privilege as were parties to any other litigation.

Appearing in person

6.78   In public law children cases, the right to *appear in court in person* will generally apply. Furthermore, the right to a 'fair trial' under Art 6 implies a right to give oral evidence. This may have considerable potential impact upon current law and practice in children's cases, as follows:

- in relation to ex parte applications such as the making of applications for emergency protection orders;
- in relation to contested interim care proceedings where at present orders are on occasion made without oral evidence being given;
- on applications for leave to be joined in care proceedings where currently a merit test has to be satisfied, and frequently oral evidence is not given;
- on application by a child for leave to make an application;
- where 'issue estoppel' is argued.

6.79   The leading case on the sub-category of issue estoppel known to the domestic courts in children cases is *Re B (Children Act Proceedings) (Issue Estoppel)*[1] in which Hale J reviewed the relevant authorities. The present balance struck between the need to achieve finality in litigation and to avoid pointless legal costs, on the one hand, and the need, on the other hand, to determine the issue of the child's welfare on the basis of well-founded findings of fact where matters of significance are in issue, nonetheless may allow of a situation in which individuals who were unrepresented in previous proceedings in which serious findings of fact were made against them are estopped from denying them in other proceedings in future. This would amount to a breach of Art 8.

Adversarial hearing

6.80   A further requirement of a 'fair trial' pursuant to Art 6 is that the proceedings should be *adversarial* in nature. One important characteritic of adversarial proceedings is that adversarial argument includes the right to cross-examine witnesses. In *McMichael v UK*[2], the lack of disclosure of vital documents to the parties amounted to a breach of their Art 6 rights and the Court found that the requirements of an adversarial trial had not been met in a children's hearing in Scotland. Although some terms used in the Articles of the Convention and by the organs of the Convention have autonomous meanings, there is potentially an inconsistency between the domestic courts' insistence that care proceedings are essentially non-adversarial in nature and the requirements of Art 6.

Reasoned judgment

6.81   Article 6 requires that a court should give *reasons for judgment*. This requirement does not imply any incompatibility with current practice or procedure.

PART B
IMPACT OF THE CONVENTION

---

1   [1997] 1 FLR 285.
2   20 EHRR 205.

THE LOCAL AUTHORITY

Intervention by the local authority to remove the child

6.82   In the important case of *W v UK*[1], which was decided before the Children Act 1989 but which retains considerable significance notwithstanding that the Court established guidelines for appropriate procedures to be adopted when children were taken into care. The Court recognised that there were circumstances in which a child could properly be removed from his family but emphasised the particular need in this sphere for protection of the interests of parents and children from arbitrary interference. The Court stated:

> '... predominant in any consideration of this aspect of the present case must be the fact that the decisions may well prove to be irreversible; thus, where a child has been taken away from his parents and placed with alternative carers, he may in the course of time establish with them new bonds which it might not be in his interests to disturb or interrupt by reversing a previous decision to restrict or terminate parental access to him. This is accordingly a domain in which there is an even greater call than usual for protection against arbitrary interferences.'

6.83   The Court nonetheless recognised the need for a margin for discretion for the local authority social services department engaged in decision making in this kind of case. The Court stated:

> 'The Court recognises that, in reaching decisions in so sensitive an area, local authorities are faced with a task that is extremely difficult. To require them to follow on each occasion an inflexible procedure would only add to their problems. They must therefore be allowed a measure of discretion in this respect.'

6.84   In the view of the Court, a fundamental requirement of procedures which adequately safeguard the interests of children and parents in such cases was that they fulfil the following test:

> 'In the Court's view, what therefore has to be determined is whether, having regard to the particular circumstances of the case and notably the serious nature of the decisions to be taken, the parents have been involved in the decision-making process, seen as a whole, to a degree sufficient to provide them with the requisite protection of their interests. If they have not, there will have been a failure to respect their family life and the interference resulting from the decision will not be capable of being regarded as "necessary" within the meaning of Article 8.'

6.85   The Court elaborated upon the importance of parental involvement in the decision-making process in the case of *McMichael v UK*[2]. The Court held that there had been a violation of Art 8 when natural parents were denied access to social work reports at a 'children's hearing' by which a Scottish local authority was seeking to take their child into care. Thus parental involvement in the decision-making process requires that they should be sufficiently informed so as to enable them to make informed decisions about the merits of the case and, inter alia, their prospects on appeal.

6.86   In *Olsson v Sweden*[3], the Court accepted that standards of care in the home of three young siblings were such that the decision to take them into care

---

1   10 EHRR 29.
2   20 EHRR 205.
3   11 EHRR 259.

was justified but the way in which the care plan was subsequently implemented, failing to promote the bonds between parents and children even though adoption was never considered by the authorities, was not 'necessary' and thus a violation of Art 8 was disclosed. Thus the authority's responsibility to behave in a manner consistent with the Convention rights of the parents is an obligation which is a continuing one which extends beyond the making of a care order to the manner of its implementation, contact arrangements and future planning and reviews thereof.

The right of the parents and their children to live together – rehabilitation

6.87   Where rehabilitation is achievable within a realistic time-scale to meet the needs of the children, it is an important aim of Art 8. The Court has made it clear that taking a child into care should normally be regarded as a temporary measure to be ended as soon as circumstances permit a return to the child's home. The consequence of this view is that measures taken to implement 'temporary' care should therefore not, either incidentally or by design, frustrate the ultimate aim of reuniting the parents and child. In the private law case of *Hokkanen v Finland*[1], it was said that there is an obligation upon the authorities to take measures to realise the parents' right pursuant to Art 8 to reunite parents and children. The Court stated that:

> 'In previous cases dealing with issues relating to the compulsory taking of children into public care and the implementation of care measures, the Court has consistently held that Article 8 includes a right for the parent to have measures taken with a view to his or her being reunited with the child and an obligation for the national authorities to take such action.'

6.88   Notwithstanding the presumption of rehabilitation, the Court attaches importance to the welfare of the child and a parent may not insist upon the Court taking a course which would have the effect of harming the child's health and development. In *Johansen v Norway*[2] the Court said:

> 'In this regard, a fair balance has to be struck between the interests of the child in remaining in public care and those of the parent in being reunited with the child. In carrying out this balancing exercise, the Court will attach particular importance to the best interests of the child, which, depending on their nature and seriousness, may override those of the parent. In particular, as suggested by the Government, the parent cannot be entitled under Article 8 of the Convention to have such measures taken as would harm the child's health and development.'

6.89   Thus the obligation to effect measures directed towards family reunification is not an absolute one. The Court has recognised the need to balance the rights of all those concerned in the decision, particularly those of the children. The obligation of a local authority is to take all necessary steps to effect rehabilitation as appear reasonable in all the circumstances of the case bearing in mind their margin for discretion.

---

1   19 EHRR 139.
2   23 EHRR 33.

The duty to promote contact – the right of the parents and the children to a continuing relationship with each other

6.90   The Court has observed that:

> 'The mutual enjoyment by parent and child of each other's company constitutes a fundamental element of family life. Furthermore, the natural family relationship is not terminated by reason of the fact that the child is taken into public care.'

The Convention and its organs therefore recognise a 'right' to contact within the fundamental rights and freedoms protected by the terms of Art 8. This is, of course, inconsistent with the approach of the domestic courts which regard contact as a right of the child rather than of the parent. The Government made a direct attempt to persuade the Court of the merits of the approach adopted in the domestic courts, which derives from the Children Act 1989, in the case of *W v UK*[1] where that argument foundered. The Court considered the submissions of the Government to the effect that following a parental rights resolution (this was a pre Children Act case) the parents had no right to access by domestic law and therefore could not sustain their complaint that their rights under Art 6(1) had been violated. The Court completely rejected that submission and concluded that:

> 'Moreover, the extinction of all parental right in regard to access would scarcely be compatible with fundamental notions of family life and the family ties which Article 8 of the Convention is designed to protect (see the Marckx judgment of 13 June 1979, Series A no. 31, p. 21, at p. 45).'

6.91   It is important to recognise that the balancing exercise the Court must conduct in determining questions of contact in this context will be to balance the right of the parents to respect for their family life with any rights which may be inconsistent with those rights, those of their children being of particular significance. The balancing exercise arises from the terms of Art 8(2) which impugns interferences by a public authority with this right (the right to respect for family and private life) except such as is in accordance with the law, and is necessary in a democratic society in the interests of, inter alia, the protection of the rights and freedoms of others. This balancing exercise does not give the children an automatically enhanced status in the process and certainly does not require that the welfare of the child should be the paramount consideration of the court.

6.92   The starting point of the balancing exercise is that the rights of the child concerned have no special status, although the child too has a right to respect for his family and private life under Art 8. The parents have rights under Art 8, which, prima facie, entitle them to a continuing relationship with their child. However, the considerations expressed by the Court in the *Johansen*[2] case are equally relevant in the case of contact. Thus if there are overriding reasons for restricting, or even in an exceptional case, for terminating, parental contact for reasons of the welfare of the child the Court would in principle countenance such an interference if following judicial scrutiny the reasons for it were 'relevant and sufficient'. Of the two, sufficiency has usually proved to be the more difficult test to satisfy.

---

1   10 EHRR 29.
2   23 EHRR 33.

Dispensing with parental consent to adoption

6.93   Closed adoption represents the most complete severance of the family ties between a child and is parents known to law. For such a severance of family ties to be effected by a court order in the face of parental opposition the organs of the Convention require overriding justification on the basis of the welfare of the child.

6.94   In *Johansen*[1], the Court was concerned with a decision by which the applicant's young daughter was taken into care and access simultaneously terminated, with a view to permanent placement for adoption. The Court found that the decision was a violation of the applicant's rights under Art 8. The Court stated that:

> 'the applicant had been deprived of her parental rights and access in the context of a permanent placement of her daughter in a foster home with a view to adoption by the foster parents. These measures were particularly far-reaching in that they totally deprived the applicant of her family life with the child and were inconsistent with the aim of reuniting them. Such measures should only be applied in exceptional circumstances and could only be justified if they were motivated by an overriding requirement pertaining to the child's best interests.'

6.95   The decision of the Court in *Keegan v Ireland*[2] made it plain that a natural father has a right to be consulted before his child is placed for adoption where family life is in existence between the father and the child.

6.96   It is not in every case of adoption, however, that the Court will find a violation of parental rights pursuant to Art 8. In the case of *Soderback v Sweden*[3], the father and mother had never cohabited. Their daughter was born in 1982. The father's contact had always been very limited, partly as a result of the mother's opposition, and partly because of the father's personal problems. The mother's husband, who had lived with the child since she was 8 months old, applied to adopt the daughter. By the time the adoption order was made, he had lived with the child for some 6½ years, 5½ of those prior to his marriage to the mother, a relationship within which de facto family ties existed. The father opposed the adoption. He sought increased access following the establishment of a stable relationship with a woman who had a child of her own. The father argued that the adoption would deprive him of family life with his daughter and was therefore an interference with his right to respect for his family life and was thus a violation of Art 8. The Court unanimously found no violation of Art 8 and expressly declined to follow the approach adopted in the *Johansen* case on the basis that it was inappropriate to do so having regard to the very different factual context in which the adoption proceedings had arisen in the two cases. The Court proceeded on the basis that the father's family ties with his daughter were sufficient for the existence of family life within the meaning of Art 8, and on that assumption, that the adoption amounted to an interference with his rights to respect for family life. It was not in doubt that the adoption was 'in accordance with the law' and pursued a legitimate aim, in formalising and consolidating the family ties between the child and her adoptive father. Nor was it doubted that the effect of the adoption, as in the *Johansen* case, would be to have the legal effect of totally depriving the applicant of family life with his daughter. The Court found that the father's

PART B
IMPACT OF THE CONVENTION

---

1   23 EHRR 33.
2   18 EHRR 342.
3   [1999] 1 FLR 250.

contact with his daughter had been infrequent and limited and at the time the adoption was granted he had not seen her for some time. In those circumstances, the Court held that the decision fell with the margin of appreciation of the State and in the light of the legitimate aim of the adoption it could not be said that the effect on the applicant's relations with the child were disproportionate.

6.97   The different attitude of the Court derived, in large part, from the different context in the which the two adoptions occurred; in the *Johansen* case the context was public care, while in the *Soderback* case, the context was private law adoption. It is interesting to note that the approach of the Court, taking as it did a more relaxed view of the effect of a private law adoption, is arguably the opposite of the approach that would be adopted by the domestic courts.

6.98   There is therefore some reason for uncertainty about the approach of the Court to domestic decisions concerning adoption, not least in the light of the fact that the possibility of post-adoption with the birth family within the domestic jurisdiction adds a further complicating factor to any attempt to predict the attitude of the Court.

Post-adoption contact

6.99   On 14 November 1995 the applicant in the case of *Clark v UK*[1] notified the Commission that he had accepted an ex gratia payment of £7,000 together with his legal costs from the Government and did not wish to pursue his complaint. Accordingly, the Commission struck out the complaint. The applicant was the father of two children who married the mother after the birth of the first child. After the separation of the parents the mother requested that the local authority take the children in care. In care proceedings contested by the father, the trial judge expressed himself impressed by the father but acquiesced in the authority's view that the children would be at risk of emotional damage if returned to the father at that time. The judge expressed the view that rehabilitation did not seem to have been explored and warned the local authority that their intended freeing application would not be a formality. There was excessive delay before the freeing application was heard during which time the local authority rejected the father's suggestion that the children be rehabilitated to him, reduced and then terminated his contact and placed the child with prospective adopters who were hostile to any post-adoption contact. The guardian's report indicated that open adoption would meet the children's needs but expressed doubt that the adopters would accept it. The judge granted the freeing order with express reluctance only upon the basis that the delay had produced a situation in which the children could not afford any new placement. The reasons for the Government's desire to settle the case can be deduced from the foregoing account. Unfortunately, the fact that the application was settled means that although the Court would, no doubt, have been able to find several instances of violation of the applicant's rights the views of the Court with regard to the merits of open adoption were not made clear.

6.100   The Court will probably be sympathetic to open adoption where it is compatible with the welfare of the children. It is further suggested that the Court will have regard to the welfare of the children in the light of the following factors, the nature of the bond with the parent, the availability of suitable placements and

---

1   Application No 23387/94.

the attitudes of the prospective adopters, the time within which it is considered that their needs must be met and the possibility of placement disruption through contact. The Court will be likely to condemn delay, lack of proper consultation with parents over future plans and any ill-thought-out decisions in relation to contact and placement which ultimately have a determinative effect. In short, the considerations the Court will have regard to are likely to be much the same as a domestic court would consider relevant to the issue but it is far from clear where the emphasis will lie.

The right to challenge the care plan

6.101   Care plans are a vital part of every local authority's strategy to meet the needs of children at risk. A judge is unlikely to make a care order unless satisfied that the authority has a plan for the future care of the child appropriate to his needs and his welfare. However, formal judicial control of the care plan begins and ends with the power of the court to allow or, alternatively, to dismiss the application of the local authority. This is obviously a very blunt instrument indeed as a means of judicial control although, apparently, a powerful one. In many cases, the power may be more apparent than real. Before a judge comes to consider the care plan in detail he will already have determined that the child concerned 'is suffering' or 'is likely to suffer' 'significant harm' as a result of unreasonable deficiencies in parental care such as will, in many cases, preclude a return to the parent's care as a realistic option.

6.102   Such a situation means that, in the absence of another viable placement within the extended family, that there is no alternative to the care system. Not infrequently, the needs of the child require some arrangement for permanency suited to his or her welfare to be effected urgently. If the judge regards the care plan as unsatisfactory in this situation his ability to control the care plan extends to adjournment of the final hearing under a further interim order if such delay can be regarded as 'planned and purposeful,' but not so as to create artificially the means to exercise a supervisory jurisdiction over matters parliament has chosen to entrust to the local authority.

6.103   In short, there is no remotely adequate means of formal judicial control of the care plan available to courts charged with the responsibility for determining such applications. Although it would be obviously incorrect to suggest that this deficiency is of practical importance in any but a minority of cases, it has aroused widespread judicial disquiet.

6.104   In the absence of any sophisticated means of judicial control of the nature and content of the care plan in the course of the care proceedings, it is a matter of concern that there are no means of control whatever available to the judge following the making of the care order. In the event that the local authority change the care plan following the making of the care order, both the court and the parents are likely to be, in practical terms, powerless. The court cannot of its own motion intervene and the only recourse open to the parents is to apply to discharge the care order or, alternatively, to apply for contact. Frequently, neither application will either be appropriate or capable of providing a remedy to 'unapproved' changes to the care plan however ill-considered and remote from the plan approved by the judge they may be.

6.105   It has been suggested by Wall J that this state of affairs is 'profoundly unsatisfactory'. That such concerns are widely felt among the designated judged and other professionals involved in the care system is clear. A broad consenses was reached among the members of the President's biennial Inter-disciplinary Conference held at Highgate House, Northampton, in September 1997, that changes to the present system are required in the final stages of the formulation of the care plan, at trial, when the care plan is controversial as between the court and the local authority, and in the subsequent implementation of the care plan. That such views exist may be highly significant when following incorporation of the European Convention the terms of Arts 6 and 8 require changes to be made to current domestic law and practice and offer the means to effect them.

6.106   In *W v UK*[1], the Court established the fundamental principle that the process of decision-making in children cases required that there should be sufficient procedural protection of parents' interests. The underlying reasoning for that decision would equally well support the conclusion that Art 8 requires that there should be sufficient procedural protection of the child's interests. With the sole exception of the local authority, none of the remaining parties to care proceedings have any formal means of control over the terms of the care plan, nor does the court. In circumstances where the Court has misgivings about the terms of care plan, it is arguable that such an administrative decision, the determination of the terms of care plan by officers of the local authority, should be subject to review by the Court. If, alternatively, the court were to make a care order having expressed reservations about the care plan of the kind that were expressed in *Clark v UK*[2], it would be open to the parents or the child (if represented either by the guardian or by another suitable representative) to argue that their Art 8 rights had been violated.

6.107   The applicant in *W v UK* had complained of the absence of remedies available to him following the decision of a local authority to terminate his contact to his child in care, and the length of the proceedings which followed. The Court held that the natural family relationship was not terminated by a child being taken into care and therefore that interferences with that relationship are violations of Art 8 rights. It is arguable that a decision by a local authority substantially to change a care plan 'approved' by the court only shortly after the care order was made would offend either the parent's or the child's Art 8 rights, or conceivably the rights of both. They could each readily argue that the circumstances afforded each of them insufficient procedural safeguards for their substantive Art 8 rights and that they were without any effective remedy contrary to the terms of Art 13. Although Art 8 contains no express procedural safeguards, the Court has determined that Art 8, nonetheless, does import into its terms the notion of 'fair procedure' where administrative decisions necessarily have the effect of interfering with family relationships protected by its terms. The Court explained the interrelationship between Art 8 and Art 6 in this regard in the course of delivering judgment in the case of *McMichael v UK*[3]:

---

1   10 EHRR 29.
2   Application No 23387/94.
3   20 EHRR 205.

'... (There is a) difference in the nature of the interests protected by Articles 6(1) and 8. Thus, Article 6(1) affords a procedural safeguard, namely the "right to a court" in the determination of one's "civil rights and obligations" (see *the Golder v. the United Kingdom* judgment of 21 February 1975, Series A no. 18, p. 18, para. 36); whereas not only does the procedural requirement inherent in Article 8 cover administrative procedures as well as judicial proceedings, but it is ancillary to the wider purpose of ensuring proper respect for, inter alia, family life (see, for example, *the B. v. the United Kingdom* judgment of 8 July 1987, Series A no. 121-B, pp. 62–74 and 75, paras. 63–65 and 68). The difference between the purpose pursued by the respective safeguards afforded by Articles 6(1) and 8 may, in the light of the particular circumstances, justify the examination of the same set of facts under both Articles (compare, for example, the above-mentioned *Golder* judgment, pp. 20–22, paras. 41–45, and *the O. v. the United Kingdom* judgment of 8 July 1987, Series A no. 120-A, pp. 28–29, paras. 65–67).

As regards the instant case, the facts complained of had repercussions not only on the conduct of judicial proceedings to which the second applicant was a party, but also on "a fundamental element of [the] family life" of the two applicants. In the present case the Court judges it appropriate to examine the facts also under Article 8.'

6.108   In the *McMichael* case, the parents had not had disclosed to them confidential social work reports and documents either before or during the 'children's hearing' in Scotland. The Court chose to examine the facts in relation to Art 8 as well as Art 6 and determined that there had been a breach of both parents' Art 8 rights without drawing distinction between them.

6.109   In addition to the arguments which would be available to parents and children to challenge the care plan available pursuant to Art 8, there would be further arguments available under Art 6(1). Particularly following the making of a care order and in relation to subsequent changes in the care plan, the Art 6(1) guarantee of the 'right to a court' in the determination of one's 'civil rights and obligations' affords the parents and children another possible means of challenge to the unapproved 'care plan'.

6.110   Where administrative decisions are directly decisive of an individual's civil rights and obligations, Art 6(1) requires the State to provide a right to challenge the decision before a tribunal with the Art 6 guarantees.

6.111   In *W v UK*[1], the Court decided that the availability of judicial review to the father to challenge a parental rights resolution was insufficient to guarantee the father's Art 6(1) rights because the court would, on such a review, confine itself to determining the question of whether the authority had acted illegally, unreasonably or unfairly and would not examine the merits. In a public law children case, the Court therefore requires that any review should be capable of examining the merits of the administrative decision complained of in order to be compatible with Art 6(1) rights. This decision therefore paves the way for guardians, for example, on behalf of the children, to be able to challenge an unsatisfactory care plan, particularly in circumstances where the court has to make a choice between a flawed care plan and an inappropriate and irresponsible parent. It would equally allow a challenge to the care plan following the making of the care order where there was a significant change made to the care plan or where there was, for example, a failure to implement the care plan or to do so in timely fashion.

---

1   10 EHRR 29.

6.112   Past decisions of the Court have illustrated a vigorous practical determination to ensure that Art 6 guarantees are made good. In *Golder v UK*[1], a prisoner was refused access to a solicitor in circumstances where he wished to bring a libel action against a prison officer. The Court held that the refusal constituted a breach of his rights under Art 6 in that it hindered his right of access to court. The Court observed:

> 'It would be inconceivable, in the opinion of the court, that Article 6 should describe in detail the procedural guarantees afforded to parties in a pending lawsuit and should not first protect that which alone makes it in fact possible to benefit from such guarantees, that is, access to a court. The fair, public and expeditious characteristics of judicial proceedings are of no value at all if there are no judicial proceedings ... It follows that the right of access constitutes an element which is inherent in the right stated by article 6. The court thus reaches the conclusion ... that article 6 secures to everyone the right to have any claim relating to his civil rights and obligations brought before a court of tribunal.'

In the light of the pivotal importance of the care plan in the life of a child subject to a care order, there is reason to believe that the domestic courts, or in default, the European Court, may find that Art 6 and Art 8 enable a challenge to the care plan in appropriate cases.

Other examples of procedural challenges

6.113   There have been a number of decisions which have considered the procedural fairness of the decision-making process in respect of parents and other family members whose relationship with the child has been the subject of interference.

6.114   In *Boyle v UK*[2], the Commission found a violation where the social services took the decision to terminate the contact of an uncle, who had been a de facto father to the child, at a case conference to which he was not invited and without seeking out his views. In contrast, where a mother complained about her child's name being placed on the child abuse register, it was held that her position had been adequately safeguarded by the opportunity to submit her views on the alleged non-accidental injury in writing to the case conference. The provision of legal representation has also been regarded as a relevant factor.

Secure accommodation

Domestic law
6.115   Secure accommodation is 'accommodation provided for the purposes of restricting liberty'. *The Children Act 1989 Guidance and Regulations Vol 4 Residential Care* (HMSO, 1991), para 8.10 states:

> 'The interpretation of the term "accommodation provided for the purposes of restricting liberty" ... is ultimately a matter to be determined by the court. However, it is important to recognise that any practice or measure which prevents a child from leaving a room or building of his own free will may be deemed by the court to constitute "restriction of liberty".'

---

1   1 EHRR 524.
2   19 EHRR 179.

It has been held that whether accommodation is 'secure' is a question of fact for the court to determine. In *Re C (Detention: Medical Treatment)*[1] Wall J held that the natural meaning of accommodation 'provided for the purpose of restricting liberty' is accommodation 'designed for, or having as its primary purpose' the restriction of liberty.

6.116 Secure accommodation orders may be made by the family proceedings court, and also in the course of criminal proceedings. The county court and High Court may also make secure accommodation orders but may only do so in the course of other proceedings. Proceedings pursuant to s 25 of the Children Act 1989 are family proceedings.

6.117 On an application under the Children Act 1989, s 25 by a local authority for the authority to place a child in secure accommodation, the welfare of the child is relevant but is not paramount. *The Children Act 1989 Guidance and Regulations Vol 1 Court Orders* (HMSO, 1991), para 5.1, states:

'Restricting the liberty of children is a serious step which must be taken only when there is no genuine alternative which would be appropriate. It must be a "last resort", in the sense that all else must first have been comprehensively considered and rejected – never because no other placement was available at the relevant time, because of the inadequacies in staffing, because the child is simply being a nuisance or runs away from his accommodation and is not likely to suffer harm in doing so, and never as a form of punishment. It is important, in considering the possibility of a secure placement, that there is a clear view of the aims and objectives of such a placement, and that those providing the accommodation can fully meet those aims and objectives. Secure placements once made, should be for only so long as is necessary and unavoidable.'

6.118 When a child is being provided with accommodation (or accommodated in care) by a local authority, the local authority may not place or keep a child in secure accommodation unless it appears either that:

– the child has a history of absconding and is likely to abscond from any other description of accommodation, and if he absconds he is likely to suffer significant harm; or that
– if he is kept in any other description of accommodation he is likely to injure himself or other persons.

6.119 A child under the age of 13 may not be placed in secure accommodation without the prior approval of the Secretary of State. Prior to the determination of an application for a secure accommodation order, a local authority may not keep a child who otherwise meets the criteria in secure accommodation for an aggregate period of more than 72 hours in anay period of 28 days. Otherwise than in criminal proceedings, secure accommodation orders may be made for up to 3 months on first application and up to 6 months on further application. A local authority must in respect of a child being kept in secure accommodation appoint at least three people to review the placement within one month of first inception of the placement and thereafter no less frequently than every 3 months. On each review, it must be established that the criteria continue to apply, that no other form of accommodation is appropriate and that the placement continues to be necessary.

---

1   [1997] 2 FLR 180.

6.120   In *Re W (Secure Accommodation Order: Attendance at Court)*[1], Ewbank J held that, on hearing an application for a secure accommodation order, the court could allow the child to be present but should do so only if satisfied that it would be in the interests of the child to be present. The judge held, in addition, that the court could under its inherent jurisdiction refuse to allow the child into court if it formed the view that the child was likely to be unruly.

Impact of the Convention

6.121   Secure accommodation orders are by definition designed to restrict liberty and are thus, prima facie, in breach of Art 5 of the Convention. When applied in a non-criminal context on an application by a local authority in the usual 'family law' context, many of the exceptions to the Article have no obvious application at all. Nonetheless, it is necessary to consider each of the exceptions to Art 5(1)(a)–(f) to see what impact incorporation is likely to have upon this aspect of family law.

6.122   Article 5(1) provides that 'nobody shall be deprived of his liberty save in the following cases and in accordance with a procedure prescribed by law'. Compliance with 'a procedure prescribed by (domestic) law' does not automatically validate a deprivation of liberty, however:

> 'The Convention here refers essentially to national law and lays down the obligation to conform to the substantive and procedural rules of national law, but it requires in addition that any deprivation of liberty should be in keeping with the purpose of Article 5 (art. 5), namely to protect the individual from arbitrariness.'

Nonetheless, the Court stated in the same case that:

> '... "Lawfulness", however, also implies that the deprivation of liberty is in keeping with the purpose of the restrictions permissible under Article 5(1) of the Convention.'

The main objective of Art 5 is to secure the liberty of the individual against arbitrary interference by a public authority. 'Liberty' means physical liberty of the person and 'security of the person' is to be interpreted in the light of the former definition.

6.123   The right to liberty is subject to the exceptions set out in Art 5(1)(a)–(f) inclusive, and which have been restrictively interpreted. It has been held that the exceptions to Art 5(1) set out in paras (a)–(f) are exhaustively listed therein.

Article 5(1)(a) applies only following 'conviction by a competent court' and thus has no bearing upon the non-criminal application of secure accommodation orders.

Article 5(1)(b) applies, inter alia, to the lawful detention of a person for non-compliance with the lawful order of a court or in order to secure the fulfilment of any obligation prescribed by law. This exception has been restrictively interpreted like the others. It has been held to apply in cases of wilful non-compliance with a lawful order of the court, such as in proceedings for civil contempt. However, it has been held that the purpose of the detention must aim to secure compliance with a 'specific and concrete obligation which he has until then failed to satisfy'. The detention must not be punitive in purpose. This

---

1   [1994] 2 FLR 1092.

exception, again, has no obvious application to secure accommodation orders applied in a non-criminal context.

6.124   Article 5(1)(d) provides 'the detention of a minor by lawful order (i) for the purpose of educational supervision or (ii) his lawful detention for the purpose of bringing him before the competent legal authority'.

In *Bouamar v Belgium*[1], a disturbed adolescent minor with a history of delinquent and aggressive behaviour was remanded to a remand prison which had no educational facilities. The Court described his predicament in these terms:

> 'he was shuttled to and fro between the remand prison at Lantin and his family. In 1980 alone, the juvenile courts ordered his detention nine times and then released him on or before the expiry of the statutory limit of fifteen days; in all, he was thus deprived of his liberty for 119 days during the period of 291 days.'

The Belgian government's submission that it had acted within the scope of Art 5(1)(d) was rejected by the Court which held that the detention was too long and that sub-paragraph (d):

> 'does not preclude an interim custody measure being used as a preliminary to a regime of supervised education, without itself involving any supervised education. In such circumstances, however, the imprisonment must be speedily followed by actual application of such a regime in a setting (open or closed) designed and with sufficient resources for the purpose.'

The case reveals the willingness of the court to put the conduct of public authorities under close scrutiny and to refuse to accept explanations for actions or procedures which are unsupported by evidence.

6.125   The second of the two permitted grounds under Art 5(1)(d) is intended to deal with a minor's detention so as to remove him from harmful surroundings. *Abbott v UK*[2] concerned a ward who was placed in secure accommodation in the course of proceedings to which he was not a party, and within which he was unrepresented. The case was settled by the Government while still before the Commission on the basis of the Government's proposals to amend the Children (Secure Accommodation) Regulations 1991[3], which had then not been brought into force, to include measures for the ward to be joined as a party. Abbott's case is therefore an example of a petition which had a direct effect upon delegated legislation in the UK.

6.126   Article 5(1)(e) and (f) have no general application in the case of secure accommodation orders.

It is thus evident that, in general, restrictions upon the liberty of minors will be, prima facie, a breach of Art 5(1) unless the particular facts of the case can be brought within one of the exceptions to the general prohibition, sub-paragraph (d) being much the most likely.

6.127   Perhaps surprisingly, the Court has, on occasion, appeared to take a robust attitude to the deprivation of liberty of children. The rationale for this view seems to be that children are almost invariably subject to restrictions upon their 'liberty' both in the context of school and in the home. In the case of *Nielsen v*

PART B
IMPACT OF THE CONVENTION

---

1   11 EHRR 1.
2   (1990) 67 DR 290.
3   SI 1991/1505.

Denmark[1], the mother of a 12-year-old boy who had sole parental rights placed the child in a closed psychiatric ward against his will. The Court found that the circumstances did not reveal a deprivation of liberty and emphasised the importance of parental rights under Art 8. The Court further emphasised the importance of the fact that the hospitalisation was carried out on medical advice, with a view to protecting the child's health and the conditions on the ward and the treatment he received were not inappropriate. The boy complained, through his father, that the hospitalisation was a deprivation of liberty since the ward was a closed one and he was unable to receive visitors without permission nor to make telephone calls and he was under almost permanent observation. He further complained that his mother's real purpose was to prevent him joining his father, a view with which the Commission evidently had some sympathy. The Commission, once again evincing more liberal sentiments than the Court, found that there was a deprivation of liberty which was not justified since the boy was not mentally ill in a real sense and the placement could not be regarded as a voluntary one.

6.128   There are real questions as to the extent to which there may be a conflict between the domestic jurisdiction in relation to the making of secure accommodation orders and the provisions of Art 5. The primary areas of potential conflict are:

–   Whether, in principle, the general circumstances in which secure accommodation orders may be imposed in non-criminal cases are compatible with the provisions of Art 5.
–   Whether the provisions of domestic law for reviewing the question of whether a secure accommodation order continues to be necessary and appropriate sufficiently safeguard the Convention rights of the minor during the currency of an order. Issues may arise under Art 5 and Art 6.
–   The willingness of the domestic court to exclude minors from court on applications for secure accommodation orders on the grounds of anticipated unruliness or in the interest of their welfare may offend the provisions of Art 6.
–   Whether the power of a local authority to place a child in secure accommodation on an interim basis may not fall within the exceptions to Art 5(1), (Art 5(4)).
–   The absence in domestic law of any remedy such as Art 5(5) requires that it should be available to the victims of breaches of Art 5.

---

1   11 EHRR 175.

Chapter 7

THE CHILD – PRIVATE LAW

7.1   The majority of Convention cases concerning family law have involved children cases. Public law cases have provided the greatest number. Private law cases are less susceptible to regulation by the organs of the Convention because disputes between parents, and other carers and relatives will, usually, involve the State only if an application has been made to court. The Commission and the Court have made it plain that in exercising their supervisory jurisdiction their proper function does not consist of substituting their view upon the merits of a case for that of the domestic authorities. They have shown great concern to ensure that procedural safeguards have been respected and that decisions have been based upon relevant and sufficient reasons. This primary focus of Convention case-law upon procedural safeguards will, following incorporation, become the responsibility of domestic courts, although it will not, of course, be theirs to exercise exclusively .

7.2   There are a small but significant number of cases which deal with the rights of parents, carers and others arising in non-conventional families.

7.3   The organs of the Convention have demonstrated a willingness, in practice, to apply the same reasoning to private law cases as to public law cases.

KEY ARTICLES

7.4   Article 6 (fair hearing); Art 8 (right to respect for family life); Art 14 (prohibition of discrimination).

Article 8: the right to respect for private and family life

7.5   Article 8(1) provides that everyone has the right to respect for his private and family life, his home and his correspondence.

7.6   Article 8(2) sets out the circumstances, in general terms, in which the State may interfere with the enjoyment of the right. It also provides that there shall be no interference by a public authority with the exercise of the right except such as is in accordance with the law and is necessary in a democratic society in the interests of national security, public safety or the economic well-being of the country for the prevention of disorder or crime, for the protection of health or morals, or for the protection of the rights and freedoms of others.

7.7   The Court has developed a practice when dealing with an issue under Art 8 of considering each of the following matters in turn:

– the scope of the right;
– the nature of the interference which is alleged to restrict the enjoyment of the right;
– the lawfulness of the interference;
– the legitimate aims of the interference;

–   the necessity for the interference in a democratic society (ie whether there
       are relevant and sufficient reasons for the interference which are proportion-
       ate to the restriction on the enjoyment of the right when taking into account
       the margin of appreciation).

RIGHTS CREATED BY ARTICLE 8

7.8   The primary objective of Art 8 is to protect individuals against arbitrary
action by public authorities[1]. Article 8 does not, however, merely prohibit certain
forms of interference by public authorities with the rights of individuals but, on
occasion, may require the State to effect measures designed to secure respect for
private life[2] even as between individuals[3].

THE EXISTENCE OF FAMILY LIFE

7.9   In the first stage in any inquiry to determine whether there has been any
interference with the right to respect for 'family life', the Convention organs
determine whether 'family life' is in existence. The Convention does not define
the concept of 'family life' and nor has the Court or the Commission attempted to
make good the deficiency. 'Family' has been interpreted widely by the European
Court and the case-law continues to expand the recognised scope of 'family life'.

In *Keegan v Ireland*[4], the Court held that:

> 'the notion of "the family" is not confined solely to marriage-based relationships and
> may encompass other de facto "family ties" where the parties are living together
> outside of marriage. A child born out of such a relationship is ipso jure part of that
> "family" unit from the moment of his birth and by the very fact of it. There thus exists
> between the child and his parents a bond amounting to family life even if at the time of
> his or her birth the parents are no longer cohabiting or if their relationship has then
> ended.'

Whether 'family life' is found to exist in the circumstances of any particular case is
a question of fact. In *X, Y and Z v UK*[5], it was held that in determining whether a
relationship can amount to 'family life' a number of factors may be relevant,
'including whether the couple live together, the length of their relationship and
whether they have demonstrated their commitment to each other by having
children together or by any other means ...'.

---

1   *Kroon v The Netherlands* 19 EHRR 263.
2   *X and Y v The Netherlands* 8 EHRR 235.
3   *Hokkanen v Finland* 19 EHRR 139.
4   18 EHRR 342.
5   [1997] 2 FLR 892, para 36.

THE RIGHTS OF THE CHILD

Family life

7.10   Where family life is found to exist the children of the family will be entitled, in their own right, to respect for their 'family life'. Because the majority of children cases are initiated by adult applicants, 'family life' has tended to be defined in terms of the adult relationships around the children, rather than upon the children and the means by which their needs are met.

7.11   However, there is a growing recognition that child applicants may be able to succeed in making a rather stronger case than an adult arguing a similar case on the basis of co-extensive rights of his own to respect for his 'family life'. The case of *Berrehab v The Netherlands*[1] is considered in some detail in Chapter 6. The rights of children under Art 8 extend to their relationships with their siblings[2].

Private life

7.12   Children also enjoy protection of their private lives under Art 8. Private life has been interpreted broadly and it includes the moral and physical integrity of the child concerned. Article 8 may involve the imposition of positive obligations upon the State including, 'the adoption of measures designed to secure a respect for private life even in the sphere of relations of individuals between themselves.'[3]. In *X and Y v The Netherlands*, the applicants were father and daughter. Dutch criminal law required any female complainant in rape proceedings to personally file a complaint. Y was 16 years of age and mentally incompetent. When she was raped in a private home for mentally disabled children there proved to be no means by which a prosecution of her attacker could legitimately be initiated. The Court held that the State had a responsibility under Art 8 to provide criminal as well as civil remedies against such attacks within the private sphere. Both the Court and the Commission have observed that 'private life' includes not only moral integrity but also the physical integrity of the person. In *Costello-Roberts v UK*[4], the Court accepted that the protection for individual physical integrity may well be wider than the protection afforded by Art 3. Therefore, Art 8 may well afford children and others greater protection from domestic violence than does Art 3. In that case the complaint was not established, not least, because the context of the complaint was a punishment inflicted at a boarding preparatory school and the very fact of placing the child at such a school necessarily involved some interference with his private life, and nor were the effects of the punishment on his physical or moral integrity sufficient to bring it within Art 8.

7.13   The protection afforded by Art 8 to 'private life' extends to protection from compulsory physical intervention such as blood tests in paternity actions.[5] Private life has also been held to include the right of access to personal records

---

1   11 EHRR 322.
2   *Moustaquim v Belgium* 13 EHRR 802.
3   *X and Y v The Netherlands* 8 EHRR 235.
4   19 EHRR 112.
5   *X v Austria* Application No 8278/78, (1979) 18 DR 154.

and information relating to a childhood in care[1] and the confidentiality of medical records[2].

7.14   Names have been held to fall within the scope of Art 8 as a means of identification and a link with family.[3] However, the margin of appreciation the Court has allowed in relation to restrictions upon permissible changes of name has been considerable[4]

Illegitimacy

7.15   The leading case on the illegitimate family is *Marckx v Belgium*[5]. The members of the 'illegitimate family' are equally entitled to enjoy the rights and freedoms guaranteed by Art 8 as members of a 'traditional' family. The applicants, a mother and her illegitimate infant daughter, complained that limitations upon the mother's capacity to give or bequeath property to her daughter violated Art 8 and Art 14. The Court held that Belgian law violated both Articles by virtue of the lack of any objective and reasonable justification for the differences in treatment between the legitimate and illegitimate family.

7.16   The Court has adopted a similar approach to that adopted in the *Berrehab* case[6] in the case of *Johnston v Ireland*[7]. In that case, a joint application by the daughter and her biological parents, the biological parents unsuccessfully argued that Art 8 protection of family life extended to the right to a formal termination of marriage. Although the parents' claim failed, the daughter's claim succeeded, based upon the disadvantageous situation in which her illegitimate status placed her, and her parents succeeded on the same ground on the basis of her success. The Court noted:

> 'As it (the Court) observed in its *Marckx*[8] judgment, "respect" for family life, understood as including the ties between near relatives, implies an obligation for the State to act in a manner calculated to allow these ties to develop normally (Series A no. 31, p. 21, § 45). And in the present case the normal development of the natural family ties between the first and second applicants and their daughter requires, in the Court's opinion, that she should be placed, legally and socially, in a position akin to that of a legitimate child.
>
> Examination of the third applicant's present legal situation, seen as a whole, reveals, however, that it differs considerably from that of a legitimate child; in addition, it has not been shown that there are any means available to her or her parents to eliminate or reduce the differences. Having regard to the particular circumstances of this case and notwithstanding the wide margin of appreciation enjoyed by Ireland in this area, the absence of an appropriate legal regime reflecting the third applicant's natural family ties amounts to a failure to respect her family life.'

---

1   *Gaskin v UK* 12 EHRR 36.
2   *Z v Finland* 25 EHRR 371.
3   *Burghartz v Switzerland* 18 EHRR 101, para 24.
4   *Stjerna v Finland* 24 EHRR 195.
5   2 EHRR 330.
6   See above.
7   9 EHRR 203.
8   See above.

THE PARAMOUNTCY PRINCIPLE

7.17   The likely impact of the Convention upon the 'paramountcy principle' set out in s 1(1) of the Children Act 1989 is considered in detail in Chapter 6.

PARENTAL RIGHTS

7.18   The likely impact of the Convention on parental rights is considered in detail in Chapter 6.

THE EXTENDED FAMILY

7.19   The likely impact of the Convention on the extended family is considered in detail in Chapter 6.

REPEATED APPLICATIONS

7.20   The relevant Article of the Convention regarding applications restricted by s 91(14) of the Children Act 1989 is Art 6, and the entitlement to a 'fair and public hearing ... in the determination of his civil rights'.

Domestic Law

7.21   Section 91(14) of the Children Act 1989 states:

> 'On disposing of any application for an order under this Act, the court may (whether or not it makes any other order in response to the application) order that no application for an order under this Act of any specified kind may be made with respect to the child concerned by any person named in the order without leave of the court.'

7.22   It has been determined that such restriction may be imposed in cases of repeated[1], vexatious or oppressive[2] applications, or other exceptional circumstances[3] but that the power to do so should be used sparingly.

7.23   In *B v B (Residence Orders: Restricting Applications)*[4], Waite LJ considered in what circumstances such a restriction should be imposed:

> 'The test that I would favour involves reading s 91(14) in conjunction with the first and most important provision in the Children Act, s 1(1), which makes the welfare of the child the court's paramount consideration when determining any question with respect to the child's upbringing.
>
> The judge must, therefore, ask him- or herself in every case whether the best interests of the child require interference with the fundamental freedom of a parent to raise issues affecting the child's welfare before the court as and when such issues arise.'

---

1   *Re R (A Minor) (Leave to Make Applications)* [1998] 2 FCR 129.
2   *Re Y (Child Orders: Restricting Applications)* [1994] 2 FLR 699.
3   *C v W (A Minor) (Leave to Apply)* [1998] 1 FCR 618.
4   [1997] 1 FLR 139.

7.24   In *Re A (Application for Leave)*[1], Thorpe LJ determined what test was appropriate to an application for leave to make a further application where a s 91(14) order had previously been imposed upon the applicant:

> '. . . I would favour the simplest of tests. Does this application demonstrate that there is any need for renewed judicial investigation? If yes, then leave should be granted. All that the court commits itself to thereby is to survey the material presented in the form of statements supporting the form C1 application and probably the contents of a report from the court welfare officer. The discretion that a court holds under the Children Act in relation to the conduct of any application relating to a child is so wide as to be almost unfettered. In appropriate cases the application may be determined at a directions appointment if the content of the statements and the court welfare officer's report indicate that the application should go no further. In other words, the grant of leave to apply is not the grant of a right to a full trial.'

Impact of the Convention

7.25   The nature and effect of the conditional bar upon applications created by s 91(14) of the Children Act 1989 has not, as yet, been directly considered by the Court. The interaction of Art 6 and the s 91(14) bar may be considered in three principal areas:

(1) the necessity for any bar to free application to the court;
(2) the nature of the s 91(14) bar;
(3) the procedures adopted by the domestic courts in determining the imposition and/or removal of such a bar.

Necessity

7.26   It is unlikely that either the domestic courts or the European Court will determine that such a bar is inconsistent with Art 6 of the Convention, in the circumstances in which it has so far been imposed. This is because the Convention itself establishes analogous powers in the Commission. Article 35, para 3 of the Convention (as to admissibility – abuse of the right to petition) itself contains provisions designed to prevent, in addition to other abuses of process, 'vexatious' and repetitious applications proceeding to full determination before the court[2]. The Convention provisions are significantly wider in scope than s 91(14) as presently interpreted by the domestic courts and extend, for example, to cases where an applicant includes abusive content in his submissions[3]. In addition, Art 37, para 1 established the power in the Commission to strike out a case from its list where the applicant does not intend to pursue his petition. Where, for example, an applicant has failed to observe the procedures of the court, failed to observe time-limits without any reasonable explanation and failed to supply requested information or even a forwarding address the petition was struck out[4].

7.27   It is also arguable that such restrictions upon application could be justified where, as is frequently the case, they are directed to the protection of a vulnerable single parent family unit from repeated hopeless applications, by reference to Art 8, respect for family life. The limits to the positive obligations

1   [1998] 1 FLR 1.
2   *M v UK* Application No 13284/87, (15 October 1987) 54 DR 214.
3   *Stamoulakatos v UK* Application No 27567/95, (15 March 1980) 20 DR 44.
4   *X v UK* Application No 10239/83, (11 April 1989) 60 DR 71.

imposed by Art 8 upon 'Public Authorities' (the State, local authority and the courts) have yet to be determined but may well extend to the duty to protect vulnerable families from the destabilising effects of applications which could be characterised as an abuse of the system.

Nature of the bar

7.28 A further reason why the s 91(14) bar is unlikely to constitute a violation of Art 6 is that the bar is not an absolute one but merely provides one further hurdle for the applicant to surmount before his application may proceed. The test established in *Re A (Application for Leave)*[1] for determining whether a further application should be allowed to proceed following a s 91(14) bar is : 'Does this application demonstrate that there is any need for renewed judicial investigation? If yes, then leave should be granted' per Thorpe LJ. The 'necessity' for a restriction upon the freedom of access to the court in children's cases of this kind is demonstrated by established authority, is fair and is in proportion to the need thus demonstrated.

Procedures

7.29 Of their very nature, orders restricting application made pursuant to s 91(14) frequently result from a judicial decision to consider making such an order first announced during the course of the hearing in which it is made. Although there are occasions when notice of an intention to seek such an order is given well before the hearing, in practice, those against whom such orders are made often have extremely limited notice that consideration is to be given to the making of such an order; little, if any, opportunity to consider what further evidence should be led or cross-examined to address the issue; and little time to consider the terms of submissions directed to the issue.

7.30 In the event that there is a serious issue of fact which is likely to be determinative, in whole or in part, of the question of whether such a bar should be imposed and there is inadequate notice of the possibility that such an order may be made, lack of opportunity to call or cross-examine relevant evidence in relation to the issue and/or time to consider the making of submissions, it is possible that Art 6(1) may provide a remedy.

7.31 Almost identical considerations arise in relation to the power of the court to make a s 8 order of its own motion in Children Act 1989 proceedings. The potential for parties to be taken by surprise, not to have appropriate opportunity to call relevant evidence, not to know the 'case' they have to meet nor to have sought relevant disclosure and thus to be prejudiced is self-evident.

If the risk of a violation of Art 6 is to be minimised in such situations, it will be necessary for the trial judge, when he identifies any possibility of making such an order to:

- alert the parties to the possibility as soon as possible;
- afford the parties the opportunity to call, recall and cross-examine evidence made freshly relevant to the issue.
- consider any application to adjourn to facilitate the calling of relevant evidence;

PART B
IMPACT OF THE CONVENTION

---

1   [1988] 1 FLR 1.

– allow the parties to make submissions in relation to the possibility of the making of such an order.

The general characteristics of a 'fair trial' and, in particular, the procedures essential to promote it have a relevance to both s 91(14) of the Children Act 1989 and the power of the court to make s 8 orders of its own motion.

FAIR HEARING

7.32 The key requirements to a fair trial within the meaning of Art 6(1) are that a party to proceedings should have knowledge of the case he has to meet, the evidence which is adduced to support it and the opportunity to challenge that evidence – 'with a view to adversarial argument' – *Barbera, Messegue and Jabardo v Spain*[1]. In that case, the Court found a violation of Art 6(1) of the Convention for the principal reason that extremely important pieces of evidence were not adequately adduced and discussed at the trial in the applicant's presence and in public. The three essential requirements of a fair trial are:

(1) a hearing in the presence of the parties;
(2) all evidence should be produced to the parties;
(3) the opportunity to challenge evidence.

It has been decided that the right to challenge evidence extends to the right to cross-examine witnesses[2].

7.33 However, in the field of family law, specifically of children's cases, although the Court has determined that 'as a matter of general principle the right to a fair – adversarial – trial "means the opportunity to have knowledge of and comment on the observations filed or evidence adduced by the other party" (see the *Ruiz-Mateos v Spain* judgment[3])', *McMichael v UK*[4] has determined that some relaxation of the composition of a classic court and its procedures may be appropriate. Nonetheless, in that case the Court plainly regarded adversarial trial as synonymous with a fair trial in the context of care proceedings which originated in a 'children's hearing' in Scotland. It was the lack of disclosure to the applicants of such vital documents as social reports which founded the violation of Art 6(1) of the Convention because that was capable of affecting their ability to influence the outcome of the hearing and to assess adequately their prospects on appeal.

7.34 It is not clear to what extent the Court's sympathy for somewhat less formal procedures in adjudicatory bodies concerned with children cases may lead to a conclusion that the opportunity to comment upon evidence in the course of submissions may suffice to satisfy the requirement of a fair trial even in the absence of opportunity to call and cross-examine witnesses.

7.35 It is at least arguable that where there are potentially determinative issues of primary fact in dispute that a decision to refuse to allow oral evidence to be adduced and cross-examined may lead to a violation of Art 6(1). The present

---

1   11 ECHR 360.
2   *X v Austria* Application No 5362/72, (1972) 42 CD 145.
3   (23 June 1993) Series A, No 262, p 25.
4   20 EHRR 205.

practice of domestic courts in dealing with such applications is to frequently take advantage of the 'almost unfettered' discretion the Children Act 1989 confers upon the court to adopt somewhat peremptory procedures.

7.36   There are a number of other areas of present practice in children cases where, presently, oral evidence is not generally given and where the right to give oral evidence implied by Art 6(1) may be relevant:

– child abduction cases[1];
– applications without notice;
– applications for leave to make an application for a s 8 order where there is no automatic right of application[2];
– applications by a child for leave to make an application;
– applications to be joined in existing Children Act 1989 proceedings.

Public hearing

7.37   The long-standing practice of hearing children cases in private has been considered by the Court of Appeal in the case of *Re PB (Hearings in Open Court)*[3]. On appeal, the current practice of hearing children cases in private was upheld not withstanding the father's specific application for the hearing to be held in open court and consideration of the provisions of Art 6. Peter Gibson LJ referred to the fact that the Article itself recognises that the right to a public trial is qualified where the interests of juveniles or the protection of private lives of the parties so requires.

Equality of arms

7.38   The principle of 'equality of arms' has been held to require:

(i)   equal treatment between a court appointed expert and an expert witness for the defence[4]; and
(ii) that parties to civil proceedings should be allowed to cross-examine witnesses[5].

7.39   The principle of 'equality of arms' may have considerable impact upon current practice in children cases in relation to expert reports where complicated medical, psychological and psychiatric issues are at large[6].

Delay: 'a fair hearing ... within a reasonable time'

7.40   Section 1(2) of the Children Act 1989 expressly sets out the general principle that delay in children proceedings is likely to be prejudicial to the welfare of the child. This is a rebuttable presumption. It has been held that delay

---

1   See the argument in *Re K (Abduction: Psychological Harm)* [1995] 2 FLR 550 in respect of Art 20 of the Hague Convention and human rights at 556C–557E, per Leggatt LJ.
2   But see *Re F and R (Section 8 Order: Grandparent's Application)* [1995] 1 FLR 524, Cazalet J held that where there are issues of fact the court should hear limited evidence from the parties to form a view on the merits of the application so as to determine whether there is a realistic possibility of a successful application.
3   [1996] 2 FLR 765.
4   *Bonisch v Austria* 9 EHRR 191, paras 32 and 33–34.
5   *X v Austria* Application No 5362/72, (1972) 42 CD 145.
6   See Chapter 3.

in conducting a final hearing may be appropriate in order to await further relevant assessment and be entirely consistent with the welfare of the child in such circumstances[1].

7.41   The Children Act 1989 establishes no specific remedy for the parties in the event of there being unreasonable delay in finally resolving the issues however such delay may have arisen and whatever the extent to which their cases may have been prejudiced thereby.

7.42   Excessive procedural delays will generally amount to a breach of Art 6(1). Neither the volume of work of the body concerned nor shortage of resources will justify excessive delay, but a purely temporary delay caused by an exceptional situation which the authorities have taken reasonably prompt action to deal with will not constitute a breach[2].

7.43   Many of the cases concerned with delay have not been family cases, nor yet children's cases. Those children cases in which the issue has been raised have shown that the Court is especially sensitive to the hazards of delay because in the absence of exceptional diligence 'there is always the danger that any procedural delay will result in the de facto determination of the issue submitted to the court before it has held the hearing'[3].

RELIGION

7.44   The likely impact of Art 14 upon discrimination on the grounds of religious belief is considered in Chapter 6.

INTERNATIONAL CHILD ABDUCTION

7.45   Incorporation of the European Convention is likely to have an impact upon English law relating to international child abduction, both in the sphere of Convention cases and 'non-Convention' cases.

The Hague Convention on the Civil Aspects of International Child Abduction 1980

7.46   The Hague Convention on the Civil Aspects of International Child Abduction 1980 is given effect in English law by the Child Abduction and Custody Act 1985 to which it is a Schedule. Article 20 of the Convention, however, was omitted from those Articles of the Convention which were included in the Schedule to the Act. Article 20 of the Convention provides that the State requested to return the child under the provisions of the Convention may refuse to do so if to order the return of the child would be inconsistent with the fundamental principles of the requested State relating to the protection of human rights and

---

1   *C v Solihull Metropolitan Borough Council* [1993] 1 FLR 290; *Hounslow London Borough Council v A* [1993] 1 WLR 291, [1993] 1 FLR 702; *Re B (A Minor) (Contact: Interim Order)* [1994] 2 FLR 269.
2   *Zimmerman and Steiner v Switzerland* 6 EHRR 17.
3   *H v UK* 10 EHRR 95, para 70.

fundamental freedoms. Although it has been said that regard can be had to the provisions of Art 20, the approach of the English courts has been hitherto to restrictively define its role. In *Re K (Abduction: Psychological Harm)*[1], Leggatt LJ said:

> 'So far as human rights are concerned, it seems to me that there is obvious objection to adopting such a construction of article 20 as would have the effect of overriding, or materially altering, the scope of any of the other articles and in particular article 13(b). It may well be that the court, as the Lord Chancellor indicated it should, will have regard to article 20 in the sense of seeking to construe other articles, such as article 13(b), in such a way as not to infringe human rights. Further than that, however, it does not go.'[2]

7.47 Article 20 clearly recognises that fundamental human rights might be compromised by making an order for the summary return of a child to the State in which he has hitherto been habitually resident. Were the English court to rely upon fundamental principles of human rights as a reason for non-return after the HRA 1998 comes into force, such decisions would be compatible with our treaty obligations in the light of Art 20. Furthermore, when the HRA 1998 comes into force the English courts will be bound to give effect to the provisions of the Child Abduction and Custody Act 1985 in a manner which is compatible with the European Convention on Human Rights. It is likely therefore that issues under the European Convention will be raised to an increasing extent by parents seeking to resist applications for the summary return of their children under the Hague Convention. Such issues may arise in a variety of forms (as described below).

Under Article 6

7.48 Issues may arise in relation to challenging evidence, the right to call oral evidence and to cross-examine. Furthermore, issues may arise, on the one hand, in relation to the peremptory nature of the proceedings, and, on the other hand, to delay in disposing expeditiously of the application. It is also possible that issues may arise as to whether there is 'equality of arms' having regard to the fact that an applicant is entitled to legal aid as of right and irrespective of means whereas a respondent to such an application is not. It is also arguable that Art 6 may enable respondents to submit successfully that they would not receive a fair trial in the courts of the requesting State and that the human rights of the respondent, the child or both of them would be compromised. Such considerations may well require an investigation of the nature of the legal system of the requesting State together with the principles the foreign court will apply[3].

Under Article 5 and Article 8

7.49 Issues may arise in relation to the effect of a return to the requesting State upon the physical and moral welfare and the security of the respondent (parent) and of the child concerned, particularly in the case of a very young child or baby or where a mother has complained of domestic violence and abuse by the father. Issues may arise in relation to the adequacy of interim arrangements for the

PART B
IMPACT OF THE CONVENTION

---

1   [1995] 2 FLR 550.
2   Ibid, at 557E.
3   See the dicta of Ward LJ in *Re JA (Child Abduction)* [1998] 1 FLR 231 at 243 suggesting that he was prepared to hold that *Re M (Abduction: Peremptory Return Order)* [1996] 1 FLR 478 was decided per incuriam.

protection of the mother and care of the child in the requesting State in the light of a number of notable failures of undertakings to achieve their object in recent years[1].

Under Article 14

7.50   In *Re W; Re B (Child Abduction: Unmarried Father)*[2], a decision of Hale J, in which she declined to find that the position of unmarried fathers in English law with regard to 'rights of custody' in international abduction proceedings, compared with that of married fathers, amounted to discrimination within the meaning of Art 14 of the Convention, but referred to the possibility that, over time, that might change.

7.51   As a result of the decision of the House of Lords in *Re J (A Minor) (Abduction; Custody Rights)*[3], unmarried fathers who have not acquired parental responsibility are acutely disadvantaged in the event that the mother removes their child to another country because they may well have 'no rights of custody' within the meaning of the Hague Convention and thus no remedy pursuant to it. Although the full impact of the decision in *Re J* has been reduced by the subsequent development of the notion of 'inchoate rights of custody'[4], unmarried fathers and their children remain at a substantial disadvantage in this regard.

'Non-Convention' abduction cases

7.52   Following the decision of the Court of Appeal in *Re P (Abduction: Non-Convention Country)*[5], such cases have been decided on the basis of the welfare test. Considerations of whether a respondent would receive a fair trial within the meaning of Art 6 may have to be explored as may the nature of the legal system of the requesting State together with the principles the foreign court will apply[6].

---

1   See Elizabeth Muirhead, 'Sending Children Back under the Hague Convention – Are Current Practices Wide of the Rules?' [1998] Fam Law 769.
2   [1998] 2 FLR 146.
3   [1990] AC 562.
4   *Re B (A Minor) (Abduction)* [1994] 2 FLR 249, CA; *Re O (Child Abduction: Custody Rights)* [1997] 2 FLR 702.
5   [1997] 1 FLR 780, CA; followed in *Re JA (Child Abduction: Non-Convention Country)* [1998] 1 FLR 231.
6   *Re JA (Child Abduction: Non-Convention Country)* [1998] 1 FLR 231.

Chapter 8

THE RIGHT TO A FAIR HEARING

8.1   Article 6 of the Convention states:

'In the determination of his civil rights and obligations or of any criminal charge against him, everyone is entitled to a fair and public hearing within a reasonable time by an independent and impartial tribunal established by law. Judgment shall be pronounced publicly but the press and public may be excluded from all or part of the trial in the interests of morals, public order or national security in a democratic society, where the interests of juveniles or the protection of private life of the parties so require, or to the extent strictly necessary in the opinion of the court in special circumstances where publicity would prejudice the interests of justice.'

8.2   The importance of Art 6 and the right to a fair trial cannot be overstated. It has long been recognised as underpinning individual rights of freedom and an essential element in the concept of the rule of law. The preamble of the European Convention for the Protection of Human Rights and Fundamental Freedoms refers to the rule of law as one of the components of the 'common heritage' of the Contracting European States. In the seminal case of *Golder v UK*[1], the Court stressed that,

'One reason why the signatory Governments decided to "take the first steps for the collective enforcement of certain of the Rights stated in the Universal Declaration" was their profound belief in the rule of law. It seems both natural and in conformity with the principle of good faith[2] to bear in mind this widely proclaimed consideration when interpreting the terms of Article 6(1) according to their context and in the light of the object and purpose of the Convention. This is all the more so since the Statute of the Council of Europe ... refers in two places to the rule of law; first in the preamble ... and secondly in Article 3 which provides that "every Member of the Council of Europe must accept the principle of the rule of law ..."'[3]

There have been more applications to the Court of Human Rights concerning this Article than for any other. The extent of its application to proceedings in the ordinary courts is great but this provision has also had substantial effect on an individual's rights as affected by administrative decisions and by administrative tribunals.

KEY PRINCIPLE: FAIRNESS

8.3   Under Art 6, the key principle is fairness. The Court's task is to ascertain whether the proceedings in their entirety were 'fair' within the meaning of Art 6(1)[4]. However, the European Court has stated that it is not within its province to substitute its own assessment of the facts for that of the national courts. Given the diversity of procedures throughout the contracting States, the Court has allowed a wide 'margin of appreciation' in this regard. The tendency has been to

---

1   1 EHRR 524, para 34.
2   Vienna Convention, Art 31(1).
3   *Golder v UK* 1 EHRR 524, para 34.
4   *Dombo Beheer BV v The Netherlands* 18 EHRR 213, para 31.

look at the end result and question whether, overall, there has been a fair trial. Whilst the Court has been careful to look at the realities of the situation to find whether there has been any conflict with the right enshrined in Art 6(1), it has also, expressly, taken into account the requirement that 'justice must not only be done but must also be seen to be done'[1].

Rights in respect of a criminal charge and family law proceedings

8.4　　Although para 1 of Art 6 guarantees the right to a fair and public hearing both for the determination of civil rights and obligations *and* for any criminal charge, paras 2 and 3 guarantee rights, theoretically, *only* for those charged with a criminal offence. Although most issues in family matters will come within the category of 'civil rights and obligations', some will fall within the category of criminal charges[2] and thus the second and third subparagraphs will automatically protect the individual during the hearing.

Under Article 6(2):
Everyone charged with a criminal offence shall be presumed innocent until proved guilty according to the law.

Under Article 6 (3):
Everyone charged with a criminal offence has the following minimum rights:

- to be informed promptly, in a language which he understands and in detail, of the nature and cause of the accusations against him;
- to have adequate time and facilities for the preparation of his defence;
- to defend himself in person or through legal assistance of his own choosing, or, if he has not sufficient means to pay for legal assistance, to be given it free when the interests of justice so require;
- to examine or have examined witnesses against him and to obtain the attendance and examination of witnesses on his behalf under the same conditions as witnesses against him;
- to have the free assistance of an interpreter if he cannot understand or speak the language used in court.

8.5　　It is not always clear when issues fall within the definition of a 'criminal charge'. This was considered in the case of *Engel v The Netherlands*[3]. Penalties for breaches of military discipline were imposed, and the Court considered the distinction between criminal and disciplinary law. It held that the classification of an offence as 'criminal' was only the starting point and that other considerations applied including:

- the nature of the offence;
- the penalty which could be imposed.

8.6　　It is arguable that the minimum standards guaranteed in criminal trials under Art 6(2) and (3) are so fundamental for the fairness of any trial that they are unlikely to be ignored in litigation in general, including civil litigation.

1　　*Delcourt v Belgium* 1 EHRR 355, para 31; but cf *Borgers v Belgium* 15 EHRR 93, para 24.
2　　Contempt and committal proceedings. For further discussion on this matter, refer to Chapter 13.
3　　1 EHRR 647.

Nevertheless, in *Dombo Beheer BV v The Netherlands*[1], the Court acknowledged that the requirements inherent in the concept of a 'fair hearing' were not necessarily the same in civil cases. It highlighted the absence of detailed provisions such as paras 2 and 3 of Art 6 applying to cases determining civil rights and obligations but concluded that 'although these provisions have a certain relevance outside the strict confines of criminal law, the contracting States have greater latitude when dealing with civil cases than they have when dealing with criminal cases'[2].

8.7   This has to be compared with an earlier case, *Albert and Le Compte v Belgium*[3], which concerned disciplinary proceedings against a doctor and his suspension from practice. The applicant had claimed a violation under Art 6(1), (2) and (3). The Court held that the civil and criminal aspects under Art 6(1) were not mutually exclusive and that it was unnecessary to decide whether there was a criminal charge in the case under the disciplinary proceedings[4]. Further, although Dr Compte relied on Art 6(2) and (3), in the opinion of the Court the 'principles enshrined therein are ... already contained in the notion of a fair trial as embodied in paragraph 1 (and) the Court (would), therefore take these principles into account in the context of paragraph 1'[5].

8.8   Article 6(2) and (3) will apply in contempt and committal proceedings[6]. It is arguable that these rights will also be imported into proceedings where, for example, allegations of abuse are made, not least because the hearing has a quasi-criminal character and findings of fact against a party would have a severe impact on any future family life[7]. In any event, it is arguable that these rights would be introduced into such proceedings under Art 6(1) even if not fully characterised as a 'criminal charge' as the implications of a finding of fact in this regard would be very severe and the courts would be keen to uphold the principle of 'fairness'. Similar considerations may apply in domestic violence proceedings where allegations of violence are made.

It is not proposed to go through the provisions of Art 6(2) and (3) and its consequent case-law in detail and reference should be made to the criminal textbooks on the subject for in-depth consideration. However, a summary of the relevant provisions and authorities are included in Chapter 13.

THE RIGHT TO A FAIR TRIAL IN THE DETERMINATION OF CIVIL RIGHTS AND OBLIGATIONS

The scope of Article 6(1)

8.9   The scope of Art 6 and its application in 'civil' matters is still unclear. There is a line of thought which holds that Art 6 should apply to any court proceedings although others feel that the distinction set out between civil and criminal cases is supposed to be a restriction of the applicability of Art 6 as a whole.

PART B
IMPACT OF THE CONVENTION

---

1   18 EHRR 213.
2   Ibid, para 32.
3   5 EHRR 533.
4   Ibid, para 30.
5   Ibid, para 30.
6   But cf *Ravnsborg v Sweden* 18 EHRR 38 and *Putz v Austria* 1996 RJD where fines imposed as a result of improper statements made during the course of the proceedings were regarded as disciplinary measures within the court's conduct of its own procedings rather than in the nature of penalties following a 'criminal charge'.
7   See *Dombho Beheer BV v The Netherlands* 18 EHRR 213, paras 31–33.

At the moment, it is the latter argument which prevails. It has been argued that if Art 6 were applicable to all administrative decisions, efficiency would have to be sacrificed. On a practical level, administrative decision-making would be unworkable if a full right of access to Court were put in place and safeguards regulated in every instance. In many Member States, including the UK, the courts are reluctant to interfere with policy decisions in the field of public administration. Unlike Arts 8–11, there is no 'necessity test' whereby the general interest can be balanced against the individual interest. The applicability of Art 6 has an 'all or nothing' test whereby the Court has considered whether the decision falls within the definition of 'civil right and obligation' or not[1].

The meaning of civil rights and obligations

8.10   The early jurisprudence seemed to make a distinction between public and private law and 'civil rights' appeared to apply to private rights alone. The starting point for the definition is the nature of the right or obligation according to the law of the Convention State[2], but that is only the starting point. The Court does not look solely at the classification of the right by the State but looks, more particularly, to the character and content of the right or obligation recognising that if applicability were dependent on the former, there would be widely differing categorisation throughout the Convention States. Further, if classification were the sole test, the State's choice of categorisation would be final on the issue and could deprive the individual of protection from a violation of Art 6.

8.11   Private law within the national legal systems appears to coincide with the concept of private law in Art 6 but it becomes more complex when looking at the relationship between the individual and the State. In a case concerning a dispute between an individual and a public authority, whether the latter has acted as a private person or in its sovereign capacity is not the determining factor[3]. The first paragraph of Art 6 will apply if there are private law features which predominate in the issue.

The case-law

8.12   Over the years, the distinction between private and public law has narrowed within Convention case-law although it is not easy to draw any consistent themes. The question was considered in *Benthem v UK*.

Benthem v UK[4]
8.13   The applicant, a garage owner, was granted a licence for the installation of a liquid petroleum gas container. Following appeal, the grant was quashed. The applicant argued that he had not had access to an independent tribunal to consider the question and thus Art 6 had been violated. The Government had argued that Art 6 did not apply because, inter alia:

–   the licence was not irrevocable;
–   this was not an instance where a previous right had been withdrawn or suspended;

---

1   But see later for the test of 'proportionality' when immunity or limitation is claimed.
2   *König v FRG* 2 EHRR 170, para 90.
3   Ibid.
4   8 EHRR 1.

- this was a right that had yet to be created;
- the carrying on of the garage business was not at stake and nothing had prevented the applicant from continuing it.

The importance of this case lies in the ordinariness of the dispute. This type of planning decision is constantly taken within each of the Convention States. If Art 6(1) was found to be applicable to this sort of decision, it would open the way for a large number of other so-called administrative decisions which are delegated by the individual States to statutory bodies to be subject to the supervision of the European Court.

8.14   By a narrow majority of nine votes to eight, the Commission felt that Art 6(1) was not applicable, acknowledging that it was clear that if Art 6(1) 'was found to be applicable in the present case, this would mean a significant extension of the application of that Article into new areas of public administration'. The Commission, unusually, decided to bring the matter before the Court because it was so strongly divided. The Court held that Art 6 was applicable.

8.15   Although the Commission referred the case to the European Court for guidance, the Court did not use the occasion to give an abstract definition of 'civil rights and obligations' but preferred to set out the factors which were not decisive rather than those which were:

- the concept of 'civil rights and obligations' cannot be interpreted solely by reference to the domestic law of the respondent State[1];
- whether or not the dispute involved the State, even acting in its sovereign capacity, was not conclusive[2];
- the character of the legislation which governs how the matter is to be determined ... and that of the authority which is invested with jurisdiction in the matter ... are of little consequence; the latter may be an ordinary court, an administrative body etc[3];
- only the character of the right at issue is relevant[4].

Feldbrugge v The Netherlands[5]
8.16   The applicant had been unemployed for some time but fell ill and ceased to register at her regional employment exchange. Under domestic law, she was entitled to 80 per cent of her daily pay in the case of unfitness for work through sickness. On 11 April 1978 the governing body of the Occupational Association of the Banking and Insurance and Wholesale Trade and Self-Employment Sector in Amsterdam decided that as from 24 March 1978 she was not entitled to sickness allowances as the Association's consulting doctor had judged her fit to resume work from that date. The applicant had appealed and there had been further medical reports but the appeals were unsuccessful. In the Netherlands, social security is managed jointly by the State (which in general confines itself to establishing the legal framework of the scheme and to overseeing coordination) and by employers and employees. The branches of the economy are divided into sectors and each sector has an 'occupational association' responsible for

1   *König v FRG* 2 EHRR 170, paras 88–89.
2   Ibid, para 90.
3   *Ringeisen v Austria* 1 EHRR 504, para 94.
4   *König v FRG* 2 EHRR 170, para 90.
5   8 EHRR 425.

implementation of the social security legislation. In this sector, the scheme was managed by the occupational association and funded by the employers and employees. In many respects, it appeared to have public law characteristics which would take it outside the scope of Art 6, that is:

- the State had assumed the responsibility of regulating the framework of the scheme and overseeing its operation;
- there was an obligation to be insured which was laid down by statute and the individual could not opt out of the benefit nor avoid making the contributions;
- there was an assumption by the State or by public or semi-public institutions of full or partial responsibility for ensuring social protection. Such a factor implied an extension of the public law domain.

8.17   Nevertheless, the Court did not consider that the above three factors were sufficient to make Art 6 inapplicable. The Court considered the following matters which brought the issue within the field of Art 6:

- the applicant was not affected in her relations with the public authorities as such but in her personal capacity as a private individual. 'She suffered an interference with her means of subsistence ... the right in question was a personal, economic and individual right, a factor that brought it close to the civil sphere ...'[1];
- the availability of health benefits was determined by reference to the terms of her former contract of employment. The contract of employment is governed by private law;
- the sickness allowance was a substitute for the salary payable under the contract; the civil character of this salary being beyond doubt;
- Dutch health insurance is similar in several respects to insurance under the ordinary law;
- in the Netherlands, the insured, themselves, participate in the financing of the scheme and have deductions made at source from their salaries. The Netherlands State was not involved in the financing of the scheme.

The Court considered all the above factors and 'evaluated the relative cogency of the features of public and private law ... and (found) the latter to be predominant. None of the various features of private law (was) decisive on its own but taken together and cumulatively they conferred on the asserted entitlement the character of a civil right within the meaning of Art 6(1) of the Convention'[2].

Ringeisen v Austria (No 1)[3]
8.18   The applicant claimed that the regional Real Property Transaction Commission was biased when it refused to approve sale of land by the applicant and had thus violated Art 6. The Austrian Government argued that Art 6 did not apply to the Commission because it was a question of administrative law and thus the individual's civil rights and obligations were not in issue. Although the Court ultimately rejected the allegation of bias and found there was no violation of Art 6 on that ground, it held, unanimously, that Art 6 was applicable to this issue

---

1   8 EHRR 425, para 37.
2   Ibid, para 40.
3   1 EHRR 455.

notwithstanding its categorisation within administrative (or public law). The Court held (against the opinion of the majority of the Commission) that:

– it was not necessary that both parties to the proceedings should be private persons[1];

– the wording of Art 6 and the French expression 'contestation sur (des) droits et obligations de caractere civil' covers all proceedings the result of which is decisive for private rights and obligations;

– the English text 'determination of ... civil rights and obligations' confirms this interpretation;

– it is the character of the legislation which governs how the matter is to be determined and whether Art 6 is applicable; and therefore

– the authority which is invested with jurisdiction in the matter (eg ordinary court or administrative court) is of little consequence as it does not conclusively determine the character of the legislation[2].

In the case itself, when the applicant exercised an option and purchased property from the third party, he had a right to have the contracts for sale approved if he fulfilled the conditions laid down in the legislation. Although the regional Commission was applying rules of administrative law, the decision was decisive for the relations in civil law between the applicant and the third parties. This was sufficient to bring the issue within Art 6.

Following the above cases, the European Court has not used Art 6 to take judicial control of all civil rights and obligations of an individual but it has extended its hold.

Case-law on the applicability of Article 6 in family law matters

Rasmussen v Denmark[3]

8.19   The applicant claimed that refusal to allow him to bring paternity proceedings because he was out of time was in breach of Art 6 (and discriminatory taken together with Art 14 because there was no such time-limit for women). The Government had argued that there was a public interest element which took the matter outside Art 6. However, the Court held that whilst it was 'true that the public interest may be affected by proceedings of this kind ... this factor (could not) exclude the applicability of Art 6 to litigation which, by its very nature, is "civil" in character. An action contesting paternity is a matter of family law; on that account alone, it is civil in character'[4].

W v UK[5]

8.20   This is a key case which could have ramifications throughout public case-law as the European Court has rejected the 'welfare paramountcy test'[6].

8.21   The applicant complained about the procedures followed by the local authority in reaching its decision to restrict and then terminate his access to his

---

1   This is in line with the concept of an incorporated body being a legal person.
2   1 EHRR 455, para 94.
3   7 EHRR 371.
4   Ibid, para 32.
5   10 EHRR 29.
6   See also Chapter 6 at paras **6.22** et seq.

child when taken into care. Under the pre-Children Act legislation there was no right to challenge such a decision in the courts on the merits of the decision and only a right to challenge by judicial review. The UK Government argued that Art 6 had no application on the grounds that:

– the matter had to constitute a legal right in the context of domestic law;
– the 'notion' of parental 'rights' over a child was outmoded and the so-called 'right' of access by a parent to his child was preferably described as a right in the child;
– the parental right was a 'rhetorical' and not a legal one;
– even if there were such a parental right at the outset, it ceased to have a separate existence on the making of the care order; the effect of the care order was to transfer to the local authority all the rights, powers and duties of the parent with respect to the child;
– the mere possibility or expectation that the local authority might, in its discretion, subsequently allow the parent to have access to the child did not constitute a 'right'[1].

8.22   The Court accepted that Art 6 (1) extended only to disputes which could be said, at least on arguable grounds, to be recognised under domestic law and 'did not guarantee any particular content for (civil) "rights and obligations" in the substantive law of the contracting States'[2]. From this it might be assumed that if there were no right of challenge within the domestic courts, Art 6 would not apply. However, the Court stated that a civil right did exist. The Government relied on the 'welfare paramountcy' test and the importance of the case lies in the rejection of this line of argument. The Government argued[3]:

– Parental rights are not denied by the legislation so much as overridden if not exercised in accordance with the welfare of the child.

– When the Courts speak of access being the right of the child, they appear not to have been asserting the absence of any parental right of access whatsoever but to have been expressing the principle that in the event of a conflict between concurrent rights of parent and child, it is the welfare of the child which should be treated as the paramount consideration.

– The making of the care order vests in the local authority nearly all the rights and duties which by law the parent has in relation to the child.

– However, a care order does not automatically deprive the parent of access to the child and the question becomes one of discretion exercised by the local authority.

– The existence of a power on the part of the local authority to decide to allow restricted or even no visits to the child by the parent does not necessarily mean that there is no longer any parental right in regard to access once the care order has been made.

– The statutes generally recognise that the continuation of parental access is generally desirable and the general policy is that the child's best interests will be best served by efforts to sustain links with the natural families. It would be

---

1   10 EHRR 29, para 72.
2   Ibid, para 73.
3   Ibid, paras 74–79.

inconsistent with this aim if the making of a care order were to divest a natural parent of all further rights and duties in regard to access.

– The effect of a care order is not to extinguish all rights and responsibilities of the natural parent in respect of the child. For example, the parent still has the right to agree to or refuse the child's adoption and there is a continuing right to seek to discharge the care order.

– The extinction of all parental right in regard to access would not be compatible with fundamental notions of family life and the family ties which Art 8 of the Convention is designed to protect.

8.23   The Government had also argued that leaving the discretion with the local authority rather than the Court was, as a matter of practice, essential, because of the number of children in care and the need to take decisions urgently and without delay through specialised social workers and as part of a continuous process. The Court was not unsympathetic to this argument but stated that 'this is an area in which it is essential to ensure the rights of individual parents are protected in accordance with Article 6(1) ... [It] does not require that all access decisions must be taken by the Courts but only that they shall have the power to determine any substantial disputes that may arise'[1].

8.24   This case is pre-Children Act 1989[2]. Nevertheless, it is questionable how parental rights can be subordinated to the interest of the child under the welfare paramountcy test in the light of *W v UK*.

Eriksson v Sweden[3]
8.25   The applicant's daughter was placed in a foster-home under the equivalent of a care order. Five years later the domestic court decided that there was no longer any need for the child to remain in public care. However, the Social Council issued a 'prohibition' on the removal of the child from the foster-home by the natural parents. The reasons for the prohibition was based on the expert opinion that the child was deeply rooted in the foster-home and a transfer to her mother's home would jeopardise her mental health and development. Access to the child was limited to a visit in the foster-home once every two months. Under the legislation at the time, there was no administrative appeal against a decision by the Social Council to restrict access.

8.26   The Government argued that there was, in effect, a right of challenge through the ability to challenge the reasons for the prohibition on removal. The Court disagreed:

> 'In cases of the present kind, the question of access is quite distinct from the question whether or not to uphold the prohibition on removal; only if sufficient access is first permitted will there be real possibilities of having the prohibition on removal lifted. The recourse available in the administrative courts in the form of a challenge to the prohibition of removal is thus not sufficient for the purpose of the mother's claim for access rights.'[4]

---

1   10 EHRR 29, para 79.
2   Which makes the welfare paramountcy test central to its approach.
3   12 EHRR 183.
4   Ibid, paras 80–81. This was also followed in the similar case of *Olssen v Sweden (No 2)* 17 EHRR 134, para 97.

8.27   Within the Children Act 1989, there is a right of challenge to local authority decisions in respect of contact (formerly access) but there are other areas of the care plan, for example choice of foster-carers, choice of treatment, therapy etc for the child which lie, in practice, wholly within the local authority's discretion. However, parental responsibility is not extinguished by the care order but is shared between the parents and the local authority[1]. Although the local authority has the power to determine the extent to which a parent or guardian of the child may meet his parental responsibility for him[2], that is subject to the restriction that it would be necessary in order to safeguard or promote the child's welfare[3]. In any event, even with parental responsibility, there are certain rights which cannot be exercised by the local authority, for example in respect of religion or appointment of a guardian[4] and other rights which can be exercised only with the consent of all others who hold parental responsibility or by Court order[5].

8.28   In the light of the Children Act 1989 provisions, the parents retain parental responsibility and retain 'rights'. Therefore, it is arguable that parents still have a 'civil right' and should be able to challenge the care plan even once the care order has been made. This may be an area which will require statutory amendment and one which has already been under consideration. Various suggestions have included the right of review and the possibility of the guardian ad litem having a limited but continuing role even after the care order has been made.

8.29   In *W v UK*[6], the Government argued in the alternative that if the applicant retained some residual right of access, there was sufficient judicial protection within domestic law to satisfy the requirements of Art 6(1). The Government referred to the right to apply for a discharge of the order or to apply for judicial review or wardship. The Court accepted that a successful challenge under one of those heads would resolve the access issue indirectly but held that whether the child should be in care and whether there should be access to him were matters to which different considerations might apply. For example, a parent may be content for the child to remain in care whilst wishing to see contact maintained or, as is more usual, there may be good reasons for challenging the decision on contact whilst having insufficient grounds to claim restoration of the child back into full parental care. In any event, judicial review would not provide the protection claimed by the Government as the courts did not review the merits of the decision but confined themselves to enquiring whether the local authority acted illegally, unreasonably or unfairly[7].

8.30   All the above applies to the care plan itself. The domestic courts are often left in a dilemma even at the time of making the care order because they have no power to change the care plan save for matters of contact and have the stark choice of making the care order with the care plan as set out or making no care order at all. At best, it is left with a power merely to influence. Even this has been severely

---

1   Children Act 1989, s 33(3)(a).
2   Ibid, s 33(3)(b).
3   Ibid, s 33(4).
4   Ibid, s 33(6).
5   Ibid, s 33(7).
6   10 EHRR 29.
7   Ibid, paras 80–83.

curtailed by the line of cases which states that the court cannot use interim care orders as a means of exercising control over the local authority or monitoring the manner in which it undertakes its duties[1].

The contrast between 'determination' and 'dispute'

The need for a dispute
8.31   In order that Art 6 should be applicable, there is a need for a dispute. It is important to note that the English draft is slightly different from the French version 'Contestation sur des droigts et obligations de caractère civil'. The word 'contestation' has no accurate equivalent translation in English and has been translated as a 'dispute' which is somewhat different from 'determination'.

8.32   Under the French text, the use of the word 'contestation' has led to the inference that the applicability of Art 6 is dependent on there being a dispute concerning a right or issue.

The case-law

8.33   The Convention case-law was considered in the following cases.

Benthem v Netherlands[2]
8.34   The Court adopted the following principles from the case-law[3]:

– Conformity with the spirit of the Convention requires that the word 'contestation' (dispute) should not be 'construed too technically' and should be 'given a substantive rather than a formal meaning'[4].

– The 'contestation' may relate not only to 'the actual existence of a ... right' but also to its scope or manner in which it may be exercised[5].

– It may concern both 'questions of fact' and 'questions of law'[6].

– The 'contestation' must be of a 'genuine and serious nature'[7].

– 'The expression "contestations sur des droits et obligation de caractère civil" covers all proceedings the result of which is decisive for such rights and obligations'[8].

– However, 'a tenuous connection or remote consequences, do not suffice for Art 6 (1) ... civil rights and obligations must be the object ... or one of the objects of the "contestation";' the result of the proceedings must be directly decisive for such a right'[9].

In the above case, on the facts the Court considered that:

---

1   *Re L (Sexual Abuse: Standard of Proof)* [1996] 1 FLR 116; *Kent County Council v C* [1993] 1 FLR 308; *Re P (Minors) (Interim Order)* [1993] 2 FLR 742; *Re S (A Minor) (Care: Contact Order)* [1994] 2 FLR 222; but cf *Buckinghamshire County Council v M* [1994] 2 FLR 506.
2   8 EHRR 1.
3   Ibid, para 32.
4   *Le Compte, Van Leuven and De Meyere v Belgium* 4 EHRR 1, para 45.
5   Ibid, para 49.
6   Ibid, para 51; see also *Albert and Le Compte v Belgium* 5 EHRR 533, paras 29 and 36.
7   *Sporrong and Lonnroth* 5 EHRR 35, para 81.
8   *Ringeisen v Austria* 1 EHRR 455, para 94 and see above.
9   *Le Compte, Van Leuven and De Meyere v Belgium* 4 EHRR 1, para 47.

– a 'genuine and serious' 'contestation' as to the actual existence of the right existed between the applicant and the Netherlands authorities;
– the grant of the licence was one of the conditions for the exercise of his activities as a businessman;
– a licence of this kind had a proprietal nature – it could be assigned to third parties;
– the grant or refusal of the licence might have had adverse effects on the value of the business and of the goodwill and also on the applicant's contractual relations with his customers and suppliers. Thus there was a direct link between the granting of the licence and the entirety of the applicant's commercial activities;
– in consequence, what was at stake was a 'civil right'.

Logan v UK[1]

8.35   The applicant claimed that there was no right to challenge the assessment by the Child Support Agency of the level of maintenance he was required to pay for his children. He did not challenge the calculation itself but argued that the agency had not taken into account the cost of exercising contact. He accepted that there was no provision under the legislation for these costs to be taken into account and, impliedly, that the agency had no discretion in this regard.

8.36   The Commission found that there was no violation of Art 6(1) because:

– there was no dispute; or
– there was no dispute of a 'genuine' or 'serious nature'[2].

This leaves open the question whether a different set of circumstances surrounding a Child Support Agency calculation might be sufficiently genuine or serious so that an inability to challenge it would amount to a violation of Art 6(1).

THE ARTICLE 6 GUARANTEES

8.37   Article 6 guarantees the following rights:

(a) the right of access to a court;
(b) the right to a fair hearing;
(c) the right to a hearing within a reasonable time;
(d) the right to an independent and impartial tribunal established by law;
(e) the right to a public hearing:
(f) the right to a public pronouncement of judgment.

(a) Right of access to court

'In the determination of his civil rights and obligations ... everyone is entitled to a ... hearing.'

8.38   Under domestic procedure, the right of access to the court is not absolute and has been limited on a number of issues, inter alia:

---

1   Application No 24875/94.
2   Ibid, para 1.

- issue estoppel;
- the requirement of leave for certain categories of parties in private and care proceedings notably grandparents, other close relatives or foster-parents or children under s 10 and s 34 of the Children Act 1989;
- the child as an applicant under s 10 of the Children Act 1989;
- barring applications under s 91(14) of the Children Act 1989;
- emergency protection orders;
- child abduction cases.

Examples of limitations to the right of access under domestic law Issue Estoppel
8.39   Article 6(1) and the right to a fair trial may be a factor when the court considers the rule of issue estoppel. In *Re B (Children Act Proceedings) (Issue Estoppel)*[1], Hale J considered the circumstances when a court would reconsider findings already made in previous proceedings:

- There is no strict rule of issue estoppel binding any of the parties in cases concerning children.

- Children proceedings are inquisitorial in nature and the court has a discretion as to how it conducts its inquiry.

- Where findings of fact are challenged in subsequent proceedings, the court would wish to be informed not only of the findings but also of the evidence upon which the findings were based. It would then be for the court to decide whether or not to allow any issue of fact to be tried afresh.

- The following factors, among others, were to be considered:
  - there was a public interest in bringing litigation to an end;
  - a matter should not be tried twice without good reason for doing so;
  - any delay was likely to be prejudicial to the welfare of the child;
  - however, the welfare of the child was unlikely to be served by relying upon findings which were erroneous;
  - the court's discretion had to be exercised so that there was justice not injustice.

- The importance of the findings were to be considered in the context of the current proceedings. If they were so important as to affect the outcome, the court might be more willing to consider a rehearing than if the findings were of a lesser or peripheral significance.

- The court would consider whether there was any reason to think that a rehearing of the issue would result in any different finding and so the court would wish to know:
  - whether the previous finding was made after a full hearing in which evidence was tested;
  - whether there was any ground upon which the accuracy of the findings could be attacked at the time;
  - if so, why there was no appeal;
  - whether there was any new evidence or information casting doubt upon the findings.

---

1   [1997] 1 FLR 285.

Although the list appears comprehensive, it still, theoretically, leaves open the possibility of a person being deprived of a full hearing within care proceedings on an issue of, for example, abuse where the facts have been determined in separate proceedings when he was not even a party. Although the factors in the above case should rule that out, anecdotal evidence suggests that applications for issue estoppel are made by local authorities relatively frequently and orders are occasionally granted.

The requirement of leave under ss 10 and 34 of the Children Act 1989

8.40   The Court has to give consideration to the factors under s 10(9) of the Children Act 1989. It should be noted that the welfare of the child is not paramount in this regard. In *Re M (Care: Contact: Grandmother's Application for Leave)*[1], the Court of Appeal equated an application for leave to apply for a s 8 order with an application for leave to apply for a s 34 order. It was held that the following test should apply:

– if the application is frivolous, vexatious or an abuse of process, it must fail;
– if the applicant fails to disclose that there is any eventual real prospect of success, or the prospect is so remote as to make the application unsustainable, then the application for leave should be dismissed;
– the applicant must satisfy the court that there is a serious issue to try and must present a good arguable case.

The requirement for leave for the child as an applicant

8.41   All the considerations under s 10(9) of the Children Act 1989 have to be taken into account. Furthermore, under s 10(8) of the Children Act 1989, the court has to be satisfied that the child has sufficient understanding to make the application.

Barring orders under s 91(14) of the Children Act 1989

8.42   Such an order is infrequent and occurs in, but is not limited to, cases where there have been repeated applications which are usually vexatious and oppressive. In *B v B (Residence Order: Restricting Applications)*[2], the Court of Appeal favoured the welfare paramountcy test holding that:

> 'The judge must ask him- or herself in every case whether the best interests of the child require interference with the fundamental freedom of a parent to raise issues affecting the child's welfare before the court as and when such issues arise.'

Emergency protection orders

8.43   The order vests parental authority in the applicant, that is, the local authority and authorises the local authority to remove the child from his parent. The test is that there is reasonable cause to believe that the child is likely to suffer significant harm if he is not removed and the court has to have the child's welfare as the paramount consideration. It is clearly an emergency measure of last resort. The limitation on the right of access lies in the fact that it can be made ex parte, that is, without the parent having notice of the proceedings.

---

1   [1995] 2 FLR 86.
2   [1997] 1 FLR 139.

Under the Convention

8.44   The 'right of access' to Court is not explicitly enshrined within the Convention; rather the entitlement to 'a fair and public hearing'. The extent of this right was considered in the case of *Golder v UK*[1] where the Court questioned whether Art 6(1) is:

> 'limited to guaranteeing in substance the right to a fair trial in legal proceedings which are already pending, or does it in addition secure a right of access to the courts for every person wishing to commence an action in order to have his civil rights and obligations determined.'[2]

This issue could be important, for example in the potential challenge of the care plan. Within the domestic courts, following the making of the care order, the care plan is only challengeable under judicial review if the local authority have acted incorrectly[3], or by application to discharge but is not challengeable on its contents, for example choice of foster-carers, placement of the children. Yet, these matters are determinative of 'civil rights' not least the right to family life. Can Art 6 provide that right of access to the Courts to determine those rights?

PART B
IMPACT OF THE CONVENTION

8.45   In the case of *Golder v UK*[4], the applicant was a prisoner. There had been a disturbance in the prison and a prison officer alleged that the applicant had been involved. Those allegations were later withdrawn but the applicant was concerned that entries on his record would affect his chances of parole. He considered the possibility of libel proceedings against the prison officer who had made the allegations and wishing to consult a solicitor, he sought the permission of the Home Secretary to do so. The Home Secretary refused. The Court noted that consultation with a solicitor was merely a preliminary step and that it was not known whether the applicant would have carried through his intention. Further, the applicant was not completely denied the opportunity to take this action as he would have been able do so once he had been freed from imprisonment.

8.46   The Court held:

> 'In civil matters one can scarcely conceive of the rule of law without there being a possibility of having access to the Courts ... The principle whereby a civil claim must be capable of being submitted to a judge ranks as one of the universally "recognised" fundamental principles of law; the same is true of the principle of international law which forbids the denial of justice. Article 6(1) must be read in the light of these principles.'[5]

The Court was concerned that if Art 6(1) were merely to be understood as concerning the conduct of an action already initiated in the Courts, it would enable an individual's rights to be extinguished by the contracting States by doing away with its courts or taking away jurisdiction to deal with certain classes of civil actions and entrusting it to organs dependent on the Government.

8.47   In the opinion of the Court, it was:

---

1   1 EHRR 524.

2   Ibid, para 25.

3   The High Court cannot exercise its inherent jurisdiction to review the merits of the actions of the local authority . See *A v Liverpool City Council* (1981) FLR 222; *Re W (A Minor) (Care Proceedings: Wardship)* [1985] 2 FLR 879. See also s 100 of the Children Act 1989.

4   1 EHRR 524.

5   1 EHRR 524, paras 34–35.

'inconceivable that Article 6(1) should describe in detail the procedural guarantees afforded to parties in a pending lawsuit and should not first protect that which alone makes it, in fact, possible to benefit from such guarantees, that is, access to Court. The fair, public and expeditious characteristics of judicial proceedings are of no value at all if there are no judicial proceedings . . . . It follows that the right of access constitutes an element which is inherent in the right stated by Article 6(1) read in its context and having regard to the object and purpose of the Convention, a law making treaty and to the principles of law.'[1]

In the light of the above principles, the Court held that:

– hindrance can contravene the Convention just like a legal impediment;
– hindrance might be a violation even if it were only of a temporary nature[2].

Limitations to the right of access
8.48   The Court also held that the right of access was not an absolute right but might have to be regulated by the State, 'regulation which may vary in time and place according to the needs and resources of the community and of individuals'[3]. The Government had argued that there were other examples which were to be found in national law limiting the right of access, notably in relation to minors or persons of unsound mind. The Court did not specifically rule on these examples but it appears that it accepted such limitations as valid[4].

The Ashingdane principles and the limitation to the right of access
8.49   In *Ashingdane v UK*[5], the Court considered the extent of any limitations on the right of access to a Court. The applicant had been committed to a mental hospital after conviction and been placed in a secure special hospital (Broadmoor). His condition improved and his return to a local psychiatric hospital was authorised by the Home Secretary but was refused by the health authority for that hospital. The applicant started legal proceedings to challenge the legality of the refusal to transfer him but the proceedings were unsuccessful because an immunity was provided for under the Mental Health Act 1959, s 141 and the action was held to be statute barred. Two years later, he was transferred to a local hospital but the applicant complained that his detention in the secure special hospital had been in breach of Art 5 and his inability to challenge the lawfulness of the refusal to transfer him had been in breach of Art 6(1).

8.50   Under the Mental Health Act 1959, s 141[6], liability in civil proceedings for breach of statutory duty under the Act was barred:

– unless the act were done in bad faith or without reasonable care;
– unless the proceedings were brought with the leave of the High Court; and
– leave would not be given unless the High Court were satisfied that there was a substantial ground for the contention that the person proceeded against has acted in bad faith or without reasonable care.

The European Court of Human Rights noted that the applicant had taken action in the High Court and the Court of Appeal and that his actions were barred by

---

1   1 EHRR 524, paras 35–36.
2   Ibid, para 29; see also *Campbell and Fell v UK* 7 EHRR 165.
3   Ibid, para 38 quoting from *Belgian Linguistic Case (No 2)* 1 EHRR 252, para 5.
4   Ibid, para 39.
5   7 EHRR 528.
6   Subsequently amended under the Mental Health Act 1983.

operation of law but that to an extent he had access to remedies that existed within the domestic court system. However, the Court questioned whether that exhausted the requirements of Art 6(1) and whether the degree of access afforded under the national legislation was sufficient to secure the individual's 'right to court having regard to the rule of law in a democratic country'[1].

8.51 The Court set out the following principles in determining whether any regulation of the right of access was legitimate:

– In laying down such regulation, the contracting States enjoy a certain margin of appreciation.

– Whilst the final decision as to the observance of the Convention's requirements rests with the Court, it is not part of the Court's function to substitute for the assessment of the national authorities any other assessment of what might be the best policy in this field.

– The limitation applied must not restrict or reduce the access left to the individual in such a way or to such an extent that the very essence of the right is impaired.

– A limitation will not be compatible with Art 6(1) if it does not pursue a legitimate aim.

– A limitation will not be compatible with Art 6(1) if there is not a reasonable relationship of proportionality between the means employed and the aim sought to be achieved[2].

8.52 In applying the above principles, the Court accepted that the mischief the legislation sought to avoid was the risk of those responsible for the care of mental patients being unfairly harassed by litigation and further recognised that such an aim was legitimate protection for staff as individuals. Although the protection for the health authority required closer scrutiny, by a majority of 6 to 1 the Court considered that the limitation of an action alleging bad faith or negligence and subject to leave of the High Court being obtained 'did not impair the very essence of Mr. Ashingdane's "right to court" or transgress the principle of proportionality'[3] and that there had been no violation.

8.53 The Court's responsibility under the Convention is to strike a fair balance between the demands of the general interest of the community and the requirements of the protection of the individual's fundamental rights. These principles reflect the process inherent in that task[4].

Privilege

8.54 *Fayed v UK*[5] is another case which shows how the European Court balances the interest of the community against the fundamental rights of the individual. Absolute or qualified privilege against action for libel brought against the Department of Trade inspectors when publishing a report on the acquisition of the House of Fraser was considered a legitimate limitation of the applicant's

1   *Ashingdane v UK* 7 EHRR 528, para 57 referring to *Golder v UK* 1 EHRR 524, paras 34–35.
2   Ibid.
3   Ibid, para 59; *Lithgow and Others v UK* 8 EHRR 329, para 194.
4   *Fayed v UK* 18 EHRR 393, para 1; *Sporrong and Lonroth v Sweden* 5 EHRR 35.
5   18 EHRR 393.

right to take proceedings to protect his reputation, particularly as the inspectors' investigation was subject to the rules of natural justice the breach of which allowed relief by judicial review. The Court accepted the community's interest in independent investigation of the affairs of large companies but whilst the inspectors were accorded broad freedom in reporting on those affairs, their performance of investigative functions was attended by not inconsiderable safeguards intended to ensure a fair procedure and the reliability of findings of fact. The Court recognised that 'limitations on access to Court might be more extensive when regulation of activities in the public sphere is at stake than in relation to litigation over the conduct of a person acting in their private capacity'[1].

Immunity/limitation of liability of local authorities

8.55   Hitherto, local authorities have been immune from actions, for example, by victims of wrongful diagnosis of abuse. In *X (Minors) v Bedfordshire County Council; M (A Minor) and Another v Newham London Borough Council and Others*[2], the House of Lords considered whether there was any local authority liability for breach of statutory duty or for breach of duty of care. In the former case, reports of possible neglect and abuse of five children had been ignored by the local authority. In the latter case, a mistaken identification by the social worker and psychiatrist of the abuser of the child had resulted in the separation of the child from her mother for one year.

8.56   The House of Lords was not considering the merits of the actions but whether the actions should be struck out. Within their judgment, they made certain assumptions, giving the plaintiffs the benefit of the doubt:

–   there were no unjusticiable policy questions involved;
–   it was not certain that all the decisions were within the ambit of the local authority's discretion;
–   on the basis that the local authority owed a direct duty of care to the plaintiffs, the damage was foreseeable; and
–   the relationship between the local authority and the plaintiffs was sufficiently proximate.

8.57   Even on the basis of these assumptions the House of Lords held that:

–   the statutory provisions under which the local authorities act did not give rise to a private law claim in damages. All the statutory provision relied upon by the authority had been made dependent upon the authority's subjective judgement and to treat such duties as being more than public duties was impossible;
–   it would not be just and reasonable to superimpose a common-law duty of care on the authority in relation to the performance of its statutory duty to protect children in circumstances where a common-law duty of care would cut across the whole system set up for the protection of children at risk;
–   where Parliament has conferred a statutory discretion on a public authority, it is for that authority, not for the courts to exercise the discretion; nothing which the authority does within the ambit of that discretion can be actionable at common law;

---

1   18 EHRR 393, para 75.
2   Both at [1995] 2 FLR 276.

– if the decision complained of falls outside the statutory discretion, it can (but not necessarily will) give rise to common law liability;
– if the factors relevant to the exercise of the discretion include matters of policy, the Court cannot adjudicate on such policy matters and therefore cannot reach the conclusion that the decision was outside the ambit of judicial discretion;
– therefore, a common-law duty of care in relation to the taking of decisions involving policy matters cannot exist;
– there would be a substantial argument in favour of imposing a duty of care if there were no other remedy for maladministration of the statutory system for the protection of children, but there is a statutory complaints system under the Children Act 1989 which provides a means to have grievances investigated though not to recover compensation. In addition, the local ombudsman would have power to investigate.

Lord Browne-Wilkinson drew upon the analogy of cases where it was argued that a common-law duty of care was imposed upon the police force when it undertook the duty to protect vulnerable members of society from wrongs done to them by others.

8.58 The European Court considered the question of public authority immunity from common-law liability in *Osman v UK*[1]. In this matter, a teacher (P) had formed an attachment to one of his pupils (O) and resented his friendship with another pupil. There were a series of unpleasant incidents amounting to serious harassment about which the police knew. Ultimately, the teacher killed O's father and the deputy headmaster's son and injured O and the deputy headmaster. The O family brought an action in negligence against the police force for failing to protect the family. The action was struck out on the ground that public policy required police immunity from suit in relation to the investigation and suppression of crime. The O family then claimed a violation of Art 6(1) on the grounds that they had been denied a right of access to a court to sue the authorities for damage caused by police negligence.

8.59 The Court referred to the *Ashingdane* principles referred to above[2] and noted that:

– whilst the Government had 'contended that the exclusionary rule of liability (was) not of an absolute nature and that its application may yield to other public policy considerations ... the Court of Appeal (had) proceeded on the basis that the rule provided a watertight defence to the police'[3];
– the Court of Appeal had proceeded on the basis that 'it was impossible to prize open an immunity which the police enjoy from civil suit in respect of their acts and omissions in the investigation and suppression of crime'.

8.60 The European Court held that such a view amounted to blanket immunity on the police[4]:

PART B
IMPACT OF THE CONVENTION

- this amounted to an unjustifiable restriction on an applicant's right to have a determination on the merits of his or her claim against the police in deserving cases;
- it must be open to a domestic court to have regard to the presence of other public interest considerations which pull in the opposite direction to the application of the rule;
- if there were blanket immunity, there would be no distinction made between degrees of negligence or of harm suffered or any consideration of the justice of a particular case;
- the proximity test provided a threshold requirement which in itself was sufficiently rigid to narrow considerably the number of negligence cases against the police which can proceed to trial;
- the applicant's case involved the alleged failure to protect the life of a child and their view that that failure was the result of a catalogue of acts and omissions which amounted to grave negligence as opposed to minor acts of incompetence;
- the applicants also claimed that the police had assumed responsibility for their safety;
- the harm sustained was of the most serious nature;
- the applicants may or may not have failed to convince the domestic court that the police were negligent in the circumstances but they were entitled to have the police account for their actions and omissions in adversarial proceedings;
- the application of the exclusionary rule in that case constituted a disproportionate restriction on the applicant's right of access to a court;
- there had been a violation of Art 6(1).

8.61   This was the unanimous judgment of the European Court and thus represents a strong view. The factors considered in the *Osman* case[1] are present on the facts in *X (Minors) v Bedfordshire County Council*[2] and it is questionable whether the dicta in *X (Minors) v Bedfordshire County Council* can stand. In particular, the relationship between a potential applicant and the local authority for negligent acts and omissions resulting in a failure to protect or a wrongful separation of child from parent is likely to pass the 'proximity test'. Similarly, the harm sustained is likely to be of a most serious nature. On the other hand, factors such as the allocation of resources and the protection of social workers from constant litigation are likely to be policy considerations pulling in the opposite direction. Nevertheless, it is likely that the *Osman* case has paved the way for further suits against the local authority for breach of statutory duty and negligence.

8.62   In the recent case of *Barrett v Enfield London Borough Council*[3], the applicant had been in care virtually all his life and was claiming that he had been the subject of negligent treatment on the part of the local authority because, inter alia, they had moved him from home to home, failed to make arrangements for his adoption, failed to provide him with proper social workers, failed to provide appropriate psychiatric advice and failed to make proper arrangements to reunite

---

1   [1999] 1 FLR 193.
2   [1995] 2 FLR 276.
3   [1999] 2 FLR 426.

him with his mother. He alleged that as a result of this treatment, he left the care of the local authority when he was 18 years old without family or attachments and suffering from a psychiatric illness leading to his having a propensity to harm himself. The local authority applied to strike out the claim on the ground that it disclosed no cause of action.

8.63　　The issue whether the claim should be struck out was considered by the House of Lords. They held that the claim should not be struck out:

> 'In the present case, the allegations … summarised are largely directed to the way in which the powers of the local authority were exercised. It is arguable (and that is all we are concerned with in this case at this stage) that if some of the allegations are made out, a duty of care was owed and was broken.'[1]

The House of Lords distinguished this set of facts from the *Bedfordshire* facts holding that in *Bedfordshire* the discretion was exercised in deciding whether or not to take a child into care, whereas in this case, discretion was exercised in the care itself when the local authority were acting in loco parentis.

8.64　　Although the House of Lords did not need to apply Art 6 of the Convention, it was pointed out by Lord Browne-Wilkinson:

> '… Bearing in mind that under the Human Rights Act 1998 Art 6 will shortly become part of English law, in such cases as these, it is difficult to say that it is a clear and obvious case calling for the striking out.'[2]

Thus, the impact of the Convention and of the Human Rights Act 1998 is likely to continue to be felt notwithstanding that it has not yet been fully incorporated.

Effective access to a fair trial: legal aid

8.65　　The right of access to a court must be an effective right in practice. In *Airey v Ireland*[3], the applicant wished to petition for judicial separation in the Irish High Court. However, she could not afford to instruct a lawyer and legal aid was not available. She claimed a violation of Art 6(1) in that her right of access to a court was effectively denied.

8.66　　The Irish Government had argued that there was no real denial of access because:

– she could have appeared before the High Court without representation and was free to do so;
– she had nothing to gain from a decree of judicial separation and so had not suffered any prejudice;
– if a violation was found in this instance, there would be an obligation to provide free legal aid in all cases concerning the determination of a 'civil right';
– the Convention should not be used so as to achieve social and economic developments in a contracting State; such developments can only be progressive;

1　　Per L Slynn of Hadley.
2　　Lord Browne-Wilkinson also stated that he confessed to finding 'the decision of the Strasbourg Court extremely difficult to understand', which gives hope to us all.
3　　2 EHRR 305.

- there was no positive obstacle emanating from the State and no deliberate attempt by the State to impede access;
- the alleged lack of access to the court stemmed not from any act on the part of the authorities but solely from the applicant's personal circumstances for which Ireland could not be held responsible under the Convention.

The Court held that the Convention is intended to guarantee not rights that are theoretical or illusory but rights that are practical and effective. This was particularly so of the right of access to the courts in view of the prominent place held in a democratic society by the right to a fair trial[1].

8.67   On the facts, the Court held that:

- it was not conclusive of the matter that there was a possibility that the applicant was free to go before the court without a lawyer[2];
- in Ireland, a decree of judicial separation was not obtainable in a district court where the procedure is relatively simple but only in the High Court;
- the procedure for instituting proceedings was very complex;
- litigation of this kind, in addition to involving complicated points of law, necessitates proof of adultery, unnatural practices or cruelty; to establish the facts, expert evidence may have to be tendered and witnesses may have to be found, called and examined;
- marital disputes often entail an emotional involvement that is scarcely compatible with the degree of objectivity required by advocacy in court;
- in the light of the above, it was improbable that someone in the applicant's position could effectively present his or her case;
- hindrance could contravene the Convention just like a legal impediment[3];
- fulfilment of duty under the Convention on occasion necessitates some positive action on the part of the State; in such circumstances, the State cannot simply remain passive and the obligation to secure an effective right of access to the courts falls within that category of duty[4];
- whilst the further realisation of social and economic rights is largely dependent on the situation – notably financial – reigning in the State, the Convention must be interpreted in the light of present-day conditions and it is designed to safeguard the individual in a real and practical way[5];
- the Convention sets forth what are essentially civil and political rights but many of them have implications of a social and economic nature.

8.68   In the UK, legal aid is routinely refused in certain cases (eg to the respondent in defended divorces or within injunction proceedings where undertakings could be given) and there is concern that in the future there will be other categories where legal aid may be refused. For example, it is feared that legal aid may not be granted to commence proceedings until mediation has been attempted. These refusals may result in a violation of Art 6(1). Although, in *Airey*, the possibility of appearing before the High Court in person was inadequate to provide the applicant in this instance with an effective right of access, that

1   2 EHRR 305, para 24; *Delcourt v Belgium* 1 EHRR 355, para 25.
2   Ibid, para 24.
3   Ibid, para 25 quoting from *Golder v UK* 1 EHRR 524, para 26.
4   Ibid, para 25.
5   Ibid, para 26.

conclusion did not necessarily follow in all cases concerning civil rights and obligations.

8.69   The Court set out why the State's obligation to provide effective access to a court fell short of providing universal free legal aid:

–   In certain eventualities, the possibility of appearing before a court in person, even without a lawyer's assistance will meet the requirements of Art 6(1); there may be occasions when such a possibility secures adequate access even to the High Court.

–   Much must depend on the particular circumstances.

–   Article 6(1) leaves to the State a free choice of the means to guarantee an effective right of access.

–   The institution of a legal aid scheme constitutes one of those means but there are others such as simplification of procedure.

–   It was not the Court's function to indicate, let alone dictate, the measure which should be taken; all that the Convention requires is that an individual should enjoy an effective right of access to the courts in conditions not at variance with Art 6(1).

–   Article 6(3) makes provision only for criminal proceedings and a finding that there was a similar obligation in respect of all disputes concerning civil rights would be too far reaching and sit ill with the fact that there is no similar clause in respect of civil litigation.

–   However, Art 6(1) may sometimes compel the State to provide the assistance of a lawyer when such assistance proves indispensable for an effective access to court either because legal representation is rendered compulsory, as is done by the domestic law of certain contracting States for various types of litigation or by reason of the complexity of the procedure or of the case [1].

8.70   Thus, the factors as applied to the *Airey* case, which would have justified legal aid, are indicative of the circumstances which would justify and necessitate the grant of legal aid in all civil litigation. However, an applicant for legal aid does not have to show that prejudice would follow from a failure to grant legal aid.

8.71   The case of *Artico v Italy* [2] concerns an application under Art 6(3), that is, in respect of a criminal charge and not civil litigation and the Court considered whether prejudice to the applicant had to exist before a violation of Art 6 could be shown. Although it is likely that prejudice would result from the vast majority of refusals of legal aid, the Court held that it was conceivable that there would be occasions when there was a violation even in the absence of prejudice [3] but stated that prejudice was not relevant under Art 6 and was relevant only in the context of Art 50 and the provision for 'just satisfaction to the injured party' [4].

---

1   *Airey v Ireland* 2 EHRR 305, para 26.
2   *Artico v Italy* 3 EHRR 1, para 35.
3   *Markx v Belgium* 2 EHRR 330, para 27.
4   Article 50 states, 'If the Court finds that a decision or a measure taken by a legal authority or any other authority of a High Contracting Party is completely or partially in conflict with the obligations arising from [the] Convention, and if the internal law of the said party allows only partial reparation to be made for the consequences of the decision or measure, the decision of the Court shall, if necessary, afford just satisfaction to the injured party.'

Case-law

8.72 The limitations of the proposition that legal aid is required to ensure an effective right of access to the courts were shown in the following cases:

WEBB v UK[1]

8.73 The applicant was subjected to affiliation proceedings. An affiliation order was made and the applicant, who had not been represented at first instance, contended that the magistrates had refused his application for blood tests and so they had reached their decision without factual evidence. He appealed and applied for legal aid. The Legal Aid Board refused on the grounds that he had not shown reasonable grounds for pursuing the appeal. He again represented himself at the appeal in the Crown Court and was allowed an adjournment to obtain blood tests (at his own expense) and to reapply for legal aid once he had the results. Following the results, the Crown Court again adjourned the matter so that he could reapply for legal aid and the judge, herself, wrote to the Legal Aid Board indicating that it would be helpful if the applicant could be legally aided if he qualified on financial grounds. Legal aid was refused again and when the matter came back to the Crown Court, the applicant was still unrepresented. His appeal was dismissed after a full hearing. He then claimed a violation of Art 6(1) on the grounds that he had been deprived an effective right of access to the court because he had not been able to be legally represented.

8.74 The Government argued that the applicant had not exhausted his domestic remedies because he could have sought judicial review of the Legal Aid Board decision. However, this argument was rejected on the grounds that such a procedure was very limited in its scope and did not provide a review of the merits of the decision.

8.75 However, the Commission found that there had been no violation on the following grounds:

– The subject of the affiliation proceedings did not, in itself, constitute a complex point of law.

– Although it was clear that rules of evidence and its presentation and interpretation to a Court are matters of legal complexity in respect of which legal advocacy is an advantage and this was reflected in the judge's letter to the Legal Aid Board, nevertheless, when the appeal did take place before another judge, he was apparently satisfied with the applicant's ability to present the appeal without legal aid.

– Although the applicant was emotionally involved in the outcome of the proceedings, both because they involved his private, personal affairs and also in the light of the financial implications following an affiliation order, these factors were not decisive in themselves.

– The question whether the applicant required legal aid in order that the hearing would be fair must be evaluated in the context of the particular proceedings in which the applicant was involved.

– There was a distinction between this and the *Airey* case in that in the latter matter the proceedings were in the High Court, involved very high fees for representation and a very complex procedure for instituting proceedings.

---

1 Application No 9353/81, (1983) 33 DR 133.

– There were, thus, significant differences in the complexity of the proceedings at issue.

– The task of the judge is never passive but includes the ultimate responsibility for ensuring the fairness of the proceedings, whether or not the parties are represented and this safeguarding principle is especially relevant in contested proceedings where one of the parties appears in person.

– The Commission's examination of the fairness of the proceedings must be based on their entirety and not on the isolated question of whether the applicant was granted legal aid.

– The Commission recognised that the aim of the merit test for legal aid was to ensure that the funds available for civil legal aid are not squandered in providing lawyers in vexatious, frivolous or other cases, where a prudent person who could personally afford the costs of litigation would be advised not to proceed and regarded this aim as legitimate[1].

– The applicant remained able to pursue his case in person and the denial of legal aid was not disproportionate to the aim sought to be achieved under the legal aid legislation.

W v FRG[2]

8.76 The applicant married a Pakistani citizen in order to enable him to obtain a residence permit in Germany. She received 8,000 DM from her husband for this service. She attempted to bring divorce proceedings and requested legal aid for that purpose claiming that she was unemployed, without any means and had spent the sum paid to her by her husband. In Germany, parties before the family courts in matrimonial matters must be represented by a lawyer. This was not the first time she had undertaken this sort of marriage arrangement and she had been told in the previous proceedings that, in principle, she should bear the cost of the divorce proceedings herself.

8.77 The domestic court rejected her application for legal aid. It accepted that the application for divorce offered sufficient prospects of success not least that because marital community between the parties was never founded. However, in the court's view, it could be expected of the applicant to bear the costs of the divorce proceedings herself and she could have held back a corresponding amount from the 8,000 DM to finance the proceedings. The Commission agreed with this approach and stated that it was not unreasonable for the German domestic court to state that the applicant was in no need of legal protection. Her experience from the previous divorce proceedings made her aware of the situation.

X v UK[3]

8.78 The applicant had been charged and convicted with terrorist offences. He alleged that after his arrest he was gravely assaulted by the police and wished to take legal proceedings against the police force. Legal aid had been granted, limited to the preparation of counsel's opinion, and the advice was given that

---

1   See also *X v FRG* Application No 3925/69.
2   Application No 11564/85, (1986) 45 DR 291.
3   Application No 8158/78, (1980) 21 DR 95.

there was a prima facie case against the police which was corroborated by the medical evidence. Notwithstanding this, the legal aid certificate was discharged.

8.79   The applicant claimed that this was a violation of Art 6(1) and that he had been denied 'access to court'. He claimed that a State may incur liability under Art 6(1) if it arbitrarily declines to grant legal aid in respect of civil claims. The Government had argued that the actions do not engage the responsibility of the State but the Commission disagreed with this, noting that:

> 'although independent of the executive, the legal aid scheme is regulated by statute (Legal Aid Act 1974) under the guidance of a Government Minister (Lord Chancellor) and involves the spending of public funds by a public body. As such, it must be considered an integral feature of the administration of justice as capable of engaging state responsibility as decisions of national courts.'[1]

However, the Commission regarded the application as manifestly ill-founded. It held that:

– where a State chooses a legal aid system to provide access to the courts, such a system can only operate effectively, given the limited resources available, by establishing machinery to select which cases should be legally aided;
– such limitations on the availability of free legal aid, common to most Convention countries, often require a financial contribution or that the proposed litigation have reasonable prospects of success;
– Art 6(1) does not require legal aid to be granted in every case irrespective of the nature of the claim or the supporting evidence;
– where an individual is refused legal aid because his proposed civil claim is either not sufficiently well grounded or is regarded as vexatious or frivolous, the burden would then fall on him to secure his 'access to court' in some other way such as bringing the action himself or seeking assistance from some other source;
– where a prisoner had been refused legal aid because his claim lacked reasonable prospects of success, such a situation would not normally constitute a denial of access to court unless it could be shown that the decision of the administrative authority was arbitrary[2].

This decision is perhaps surprising given the existence of counsel's opinion on the prospects of success, but the Commission took the view that the decision of the Legal Aid Committee was based on a proper examination of the evidence and the Committee's conclusion that there was a lack of corroborative evidence as to how the injuries were actually received could not be described as arbitrary.

WINER v UK[3]

8.80   The applicant sought to commence proceedings for defamation following the publication of a book. He obtained initial advice under the legal aid scheme and was informed that parts of the book were 'obviously libellous' but that he would require £20,000 to engage the services of a lawyer with defamation expertise, legal aid being unavailable for such matters. The applicant commenced action without the benefit of legal assistance. Eventually, a sum of £5,000 was offered to the applicant in full and final settlement and he was advised to take the

---

1   Application No 8158/78, para 14.
2   Ibid, para 16.
3   Application No 10871/84, 48 DR 154.

offer as he was lacking in funds to take the matter any further. He accepted the offer but claimed that he had been denied an effective right of access to court because legal aid was not available. Before the Commission the Government argued:

– That defamation proceedings were excluded from the scope of the Legal Aid Act 1974 on the basis that experience had shown that they were among a class of action in which there was most room for bringing vexatious, frivolous, unmeritorious or unnecessary claims.

– A requirement that the State provide legal aid for proceedings of this sort was a totally unjustifiable use of public money in an area in which resources were limited and in which there were other competing claims possessing much greater merit[1].

The applicant countered these submissions arguing that:

– This area of law was extremely complicated and the facts were also of unusual complexity.

– He accepted that checks and balances were necessary in a system of legal aid, but pointed out that a bar on the granting of legal aid for even the most meritorious action by a poor plaintiff against a wealthy defendant was tantamount to granting a licence to the unscrupulous to defame and perhaps ruin the impecunious. This would amount to a consequential breach of Art 14[2].

The Commission considered that the applicant had not been deprived of a right to access to court:

– It was not unreasonable to impose conditions on the availability of legal aid involving, inter alia, the financial situation of the litigant or the prospects of success of the proceedings.

– Given the limited financial resources of most civil legal aid schemes, it is not unreasonable to exclude certain categories of legal proceedings from this form of assistance.

– The fact that the English legal aid scheme excludes assistance in defamation proceedings had not been shown to be arbitrary in the present case.

– The facts show that the applicant did have access to the court as a litigant in person, albeit inexperienced. This was borne out by the settlement which was neither derisory nor unreasonable[3].

MUNRO v UK[4]

8.81   This was another defamation case where the applicant had been denied legal aid. Its importance lies in the distinction drawn by the Commission between defamation and family proceedings:

– The nature of defamation action is to protect an individual's reputation.

---

1   Application No 10871/84, 48 DR 163.
2   Ibid at 167.
3   Ibid at 171–172.
4   52 DR 158.

–   An application for judicial separation[1] regulates the legal relationship between two individuals and may have serious consequences for any children of the family.

In the light of the above cases, there may be a claim that a right to access has been violated if legal aid is refused in, for example, domestic violence and injunction proceedings where refusal is based on the fact that the respondent can give undertakings[2].

Right of access to a court: the limitation period

8.82   Limitation periods in personal injury cases are a legitimate limitation to the right of access to a court under Art 6(1).

STUBBINGS AND OTHERS v UK[3]

8.83   The applicants were all adult women who had been sexually abused during their childhood. The applicants suffered psychological problems and some had not made the connection between their problems and their sexually abusive experiences whilst others had blocked out the memory of the abuse until therapy had been undertaken. In all cases, the proceedings were instituted over 6 years after 'the date of knowledge' of the causal link between the abuse and the psychological damage and so were time barred under English law. The applicants claimed that they had been deprived access to the courts because of the limitation period.

8.84   The European Court referred to the *Ashingdane* principles[4] and held that the limitation period did not violate Art 6(1) because:

–   limitation periods serve several important purposes, namely, to ensure legal certainty and finality, to protect potential defendants from stale claims which might be difficult to counter and to prevent injustice which might arise if courts were required to decide upon events which took place in the distant past on the basis of evidence which might have become unreliable and incomplete because of the passage of time;

–   the English law of limitation allowed the applicants 6 years from their eighteenth birthdays in which to initiate civil proceedings;

–   a criminal prosecution could still be brought at any time and, if successful, a compensation order could be made, thus the very essence of the applicants' right of access to a court was not impaired;

–   the time-limit was not unduly short and was longer than the extinction periods for personal injuries set by some international treaties;

–   the rules applied were proportionate to the aims sought to be achieved when it is considered that if the applicants had commenced actions shortly before the expiry period, the courts would have been required to adjudicate on events which had taken place approximately 20 years earlier;

---

1   See *Airey v Ireland* 2 EHRR 305.
2   See Chapter 13 for more detailed consideration of this aspect.
3   23 EHRR 213.
4   7 EHRR 528, para 48.

- the contracting States properly enjoy a margin of appreciation in deciding how the right of access to court should be circumscribed. It was clear that the UK had devoted a substantial amount of time to the consideration of these questions[1].

However the Court also noted that:

> 'there has been a developing awareness in recent years of the range of problems caused by child abuse and its psychological effects on victims, and it is possible that the rules on limitation of actions applying in Member States of the Council of Europe may have to be amended to make special provision for this group of claimants in the near future.'[2]

Although the Court accepted that it should not substitute its own view for that of the State authorities as to what would be the most appropriate policy in this regard, the Convention is a 'living instrument' and the above comment could be seen as an indication that a similar claim in the future might have more success.

Right of access to the court: clarity of the legislation

8.85 The legislation has to be sufficiently clear to enable an applicant to challenge an administrative act that was a direct interference with his rights.

DE LA PRADELLE v FRANCE[3]

8.86 The applicant was the owner of land which the Ministry of the Environment wished to designate as an area of outstanding beauty and public interest. Amongst other matters, this would prevent the applicant from making any changes on his land. The applicant had planned to convert a long-disused hydroelectric dam into a self-contained miniature power station and had previously obtained planning permission to do so. He opposed the making of any decree in respect of the Ministry's designation and wished to appeal the decree itself. However, having waited for the decree to be notified to him, he was then informed that time for the appeal had started to run from the date of publication of the decree and not from the later notification. The applicant claimed that the complexities of the limitation period imposed by the legislation were such as to violate his right of access to the court. The Court agreed with the applicant stating that:

- (It could not) but be struck by the extreme complexity of the positive law resulting from the legislation on the conservation of places of interest taken together with the case-law on the classification of administrative acts.

- Such complexity was likely to create legal uncertainty as to the exact nature of the decree ... and as to how to calculate the time-limit for bringing an appeal.

- The applicant was entitled to expect a coherent system that would achieve a fair balance between the authorities' interests and his own.

- In particular, he should have had a clear, practical and effective opportunity to challenge an administrative act that was a direct interference with his right of property[4].

---

1   23 EHRR 213, paras 49–53.
2   Ibid, para 54.
3   (1992) Series A, No 253-B.
4   Ibid, paras 33–35.

(b) Right to a fair hearing

8.87   The fair hearing guarantee includes:

– the principle of equality of arms;
– access to evidence;
– freedom from self-incrimination;
– right to a public hearing and a hearing in one's presence;
– reasons for judgment.

Many of these principles overlap and there is a common thread throughout the case-law that these principles underpin the practice that court proceedings are adversarial in nature.

Equality of arms

8.88   The principle of the right to a 'fair trial' has been associated with the concept of an 'adversarial' hearing. This is particularly relevant in family cases where there has been a shift towards a non-adversarial or inquisitorial hearing. In the case of *Dombo Beheer BV v The Netherlands*[1] the Court held that the requirement of 'equality of arms', in the sense of a 'fair balance', between the parties applied in principle to civil cases. This implied:

> 'that each party must be afforded a reasonable opportunity to present his case – including his evidence – under conditions that do not place him at a substantial disadvantage vis-à-vis his opponent.'

However, the court was also clear that it was up to the national authorities to ensure in each individual case that the requirements of a 'fair hearing' were met[2].

8.89   Nevertheless, justice must also be seen to be done. In two cases, 20 years apart, the European Court of Human Rights considered similar points as to the role and impartiality of the 'procureur general's' department in criminal proceedings[3]. The cases show how the principles adopted by the Court have developed over the years. In *Delcourt v Belgium*[4], the Court held that there was no impartiality in the role but referred to a number of considerations which would understandably give the litigant a feeling of inequality. Even so, the Court held that there was no violation of Art 6(1) but those considerations:

> 'are of a certain importance which must not be underestimated. If one refers to the dictum "justice must not only be done; it must also be seen to be done", these considerations may allow doubts to arise about the satisfactory nature of the system in dispute. They do not, however, amount to proof of a violation of the right to a fair hearing. Looking behind appearances, the Court does not find the realities of the situation to be in any way in conflict with this right.'

Just over 20 years later, in *Borgers v Belgium*[5], a similar point arose. Although the Court upheld the validity of the findings in *Delcourt v Belgium* as to the independence and impartiality of the 'procureur general's' department, it

---

1   18 EHRR 213, para 33.
2   Ibid.
3   Although these matters were criminal cases, the application was brought under Art 6(1) and not Art 6(2) and (3). It is submitted that the same principles apply to disputes concerning civil rights and obligations.
4   1 EHRR 355, para 31.
5   15 EHRR 92.

questioned whether the proceedings respected the rights of the defence and the principle of equality of arms which were features of the wider concept of a fair trial. The Court commented that 'this [had] undergone a considerable evolution in the Court's case-law notably in respect of the importance attached to appearances and to the increased sensitivity of the public to the fair adminis-tration of justice'[1]. On similar facts, a violation of Art 6(1) was found. In spite of the acknowledgement of the validity of the judgment of the earlier case, in reality, *Borgers* reverses *Delcourt* and is a good example of the 'living' character of the Convention. From this it can be argued that:

– it is unnecessary to show an actual absence of equality;
– an appearance of inequality may violate the Convention even if there is no inequality in fact;
– previous findings/precedents that certain procedures are fair are not necessarily conclusive. Fairness is a concept which reflects the standards of the times and can change as public attitude changes.

RULES OF EVIDENCE AND PROCEDURE

8.90   The wide variations between the common and civil legal systems throughout the Convention States prevent a standard set of rules and Art 6(1) does not set down any rules of procedure and evidence. In *Schenk v Switzerland*[2], a case involving the admissibility of an illegally taped telephone conversation, the Court held that rules of evidence were 'primarily a matter for regulation under national law'[3]. One breach does not necessarily violate Art 6(1) if the trial as a whole is fair.

PROCEDURE

8.91   Article 6 guarantees the right of a defendant to participate effectively in a criminal trial although that right may be exercised adequately through his legal representation. In *Schenk v Switzerland*[4], the applicant had been charged with serious sexual offences against a young girl. She gave evidence during the trial but the applicant could not hear her because her voice was so soft. However, no complaint had been made during the trial. The Court considered the rights guaranteed under Art 6 including Art 6(3) and held that the applicant had been adequately represented by experienced counsel and solicitor who had no difficulty following the proceedings and who would have had every opportunity to discuss with the applicant any points that arose out of the evidence which did not already appear in the witness statements.

8.92   Further, the fact that the procedure adopted would have breached Art 6(3)[5] in a criminal case does not mean there has been a violation in a trial for the determination of civil rights even if similar procedures have been adopted. For example, in the case of *X v Austria*[6], the applicant sought a new hearing on the basis that he had not been allowed to call and cross-examine a witness. Such a right is enshrined in Art 6(3) in criminal cases. However, the Commission held that

---

1   15 EHRR 92, para 24.
2   13 EHRR 242.
3   Ibid, para 46.
4   Ibid.
5   The minimum rights held by anyone charged with a criminal offence.
6   Application No 5632/72.

there was no violation of Art 6(1) because the domestic court had carefully considered the possible benefit of complying with the applicant's request and concluded that the evidence sought would not be relevant nor would it be of assistance in determining any of the matters in dispute in the case. Although the Commission considered the matter in the light of Art 6(1), it stated that the rights under Art 6(3) 'do not apply as such to the determination of civil rights and obligations'.

8.93   In *Feldbrugge v The Netherlands*[1], the applicant had appealed against a decision to terminate her statutory sickness allowance. She complained that there had been a violation of Art 6(1) because of the procedures adopted. The Court agreed[2]:

–   The procedure adopted did not allow proper participation of the contending parties at any rate during the final and decisive stage of the procedure.

–   The applicant was not heard nor was she asked to file pleadings.

–   Neither she nor her representative was afforded the opportunity to consult the evidence in the file, in particular the two reports (which were the basis of the decision) drawn up by the permanent experts.

–   She was allowed to formulate her objections to the reports.

–   Although the experts examined the applicant and she was given the opportunity to formulate any comments she might have had, this did not cure the defect.

Access to evidence

8.94   In *Edwards v UK*[3], the Court considered that it is 'a requirement of fairness under Art 6(1), indeed one which is recognised under English law, that the prosecution authorities disclose to the defence all material evidence for or against the accused'. Although this was in the context of a criminal trial, the Court had stated that the minimum rights in Art 6(3) are specific aspects of the right to a fair trial set forth in Art 6(1). In the light of this, it is arguable that such disclosure is required in civil cases where the allegations have a criminal character, for example domestic violence proceedings or where there are committal proceedings.

8.95   Unlawfully obtained evidence, for example documents stolen during ancillary relief proceedings, will not necessarily result in a breach of Art 6. In the case of *Schenk v Switzerland*[4], the applicant was involved in protracted divorce proceedings and decided to murder his wife. He paid Mr Pauty to do the deed but Mr Pauty decided to inform the wife and the judicial authorities of his 'assignment.' Thereafter, Mr Pauty connected a tape recorder to his telephone and recorded Mr Schenk's call when he rang to query whether the assignment had been completed. Mr Schenk was duly arrested, tried and convicted. He applied to the European Court arguing that the use of unlawfully obtained evidence in his trial amounted to a violation. The Court held that there was no violation. It held that:

---

1   8 EHRR 425.
2   Ibid, para 44.
3   15 EHRR 417, para 36.
4   13 EHRR 242.

- the Court could not exclude, as a matter of principle and in the abstract that unlawfully obtained evidence may be admissible;
- it had only to ascertain whether the trial as a whole was fair;
- it took into account that the tape recording of the conversation was not the only evidence upon which the court relied to convict the applicant[1].

APPEALS

8.96   An apparent defect in the proceedings which would otherwise result in a violation of Art 6 may be remedied through the process of appeal. In *Edwards v UK*[2], the applicant had appealed against his conviction to the Court of Appeal. He complained that the police had not disclosed all the material evidence which had given rise to a defect in the trial proceedings. There he had the opportunity to ask the appellate court to hear fresh evidence and to cross-examine the police witnesses but the applicant had not asked the court to do so. Although the European Court agreed with the applicant that the trial at first instance had been defective which would have amounted to a breach of Art 6, the defects were cured by the subsequent procedure of the Court of Appeal and there was, therefore, no violation[3].

THE DISTINCTION BETWEEN THE ADVERSARIAL AND THE INQUISITORIAL APPROACH

8.97   The nature of the trial in family proceedings was referred to in *McMichael v UK*[4]. The Government had explained that the function of determining what measures of care would be in the best interests of the child had been conferred on the children's hearing rather than the ordinary courts because the legislature believed that this function was likely to be exercised more successfully by an adjudicatory body of three specially trained persons with substantial experience of children, following a procedure which is less formal and confrontational than that of the ordinary courts. The Court accepted:

> 'that in this sensitive domain of family law there may be good reason for opting for an adjudicatory body that does not have the composition or procedures of a court of law of the classic kind[5]. Nevertheless, notwithstanding the special characteristics of the adjudication to be made, as a matter of general principle the right to a fair – adversarial – trial "means the opportunity to have knowledge of and comment on the observations filed or evidence adduced by the other party."'[6]

8.98   In the above case, the parents in care proceedings did not receive all the reports or documents which had been produced to the hearing, although they were informed of the substance of the documents and were able to cross-examine all the witnesses and to lead their own evidence. The lack of disclosure of 'such vital documents' was capable of affecting the ability of participating parents not only to influence the outcome of the children's hearing in question but also to assess their prospects of an appeal to a higher court. In the circumstances, the

---

1   13 EHRR 242, para 46.
2   15 EHRR 417.
3   Ibid, para 38.
4   20 EHRR 205.
5   See also *X v UK* 4 EHRR 188 where the habeas corpus procedures were reviewed in respect of convicted criminals who were treated also as mental patients and kept in secure custody and found to be in violation of Art 5(4).
6   *Ruiz Mareos v Spain* 16 EHRR 505, para 63.

failure to disclose these documents amounted to a violation of Art 6(1). Other matters including the mother's attendance at one hearing, heavily sedated and unrepresented and the refusal of an adjournment for the purpose of obtaining a psychiatric report contributed to the court's findings that the requirement of an adversarial trial had not been fulfilled[1].

8.99 From this, it can be seen that adopting a non-adversarial approach is not unacceptable within Art 6 but care must be taken to ensure that parents' rights as guaranteed by Art 6(1) are upheld. The approach of the UK courts has, on occasions, been to import the 'welfare paramountcy test' as the guiding principle in the procedures adopted by the court[2]. It is arguable that in the light of *McMichael v UK*, that is going too far.

8.100 However, *McMichael v UK* has to be contrasted with *Hendriks v The Netherlands*[3] where the report of the Council for the Protection of Children, upon a general directive of the Secretary of State, was not handed over to the applicant because such reports generally contain information on persons other than the applicants and the privacy of such persons could be infringed if such information was released. Under the directive, the Council could object to the applicant seeing the report at all although, in principle, the applicant could have access to the report at the Council's offices. If a lawyer were to represent the applicant, he would receive a copy of the report which he would only be allowed to discuss with his client. The Commission did not exclude that the applicant may be prejudiced if he could keep a copy of the report, the more so, if he did not have a lawyer. However, on the facts the applicant did have adequate access to the report and 'the contents were sufficiently familiar to the applicant to enable him to prepare his case in detail with his lawyer and that the principle of "equality of arms" [had] therefore been respected'[4].

EXPERT'S REPORTS

8.101 The role of experts and experts' reports in family cases has proved controversial over the years. The UK courts have made it clear that there can be no trial by experts and that the experts cannot usurp the judge's role. Nevertheless, it would be difficult to claim that the reports do not have a strong influence on the court's approach, particularly if it has been produced by jointly instructed experts or by the court-appointed welfare officer.

8.102 In the case of *Bonisch v Austria*[5], a violation of Art 6 was found where there was unequal treatment between the court-appointed expert and the expert witness for the defence in a criminal case. The inequality was stark. The court-appointed expert had earlier drafted a report leading to the defendant's prosecution and the defendant felt that he was biased. The court-appointed expert could attend throughout the hearings, put questions to the defendant and to witnesses and comment on their evidence at the appropriate moment. The defendant's expert witness was not allowed to appear before the court until he gave evidence; he was examined both by the judge and the court-appointed expert and, thereafter, was relegated to the public gallery. All this is far removed from the

---

1   *McMichael v UK* 20 EHRR 205, para 83.
2   See **8.106** et seq on subject of disclosure.
3   5 EHRR 223.
4   Ibid, para 144.
5   9 EHRR 191.

use of experts in family cases (although perhaps not quite so far removed in the case of the court-appointed welfare officers). However, in the above case the court also held that there was a violation of Art 6(1) because the defendant had 'little opportunity ... to obtain the appointment of a counter-expert'[1]. This case has to be seen in the context of the court, in this instance, as part of a civil system of justice where the court itself has an inquisitorial role.

8.103 In contrast, in the case of *H v France*[2], a medical-negligence case, the Court had refused to allow the applicant to obtain a medical report to prove a causal link between his condition and the act of a medical practitioner. Before the European Court, the French Government contended that the requirements of a 'fair trial' could not include an obligation on the court trying the case to order an expert's report to be given or any other investigative measure to be taken solely because a party sought it and that it was for the court to judge whether the measure requested would serve any useful purpose. The Court agreed with this proposition but added the caveat that 'it must, however, ascertain whether the proceedings as a whole were fair as required by Art 6(1)'[3]. On the facts, it was held that the administrative court was entitled to take the view that it had sufficient information for it to be able to give judgment on the basis of its preliminary examination of the case and the evidence before it. The fact that it did not accede to the applicant's request for an expert's report did not infringe the applicant's right to a fair trial.

8.104 Although litigants are not bound by the experts and have a right to cross-examine, an inability to instruct their own expert may, in a very practical way, severely limit this right and, further, the right to adduce their own case. The domestic courts have been anxious to avoid the proliferation of experts and, in particular, to prevent 'shopping around' for an opinion. Nevertheless, in certain circumstances, Art 6(1) may be one factor in any application by a litigant for his own expert notwithstanding that there are already jointly instructed experts within the case[4].

ERIKSSON v SWEDEN[5]

8.105 The applicant complained that the administrative court took their decisions without having before them any opinion from an independent medical expert, and that she was herself unable to challenge the evaluations of the Social Council's experts as she was not allowed to have her child examined by an expert of her own choice. The Court held that there was no violation considering that 'proper steps were taken to obtain sufficient expert medical opinion for the purposes of the proceedings' and, accordingly, taking the proceedings as a whole, they were not incompatible with Art 6(1)[6].

Freedom from self-incrimination
8.106 It is arguable that Art 6(1) may affect the practice of disclosure of reports within Children Act 1989 proceedings. The High Court has held that parties in family proceedings are under a duty to make voluntary disclosure of all

---

1   9 EHRR 191, para 34.
2   12 EHRR 74.
3   Ibid, para 61.
4   See also *Hentrich v France* 18 EHRR 440, paras 53–56.
5   12 EHRR 183.
6   Ibid, paras 74–75.

matters likely to be material to the welfare of the child even if adverse to their own particular case [1]. This was further considered by the House of Lords in the case of *Re L (A Minor) (Police Investigation: Privilege)* [2]. In the majority judgment, Lord Jauncey of Tullichettle made a distinction between legal professional privilege (privilege attaching to communications between client and solicitor) and litigation privilege (privilege attaching to reports by third parties prepared on the instructions of a client for the purposes of litigation). The House of Lords held that [3]:

–   family proceedings were primarily non-adversarial and investigative as opposed to adversarial, therefore the notion of a fair trial between opposing parties assumed far less importance;

–   litigation privilege was not so much overridden in these sort of cases but did not arise in the first place;

–   there was no need to decide the point whether there was a duty on a party to care proceedings to disclose *all* matters likely to be material to the welfare of the child;

–   there was no need to decide the point whether a party may avoid disclosure of an adverse report because he may have a claim to privilege against self-incrimination. On the facts, the appellant had filed the report and thus had waived her claim.

The minority judgment was set out by Lord Nicholls of Birkenhead. He rejected the view that family proceedings were necessarily different from others on the basis of the description that they were non-adversarial [4]:

'the answer to the present question turns on what are the requirements of procedural fairness in the conduct of family proceedings . . . Fairness is a universal requirement in the conduct of all forms of proceedings, inquisitorial as much as adversarial, although the requirements of fairness vary widely from one type of proceedings to another. The requirements depend upon matters such as the nature of the proceedings, the subject matter being considered, the rules governing the conduct of the proceedings, the parties involved, the composition of the tribunal and the consequences of the decision. The distinction between the adversarial and inquisitorial nature of the proceedings is no more than one of these elements, although sometimes a very important element. The crucial question is not whether and to what extent, the proceedings are inquisitorial rather than adversarial. The question to be addressed is what is required if the proceedings are to be conducted fairly.'

Lord Nicholls referred to the European Convention on Human Rights and doubted whether a parent who was denied the opportunity to obtain legal advice in confidence would be accorded a fair hearing under Arts 6(1) and 8. In his view, legal professional privilege and litigation privilege were integral parts of a single privilege [5].

8.107   In the light of the incorporation of the Convention into domestic law, it is arguable that the minority opinion in *Re L (A Minor) (Police Investigation: Privilege)*

---

1   *Essex County Council v R* [1993] 2 FLR 826 at 828–829; *Re DH (A Minor) (Child Abuse)* [1994] 1 FLR 679 at 703–704; *Oxfordshire County Council v P* [1995] 1 FLR 552 at 557–558.
2   [1997] AC 16. Note that this case is the subject of an application to the European Court of Human Rights and a decision is still awaited.
3   Ibid at 27–29.
4   Ibid at 31–32.
5   Ibid at 32–33.

is correct and there is no duty to disclose all reports. It is submitted that this argument is strengthened by the fact that the paramountcy principle may not govern most matters or procedures[1] in family proceedings and, in addition, the child is safeguarded by the fact that there is no property in a witness and the expert could be called by any party or, indeed, by the court to give evidence on the issue before the court.

8.108   Further, an obligation to disclose all reports on all matters likely to be material to the welfare of the child could place a party at risk of self-incrimination. The House of Lords accepted that disclosure of reports would amount to an infringement of the privilege against self-incrimination[2].

8.109   Nevertheless, it is also arguable that if there is to be 'equality of arms', it is equally open to the local authority to argue that there is no need to disclose all material adverse to its case. Nevertheless, that argument is unlikely to succeed because the local authority would have similar duties to the prosecution in criminal cases especially where there are allegations of abuse and the family proceedings have a quasi-criminal element introduced into them. In any event, the local authority has a duty to disclose all relevant information because of the nature of their functions and their duties under domestic legislation and under Art 8 of the Convention[3].

SAUNDERS v UK

8.110   The question of self-incrimination was raised before the European Court in the case of *Saunders v UK*[4]. The applicant was the director and chief executive of Guinness plc. A takeover battle resulted in a victory for Guiness but the conduct of the battle caused concern and an investigation by the Department for Trade and Industry was ordered. Under the DTI rules, the applicant was required to answer all questions put to him and a failure to do so making him liable to punishment as if he had been guilty of contempt of court. The applicant was subsequently charged with several counts of false accounting and conspiracy charges and the answers given by the applicant to the DTI inspectors were used by the prosecution during the trial.

8.111   The applicant claimed that there had been a violation of Art 6 and that it was implicit in the right to a fair trial as guaranteed by Art 6(1) that there was a right of an individual not to be compelled to contribute incriminating evidence to be used in a prosecution against him. The Court agreed with the applicant. The Government had argued that only statements which were self-incriminating could fall within the privilege. However, the Court held that the scope of privilege was somewhat wider:

> 'Testimony obtained under compulsion which appears on its face to be of a non-incriminating nature – such as exculpatory remarks or mere information on questions of fact – may later be deployed in criminal proceedings in support of the prosecution case, for example to contradict or cast doubt upon other statements of the accused or evidence given by him during the trial or otherwise to undermine his credibility ... It follows that what is of the essence in this context is the use to which evidence obtained under compulsion is made in the course of the criminal trial.'[5]

---

1   See *W v UK* 10 EHRR 29.
2   In *Re L* (above) at 28–29.
3   See *Feldbrugge v The Netherlands* 8 EHRR 425; *Edwards v UK* 15 EHRR 417; *H v France* 12 EHRR 74.
4   23 EHRR 313.
5   23 EHRR 313, para 71.

Thus, the right seems to extend to all incriminating evidence and not simply self-incriminating.

8.112   Although the European Court was considering privilege in the context of a criminal trial, the same guarantees may also apply within civil matters under the principle of 'fairness', especially if the effects of a finding against a party would have serious implications. For example, disclosure of forensic reports in cases of serious abuse do not affect the relationship of the party to his family alone. In certain circumstances, the court will allow such reports to be disclosed to the police resulting in criminal charges being preferred.

8.113   If there is a claim in privilege not to disclose material which tends to incriminate (rather than merely directly self-incriminating), it is arguable that parties in family proceedings may avoid disclosure of some expert reports under that claim.

FUNKE v FRANCE [1]

8.114   Customs officers made a search of the applicant's home and seized documents in order to obtain particulars of overseas assets held by him and his wife. The seizure did not lead to criminal proceedings but did lead to parallel proceedings for disclosure of documents and interim orders. Following subsequent disclosure, the applicant was charged, convicted and fined for failure to provide the customs authorities with statements of his overseas bank accounts. The applicant, through his wife, claimed that this had violated Art 6(1) and Art 6(2) (presumption of innocence). The Government had argued that under the regime of French customs and exchange control, the disclosure of documents was not to facilitate a prosecution but to implement the (tax) legislation. The Commission which compared the obligation to a taxpayer's duty to supply information about his wealth and income approved this argument. The European Court disagreed and held that 'the special features of customs law cannot justify such an infringement of the right of anyone "charged with a criminal offence" . . . to remain silent and not to contribute to incriminating itself'[2].

8.115   Although this case was considered under the scope of 'a criminal charge', the Court limited its deliberations to Art 6(1) and found it unnecessary to consider any of other guarantees specifically applicable to criminal charges under Art 6 and specifically found it unnecessary to consider Art 6(2).

8.116   In the light of this, it is arguable that the judgment is equally applicable to 'the determination of civil rights and obligations'. It is further arguable that the domestic court's view that all material should be disclosed for the purposes of determining the issue of the welfare of the child will have to be reconsidered, particularly where it has to be balanced against the effect of any determination on the reputation, character and status of one of the parties where, for example, allegations of abuse are made.

8.117   Under domestic procedure, the duty to disclose extends to, for example, ancillary relief proceedings. It is unlikely that this will change because the purpose of the disclosure is not to incriminate but to facilitate the manner in

---

1   16 EHRR 297.
2   Ibid, para 44.

which the Court can determine a fair distribution of assets on the breakdown of a marriage.

The right to a public hearing and a hearing in one's presence

'IN THE DETERMINATION OF HIS CIVIL RIGHTS AND OBLIGATIONS ... EVERYONE IS ENTITLED TO A ... PUBLIC HEARING ...'

8.118   The right to a public hearing[1] is explicitly guaranteed under Art 6(1) and it is arguable that the right to a hearing in one's presence and, flowing from that, the right to an oral hearing, is implicit under the Convention to ensure a public hearing. Under English law, the hearing of oral evidence is implicit in the Family Proceedings Rules 1991[2] but there are occasions when the court has determined that it was not necessary or was not appropriate to have a full oral hearing. In *Re B (Minors) (Contact)*[3], Butler Sloss stated:

'There is a spectrum of procedure for family cases from the ex parte application on minimal evidence to the full and detailed investigations on oral evidence which may be prolonged. Where on that spectrum a judge decides a particular application should be placed is a matter for his discretion. Applications for residence orders or for committal to the care of the local authority or revocation of a care order are likely to be decided on full oral evidence, but not invariably. Such is not the case on contact applications which may be and are heard sometimes with and sometimes without oral evidence or with a limited amount of oral evidence ... The considerations which should weigh with the court include:

(1)   whether there is sufficient evidence upon which to make the relevant decision;
(2)   whether the proposed evidence (which should be available at least in outline) which the applicant for a full trial wishes to adduce is likely to affect the outcome of the proceedings;
(3)   whether the opportunity to cross-examine the witnesses for the local authority, in particular ... expert witnesses, is likely to affect the outcome of the proceedings;
(4)   the welfare of the child and the effect of further litigation ...;
(5)   the prospects of success of the applicant for a full trial;
(6)   does the justice of the case require a full investigation with oral evidence?'

8.119   Although there have been cases where the courts have criticised proceedings where oral evidence has been limited or absent[4], the criticism has been levelled either at the lack of even-handedness or the absence of *any* evidence rather than an absence of *oral* evidence. However, there have been cases where oral evidence has not been allowed, inter alia:

---

1   See **8.171**.
2   See, for example, FPR 1991, r 4.16. There is a presumption that the parties will attend all hearings and direction appointments although attendance can be dispensed with if it is in the interests of the child and the party is represented by a guardian ad litem or solicitor, FPR 1991, r 4.17(a) – filing of written statements of the oral evidence and FPR 1991, r 4.20 – keeping a note of the oral evidence.
3   [1994] 2 FLR 1.
4   In *Re F (A Minor) (Care Order: Procedure)* [1994] 1 FLR 240, the magistrates' court heard evidence of the local authority but refused to hear evidence from the father. Wall J said the court should have heard evidence from both sides or neither side. In *S v Merton London Borough* [1994] 1 FCR 186, the magistrates had heard no evidence and refused to read any documentation before making a care order. The case was dealt with on submissions. On appeal, Ward J held that there must be some evidence (and submissions do not constitute evidence) on which a decision could be made.

– *Re S and P (Discharge of Care Order)*[1]. The family proceedings court was held to be entitled to dismiss an application to discharge a care order after hearing the evidence for the applicant, mother, when the application was being opposed by the local authority and the guardian ad litem because the evidence could get no better for the applicant after that point. The court had correctly considered whether a prima facie case had been made out.

– *Re B (Contact: Stepfather's Opposition)*[2]. A father had applied for contact but his application was dismissed by Johnson J at the directions hearing (where the father was represented but not present and had no notice of the proposal to dismiss the application) because the stepfather was threatening to reject the child and the mother if the matter proceeded. The decision was upheld on appeal during which the father had been allowed to adduce fresh evidence.

8.120   Many of the Convention cases are the result of criminal charges where 'it flows from the notion of a fair trial that a person charged with a criminal offence should, as a general principle, be entitled to be present at the trial hearing'[3]. In *T v Italy*[4], the Court stated that in criminal trials, 'although not expressly mentioned in paragraph 1, the object and purpose of the Article taken as a whole show that a person charged with a criminal offence is entitled to take part in the hearing'. In that case, it was held that:

> 'indirect knowledge of a prosecution against him was insufficient and that to inform someone of a prosecution brought against him is a legal act of such importance that it must be carried out in accordance with procedural and substantive requirements capable of guaranteeing the effective exercise of the accused's rights ... Vague and informal knowledge cannot suffice'[5].

In this case the applicant was convicted in absentia of the rape of his daughter when he had skipped the country and been untraceable for a number of years. It was held that the conviction in his absence was a violation. It is arguable that this would be a factor in any hearing of committal proceedings and could also be a factor in any proceedings where there are criminal characteristics in the allegation being made, for example allegations of assault in injunction proceedings.

8.121   In the same way that a right of access to the court impliedly guarantees a right to effective access and, in certain circumstances, legal aid, the right to a hearing in one's presence impliedly guarantees a right to participate effectively[6]. Furthermore, the right to a hearing in one's presence is linked to the right to adversarial argument and has been accepted as such as a principle in criminal cases[7].

8.122   The right to a hearing in one's presence is not as clear in civil proceedings but it appears that there is such a right where:

---

1   [1995] 2 FLR 782. It should be noted that the mother had no opportunity to cross-examine the local authority witnesses or the guardian ad litem.
2   [1997] 2 FLR 579.
3   *Ekbatani v Sweden* 13 EHRR 504 at para 25. See also *Barbera, Messegue and Jabardo v Spain* 11 EHRR 360, para 78 where it was stated that 'all the evidence must in principle be produced in the presence of the accused at a public hearing with a view to adversarial argument'.
4   (1992) Series A, No 245-C, para 26.
5   Ibid, para 28.
6   See *Stanford v UK* (1984) Series A, No 282-A.
7   *Barbera, Messegue and Jardabo v Spain* 11 EHRR 360, para 81.

– an assessment of a party's conduct is involved[1];
– the personal character and manner of life are involved[2].

AN ASSESSMENT OF THE PARTY'S CONDUCT IS INVOLVED

8.123 In *Muyldermans v Belgium*[3], the applicant was an accountant in the Belgian Post Office. Money disappeared from the cashier's desk over which the applicant was in charge. The Post Office authorities determined, in administrative, non-adversarial and closed proceedings in the absence of the applicant, that she should reimburse the Post Office. The Commission stated that 'although the right to appear in person in a civil case is not, as such, guaranteed by the Convention, it may, in particular circumstances, be implied in the right to a fair hearing'[4]. The Commission noted that the audit court did not hear her or summon her to appear nor was she invited to make supplementary observations notwithstanding that the hearing was concerned with the applicant's personal conduct. The Commission's view that there had been a violation of Art 6(1) was based on the finding that:

> 'the procedure followed ... was clearly not adversarial although this is one of the principal guarantees of a judicial procedure ... Since the applicant's personal conduct directly contributed to the formation of the Audit Court's opinion ... the right to a fair hearing in the particular circumstances of the case, necessitated direct consideration by the Court of the applicant's grounds of defence.'[5]

In the event, the matter was not heard by the European Court. It was struck out of the list because the Belgian Government had come to a settlement with the applicant and a bill had been introduced to amend the offending procedure to include adversarial and public hearings in cases of this type and there was no remaining reason of public policy necessitating a decision on the merits[6].

THE PERSONAL CHARACTER AND MANNER OF LIFE IS INVOLVED

8.124 In *X v Sweden*[7], a father who was resident in Germany was seeking access to his child in Sweden. He was informed that his son was only being taught in the Swedish language in which he, himself, was unable to correspond with his son. The father applied for an entry permit into Sweden so that he could attend the Court in the access proceedings but the permit was refused. The Court also declined to make an order that the father's personal appearance was necessary. As an alternative, it was agreed by his counsel that the father could attend at a German court and submit his evidence on oath there. The father withdrew instruction from his counsel on the grounds that he had no authority to make that agreement. The father attended the German court but declined to answer any questions. He claimed that he was entitled to be present at the hearing for access and the refusal to allow him entry to Sweden for those purposes deprived him of the right to a fair hearing.

8.125 The Court agreed that there was a violation of Art 6(1) and stated:

---

1   *Muyldermans v Belgium* 15 EHRR 204.
2   *X v Sweden* Application No 434/58, (1959) 2 YB 354.
3   15 EHRR 204. Note, this matter falls under the category of 'civil rights and obligations' because the audit court was determining the applicant's liability to reimburse the post office rather than judging whether she was guilty of a criminal offence.
4   Ibid, para 62.
5   Ibid, para 64; see also *Feldbrugge v The Netherlands* 8 EHRR 425, para 44.
6   Ibid, para 20.
7   Application No 434/58, (1959) 2 YB 354 at 370 and 372.

- The right to be present in person in civil proceedings is not guaranteed by Art 6(1) or by any other provision of the Convention.

- In certain classes of cases or in certain sets of circumstances, the right to a fair hearing guaranteed by Art 6(1) implies a right to be present in person at the hearing of the case.

- One class of case in which this appears to arise with some particular force is a case where the personal character and manner of life of the party concerned directly relevant to the formation of the Court's opinion on the point which it is called upon to decide.

- A case in which a parent, following upon a divorce, makes an application to the Court for a right of access to a child of the marriage is without doubt a case of this kind[1].

The Court gave full weight to the fact that the father was legally represented and that arrangements had been made to give evidence on oath which would then be transmitted to the Swedish Court. However, it was still arguable that he was under a substantial disadvantage vis-à-vis his wife who was in a position to attend the court hearings and impugn in court, his personal character and manner of life.

8.126   In *X v Austria*[2], custody of the applicant's twin daughters had been awarded to his ex-wife. On appeal by the applicant, the matter was referred back to the court at first instance and following three psychiatric opinions, the decision was confirmed. The applicant appealed again claiming that the court had failed to hear from the children themselves. The court at first instance then heard the children in the absence of both parents and decided that there was no basis for revoking its earlier decision.

8.127   The Commission observed that the fairness of civil proceedings must be judged on the basis of the development of the case as a whole and that an isolated incident cannot be seen as interfering with the principle of fairness unless it might have substantially affected the overall conduct of the proceedings or their result. The only question was whether the children's evidence had been obtained in such a manner that the applicant's right to a fair hearing was thereby impaired.

8.128   The Commission referred to the fact that:

- these were non-contentious civil proceedings and as such were conducted in a very flexible way with the judge having a wide discretion as to the circumstances in which he collects evidence;
- it was not excluded that the parties could be present during the children's evidence but the fact that the judge refrained from exercising his discretion in that sense did not amount to a breach of the principle of a fair hearing;
- since it was the purpose of the hearing to determine with which parent the children wished to stay, it may have been the proper course to exclude the influence of both parents;
- the applicant was not treated less favourably than his ex-wife and so there was no violation of the fundamental principle of equality of arms[3].

---

1   Application No 434/58, (1959) 2 YB 354 at 370.
2   Application No 8893/80, 31 DR 66.
3   Application No 8893/80, all at p 68.

The right to a hearing in one's presence or to an oral hearing is not an absolute right. The Court will look at the overall fairness of the proceedings.

THE CASE-LAW

8.129   In the following cases, a violation of Art 6(1) was found on the grounds of failure to provide a hearing in the presence of the applicant or a failure to provide an oral hearing:

–   *Ekbatani v Sweden*[1]. The Court of Appeal upheld the conviction of the applicant without an oral hearing. The Court noted that it had held on a number of occasions that 'providing there has been a public hearing at first instance, the absence of "public hearings" before a second or third instance may be justified by the special features of the proceedings at issue'. In this case, there were no special features to justify such a course and, moreover, the Court of Appeal had to make a full assessment of the question of the applicant's guilt or innocence.

–   *Fredin v Sweden (No 2)*[2]. The applicant had been refused a special extraction permit for his gravel pit and had sought a review by the Supreme Administrative Court. He also sought an oral hearing but this was refused. It was held that:

> 'it was clearly established under the existing case-law that in proceedings before a court of first and only instance the right to a "public hearing" in the sense of Art 6(1) may entail an entitlement to an "oral hearing."'

The Court did not consider when such an entitlement would follow as of right but held that, in the circumstances, where the Supreme Administrative Court was acting as the first and only judicial instance in contested proceedings which raised issues of both facts and law, a refusal to have an oral hearing amounted to a violation of Art 6(1).

8.130   In the following cases the Court held that there was no violation of Art 6(1) based on the applicant's claim that there was no hearing in his presence or no oral hearing:

–   *Axen v Germany*[3]. The German Federal Court of Justice considered a civil appeal. This court had brought in a temporary measure to reduce the workload whereby it could determine an appeal on points of law if it unanimously considered that the appeal was ill founded and that an oral argument was unnecessary. The parties had to be informed and asked for their views. If the court was minded to reverse the lower court's decision, an oral hearing was compulsory under German law. The Court held there was no violation because the Federal Court of Justice had restricted its considerations to points of law.

–   *Monnell and Morris v UK*[4]. The Court of Appeal considered an application for leave to appeal against conviction and sentence. The applicants were not

1   13 EHRR 504, paras 31 to 32; see also *Helmers v Sweden* 15 EHRR 285 where there is similar dicta in a civil case for damages for defamation which had been taken out in conjunction with a private prosecution for defamation. The proceedings were thus joint criminal and civil proceedings.
2   13 EHRR 784, para 21.
3   6 EHRR 195.
4   10 EHRR 205.

present and not represented. Leave was not given and the applicants' time spent in custody pending appeal was ordered not to count towards their total sentence on the grounds that their appeal was unmeritorious ('the loss of time direction'). It was held that there was no violation for want of an oral hearing because[1]:

- at first instance, the applicants had received the benefit of a fair trial which satisfied the requirement of an oral hearing;
- the Court of Appeal does not rehear the case on the facts, no witnesses are called even though the grounds of appeal involve questions of fact as well as law;
- the court's power to direct 'loss of time' was legitimate in the interests of the proper administration of justice as a way of ensuring that unmeritorious appeals did not clog up the system;
- the principle of equality of arms was respected in that the prosecution, like the two accused, was not represented;
- they had the benefit of free legal advice on appeal and chose to ignore the advice that there were no reasonable prospects of successfully appealing. Furthermore, they were aware of the risk of 'loss of time' orders;
- they were afforded the opportunity to make written submissions;
- there was no cause to doubt that there had been a proper evaluation of the applicants' case.

WAIVER OF THE RIGHT TO A HEARING IN ONE'S PRESENCE/ORAL HEARING

8.131   In the case of *Poitrimol v France* which concerned a criminal trial and conviction of the applicant for the offence of absconding with his children in breach of the custody order, it was held that:

> 'proceedings held in an accused's absence are not incompatible with the Convention if the person concerned can subsequently obtain from a court which has heard him a fresh determination of the merits of the charge in respect of both law and fact.'[2]

Further it was held that:

> 'it is an open question whether this latter requirement applies when the accused has waived his right to appear and to defend himself but at all events such a waiver must, if it is to be effective for Convention purposes, be established in an unequivocal manner and be attended by minimum safeguards commensurate to its importance.'[3]

A violation was found. The applicant had been given notice of the hearing and had clearly expressed his wish not to attend. On that basis there should have been no finding of a breach of the Convention. However, a violation was found because the applicant had also expressed an intention to be legally represented but had been deprived of such entitlement once he had failed to appear at the appeal proceedings.

Reasons for judgement

8.132   Although a reasoned judgment is not explicitly referred to under Art 6, it is implicit in the requirement of a fair trial because:

---

1   *Monnell and Morris v UK* 10 EHRR 205, paras 57–70.
2   *Poitrimol v France* 18 EHRR 130, paras 30–32.
3   Ibid, para 31.

- it places the tribunal 'under a duty to conduct a proper examination of the submissions, arguments and evidence adduced by the parties without prejudice to its assessment of whether they are relevant to its decision[1];
- 'the silence of the ... Court could give rise to doubts as to the scope of the examination conducted by that court'[2];
- 'it makes it possible for the accused to exercise usefully the rights of appeal available to him'[3].

8.133 In *Van der Hurk v The Netherlands*[4], the applicant was a farmer who had been allocated a milk production quota. His claim for a higher quota was rejected as was his subsequent appeal. He claimed that there had been a violation of Art 6(1) because, inter alia, the tribunal had refused to consider the applicant's method of calculation in support of his claim and, therefore, did not or did not sufficiently deal with various arguments advanced by him. The Court held that there was no violation, that the tribunal had given adequate consideration to the matter and that:

> 'Article 6(1) obliges courts to give reasons for their decisions, but cannot be understood as requiring a detailed answer to every argument.'[5]

8.134 This should be contrasted with the case of *Hiro Balani v Spain*[6]. A Japanese company tried to obtain the removal of the applicant's trademark from the industrial property register. At first instance the company's claim was dismissed. On appeal, the Supreme Court quashed the judgment of first instance rejecting two of the submissions made by the applicant but making no reference to the third. The applicant claimed that she had not had a fair hearing in breach of Art 6(1). The applicant's family had registered a large number of trademarks over the years and frequently been involved in litigation concerning the trademarks in question. Before the European Court, the Government claimed that the third submission had already been elucidated in a decision given only one year before concerning the same parties and the same subject matter. The European Court held that this was irrelevant and that the applicant's claim was well founded. It referred to *Van der Hurk v The Netherlands* and the fact that there was no need to give a detailed answer to every argument but stated:

> 'the extent to which this duty to give reasons applies may vary according to the nature of the decision. It is moreover necessary to take into account, inter alia, the diversity of the submissions that a litigant may bring before the courts and the differences existing in the Contracting States with regard to statutory provisions, customary rules, legal opinion, and the presentation and drafting of judgments. That is why the question whether a court has failed to fulfil the obligation to state reasons ... can only be determined in the light of the circumstances of the case.'[7]

1 *Van der Hurk v The Netherlands* 18 EHRR 481, para 59.
2 *Hiro Balani v Spain* 19 EHRR 566, para 25.
3 *Hadjianastassiou v Greece* 16 EHRR 219, para 33; *H v Belgium* 10 EHRR 339, para 53; see also *C v Italy* Application No 10889/84, (1988) 56 DR 40 where it was stated that time for an application started to run only when the applicant was able to acquaint himself with the reasons for judgment, ie when they were made public.
4 18 EHRR 481.
5 Ibid, para 61.
6 19 EHRR 566.
7 Ibid, para 27.

In this case, the fact that the Supreme Court was silent on the applicant's submission made it impossible to ascertain whether the Supreme Court simply neglected to deal with the submission or whether it intended to dismiss it and, if that were its intention, what its reasons were for so deciding.

8.135   In the case of *H v Belgium*[1], the applicant was a disbarred advocat who had sought, unsuccessfully, to be restored. Belgian law permitted a disbarred advocat to seek readmission after 10 years if 'exceptional circumstances' warranted it. There was no definition of 'exceptional circumstances' which could be obtained either from the relevant provision or from previous decisions of the tribunal. The application to be restored to the roll was rejected but the decision merely noted that there were no such circumstances without explaining why the circumstances relied on by the applicant were not to be regarded as exceptional. The European Court, in declaring that there had thus been a violation, felt that the very lack of precision in the definition made it all the more necessary to give reasons on the issue in question.

8.136   The importance of a reasoned judgment can be seen in the case of *De Moor v Belgium*[2] where the applicant was seeking to be enrolled as a pupil advocate. Reasons were given in the judgment but it was held that the proceedings had violated Art 6(1) and were unfair in that the reasons given showed that the rejection of the applicant's case was not a legally valid one in that it did not fall within the scope of the applicable legislation.

(c) Right to a trial within a reasonable time

'In the determination of his civil rights and obligations . . . everyone is entitled to a . . . hearing within a reasonable time by (a) . . . tribunal'

8.137   Right to a trial within a reasonable time is specifically guaranteed under Art 6(1). Under s 1(2) of the Children Act 1989, 'in any proceedings in which any question with respect to the upbringing of a child arises, the court shall have regard to the general principle that any delay in determining the question is likely to prejudice the welfare of the child.' The Convention guarantees protection to *all* parties to court proceedings from excessive procedural delays[3] and 'underlines the importance of rendering justice without delays which might jeopardise its effectiveness and credibility'[4].

8.138   In civil cases, time runs from the institution of the relevant court procedure[5], although as stated in *Golder v UK*[6] 'it is conceivable . . . that in civil matters the reasonable time may begin to run, in certain circumstances, even before the issue of the writ commencing proceedings before the court to which the plaintiff submits the dispute'. This was the case in *König v FRG*[7] where the applicant, a medical practitioner, had his authorisation to practise medicine and run a clinic withdrawn. Mr Konig lodged an objection to the withdrawal and later commenced proceedings to challenge the decision of the authorising authority.

---

1   10 EHRR 339.
2   18 EHRR 372.
3   *Stögmüller v Austria* 1 EHRR 155, p 40.
4   *H v France* 12 EHRR 74; *Moreira de Azevedo v Portugal* 13 EHRR 721, para 74.
5   *Darnell v UK* 18 EHRR 205.
6   1 EHRR 524, para 32.
7   2 EHRR 170.

It was held that time did not start to run at the moment of the institution of proceedings but before that from the time the applicant lodged his objection against withdrawal of the authorisation.

8.139   In criminal proceedings, which would include proceedings for contempt and committal, time runs from when the charge is brought against a defendant although, again, it can predate this if the defendant's situation has been 'substantially affected' as a result of the measure taken against him[1].

8.140   As regards the period to which Art 6 is applicable, there is no difference between criminal and civil matters and it covers the whole of the proceedings including appeals and ends at the date of the giving of judgment[2]. In civil cases, subsequent enforcement proceedings may be taken into account.

8.141   It is submitted that in family public law cases, time could begin to run, for example, when:

–   the case conference decides that care proceedings are to be taken, particularly if allegations of abuse are made;
–   when the local authority indicates that the plan for the children is that they are to be placed for adoption;

8.142   The reasonableness of the duration of the proceedings covered by Art 6(1) must be assessed in each case according to its circumstances. The Court takes the following criteria into account:

–   the complexity of the case;
–   the conduct of the applicant;
–   the conduct of the authorities[3];
–   what was at stake for the applicant[4].

The complexity of the case
8.143   In *Union Alimentaria Sanders SA v Spain*[5], the Government tried to excuse the delay claiming that there were several defendants with different claims against them, the claims based on the principle of subrogation raised delicate legal problems and the file amounted to 1,400 pages. The Court disagreed pointing out that only one of the defendants appeared before first instance court simplifying the task. However, in *H v UK*[6], the proceedings were described as 'somewhat complex' because:

–   there were several parties including the natural parents, the prospective adopters, the Official Solicitor and the local authority;
–   a considerable amount of evidence had to be collected and filed[7];
–   the assessment of the court was a most difficult task.

PART B
IMPACT OF THE CONVENTION

---

1   See *Ewing v UK* (1988) 56 DR 71, para 145. Time started to run when the applicant was arrested and informed that he was suspected of committing offences of fraud. At this stage the applicant was also deprived of his liberty for a short period and this was also taken into account in determining the commencement of the period taken into account.
2   *Trevisan v Italy* (1993) Series A, No 257–F.
3   See, inter alia, *König v FRG* 2 EHRR 170, all at para 99.
4   Ibid, para 111.
5   12 EHRR 24.
6   10 EHRR 95.
7   Ibid, para 72.

The conduct of the applicant

8.144   In civil proceedings the parties must show due diligence[1]. However, even if within domestic procedural law, the responsibility for the progress of the proceedings lies with the parties. The Court has held that:

'this does not absolve the domestic courts from ensuring compliance with the requirements of Art 6 concerning time. The applicant is required only to show diligence in carrying out the procedural steps relevant to him, to refrain from using delaying tactics and to avail himself of the scope afforded by domestic law for shortening the proceedings. He is under no duty to take action which is not apt for that purpose.'[2]

The conduct of the authorities

8.145   Although the Court will take into account the defendant's behaviour in civil litigation, it is only delays attributable to the State which may justify its finding a failure to comply with the requirements of 'reasonable time'[3]. In effect, the Convention requires the domestic courts to be proactive in managing the conduct of the caseload to ensure that the parties obtain a decision within a reasonable time. However, too much judicial activity can lead to a violation as much as too little[4].

8.146   An error by the court leading to appeal proceedings and consequent delay may, in combination with other factors, be taken into account in the determination of the reasonableness of the relevant period in spite of the argument against that it would be tantamount to acknowledging that there is a right to error-free court decisions[5].

8.147   The Convention places a duty on the contracting States to organise their legal systems so as to allow the courts to comply with the requirements of Art 6(1) including that of a trial within a reasonable time. A temporary backlog of business does not involve liability on the part of the contracting States provided that they take, with the requisite promptness, remedial action to deal with an exceptional situation. Acceptable expedients can include choosing to deal with cases in a particular order based on the degree of urgency and importance and on what is at stake for the individual concerned. However, if the backlog is prolonged and becomes a matter of structural organisation, such temporary expedients are no longer sufficient and the State will not be able to postpone further the adoption of effective measures[6]. In effect, if the backlog ceases to be temporary, a genuine willingness to tackle the problem will be insufficient if the practical arrangements are inadequate not least because the urgency of a case increases

---

1   *Pretto v Italy* 6 EHRR 182, para 33.
2   *Union Alimentaria Sanders SA v Spain* 12 EHRR 24, para 35; cf *Monnet v France* 18 EHRR 27.
3   *Buchholz v FRG* 3 EHRR 597, para 49; *H v France* 12 EHRR 74, para 55; *H v UK* 10 EHRR 95, para 71.
4   *Bock v Germany* 12 EHRR 247.
5   Ibid, para 44, although the delay attributable to this factor was not of an unreasonable length, being some 2½ months to appeal.
6   *Zimmerman and Steiner v Switzerland* 6 EHRR 17, paras 29–31; see also *Neves e Silva v Portugal* 13 EHRR 535, paras 43–46.

with time. The expedients become increasingly inadequate if the increase in workload was foreseeable[1].

8.148   However, if the State is aware of the backlog, fully conscious of its responsibilities in the matter and has made adequate efforts to expedite the conduct of business, even if the action has to take time to have effect and has not in fact assisted the applicant, the delay may not exceed a reasonable time within the meaning of Art 6(1)[2]. Similarly, if the system of courts and remedies produces a procedural maze, it is for the State alone to draw conclusions and, if need be, to simplify the system with a view to complying with the Convention[3].

What was at stake for the applicant?

8.149   In the case of *Bock v Germany*[4], the German courts took 9 years to resolve divorce proceedings when the wife of the applicant cast doubt on the applicant's mental state and his ability to conduct proceedings. In the event, there were five reports attesting to Mr Bock's soundness of mind against one report whose author had been disqualified for bias. The European Court commented on the domestic court's 'excessive amount of activity which focussed on the petitioner's mental state'. The Court took into consideration:

–   that the case concerned matters central to the enjoyment of private and family life, namely relations between spouses as well as between the parents and their children;

–   the personal situation of the applicant who, for some 9 years, suffered by reason of the doubts cast on the state of his mental health which, subsequently, proved unfounded. This represented a serious encroachment on human dignity[5].

The criteria can be cumulative and the Court may find that the length of the proceedings is reasonable taking all the factors into account notwithstanding that one of the criteria, taken on its own, would not justify the length of the proceedings[6].

8.150   The following periods have been considered unreasonable:

–   Eleven years to determine whether authorisation to practise medicine and run a clinic should have been withdrawn. Notwithstanding that some element of the delay had been attributable to the applicant himself, the time was unreasonable taking into account that the whole of the applicant's livelihood was at stake[7].

1   *Union Alimentaria Sanders SA v Spain* 12 EHRR 24, paras 38–41 where the Court acknowledged the difficulties of the Spanish Government following the restoration of democracy but pointed out that Spain undertook to reorganise its judicial system in such a way as to comply with the requirements of Art 6.
2   *Buchholz v FRG* 3 EHRR 597, paras 61–63.
3   *König v FRG* 2 EHRR 170, para 100.
4   12 EHRR 247.
5   Ibid, para 48.
6   *Buchholz v FRG* 3 EHRR 597, para 55.
7   *König v FRG* 2 EHRR 170.

–   Three-and-a-half years' delay in the hearing of an action for compensation
    for noise and air pollution. The backlog of cases became prolonged and a
    matter for structural organisation[1].

–   Seven-and-a-half years for an action against a public hospital for damages[2].

8.151   The following periods have been considered reasonable:

–   Five years to determine unfair dismissal proceedings. The State had taken
    remedial action to deal with a temporary backlog[3].

–   Contact proceedings in an 'implacable hostility' case taking periods of 6, 1½
    and 7 months respectively[4].

Case-law

8.152   The approach of the European Court of Human Rights can be seen in
the following 'family' cases:

MONNET v FRANCE[5]

8.153   The applicant's wife brought judicial separation proceedings. Five
months later, the applicant lodged a cross-petition for divorce and 19 months later
submitted grounds in support. The wife had to be directed by the court to file her
reply 11 months later. The divorce was pronounced 3½ years after the original
petition. The applicant appealed the pronouncement of divorce and later sought
an adjournment of the appeal because he had filed his submissions late. During
this time, the court had made orders in respect of custody of the children and
maintenance which the applicant appealed and, of its own motion, dismissed the
petition and cross-petition. The applicant appealed this as well. The proceedings
ended with the dismissal of his appeal some 7 years after the wife's original
petition. There had been no pronouncement of divorce or judicial separation.

8.154   The Commission decided that there had been a breach of Art 6(1).
Although the exercise of the right to a hearing was subject to the due diligence of
the applicant, that principle could not absolve the judge from seeing that the trial
progressed within a reasonable time[6] and felt that 'in proceedings concerning
civil status, the judicial authorities must show particular diligence'[7]. Accordingly,
they found that there had been a violation.

8.155   The Court found that there had been no violation although it agreed
with the principles applied by the Commission. The applicant claimed that he had
simply done no more than have recourse to the different means available to him to
secure the best protection of his interests which included a number of
interlocutory applications in respect of the issues of custody of the children and
maintenance. The Court found that the applicant or his wife had been the major
cause of the slow progress of the proceedings:

–   The majority of his submissions were filed late.

1   *Zimmerman and Steiner v Switzerland* 6 EHRR 17.
2   *H v France* 12 EHRR 74.
3   *Bucholz v FRG* 3 EHRR 597.
4   *Hendriks v The Netherlands* 5 EHRR 223 (see below).
5   18 EHRR 27.
6   Ibid, para 31; see also, inter alia, *Martens Moreira v Portugal* 13 EHRR 517, para 46.
7   Ibid, para 35 cf *Bock v Germany* 12 EHRR 247, para 49.

- He changed his lawyer on a number of occasions.

- The social enquiry report had taken a year to complete but the expert appointed had encountered all manner of difficulties in dealing with Mr and Mrs Monnet who were bitterly divided on the question of the children and the time was not unreasonable in view of the consequences of the report.

- During the ancillary relief proceedings an accountant's report had been ordered to look at the applicant's income. The report was filed one year later. However, the applicant was ordered to pay a deposit towards the cost of the report and this sum was not paid for 8 months.

The Court held, unanimously, that there had been no violation of Art 6(1).

HOKKANEN v FINLAND [1]

8.156   The applicant agreed that his daughter should be looked after by her maternal grandparents following the death of his wife. The grandparents subsequently refused to return the child to her father and disobeyed court orders in respect of access and custody. The appeal court eventually transferred custody to the grandparents and refused to order access against the wishes of the child. The proceedings which were the subject of the applicant's complaint took 18 months. The applicant submitted that the proceedings had been unduly delayed by the fact that the district court had twice suspended them for no pressing reasons, the second time for a period of 6 months. In addition, the extensive investigations requested by the district court were unnecessary as they were based exclusively on material already available to it.

8.157   The Court held that there had been no breach of the 'reasonable time requirement' for the following reasons:

- The importance of what was at stake to the applicant had to be taken into account.

- Although it is essential for custody cases to be dealt with speedily, there was no reason to criticise the district court for having suspended the proceedings twice in order to obtain expert opinions on the issue before it.

- The difficulties encountered by the social welfare authorities encountered as a result of the grandparents' refusal to allow the child to be subjected to investigation and to take part in related interviews must not be overlooked.

- Irrespective of whether there were sufficient reasons for suspending the hearing for as long as 6 months, it had to be noted that the overall length of the proceedings was approximately 18 months which, in itself, is not excessive for proceedings comprising three judicial levels.

HENDRIKS v THE NETHERLANDS [2]

8.158   The applicant had claimed contact with his son but this had been refused by the court on the ground that the mother's lack of co-operation would lead to tensions within the family which would harm the child's interests. The applicant had appealed. In all, the proceedings had taken 6 months, 1½ months and 7 months respectively.

8.159   The Commission took the view that the length of the proceedings had not violated the 'reasonable time' guarantee:

−   In order to keep parents and children concerned no longer than necessary in uncertainty, proceedings relating to a parent's access to his child should not be unduly prolonged.

−   On the other hand, the decision to be taken requires careful examination of the family situation.

−   The preparation of the report involved time-consuming contacts with the parties concerned.

−   The chances of reaching an agreed arrangement had to be ascertained[1].

H v UK[2]
8.160   The applicant complained about the length of court proceedings regarding access to her child who had been taken into the care of the local authority. The proceedings had taken 2 years 7 months and had included an appeal to the Court of Appeal and an application for leave to appeal to the House of Lords. The Court held that there had been a violation of the 'reasonable time' right under Art 6(1)[3]:

−   The Court accepted that the case was 'somewhat complex'[4].

−   Although the applicant had allowed 17 months to elapse from the High Court's order terminating her access before she referred the matter back to court, she had deferred an approach to the courts so that she could show that her health had improved and that she had a stable home.

−   As soon as her condition had improved, she had made persistent attempts to settle the matter amicably with the local authority.

−   In any event, her delay in instituting proceedings was not decisive. The Court had to assess the reasonableness of the length of the proceedings as they actually took place. The period under consideration ran from when the applicant, in fact, instituted proceedings.

−   The applicant's lawyer had delayed seeking an order that the local authority should file its evidence for 4 months. However, during that interval, he had pressed the local authority on that issue and he was entitled to rely on their assurances.

−   It was only when the local authority filed its evidence that it became clear that the child had already been placed for adoption and it was, therefore, only then that the true degree of urgency was apparent to the applicant.

−   The time taken by the prospective adopters between notifying the local authority of their intention to apply for adoption and the application was not unreasonable. An application for adoption is clearly a step of far-reaching implications and it cannot be taken hastily.

1   5 EHRR 223, paras 136 and 137.
2   10 EHRR 95.
3   Ibid, paras 70–85.
4   Ibid, para 72.

– The local authority took no steps to ensure that the summons for adoption was issued promptly by the prospective adopters but the Court accepted that it could not force their hand.

– Although the Official Solicitor had been involved from the outset in 1978 and did not complete his inquiries until May 1980, he was unable to start work until all the evidence had been filed including that of the local authority and the prospective adopters. That had not happened until January 1980. He had acted with all reasonable promptness.

– The fact that the local authority did not inform the applicant or the Official Solicitor that the child had been placed for adoption was inexplicable. Such information would have enabled the parties to regulate their conduct in the proceedings more effectively.

– The 5-month delay in the local authority filing its evidence was deplorable and seriously prejudicial to the applicant. The fact that the result might have been the same had the evidence been filed more quickly is not the point. The Court must look at the length of the proceedings and the outcome of the proceedings is not decisive in this context.

– The obligations of the local authority included that of ensuring that the proceedings were conducted with reasonable speed and in the child's interests.

– The importance of what was at stake for the applicant.

– The proceedings were decisive for the future relations between the applicant and her child.

– The proceedings had a particular quality of irreversibility involving what the High Court graphically described as the 'statutory guillotine' of adoption.

– The authorities are under a duty to act with exceptional diligence as there is always the danger that any procedural delay will result in the de facto determination of the issue submitted to the court before it has held its hearing.

In the following cases, it was found that the reasonable time guarantee had not been violated:

– *Olssen v Sweden*[1]. Thirteen months for care proceedings which involved three levels of jurisdiction.

– *Johanssen v Norway*[2]. Twenty-one months for care proceedings involving three administrative and two judicial levels.

(d) Right to an independent and impartial tribunal

'In the determination of his civil rights and obligations ... everyone is entitled to ... a hearing ... by an independent and impartial tribunal established by law'

8.161   Article 6(1) guarantees the right to a hearing before an independent and impartial tribunal established by law.

---

1   11 EHRR 259.
2   23 EHRR 33.

PART B
IMPACT OF THE CONVENTION

Tribunal

8.162   The word 'tribunal' is not necessarily to be understood as signifying a court of law of the classic kind, integrated within the standard judicial machinery of the country. It may comprise a body set up to determine a limited number of specific issues, provided that it offers appropriate guarantees[1] of independence and impartiality. According to the European Court case-law, a 'tribunal' is characterised by its judicial function, that is, determining matters within its competence on the basis of rules of law and after proceedings conducted in a prescribed manner. The fact that the tribunal may also have supervisory functions does not undermine the adjudicatory role. Such plurality of powers cannot in itself preclude an institution from being a tribunal in respect of some of them[2].

Independent tribunal

8.163   In assessing the independence of the tribunal, consideration is given to the guarantees designed to shield the members of the tribunal from outside pressures[3]. The tribunal must be independent of the executive in its functions and as an institution ensuring that justice is seen to be done[4]. In determining whether a body can be considered to be 'independent' – notably of the executive and the parties of the case – attention is given to[5]:

- the manner of appointment of its members;
- the duration of the members' term of office;
- the existence of guarantees from outside pressures;
- whether the body gives an appearance of independence.

The fact that the body has supervisory as well as adjudicatory roles is not fatal to its independence[6].

8.164   In *Van der Hurk v The Netherlands*[7], the Court stressed that 'independence' was underpinned by the 'power to give a binding decision which may not be altered by a non-judicial authority to the detriment of an individual party'.

Impartial tribunal

8.165   Impartiality denotes absence of prejudice or bias. Its existence can be tested in two ways through the subjective and the objective approach. Under the subjective approach, the personal conviction of a given judge in a given case is assessed. Personal impartiality is to be presumed until there is proof to the contrary[8]. However, it is not possible to confine the matter to the subjective approach alone. The objective approach has to be taken into account. As the Court stated in *Piersack v Belgium*[9]:

'In this area even appearance may be of a certain importance. Any judge in respect of whom there is a legitimate reason to fear a lack of impartiality must withdraw. What is

---

1   *Lithgow v UK* 8 EHRR 329, para 201.
2   *H v Belgium* 10 EHRR 339, para 50.
3   *Piersack v Belgium* 5 EHRR 169, para 27.
4   *Campbell and Fell v UK* 7 EHRR 165, para 77.
5   Ibid, para 78; *Belilos v Switzerland* 10 EHRR 466.
6   *Campbell and Fell v UK* (above), para 81.
7   18 EHRR 481, para 45.
8   Inter alia, *Piersack v Belgium* 5 EHRR 169, para 27; *Campbell and Fell v UK* 7 EHRR 165, para 84.
9   5 EHRR 169, para 30.

at stake is the confidence which the courts must inspire in the public in a democratic society.'

However, this does not mean that a judge who has been involved at a previous point in the proceedings cannot be the judge at the trial itself. The questions a judge has to answer when taking pre-trial decisions are not the same as those which are decisive for his final judgment.

8.166   The example given in *Hauschildt v Denmark*[1] was the decision of the judge whether to remand in custody or not and other pre-trial decisions of this kind:

> 'when the judge summarily assesses the available data in order to ascertain whether, prima facie the police have grounds for their suspicion; when giving judgment at the conclusion of the trial he must assess whether the evidence that has been produced and debated in court suffices for finding the accused guilty. Suspicion and formal finding of guilt are not to be treated as being the same.'

The Court held that the mere fact that a trial judge or an appeal judge has also made pre-trial decisions does not, of itself, justify fears as to his impartiality. In the light of this, there would appear to be no problem if the same judge hears the interim and the full care proceedings as long as the opportunity is given:

– to have a full hearing at the interim stage if requested;
– to challenge the findings of the interim care order at the final hearing if there is, for example, further evidence.

8.167   However, it should be noted that in the *Hauschildt* case, the judge, at the pre-trial stage, had to make decisions on the basis that he was convinced that there was 'a very high degree of clarity of guilt'. In those circumstances, the distinctions between the issues the judge had to apply at the pre-trial stage and those he had to try when giving judgment at the trial became tenuous and the impartiality of the court in question was capable of appearing open to doubt[2].

8.168   The role of the local authority case conferences may have to be reconsidered in the light of the Convention. On the whole, the functions of the case conferences are either investigative or simply a part of the management of the local authority's executive functions. However, the case conferences also determine whether a child should be placed on the Child Protection Register. It is arguable that this is a determination of parents' rights and is subject to judicial review only if the local authority has acted arbitrarily. If so, the structure and organisation of the case conference has to be such as to guarantee the parent a fair hearing by an independent and impartial tribunal. Taking into account the membership of the case conference and the fact that the chairman is also part of the social work team, at the very least, the appearance of independence and impartiality is open to doubt.

8.169   In *Fayed v UK*[3], the applicants challenged the impartiality and independence of the Department of Trade inspectors. It was held that the functions of the inspectors were essentially investigative and their report did not determine the Fayeds' civil rights and obligations. Nevertheless, even on that basis, the Court

---

1   12 EHRR 266, para 50.
2   Ibid, para 53.
3   18 EHRR 393.

underlined the fact that their investigative functions were 'attended by not inconsiderable safeguards intended to ensure a fair procedure and the reliability of findings of fact'[1].

Appeals

8.170   The obligation to be impartial does not lead to a general rule that when a superior court sets aside an administrative or judicial decision, it is bound to send the case back to a different jurisdictional authority or to a differently composed branch of that authority[2]. The procedure adopted on appeal may remedy any defect at first instance which would otherwise amount to a violation of Art 6[3].

(e) Right to a public hearing

'In the determination of his civil rights and obligations or of any criminal charge against him, everyone is entitled to a ... public hearing'
8.171   The right to a public hearing is expressly enshrined within the Convention[4]. It is linked with a number of other rights, notably:

–   the right to a hearing in one's presence;
–   the right to have oral argument.

8.172   There are exceptions to this right specifically stated within Art 6(1). The exception is that the press and public may be excluded from all or part of the trial on one of the following grounds:

–   in the interests of morals, public order or national security in a democratic society;
–   where the interests of juveniles or the protection of private life of the parties so require;
–   to the extent strictly necessary in the opinion of the court in special circumstances where publicity would prejudice the interests of justice[5].

8.173   It is likely that all family proceedings would fulfil the requirements of the exception falling either under:

–   the interests of juveniles; or
–   the protection of private life of the parties.

Nevertheless, it is open to the parties to request a public hearing if they so choose.

8.174   The position according to UK legislation is set out in *Re PB (Hearings in Open Court)*[6]. The case involved residence proceedings in respect of a 5-year-old boy. The father applied for the whole case to be heard in open court and cited the Convention in support of that application. The judge at first instance decided that the proceedings should be heard in private but gave leave to appeal on the issue.

---

1   18 EHRR 393, paras 78–79.
2   *Ringeisen v Austria (No 1)* 1 EHRR 455, para 97.
3   See *Edwards v UK* 15 EHRR 417, paras 36–38.
4   See also *Ringeisen v Austria* 1 EHRR 455, para 98.
5   All enshrined within the second paragraph of Art 6(1).
6   [1996] 2 FLR 765.

The Court of Appeal, consisting of Butler-Sloss, Gibson and Thorpe LJJ dismissed the appeal on the following grounds:

–   Rule 4.16 of the Family Proceedings Rules 1991 governs hearings under the Children Act 1989. Rule 4.16(7) states:

> 'Unless the court otherwise directs, a hearing of, or directions appointment in, proceedings to which this Part applies shall be in chambers.'

–   There is a wide divergence of practice in other countries extending from the entire proceedings in private to the entire proceedings in public with some other countries hearing evidence in private but judgment in open court or the discretion of the court to hear part or the whole case in private.

–   The present procedures in family proceedings are in accordance with the spirit of the convention[1].

–   The long-established practice has been and remains to hear the whole proceedings in private.

–   In the High Court which hears the more difficult cases and those which create public interest, judgment will often be given in public either in part or in whole where the court believes there to be a public interest in the case or to give guidance to practitioners.

–   The difference in procedure of the various courts in child cases in relation to admission of the public, of the press and the right to report proceedings have been usefully set out in a consultation paper *Review of Access to and Reporting of Family Proceedings* provided by the Lord Chancellor's Department in August 1993.

–   The courts are bound by r 4.16(7) to hear child cases generally in private. Paragraph (7) of r 4.16 allows for all or part of the case to be heard in public.

–   In the light of the long-established practice, judges will only rarely hear the evidence relating to the welfare of a child in public.

8.175   The underlying principle of Art 6(1) is the protection of litigants and the public scrutiny of the courts' proceedings. It has been stated by the European Court in *Sutter v Switzerland*[2] that:

> 'the public character of proceedings before the judicial bodies referred to in Article 6(1) protects litigants against the administration of justice in secret with no public scrutiny; it is also one of the means whereby confidence in the courts, superior and inferior, can be maintained. By rendering the administration of justice visible, publicity contributes to the achievement of the aim of Article 6(1), namely a fair trial, the guarantee of which is one of the fundamental principles of any democratic society within the meaning of the Convention.'[3]

However, the rule that there should be a public hearing is not absolute and regard is given to the diversity of the court proceedings in the Member States and the Court stated that:

PART B
IMPACT OF THE CONVENTION

---

1   At the time of judgment, the UK was a signatory to the Convention but it had not yet been incorporated into domestic law.
2   6 EHRR 272.
3   Ibid, para 26; see also *Werner v Austria, Szücs v Austria* 26 EHRR 313, para 45.

'the formal aspect of the matter is of secondary importance as compared with the purpose underlying the publicity requirement by Art 6(1). The prominent place held in a democratic society by the right to a fair trial impels the Court, for the purposes of the review which it has to undertake in this area, to examine the realities of the procedure in question.'[1]

In the case in question, the applicant had appealed against a sentence of 10 days' imprisonment for insubordination and breach of military service regulations (his hair was too long). The appeal court heard his case in private. It was held that there was no violation because the hearing before the first instance tribunal had been held in public and the appeal was only hearing points of law.

The exceptions

8.176   The following have been held to be reasonable grounds for avoiding a public hearing:

– Disciplinary proceedings concerning convicted prisoners. To require these proceedings to be held in public would for reasons of public order and security 'impose a disproportionate burden on the authorities of the State'[2].

– A hearing in respect of an invalidity pension which was stopped after the birth of the applicant's child on the basis that she was able to look after her child and home. It was held that the dispute was highly technical and better dealt with in writing than in oral argument. Its private medical nature would have deterred the applicant from seeking to have the public present. Furthermore, there were demands of efficiency and economy and systematically holding hearings could be an obstacle to particular diligence required in social security cases and could ultimately prevent compliance with the reasonable time requirement of Art 6(1)[3].

Waiving the right to a public hearing

8.177   Although the right to a public hearing is enshrined in Art 6(1), it does not prevent a person from waiving, of his own free will, either expressly or tacitly, his entitlement to a public hearing. However, a waiver must be made:

– in an unequivocal manner; and
– must not run counter to any important public interest[4].

8.178   In *Hakansson and Sturesson v Sweden*[5], the applicants were appealing against the refusal of a permit in respect of the use of land. There was provision within the legislation for a public hearing although the proceedings were held in private. There was no express waiver of the right to a public hearing by the applicants and the Court had to consider whether there was a tacit waiver. It was held that the applicants could have asked for a public hearing if they had felt that it was important to them. As they had not done so, there was a tacit waiver of this right. However, the view of the applicants is not the end of the matter. The Court also had to consider whether there were any questions of public interest which

---

1   *Sutter v Switzerland* 6 EHRR 272, para 27.
2   *Campbell and Fell v UK* 7 EHRR 165, paras 86–88.
3   *Schuler-Zgraggen v Switzerland* 16 EHRR 405, para 58.
4   *Hakansson and Sturesson v Sweden* 13 EHRR 1, para 66; see also *Schuler-Zgraggen v Switzerland* 16 EHRR 405, para 58.
5   13 EHRR 1.

could have made a public hearing necessary. In the event, the Court held that there were no such questions and, accordingly, there was no violation of Art 6(1).

8.179   In *Pauger v Austria*[1], the applicant was appealing to the constitutional court that transitional provisions under which he was granted only a reduced pension were unconstitutional. The constitutional court does not normally hear parties unless one of them expressly asks it to do so. The applicant was a professor in public law and was familiar with the court's procedure. Consequently, he could be expected to ask for a public hearing if he wished and the fact that he did not do so amounted to a tacit waiver. The court went on to decide that there was no public interest sufficient to warrant a public hearing[2].

8.180   The above cases can be contrasted with the case of *Werner v Austria* where the applicant was seeking compensation for detention following arrest. At the hearing he did not expressly ask for it to be made public. The relevant provisions did not expressly rule out holding a public hearing, but it was established in practice that public proceedings were never held. The Court held that the applicant could not be blamed for not having made an application which had no prospects of success. Consequently, there was no tacit waiver and there was a breach of Art 6(1).

8.181   In the light of the above cases, the procedure of the family courts and the practice of having private hearings will fall within the exceptions under Art 6(1). However, if it becomes an issue, the very fact that it is the general practice and the likelihood that any request for a public hearing is likely to be met with a refusal, it is arguable that a waiver would have to be clear and unequivocal and that a tacit waiver would not suffice.

(f) Right to a public pronouncement of judgment

'Judgment shall be pronounced publicly . . .'
8.182   Under Art 6(1), there is express provision for the public pronounce-ment of judgment. Although the provision appears in the second sentence of Art 6(1), it should be noted that there are no exceptions to this rule, unlike the right to a public hearing. In *Campbell and Fell v UK*[3], the UK Government had argued that the exceptions were imported into the right to a public pronounce-ment of judgment. However, the Court disagreed stating that there was no implied limitation.

8.183   Arguably, this will affect all family proceedings where the judgments are, on the whole, delivered in private at the end of private proceedings. This was recognised in *Re PB (Hearings in Open Court)*[4], where the court made a distinction between the question of a public hearing and the pronouncement of judgment:

–   The judgment is in a somewhat different position and it may be that the practice of giving judgment in private is partly due to the parties not asking for it to be heard in public and partly because in the county court, where the vast majority of children cases are heard, it is less likely that there will be issues of public interest.

– Where issues of public interest do arise it would seem entirely appropriate to give judgment in open court provided that, when desirable in the interests of the child, appropriate directions are given to avoid identification.

– If the case raises issues of principle or of law, the judgments are increasingly provided to the law reporters and are published in a large number of law reports which report family cases. But the majority of cases are of no interest to anyone beyond the parties and their families[1].

– The Court has power to give judgment publicly and in exercising its discretion it can take into account the provision of Art 6(1) that judgment should be pronounced publicly, though if so pronounced, it should be done in such a way as to avoid detriment to the child[2].

8.184	In spite of the express provision, the European Court has regard to the diversity of legal systems amongst the Member States and has taken a practical stance. In the case of *Pretto v Italy*[3], the Court highlighted the protection afforded to litigants by the public pronouncement of judgment but stated:

'Many member states have a long standing tradition of recourse to other means besides reading out aloud, for making public the decisions of all or some of their courts, for example, deposit in a registry accessible to the public ... The Court does not feel bound to adopt a literal interpretation. It considers that in each case the form of publicity to be given to the judgment under the domestic law of the Respondent State must be assessed in the light of the special features of the proceedings in question and by reference to the object and purpose of Article 6(1). In this instance, the judgment was not delivered in open court but could be obtained by anyone upon application to the court registry.'[4]

8.185	In contrast, in the case of *Werner v Austria; Szücs v Austria*[5], which concerned two applicants' claims for compensation following detention after arrest, the Court held that there had been a violation of Art 6(1). There had been no public pronouncement of judgment:

– The decisions of the domestic court were served on the applicant and not delivered in public sittings.

– A third party could be given leave to inspect the files and obtain a copy of the judgment if he shows a legitimate interest.

– Such leave is granted only at the discretion of the relevant court and so the full texts are not made available to everyone.

8.186	Furthermore, the Government had argued that there was no violation of Art 6(1) because the court had taken into account the question of continuing suspicion of the applicant's involvement in crime when determining whether compensation was payable. The Government argued that a public pronounce-

---

1	All within the judgment of Butler Schloss LJ at p 767 onwards.
2	As per Gibson LJ at p 770.
3	6 EHRR 182, paras 21 and 26–28.
4	Ibid, paras 26–27; see also *Axen v Germany* 6 EHRR 195, *Sutter v Switzerland* 6 EHRR 272, paras 33–34.
5	26 EHRR 313, paras 54–60.

ment of the judgment would breach the principle of the presumption of innocence as the judgment contained statements expressing a lingering suspicion against the applicant. The Court held that it could not see why it was necessary for the relevant courts to make such statements which would breach the principle of the presumption of innocence. On the other hand, it may be of importance to the person concerned that the fact that the suspicion concerning him had been dispelled should be brought to the knowledge of the public.

STATUTORY DUTY

8.187   This question will be considered more fully under local authorities' duties under the Children Act 1989[1], but it is worth a brief study here.

8.188   Parents have a number of routes by which they can enforce their rights under the Education Acts, for example judicial review, statutory appeals, actions in negligence against professional for which local education authorities are vicariously liable, complaints to the local ombudsman or, in respect of independent schools, on occasion, claims in contract. The question whether a claim for breach of statutory rights would lie was considered in *X v Bedford County Council*[2]. The House of Lords considered five appeals in all, two of which fell under the Children Act 1989 and the remaining three under the Education Acts[3]. It was held that:

–   where Parliament has conferred a statutory discretion on a public authority, it is for that authority, not for the courts to exercise the discretion;

–   nothing which the authority does within that discretion is actionable at common law;

–   if the decision complained of falls outside the statutory discretion, it *can* (but not necessarily will) give rise to common law liability;

–   if the factors relevant to the exercise of the discretion include matters of policy, the Court cannot adjudicate on such policy matters and therefore cannot reach the conclusion that the decision was outside the ambit of statutory discretion;

–   a common law duty of care in relation to the taking of decisions involving policy matters cannot exist;

–   a common law duty of care cannot be imposed on a statutory duty if the observance of such common law duty of care would be inconsistent with, or have a tendency to discourage, the due performance by the local authority of its statutory duties[4].

8.189   In the above case, Lord Browne-Wilkinson considered whether it was right to superimpose on the statutory machinery for the investigation and treatment of the plaintiff's special educational needs a duty of care to exercise the statutory discretion carefully. The Court held that it was not right on the grounds that:

–   the exercise of the discretion involves the close participation of the parents who are themselves under a duty to cause the child to receive 'efficient full-time education suitable to his ... ability and aptitude' under s 36 of the Education Act 1944;

---

1   See Chapter 10.
2   [1995] 2 FLR 276.
3   *E (A Minor) v Dorset County Council; Christmas v Hampshire County Council* [1995] 2 AC 685.
4   [1995] 2 FLR 276 at 290.

- the number of cases which could be brought would be very small but there would be a very real risk that many hopeless (and possibly vexatious) cases will be brought, thereby exposing the authority to great expenditure of time and money in their defence;
- in most of the above cases, there would be an alternative remedy by way of claim against the authority on the grounds of its vicarious liability for the negligent advice on the basis of which it exercises its discretion[1].

This question has been considered in the case of *Hill v Chief Constable of West Yorkshire*[2], and it was similarly held that no duty of care was owed to the plaintiff by the West Yorkshire police on grounds of public policy and that the necessity for defending proceedings, successfully or unsuccessfully, would distract the policeman from his duties.

8.190   In *Osman v UK*[3], the question of police immunity from actions in negligence was considered by the European Court of Human Rights in the light of Art 6 of the Convention. Article 6 states (to the extent that it is relevant to this question): 'In the determination of his civil rights and obligations ... everyone is entitled to a ... hearing by [a] ... tribunal ...'.

8.191   The Court held that there had been a violation of Art 6 because:

> 'the Court of Appeal proceeded on the basis that the rule provided a watertight defence to the police and that it was impossible to prise open an immunity which the police enjoy from civil suit in respect of their acts and omissions in the investigation and suppression of crime ... It must be open to a domestic court to have regard to the presence of other public interest considerations which pull in the opposite direction to the application of the rule. Failing this, there will be no distinction made between degrees of negligence or of harm suffered or any consideration of the justice of a particular case.'[4]

8.192   In the light of the *Osman* judgment, it may be that the decision *in X v Bedfordshire County Council*, excluding the courts from consideration of the effects of policy decisions, will no longer stand as being a disproportionate restriction on an applicant's right of access to a court. If an applicant is entitled to have the police account for their actions and omissions in adversarial proceedings, an applicant may be similarly entitled in respect of an education authority.

---

1   [1995] 2 FLR 290 at 313.
2   [1989] AC 53.
3   [1999] 1 FLR 193.
4   Ibid, at 232.

Chapter 9

ACCESS TO INFORMATION

9.1 The organs of the Convention have not attempted any general definition of 'personal information', nor has any detailed analysis been conducted as to what categories of 'personal information' may be protected by Art 8 or Art 10. In *Friedl v Austria*[1], although no violation of Art 8 was established, the Commission considered that the personal data which related to the establishing of the applicant's identity by the police fell within Art 8.

9.2 No general right of access to 'personal information' retained by public bodies has yet been enunciated by the organs of the Convention. The leading case in this area is that of *Gaskin v UK*[2], in which the applicant had sought unsuccessfully through the domestic courts to gain access to his personal files maintained by a local authority in relation to his childhood in care. The Court found that he had suffered a violation of his Convention rights under Art 8.

9.3 Although the freedom to receive and to impart information pursuant to Art 10 might arguably include 'personal information', the scope of the right has been interpreted relatively narrowly to date in a way which suggests that it relates only to information which others wish to pass on. Article 10 is very far from establishing a general right to information and there is some reason to believe that the organs of the Convention consider that a right of access to 'personal information', where appropriate, should be available under Art 8 rather than Art 10.

9.4 Article 13 also has a role to play in this sphere. The case of *Friedl v Austria*[3] illustrates this point. Although the Commission found no breach of the applicant's Art 8 rights in the gathering of 'personal data' about him by the police for the purpose of establishing identity, a substantial majority of the Commission considered that the absence of a domestic remedy in respect of the substance of that complaint constituted a violation of his Convention rights pursuant to Art 13[4]. The case was the subject of a 'friendly settlement' before reaching a determination on the merits by the Court.

KEY ARTICLES

9.5 Article 8 (right to respect for family and private life).

Article 10 (freedom of expression and to impart and to receive information).

---

1   (1994) Series A, No 305–B, p 20.
2   Ibid.
3   (1994) Series A, No 325–B; 21 EHRR 288.
4   See also the *Leander* case, 9 EHRR 433, paras 74 and 84, in which the Court rejected complaints of breaches of Arts 8 and 10 but only very narrowly rejected a complaint pursuant to Art 13 by a 4:5 majority.

KEY CASES

9.6   *Gaskin v UK* 12 EHRR 36.

Open Door and Dublin Well Woman v Ireland 15 EHRR 244.

RECEIVE AND IMPART INFORMATION AND IDEAS

9.7   The organs of the Convention have not developed a clear jurisprudence in relation to this aspect of Art 10; 'the right to receive and impart information and ideas'. In the *Gaskin*[1] case the Commission held that the applicant had no right as against the authority to demand personal information if the authority was unwilling to impart it. The Court confirmed the general accuracy of that assertion, without expressly endorsing the suggestion that that would invariably be the case. The court said[2]:

> 'The Commission found that Article 10 did not, in the circumstances of the case, give the applicant a right to obtain, against the will of the local authority, access to the file held by that authority. The Government agreed.
>
> The Court holds, as it did in its aforementioned Leander judgment, that "the right to freedom to receive information basically prohibits a Government from restricting a person from receiving information that others wish or may be willing to impart to him" (Series A no. 116, p. 29, para. 74). Also in the circumstances of the present case, Article 10 does not embody an obligation on the State concerned to impart the information in question to the individual.'

9.8   The emphasis the Court placed upon the words 'in the circumstances of the present case' in the final sentence of the passage cited may imply that the Court was anxious not to appear to rule out completely developments in this area. However, the Court specifically rejected Mr Gaskin's complaint of a breach of Art 10 rather than simply declining to consider that aspect of his complaint on the basis that it was unnecessary to do so in circumstances where the Court had found a violation of the terms of Art 8 sufficient to sustain the substance of his complaint.

9.9   In a very different case, *Guerra and Others v Italy*[3], the Court found a violation of Art 8 where the authorities had failed to provide local people with information about the risks to their health from a chemical factory. The Court found no violation of Art 10 in the same circumstances. The freedom to receive information basically prohibited a government from restricting a person from receiving information that others wished or might be willing to impart to him – that freedom could not be construed as imposing on the State, on the basis of the facts of the case, positive obligations to collect and disseminate information to local people of its own motion.

9.10   These two cases suggest that the Court will prefer to deal with issues relating to access to information, where possible, by means of Art 8 rather than Art 10.

---

1   12 EHRR 36.
2   Ibid, paras 51 and 52.
3   Application No 1998116/1996/735/932 (19 February 1998).

9.11   The important case of *Open Door and Dublin Well Woman v Ireland*[1] is an example of a violation of Art 10 where a court injunction prevented, in perpetuity, the dissemination of information and non-directive counselling to pregnant women in Ireland by the applicants. The Court determined that the real question in issue was 'whether the restrictions on the freedom to impart and receive information contained in the relevant part of the injunction are necessary in a democratic society for the legitimate aim of the protection of morals'. The Court stated that:

> 'The Court cannot agree that the State's discretion in the field of the protection of morals is unfettered and unreviewable ... However this power of appreciation is not unlimited. It is for the Court, in this field also, to supervise whether a restriction is compatible with the Convention.'[2]

The Court continued:

> 'Accordingly, the Court must examine the question of "necessity" in the light of the principles developed in its case-law (see, inter alia, the *Observer and Guardian v the United Kingdom* judgment of 26 November 1991, Series A no. 216, pp. 29–30, para. 59). It must determine whether there existed a pressing social need for the measures in question and, in particular, whether the restriction complained of was "proportionate to the legitimate aim pursued".'[3]

The Court ultimately found that the ban was disproportionate to the legitimate ends pursued, because:

> 'The Court is first struck by the absolute nature of the Supreme Court injunction which imposed a "perpetual" restraint on the provision of information to pregnant women concerning abortion facilities abroad, regardless of age or state of health or their reasons for seeking counselling on the termination of pregnancy.'[4]

9.12   The Court also took note of the fact that the corporate applicants gave advice and counselling which 'neither encouraged nor advocated abortion' but merely explained the available options. Equally relevant was the fact that the same information was available both from other sources in Ireland and by telephone from elsewhere, but in a manner not supervised by qualified personnel and thus less protective of women's health.

9.13   The Court declined to consider the complaints of violations of Art 8 rights which arose on the same facts declaring that in the light of the finding in relation to Art 10 it was unnecessary to do so. Furthermore, because the Art 8 complaints had not all been raised before the Commission and had thus not been declared admissible there was an issue as to whether the Court had jurisdiction to entertain them in any event.

9.14   Article 10 has not as yet provided the means of access to information where the public body controlling it was unwilling to allow an applicant to have access to it. Nor has Art 10 as yet been used by Court or the Commission to impugn the denial of access to 'private information'. However, the decision in the *Open Door* case can perhaps be seen as evidence of the Court taking its first cautious and

---

1   15 EHRR 244.
2   Ibid, para 68.
3   Ibid, para 72.
4   Ibid, para 73.

tentative steps towards deriving a general right of access to information from Art 10.

ARTICLE 8

9.15   Article 8 states:

'Everyone has the right to respect for his family and private life, his home and his correspondence.

There shall be no interferences by a public authority with the exercise of this right except such as is in accordance with the law and is necessary in a democratic society in the interests of national security, public safety or the economic well-being of the country, for the prevention of disorder or crime, for the protection of health or morals, or for the protection of the rights and freedoms of others.'

GASKIN v UK

9.16   In the case of *Gaskin v UK*[1], the Court found that in certain circumstances the State had an obligation to act positively in order to afford appropriate respect for 'family and private life' by requiring a local authority to allow an individual to have access to personal information stored by the authority about his childhood in its care.

9.17   The relevant proceedings in the domestic courts began as something of a 'fishing expedition'. In 1979 the applicant, wishing to bring proceedings against the local authority for damages for negligence, made an application under s 31 of the Administration of Justice Act 1970 for discovery of the local authority's case records made during his period in care. Section 31 of the 1970 Act provides, inter alia, that the High Court shall have power to order such disclosure to a person who is likely to be a party to legal proceedings for personal injuries.

9.18   The application was heard by the High Court on 22 February 1980. The local authority objected to the grant of discovery of the records on the ground that disclosure and production would be contrary to the public interest. The records contained contributions from medical practitioners, school teachers, police and probation officers, social workers, health visitors, foster-parents and residential school staff. The authority maintained that the contributions were treated in strict confidence and that such was necessary to ensure that the authority obtained records which were as full and frank as possible. It was suggested that if discovery were to be ordered that the public interest in the proper conduct of the care system would be jeopardised because future contributors would be reluctant to be completely frank.

9.19   The Court noted that the judge did not read the records in question, but balanced the public interest in maintaining an efficient child-care system with the applicant's private interest in receiving access to his case records for the purpose of the proposed litigation. Referring to *Re D (Infants)*[2], in which Denning MR held

1   12 EHRR 36 at paras 36–37.
2   [1970] 1 WLR 599.

that case records compiled pursuant to reg 10 of the Boarding-Out of Children Regulations 1955[1], were regarded as private and confidential, he concluded:

> 'I am left in no doubt that it is necessary for the proper functioning of the child care service that the confidentiality of the relevant documents should be preserved. This is a very important service to which the interests – also very important – of the individual must, in my judgment, bow. I have no doubt that the public interest will be better served by refusing discovery and this I do.'

9.20 On appeal the decision of the High Court was affirmed by the Court of Appeal. The Court of Appeal took the view that the High Court had correctly judged the competing interests. The court also indicated that there might be cases where it was appropriate for the court to examine the documents concerned, where it could not determine otherwise how to decide the issue and there were 'grave doubts' on which side of the balance the competing public/private interests lay. The Court of Appeal was confident, however, that such 'grave doubts' did not exist in the *Gaskin* case. Leave to appeal to the House of Lords was refused.

9.21 Eventually, of the applicant's entire case record, consisting of some 352 documents contributed by 46 persons, copies of 65 of them, supplied by 19 persons, were sent to the applicant's solicitors on 23 May 1986. These were documents whose authors had consented to disclosure to the applicant. Those contributors who refused to waive confidentiality, although not asked to give reasons, stated, inter alia, that third-party interests could be harmed; that the contribution would be of no value if taken out of context; that professional confidence was involved; that it was not the practice to disclose reports to clients; and that too great a period of time had elapsed for a letter or report still to be in the contributor's recollection. Nonetheless, Mr Gaskin complained to the European Court that he had been denied access to the substantial balance of his personal record.

9.22 The Court stated[2]:

> 'In the opinion of the Commission "the file provided a substitute record for the memories and experience of the parents of the child who is not in care". It no doubt contained information concerning highly personal aspects of the applicant's childhood, development and history and thus could constitute his principal source of information about his past and formative years. Consequently lack of access thereto did raise issues under Article 8.
>
> The Court agrees with the Commission. The records contained in the file undoubtedly do relate to Mr. Gaskin's "private and family life" in such a way that the question of his access thereto falls within the ambit of Article 8.'

9.23 However, the impact of this judgment was reduced by the concluding words of the paragraph:

> 'This finding is reached without expressing any opinion on whether general rights of access to personal data and information may be derived from Article 8(1) of the Convention. The Court is not called upon to decide in abstracto on questions of general principle in this field but rather has to deal with the concrete case of Mr. Gaskin's application.'

---

1   SI 1955/1377.
2   12 EHRR 36 at paras 36–37.

9.24   The Government had sought to distinguish the *Leander* case in submissions to the Court because although in that case no violation of Art 8 was established, nevertheless Sweden was found to have interfered with Art 8 rights 'by compiling, storing, using and disclosing private information about the applicant in that case'. The Government argued that the circumstances in the *Gaskin* case were very different as the Court acknowledged in the following passage of the judgment:

> 'Indeed, by refusing him complete access to his case records, the United Kingdom cannot be said to have "interfered" with Mr Gaskin's private or family life. As regards such refusal, "the substance of [the applicant's] complaint is not that the State has acted but that it has failed to act" (see the Airey judgment of 9 October 1979, Series A no. 32, p. 17, para. 32).'

The Court then reiterated the policy of the Court in determining in what circumstances it would be right to impose such positive duties upon the State. The Court said it sought to strike a fair balance between the general interests of the community and the interests of the individual bearing in mind, to some extent, the aims set out in the second paragraph of Art 8, although they were framed in terms of validating 'interferences' rather than necessarily indicating the proper context within which positive obligations should be imposed upon the State.

9.25   In this passage, the Court expressed the crucial factors supporting the judgment that there had been a violation of Mr Gaskin's Art 8 Convention rights [1];

> 'In the Court's opinion, persons in the situation of the applicant have a vital interest, protected by the Convention, in receiving the information necessary to know and to understand their childhood and early development. On the other hand, it must be borne in mind that confidentiality of public records is of importance for receiving objective and reliable information, and that such confidentiality can also be necessary for the protection of third persons. Under the latter aspect, a system like the British one, which makes access to records dependent on the consent of the contributor, can in principle be considered to be compatible with the obligations under Article 8, taking into account the State's margin of appreciation. The Court considers, however, that under such a system the interests of the individual seeking access to records relating to his private and family life must be secured when a contributor to the records either is not available or improperly refuses consent. Such a system is only in conformity with the principle of proportionality if it provides that an independent authority finally decides whether access has to be granted in cases where a contributor fails to answer or withholds consent. No such procedure was available to the applicant in the present case.
>
> Accordingly, the procedures followed failed to secure respect for Mr. Gaskin's private and family life as required by Article 8 of the Convention. There has therefore been a breach of that provision.'

Domestic law

9.26   Domestic law in relation to access to personal files has changed since the *Gaskin* case was decided by the European Court. Presently, the domestic law in relation to access to 'personal files' is set out in the Access to Personal Files Act 1987 and regulations made thereunder. By s 1(1) of the Act it is provided that:

---

1   12 EHRR 36 at para 41.

'Subject to the provisions of this Act and regulations under section 3, any authority keeping records containing personal information which is accessible personal information for the purposes of this Act shall have such obligations as regards access to, and the accuracy of, that information as are imposed by the regulations.'

The obligations of 'authority' are expressly limited by the ambit of s 21 of the Data Protection Act 1984 to the extent that they would be inconsistent with its terms. Otherwise, the principal limitations upon the right of access to 'personal files' is as set out in the regulations: Access to Personal Files (Social Services) Regulations 1989[1]; Access to Personal Files (Housing) Regulations 1989[2].

9.27   'Personal files' and 'accessible personal files' are defined in s 2 of the Act:

'2(2) "Personal information" means information which relates to a living individual who can be identified from that information (or from that and other information in the possession of the authority keeping the record) including any expression of opinion about the individual but not any indication of the intentions of the authority with respect to that individual.

(3) Subject to subsection (4) below, information is "accessible personal information" for the purposes of this Act if it is held in a record kept by an authority specified in the Table in Schedule 1 to this Act or, as respects Scotland, Schedule 2 to this Act and is information of a description specified in that Table in relation to that authority; and any obligation to give access to information is an obligation to give access to the individual who is the subject of it or is, under that Schedule, to be treated as such.'

Schedule 1 to the Act contains the Schedule referred to in the subs 2(3) referred to above. There are two categories of 'authority' specified, local social services authorities and local Housing Act authorities, with respect to personal information held for any purpose of the authority's respective social services or Housing Act functions.

9.28   The Access to Personal Files (Social Services) Regulations 1989[3], create a general right of access to 'accessible personal files,' by reg 2, subject to restrictions set out in regs 3, 4, 8 and 9.

9.29   Regulation 3 simply requires that an applicant should make a request for information in writing to the relevant authority and that he or she should pay a small fee (less than £10).

9.30   Regulation 4 absolves the authority from any obligation to provide such information unless it is provided with sufficient information to satisfy itself of the identity of the applicant and to locate the information sought.

9.31   Regulation 5 provides as follows:

'**Another individual involved**

If any accessible personal information in respect of which a local social services authority have received a request under regulation 3 contains information relating to another individual who can be identified from that information (other than an individual to whom regulation 8(5)(b) or regulation 9(3)(a) applies), the local social services authority, within 14 days of receiving the request under regulation 3, or, if later, of receiving the information referred to in regulation 4, shall in writing inform

---

1   SI 1989/206.
2   SI 1989/503.
3   SI 1989/206.

that other individual of the request and that the accessible personal information contains information relating to him and ask that other individual whether he consents to the information relating to him being disclosed to the person making the request.'

9.32   Regulation 9 sets out circumstances that either absolve the authority of the duty to disclose information or limit its responsibility to do so. The obligation of the authority to disclose will be merely limited where the objects of the exceptions can be met by editing the documents concerned.

9.33   The limitations set out in reg 9, are as follows:

Regulation 9(2) – where serious harm to the physical or mental health of the applicant or any other person would be caused.

Regulation 9(3) – where the identity of another individual (who has not consented to the disclosure of the information) (not being an employee of the authority) would be likely to be disclosed to or deduced by the applicant.

Regulation 9(4) – where the information is held by the authority for the purpose of the apprehension and detection of offenders or the prevention of crime and disclosure would be likely to prejudice either or both.

Regulation 9(5) – where the information consists of a report given or to be given to the court by the local social services authority in the course of any proceedings to which the Magistrates' Courts (Children and Young Persons) Rules 1988[1] apply where, in accordance with the provision of those Rules, the information may be withheld by the court in whole or in part from the individual who is the subject of the information.

Regulation 9(7) – where the information sought is such that legal professional privilege could be claimed in respect of it in legal proceedings.

Regulation 9(6) – where the information sought consists of information the disclosure of which is prohibited or restricted by:

(a) s 50 or s 51 of the Adoption Act 1976;
(b) reg 11 of the Education (Special Educational Needs) Regulations 1983, SI 1983/29;
(c) reg 6 or reg 14 of the Adoption Agencies Regulations 1983, SI 1983/1964; rr 9, 21, 22 or 53 of the Adoption Rules 1984, SI 1984/265, or rr 9, 21, 22 or 32 of the Magistrates' Courts (Adoption) Rules 1984, SI 1984/611.

9.34   Finally, reg 11 provides for the means to review the decisions of local authorities in discharging their responsibilities created by the Act and the regulations made thereunder. A disappointed applicant may, by notice in writing, require the decision to limit or refuse access be reviewed by a committee of three members of that authority appointed for that purpose. In the event that an applicant remains dissatisfied with the outcome of any such review, he may apply for judicial review.

Summary of the effect of the *Gaskin* case

9.35   The Court was plainly not prepared to make any general pronounce-ment of universal entitlement to access to archived personal records held by the

---

1   SI 1988/913.

State and public bodies. However, it is possible to indicate the major criteria that any court seized of such an issue in future is likely to consider as important qualifications for such a complaint:

–   That the complaint arises in relation to records or information of relevance to the 'private and family life' of the applicant (it will arguably be extended to 'home and correspondence', as well).

–   Where the importance of the access to the information for the individual can properly be described as 'vital', on the basis that fundamental and essential aspects of his or her private life or family life would be illuminated by such disclosure.

–   Where there are no equally pressing considerations of public interest arguing against disclosure.

–   Where there are no equally pressing considerations involving another individual's interests arguing against disclosure. (This is not exemplified by the case-law but arises, arguably, on the basis of the Court's willingness to have some regard to aims set out in the second limb of Art 8 when considering the imposition of positive obligations.)

–   Where there are no equally pressing considerations involving the applicant's own interest, particularly if still a minor, arguing against disclosure. (Once again, this is not exemplified by the case-law but arises, arguably, on the basis of the Court's willingness to have some regard to aims set out in the second limb of Art 8 when considering the imposition of positive obligations.)

9.36   However, in a system such as that in place in the UK, dependent upon the consent of the contributor before disclosure will be authorised, the Court has said that it is essential that an applicant should have access to an 'independent authority' as an arbiter in the event of dispute, otherwise the system will breach the principle of proportionality and not be compliant with the obligations of the State under the Convention. In England, the ultimate remedy available to a dissatisfied applicant is to seek a judicial review of the local authority's decision.

9.37   Examples of the individual's interest being regarded as sufficiently serious to satisfy the requirements for imposition of a positive obligation upon the State are the following.

Gaskin v UK[1]:
See above.

X & Y v The Netherlands[2]
A case involving serious infringement of physical and moral integrity, a rape.

B v France[3]
A transsexual case in which the refusal of the French authorities to recognise Miss B's changed sexual identity by, for example, permitting amendment to her birth certificate, gave rise to acute interference with her private life on a daily basis. The

---

1   12 EHRR 36.
2   8 EHRR 235.
3   16 EHRR 1.

Rees[1] and *Cossey*[2] cases were distinguished in that in England a birth certificate is regarded as an historical record of accepted fact at the time of the birth and thereafter immutable while in France it is possible to amend a birth certificate at any time during life without any need to amend primary legislation.

Guerra and Others v Italy[3]

In which the applicants, all residents of an area close to a chemical factory, had waited, right up until production of fertilisers had ceased in 1994, for essential information that would have enabled them to assess risks they and their families might run if they continued to live at Manfredonia, a town particularly exposed to danger in event of an accident at a factory. The Ministry for the Environment and Ministry of Health had jointly adopted conclusions of a safety report submitted by the factory; they had provided the prefect with instructions as to an emergency plan, which he had drawn up in 1992, together with the measures required for informing the local population. Three years later the information had still not been disseminated to the local population or to their district council. The risk of severe environmental pollution might affect individuals' well-being and prevent them from enjoying their homes in such a way as to affect their private and family life.

9.38   Examples of where the interferences with the individual's rights were not regarded as sufficiently serious as to found a violation on the basis of the failure of a State to recognise a positive obligation to include the following:

Costello-Roberts v UK[4]

A corporal punishment case. The punishment, one blow with a rubber gym shoe over the boy's trousers, not causing any injury, was insufficiently severe (to found a violation of Art 8). In any event, his placement in a boarding preparatory school in England restricted the ambit of his private life.

The Rees[5] *and Cossey*[6] *cases*

Transsexual cases. Expressly distinguished in *B v France*[7] on the basis of the different characteristics of birth certificates in the two jurisdictions. The rights claimed by the applicants were too 'controversial' (ie there was insufficient consensus as to whether to afford transsexuals such rights among the contracting States).

9.39   Where important national interests are claimed to conflict with the rights of the individual, the Court may consider that to be a significant contra-indication to the imposition of a positive duty upon the State. Examples of such considerations include the following.

---

1   9 EHRR 56.
2   13 EHRR 622.
3   Application No 116/1996/735/932 (19 February 1998).
4   19 EHRR 112.
5   See above.
6   See above.
7   See above.

The Leander case[1]
Where legitimate public interest in matters of national security and the security of important military installations were said, potentially, to be at stake.

Abdulaziz and Others v UK[2]
Where vital State interests in immigration control were concerned.

POSSIBLE AREAS OF IMPACT UPON DOMESTIC LAW AND PRACTICE

9.40   One of the principal problems posed by the domestic system of disclosure created by the Access to Personal Files (Social Services) Regulations 1989[3] is that criteria for disclosure do not reveal, in any particular case, without recourse to the personal files themselves, whether they should be disclosed in whole or in part, edited or otherwise. Thus an applicant initially is dependent upon the officers of the respondent authority discharging their duties under the legislation properly without any means to determine for him or herself whether that has been done in fact. Where significant numbers of applicants are likely to be people who are distrustful and antagonistic towards such authorities and where the review system lacks true independence, the Court may regard it as in breach of the principal of proportionality, unduly restrictive and lacking in independent control. However, the final remedy available to a disappointed applicant is to apply for judicial review.

Personal history and background

The 'right' of a child, permanently placed outside the natural family, to information about his or her personal history and background together with that of the natural family
9.41   Although there are superficial similarities between a case in this category and the factual context which was considered in the *Gaskin* case there are also potentially significant differences:

– the age of the applicant and welfare considerations if he or she is still a minor;
– the influence of notions of the 'permanency' of placement, particularly if the placement is by means of adoption, on the view of the court;
– the interests of the natural family, particularly in the case of an adoptive placement.

There are special rules in domestic law as to the disclosure of the birth records of adopted children to such a child on his or her own application after attaining the age of 18 (Adoption Act 1976, s 51). There are also special provisions under s 51A of that Act for disclosure to adopted children over the age of 18 of the names and addresses of such members of their natural family who may be willing to allow their names to remain on the contact register. These rules provide for the disclosure of fundamental information (birth records) if available, and somewhat

---

1   (1987) Series A, No 116.
2   (1985) Series A, No 94.
3   SI 1989/206.

more information as to the identity of members of the natural family where they are willing, but not more than that. Alternatively, or additionally, an application could be made to the Court which made the adoption order pursuant to r 53(4) of the Adoption Rules 1984[1] for the leave of the court to inspect or copy the court's files.

9.42   In the case of an adoptive placement, the Access to Personal Files (Social Services) Regulations 1989[2] would have no relevance because of the exclusions pursuant to reg 9(6) but would apply in the case of other forms of placement.

9.43   The circumstances in which such applications may be made are likely to vary so widely that it is not possible to indicate any but the most general differences incorporation may produce.

Local authority records

The 'right' of the child to have access to confidential social services records about a period spent in the care of a local authority
9.44   This is in essence the factual context of which the Court was seized in the *Gaskin* case. Such an issue might arise where the applicant was significantly younger than Gaskin, for example, while such an applicant was still a minor. The underlying issues which inform the domestic regulations all represent 'aims' which would be regarded as legitimate grounds for restriction under the Convention.

Knowledge of child's background

The 'right' of prospective adopters/foster-carers to information on the child's history and family background
9.45   Under Art 8, the organs of the Convention would be likely to determine that family life was not 'in existence'. The case-law of the organs of the Convention has shown no willingness on part of the Court or of the Commission to anticipate the development of family life and to hold that respect must be shown for family life prospectively. However, 'private life' under Art 8 includes the right to establish and develop relationships with other human beings. In *Niemietz v Germany*[3], the Court said:

> '. . . it would be too restrictive to limit the notion (of private life) to an "inner circle" in which the individual may live his own personal life as he chooses and to exclude therefrom entirely the outside world not encompassed within that circle. Respect for private life must also comprise to a certain degree the right to establish and develop relationships with other human beings.'[4]

9.46   It is arguable, therefore, that personal information that may be necessary to assist prospective adopters and foster-carers to understand children entrusted to their care and to avoid dangers which they would otherwise be unaware of should be disclosed to them pursuant to the terms of Art 8. Domestic law at

---

1   SI 1984/265.
2   SI 1989/206.
3   16 EHRR 97.
4   Ibid, para 29.

present requires that they should trust to the good sense of the local authority or adoption agency to impart all relevant information to them or otherwise to attempt to obtain information by means of the regulations, a course which few, if any, are likely to feel able to take.

Social services records

The 'right' of a natural parent to disclosure of social services records in relation to his or her child

9.47 On the assumption that it is current information about the child which is likely to be sought by the parent rather than merely historical records relating to the original removal of the child from the birth family, it is questionable to what extent 'family life', in the absence of continuing contact, would be said to subsist, if at all. Similarly, in such circumstances, it is questionable to what extent respect for the 'private life' of the applicant will be considered relevant. Such an application, one must assume, would be most likely following a decision of a court to deny the applicant contact, even indirect contact, with his or her child. The more profitable Convention point in such circumstances may well lie in a challenge to that decision. An application to the local authority for access to personal information, even were the court to decide that the applicant could bring him or herself within the sphere of Art 8 rights, would be likely to be regarded as an attempt to circumvent judicial protection of the rights of the child and the placement family imposed by restrictions upon contact and the nature of the primary orders under which the placement had been effected. In short, in those cases where the parent has reason to apply, the courts are likely to have the greatest sympathy with the need to absolve the authority from responsibility for disclosure of personal files.

9.48 In the case of a child placed by way of adoption, an application could be made to the court which made the adoption order pursuant to r 53(4) of the Adoption Rules 1984[1] for the leave of the court to inspect or copy the court's files. The Rules do not indicate the basis upon which the discretion to give leave should be exercised and neither is there any reported authority on the point. However, there is authority in relation to applications made pursuant to s 50(5) of the Adoption Act 1976 for disclosure of information on the Adopted Children Register. In the case of an application by a parent, Sir Stephen Brown P said, obiter, in relation to such an application that for such an application to succeed the applicant would have to show an exceptional need to know the information[2]. In the case of *Re H (Adoption: Disclosure of Information)*[3] an application by a half-sibling succeeded on one of the grounds that information about her medical condition which would be of benefit to her adopted half-sibling might then be passed on.

---

1   SI 1984/265.
2   *D v Registrar General* [1997] 1 FLR 715.
3   [1995] 1 FLR 236.

Disclosure of records and public interest immunity

The 'right' of the natural parents to protection from disclosure of information; public interest immunity and self-incrimination

9.49   In general, the primary protection for a natural parent from disclosure of information from social services files concerning him or her is in present domestic law that afforded by the Access to Personal Files (Social Services) Regulations 1989[1]. Regulation 9(3) applies, where a person identified in the files or identifiable, should they be disclosed, has been given notice of the application by the authority and has not consented to disclosure the authority is relieved of the obligation to disclose copies of the files unless they can be suitably edited to prevent such identification.

9.50   Article 8(2) of the Convention identifies as some of the legitimate aims of interference with the Art 8 rights and freedoms, 'the protection of health or morals, or for the protection of the rights and freedoms of others'. It is by reason of those words that the protection of all third party rights other than those of the applicant are brought into the balancing exercise when a claimed breach of Art 8 rights is being considered by the Court. Therefore, potentially, the Convention itself allows the same kind of protection of third party rights, including those of natural parents, as presently are set out in domestic law. It is not yet clear whether the emphasis will be different following incorporation.

SELF-INCRIMINATION

Domestic law

9.51   Section 98 of the Children Act 1989 provides as follows:

'(1) In any proceedings in which a court is hearing an application for an order under Part IV or V, no person shall be excused from –

(a)   giving evidence on any matter; or
(b)   answering any question put to him in the course of his giving evidence, on the ground that doing so might incriminate him or his spouse of an offence.

(2) A statement or admission made in such proceedings shall not be admissible in evidence against the person making it or his spouse in proceedings for an offence other than perjury.'

The phrase 'statement or admission' includes written statements of evidence filed in the proceedings[2] and any statement or admission made to the guardian ad litem in the course of his or her investigation[3].

9.52   Section 98(2) of the Children Act 1989 protects the author of a statement or admission made in care proceedings from that statement being 'admissible in evidence' against him or his spouse in criminal proceedings. It should be noted that nothing in s 98 prevents the disclosure of such material to the police or other agencies.

---

1   SI 1989/206.
2   Children Act 1989, s 98(2).
3   *Oxfordshire County Council v P* [1995] 1 FLR 552.

9.53   The factors identified as significant in determining whether to order disclosure have included the following[1]:

– the welfare and the interest of the child concerned and of other children generally;
– the public interest in the administration of justice and the prosecution of serious crime;
– the seriousness of the offence(s) alleged and the probative value of the evidence concerned;
– the importance of encouraging frankness in children cases and the relevance of confidentiality in achieving that end;
– the importance of encouraging inter-agency co-operation;
– 'fairness' to the person incriminated by the material and/or others who would be affected by disclosure of it;
– previous disclosure in the same case.

9.54   The privilege against self-incrimination in care proceedings has recently been considered by the House of Lords in the case of *Re L (Police Investigation: Privilege)*[2] in which it was determined that where a party has voluntarily initiated a process which led to the preparation and filing of an expert report she can be said to have waived the right to privilege against self-incrimination and the report may quite properly be ordered subsequently to be disclosed to the police. The case illustrates how easily the privilege against self-incrimination may be lost, unknowingly and without any actual intention so to do by a party claiming such privilege in care proceedings. It further illustrates the restriction upon litigation privilege in care proceedings where the same can be said to be inconsistent with the principle of the paramountcy of the welfare of the child and thus to have no place. However, in a strong dissenting judgment Lord Nicholls maintained that legal professional privilege was an established ingredient of the right of a party to a fair hearing and a right to present his or her case and to call evidence. There was no reason why parties to family proceedings should not be as much entitled to a fair hearing with the same safeguards as were accorded to parties to other court proceedings. Indeed, it was doubtful whether a parent who was denied the right to obtain legal advice in confidence was accorded the fair hearing to which he was entitled under Art 6(1) read in conjunction with Art 8 of the European Convention for the Protection of Human Rights and Fundamental Freedoms.

9.55   The present domestic system allows material, including statements and admissions made in written statements which tend to incriminate the author of them, to be disclosed to third parties, including the police, for purposes which may include the preparation of a prosecution, with the leave of the court. The safeguard for the author of such a statement is that such material will not be admissible in criminal proceedings involving him or his wife save in respect of an offence of perjury.

---

1   *Re EC (Disclosure of Material)* [1996] 2 FLR 725 concerning disclosure by a local authority to the police and *Re V (Sexual Abuse: Disclosure); Re L (Sexual Abuse: Disclosure)* [1999] 1 FLR 267 CA, concerning disclosure of such material by a local authority to other organisations for the protection of children.
2   [1996] 1 FLR 731.

Impact of incorporation

9.56   There is a potential inconsistency between domestic law in this regard and the terms of Art 6(1) and the case-law of the organs of the Convention.

9.57   In the case of *Saunders v UK*[1], which concerned the use to which statements made by the accused to DTI inspectors (whose enquiries he was obliged to answer) were subsequently put in the course of his criminal trial. The Court said:

> 'Although not specifically mentioned in Art 6 of the Convention, the right to silence and the right not to incriminate oneself are generally recognized international standards, which lie at the heart of the notion of a fair procedure under Art 6.'

The Court specifically rejected the submission that only statements which are directly self-incriminating could fall within the privilege against self-incrimination. The Court determined that whether a particular applicant can claim to have been subject to compulsion to incriminate himself to such an extent so as to render the proceedings unfair and a violation of Art 6 will depend upon an assessment of the circumstances of each case as a whole[2].

Public interest immunity

9.58   An issue in relation to Convention rights could arise in connection with public interest immunity. For example, where a party in care proceedings, as one of several persons under suspicion of child abuse within those proceedings, had a direct interest in obtaining disclosure of material held by the police which tended to incriminate one of the others under suspicion in the care proceedings in relation to the alleged abuse. Such considerations are already factors to which it is established that the domestic courts should have regard and the potential for incompatibility in this instance is slight.

---

1   23 EHRR 313, para 68.
2   See also *Fayed v UK* 18 EHRR 393 and Chapter 8.

Chapter 10

LOCAL AUTHORITY DUTIES

10.1   The majority of family law cases concerning Convention rights have involved public law. The removal of children from their families by local authorities together with consequential decisions in relation to their placement and their contact with their natural families have provided the basis of numerous complaints. Such complaints have usually been prompted by the belief that the local authority has acted prematurely or unreasonably having regard to the sensitivity and complexity of the issues involved. Many of the successful complaints have concentrated upon a lack of procedural fairness.

10.2   However, it is clear that the Convention, in addition to providing a means of restraint upon unnecessarily harsh and insensitive behaviour by the State and local authorities in the field of family law, may also require the State and local authorities to act positively to support Convention rights. It is with the positive duties of local authorities and their present immunity from suit that this chapter is concerned.

10.3   The duty of local authorities and the State to act so as to promote or support Convention rights is a developing aspect of the jurisprudence of the European Court. The case-law of the Commission and the Court has dealt with subject areas as they have arisen, tending to focus narrowly on the facts in issue and has not therefore created a sharply defined and comprehensive line of jurisprudence. The boundaries to potential developments in this field are far from clear but further development is inevitable and likely to be significant.

THE DUTY TO ACT

Key Articles

10.4   Article 3, protection from torture and inhuman or degrading treatment; Article 6 (1), the right to a fair trial; and
Article 8, the protection of private and family life, home and correspondence.

Article 3

Key cases: Article 3
10.5   *A v UK* [1998] 2 FLR 959.
Costello Roberts v UK 19 EHRR 112.
Y v UK 17 EHRR 233.
Warwick v UK Application No 9471/81 (Rep), (18 July 1986) 60 DR 5, paras 86 and 87.
Tyrer v UK 2 EHRR 1.

10.6   Article 3 has been the principal means of raising complaints of breaches of Convention rights arising from corporal punishment both at home and in school. The contribution of the UK to this line of authority has been substantial. The most significant case in establishing the responsibilities of the State 'to take measures designed to ensure that individuals within their jurisdiction are not subjected to torture or inhuman or degrading treatment or punishment, including such ill-treatment administered by private individuals' is *A v UK* (above). The judgment of the Court continued:

> 'Children and other vulnerable individuals, in particular, are entitled to State protection, in the form of effective deterrence, against such serious breaches of personal integrity (see, *mutatis mutandis*, the *X & Y v. the Netherlands* judgement of 26 March 1985, series A no. 91, pp. 11–13, 21–27; the *Stubbings and others v the U.K.* judgment of 22 October 1996, Reports 1996-IV, p. 1505, 62–64; and also the United Nations Convention on the Rights of the Child, Articles 19 and 37).'

The facts of the case were as follows. A was aged 9 when he was beaten repeatedly with a garden cane with considerable force by his step-father. He suffered significant bruising as a result. His step-father was subsequently charged with assault occasioning actual bodily harm. At his trial it was not disputed that he had caned A on a number of occasions, but in his defence it was argued that such punishment was reasonable in the light of A's difficult and disobedient behaviour. The jury acquitted A's step-father of assault. There was some history of similar behaviour by the step-father towards A. Earlier, in May 1990, A and his brother had been placed on the local child protection register because of 'known physical abuse'. A's step-father, who was at that time A's mother's cohabitant, who she subsequently married, was given a police caution after he admitted hitting A with a cane. Both boys' names were removed from the child protection register in November 1991 before the incident which gave rise to this case.

10.7   The reference made by the Court to the case of *X and Y v The Netherlands*[1] together with the Court's express reference to 'effective deterrence' makes it clear that the primary reason for the decision of the court was that despite the fact that A had suffered ill-treatment of a sufficient level of severity so that it fell within the scope of the prohibition imposed by Art 3, A's step-father had been acquitted by the verdict of the jury and the (criminal) law did not provide sufficient protection to A (in the form of deterrence) against such treatment. The judgment was reinforced by the UK Government's acceptance that the law (s 47 of the Offences Against the Person Act 1861) failed to provide sufficient protection to children and should be amended.

10.8   The focus upon the inadequacy of the criminal law arose from the facts of the case. The Government originally submitted before the Commission that the fact that the domestic criminal law could, in theory, have protected the child by resulting in the conviction and punishment of the step-father, should, it was argued, absolve the State of any further responsibility. The Commission did not accept such a submission and held that Art 3, when read in conjunction with Art 1 (which provides that the signatory countries shall secure to their inhabitants all the rights and freedoms of the Convention), imposed positive duties upon the State to put in place effective measures to protect individuals from inhuman or degrading treatment.

10.9   The UK Government was candid in making submissions to the Court which accepted the reasoning and conclusion of the Commission that there had been a violation of Art 3. However, they asked the Court to confine itself to

---

1   8 EHRR 235.

considering the facts of the case without making any general statement about the corporal punishment of children. Although the Court reviewed the scope of both criminal and civil remedies to such conduct available in the UK in the course of delivering judgment, the Court's reasoning that there had been a violation of Art 3 was based upon the inadequacy of the criminal law in protecting children and focused upon the facts of the case, as is the general policy of the Court.

10.10   In a manner consistent with its usual practice, in the light of the finding that there had been a violation of Art 3, the Court announced that it was not necessary to consider A's further complaints of violations of Arts 8, 13 and 14.

10.11   The principles derived from the case could have far-reaching implications if applied to public law child care cases. It may, for example, be possible to successfully argue that a local authority should have intervened, or intervened at an earlier stage, in a case where children have suffered ill-treatment amounting to inhuman or degrading treatment under Art 3[1]. Many of the varieties of child abuse which feature in domestic public law cases, such as physical, emotional and sexual abuse would qualify if of a sufficient degree of severity to amount to violations of Art 3.

10.12   The significance of the positive duties of the State and, arguably, of local authorities, to take steps to protect individuals from inhuman and degrading treatment is the greater because Art 3 is expressed in unqualified terms, from which there may be no derogation. It purports to be an absolute guarantee of the freedom it protects[2]. It is also one in respect of which the State, by Art 1, has agreed as follows:

'*Article 1*

The High Contracting Parties shall secure to everyone within their jurisdiction the rights and freedoms defined in Section I of this Convention.'

10.13   The nature of the conduct prohibited by Art 3 has been illuminated by a number of UK cases. 'Torture' has been defined as 'deliberate inhuman treatment causing very serious and cruel suffering'[3]. 'Ill-treatment', as the Court frequently re-asserts, must attain a minimum level of severity if it is to fall within the scope of Art 3[4]. The standard of severity 'depends on all the circumstances of the case, such as the nature and context of the treatment, its duration, its physical and mental effects and, in some instances, the sex, age and state of health of the victim'[5]. 'Degrading treatment' is treatment which grossly humiliates or degrades[6] or which rouses in the victim feelings of fear, anguish and inferiority capable of humiliating and debasing him and possibly breaking his physical or moral resistance[7].

10.14   In *Y v UK*[8], in which a schoolboy was caned by his headmaster who administered four strokes of the cane over the boy's trousers which caused wheals,

PART B
IMPACT OF THE CONVENTION

---

1   See, below, the discussion of the interrelationship of Art 3 and s 31 of the Children Act 1989.
2   *Ireland v UK* 2 EHRR 25, para 163.
3   Ibid.
4   *A v UK* [1998] 2 FLR 959.
5   Ibid.
6   *The Greek Case* (the Greek case) (1969) 12 YB 186.
7   *Ireland v UK* 2 EHRR 25.
8   17 EHRR 233.

heavy bruising and swelling across his buttocks, the Commission held that there had been a violation of Art 3. In another case involving corporal punishment in school, *Warwick v UK*[1], the Commission attached particular importance to the combination of punishment which caused physical injury to a 16-year-old female pupil of marriageable age, with the particular circumstances of its infliction by a male teacher in the presence of another male teacher. The Commission again found a violation of Art 3 even though the girl had suffered 'only' one stroke with a cane on her hand, albeit one which resulted in two large bruises.

10.15 Another UK case, *Costello-Roberts v UK*[2], produced a contrasting result. The Court held, by a narrow majority of four votes to five, that corporal punishment inflicted upon a 7-year-old pupil at an independent preparatory school by his headmaster did not violate either Art 3 or Art 8. Neither the nature of the punishment itself, three whacks on the bottom administered by a rubber-soled gym shoe over his shorts not resulting in any physical injury, nor the fact that the sentence had been announced 3 days before it was imposed, not yet that it 'automatically' followed the acquisition of his fifth demerit mark for minor acts of misconduct sufficed to satisfy the minimum level of severity required for a violation of Art 3. It was for that reason alone that the complaint failed and not because, as the Government had argued, the responsibilities of the State were not engaged because the English legal system had adequately secured the rights guaranteed by Art 3 and 8 of the Convention by prohibiting the use of any corporal punishment which was not moderate or reasonable.

10.16 The Court distinguished its judgment in *Tyrer v UK*[3] (a Manx case) by observing that for a punishment to be 'degrading' to a sufficient extent to be in breach of Art 3 'the debasement involved must attain a particular level of severity and must in any event be other than that usual level of humiliation inherent in any punishment'. Mr Tyrer was a young man sentenced in the juvenile court to three strokes of the birch on his bare bottom. His punishment was inflicted 3 weeks after he was sentenced in a local police station in the presence of three male police officers, two of whom restrained him while the third administered the punishment.

10.17 There is significant interrelationship between Art 3 and Art 8 which has not yet been clarified by the case-law. In the *Costello-Roberts* case[4], the applicant argued that his punishment violated not only his Art 3 rights but also had given rise to a breach of his Art 8 right to respect for his private life. His submissions persuaded a majority of the Commission on the basis of the consistent case-law of the Convention organs that 'private life' extended to a person's physical and moral integrity. The Commission, in particular, took the view that the protection afforded by Art 8 in the sphere of protection of physical integrity could be wider than that afforded by Art 3. The Court did not agree with the Commission that, in the particular circumstances of the case, there had been a breach of Art 8 but did so on the grounds that in the view of the Court the punishment sustained by the applicant did not involve any sufficiently adverse effect upon his physical or moral integrity to bring it within the prohibition contained in Art 8 having regard to the

---

1   Application No 9471/81 (Rep), (18 July 1986) 60 DR 5.
2   19 EHRR 112.
3   2 EHRR 1.
4   19 EHRR 112.

fact that 'the sending of a child to school necessarily involves some degree of interference with his or her private life'[1]. The applicant in *A v UK* was also anxious to explore the relationship between Art 3 and Art 8 but the Court upon finding a violation of Art 3 declined, notwithstanding his request, to consider whether his ill-treatment amounted to a breach of Art 8 on the basis that it was not necessary in the circumstances to do so[2].

Article 8

Key cases: Article 8
10.18   *X and Y v The Netherlands* (1985) Series A, No 91, judgment.

10.19   There is a possibility that a variety of forms of child abuse may constitute violations of Art 8 even where they do not constitute breaches of Art 3, as a result of failing to attain the minimum level of severity required[3]. The Government as a signatory to the Convention has agreed by Art 1 to secure to everyone within the jurisdiction the rights and freedoms secured by Art 8.

10.20   Article 8(1), unlike Art 3, is not unqualified in its terms. Article 8(2) provides that there shall be no interference by a public authority with the exercise of this right except such as is in accordance with the law and is necessary in a democratic society in the interests of national security, public safety or the economic well-being of the country, for the prevention of disorder or crime, for the protection of health or morals, or for the protection of the rights and freedoms of others.

10.21   In the case of *X and Y v The Netherlands*[4], the Court held that the State was under a positive duty to adopt measures to protect the applicant from the kind of wrongdoing which had been inflicted upon her. The facts of the case pressed to the conclusion that it was the provisions of the Dutch criminal law which afforded her insufficient protection but the principles involved may point to a considerably wider significance. Mr X had a mentally handicapped daughter, Y, who lived in a privately run home for mentally handicapped children. On the day following her sixteenth birthday, she was raped by B, the son-in-law of the directress of the establishment. The trauma caused by these events led to Y developing a major mental disturbance. Despite the efforts of X, Y's father, to ensure that criminal proceedings were initiated against B, the public prosecutor's office provisionally decided not to open proceedings against B, provided that he did not commit a similar offence within the next 2 years. Mr X appealed against that decision to the Arnhem Court of Appeal; he requested that the court should direct criminal proceedings be commenced against B. On its exceptional facts the case exposed a minor but significant lacuna in Dutch criminal law.

10.22   The Arnhem Court of Appeal decided that there was no effective substitute for a complaint lodged by Y herself, since she was over 16, even though the police and her father regarded her as incapable of doing so, and that since no one else was legally empowered to file a complaint the court could not direct that

PART B
IMPACT OF THE CONVENTION

---

1   19 EHRR 112, para 36.
2   Ibid, paras 25–28.
3   See the discussion of *A v UK* and *X and Y v The Netherlands* (below).
4   (1985) Series A, No 91.

proceedings be commenced by means of a broad interpretation of the law to the detriment of B.

10.23   The European Court found that there had been a violation of Art 8 by the State in that, 'the protection afforded by the civil law in the case of wrongdoing of the kind inflicted on Miss Y is insufficient. This is a case where fundamental values and essential aspects of private life are at stake. Effective deterrence is indispensable in this area and it can be achieved only by criminal law provisions; indeed, it is by such provisions that the matter is normally regulated.'[1] Having found a violation of Art 8 in relation to Y the Court did not proceed to consider her further complaints that her rights pursuant to Articles 3, 13 or 14 had been violated.

10.24   Once again, the interrelationship of the Articles of the Convention can be seen in the judgment of the Court. Although complaint of a breach of Art 13 might be seen as that most appropriate to the essential facts of the case, in fact, the Court found a violation of Art 8 on the basis that there was no adequate means under Dutch criminal law available to the applicant to obtain a remedy, and having done so, declined to consider her other complaints.

10.25   The combined effect of the judgments of the European Court in the cases of *A v UK* and *X and Y v The Netherlands* is that the State has positive obligations, in certain circumstances, to protect Convention rights by providing an appropriate and effective means by which their breach by private individuals may be deterred. It is possible to argue that the principle which emerges from these cases is that the organs of the State have a responsibility to secure for everyone within the jurisdiction, particularly the most vulnerable members of society, the fundamental freedoms guaranteed by Arts 3 and 8 as to protection from ill-treatment and protection of moral and physical integrity by taking positive and effective measures to deter and restrain such conduct.

10.26   If the same principles were to be applied to local authorities in child-care cases where children had suffered a sufficient level of ill-treatment for there to be a violation of either Art 3 or Art 8, and an authority had either failed to make a decision, decided not to take action, failed to take effective action or had only taken appropriate action after unreasonable delay, it is arguable that there could be a breach of the Convention rights of the child victims.

10.27   The interrelationship between ill-treatment prohibited by Art 3, inter-ference with physical and moral integrity prohibited by Art 8 and the 'threshold criteria' of s 31 of the Children Act 1989 has not yet been explored in the case-law. Clearly, it would be easier to argue a case where the complaint lay against a local authority for failing to act if that failure was one which had allowed inhuman treatment of children to continue, rather than some lesser form of ill-treatment prohibited by Art 8.

10.28   It is in the nature of social work that local authorities are rarely in a position to act pre-emptively so as to avoid any harm befalling a child and are frequently criticised when they seek to do so. In the majority of public law cases the nature of the jurisdiction dictates that local authorities have to react to the discovery of significant harm which has already occurred in order to prevent

---

1   (1985) Series A, No 91, para 27.

further harm. If it were to be decided that complaints about local authorities failing to act effectively, expeditiously or at all were capable, in principle, of amounting to a violation of the Convention, whatever court had the responsibility of deciding such a case on its facts, would undoubtedly give the local authority concerned considerable latitude in the exercise of its discretion in determining how and when to act in the matter of taking a child into care. It is likely that a violation would not be found except where the inaction of the local authority amounted to sustained professional negligence.

Article 6

Key cases: Article 6
W v UK 10 EHRR 29

10.29 Article 6 applies to family public law decisions such as placing children in care, involving parental contact, fostering and adoption, where State action is directly determinative of the right.

10.30 In the sphere of administrative decisions, where they are decisive of rights and obligations, Art 6 requires that the State should provide a right to challenge those decisions before a tribunal which conforms with the Art 6 guarantees.

10.31 In the case of *W v UK*[1], an applicant father complained that a local authority had made and implemented decisions to initially restrict his contact with his child in care and eventually to terminate it. He additionally complained that he had no effective remedy against those decisions and about the length of the related wardship proceedings. The case pre-dated the Children Act 1989 and the situation described in the case would not give rise to the same issues today. However, the principles derived from the judgment of the Court still have considerable bearing upon public law cases.

10.32 The Government argued before the Court that Art 6(1) could have no application because no 'right' was in issue. The Government submitted that Art 6 could have application only where 'a right', was recognised by domestic law, and that the notion of a parent having 'a right' to contact with a child was outmoded and better recognised as a right of the child rather than that of the parent. In any event, it was argued, 'the right' if it existed at all was a 'rhetorical' one and not a 'legal' right, and, such 'a right' could not survive a parental rights resolution which passed all parental rights to local authority, subject only to very limited exceptions. The Court firmly rejected those submissions, while accepting that under English law access to children in care was a matter for the local authority's discretion, it took note of the fact that a parent retained a number of positive rights to make application to the court following a parental rights resolution and further observed that 'the extinction of all parental right in regard to access would scarcely be compatible with fundamental notions of family life and the family ties which Art 8 of the Convention is designed to protect'[2]. The Court rejected the submission that an application for judicial review would afford the father an

---

1   10 EHRR 29.
2   Ibid, para 77.

appropriate remedy 'in a case of this kind', and held that what was required was recourse to a court with jurisdiction to examine the case on its merits.

10.33 The Court also held that there had been a violation of Art 8 on the basis that the authority had 'failed to put the parents properly in the picture before firm decisions were taken by the Authority' at a time when the child had been placed with long-term foster-carers and no contact was taking place; a period the Court characterised as crucial in the child's road to adoption.

10.34 The Court's insistence upon the continuing need for openness on the part of the authority in its dealings with parents in relation to matters within the discretion of the authority at a time when the child was in the care of the authority to some extent mirrors the decision of the Court in the *McMichael* case [1]. There the Court found a breach of Art 6 when the applicants had been unable to see confidential social work reports submitted before and during care proceedings concerning their children on the basis that, arguably, the absence of such disclosure may have affected their ability to influence the outcome of the proceedings and also to assess their prospects on appeal.

10.35 The approach of the Court places positive obligations upon local authorities to consult with parents in a meaningful way both before and after the making of care orders. The process of consultation must be meaningful and timely and the parents must be properly informed so as to be able to make properly informed decisions. In addition, the decision creates the possibility that Art 6 may provide a means by which the administrative discretion of the local authority may be challenged, particularly where the court is confronted with the need to choose between an unsatisfactory care plan or refusing to make an otherwise justified care order [2].

BREACH OF DUTY: *X (Minors) v Bedfordshire County Council*

10.36 The decision of the House of Lords in the *Bedfordshire* case [3] concerned five separate appeals linked by common issues of principle. In each of the cases, the plaintiffs alleged that they had been injured by local authorities in their carrying out of functions imposed upon them by statute.

10.37 In the two 'abuse' cases, of which the *Bedfordshire* case was one, the issue was whether any private law claim could arise in damages from the manner in which a local authority had carried out its duties towards children, pursuant to the Children Act 1989, 'in respect of whom they receive reports of neglect or ill-treatment'.

10.38 The children in both the 'abuse' cases made claims against the local authorities for breach of statutory duty and breach of the common law duty of care. The mother and child in the second 'abuse' case, the *Newham* case, based their cases on the allegation that a social worker and a psychiatrist individually owed a duty of care to them for breaches of which the authority was vicariously liable.

---

1 *McMichael v UK* 20 EHRR 205.
2 See Chapter 6 for further discussion of this issue.
3 [1995] 2 FLR 276.

10.39 The local authorities accepted that the plaintiffs satisfied both the 'proximity' test and that of forseeability of harm in relation to the issue of whether there was a common law duty of care owed to them. The local authorities submitted that it was not just and reasonable in all the circumstances to impose liability. The claims were struck out at first instance and appeals to the Court of Appeal were dismissed. The plaintiffs appealed to the House of Lords.

10.40 In the other three cases, the 'education' cases, claims were based upon breach of statutory duty and negligence. In the first case the claim was founded upon the allegation that the authority had failed to make proper provision for the plaintiff, a boy with special educational needs, as required by the Education Act 1981. He further made a claim based upon alleged vicarious liability of the authority for the negligence of professionals employed by them, which was also the basis of the claim in the second 'education' case. The third education case was a claim based primarily upon negligence and breach of statutory duty.

10.41 The House of Lords' judgment established that 'abused' children and children with special educational needs, on any view amongst the most vulnerable and disadvantaged members of society, could not succeed with private law claims for damages against local authorities in respect of either the breaches of statutory duty alleged or a common law duty of care in carrying out their statutory duties.

10.42 The claim, in the second 'abuse' case, that the authority was vicariously liable for the negligent acts of the social worker and the psychiatrist, was rejected on the basis that neither had assumed a professional duty of care to the plaintiffs, they had been retained to advise the authority. Furthermore, it was held that the psychiatrist would be protected from liability in negligence by the doctrine of witness immunity.

10.43 Even the most terse statement of the facts of the cases illustrates the seriousness of the allegations and of the consequences to the children. In the *Bedfordshire* case, repeated reports about five children thought to be abused and neglected were made to the local authority by a variety of professionals, including their doctor and their head teacher. These, together with reports from neighbours and relatives were disregarded for 5 years. However, the local authority disputed the allegations. In the *Newham* case, social workers believed a girl was at risk of sexual abuse. An elementary mistake as to the identity of the alleged abuser, made by the social worker and psychiatrist in the case led to the child being separated from her mother for one year. However, the local authority disputed the allegations.

10.44 The 'education' cases did establish that there were some limited circumstances in which liability might be established:

– where a local authority provided a service beyond that required of it by its statutory duty and did so negligently;
– where there was a possibility of an authority being liable vicariously for torts committed by their servants on the ordinary principles;
– where the claim could be characterised as a pure common law claim against an individual (eg a headmaster or an educational adviser).

In the light of the subsequent judgment of the European Court in *Osman v UK*[1], it is very much open to question as to whether the extensive immunity of local authorities from private law actions for damages based upon negligent perform-ance of their statutory duties can be sustained. The facts of the case are set out in the case summaries in Part C.

10.45   A private law action for damages brought by Mrs Osman and her son against the Commissioner of the Metropolitan Police alleging negligence was struck out by the Court of Appeal[2] on the basis that, in the light of previous authorities, in particular the case of *Hill v Chief Constable of West Yorkshire*[3], no action could lie against the police in negligence in the investigation and suppression of crime on the grounds that public policy required immunity from suit in such circumstances. The Court of Appeal refused leave to appeal to the House of Lords.

10.46   The European Court held that the rule that no action could lie against the police for their negligence in the investigation and suppression of crime was a disproportionate restriction on the right of access to a court and thus in breach of Art 6. In making that decision the court observed, inter alia:

> '... it would appear to the Court that in the instant case the Court of Appeal proceeded on the basis that the rule provided a watertight defence to the police and that it was impossible to prise open an immunity which the police enjoy from civil suit in respect of their acts and omissions in the investigation and suppression of crime.'

and,

> 'The Court would observe that the application of the rule in this manner without further inquiry into the existence of competing public interest considerations only serves to confer a blanket immunity on the police for their acts and omissions during the investigation and suppression of crime and amounts to an unjustifiable restriction on an applicant's right to have a determination on the merits of his or her claim against the police in deserving cases.
>
> In its view, it must be open to a domestic court to have regard to the presence of other public interest considerations which pull in the opposite direction to the application of the rule. Failing this, there will be no distinction made between degrees of negligence or of harm suffered or any consideration of the justice of a particular case.'

and,

> 'For the Court, these are considerations which must be examined on the merits and not automatically excluded by the application of a rule which amounts to the grant of an immunity to the police.'[4]

10.47   The primary reasons why the judgment of the European Court in the *Osman* case[5] threaten local authority immunity in their conduct of their statutory responsibilities are as follows:

–   There is a very strong analogy between the immunity of the police from suit in respect of negligence in the investigation and suppression of crime and that of local authorities in performing their statutory duties imposed by the

---

1   [1999] 1 FLR 193.
2   *Osman and Another v Ferguson and Another* [1993] 4 All ER 344.
3   [1989] AC 53.
4   [1999] 1 FLR 193 at 232.
5   [1993] 4 All ER 344.

Children Act 1989. This was remarked upon by Lord Browne-Wilkinson who delivered the leading judgment in the *Bedfordshire* case:

> 'To my mind, the nearest analogies are the cases where a common-law duty of care has been sought to be imposed upon the police (in seeking to protect vulnerable members of society from wrongs done to them by others) or statutory regulators of financial dealings who are seeking to protect investors from dishonesty. In neither of those cases has it been thought appropriate to superimpose on the statutory regime a common-law duty of care giving rise to a claim in damages for failure to protect the weak against the wrongdoer: see Hill.'[1]

– There was no investigation of competing public interest considerations in the *Bedfordshire* case which might have militated in favour of a different decision, just as there had not been in the *Osman* case. In relation to matters of public policy the judgments were informed by judicial experience and prejudices rather than evidence – a feature of which the Court was highly critical in the *Osman* case.

– There was no investigation of the merits of the claims, of the degree of negligence involved nor of the harm suffered or of the justice of a particular case.

PUBLIC POLICY AND LOCAL AUTHORITY IMMUNITY

10.48   The entire explanation for local authority immunity in respect of negligence in carrying out their statutory duties is one of public policy. In the *Bedfordshire* case, Lord Browne-Wilkinson acknowledged that the first two of the three necessary factors to establish liability were accepted by the local authority, sufficient proximity in the relationship between the authority and the plaintiffs and forseeablity of harm, and thus based his judgment upon the view that the third factor, the question of whether it was just and reasonable in all the circumstances to impose such a duty of care, was neither accepted by the authority nor satisfied in practice. He acknowledged the similarity of his views to those of the Master of the Rolls, who delivered the leading judgment in the case in the Court of Appeal[2]. They agreed about the test to be applied:

> 'Is it, then, just and reasonable to superimpose a common-law duty of care on the local authority in relation to the performance of its statutory duties to protect children? In my judgment it is not. The Master of the Rolls took the view, with which I agree, that the public policy consideration which has first claim on the loyalty of the law is that wrongs should be remedied and that very potent counter-considerations are required to override that policy: [1994] 2 WLR 554 at p 572F. However, in my judgment there are such considerations in this case' Lord Browne-Wilkinson[3].

10.49   He gave four reasons for that judgment:

> 'First, in my judgment a common-law duty of care would cut across the whole statutory system set up for the protection of children at risk. As a result of the ministerial directions contained in *Working Together* the protection of such children is not the

---

1   [1989] AC 53.
2   [1994] 2 WLR 554.
3   [1995] 2 FLR 276 at 301.

exclusive territory of the local authority's social services. The system is interdisciplinary, involving the participation of the police, educational bodies, doctors and others. At all stages the system involves joint discussions, joint recommendations and joint decisions. The key organisation is the Child Protection Conference, a multidisciplinary body which decides whether to place the child on the child protection register. This procedure by way of joint action takes place, not merely because it is good practice, but because it is required by guidance having statutory force binding on the local authority. The guidance is extremely detailed and extensive: the current edition of *Working Together* runs to 126 pages. To introduce into such a system a common-law duty of care enforceable against only one of the participant bodies would be manifestly unfair. To impose such liability on all the participant bodies would lead to almost impossible problems of disentangling as between the respective bodies the liability, both primary and by way of contribution, of each for reaching a decision found to be negligent.

Secondly, the task of the local authority and its servants in dealing with children at risk is extraordinarily delicate. Legislation requires the local authority to have regard not only to the physical well-being of the child but also to the advantages of not disrupting the child's family environment: see, for example, s 17 of the 1989 Act. In one of the child abuse cases, the local authority is blamed for removing the child precipitately: in the other, for failing to remove the children from their mother. . . .

Next, if a liability in damages were to be imposed, it might well be that local authorities would adopt a more cautious and defensive approach to their duties. For example, as the *Cleveland Report* makes clear, on occasions the speedy decision to remove the child is sometimes vital. If the authority is to be made liable in damages for a negligent decision to remove a child (such negligence lying in the failure properly first to investigate the allegations) there would be a substantial temptation to postpone making such a decision until further inquiries have been made in the hope of getting more concrete facts. Not only would the child in fact being abused be prejudiced by such delay: the increased workload inherent in making such investigations would reduce the time available to deal with other cases and other children. The relationship between the social worker and the child's parents is frequently one of conflict, the parent wishing to retain care of the child, the social worker having to consider whether to remove it. This is fertile ground in which to breed ill feeling and litigation, often hopeless, the cost of which both in terms of money and human resources will be diverted from the performance of the social service for which they were provided. The spectre of vexatious and costly litigation is often urged as a reason for not imposing a legal duty. But the circumstances surrounding cases of child abuse make the risk a very high one which cannot be ignored. If there were no other remedy for maladministration of the statutory system for the protection of children, it would provide substantial argument for imposing a duty of care. But the statutory complaints procedures contained in s 76 of the 1980 Act and the much fuller procedures now available under the 1989 Act provide a means to have grievances investigated, though not to recover compensation. Further, it was submitted (and not controverted) that the local authorities ombudsman would have power to investigate cases such as these.'

Finally, your Lordships' decision in [*Caparo Industries v Dickman* [1990] AC 605] lays down that, in deciding whether to develop novel categories of negligence the court should proceed incrementally and by analogy with decided categories.'

and

'In my judgment, the courts should proceed with great care before holding liable in negligence those who have been charged by Parliament with the task of protecting society from the wrongdoings of others.'

10.50 However, there are suggestions of *some* considerations of public policy which tend towards an opposite view to be found in the judgment of Sir Thomas Bingham MR in the Court of Appeal:

> 'I cannot accept, as a general proposition, that the imposition of a duty of care makes no contribution to the maintenance of high standards. The common belief that the imposition of such a duty may lead to overkill is not easily reconciled with the suggestion that it has no effect' (referring to the claim against the psychiatrist).[1]

and,

> 'One argument on public policy was addressed to us which seemed to have more relevance to the local authority than to the health authority and the psychiatrist. If a duty of care were imposed on the local authority, and claims such as the child's were permitted to continue, the already over-stretched resources of local authorities, human and financial, would be diverted from the valuable purpose of looking after children and wasted on the sterile processes of litigation. One must accept that this must, to a greater or lesser extent, be so, and a somewhat similar argument found favour in *Hill v Chief Constable of West Yorkshire* [1989] AC 53 at p 63G. But this is an argument frequently (and not implausibly) advanced on behalf of doctors; it has not prevailed. Other professions resist liability on the ground that it will in the end increase the cost to the paying customer; that resistance has not on the whole been effective either. Save in clear cases, it is not for the courts to decide how public money is best spent nor to balance the risk that money will be wasted on litigation against the hope that the possibility of suit may contribute towards the maintenance of the highest standards.'[2]

Barrett v London Borough of Enfield[3]

10.51 The House of Lords have recently considered an appeal by the plaintiff, in the *Barrett* case against an order, upheld by the Court of Appeal, striking out his action for damages against the defendant council as disclosing no cause of action. The plaintiff was made the subject of a care order to the defendant council when he was 10 months old and he remained in their care until he was 17 years of age. He alleged that the defendant council's treatment of him while in their care was negligent and that as a consequence he suffered personal injury.

10.52 The plaintiff argued that the relationship between the defendant council and himself which arose as a result of the care order was such as to create a common law duty of care. He complained that the defendant council breached that duty in a number of respects in failing to safeguard his welfare after the making of the care order. He alleged that the combined effect of a series of failures by the defendant council to safeguard adequately his welfare left him, on leaving care, without family, or other attachments, and suffering from a psychiatric illness with an associated alcohol problem and a propensity for self-harm.

10.53 The House of Lords was unanimous in allowing Barrett's appeal. The primary reasons for the decision lay in the fact that the nature of the claim made was distinguishable from that made by the children in the *Bedfordshire* case in the sense that it did not relate to the particularly difficult area of the exercise of local

---

1   [1994] 1 FLR 449 at 462.
2   Ibid, at 467.
3   [1999] 2 FLR 426.

authority discretion as to whether to initiate proceedings to take children into care but rather to the duties of a local authority in respect of a child already in its care.

10.54   However, the case allowed the House of Lords an opportunity of considering the judgment of the European Court in the *Osman*[1] case. In the course of a judgment with which two other members of the court specifically agreed, Lord Browne-Wilkinson, while critical of the decision in the *Osman* case, said:

> 'In view of the decision in the Osman case it is now difficult to foretell what would be the result in the present case if we were to uphold the striking out order. It seems to me that it is at least probable that the matter would then be taken to Strasbourg. That court, applying its decision in the Osman case if it considers it to be correct, would say that we have deprived the plaintiff of his right to have the balance struck between the hardship suffered by him and the damage to be done to the public interest in the present case if an order were to be made against the defendant council. In the present very unsatisfactory state of affairs, and bearing in mind that under the Human Rights Act 1998 Art 6 will shortly become part of English law, in such cases as these it is difficult to say that it is a clear and obvious case calling for striking out.

> For these reasons in my judgment this action should proceed to trial...'.

It is clear, therefore, that a majority were prepared to consider, anticipating the date of effective incorporation pursuant to the Human Rights Act 1998, and to decide the instant case in such a way as to ensure, at least for the time being, that the judgment of the House of Lords was congruent with the decision of the European Court in the *Osman* case.

THE FUTURE

10.55   The children in the *Bedfordshire* case have petitioned the European Court on the grounds, inter alia, that their Convention rights, to a determination of their claims on their merits, under Art 6(1), have been infringed. The decision of the Commission that their complaint of breach of Art 6 is admissible followed the lines of the similar decision in the *Osman* case and to some extent therefore supports the inference that there are substantial grounds for the belief that the European Court may find that their Convention rights have been violated.

10.56   Clearly, even if local authorities were to lose their immunity from actions in negligence in respect of their performance of their statutory duties in relation to child care, the margin of discretion they would be allowed before, on the facts of a particular case, they were found liable would be very considerable indeed. Any court dealing with such a case would inevitably be mindful of the difficult and delicate balancing exercise which a local authority must conduct when considering when and how to remove children from their homes against a background, frequently, of inadequate information, differences of opinion and of conflicts with, and between, the parents.

10.57   Notwithstanding the strictures of the European Court upon judicial and administrative delays in other jurisdictions, it appears unlikely that the

---

1   [1993] 4 All ER 344.

Court's judgment on the merits of the *Bedfordshire* petition will be delivered before Spring 2001.

10.58 The potential significance of the decision of the European Court in the *Bedfordshire* case is considerable. There are a range of cases which involve the immunity of public bodies in respect of their conduct of statutory responsibilities which may be affected by the judgment. They include, for example, the fire service as well as the police force and local authorities.

10.59 The issues which may arise in relation to local authorities are, potentially, far more extensive than those which arise pursuant to the Children Act 1989. There are a number of other spheres of activity in which local authorities have statutory obligations which presently do not give rise to any duty of care and, consequently, therefore no right to claim damages in respect of breach. Future failures of local authorities to carry out their responsibilities reasonably competently in matters of public health, education and in relation to their responsibilities pursuant to the Housing Act 1996, could be susceptible to private law actions for damages.

Chapter 11

THE FAMILY

(A) MARRIAGE

11.1 Marriage is the only relationship identified by the Convention as requiring separate treatment. Not only is the right to marry guaranteed by Art 12 but it is also singled out as the only relationship within which the right to found a family is specifically guaranteed. The special status of marriage within the Convention has its origin in the terms of Art 12 but resonances of that status are found in a number of other areas, particularly within the sphere of family life under Art 8. For example, married couples may legitimately be treated differently from unmarried couples for the purpose of taxation because their status is not analogous and marriage relates to a 'special regime of rights and obligations'[1], while discrimination in favour of married fathers in conferring upon them automatic parental rights compared with the different status of unmarried fathers in that regard, the Court has determined, is objectively and reasonably justified[2].

11.2 Article 12 heavily qualifies the right to marry which it purports to guarantee by its reference to the right being exercisable 'according to the national laws governing the exercise of this right'. Widely recognised limitations such as capacity, consanguinity, consent and the prevention of bigamy are highly likely to be compatible with the Convention. In *Rees v UK*[3] the Court determined that the right to marry:

> '... shall be subject to the national laws of the contracting states, but ... the limitations thereby introduced must not restrict or reduce the right in such a way or to such an extent that the very essence of the right is impaired.'

The Court has interpreted the right to marry guaranteed by Art 12 as referring to the traditional model of marriage, as a union between persons of the opposite biological sex[4]. Much of the case-law of the Convention organs in this sphere has concerned challenges to the traditional model of marriage by transsexuals and homosexuals seeking to extend the scope of the guarantee to embrace non-conventional relationships. To date, such challenges have been, in most important respects, unsuccessful.

Key Articles

11.3

> *'Article 12*
>
> Men and women of marriageable age have the right to marry and to found a family according to the national laws governing the exercise of that right.'

---

1   *Lindsay v UK* Application No 11089/84, (11 November 1986) 49 DR 181.
2   *McMichael v UK* (1995) Series A, No 307-B.
3   *Rees v UK* 9 EHRR 56.
4   Ibid.

'Article 14

The enjoyment of the rights and freedoms set forth in this Convention shall be secured without discrimination on any ground such as sex, race, colour, language, religion, political or other opinion, national or social origin, association with a national minority, property, birth or other status.'

Key cases

11.4   *Airey v Ireland* 2 EHRR 205; *Rees v UK* 9 EHRR 56; *Johnston v Ireland* 9 EHRR 203; *F v Switzerland* 10 EHRR 411; *Cossey v UK* 13 EHRR 622.

The right to marry

11.5   The Court has been consistent in enunciating the principle that although Art 12 provides that the exercise of the right to marry is subject to the national laws of the contracting States, those laws must not interfere with the right in such a way or to such an extent that the very essence of the right is impaired[1]. Although it is easy to see how that principle has been derived from Art 12 it is less easy to follow the logic of the application of the principle in the case-law of the Court. In the *Rees*[2] case the applicant, a female to male transsexual, complained that his Convention rights pursuant to Arts 3, 8 and 12 had been violated. The applicant complained that he could not have his birth certificate altered so as to unequivocally record his current gender. The Commission found his complaints of breaches of Art 8 and Art 12 admissible but not his complaint of breach of the terms of Art 3. The Commission reported unanimously that the applicant's rights under Art 8 had been violated but not those under Art 12. The Court disagreed with the Commission and held that there had been no breach of the applicant's Convention rights under Art 8 or Art 12. In relation to Art 12 the Court's reasoning was as follows[3]:

'In the Court's opinion, the right to marry guaranteed by Article 12 refers to the traditional marriage between persons of opposite biological sex. This appears also from the wording of the Article which makes it clear that Article 12 is mainly concerned to protect marriage as the basis of the family.

Furthermore, Article 12 lays down that the exercise of this right shall be subject to the national laws of the Contracting States. The limitations thereby introduced must not restrict or reduce the right in such a way or to such an extent that the very essence of the right is impaired. However, the legal impediment in the United Kingdom on the marriage of persons who are not of the opposite biological sex cannot be said to have an effect of this kind.'

11.6   In the important case of *F v Switzerland*[4], the applicant complained that his Convention rights had been violated by the imposition of a temporary prohibition upon re-marriage following his third divorce. Pursuant to Art 150 of the Swiss Civil Code, the Lausanne Civil Court, on granting his wife's cross-petition for divorce and dismissing his own petition, found that he was solely at fault for the breakdown of his third marriage and imposed a 3-year prohibition

---

1   *Rees v UK* 9 EHRR 56.
2   Ibid.
3   Ibid, paras 49 and 50.
4   10 EHRR 411.

upon his re-marriage. The applicant unsuccessfully appealed the imposition of the ban to the Swiss Federal Court.

11.7 The European Court reviewed the then current state of Swiss law in relation to such temporary prohibitions upon marriage and took note of the following features of the law:

– That Art 54 of the Swiss Federal Constitution guaranteed that marriages celebrated abroad in accordance with local laws would be recognised throughout the Confederation.

– That the temporary prohibition upon the remarriage of the party 'at fault' following divorce pursuant to Art 150 had been made more flexible by the case-law of the Swiss Federal Court which had decided that courts 'should not impose a prohibition on remarriage unless the fault committed is of exceptional gravity and has also played a decisive role in the breakdown of the marriage'.

– That proposals for law reform in Switzerland recognised that the prohibition might so readily be circumvented by celebrating abroad what would then be regarded as a valid marriage in Switzerland, irrespective of any prohibition upon marriage imposed under Swiss law, that the measure (the Art 150 temporary prohibition) was therefore ineffective, offensive and should be deleted from the Civil code.

11.8 The Court rejected the case of the Swiss Government and found a violation of Art 12 despite acknowledging, as the Government contended, that the stability of marriage is a legitimate aim in the public interest, the Court doubted that the particular means adopted were appropriate to achieving that objective. The Court's summary of its findings was that the temporary prohibition 'affected the very essence of the right to marry' and was 'disproportionate to the legitimate aim pursued'.[1]

11.9 Thus even a temporary prohibition upon marriage may amount to a breach of Convention rights under Art 12. Three features of the case particularly influenced the Court's judgment:

(1) That the temporary prohibition upon remarriage under Swiss law was unusual, if not unique, among the contracting States.

(2) That the law had been criticised by a respected law reform group in Switzerland and its impact reduced by the case-law developed by the Swiss Federal Court.

(3) That the temporary prohibition was ineffective in promoting its legitimate aim and disproportionate.

11.10 The Commission has found complaints relating to delay consequent upon procedural requirements inadmissible in two French cases: in *Vadbolski and Demonet v France*[2] and *Sanders v France*[3]. However, in *Hamer v UK*[4] and in *Draper v*

1   10 EHRR 411, para. 40.
2   Application No 22404/93, (12 October 1994).
3   Application No 31401/96, (16 October 1996).
4   Application No 7114/75, (13 December 1979) 24 DR 5.

PART B
IMPACT OF THE CONVENTION

UK[1] the issue concerned the refusal of the UK prison authorities to permit two serving prisoners to marry during the course of their sentences (one was serving a sentence of 5 years and the other a life sentence). That fact that they would not have been able to cohabit or consummate their marriages during the remaining course of their respective sentences was regarded by the Commission as irrelevant. The Commission found that the delay which would be imposed upon them by having to wait until the end of their sentences in order to marry their girlfriends affected the substance of their right to marry and constituted a violation of their Convention rights.

11.11   In general, the organs of the Convention have not found the Convention rights of heterosexual couples pursuant to Art 12 violated by anything less than direct, if temporary, prohibitions upon their right to marry. Provisions of national law which establish conditions precedent for marriage, in relation to such matters as age[2], bigamy and polygamy[3] have not been regarded as a violation of Art 12 rights.

Homosexuals

11.12   Although in some respects the impact of decisions by the organs of the Convention have had some liberalising effects upon the law affecting homo-sexuals[4], the combination of the conservatism of the ideology underlying Art 12 and the conservatism of the Court's interpretation of it has ensured that the right to marry under the Convention is not one which is shared with the gay community. The Court's judgment in the *Rees* case[5], which concerned a transsexual, included the unqualified assertion that the right to marry guaranteed by Art 12 'refers to the traditional marriage between persons of the opposite biological sex'. The Court has consistently followed that interpretation of Art 12 ever since. Art 12 does not therefore create a right for homosexuals to marry one another.

Transsexuals

11.13   Marriage is defined in English law as the voluntary union for life of one man and one woman. A purported marriage is void ab initio in the event that the parties are not respectively a man and a woman[6], and is voidable if the marriage is incapable of consummation[7].

11.14   In the leading UK case of *Corbett v Corbett otherwise Ashley*[8], Ormerod J held that marriage is a union between a man and a woman and that the only criteria for determining a person's sex for the purpose of capacity to marry was to have regard to chromosomal, gonadal and genital factors. Where each of those factors were congruent, psychological factors and surgical interventions were irrelevant. Thus in the UK, sex rather than gender is treated as the determinant of whether the parties to a marriage are respectively male and female. In the event that they are not the marriage is void.

---

1   Application No 8186/78, (10 July 1980) 24 DR 72.
2   *Khan v UK* Application No 11579/85, (7 July 1986) 48 DR 253.
3   *Bibi v UK* Application No 19628/92, (29 June 1992) unpublished.
4   *Dudgeon v UK* (1981) 4 EHRR 149 and *Sutherland v UK* Application No 25186/94.
5   9 EHRR 56, p 4 quoting paras 49 and 50.
6   Matrimonial Causes Act 1973, s 11.
7   Ibid, s 12.
8   [1971] P 83; [1970] 2 All ER 33.

11.15   In an increasing number of other jurisdictions, transsexuals have the right to marry persons who are, at the time of the marriage, of the opposite sex. Such jurisdictions include other European nations such as Germany, the Netherlands, Sweden and Italy, certain of the states of the USA as well as Australia and New Zealand. Nonetheless, the English law on this issue has been found to be compatible with the Convention[1] although the Court did indicate that this was an area which may well need to be reviewed in future even in the course of dismissing the complaint in the *Rees* case[2]:

> 'The Convention has always to be interpreted and applied in the light of current circumstances (see, mutatis mutandis, amongst others, the Dudgeon judgment of 22 October 1981, Series A no. 45, pp. 23–24, paragraph 60). The need for appropriate legal measures should therefore be kept under review having regard particularly to scientific and societal developments.'

11.16   In the *Rees* case, the Court considered complaints of violation of the applicant's Convention rights pursuant to Art 8 and Art 12. The Court treated the complaint of breach of the right to respect of the applicant's private life under Art 8 as the principle one, which was based upon the refusal of the UK Government to allow his birth certificate to be altered to reflect his changed sex. The Court noted that there was little consensus among the contracting States in relation to this area and that, as a consequence, States enjoyed a wide margin of appreciation. What was ultimately decisive in the Court's rejection of the applicant's complaint under Art 8 was the Court's view that a UK birth certificate is a record of historical fact only rather than a document which purports to demonstrate current status. In the light of the Court's view of the administrative difficulty of changing the system in the UK and the general significance of doing so and having regard to the margin of appreciation, the Court found no breach of Art 8 by a majority of 12:3. In rejecting the applicant's complaint pursuant to Art 12, the Court was unanimous.

11.17   The *Rees* case was decided in 1986. In 1990, the Court reconsidered the same issues in *Cossey v UK*[3]. Miss Cossey was a male to female transsexual who had a male partner who wished to marry her and had previously participated in a ceremony of marriage which was declared void. A majority of the Court (10:8, Art 8, 14:4, Art 12) refused to accept that there were any material facts which distinguished her case from the *Rees* case and, accordingly, rejected her complaints of breaches of her Convention rights under Art 8 and Art 12. The Court followed its reasoning in the *Rees* case while accepting Miss Cossey's submission that it was not obliged to do so should it find cogent reasons for a different judgment on the issues. In relation to her complaint of violation of Art 12 and her contention that she could not realistically marry at all, the Court observed that her inability to marry a woman did not stem from any legal impediment and that her inability to marry a man arose as result of 'criteria adopted by English law (which) are in this respect in conformity with the concept of marriage to which the right guaranteed by Art 12 refers'[4].

---

1   *Rees v UK* 9 EHRR 56; *Cossey v UK* [1991] 2 FLR 492.
2   9 EHRR 56.
3   [1991] 2 FLR 492.
4   [1991] 2 FLR 492 at 504G.

11.18 In *B v France*[1], which was decided by the Court in 1990, it held by a majority (of 15:6) that the right to respect for the private life of a post-operative male to female transsexual had been violated by the refusal on the part of the French Government to permit rectification of her birth certificate to reflect her female sex and to allow her to bear unequivocally female forenames. Although Miss B's complaint before the Commission included an alleged violation of Art 12, as well as Art 8, because she wished to marry her male partner, the Commission held that her Art 12 complaint was inadmissible as a result of her failure to exhaust domestic remedies. The Court held that there was as yet insufficient consensus among the States of the Council of Europe on this question to justify the Court reconsidering its decisions in the *Rees* and *Cossey* cases but distinguished them on the basis that there were significant differences between France and England in the legal nature of birth certificates, in particular, and in respect of their law and practice in relation to civil status, change of forenames and of identity documents.

11.19 In two subsequent decisions of the Court concerned with transsexuals, both involving complaints of breaches of the right to respect for private life, there have been distinct signs of growing sympathy with such complaints and of impatience with the failure of the UK Government to keep domestic law in this area under review[2]. However, the Court has consistently been more firm in the opinion that transsexuals may not avail themselves of a remedy under Art 12 when national law denies them opportunity to marry in their adopted sexual identity than it has in rejecting complaints that proper respect for their private or family life had been denied them. It is therefore likely that growing momentum for reform will meet with more success, at least initially, in the sphere of Art 8 and Art 14 than in relation to Art 12. In relation to the latter the concept of family values which underpins Art 12 is very much in the conservative tradition and the Court has been consistently conservative in its interpretation.

11.20 On 30 July 1998, in the case of *Sheffield and Horsham v UK*[3], the Court again reiterated the reasons given in Miss Cossey's case for the rejection of claimed violations of the rights of transsexuals to marry pursuant to Art 12. The Government had argued, inter alia, in relation to Miss Horsham's concern that she intended to marry her partner in the Netherlands but feared that she would be unable to settle in the UK because it was doubtful that the validity of such a marriage would be recognised in the UK. Were that to be the case, it would expose our domestic law to the same kinds of criticisms as were raised in *F v Switzerland*[4], by the ease with which a temporary ban upon remarriage under Swiss law could be circumvented by a marriage contracted abroad.

11.21 The primary obstacle to reform of the law in relation to marriage is the decision in *Corbett v Corbett*[5]. Recently, in *S-T v J*[6], Ward LJ raised the possibility that a future court might be able to place greater emphasis upon gender than

---

1   [1992] 2 FLR 249.
2   See *X, Y and Z v UK* [1997] 2 FLR 892, in which it was recognised that 'family life' was in existence for the purpose of arguing a complaint of violation of Art 8; see also *Sheffield and Horsham v UK*, [1998] 2 FLR 928, in particular para 60 of the opinion of the Court and para 1 of the concurring opinion of Sir John Freeland.
3   Ibid.
4   10 EHRR 411.
5   [1971] P 83; [1970] 2 All ER 33.
6   [1998] 1 All ER 431.

biological sex in determining whether a person were male or female, having undertaken a review of the relevant domestic law and the European Court. The possibility was raised without any conclusion being expressed on the basis that the present statutory formulation of the ground for nullity of marriage may permit a court to rely upon developing medical knowledge to depart from the judgment in *Corbett*. Since it is marriage which is the pre-eminent focus of the protection of family life under Art 8, such an approach would transform the law concerning marriage for transsexuals and would entitle them to access, in the most complete way, the protection afforded to family life under the Convention.

11.22   The dicta of Ward LJ in *S-T v J*[1] hint at a possible willingness on the part of our judges to be considerably less conservative in their interpretation of the law than the European Court has been. It has frequently been suggested that the doctrine of the margin of appreciation, which has in this sphere encouraged a conservative and cautious interpretation of the Convention, would be likely to be less influential in the judgment of our own judges, who are better placed to determine the domestic impact of their decisions than the judges of the European Court. If, pursuant to Art 14, non-discrimination on the ground of 'sex' were to be interpreted as including sexual orientation in the same way that the United Nations Human Rights Committee has interpreted Art 26 (right to non-discrimination) of the International Covenant on Civil and Political Rights in the Australian case of *Toonen*[2], it would be necessary to reconsider the present interpretation of Art 12 so as to ensure conformity.

Dissolution of marriage

11.23   In *Johnston v Ireland*[3], the Court held that applicants could not derive a right to divorce from the terms of Art 12. The Court said that:

> 'The Court agrees with the Commission that the ordinary meaning of the words "right to marry" is clear, in the sense that they cover the formation of marital relationships but not their dissolution. Furthermore, these words are found in a context that includes an express reference to "national laws"; even if, as the applicants would have it, the prohibition on divorce is to be seen as a restriction on capacity to marry, the Court does not consider that, in a society adhering to the principle of monogamy, such a restriction can be regarded as injuring the substance of the right guaranteed by Art 12 .'

Although the Court accepted that the Convention should be given an evolutive interpretation and account should be taken of developments in society with regard to the general availability of divorce, in this instance they were irrelevant given the clear evidence of the intention of the original drafters of the Convention revealed by the 'travaux preparatoires' deliberate omission of any reference to the dissolution of marriage. The applicant's inability to secure a divorce from his first wife in order that he might marry the woman by whom he had had a child and with whom he had lived for 8 years did not avail either of a successful complaint under Art 12, nor under Art 8 on their own account, but the resultant status of their child under Irish law did reveal a lack of respect for their family life and, consequently, a breach of the Convention rights of each of them under Art 8.

PART B
IMPACT OF THE CONVENTION

---

1   [1998] 1 All ER 431.
2   CCPR/C/50D/488/1992.
3   9 EHRR 203.

11.24 In *Airey v Ireland*[1], the lack of an accessible procedure for judicial separation in Eire revealed a breach of the applicant's Convention rights under Art6(1) and Art8. The very high costs of the proceedings combined with an absence of legal aid, complex procedure and an emotional involvement on the part of the applicant which led to it being unreasonable to expect the applicant to present her own case all contributed to such a finding.

(B) FAMILY LIFE

The right to found a family

11.25 In the *Rees* case[2], the Court held that Art12 refers to the traditional marriage between persons of the opposite sex. The Court added that the wording of the Article makes it clear that Art 12 is mainly concerned to protect marriage as the basis of the family. As in the case of the right to marry the right to found a family is made subject to the national laws of the contracting States by the terms of Art 12. Even though the State is obliged to refrain from interfering with the right of a couple to found a family, the State is not burdened with a positive obligation to provide opportunities, for example, for a couple to found a family by instituting conjugal visits for serving prisoners[3]. The same rule was applied where the Commission decided that serving prisoners should be allowed to marry while in prison despite the fact that they would have been unable to consummate their marriages (as a result of the prison authorities denying them any opportunity to do so during the currency of their sentences), an aspect of the matter which was regarded by the Commission as irrelevant[4]. The right to found a family is absolute to the extent that the State has no right to interfere with it[5].

The unmarried single person: adoption and artificial reproduction

11.26 The right to found a family includes founding a family by adoption, although such an adoption will be governed by national laws regarding adoption. Conditions imposed upon adoptions by national law may be subjected to the scrutiny of the Court and the Commission under the Convention[6].

11.27 The applicants in the *Marckx* case[7], a mother and her illegitimate daughter, complained of the differences in the status of legitimate and illegitimate children, particularly in connection with rights of inheritance, under Belgian law. A number of complaints were pursued by them, two of which related to Art 12. They claimed that the Belgian Civil Code failed to respect the right of a mother not to marry, which, they argued, is inherent in the guarantee embodied in Art 12. They further argued, as a secondary submission under Art 12, that in order to confer on the daughter the status of a 'legitimate' child, her mother would have to legitimate her and, hence, to contract marriage. The Court dealt

---

1 2 EHRR 205.
2 9 EHRR 56.
3 *X and Y v Switzerland* Application No 8166/78, (3 October 1978) 13 DR 241.
4 See *Hamer v UK* Application No 7114/75, (13 December 1979) 24 DR 5 and *Draper v UK*, Application No 8186/78, (10 July 1980) 24 DR 72.
5 *X v UK*, Application No 6564/74, (21 May 1975) 2 DR 105.
6 *X and Y v UK* Application No 7229/75, (15 December 1977) 12 DR 32.
7 *Marckx v Belgium*, 2 EHRR 330.

with the first submission on the basis that there was no legal obstacle to the mother either marrying or choosing to remain single and that, consequently, there was no need to determine whether the Convention establishes a right not to marry. Furthermore, the Court refused to accept the submission of the applicants that Art 12 should be construed as requiring that all the legal effects attaching to marriage should apply equally to situations that are in certain respects comparable to marriage, holding that such considerations fell outside the scope of Art 12.

11.28 Unmarried people may not successfully claim a right to adopt under the Convention[1], nor does it appear that the State is obliged to provide a system of adoption at all, or if it does, to provide any particular system of adoption, or even to recognise a foreign adoption order.

11.29 Forms of artificial or assisted reproduction may well give rise to issues under the Convention. Such issues may arise under Art 12, and Art 12 in conjunction with Art 14. The State may be involved in determining what techniques may be employed, in what circumstances and also in determining to whom they should be available. Article 12 could be interpreted so as to impose a positive obligation upon the State to legislate so as to permit particular techniques of artificial reproduction which would not otherwise be lawful. Although at present it is difficult to anticipate that the Convention would be at all likely to provide a mechanism by which a positive obligation was imposed upon the State to fund such treatments and make them available to married couples, it is entirely possible that the combined effects of arbitrariness, unevenness of provision and discriminatory practices within the NHS might well form the basis of complaints under Art 12 and Art 14. Article 12 and the right to found a family may also raise issues in relation to compulsory sterilisation or abortion.

Discrimination

11.30 *Marckx v Belgium*[2] explained the nature of the concept of discrimination recognised by the Court pursuant to the Convention:

> 'A distinction is discriminatory if it has no objective and reasonable justification, that is, if it does not pursue a legitimate aim or if there is not a reasonable relationship of proportionality between the means employed and the aim sought to be realised.'[3]

The list of the grounds upon the basis of which discrimination is prohibited, as set out in Art 14, is not exhaustive[4]; the list is introduced with the words 'such as', and continues, 'sex, race, colour, language, religion, political or other opinion, national or social origin, association with national minority, property, birth or other status'. Article 14 is concerned to prohibit discrimination on the grounds of personal status.

11.31 The words of the Article make clear that 'the enjoyment of the rights and freedoms set forth in this Convention shall be secured without discrimination ...', and that therefore Art 14 applies only to discrimination which affects enjoyment of the rights and freedoms of the Convention.

---

1 *X v Belgium and Netherlands* Application No 6482/147, (1975) 7 DR 75.
2 2 EHRR 330.
3 Ibid, para 33.
4 *James v UK* 8 EHRR 123, para 74.

11.32   In order to successfully make out a complaint of violation of Art 14 an applicant must be able to demonstrate that:

–   he has been subjected to treatment which was different from the treatment of others in an analogous position;
–   the difference in treatment relates to one of the rights and freedoms established by the Convention;
–   the difference in treatment cannot be objectively and reasonably justified, having regard to the doctrine of proportionality and the margin of appreciation.

Difference in treatment

11.33   A number of important family relationships have been held not to be analogous with one another for the purposes of a complaint under Art 14:

–   a married couple with an unmarried couple[1];
–   a natural father with a natural mother[2];
–   a natural father and a married father concerning rights in relation to children[3];
–   a stable lesbian relationship with family life[4].

Although *McMichael v UK*[5] concerned Scottish domestic law, that law is sufficiently similar to English law in relation to parental responsibility for it to be highly likely that English law relating to parental responsibility would at present comply with Arts 8 and 14 of the Convention.

11.34   A natural father who does not have parental responsibility will be potentially disadvantaged in a number of respects in domestic private law:

–   his consent is not required before his child may be removed from the jurisdiction;
–   he may not be able to establish a breach of a 'right of custody' within the meaning of the Hague Convention on the Civil Aspects of International Child Abduction;
–   he may be deprived of parental responsibility, should he have acquired it, by court order following an application under the Children Act 1989, s 4(3).

In matter of adoption and freeing, an unmarried father without parental responsibility will also be at a potential disadvantage since there is no absolute requirement that he be allowed a role in the process.

11.35   English law relating to parental responsibility is at present under review[6]. As the importance and prevalence of marriage diminishes, it is becoming more likely that at some time in the future English law relating to parental responsibility, should it continue to discriminate against unmarried men in relation to their children, will violate Art 14.

---

1   *Lindsay v UK* Application No 11089/84 (Dec), (11 November 1986) 49 DR 181.
2   *MB v UK* (6 April 1994) 77-A DR 108; *Rasmussen v Denmark* 7 EHRR 371.
3   *McMichael v UK* 20 EHRR 205, para 98.
4   *S v UK* Application No 11716/85, (1986) 47 DR 274.
5   20 EHRR 205.
6   Consultation Paper, *1. Court Procedures for the Determination of Paternity; 2. The Law on Parental Responsibility for Unmarried Fathers* (LCD, March 1998).

11.36   It is arguable that discrimination on the grounds of sexual orientation against same sex couples compared with heterosexual couples would offend Art 14 in conjunction with Art 8. There is no direct authority on the point; in the case of *Dudgeon v UK*[1], the Court declined to consider the applicant's complaint under Art 14 as a separate issue after it held that the criminalisation of homosexual acts in private was a breach of Art 8.

The relationship between Article 14 and Article 8
11.37   Article 14 is intended to safeguard access to and enjoyment of the rights and freedoms guaranteed by the other Articles of the Convention. Where it is possible to resolve the substance of a complaint by a finding that there has been a breach of the terms of one of the substantive Articles, it is the usual practice of the Court to do so. When the Court is able to do so, it usually finds that it is unnecessary to consider Art 14 as a separate issue.

11.38   A clear exception to that general rule is the case of *Hoffman v Austria*[2], where the Court held that the applicant mother had been denied custody as a result of discrimination on religious grounds, found a breach of Art 14 considered in conjunction with Art 8 and declined to consider Art 8 as a separate issue.

Justification
11.39   A difference of treatment may be justified, if it pursues a legitimate aim, and if the means employed to achieve it are reasonably proportionate to the aim sought to be realised. Additionally, there must be an objective and reasonable justification for the difference in treatment which will depend upon the individual facts of the case and the margin of appreciation. An example of this process of reasoning is to be found in the case of *McMichael v UK* in relation to the issue of the Scottish law of parental responsibility[3].

> 'As explained by the Government, the aim of the relevant legislation, which was enacted in 1986, is to provide a mechanism for identifying "meritorious" fathers who might be accorded parental rights, thereby protecting the interests of the child and the mother. In the Court's view, this aim is legitimate and the conditions imposed on natural fathers for obtaining recognition of their parental role respect the principle of proportionality. The Court therefore agrees with the Commission that there was an objective and reasonable justification for the difference of treatment complained of.'

The right to respect for private and family life [4]

Article 8
11.40   Article 8(1) provides that everyone has the right to respect for his private and family life, his home and his correspondence.

Article 8(2) sets out the circumstances, in general terms, in which the State may interfere with the enjoyment of the right. It also provides that there shall be no interference by a public authority with the exercise of the right except such as is in

---

1   4 EHRR 149.
2   17 EHRR 293, paras 36 and 37.
3   20 EHRR 205.
4   A detailed discussion of the balancing exercise under Art 8(2) and its relationship with the paramountcy of the welfare of the child is set out in Chapter 6.

accordance with the law and is necessary in a democratic society in the interests of national security, public safety or the economic well-being of the country for the prevention of disorder or crime for the protection of health or morals, or for the protection of the rights and freedoms of others.

11.41   The Court has developed a practice when dealing with an issue under Art 8 of considering each of the following matters in turn:

- the scope of the right;
- the nature of the interference which is alleged to restrict the enjoyment of the right;
- the lawfulness of the interference;
- the legitimate aims of the interference;
- the necessity for the interference in a democratic society (ie whether there are relevant and sufficient reasons for the interference which are proportionate to the restriction on the enjoyment of the right when taking into account the margin of appreciation) [1].

The scope of the rights created by Article 8

11.42   The primary objective of Art 8 is to protect individuals against arbitrary action by public authorities. In *Kroon v The Netherlands*[2], the Court stated:

> 'The Court reiterates that the essential object of Article 8 is to protect the individual against arbitrary action by the public authorities. There may in addition be positive obligations inherent in effective "respect" for family life. However, the boundaries between the State's positive and negative obligations under this provision do not lend themselves to precise definition. The applicable principles are nonetheless similar. In both contexts regard must be had to the fair balance that has to be struck between the competing interests of the individual and of the community as a whole; and in both contexts the State enjoys a certain margin of appreciation.'

The imprecision of the language employed in the text of the Article and the determined avoidance by of the organs of the Convention of definitive interpretation of the various components of the 'respect for family life' have left the extent and substance of the rights protected by Art 8 shrouded by a degree of imprecision. It is that same imprecision that the Convention organs have taken advantage of in order to be able to give the Articles of the Convention an evolutive interpretation responsive to the changing needs of society.

11.43   'Public authorities' not only include local authorities whose interventions in private and family lives falls within the ambit of Art 8, but also includes the courts.

The existence of family life

11.44   In the first stage of any inquiry to determine whether there has been any interference with the right to respect for 'family life' the Convention organs determine whether 'family life' is in existence. 'Family' has been interpreted widely by the European Court and the case-law continues to expand the recognised scope of 'family life', taking into account the nature of rapidly developing European attitudes.

---

1   A more detailed description of these criteria is set out in Chapter 6.
2   *Kroon v The Netherlands* 19 EHRR 263.

11.45 In *Keegan v Ireland*[1], the Court held that an unmarried father who had no parental rights sought custody of his child who had been placed for adoption by the mother without his knowledge. He had enjoyed a relationship of approximately 2 years' duration with the mother. They had at one time planned to marry but they parted before the child was born. He had seen the baby on only one occasion. The Court held that the nature of the parental relationship meant that the father had a 'family life' with his child 'from the moment of the birth'.

11.46 Whether 'family life' is found to exist in the circumstances of a particular case is a question of fact. In *X, Y and Z v UK*[2], it was held that in determining whether a relationship can amount to 'family life' a number of factors may be relevant, 'including whether the couple live together, the length of their relationship and whether they have demonstrated their commitment to each other by having children together or by any other means ...'.

The rights of the child

11.47 The rights of the child are considered in detail in Chapter 6.

Parental rights

11.48 Parental rights are considered in detail in Chapter 6.

The rights of the extended family

11.49 The rights of the extended family are considered in detail in Chapter 6.

Relationships beyond the natural and extended family

11.50 The Convention has also been held to apply to the relationship between the adopted child and adoptive parents[3]. 'Family life' has also been held to include the relationship between a foster-parent and foster-child, although the Court noted that the content of family life may depend on the nature of the fostering arrangements[4].

The home

Article 8 guarantees the right to respect for the home
11.51 The right is not a positive right giving rise to an entitlement to a home but rather a right to occupy the home and not be expelled or evicted[5]. It includes the right to peaceful enjoyment of the home[6].

11.52 What may amount to a 'home' has been subject to extremely broad interpretation in the case-law of the Convention. Unsurprisingly, the usual interpretation is that 'home' is where one lives on a settled basis. The guarantee to respect for a 'home' may, however, extend to an intended place to live. In *Gillow v*

PART B
IMPACT OF THE CONVENTION

---

1   18 EHRR 342.
2   [1997] 2 FLR 892.
3   *X v France* Application No 9993/82, (1982) 31 DR 241.
4   *Gaskin v UK* 12 EHRR 36, para 49; also *X v Switzerland* Application No 8257/78 (Dec), (10 July 1978) 13 DR 248.
5   *Wiggins v UK* Application No 7456/76, (1978) 13 DR 40; *Cyprus v Turkey* 4 EHRR 282.
6   *Arrondelle v UK* Application No 7889/77, (1982) 26 DR 5.

UK^1, the applicants had been refused permission to reside in their house on Guernsey. The Court acknowledged a legitimate interest on the part of the State in controlling the population on the island but in the absence of a pressing social need for the restriction and in the light of the fact that the authorities had failed to have sufficient regard to the personal circumstances of the applicants, who had always intended the house to be their home despite a very long period of absence, a breach of Art 8 was found to have occurred . However, in *Buckley v UK*[2], which involved an unsuccessful challenge by the applicant gypsy to the refusal of planning permission for her to maintain a home on her land which she had established without prior permission, the Court took note of the fact that there was a procedure by which the competing interests could be properly assessed and the planning inspectors had made their decision on the basis of relevant and sufficient reasons. The Court expressed the view that in the sphere of planning controls national authorities are better placed to assess relevant criteria of local importance.

11.53   The guarantee of respect for 'home' may even extend to office premises in some circumstances. In *Niemitz v Germany*[3], where the applicant lawyer's offices were searched pursuant to a warrant in order to obtain information about the identity and whereabouts of a third party, the Court interpreted 'home' as including professional or business premises[4] and held that there had been a violation of Art 8. The search had not been accompanied by any special procedural safeguards such as an independent observer and, more importantly, it impinged upon professional secrecy (or legal professional privilege) of a lawyer to an extent which was disproportionate[5]. It has been in the context of searches by the various limbs of the State authorities that much of the case-law in relation to the right of respect for the home has been generated.

11.54   Any interferences with the 'home' must conform with the requirements set out in para 8(2) of Art 8. Searches should therefore be 'lawful' and be attended by appropriate safeguards against arbitrariness and abuse[6]. The right affords protection against entry by the authorities pursuant to powers of arrest, search and seizure. Article 8(2) places the burden on the authorities to justify such interferences.

11.55   In *Chappell v UK*[7], the applicant unsuccessfully challenged the making of an *Anton Piller* order. The element of judicial supervision was decisive in that case, although even when a search is authorised by a court order it is necessary for the powers thus granted to be kept within identifiable limits if compliance with the Convention is to be achieved[8].

11.56   In *McLeod v UK*[9] where, in contempt of court, the wife had failed to deliver up certain property to the husband and the husband went to her home

---

1   11 EHRR 335, para 46.
2   23 EHRR 101, para 54.
3   16 EHRR 97.
4   Ibid, para 31.
5   Ibid, para 37.
6   See *Botka and Paya v Austria* Application No 15882/89 Austria, (29 March 1993) 74 DR 48.
7   *Chappell v UK* 12 EHRR 1.
8   See the *Niemitz* case (above).
9   [1998] 2 FLR 1048.

accompanied at his solicitor's request by police officers to collect his property, the Court found that the entry into her home was disproportionate to the legitimate aim of preventing breach of the peace; the Court found that the police had failed to look at the court order which did not entitle the husband to collect the property concerned, and, in any event, they should not have entered her home, once it was clear that she was not present.

Correspondence

Article 8 guarantees the right to respect for correspondence

11.57   In *Klass v FRG*[1], telephone-tapping was held to constitute a violation of Art 8. This provision may, therefore, in future be relevant in those cases where taped telephone conversations are sought to be adduced in evidence, for example, in private law cases and ancillary relief applications.

11.58   In *Andersson v Sweden*[2], the social welfare authorities had prohibited all contact between the applicant mother and son, including all correspondence and telephone conversations. The Commission found that 'telephone conversations between family members are covered by the notions of "family life" and "correspondence" within the meaning of Article 8'[3] and that there had been a breach of Art 8.

PART B
IMPACT OF THE CONVENTION

---

1   2 EHRR 214.
2   14 EHRR 615.
3   Ibid, para 72.

Chapter 12

PROPERTY AND ANCILLARY RELIEF

(A) SPOUSES

Generally

12.1   Although there is currently no reported Convention case-law which deals expressly with ancillary relief applications[1], the Convention guarantees which are most likely to be relevant are Art 6 (a right to a fair trial), Art 8 (a right to respect for private and family life), Art 14 (freedom from discrimination) and Art 1 of the First Protocol (a right to property). Article 5 of the Seventh Protocol (equality of rights of spouses) has for the present been omitted from the Human Rights Act 1998. The Government has, however, expressed a continuing commitment to its ratification and, as it is likely to have important ramifications in the field of ancillary relief, it is discussed below.

Equality of rights of spouses

12.2   Article 5 of the Seventh Protocol provides:

> 'Spouses shall enjoy equality of rights and responsibilities of a private law character between them, and in their relations with their children, as to marriage, and in the event of its dissolution. This Article shall not prevent states from taking such measures as are necessary in the interests of children.'

The reason given for omitting Art 5 of the Seventh Protocol from the Human Rights Act 1998 is that the Government has anticipated 'a difficulty ... because a few provisions of our domestic law, for example in relation to the property rights of spouses, could not be interpreted in a way which is compatible with Protocol 7. The Government intends to legislate to remove these inconsistencies when a suitable opportunity occurs, and then to sign and ratify the Protocol'[2].

The 'difficulty'

12.3   What the White Paper does not do is identify 'the difficulty' nor 'the few provisions of our domestic law' which could be incompatible with the Seventh Protocol. The following provisions of our domestic law have since been highlighted by the Government as being potentially incompatible in that they give the wife more favourable rights:

–   The common law duty of a husband to maintain his wife where there is no similar duty laid on a wife to maintain her husband.

–   The presumption of advancement between husband and wife whereby, subject to evidence to the contrary, if a husband transfers property to his wife he is presumed to be making her a gift; whereas if a wife transfers property to her husband, the presumption is that no gift is intended.

---

1   *Dart v Dart* [1996] 2 FLR 286 reached the Commission where the complaint was dismissed as inadmissible without the grounds being made public.

2   White Paper: *Rights Brought Home*, para 4.15.

– Section 1 of the Married Women's Property Act 1964 relating to money and property derived from a housekeeping allowance, whereby, subject to evidence to the contrary, if a husband pays a housekeeping allowance to his wife, any savings or property derived from that allowance belong to the husband and wife in equal shares; whereas if a wife pays a housekeeping allowance to the husband, then the property belongs to the wife only.

The Married Women's Property Act 1882 also does not provide equal opportunities for husbands and is, therefore, another potential candidate for amendment.

12.4   However, it is the possible amendment or substitution of s 25 of the Matrimonial Causes Act 1973 which will be of particular concern to family practitioners. Section 25 has long provided our domestic law with a flexible, discretionary approach to the diverse financial situations arising on the breakdown of a marriage. What s 25 does not do is express the objective of promoting the equality of rights and responsibilities between the spouses. There is, in fact, no current statutory objective and it has been left to the court to define the judge's ultimate aim as being 'to do that which is fair, just and reasonable between the parties'[1].

12.5   Section 25 has been the subject of recent scrutiny by the Lord Chancellor's Ancillary Relief Advisory Group chaired by Thorpe LJ. The Advisory Group's recommendation was to wait and see how the many reforms imminent in family law work out in practice before implementing further changes. It did not consider, nor was asked to consider, issues arising from the ratification of the Seventh Protocol.

12.6   It is significant to note that, in a response to the Government proposals on ancillary relief reform by the 17 judges of the Family Division (which they made by way of submission to the Lord Chancellor's Ancillary Relief Advisory Group)[2], there was unanimous opposition to any introduction of equality in the division of assets as a governing principle, even subject to departures. Some of the judges suggested that consideration be given to the re-amendment of the 1973 Act so as to cast a duty on the court to consider whether it would be practicable and just to exercise its powers under the capital provisions so as to divide the joint assets equally. Subject to the same caveat, others put forward the possibility of the re-introduction of concluding words into s 25(2); one of the various possible principles being to require the court to so exercise its powers as to place each party, so far as it is practicable and just so to do, in a position of economic security commensurate with that of the other. A third group had prima facie reservations about each[3]. Their provisional feeling was that the introduction of the principle of equal division 'would be adverse to the interests of most women ... The older woman following a long marriage during which the man amassed more than (say) £5m, would clearly benefit from such a change. But the average wife, currently awarded the whole of the £50k equity in order to house the children, would be, at least, more vulnerable. Some such awards are arguably unfair on husbands. But to find the right balance is acutely difficult'[4].

---

1   *White v White* [1998] 2 FLR 310 at 316H–317C, per Thorpe LJ.
2   [1999] Fam Law 159, per Wilson J.
3   Ibid, at 161.
4   Ibid.

12.7 Notwithstanding the Advisory Group's recommendation, in November 1998 the Government published a Green Paper *Supporting Families* which heralds radical proposals for reform of ancillary relief law including:

–   The objective that the court should 'exercise its powers so as to endeavour to do that which is fair and reasonable between the parties and any child of the family'[1].

–   'Having dealt with the needs of the children and the housing needs of the couple and having taken into account a nuptial agreement, the court would then divide any surplus so as to achieve a fair result, *recognising that fairness will generally require the value of the assets to be divided equally between the parties*' (emphasis added).

The inclusion of the proposal that the 'equal division of the value of the assets' should be 'a general requirement of fairness' may provide a signal that s 25, as presently drafted, may also be viewed by the Government as one of those 'few provisions in our domestic law which could be incompatible with Protocol 7'.

The European approach

12.8 There is at present no Convention case-law which acts as a pointer to the interpretation of the Seventh Protocol, Art 5. However, the explanatory memorandum to the Protocol does say that Art 5 'should not be understood as preventing the national authorities from taking due account of all relevant factors when reaching decisions with regard to the division of property in the event of the dissolution of marriage'[2]. This not only provides a comforting ring of familiarity with the words 'taking due account of all the relevant factors' but also reinforces the view that a wide margin of appreciation applies. A common interpretation has been:

> 'The fact that the Protocol is concerned with equality of rights and responsibilities of spouses does not, of course, mean that either in their relations with their children, or in other matters, they must divide everything between the spouses equally. For, apart from the fact that the interests of the children may dictate a different result, Article 5 is not intended to prevent the authorities from taking all relevant factors into account when deciding on the division of the matrimonial property in the event of a dissolution of marriage'[3].

Again, it is interesting to note the similar emphasis given in the response of the judges of the Family Division to Government proposals[4] on the interests of the children:

> 'Our view is that the principle of primacy for the children (in s 25(1)) is valuable and we question how any principle of equal asset division can be reconciled with (the principle of equal division). Either the principle of equal division would be subordinate, in which case its effect would be severely emasculated; or the two principles would stand together, in which case their frequent clashes might not easily be resolved; or the children principle would become subordinate which, we sense, would be as unacceptable to the public as ourselves'.

---

1   This largely reproduces the court's definition of the judge's ultimate aim referred to in *White v White* (above).

2   Paragraph 38.

3   A H Robertson and J G Merrill *Human Rights in Europe: A Study of the European Convention on Human Rights* 3rd edn (Manchester UP, 1995).

4   [1999] Fam Law 159 at 161.

12.9   It is, therefore, arguable that Art 5 should simply be interpreted as treating parties on the basis of an equal footing in the application before the court rather than imposing a requirement of 'equal division' in every case. The latter approach could be seen as a blunt instrument in such circumstances as a very short childless marriage or where most of the wealth is inherited from one party or in the context of pension sharing. On the other hand, it would redress the disparity which arises for the wives of wealthy husbands in the 'big money' cases where the traditional approach has been to look no further than her 'reasonable require-ments'[1] and would generally introduce 'certainty'.

12.10   It may be significant that, although there is not yet a consensus approach in the other Convention States, there is a clear trend developing in, for example, such other European countries as Iceland, Norway and Sweden, towards equal division providing the starting point in ancillary relief applications. So the question which is likely to arise is: has the currently wide margin of appreciation in this area narrowed so far as to oblige our domestic law to follow suit and introduce the notion of equal division of assets as a starting point in our domestic law?

12.11   If the answer is 'Yes', and the amending legislation were to require the objective of achieving financial equality between the parties, this will not only bring about a fundamental shift in our domestic law but also revolutionise our current approach to ancillary relief applications. The fall-out will also include applications under the Inheritance (Provision for Family and Dependants) Act 1975, as amended, and the provisions relating to pension sharing under the Matrimonial Causes Act 1973 when amended as proposed by the Welfare Reform and Pensions Bill 1999.

The right to property

12.12   Article 1 of the First Protocol provides that every natural or legal person is entitled to the peaceful enjoyment of his possessions. It comprises three rules.

(1) The first lays down the principle of peaceful enjoyment of property.

(2) The second covers deprivation of possessions and subjects it to certain conditions.

(3) The third recognises that the contracting States are entitled, amongst other things, to control the use of property in accordance with the general interest, by enforcing such laws as they deem necessary for the purpose[2].

The rules are not distinct in the sense of being unconnected: the second and third rules are concerned with particular instances of interference with the right to peaceful enjoyment of property and must therefore be construed in the light of the general principle laid down in the first rule[3].

12.13   Although the Article refers to peaceful enjoyment of possessions rather than a right of property, the Court has held that 'Article 1 is in substance

---

1   *Dart v Dart* [1996] 2 FLR 286; *Conran v Conran* [1997] 2 FLR 615; in contrast *White v White* [1998] 2 FLR 310 where it was held that the fact that the parties had traded as equal partners was the dominant feature of the case.

2   *Sporrang and Lonroth v Sweden* 5 EHRR 35, para 61; *Mellacher v Austria* 12 EHRR 391, para 42.

3   *Lithgow v UK* 8 EHRR 329, para 106.

guaranteeing the right of property'[1]. 'Possessions' has been widely interpreted to include all forms of interest in land and will also cover matrimonial assets.

12.14 Although at first blush Art 1 has all the hallmarks of making a major impact in the field of matrimonial property and finance, a second look shows that, to date, Art 1 has had very limited application in practice. There are no reported Convention cases which give any guidance as to how the First Protocol, Art 1 would impact upon ancillary relief applications.

12.15 Article 1 of the First Protocol has, however, been considered in the context of (a) pensions, and (b) inheritance. In respect of inheritance, it should be noted that violations have been found only where there has been a discriminatory element and it has been taken in conjunction with Art 14, and its impact upon our domestic inheritance law is likely to be marginal.

Pensions

12.16 According to the Commission's case-law, the right to a pension is not, as such, guaranteed by the Convention under Art 1 of the First Protocol[2]. However, in respect of private pension schemes where the pension is based on a private contract arranged by a financial institution or by a private insurance company and entered into by an individual in his own right, this is classified as a property right within the meaning of Art 1 of the First Protocol

12.17 Further, in respect of occupational pension schemes the Commission has considered that the right to a pension which is based on employment can in certain circumstances be assimilated to a property right; for example where special contributions have been paid or the employer has given a more general undertaking to pay a pension on conditions which can be considered part of the employment contract[3].

12.18 As to statutory schemes, the Commission has held that this provision does guarantee to persons who have paid contributions to a social insurance system the right to derive benefits from the system. However, it cannot be interpreted as an entitlement to a pension of a particular amount. The Commission found in this respect:

> 'The operation of a social security system is essentially different from the management of a private insurance company. Because of its public importance, the social security system must take account of political considerations, in particular those of financial policy. It is conceivable, for instance, that a deflationary trend may oblige the state to reduce the nominal amount of pensions. Fluctuations of this kind have nothing to do with the guarantee of ownership as a human right'[4].

12.19 In an earlier Commission case concerning Dutch social insurance legislation, the Commission had concluded that:

---

1   *Marckx v Belgium* 2 EHRR 330, para 63.
2   *Muller v Austria* Application No 5849/72 (16 December 1974), (1975) 1 DR 46; *X v Austria* Application No 7624/76 (Dec), (6 July 1977) 99 DR 100; *JW and EW v UK* Application No 9776/82, (3 October 1983) 34 DR 153.
3   Application No 10671/83 (Dec), (4 March 1985) (unpublished); *Stigson v Sweden* Application No 12264/86, (1988) 57 DR 131.
4   *Muller v Austria* (above); *Dorner v Austria* Application No 25044/94.

'There is ... no relationship between the contributions made and the pension received in the sense that the amounts paid by the insured person are accumulated with a view to covering the pension benefits accruing to him when reaching pensionable age. Consequently, a person does not have, at any given moment, an identifiable share in the fund claimable by him but he has an expectancy of receiving old age or survivors pension benefits subject to the conditions envisaged by the Acts concerned.'[1]

12.20 Potential areas where the First Protocol, Art 1 may have an impact in respect of pensions include: (a) discrimination issues under Art 14, taken in conjunction with the First Protocol, Art 1, where gender-based differences arise under pension schemes[2]; and (b) pension sharing orders when the amendments to the Matrimonial Causes Act 1973 proposed in the Welfare Reform and Pensions Bill 1999 are implemented[3].

Inheritance

12.21 The limitations of Art 1 of the First Protocol are amply demonstrated by the Court's approach in *Marckx v Belgium*[4]. The applicants, Paula Marckx and her infant daughter, Alexandra, complained that the illegitimacy laws in Belgium which placed limitations on: (a) the mother's capacity to give property to her daughter inter vivos or bequeath property to her by will; and (b) the child's capacity to take the property or inherit it on intestacy or by will infringed Art 1 of the First Protocol alone and together with Art 14.

12.22 As to Alexandra's rights, the Court excluded Art 1 of the First Protocol on the basis that:

'this Art does no more than enshrine the right of everyone to peaceful enjoyment of "his" possessions, that consequently it applies only to a person's existing possessions and does not guarantee the right to acquire possessions whether on intestacy or through voluntary dispositions.'[5]

12.23 As to her mother's rights, in respect of Art 1 of the First Protocol taken alone, the Court recognised that 'the right to dispose of one's property constitutes a traditional and fundamental aspect of the right of property'. However, it went on to hold that the second paragraph of Art 1 which authorises a contracting State to 'enforce such laws as it deems necessary to control the use of property in accordance with the general interest' sets the contracting States up as sole judges of the 'necessity' and that 'the general interest' may in certain circumstances induce a legislature to 'control the use of property' in the area of dispositions inter vivos or by will. In consequence, it found that the limitation complained of by the mother was not itself in conflict with the First Protocol.

12.24 The Court did, however, find a breach of Art 14 taken in conjunction with Art 1 of the First Protocol with respect to the mother. As the limitation

---

1   *X v The Netherlands* Application No 4130/69, (20 July 1971), (1972) 38 CD 9.

2   *Van Raalte v The Netherlands* 21 February 1997 RJD, 1997–1 No 39; in contrast *Vos v The Netherlands* Application No 10971/84 (Dec), (10 July 1985) 43 DR 190.

3   The Welfare Reform and Pensions Bill is likely to be implemented in 2000; see *Willis v UK* Application No 36042/97; *Cornwall v UK* Application No 36578/97 and *Leary v UK* Application No 38890/97.

4   2 EHRR 330.

5   Ibid, para 50.

applied only to unmarried and not to married mothers, the Court considered it to be discriminatory and failed to see on what 'general interest' or on what objective and reasonable justification a State could rely to limit an unmarried mother's right to make gifts or legacies in favour of her child when at the same time a married woman is not subject to any similar restriction.

12.25   In *Inze v Austria*[1], the Court found there was a violation of Art 14 taken together with Art 1 of the First Protocol where Austrian law on intestacy gave precedence to a legitimate child over an illegitimate child in the attribution of their deceased mother's farm. Although the applicant did not allege a violation of Art 1 of the First Protocol taken alone, the Court still had to consider whether the facts of the case fell within the ambit of the First Protocol, Art 1 for the purposes of Art 14. It distinguished the case from the *Marckx* case on the grounds that in the latter the complaint concerned a potential right to inherit, whereas in the instant case the applicant had already acquired by inheritance a right to a share in his mother's estate. Although the Court found that Art 1 of the First Protocol was applicable, it emphasised that 'Article 1 of Protocol No 1 did not entitle the applicant to inherit the farm specifically'[2].

12.26   Under Art 1 of the First Protocol it is not, therefore, for the court to determine who should inherit. This further demonstrates its limited application. Moreover, in our domestic law the former distinctions between the legitimate and illegitimate child are in the process of disappearing from our legal landscape, following the passing of s 1 of the Family Law Reform Act on 4 April 1988. Further, 'child' under s 25 of the Inheritance (Provision for Family and Dependants) Act 1975 is defined as including 'an illegitimate child and a child – ventre sa mere at the death of the deceased' and in *Re McC (A Minor)*[3] provides an illustration of how the domestic court treated as equal the claims of an illegitimate child and his legitimate half-brother.

12.27   It is, therefore, very unlikely that the inheritance issues raised in the *Marckx* and *Inze* cases under Art 14 taken in conjunction with Art 1 of the First Protocol will arise in our domestic law.

(B) COHABITANTS

Heterosexual cohabitants

Domestic law

12.28   Our domestic law distinguishes between spouses and cohabitants. Changing social attitudes in respect of cohabitants have already had some impact upon our domestic law. For example, succession to a secure tenancy under the Housing Acts or to a statutory or protected tenancy under the Rent Acts has now been extended to include 'someone living with him or her as wife or husband'. The new s 1A of the Inheritance (Provisions for Family and Dependants) Act 1975 ('the Inheritance Act') (inserted by s 2 of the Law Reform (Succession) Act 1995),

---

1   10 EHRR 394; see also *Cierva Osorio de Moscoso v Spain* Application No 41127/8, 41503/98, 41717/98 and 45726/99; *Nazvrek v France* Application No 34406/96 (4 May 1999).

2   Ibid, para 47.

3   [1985] AC 528.

which defines the class of cohabitant able to apply to the court for financial provision out of the estate of the deceased partner, is a recent example. Section 1A now provides:

'This subsection applies to a person if ... the person was living –

in the same household as the deceased, and
as the husband or wife of the deceased.'

This now obviates the cohabitant having to satisfy the dependency test in s 1(1)(e) as pre-requisite for locus standi to make an application for financial provision under the Inheritance Act.

12.29   Although cohabitants have enjoyed certain protection under the Domestic Violence and Matrimonial Proceedings Act 1976 in the context of the cohabitants' home (which is preserved and enlarged by Part IV of the Family Law Act 1996), cohabitants nevertheless (by way of example):

–   remain excluded from the ancillary relief provisions of the Matrimonial Causes Act 1973 as these are consequent upon decree of nullity, divorce or judicial separation; the cohabitants' recourse has been to look to the law of trusts to determine their property rights;
–   remain excluded from the matrimonial home rights under s 30 of the Family Law Act 1996 which provide protection for a spouse who would otherwise have no legal right to occupy the matrimonial home; cohabitants cannot have matrimonial home rights as such rights can arise only as the result of the marriage. Cohabitants and former cohabitants do have some protection in relation to certain tenancies[1] and in respect of mortgage possession proceedings[2];
–   do not enjoy the privileged position of a husband or wife under ss 1(2)(a) and 3(2) of the Inheritance (Provision for Family and Dependants) Act 1975.

12.30   Although there are Governmental moves afoot to provide some, as yet unspecified, form of statutory system for regulating cohabitants' rights and responsibilities in relation to their financial affairs on the termination of the relationship, some of the questions which may arise under the Human Rights Act 1998 in the meantime are whether our present law, which (a) confines 'ancillary relief adjustment rights' to spouses, and (b) accords preferential treatment to spouses under the Inheritance Act provisions and, therefore, clearly discriminates against cohabitants, is vulnerable to challenge as constituting a violation of one or more of the guaranteed rights under the Convention ('the discriminatory argument').

Convention law

12.31   Although Art 14 guarantees the Convention rights and freedoms 'without discrimination on any ground such as sex, race ... or other status', it can only be taken into account when taken in conjunction with another Article and is not free-standing. Article 5 of the Seventh Protocol applies only to spouses and,

---

1   Family Law Act 1996, s 36; Housing Act 1985, s 85(5A) and Housing Act 1988, s 9(5A); an order under s 36 gives protection to cohabitants which was denied in *Colin Smith Music Ltd v Ridge* [1975] 1 WLR 463.
2   Family Law Act 1996, ss 54–56.

therefore, does not provide the catalyst necessary to trigger the discriminatory argument under Art 14.

12.32 The Strasbourg Court has not shown any enthusiasm for applying Arts 8 and 14 together to assist the unmarried applicant to claim similar property rights in the family home to those where the couple were married.

12.33 In a recent Commission case, *Saucedo Gomez v Spain*[1], the applicant, who was already married, cohabited with her partner from 1974 to 1992. She could not marry him because, at the time, divorce was not allowed in Spain. The applicant, her daughter and her partner all lived together in the partner's accommodation. The relationship broke down. Her application for an order granting her the use of the family home and pecuniary provision was dismissed and her appeal was dismissed on the grounds that: (a) the right claimed by the applicant could arise only where a couple were married; (b) cohabitation could not be equated with marriage, particularly as no children had been born of this cohabitation; and (c) the applicant could have regularised her marital position when divorce became available in 1981. The applicant's contention before the Commission was that the decisions of the courts on these grounds constituted discriminatory treatment and infringed her right to respect for family life.

12.34 The Commission ruled that the decisions complained of did not result in discriminatory interference with the applicant's right to respect for family life. It held that, although there was no doubt that the existence of a family life may be assumed in the case of a couple who lived together for 18 years, the differences in treatment between spouses and cohabitees with regard to the granting of the family home pursued a legitimate aim and could be objectively and reasonably justified as protection of the traditional family. The discrimination was not disproportionate, especially because the applicant freely decided not to benefit from the advantages inherent in the status of spouse by not regularising her position with her partner.

12.35 It went on to say that it was not for the court to dictate or indicate to States the measures that should be taken with regard to the existence of stable relationships between men and women who live together as a couple without being married. This is a question on which states enjoy a margin of discretion: that they are free to decide what measures to take provided they meet the requirement of respect for family life.

12.36 As the Convention law stands at present, the prospects for the discriminatory argument in relation to cohabitants look distinctly unpromising. However, the law is dynamic and evolutive and it is, therefore, possible that in the future changing social attitudes may provide the impetus to roll back the covers and expose the discrimination against the unmarried to the full glare of the Convention rights and guarantees.

---

1 Application No 37784/97 (Dec) (19 January 1998).

Homosexual cohabitants

Domestic law

12.37   In *R v Ministry of Defence ex parte Smith*[1], where the four applicants were discharged as serving members of the armed forces on the sole ground of their sexual orientation and challenged the decision in judicial review proceedings on the grounds that it was, inter alia, contrary to Art 8, Sir Thomas Bingham MR (as he then was) said:

> 'There can be no doubt that public attitudes to homosexuals and homosexuality have in the past varied widely from country to country and within the same country at different times, and among different social groups in the same country. Almost any generalisation can be faulted. But there has in this country been a discernible trend, over the last half century or so, towards a greater understanding and greater tolerance of homosexuals by heterosexuals, and towards greater openness and honesty by homosexuals ... I regard the progressive development and refinement of public and professional opinion at home and abroad ... as an important feature of this case. A belief which represented unquestioned orthodoxy in year X may have become questionable by year Y and unsustainable by year Z.'[2]

12.38   The Court of Appeal went on to dismiss the applicants' appeals. Although the relevance of the Convention was merely treated as background to the complaint of irrationality and the Court declined to proffer any answers relating to any future liability under the Convention, nevertheless this case provided a landmark example of domestic judicial recognition and expression of the major changes in public attitudes towards homosexuality that have already taken place in our generation[3].

12.39   The future potential was further signalled in the powerful dissenting judgment of Ward LJ in *Fitzpatrick v Sterling Housing Association*[4]. The tenant of a flat lived with the appellant in a stable and permanent homosexual relationship. When the tenant died, the appellant applied to the respondent landlord to take over the tenancy and was refused. The question which arose was whether the surviving partner in a permanent homosexual relationship could claim succession rights under the Rent Act 1977 in respect of which the deceased partner was a protective tenant. The majority of the Court of Appeal held that the phrase 'living with the original tenant as his or her wife or husband' within the meaning of Sch 1, para 2(2) to the Rent Act 1977 applied only to heterosexual relationships. They further went on to hold that the appellant was not 'a person who was a member of the original tenant's family' within the meaning of para 3(1) of the same Schedule. Waite LJ (in the majority) said:

> 'If endurance, stability, interdependence and devotion were the sole hall-marks of family membership, there could be no doubt about this case at all. Mr Fitzpatrick and Mr Thompson lived together for a longer period than many marriages endure these days. They were devoted and faithful, giving each other mutual help and support in a life which shared many of the highest qualities to be found in heterosexual

---

1   [1996] QB 517.

2   Ibid, at 552E–F and 554 at C–D.

3   The four applicants have subsequently complained to the Strasbourg Court which held that there had been a violation of their right to respect for private life (*Lustig-Praen and Becket v UK and Smith and Grady v UK* (1999) *The Times*, 11 October).

4   [1998] 1 FLR 6 at 25H–42D.

attachments, married or unmarried. To adopt an interpretation of the statute that allowed all sexual partners, whether of the same or opposite sex, to enjoy the privilege of succession to tenancies protected by the Rent Acts would, moreover, be consistent not only with social justice but also with the respect accorded by modern society to those of the same sex who undertake a permanent commitment to a shared life.

The survey which I have undertaken ... shows, however, that the law in England regarding succession to statutory tenancies is firmly rooted in the concept of the family as an entity bound together by ties of kinship (including adoptive status) or marriage. The only relaxation ... has been a willingness to treat heterosexual cohabitants as if they were husband and wife. *That was a restrictive extension, offensive to social justice and tolerance because it excludes lesbians and gays. It is out of tune with modern acceptance of the need to avoid any discrimination on the ground of sexual orientation.* In that respect I wholly agree with the comments of Ward LJ ... They are changes which will certainly need to be made, if Parliament is to fulfil its function of reflecting the spirit of our times – in particular the spirit which recognises the value of abiding realtionships, the heterosexual, the lesbian, the gay – or even those which are not sexually based at all' (emphasis added) [1].

Ward LJ (dissenting) said:

'In my judgment our society has shown itself to be tolerant enough to free itself from the burdens of stereotype and prejudice in all their subtle and ugly manifestations. The common man may be disapproving of the homosexual relationship which is not for him but, having shrugged his shoulders, he would recognise that the relationship was to all intents and purposes a marriage between those partners. They lived a life akin to that of any husband and wife. They were so bound together that they constituted a family.'

12.40 This judgment stands as a beacon for the future as a striking example of how, once the Human Rights Act 1998 is implemented, it will be our judiciary who will be at the cutting edge in tackling the controversial social issues (currently avoided by the Strasbourg Court) and developing the Convention law in imaginative and innovative ways to reflect changing social attitudes.

12.41 Domestic legislation has made a start in acknowledging homosexual cohabitants in the following limited context: Part IV of the Family Law Act 1996 which gives comparable protection from domestic violence to homosexual and heterosexual cohabitants [2].

Convention law
12.42 The present position under Art 8 is that, despite the modern evolution of attitudes towards homosexuality, a stable homosexual relationship between two men or two women does not yet fall within the scope of the right to respect for family life [3].

12.43 However, on 8 February 1994 the European Parliament did resolve to sweep away any unequal treatment based on sexual orientation, and a number of European countries including Holland, Hungary, Sweden, Norway, Denmark, Greenland and Iceland, have taken some first steps in that direction by permitting homosexual couples to enter into agreements regulating their property and inheritance rights in the same way that heterosexual cohabitants can.

---

1   Ibid. at 19E–H and 20F.
2   Family Law Act 1996, s 62(3).
3   *X & Y v UK* [1997] 2 FLR 892 and *Kerkhoven v Netherlands* Application No 15666/89.

12.44 These steps may be tentative but they at least illustrate how the European States are beginning to move in response to a growing understanding and social tolerance towards homosexual relationships. In the event that the right to marry under Art 12 was ever extended to homosexual marriages, then this may even open up the way to claims for ancillary relief.

(C) CHILDREN

Domestic law

12.45 Under s 25(1) of the Matrimonial Causes Act 1973, it is the court's duty in deciding whether to exercise its powers under s 23, s 24 or s 24A and in what manner to give first consideration to the welfare, while a minor, of any child of the family who has not attained the age of 18. In *M v B (Ancillary Proceedings: Lump Sum)*[1], the Court of Appeal expressed the child's welfare in the context of the parties' housing needs as follows:

> 'In all these cases it is one of the paramount considerations, in applying the s 25 criteria, to endeavour to stretch what is available to cover the need of each for a home, particularly where there are young children involved. Obviously the primary carer needs whatever is available to make the main home for the children, but it is of importance, albeit it is of lesser importance, that the other parent should have a home of his own where the children can enjoy their contact time with him. Of course there are cases where there is not enough to provide a home for either. Of course there are cases where there is only enough to provide one. But in any case where there is, by stretch and a degree of risk-taking, the possibility of a division to enable both to rehouse themselves, that is an exceptionally important consideration and one which will inevitably have a decisive impact on outcome.'

12.46 In *Piglowska v Piglowski*[2], Lord Hoffmann, after citing this passage in *M v B*, said:

> 'I do not doubt for a moment the sound sense of these remarks. That was a case in which the couple had two children aged 10 and 6 and the question was whether the wife should have a house which cost £210,000, leaving the husband without enough to buy a property of his own, or a house costing £135,000, leaving the husband £75,000 to buy a property of his own. The Court of Appeal held that the second approach was correct. This is a useful guideline to judges dealing with cases of a similar kind.'[3]

Convention law

12.47 The right to respect for family life under Art 8 recognises the parents' right to contact[4] and the Convention is, therefore, likely to reinforce the approach taken by the Court of Appeal in *M v B*[5]. Consequently, this opens up the way to a strengthened argument in the future that the court in determining the

---

1   [1998] 1 FLR 53 at 60 E–G.
2   [1999] 2 FLR 763.
3   It should be noted that Lord Hoffmann went on to say: 'But to cite the case as if it laid down some rule that both spouses invariably have a right to purchased accommodation is a misuse of authority'.
4   *Hendriks v The Netherlands* 5 EHRR 233, paras 94–95; *B v UK* 10 EHRR 87, para 60; *Peter Whitear v UK* [1998] 3 EHRLR 291.
5   [1998] 1 FLR 53.

division of the parties' income and assets in an ancillary relief application involving minor children should have regard as 'exceptionally important' factors as to how best to secure not only for the child his right to enjoy contact with the parent who is not the primary carer but also to secure for the secondary parent his right of contact with his child.

12.48 It is interesting to note that the Government's Green Paper *Supporting Families* foreshadows this approach by making its first guiding principle 'to promote the welfare of any child of the family under the age of 18 by meeting the housing needs of any children and the primary carer, and of the secondary carer; *both to facilitate contact and to recognise the continuing importance of the secondary carer's role*' (emphasis added).

12.49 A contact argument was, however, raised in the context of the Child Support Act 1991 in *Logan v UK*[1], where the father applicant contended that the amount of maintenance he was required to pay under the Act left him with insufficient money to enable him to maintain reasonable contact with his children in violation of Art 8 of the Convention. He submitted that this restriction impeded the development of his relationship with his children and disclosed a failure to respect that relationship. The Commission noted that the relevant legislation, in so far as it sought to regulate the assessment of maintenance payments from absent parents, did not by its very nature affect family life. Nor in the light of the factual information supplied by the applicant regarding his income and expenses, including the cost of visiting his children every fortnight, did the Commission consider that the applicant had shown that the effect of the operation of the legislation in his case was of such a nature and degree as to disclose any lack of respect for his rights under Art 8. In the circumstances, the Commission did not find it necessary to go on to consider whether, had there been an interference, it would have been justified within the meaning of Art 8(2) of the Convention and rejected this part of his application. The Art 8 point in *Logan v UK*, therefore, turned upon its particular facts and the case does not rule out the possibility of a violation where it can be demonstrated that the operation of the legislation is of such a nature and degree that it prevents or so substantially restricts contact as to amount to a lack of respect for family life.

12.50 In the *Logan* case, the father also complained of a violation of Art 6(1) of the Convention as he was unable to challenge the maintenance assessment before a court. The Commission rejected his complaint. It recalled that Art 6 (1) applies only to disputes over rights and obligations which can be said, at least on arguable grounds, to be recognised under domestic law and that the dispute must be 'genuine and of a serious nature'. It noted that the applicant accepted that the maintenance assessment was calculated correctly under domestic law and that it was uncontested that there was no scope under the applicable provisions for costs of access visits to be taken into account in the assessment. In these circumstances the Commission found that there was no dispute of a 'genuine' or 'serious nature' as to any civil right or obligation[2].

---

1   22 EHRR 178 CD.
2   Article 6 of the Convention.

(D) PROCEDURE

12.51　　As ancillary relief applications concern disputes over private rights and, therefore, are proceedings within the scope of Art 6, they must comply with its requirements. In summary, the principal Art 6 guarantees which will apply particularly to ancillary relief applications are:

- the 'fair hearing' guarantees;
- the right of access to a court;
- the right to a hearing within a reasonable time;
- the right to a public hearing and the public pronouncement of judgment.

The potential areas of impact include possible challenges to:

- hearing ancillary relief applications in chambers. In the European Court, cases concerning family law are heard in public, although the parties can be referred to by initials so as to preserve their anonymity;
- the 'millionaire's defence' which limits the wife's access to documentation [1];
- the 'full and frank disclosure' rule [2] as arguably infringing the freedom from self-incrimination [3]. It should be anticipated, however, that any such challenge is likely to meet stiff judicial resistance;
- evidence obtained clandestinely such as taped telephone calls. However, in *Schenk v Switzerland* [4], the European Court noted that Art 6 does not lay down any rules on the admissibility of evidence as such, which is therefore primarily a matter for regulation under national law and thus the guiding principle must be to ascertain whether the hearing as a whole is fair;
- orders which may make mediation a compulsory preliminary or alternative to litigation or if legal aid were to be withheld until mediation had been attempted;
- delay which all too frequently occurs in ancillary relief application. However, since 1 October 1996 there has been a pilot scheme to evaluate new rules for ancillary relief applications which emphasise judicial control of the application in accordance with the general philosophy of the new Civil Procedure Rules 1998 and impose strict time-limits. The Art 6 guarantee of a hearing within a reasonable time will reinforce this approach.

1　　*Thyssen-Bornemisza v Thyssen-Bornemisza (No 2)* [1985] FLR 1069; *Van G v Van G (Financial Provision: Millionaire's Defence)* [1995] 1 FLR 328.

2　　*Jenkins v Livesey (formerly Jenkins)* [1985] FLR 813.

3　　*Saunders v UK* 23 EHRR 313.

4　　13 EHRR 242.

Chapter 13

DOMESTIC VIOLENCE

DOMESTIC LAW

13.1   Under the Family Law Act 1996, the victims of domestic violence are able to obtain protection through the courts. Occupation orders can be granted under ss 30 to 40 and those orders grant or take away the right to occupy a property. The Act sets out various factors which should be considered when making an order. There are different factors to be taken into account dependent on the status of the parties in respect of the property[1]. The court must take into account 'any relevant child' and must make an order if a 'balance of harm' test is satisfied[2]. Under s 41 of the Family Law Act 1996, where the court is required to consider the relationship between the parties, the court 'is to have regard to the fact that (the parties) have not given each other the commitment involved in marriage'. There are similar provisions under the Trusts of Land and Appointment of Trustees Act 1996.

13.2   Sections 42 to 45 enable the court to provide protection to a party by making a non-molestation order. These sections also specifically provide for an ex parte order[3] and for undertakings to be given. However, a power of arrest cannot be attached to an undertaking and the court is specifically forbidden from accepting an undertaking if a power of arrest would have been attached to the order[4].

13.3   Under s 47, it is mandatory for the court to attach a power of arrest if:

–   the court makes the relevant order, ie an occupation order or non-molestation order; and
–   the respondent has used or threatened violence against the applicant or a relevant child; and
–   the court is not satisfied that the applicant and/or the child will be adequately protected without attaching a power of arrest[5].

THE RIGHT TO PROPERTY

13.4   Under Art 1 of the First Protocol:

'Every natural or legal person is entitled to the peaceful enjoyment of his possessions. No one shall be deprived of his possessions except in the public interest and subject to the conditions provided for by law and by the general principles of international law.

The preceding provisions shall not, however, in any way impair the right of a State to enforce such laws as it deems necessary to control the use of property in accordance

PART B
IMPACT OF THE CONVENTION

---

1   Eg whether either or both of the parties have or have had a right to occupy.
2   Sections 33(7), 35(8). But cf ss 36(7) and 38(4) where the 'balance of harm' test is not determinative but simply a factor to be taken into account.
3   Family Law Act 1996, s 45.
4   Ibid, s 46.
5   Ibid, s 47(2).

with the general interest or to secure the payment of taxes or other contributions or penalties.'

Similar provisions are available under the Trusts of Land and Appointment of Trustees Act 1996 (TOLATO).

13.5   The drafting allows the State a wide measure of latitude in its legislation regarding property. There is no case-law in respect of occupation orders within domestic violence proceedings but the case-law in respect of property rights in general may point to the approach the courts should take.

13.6   One of the leading cases is that of *Sporrong and Lonnroth v Sweden*[1]. The points raised in the judgment include:

–   Regulation of property rights falling short of expropriation and where ownership remains is unlikely to amount to a deprivation of property but may involve an interference with the peaceful enjoyment of possessions[2].

–   The Court must determine whether a fair balance was stuck between the demands of the general interest of the community and the requirements of the protection of the individual's fundamental rights. The search for this balance is inherent in the whole of the Convention and is also reflected in the structure of Art 1[3].

It is submitted that the factors which the court has to consider under ss 33 to 41 would fulfil the 'fair balance' test.

THE RIGHT TO RESPECT FOR PRIVATE AND FAMILY LIFE

13.7   Under Art 8 of the European Convention:

'1. Everyone has the right to respect for his private and family life, his home and his correspondence.

2. There shall be no interference by a public authority with the exercise of this right except such as in accordance with the law and is necessary in a democratic society in the interests of national security, public safety or the economic well-being of the country, for the prevention of disorder or crime, for the protection of health or morals, or for the protection of the rights and freedoms of others.'

It is highly likely that an occupation order (and to some extent a non-molestation order) will interfere with the respondent's right to family life. However, even if an order is made, there will be no breach of the Convention if the order fulfils one of the exceptions under the second paragraph of Art 8. It is not proposed to go into this in detail[4] but it is arguable, on common sense grounds alone, that the domestic violence provisions under the Family Law Act 1996 would fall within the ambit of:

–   public safety; or
–   prevention of disorder or crime; or

---

1   5 EHRR 35.
2   Ibid, para 63.
3   Ibid, para 69.
4   See **11.40** et seq for a fuller argument on the right to family life.

- protection of health or morals; or
- protection of rights and freedoms of others.

FREEDOM FROM DISCRIMINATION IN RESPECT OF PROTECTED RIGHTS

13.8 Under Art 14 of the Convention:

'The enjoyment of the rights and freedoms set forth in this Convention shall be secured without discrimination on any ground such as sex, race, colour, language, religion, political or other opinion, national or social origin, association with a national minority, property, birth or other status.'

Where the parties are cohabitants rather than spouses, the Family Law Act 1996 specifically enjoins the court 'to have regard to the fact that [the parties] have not given each other the commitment involved in marriage'[1]. There is a clear discrimination between those who are married and those who cohabit. Can it be argued that the legislation violates Art 14? In the *Belgian Linguistic Case (No 2)*[2], the Court held that the 'principle of equality of treatment' is violated if the distinction has no objective and reasonable justification[3]. In the case of *Lindsay v UK*[4], a couple argued that the UK taxation system favoured couples who were married over couples who were not married, in breach of Art 14. The Commission said that such an application was manifestly ill-founded on the grounds that:

- the two situations were not analogous;
- although in some fields the de facto relationship of cohabitees is now recognised, there still exist differences in legal status and legal effects;
- marriage continues to be characterised by a corpus of rights and obligations which differentiate it markedly from their situation of a man and woman who cohabit[5].

At present, therefore, it is likely that no breach under Art 14 would be found. However, as time passes, and cohabitation becomes more widespread, the distinction may well go further than the de facto recognition and an application against discrimination may succeed.

COURT PROCEDURE AND THE RIGHT TO A FAIR TRIAL UNDER ARTICLE 6

13.9 Under Art 6, a person is guaranteed a fair trial in any court proceedings involving:

- 'the determination of his civil rights and obligations'; or
- 'any criminal charge against him'[6].

---

1   Family Law Act 1996, s 41, although this section applies only in certain limited circumstances.
2   1 EHRR 252.
3   Ibid, para 34.
4   49 DR 181.
5   Ibid, p 193.
6   Article 6(1).

In either category, the guarantees under Art 6(1) apply. Such guarantees are considered more fully in the chapter on the right to a fair trial but Art 6(1) explicitly includes the following rights:

- right of access to a court;
- right to a fair hearing;
- right to a hearing within a reasonable time;
- right to an independent and impartial tribunal established by law;
- right to a public hearing;
- right to a public pronouncement of judgment.

13.10   Further rights under Art 6(2) and (3) are guaranteed if the proceedings fall within the category of a 'determination ... of a criminal charge'. Within domestic violence proceedings, there are two potential stages, either of which may fall within this definition:

(1) imposition of a non-molestation or occupation order following a finding that an assault or threat of an assault has occurred;
(2) committal proceedings in the event of a breach of the above order.

Determination of a criminal charge [1]

13.11   In domestic violence proceedings, the court is given the task of deciding whether or not allegations of assault or threats of assault have been proved. Such allegations could, as easily, form the basis of a criminal offence to be dealt with in the criminal courts. Although domestic violence proceedings are dealt with in the civil courts this does not necessarily mean that such proceedings fall outside the 'determination ... of a criminal charge'. The label given to such proceedings by the contracting State is only one aspect of the categorisation and the European Court of Human Rights looks to the reality of the proceedings and not simply at the given classification. The Court applies three criteria in deciding whether the offence is 'criminal' within Art 6(1):

(1) the classification of the offence by the contracting State;
(2) the nature of the offence;
(3) the severity of the possible penalty.

The criteria are not cumulative and the application of any one of the above can bring the proceedings within the classification of a criminal charge for purposes of Art 6 of the Convention.

The classification of the offence under domestic law – 'the autonomy argument'

13.12   Contracting States have argued that the classification each State gives to the 'offence' is determinative as to whether it was 'criminal' or not. This was described as the 'autonomy argument' [2]. However, the European Court of Human Rights has taken a different approach. If the contracting State designates an offence as 'criminal' then the European Court respects such classification under the Convention as well and the offence is covered specifically by all the subparagraphs of Art 6. However, if the offence is not designated as 'criminal' by the contracting state, this is not the end of the matter. The Court will not consider

---

1   See also Chapter 8.
2   *Engel and Others v The Netherlands* 1 EHRR 647.

itself bound by such classification and will consider the matter further under the other two criteria. 'In short, the "autonomy" of the concept of "criminal" operates, as it were, one way only'[1].

The nature of the offence
13.13 Two aspects are considered:

(1) whether the 'offence' applies in general or whether it applies to a specific and restricted group;
(2) the purpose of the offence.

Application of the offence – general or specific
13.14 If the 'offence' and subsequent proceedings apply only to a specific or restricted group of people, for example a profession, it is more likely, although not automatic, that the regulation will be considered, for example, a disciplinary matter rather than a 'criminal charge'. It may, in these circumstances, still fall within the 'determination of a civil right and obligation'[2].

The purpose of the offence
13.15 This was considered in the case of *Ozturk v Germany*[3]. The German Government had 'decriminalised' certain offences, notably in the road traffic sphere. The applicant, who was Turkish speaking, was charged with causing an accident through careless driving and was fined 60 DM and ordered to pay costs and fees (including the interpreter's fees) of 13 DM. He claimed that this was a criminal charge and that he was, thus, entitled to an interpreter. He further claimed that the order that he bear the costs of the interpreter was in breach of Art 6(3)(e). The Court considered the amount involved to be small and further recognised that the German Government's attempt to decriminalise offences with the consequent advantage to the individual represented 'more than a simple change in terminology'[4]. Nevertheless, the Court felt that it mattered little whether the legal provision contravened by the applicant was aimed at protecting the rights and interests of others, or solely at meeting the demands of road traffic. It held that these two ends were not mutually exclusive and that,

> 'Above all, the general character of the rule and the purpose of the penalty, being both deterrent and punitive, suffice to show that the offence in question was, in terms of Art 6, criminal in nature.'[5]

The following points can be drawn from the judgment:

– Although the offence was minor and hardly likely to damage the reputation of the individual, there was nothing in Art 6 which required a criminal offence to be of a serious nature.

– Indeed, it would contravene the purpose of Art 6 if States could remove categories of offences from the protection of Art 6 only on the ground that they were petty.

---

1   *Engel and Others v The Netherlands*, 1 EHRR 647, para 81.
2   See *Albert and Le Compte v Belgium* 5 EHRR 533 and below.
3   6 EHRR 409.
4   Ibid, para 53.
5   Ibid.

–   Furthermore, the conduct of the applicant and the provision allegedly contravened were regarded by the majority of contracting States as criminal in nature.

–   The above decision was made by a majority of 13 votes to 5. The dissenting voices were strong and felt that insufficient recognition had been given to the development of decriminalisation which would end the stigma of criminality in this regard. For the minority, such recognition would take such provisions outside the ambit of criminal charges.

The severity of the penalties

13.16   It is not the penalty actually imposed which is relevant, but the highest penalty applicable which is the decisive factor.

13.17   In *Demicoli v Malta*[1], the maximum sentence which could have been imposed was a custodial sentence of 60 days or a fine not exceeding 500 lira. Although the penalty actually imposed amounted to a fine of 250 lira, 'what was at stake was thus sufficiently important to warrant classifying the offence with which the applicant was charged as a criminal one'[2].

13.18   The case of *Campbell and Fell v UK*[3] concerned the loss of remission for breach of disciplinary provisions within prison. The Court held that the practice of remission created the justifiable expectation on the prisoner's mind of an earlier release and, therefore, the loss of a prospect of a reduction of sentence amounted to a deprivation of liberty. In the circumstances, the parallels between the 'disciplinary proceedings' and the sentencing procedures within the criminal courts placed it firmly within the 'determination of a criminal charge'.

13.19   The approach of the European Court can be seen in the leading case of *Engel and Others v The Netherlands*[4]. The case concerned five conscript soldiers in different non-commissioned ranks in The Netherlands armed forces. Various penalties had been imposed upon them for offences against military discipline. The soldiers applied to the European Court claiming that the proceedings taken against them had violated Art 6[5]. The Government had argued that the proceedings were disciplinary and did not come within the scope of Art 6 as they did not involve a determination of either a criminal charge or of a determination of civil rights and obligations.

13.20   The Court stated that the designation of the offences as a matter of disciplinary law or of criminal law was only the starting point[6]. The Court accepted that, in general, there were substantial advantages for the individual if the offence were designated disciplinary rather than criminal, for example, in sentencing which was usually less severe, did not appear on a person's criminal record and entailed more limited consequences. On the other hand, criminal proceedings were ordinarily accompanied by fuller guarantees[7]. It was matter of choice for the State if it chose to classify the offence under the criminal law but a designation

---

1   14 EHRR 47.
2   Ibid, para 34.
3   7 EHRR 165.
4   1 EHRR 647.
5   They also claimed a loss of liberty in violation of Art 5.
6   1 EHRR 647, para 82.
7   Ibid, para 80.

under disciplinary law entailed more careful scrutiny to 'ensure that the disciplinary does not encroach on the criminal'.

13.21 As for the remaining two criteria, the Court held that 'the very nature of the offence is a factor of greater import', accepting that an offence concerning the operation of the armed forces, that is, a matter of internal regulation, was, in principle, capable of being designated disciplinary rather than criminal by the State. However, 'supervision by the court (did) not stop there (and) would generally prove to be illusory if it did not also take into consideration the degree of severity of the penalty that the person risks incurring'[1]. It is likely that an 'offence' which results or could result in the deprivation of liberty will belong to the criminal sphere 'except those which by their nature, duration or manner of execution cannot be appreciably detrimental'[2].

13.22 In *Engel*, the range of penalties available give an indication of the Court's view whether or not a charge fell within the criminal arena or not. Mr Engel's 2 days' strict arrest which was served by being locked in a cell both day and night and therefore excluding performance of normal duties fell short of that severity of penalty to bring the offence within the criminal law, although it was only the shortness of the sentence which led to its exclusion. The Court did not indicate how long a penalty was required to bring the offence with the criminal classification although the sentence could, potentially, have continued for 14 days.

13.23 Mr van der Wiel's 4 days' light arrest was not considered a deprivation of liberty. Under light arrest, servicemen were confined to their premises or military buildings during off-duty hours, but were not locked up and continued to perform their duties.

13.24 Committal to a disciplinary unit was considered to be a penalty the severity of which brought the offence within the criminal class. It represented the most severe penalty under military law in The Netherlands. The length of sentence could range from 3 to 6 months. Those sentenced in this way were unable to leave the unit for the first month or more, were not separated from those who were sentenced under the criminal law and were locked in their cells at night.

13.25 Although the penalties imposed may have been less than the maximum, the 'final outcome ... cannot diminish the importance of what was initially at stake'[3]. Thus, although the general form of the proceedings were similar and disciplinary in nature, the differences between the penalties which could have been imposed, led the Court to distinguish between the applicants and to their entitlement to protection from Art 6.

DOMESTIC VIOLENCE PROCEEDINGS

13.26 Thus it can be seen that the fact that the proceedings take place within the civil court is only the starting point that the proceedings are for the

---

1   1 EHRR 647, para 82.
2   Ibid, para 82.
3   Ibid, para 85.

determination of civil rights and obligations rather than the determination of a criminal charge. The nature of the allegations within domestic violence proceedings would suggest that the hearing more readily fits within the criminal arena. However, the outcome of the proceedings, that is, the imposition of a non-molestation order or an occupation order may have serious implications but it is arguable that it is less in the nature of a penalty or a deterrent (although it may have that effect) rather than a form of protection for the person making the allegations or for children within the same household. In the light of this, although it is arguable that the proceedings could fulfil the criteria of the determination of a criminal charge and are thus covered by all the provisions under Art 6, it is likely that they fit more readily within the classification of a 'determination of civil rights and obligations'. However, the fact that 'civil rights and obligations' are at issue, does not exclude that the proceedings have a criminal character.

Committal proceedings for contempt of court

13.27   The question whether proceedings for contempt of court fall within the definition of 'determination of a criminal charge' has come before the European Court. In the case of *Ravnsborg v Sweden*[1], the applicant had, on three separate occasions made improper and colourful statements[2] in written observations lodged by him in proceedings before the Swedish courts. Three fines of 1,000 Swedish Kroner[3] had been imposed for the Swedish equivalent of contempt of court but the applicant had not been given a hearing. The applicant claimed that the proceedings were in the nature of a determination of a criminal charge and there had been a breach of Art 6. The Court held that Art 6 did not apply for the following reasons:

–   *Legal classification:* it was not established that under Swedish law, the proceedings were classified as criminal. However, this was only the starting point.

–   *Nature of the offence:* the rules relating to the court's conduct of its own proceedings including sanctions were more akin to disciplinary proceedings than a criminal charge.

–   *The nature and degree of severity of the penalty:* the fine was neither sufficiently large nor convertible into a term of imprisonment (except in limited circumstances and after judicial proceedings) to warrant its classification as criminal.

13.28   Similar considerations were adopted in the case of *Putz v Austria*[4] where, during criminal proceedings involving, inter alia, bankruptcy charges, several fines were imposed on the applicant for disrupting court proceedings. The Court held that Art 6 did not apply because the imposition of the fines did not amount to a determination of a criminal charge for the following reasons:

---

1   18 EHRR 38.
2   Such statements included, inter alia, a description of the Board as 'a basket of municipal rotten eggs of different colours with a common denominator and overriding ideology, namely fascism' and of a certain member of the district court as having a 'far reaching tendentiously fascist way of presiding' over the court.
3   This was also the maximum fine which could be imposed.
4   (1996) RJD 1996–I No 4.

– It was not established that in the legal system the provisions covering disruptions of court proceedings belonged to criminal law.

– The rules enabling a court to sanction disorderly conduct was a common feature of the legal systems of most contracting States – such rules and sanctions derive from the inherent power of a court to ensure proper and orderly conduct of its own proceedings. The measures ordered by the court under such rules were more akin to the exercise of disciplinary powers than to the imposition of a punishment for commission of a criminal offence and the proscribed conduct in question therefore fell outside the ambit of Art 6.

– The fines imposed were not entered onto the criminal record. The fines could be converted into a term of imprisonment if unpaid and an appeal lay against such decisions. However, the term of imprisonment could not exceed 10 days. Consequently, what was at stake for the applicant was not sufficiently important to warrant classifying the offences as 'criminal'.

13.29 These should be contrasted with another case involving contempt of court proceedings. In the case of *Weber v Switzerland*[1] the applicant, a journalist, had lodged a complaint initiating criminal proceedings against another person. He was not a party to those criminal proceedings. He later revealed information in breach of confidence about the conduct of the judicial investigation resulting from the complaint and was convicted under Swiss law under the Swiss equivalent of contempt of court proceedings. Although it was not classified as a criminal offence under Swiss law, it nevertheless fell under Art 6 as a determination of a criminal offence because:

– A distinction was drawn between acts by judges, lawyers and those closely associated with the functioning of the courts (who were liable to disciplinary measures on account of their profession) and parties who only take part in the proceedings as people subject to the jurisdiction of the courts and therefore not within the disciplinary sphere of the judicial system.

– The offence potentially affected the whole of the population.

– The fine of 500 Swiss francs could be converted into a term of imprisonment in certain circumstances and, thus, what was at stake was sufficiently important to warrant classifying the offence with which the applicant was charged as criminal under the Convention.

13.30 In many respects, the differences between *Weber* on the one hand and *Ravnsborg* and *Putz* on the other are unclear, but it is arguable that contempt of court proceedings for disruptive behaviour fall within the general power of the court to administer the general conduct of its own proceedings.

13.31 However, it is submitted that committal proceedings for contempt, where there has been a breach of an non-molestation or occupation order, is likely to be treated differently because:

PART B
IMPACT OF THE CONVENTION

---

1   12 EHRR 508.

–   Classification within domestic law: a criminal standard of proof has to be satisfied before the allegation of breach of non-molestation order can justify a committal[1].

–   Nature of the offence: committal proceedings are directed against any person who disobeys an order of the court. As such, the proceedings do not fall within mere disciplinary proceedings but are directed against the population at large.

–   Nature and severity of the penalty: both fines and a term of imprisonment can be imposed. The terms of imprisonment can be severe (up to 2 years under the Contempt of Court Act 1981) and are not limited to a failure to pay the fines but can be imposed in their own right.

13.32   In the case of *Harman v UK*[2] the applicant, a solicitor working for the National Council for Civil Liberties, represented Mr Williams against the Home Office. Mr Williams sought disclosure of certain documents. The Home Office sought assurance from the applicant that the documents disclosed would only be used for purposes of the court hearing, would not be disseminated any wider and would not be used generally for purposes of the National Council. Such assurances were given by the applicant. During the trial certain parts of the documents were read out to the court. Following the court hearing a journalist approached the applicant and asked to see the documents. The journalist was given sight of those parts of the document which had been read out in court. Contempt of court proceedings were taken against the applicant by the Home Office. The court found that there had been a contempt of court although accepted that the applicant had acted in good faith and there was no penalty imposed. The applicant appealed the decision to the Court of Appeal and the House of Lords but failed. During the course of the House of Lords judgment, Lord Keith stated:

> 'The implied obligation not to make improper use of discovered documents is, however, independent of any obligation existing under the general law relating to confidentiality. It affords a particular protection accorded in the interests of the proper administration of justice. It is owed not to the owner of the documents but to the court and the function of the court in seeing that the obligation is observed and is directed to the maintenance of those interests and not to the enforcement of the law relating to confidentiality.'

13.33   The applicant brought the matter to the European Court of Human Rights claiming that there had been a breach of Arts 10 (freedom of speech) and 7 claiming that she had, in substance been found guilty of a criminal offence notwithstanding that the Home Office had taken proceedings for civil contempt and, further, that the offence was not one which had previously been known in law. Thus the issue whether contempt proceedings fell within the ambit of a 'determination of a criminal charge' fell to be considered by the Commission. In fact the opinion of the Commission is not particularly helpful and does not indicate its view one way or the other. However, the Commission declared that

---

1   *Smith v Smith* [1991] FCR 233 and *Dean v Dean* [1987] 1 FLR 517 where Dillon LJ cited the case of *Re Bramblevale Ltd* [1969] 3 All ER 1062 at 1071 and quoted Lord Denning's statement that 'contempt of court is an offence of a criminal nature. It must be satisfactorily proved. To use the time-honoured phrase it must be proved beyond reasonable doubt'.

2   (1984) 38 DR 53.

question was a matter which 'raises important and complex issues under the Convention which should be determined in an examination of the merits of the case. [The Commission] does not consider that the application can as a whole be rejected as manifestly ill-founded'.

13.34 Unfortunately, the issue was the subject of a friendly settlement and so was not considered by the Court. However, it can, at least, be inferred from the opinion of the Commission that the categorisation of contempt proceedings is unclear.

Implications of committal proceedings falling within the determination of a criminal charge

13.35 If committal proceedings are classified as the determination of a criminal charge, this does not mean that the proceedings are no longer civil proceedings. It simply results in the application of *all* paragraphs of Art 6 including paras (2) and (3). However, for these purposes the distinction between a determination of a criminal charge and the determination of civil rights and obligations may prove to be academic.

Albert and Le Compte v Belgium[1]

13.36 This case also involved disciplinary proceedings against two doctors. At issue was whether the applicants were to be allowed to continue to practise or not. Deprivation of liberty was not in issue. Nevertheless, the question was raised whether the hearing fell within the determination of a criminal charge or the determination of civil right and obligations or, indeed, either.

13.37 The Court held that, for its part, it did not believe that the two aspects, civil and criminal, of Art 6(1) were necessarily mutually exclusive and did not consider it necessary to decide whether there was a criminal charge. The Court regarded Art 6(2) and (3) and the principles enshrined as already contained in the notion of a fair trial as embodied in Art 6(1) and took those principles into account.

13.38 It is arguable that in both injunction and committal proceedings, the nature of the allegations would, at the very least, bring the proceedings within a quasi-criminal sphere. In that light, it would be desirable for the domestic courts to take account of all the Art 6 guarantees within whichever category the proceedings strictly fall.

13.39 Under Art 6, the Convention further guarantees in criminal proceedings:

–   the presumption of innocence (Art 6(2));
–   the right to be informed of the accusation (Art 6(3)(a));
–   the right to have adequate time and facilities for the defence (Art 6(3)(b));
–   the right to defend oneself, to have representation and legal aid (Art 6(3)(c));
–   the right to call and cross-examine witnesses (Art 6(3)(d));
–   the right to an interpreter (Art 6(3)(e)).

---

1   5 EHRR 533.

The presumption of innocence

13.40   Under Art 6(2) 'Everyone charged with a criminal offence shall be presumed innocent until proved guilty according to law'.

13.41   This is a specific aspect to 'the right to a fair trial' and enshrines a fundamental principle in virtually all systems of criminal procedure. In the leading case of *Barbera, Messegue and Jabardo v Spain*[1], the Court stated:

> 'Paragraph 2 embodies the principle of the presumption of innocence. It requires, inter alia, that when carrying out their duties, the members of a court should not start with the preconceived idea that the accused has committed the offence charged; the burden of proof is on the prosecution and any doubt should benefit the accused. It also follows that it is for the prosecution to inform the accused of the case that will be made against him, so that he may be prepare and present his defence accordingly, and to adduce evidence sufficient to convict him.'[2]

The principles stated above are reflected in the principles enunciated in Art 6(1) and in the subparagraphs of Art 6(3). As such, a finding that there has been a violation of any other paragraph will obviate any need to consider further whether there are any violations of Art 6(2).

13.42   Quite apart from these aspects of the criminal trial, the presumption of innocence also concerns the treatment of the accused person and the conclusions which can be drawn from the authorities' attitude towards him. This was exemplified in the case of *Minelli v Switzerland*[3]. Minelli, a journalist, published an article accusing a company and its director of fraud. In 1972, the company and the director instituted a prosecution for defamation. Those proceedings were adjourned in 1974 to await the outcome of a prosecution against another journalist, Fust, who had written a similar article. Fust was convicted but in 1976 the domestic court decided that the proceedings against Minelli could not be heard because they were out of time. However, notwithstanding the acquittal, the court ordered Minelli to pay two-thirds of the investigation of the trial and investigation costs and to compensate the private prosecutors for their expenses. The court considered that Minelli would 'in all probability' have been convicted without the protection of the time bar.

13.43   The Government argued that there had been no finding of guilt but that the conduct of the applicant had only been taken into account on the question of apportionment of costs. The Commission and the Court said that the distinction was not material and that the importance lay in the opinion reflected in the judgment. The Court held,

> '... the presumption of innocence will be violated if, without the accused's having previously been proved guilty according to the law and, notably, without his having had the opportunity of exercising his rights of defence, a judicial decision concerning him reflects an opinion that he is guilty. This may be so even in the absence of any formal finding; it suffices that there is some reasoning suggesting that the court regards the accused as guilty.'[4]

---

1   11 EHRR 360.
2   Ibid, para 77.
3   5 EHRR 554.
4   Ibid, para 37; see also *I and C v Switzerland* Application No 10107/82, (1986) 48 DR 35.

13.44 Whilst this case concerned the question of costs, it is arguable that the judgment has broader application. Within domestic violence proceedings, the court may accept undertakings and frequently does so without prejudice as to the facts particularly in instances where the respondent is unrepresented[1]. However, as stated above[2], the court cannot attach a power of arrest to undertakings and is specifically prevented from accepting undertakings where a power of arrest would be attached to an order[3]. Lack of court time frequently prevents full consideration of the facts, thus preventing a power of arrest being attached and necessitating an adjournment. Undertakings are theoretically impossible in the circumstances because of the necessity to consider ordering a power of arrest. It is anecdotal evidence only, but there are reports that, on occasions, the court treats the hearing as ex parte, and, although the respondent is present, the court will order a power of arrest on the basis of the applicant's evidence alone. It is clear that this practice breaches a number of principles under Art 6 including the presumption of innocence.

The guarantees under Article 6(3)
13.45 As stated in the case of *Adolf v Austria*, 'Article 6(3) merely exemplifies the minimum guarantees which must be accorded to the accused in the context of a "fair trial" referred to within Article 6(1)'[4]. The approach of the Commission to the Art 6(3) standards is shown in the case of *Can v Austria*:

> 'They exemplify the notion of a fair trial ... but their intrinsic aim is always to ensure or contribute to ensuring the fairness of the criminal proceedings as a whole. The guarantees enshrined in Article 6(3) are therefore not an aim in themselves, and they must accordingly be interpreted in the light of the function which they have in the overall context of the proceedings.'[5]

Conduct falling short of any one of the guarantees does not necessarily result in a violation of Art 6. The Court would take an overall view of the proceedings before deciding whether they were fair.

The right to be informed of the accusation
13.46 Under Art 6(3)(a) everyone charged with a criminal offence has the right 'to be informed promptly, in a language which he understands and in detail, of the nature and cause of the accusation against him'.

13.47 This provision overlaps with Art 5(2) which provides similar protection for those being detained pending trial and with Art 6(3)(b) the right to adequate time and facilities in order to prepare a defence.

PROMPTLY
13.48 There is no case which sets out clearly the interpretation of 'promptly' but, by necessity, there has to be sufficient time for the defendant/respondent to prepare his defence. The information has to be received by the person charged. In

---

1   The respondent is frequently unrepresented in these proceedings because the Legal Aid Board will not grant legal aid considering that the proceedings can be satisfactorily compromised by undertakings without any findings of fact.
2   See **13.1**.
3   Family Law Act 1996, s 46.
4   4 EHRR 313.
5   8 EHRR 121, para 15.

C v Italy[1], notification was sent by the investigating judge to the address of the defendant. Someone else signed the notification and the defendant claimed that he had not received it. This was held to be inadequate notification for purposes of the Convention although there was, ultimately, no violation, the error being corrected by service of the information providing the defendant with 4 months to prepare his defence 'which is the principle underlying Art 6(3)(a) of the Convention'[2].

IN DETAIL
13.49   In the case of *Brozicek v Italy*[3], the only detail required was that the information 'listed the offences of which he was accused, stated the place and the date thereof, referred to the relevant Article of the Criminal Code and mentioned the name of the victim'[4]. The Court did not consider it necessary to give any detail about the evidence. In the later case of *Gea Catalan v Spain*[5], the Commission emphasised that 'the accused is entitled to be informed not only of the cause of the accusation i.e. the material facts alleged against him which form the basis of the accusation but also the nature of the accusation i.e. the legal classification of these material facts'[6]. Nevertheless, minute detail is not required[7].

13.50   In committal proceedings for breach of an injunctive order, the summons or notice must 'list the ways in which it is alleged that the order or undertaking has been disobeyed or broken'[8]. If properly drafted[9], the summons or notice will comply with the requirements of Art 6(3)(a) as will the warrant for arrest under s 47(8) of the Family Law Act 1996[10]. There is no requirement for any particular form[11].

IN A LANGUAGE WHICH HE UNDERSTANDS
13.51   In the case of *Brozicek v Italy*[12], a German national was charged in Italy. The Italian authorities wrote him in Italian and the applicant replied with a request that they write to him in a language which he could understand. The authorities continued to write to him in Italian. The Court found that there was a violation of Art 6(3)(a) because they were not in a position 'to establish that the applicant in fact had sufficient knowledge of Italian to understand . . . the purport of the letter notifying him of the charges brought against him'.

13.52   This case should be contrasted with the case of *Kamasinski v Austria*[13], when an American national was tried in Austria on charges of fraud. The applicant claimed that the trial was unfair because only the titles of the crimes alleged were

---

1   Application No 10889/84, (1988) 56 DR 40.
2   Ibid at 59.
3   12 EHRR 371.
4   Ibid, para 42.
5   20 EHRR 266.
6   Ibid, para 29 and see also *Chichilian and Ekindjian v France* 13 EHRR 553.
7   *X v FRG* 1169/61, 6 YB 520 at 584.
8   *Harmsworth v Harmsworth* [1988] 1 FLR 349 at 354D–355B.
9   Ie particularising the allegation of the breach of the injunction or undertaking. See also
      Williams v Fawcett [1985] 1 All ER 787 which referred to various practice and drafting errors
      which could occur. These have largely been resolved following the amendment of Form N78.
10   *Erdogan v Turkey* Application No 14723/89, 73 DR 81.
11   Ibid.
12   12 EHRR 371.
13   13 EHRR 36.

made known to him in English but not the material substance upon which the crimes were founded. The Court accepted that whilst para 3(a):

> '... did not specify that the relevant information should be given in writing or translated in written form for a foreign defendant, it does point to the need for special attention to be paid to the notification of the "accusation" to the defendant. An indictment plays a crucial role in the criminal process, in that it is from the moment of its service that the defendant is formally put on written notice of the factual and legal basis of the charges against him. A defendant not conversant with the court's language may in fact be put at a disadvantage if he is not also provided with a written translation of the indictment in a language he understands.'[1]

13.53 In the event, the Court decided that there had been no violation because:

– the indictment was a relatively uncomplicated document of six pages;
– the defendant had been questioned at length and in the presence of interpreters by the police and then the investigative judge and thus must have been aware in sufficient detail of the accusations levelled against him;
– as a result of oral explanations given to him in English, he had been sufficiently informed of the nature and cause of the accusation against him for purposes of Art 6(3)(a).

It is noteworthy that the interpretation at the trial was not simultaneous but 'consecutive and summarising'. In particular, questions put to the witnesses were not interpreted. Nevertheless, the interpretation was considered adequate and it was not substantiated that the applicant was unable to understand the evidence being given against him or to have witnesses examined or cross-examined on his behalf.

The right to have adequate time and facilities for the defence
13.54 Under Art 6(3)(b) everyone charged with a criminal offence has the right 'to have adequate time and facilities for the preparation of his defence'. As stated above, there is an overlap with Art 6(3)(a) but there is also an overlap with Art 6(3)(c) and the right to legal aid and assistance.

ADEQUATE TIME
13.55 This guarantee has to be considered in the light of the nature and the complexity of the case.

13.56 In the case of *Murphy v UK*[2], the applicant complained that he had insufficient time to instruct his barrister because he was 'only granted a dock brief ten minutes before he was due to appear'. The Government denied that this was the case but also claimed that even if it had been the case, counsel could have applied for an adjournment if he so wished which would certainly have been granted. The Commission agreed with the Government's submissions and found that the application was ill-founded.

13.57 In *Campbell and Fell v UK*[3], 5 days' notice of the charges and less than one day's notice of the report were found to be sufficient not least because there had

---

1   13 EHRR 36, para 79.
2   43 CD 1.
3   7 EHRR 165.

been no application for an adjournment. In this case, it was implicit that the Commission accepted that counsel could be briefed at short notice and had the skills and expertise to cope with shortness of time coupled with a remedy of an adjournment if necessary.

13.58   This provision also applies to appeal hearings. In the case of *Had-jianastassiou v Greece*[1], notice of appeal had to be given within 5 days of the order. At that stage, the applicant had not had sight of the written judgment and thus his appeal was restricted to the points of law which he had been able to hear or gather during the hearing and he could do no more than make general references as a basis for appeal. A breach of the Convention was found.

13.59   Within domestic proceedings, the legal representatives take a note of judgment and this is regarded as sufficient to enable grounds of appeal to be drafted. It is likely that this practice would not violate the Convention, particularly as there is usually provision for amending the grounds of appeal once the full judgment has been obtained. However, this may not be sufficient for the unrepresented party who may wish to appeal the decision and will, at best, have gathered only the gist of the salient points of law and facts.

13.60   Most cases regarding time under Art 6 concern a failure to provide a hearing within a reasonable time under Art 6(1) rather than providing too short a time. The majority of cases under this provision relate to the adequacy of facilities.

FACILITIES

13.61   The provision recognises the right of the accused to have at his disposal all relevant elements for the purposes of exonerating himself or of obtaining a reduction in penalty[2]. In *Jespers v Belgium*[3], the Commission took the view that 'facilities' included the opportunity to acquaint himself with the results of investigations carried out throughout the proceedings and that a right of access to the 'prosecution file' although not specifically guaranteed could be inferred from Art 6(3)(b). However, the word 'adequate' limited such right to those facilities which assist or may assist in the preparation of the defence. It does not give a general right to trawl through all the other party's papers and documentation but is designed to 'help establish ... the equality necessary for a fair trial and that consequently the principle of the equality of arms was grounded in it'[4]. To this end, such access can legitimately be restricted to the defendant's lawyer[5].

Access to a lawyer

13.62   Although not specifically mentioned, access to facilities would be meaningless if inadequate time was allowed for preparation and consultation between client and legal representative. In the case of *Campbell & Fell v UK*, the Court had pointed out that 'a lawyer could scarcely "assist" his client – in terms of sub-paragraph (c) – unless there had been some consultation between them. This latter consideration leads the Court to the conclusion that the "facilities" contemplated by sub-paragraph (b) were not afforded'[6]. Whilst in *Krocher &*

---

1   16 EHRR 219.
2   *Jespers v Belgium* 27 DR 61; see also *Bricmont v Belgium* 12 EHRR 217.
3   27 DR 61.
4   Ibid, para 70.
5   *Kremzow v Austria* 17 EHRR 322, para 52 and *Kamasinski v Austria* 13 EHRR 36.
6   7 EHRR 165, para 99.

Moller v Switzerland[1], 'the possibility for the accused to communicate with his lawyer is a fundamental part of the preparation of his case'.

Right to defend oneself, to have representation and legal aid

13.63   Under Art 6(3)(c), the Convention guarantees the right 'to defend himself in person or through legal assistance of his own choosing or, if he has not sufficient means to pay for legal assistance, to be given it free when the interests of justice so require'. Thus this provision guarantees three separate rights. The aim of these guarantees is to ensure that the defendant has the benefit of an effective defence which is both practical and effective and ensures that there has been a fair trial[2]. The right should extend not only to the court hearing but also to the preliminary inquiries, particularly where inferences can be drawn from silence or from responses to police questions[3].

The right to defend oneself in person

13.64   This is not an absolute right and depends on the proceedings in question. In general, any proceedings which involve a question of fact will provide justification for the presence of the accused and the right to defend himself if he so chooses. In the case of *Kremzow v Austria*[4], involving an appeal against sentence, it was held that the possibility of the court increasing the sentence from 20 years to life imprisonment and attributing a motive to him for his offending, and that 'where evaluations of this kind were to play such a significant role and where their outcome could be of major detriment to him, it was essential to the fairness of the proceedings that he be present during the hearing of the appeals and afforded the opportunity to participate in it together with his counsel'[5].

13.65   This requirement is reflected in domestic violence proceedings and, particularly, in committal proceedings where the respondent has to be served personally with the notice of committal.

The right to appoint a lawyer of one's own choosing

13.66   If the defendant is not to be present either by choice or by operation of procedure, he is entitled to be represented by a lawyer of his own choosing[6]. In *Pakelli v Germany*, the Government had argued that the rights of a defendant to defend himself or to have representation were in the alternative but the Court held that the use of the word 'or' in the English text to link the two rights was different from the French text which utilised the word 'et', the Court preferring the latter text[7]. Although the Court accepted that the issues of the case were not complicated and the result would not have serious consequences for Mr Pakelli

---

1   Application No 8463/78, para 14.

2   *Goddi v Italy* 6 EHRR 457, para 27.

3   *John Murray v UK* 22 EHRR 29.

4   17 EHRR 322.

5   Ibid, para 67.

6   *Pakelli v Germany* 6 EHRR 1; see also *Lala v The Netherlands* 18 EHRR 586, para 52 where it was stated that the appointment or otherwise of a lawyer could not be used as a tool to secure the presence of the defendant in an instance where the defendant deliberately chose not to attend to avoid arrest on further charges.

7   6 EHRR 1, para 31.

because there would have been no aggravation of the decision complained of, the decision itself could have had some importance in the development of case-law.

> 'In these circumstances, it goes without saying that the appearance of the appellant would not have compensated for the absence of his lawyer: without the services of a legal practitioner, Mr Pakelli could not have made a useful contribution to the examination of the legal issues ...'[1].

13.67   Article 6(3)(c) does not merely guarantee legal assistance but *effective* legal assistance thus reflecting the general right in Art 6(1) as stated in *Airey v Ireland*[2]. In the case of *Artico v Italy*[3], the State-appointed lawyer did not want to act for the defendant and excused himself on grounds of ill-health and too much work. The Government argued that they had put in place a system whereby a legal representative was nominated and upon that, its responsibility ended. The Court emphasised that 'when compliance with paragraph 3 is being reviewed, its basic purpose must not be forgotten, nor must it be severed from its roots'[4]. It continued that:

> 'The Court recalls that the Convention is intended to guarantee not rights which are theoretical or illusory but rights that are practical and effective; this is particularly so of the rights of the defence in view of the prominent place held in a democratic society by the right to a fair trial from which they derive ... Article 6 (3) (c) speaks of "assistance" not of "nomination". Again mere nomination does not ensure effective assistance, since the lawyer appointed for legal aid purposes may die, fall seriously ill, be prevented for a protracted period from acting or shirking his duties. If they are notified of the situation, the authorities must either replace him or cause him to fulfil[5] his obligations.'

13.68   It is implicit that the State authorities cannot remain passive in ensuring a fair trial through proper representation. Even if there is legitimate reason for a defendant to be without representation or to be absent, the authorities, through the Courts, have a watching brief to ensure that circumstances do not change so that representation becomes necessary[6].

13.69   Free communication between defendant and lawyer is implicit under subpara (c) although not expressly stated[7] and any hindrance in such communication has been carefully scrutinised and limited[8].

13.70   Article 6(3)(c) does not entitle the defendant to choose his own counsel where legal aid is granted. In *Croissant v Germany*[9], the defendant had been granted legal aid and had been assigned three counsel. The defendant objected to one of them stating that he had been assigned to ensure that the proceedings ran without interruption rather than to act in his interests. As there was no evidence to show that the relationship was so strained as to make a proper defence impossible, there was no violation of Art 6(3)(c) although 'the court

---

1   *Pakelli v Germany* 6 EHRR 1, para 38.
2   2 EHRR 305.
3   3 EHRR 1.
4   Ibid, para 32.
5   Ibid, para 33.
6   *Goddi v Italy* 6 EHRR, para 31.
7   *S v Swizerland* 14 EHRR 670.
8   See *Golder v UK* 1 EHRR 524.
9   16 EHRR 135.

should, as a rule, endeavour to choose a lawyer in whom the defendant places confidence'[1].

Free legal assistance

13.71   This is not an absolute right and its availability depends on the defendant either having 'insufficient means' or 'in the interests of justice'.

13.72   Legal aid may be essential even if the case of appeal is hopeless and even where counsel has so advised[2]. In the case of *Quaranta v Switzerland*[3], the Court set out the criteria for determining when the 'interest of justice' applies[4]:

– the seriousness of the offence;
– the potential severity of sentence;
– the complexity of the case;
– whether the defendant's appearance without the assistance of a lawyer could enable him to present his case in an adequate manner.

In this case, a maximum sentence of 6 months and the possible suspension of a period of probation justified the granting of legal aid 'in the interests of justice'. However, legal aid is a limited resource and does not entitle the defendant to endless conferences particularly if the legal representative considers further consultation to be unnecessary[5].

13.73   In domestic violence proceedings, there has been a growing tendency for legal aid to be refused for respondents on the basis that an undertaking can be given by him 'without prejudice as the facts'. It is at least arguable that legal aid should be granted to all parties in these circumstances under Art 6(3)(c) as well as the right to a fair trial and the principle of equality of arms.

The right to call and cross-examine witnesses

13.74   Under Art 6(3)(d) the defendant has a right 'to examine or have examined witnesses against him and to obtain the attendance and examination of witnesses on his behalf under the same conditions as witnesses against him'. The purpose of this provision is to put the defendant on the same footing as the other party ensuring the principle of 'equality of arms'. However, the right is not absolute and the authorities, through the courts, have a right to determine whether such a witness would be relevant[6]. Further, there is no violation if the defendant does not give the period of notice required by domestic law and the witness fails to attend[7].

13.75   'Witnesses' has an autonomous meaning and includes statements which are used by the court or read out at the hearing. This provision covers unchallenged evidence because the witness could not attend for some reason and hearsay evidence.

---

1   16 EHRR 135, para 7.
2   *Granger v UK* 12 EHRR 469.
3   (1991) Series A, No 205.
4   Ibid, paras 32–38. See also *Granger v UK* 12 EHRR 469; *Boner v UK* 19 EHRR 246; and *Maxwell v UK* 19 EHRR 97.
5   *M v UK* Application No 9728/82, (1984) 36 DR 155.
6   *Bricmont v Belgium* 12 EHRR 217.
7   *X v UK* Application No 4042/69.

13.76   The case of *Asch v Austria*[1] involved a criminal trial but, on the facts, could apply equally to injunction or committal proceedings. Following an alleged assault by the applicant, his cohabitant fled the home and took refuge with her mother. She made complaints to the police and there was medical evidence that she had suffered bruising and had been hit with a belt. The following day the parties reconciled and the cohabitant wished to withdraw her complaint. In injunction proceedings, that would have been the end of the matter, but within committal proceedings, the issue was whether the respondent had committed contempt against the court. As such, the wishes of the cohabitant were not necessarily decisive.

13.77   The Commission considered that:

–   the reading out of statements on which the judgment is later based cannot of itself be regarded as being inconsistent with Art 6(1) and (3)(d) of the Convention;
–   on the one hand, a person charged must have the opportunity to examine or have examined witnesses against him, particularly if he has not had the opportunity at an earlier stage in the proceedings;
–   on the other hand, it does not give an unlimited right to obtain the appearance of and examine witnesses in court;
–   however, where the court relies, in the main, on such statements, the rights of the defence would be substantially restricted and would violate Art 6(3)(d).

In the event, the reliance on the cohabitant's statement by the court and the defendant's inability to cross-examine her resulted in a violation of the Convention. It is arguable that this would also be true in committal proceedings

13.78   There was a similar result in *Unterpertinger v Austria*[2], where statements of the wife and step-daughter were read out. They did not wish to give evidence for fear of intimidation. Again, the findings of the court were mainly based on these statements which the defendant had been unable to challenge by cross-examination. The use of these statements was held to be in violation of Art 6(3)(d), although it was stated that this provision made allowance for the special problems that may be entailed by a confrontation between someone charged with a criminal offence and a witness from his own family and is calculated to protect such a witness by avoiding his being put in a moral dilemma which 'was manifestly not incompatible with Article 6(1) and (3)(d) of the Convention'[3].

The right to an interpreter

13.79   Under Art 6(3)(e) the defendant has the right 'to have the free assistance of an interpreter if he cannot understand or speak the language used in court'. Unlike the right to free assistance under Art 6(3)(c), there is neither means test nor a requirement that it is in the interests of justice. The only requirement is that the defendant cannot understand or speak the language.

---

1   15 EHRR 597.
2   13 EHRR 175.
3   Ibid, para 30.

13.80 The interpretation of questions of the witnesses does not have to be concurrent but can be 'consecutive and summarising'[1]. Although this provision does extend to pre-trial proceedings and the translation of documents it does not entail the translation of every document but only those which would enable the defendant to have a full understanding of the proceedings[2]. Further, the availability of bilingual counsel will, to some extent, obviate the need for full translation or interpretation[3].

DOUBLE JEOPARDY

13.81 Article 4 of the Seventh Protocol protects an individual from being tried or punished again in criminal proceedings under the jurisdiction of the same State for an offence for which he has already been acquitted or convicted. It is arguable that, under this provision, a person who was subject to committal proceedings would escape liability for a trial within criminal proceedings based on the same facts and vice versa.

13.82 The Seventh Protocol has not been ratified by the UK nor will it be incorporated into UK law by virtue of the Human Rights Act 1998. However, it is likely that the UK Government will incorporate it into law soon. In the White Paper *Rights Brought Home*[4], it was stated that:

> 'In general, the provisions of Protocol 7 reflect principles already inherent in our law. In view of concerns in some of these areas in recent years, the Government believes that it would be particularly helpful to give these important principles the same legal status as other rights of the Convention by ratifying and incorporating Protocol 7. There is, however, a difficulty with this because a few provisions of our domestic law... could not be interpreted in a way which is compatible with Protocol 7[5]. The Government intends to legislate to remove these inconsistencies, when a suitable opportunity occurs and then to sign and ratify the Protocol.'

13.83 Although the Seventh Protocol is not to be incorporated, this does not mean that Art 6 and the right to a fair trial requires that a person should not be tried twice for the same offence. The Commission has left the question open.

13.84 The effect of Art 4 of the Seventh Protocol can be seen in the case of *Gradinger v Austria*[6]. The applicant killed a cyclist whilst driving and was convicted of causing death by negligence. Although he had been drinking, his level of alcohol was below the prescribed limit for the more serious offence of being under the influence of alcohol. However, a medical report showed that he was in fact over the limit and he was fined by the administrative authorities for driving under the influence of alcohol. It was held that there was a violation of Art 4 of the Seventh Protocol and the Commission commented strongly that this provision would be ineffective if the contracting State could prosecute individuals under nominally different offences.

---

1   *Kamasinski v Austria* 13 EHRR 36.
2   *Unterpertinger v Austria* 13 EHRR 175, para 74 and see also *Luedicke, Belkacem and Koc v Germany* 2 EHRR 149.
3   *Kamasinski v Austria* 13 EHRR 36.
4   Cm 3782.
5   Eg the ancillary relief provisions under the Matrimonial Causes Act 1973, ss 23–25, which might be affected by Art 5 of the Seventh Protocol.
6   (1995) Series A, No 328–C.

13.85 The Government had argued that the provision relied on by the applicant could not be invoked because, under Austrian law and the reservation, the declaration limited the scope exclusively to 'criminal proceedings' thereby excluding disciplinary and administrative proceedings. The Government argued that the two sets of proceedings pursued different aims – the first to penalise homicide committed while under the influence of alcohol, the second to ensure the smooth flow of traffic. However, the court held that because 'both impugned decisions were based on the same conduct', accordingly, there was a breach of Art 4 of the Seventh Protocol[1].

13.86 This may run counter to the approach in the domestic courts where committal proceedings are regarded as independent from criminal proceedings even if arising from the same facts. In *Smith v Smith*[2], the court reduced a sentence for contempt of court on appeal. Criminal proceedings were pending. The Court of Appeal held that it was important to avoid double punishment and that the sentence (12 months) was too great in the circumstances. However, the court had to punish the contempt and not take into account the criminal aspects of the case which would be dealt with in another court. The court was emphasising the distinction between criminal and contempt proceedings.

13.87 Similarly, in the case of *Szczepanski v Szczepanski*[3], the husband applied for an adjournment pending the outcome of the criminal case. The judge refused and sentenced the respondent to 12 months' imprisonment for contempt. On appeal, it was emphasised that it was well established that courts had an inherent jurisdiction to enforce their own orders and that this was quite separate from any criminal proceedings even when they arose out of the same set of facts.

13.88 If and when the Seventh Protocol is incorporated, it may be arguable that a party should not be tried twice even if under the guise of contempt and criminal proceedings.

ARREST

Domestic law

Power of arrest

13.89 Under the Family Law Act 1996, the Court shall attach a power of arrest to an occupation order or a non-molestation order where it appears to the court that the respondent has used or threatened violence against the applicant or a relevant child[4]. The provision is mandatory unless the court is satisfied that in all the circumstances of the case the applicant or child will be adequately protected without such a power of arrest[5].

13.90 Under s 47(6), if the power of arrest is attached to a provision of the order, a constable may arrest without warrant a person whom he has reasonable cause for suspecting to be in breach of the provision. If the respondent is arrested,

1   Paragraphs 54 and 55.
2   [1991] FCR 233.
3   [1985] FLR 468.
4   Family Law Act 1996, s 47(2).
5   Ibid.

he must be brought before the relevant judicial authority within the period of 24 hours beginning at the time of his arrest[1] and if the matter is not disposed of forthwith, the respondent may be remanded[2]. If it is not convenient for the respondent to be brought to a courtroom, he may be brought before a relevant judicial authority at any convenient place but as the liberty of the respondent is involved the press and public should be permitted to be present unless security makes this impracticable. The order should then be announced in open court at the earliest opportunity which should be the next listed sitting of that court[3].

Warrant of arrest

13.91   If a power of arrest has not been attached to any provisions of an occupation or non-molestation order, then the applicant can apply to the court for a warrant of arrest if he considers that the respondent has not complied with the order[4]. The court shall not issue a warrant unless the application is substantiated on oath and the court has reasonable grounds for believing that the respondent has failed to comply with the order[5]. As with the power of arrest, if a person is brought to court under the warrant of arrest and the court does not dispose of the matter forthwith, the court has power to remand him[6].

Convention law

13.92   Once the respondent has been brought to court under a power of arrest or a warrant of arrest, the subsequent proceedings are governed by Art 6 and all the aspects of a fair trial. However, the arrest itself will fall under the provisions of Art 5 which guarantees the right to liberty and security of person. It is unlikely that any breach of Art 5 would not also breach the provisions of domestic law but the Convention provides a further layer of protection and is another potential argument in the advocate's armoury if a breach of procedure is alleged.

13.93   As such, it is not proposed to go through the provisions of Art 5 and its consequent case-law in detail and reference should be made to the criminal textbooks on the subject for in-depth consideration. However, a summary of the relevant provisions and authorities will be included here.

Meaning of 'arrest'

13.94   Where a policeman indicates that a person is not free to leave, either by words or conduct, this will amount to an arrest for purposes of Art 5. Under Art 5:

> 'Everyone has the right to liberty and security of person. No one shall be deprived of his liberty save in the following cases and in accordance with a procedure prescribed by law.'

13.95   Under the subsequent subparagraphs, the Convention sets out the exceptions to the right to liberty.

---

1   Family Law Act 1996, s 47(7)(a).
2   Magistrates' Courts Act 1980, ss 128, 129 and Family Law Act 1996, Sch 5.
3   President's Direction 17 December 1997 (Family Law Act 1996, Part IV) [1998] 1 FLR 496.
4   Family Law Act 1996, s 47(8).
5   Ibid, s 47(9).
6   Ibid, s 47(10); Magistrates' Courts Act 1980, ss 128, 129 and Family Law Act 1996, Sch 5.

Detention for non-compliance with a court order

13.96   Article 5(1)(b) provides the following exception to Art 5(1):

> 'the lawful arrest or detention of a person for non-compliance with the lawful order of
> a court or in order to secure the fulfilment of any obligation prescribed by law.'

This allows for detention of a person for failure to comply with a court order which
has already been made against him. This would include cases of civil contempt and
committal proceedings.

13.97   The detention is permitted only to compel the person to fulfil a specific
and concrete obligation which he has until then failed to satisfy[1]. It follows that the
order must be clear and specific. A general obligation, for example, 'to change
your behaviour' will not be sufficiently precise[2].

Detention on suspicion of having committed a criminal offence

13.98   The exception under Art 5(1)(c) provides for:

> 'the lawful arrest or detention of a person effected for the purpose of bringing him
> before the competent legal authority on reasonable suspicion of having committed an
> offence or when it is reasonably considered necessary to prevent his committing an
> offence or fleeing after having done so.'

This permits arrest and detention for suspects within the criminal justice system
but also under the powers or arrest with or without warrant under s 47 of the
Family Law Act 1996.

Definition of 'reasonable suspicion'

13.99   For reasonable suspicion to exist, it is not necessary to show that the act
complained of has, in fact, occurred or that the arrested person has committed it.
However, the test is objective and a police officer acting on an honestly held
suspicion is not sufficient. In the case of *Fox, Campbell and Hartley v UK*[3], the Court
held:

> 'The "reasonableness" of the suspicion on which an arrest must be based forms an
> essential part of the safeguard against arbitrary arrest and detention which is laid
> down in Article 5(1)(c). The Court agrees with the Commission and the Government
> that having a "reasonable suspicion" presupposes the existence of facts or information
> which would satisfy an objective observer that the person concerned may have
> committed the offence. What may be regarded as "reasonable" will however, depend
> on all the circumstances.'

Reasons for arrest

13.100   Under Art 5(2):

> 'Everyone who is arrested shall be informed promptly, in a language which he
> understands, of the reasons for his arrest and of any charge against him.'

This echoes the provision under Art 6(3)(a) when a person is charged. However,
the basis of arrest does not require the same amount of detail as upon charge.

---

1   *Angel v The Netherlands* 1 EHRR 647, para 69.
2   *Ciulla v Italy* 13 EHRR 346.
3   13 EHRR 157.

13.101 The purpose and extent of Art 5(2) was set out in the leading case of *Fox, Campbell and Hartley v UK*[1]:

– Paragraph (2) of Art 5 contains the elementary safeguard that any person arrested should know why he is being deprived of his liberty.

– This provision is an integral part of the scheme of protection afforded by Art 5.

– Any person arrested must be told the essential legal and factual grounds for his arrest.

– The language used should be simple and non-technical.

– The purpose of this provision is to enable the arrested person to apply to a court to challenge its lawfulness in accordance with Art 5(4).

– Whilst the information must be conveyed promptly, it need not be related in its entirety by the arresting officer at the very moment of the arrest.

– Whether the content and promptness of the information conveyed is sufficient, is to be assessed in each case according to its special features.

In the above case, the applicants had been arrested on suspicion of terrorist acts. On arrest they were told of the statutory provision under which they were being held but not informed of the factual basis of the arrest. Although the Court found that there was an initial failure, this was made good because the suspects were able to gather the factual basis from the subsequent interrogations. In any event, a gap of 7 hours between arrest and the giving of all the information was regarded as sufficiently 'prompt' although this decision has been heavily criticised as an 'unacceptable dilution of a basic guarantee'[2].

13.102 It is unnecessary for the information to be conveyed in any particular way. It does not have to be in writing nor does the warrant have to be shown.

Trial within a reasonable time
13.103 Under Art 5(3):

> 'Everyone arrested or detained in accordance with the provisions of paragraph (1)(c) of this Article shall be brought promptly before a judge or other officer authorised by law to exercise judicial power and shall be entitled to trial within a reasonable time or to release pending trial. Release may be conditioned by guarantees to appear for trial.'

In the case of *Brogan v UK*[3], it was stated that:

> 'The assessment of promptness has to be made in the light of the object and purpose of Article 5. The Court has regard to the importance of this Article in the Convention system: it enshrines a fundamental human right namely the protection of the individual against arbitrary interference by the State with his right to liberty. Judicial control of interferences by the executive with the individual's right to liberty is an essential feature of the guarantee embodied in Article 5(3) which is intended to minimise the risk of arbitrariness'[4].

---

1   13 EHRR 157, para 40.
2   Harris, Warbrick and O'Boyle, *The European Convention on Human Rights* (Butterworth Law, 1994).
3   11 EHRR 117.
4   Ibid, para 58.

13.104   Under a power of arrest, the arrested person has to be brought before
the court within 24 hours[1]. There is no similar provision under s 47 of the Family
Law Act 1996 for those arrested under a warrant, although s 41 of Police and
Criminal Evidence Act 1984 lays down the principle that a person should not be
held without charge for more than 24 hours. In the case of *Brogan*, a gap of 4 days
and 6 hours before the arrested person was brought before the court was
considered too long. There are no guidelines within the cases as to precise
meaning of 'prompt' and the Court in *Brogan* left the issue open stating that there
was 'no call to determine ... whether in an ordinary criminal case any given
period, such as four days, in police or administrative custody would as a general
rule be capable of being compatible with the first part of Article 5(3)'[2]. It is
arguable that the same considerations (although not the time scales) apply under
this provision as under the 'reasonable time' requirement under Art (1)[3].

---

1   Family Law Act 1996, s 47(7).
2   11 EHRR 117, para 60.
3   See **13.9**.

Chapter 14

EDUCATION

14.1   The system of education in the UK has been established by statutes going back to 1870. The Education Act 1944 was the most significant development in that process of establishing the right to free education. The purpose of the Act was set out in s 7:

> '... it shall be the duty of the local education authority for every area, so far as their powers extend, to contribute towards the spiritual, moral, mental and physical development of the community by securing that efficient education ... shall be available to meet the needs of the population of their area.'

14.2   The Education Act 1944 largely anticipated the rights created under the Convention as have subsequent Education Acts which have, inter alia, increased parental choice of schools, increased the opportunity for parental involvement in schools and amended the statutory process to safeguard children with special needs.

14.3   In addition, the Convention has influenced subsequent UK legislation even before its incorporation into English law because successive Governments have taken notice of adverse decisions from the European Court and acted accordingly, for example with regard to corporal punishment in schools.

14.4   Article 2 of the First Protocol of the European Convention on Human Rights provides:

> 'No person shall be denied the right to education. In the exercise of any functions which it assumes in relation to education and to teaching, the State shall respect the rights of parents to ensure such education and teaching in conformity with their own religious and philosophical convictions.'

As can be seen, it is formulated in two sentences, and is often discussed in terms of the 'fundamental principle' in the first sentence, and the additional requirements of the second sentence.

BACKGROUND

14.5   To have a full understanding of this Article, it is helpful to consider the wording in the light of earlier provisions. Article 26 of the Universal Declaration of Human Rights which was formulated after the war proposed a positive right to education. It also provided that elementary education should be free and compulsory, technical and professional education generally available and higher education equally accessible on the basis of merit. Under para 5 of Art 26 it was clear that the aim was to give parents a prior right to choose the kind of education to be given to their children. The original text of the European Convention as proposed in 1950, again gave a positive right, 'Every person has the right to education' and continued that the State should not trespass on the right of parents to ensure the religious and moral education and teaching of their children in conformity with their own religious and philosophical convictions. However, it was felt that this went too far and, moreover, was impracticable to implement. The States contracting to the Convention decided to refer back the right to education for further consideration because of the difficulties in drafting and interpretation and because of doubt that this right was an essential obligation of a democratic country. In any event, if it were a positive duty on the State not only to provide education but to do so in conformity with parents' wishes, religious and philosophical convictions, it would not be easy to see where any limits could be drawn, raising the spectre of endless disputes and damaging controversies in some countries between State and Church over support for the Church schools.

14.6   The right to education, the most significant part of the proposal, was not rejected and is still the policy of the Council of Europe and the consequence of the reference back was a negatively phrased formulation whereby the individual is not denied the right of access to education.

Right of individuals

14.7   In the light of this wording, the question arose as to whether the Article conferred any right which individuals could invoke. This issue was considered in the *Belgian Linguistic Case (No 2)*[1].

14.8   The applicants were French-speaking parents who lived in Flemish localities in Belgium where the Flemish language prevailed. Under Belgian legislation, the schools in Flemish areas taught in Flemish[2]. The effective choice was that the children could go to a Dutch-speaking school and be brought up speaking a different language from their parents or go to a French-speaking school some distance away (referred to as 'scholastic emigration'). These children were also denied access (because of residence) to the French language schools in the six communes on the Brussels periphery which were subject to special status as regards use of language. In practice, there was no similar obstacle for Dutch-speaking children. The parents alleged that it was a violation of Art 8 (the protection of private and family life, home and correspondence), Art 14 (freedom from discrimination) and Art 2 of the First Protocol.

14.9   The Court held unanimously that in respect of five out of the six questions referred to the Court, there had been no breach of Arts 8, 14 or 2 of the First Protocol but by a majority of only one (8 : 7) that there had been a breach of Art 14 in conjunction with Art 2 of the First Protocol in respect of a narrow point. The violation of the Convention based on discrimination lay not in the inability per se of the children to attend the French-speaking school but that the Dutch speaking children had no such problem. Other complaints of unequal treatment were dismissed, the Court accepting the aim of promoting linguistic unity within the regions and knowledge of the normal language of the region as in the public interest and not disclosing any discrimination[3].

14.10   The Court provided guidance on the scope of Art 2 of the First Protocol and held that individuals could invoke the Convention to protect their right to education. In spite of the negative formulation, the provision uses the term 'right' and speaks of a 'right to education'. Similarly, the preamble to the First Protocol

---

1   1 EHRR 252.

2   The reverse situation applies in the Walloon region of Belgium where the French language prevails.

3   See under Art 14 at para **14.87**.

specifies that the object of the Protocol lies in the collective enforcement of 'rights and freedoms'. In spite of the negative formulation, the Court had no doubt that Art 2 did enshrine a right.

Negative formulation

Nevertheless, the negative formulation was relevant.

> 'The negative formulation indicates .... that the Contracting parties do not recognise such a right to education as would require them to establish at their own expense, or to subsidise, education of any particular type or at any particular level.'[1]

This has implications when considering the second sentence of the Protocol and further when considering special needs education.

14.11 The judgment impliedly guarantees a right to be educated in the national language or one of them but 'in no way guarantees the right to be educated in the language of one's parents by the public authorities or with their aid. Furthermore, in so far as the legislation leads certain parents to separate themselves from their children, such separation is not imposed by the legislation; it results from the choice of the parents ...'[2].

14.12 However, the State must guarantee a right of access to educational institutions as they exist at any given time and the individual has the right to obtain official recognition of the studies he has completed in order to ensure an 'effective' education[3]. Whilst the State need not guarantee the right of parents to have their children educated as they wished, it should, in principle, guarantee the right of persons to have equal access to the means of instruction existing at a given time, subject to objectively necessary criteria. This might entail some positive obligations on the State. Such obligations are limited and do not extend, for example, to the automatic provision of subsidies for private education schools[4]. The Court also recognised that the provision of education might require 'regulation which may vary in time and place according to the needs and resources of the community'[5]. However, such regulation should never injure the substance of the right to education nor conflict with other rights enshrined in the Convention.

14.13 The Court emphasised that the aim of the Convention was the protection of fundamental human rights, particularly in an age when social and technical developments offered the State considerable possibilities for regulating the exercise of those rights. There has to be a just balance between the protection of the general interest of the Community and the respect due to fundamental human rights, although particular importance has to be attached to the latter[6].

PART B
IMPACT OF THE CONVENTION

---

1   *Belgian Linguistic Case (No 2)* 1 EHRR 252, para 3.
2   Ibid, para 7.
3   Ibid, para 4.
4   *Verein Gemeisen Lernen v Austria* 20 EHRR 78 CD.
5   *Belgian Linguistic Case (No 2)* 1 EHRR 252, para 5.
6   Ibid, para 5.

DECISIONS OF LOCAL EDUCATION AUTHORITIES

Financial provision

14.14   In the past, the Commission has rejected a number of complaints against the actions of education authorities which have included:

X and Y v UK[1]
14.15   A refusal by the education authority to provide grants or financial support for children to attend at a private school.

Cohen v UK[2]
14.16   A refusal by the education authority to pay the cost of travel to the school of the parents' choice where another school was available locally which would provide equivalent educational facilities but which was not the favoured school of the parents.

Choice

W & DM and M & HI v UK[3]
14.17   The inability of the education authority to ensure admission to single sex, selective grammar schools where such schools were oversubscribed.

X v UK[4]
14.18   A rejection of an application by parents in Northern Ireland who did not want their children to be educated in either a Roman Catholic school or the overwhelmingly Protestant State schools but in an 'integrated' school. Article 2 did not impose an obligation on a State to establish or to subsidise education of a particular type.

Application No 11644/85 UK[5]
14.19   A rejection of an application by parents that their children should go to a certain school. The school had been closed down. Part of the Commission's view was based on the fact that the children could attend another school less than one mile away.

14.20   In the light of the above decisions, the Convention is unlikely to provide any basis for a complaint when children are unable to attend the school of their parents' first choice. Again, this may have implications for special needs children.

Higher education

14.21   Although the intention of the Convention was primarily to guarantee elementary education, the wording of Art 2 does not exclude higher education. Certainly, the Commission has considered itself to be competent to consider the matter even if the complaints have been rejected:

---

1   Application No 9461/81 UK, (1983) 31 DR 210.
2   21 EHRR 104.
3   Application No 10228–9/82 UK, (1984) 37 DR 96; 7 EHRR 135.
4   (1978) 14 DR 179.
5   Unpublished.

X v UK[1]

14.22 The Commission rejected a complaint by a 27-year-old applicant against a decision that he was unable to continue his technological studies from prison. The Commission concluded that Art 2 of the First Protocol was not necessarily concerned with advanced studies such as technology and accepted the probability that the prison had no facilities for its study. The Commission decided that the prison authorities had not, therefore, failed to observe the obligations of Art 2.

Glazewska v Sweden[2]

14.23 A doctor qualified in Poland wished to practise in Sweden but was required to undergo further education. Such facilities did not exist. The application was not admissible, there being no obligation on the State to provide for specific forms of higher education which were not otherwise available in the State.

Exclusion

15 Foreign Students v UK[3]

14.24 Foreign students expelled from the UK could not rely on Art 2 of the First Protocol granting them a right to stay in this country. An alien's right to stay in a country was independent of his right to education and did not protect or include this latter right.

14.25 The refusal of permission was not an interference with the right to education but a control of immigration falling outside the scope of Art 2. The applicants conceded that the UK was not obliged to organise education 'for all and sundry'. Nevertheless, it is implicit from the above case that once a person is entitled to enter the country, he is to be treated the same as everyone else and that includes a right not to be denied access to education. As a 'right' does exist, it is secured by reason of Art 1 of the Convention to everyone within the jurisdiction of a contracting State[4]. The Commission hints at the possibility of a different decision if the applicants could show that deportation from the UK would mean that they could not obtain education elsewhere. However, even this was tempered by the comment that Art 2 was concerned primarily with elementary education and not necessarily with advanced studies.

Sulak v Turkey[5]

14.26 Expulsion from the educational institution on disciplinary grounds did not breach Art 2 of the First Protocol because it did not injure the substance of the right even though expelled students were prevented from enrolling in another higher education institution to pursue studies.

14.27 However, it may be that expulsion of a pupil from school would go to the substance of the right; it is likely that the severity of the measure would be considered in the light of the reasons for and the events leading up to the expulsion including the procedures adopted. Similarly suspension of a pupil from school may entail a denial of the right to education if the length of the suspension

1   (1975) 2 DR 50.
2   (1985) 45 DR 300.
3   Application No 7671/76, (19 May 1977) 9 DR 185.
4   *Belgian Linguistic Case (No 2)* 1 EHRR 252, para 3.
5   Application No 24515/94, (17 January 1996) 84A DR 98.

was found to be excessive in relation to the original complaint, or if any condition of return to school was unreasonable or subject to acceptance of conditions which conflicted with other rights enshrined in the Convention [1].

Selection

14.28 Equally, the right not to be denied access to education can be subject to conditions, for example suitability or qualifications. There have been no cases specifically questioning the selection procedures for higher education institutions but the Court would be competent to consider the matter if such a complaint arose. In *Patel v UK* [2], the Commission accepted that higher education facilities were limited and, as a corollary, it was not incompatible with Art 2 of the First Protocol to restrict access to those students who have attained the academic level required to benefit most from the courses offered.

THE UK RESERVATION

14.29 Upon signing the First Protocol, the UK entered a reservation to Art 2 stating:

> '. . . in view of certain provisions of the Education Acts in force in the United Kingdom, the principle affirmed in the second sentence of Article 2 is accepted by the United Kingdom only so far as it is compatible with the provision of efficient instruction and training, and the avoidance of unreasonable public expenditure.'

14.30 The reservation has been preserved by the Human Rights Act 1998, s 15. In essence, the reservation reflects the wording of s 9 of the Education Act 1996 the terms of which are, in effect, identical with the terms of s 76 of the Education Act 1944 [3]:

> 'In exercising or performing all their respective powers and duties under the Education Acts, the Secretary of State, local education authorities and the funding authorities shall have regard to the general principle that pupils are to be educated in accordance with the wishes of their parents, so far as that is compatible with the provision of efficient instruction and training and the avoidance of unreasonable public expenditure.'

14.31 The reservation is subject to review every 5 years, at which time the appropriate Minister must lay a report before each House of Parliament. It is open for the reservation to be withdrawn, but in the White Paper [4] the Government concluded that the reservation should be kept in place because it did not affect the right to education in Art 2 nor deny parents the right to have account taken of their religious and philosophical convictions. It stated that the purpose of the reservation is to recognise that in the provision of State-funded education a balance must be struck in some cases between the convictions of parents and what is educationally sound and affordable.

14.32 At first consideration, it is unclear whether continuation of the reservation will result in any change in the application of the statutory provisions

---

1   *Campbell and Cosans v UK* 4 EHRR 293, para 41.
2   (1980) 23 DR 228; 4 EHRR 256.
3   Education Act 1944, s 76 as re-enacted by the Education Act 1996, s 9.
4   White Paper *Rights Brought Home* (Cm 3782, para 4.6).

but, so far, the European Court has not decided any application with reference to the reservation in spite of the Government's pleading to the contrary. When the matter has arisen, it has been decided in favour of the UK on other grounds or by holding that the reservation was not applicable in the circumstances[1].

SECOND SENTENCE

14.33   The second sentence of Art 2 of the First Protocol does not give a separate right but rather has to be read together with the first sentence[2]. In addition, the whole of Art 2 of the First Protocol should be read in conjunction with Art 8 (right to respect for a person's private and family life), Art 9 (right to freedom of thought, conscience and religion and to manifest one's religion or beliefs) and Art 10 (right to freedom to receive and impart information and ideas)[3].

14.34   The aim of Art 2 was set out in *Kjeldsen, Busk Madsen and Pedersen*[4] as:

'... safeguarding the possibility of pluralism in education which possibility is essential for the preservation of the "democratic society" as conceived by the Convention. In view of the power of the modern State, it is above all through teaching that this aim must be realised.'[5]

14.35   It is to be noted that:

– there is no absolute right to have children educated in accordance with parents' religious or philosophical convictions but only a right to have such convictions respected[6];
– it is the right of everyone not to be denied education but the Convention proclaims the right of parents alone to have their religious and philosophical convictions respected in the field of education[7];
– the duty to respect religious and philosophical convictions rests on the State;
– the State's duty to respect religious and philosophical convictions has to be in the exercise of *any* functions which it assumes in relation to education and to teaching.

Meaning of religious and political conviction

14.36   The Court has avoided defining 'conviction' but has said in *Campbell and Cosans v UK*[8] (an application involving the question of corporal punishment) that:

'in its ordinary meaning the word "convictions", taken on its own is not synonymous with the words "opinions" and "ideas", such as are utilised in Article 10 of the Convention ...; it is more akin to the term "beliefs" appearing in Article 9 ... and

1   See, for example, *Campbell and Cosans v UK* 4 EHRR 293, para 37.
2   *Kjeldsen, Busk, Madsen & Pedersen v Denmark* 1 EHRR 711 at 730, paras 50 and 52.
3   Ibid, para 52.
4   Ibid.
5   Ibid, para 50.
6   *Family H v UK* Application No 10233/83 (Dec), (6 March 1984) 37 DR 105.
7   *Campbell and Cosans v UK* 4 EHRR 293, para 40; see Art 25 on who can address petitions.
8   4 EHRR 293.

denotes views that attain a certain level of cogency seriousness, cohesion and importance.'[1]

14.37　　In the same case, 'philosophical convictions' were regarded as 'not capable of exhaustive definition' covering a wide spectrum from 'a fully fledged system of thought or, rather loosely, to views on more or less trivial matters'[2]. However, within the context of that case, philosophical convictions denoted '... such convictions as are worthy of respect in a democratic country and are not incompatible with human dignity; in addition, they must not conflict with the fundamental right of the child to education'[3]. Applications based on a violation of 'philosophical convictions' have included:

– 　A claim to choose between the different types of curriculum; specifically to choose between modern and elementary school arithmetic. Not surprisingly, the Commission held that the application was inadmissible as showing no failure on the part of the State to respect those convictions. It left open whether such a choice fell within the definition, although made its scepticism clear[4].

– 　A claim that parents should be allowed to send their children to a single sex grammar school. The Commission held that the comprehensive system did not deny the parents their major role in the education of their children, in particular the transmission of their values or philosophical convictions[5].

– 　Claims relating to the use of corporal punishment in schools.

14.38　　In a number of cases, the State's views of the child's needs clashed with the parents' plans for their child's education and the State's view has prevailed on the ground that the child's right of education was of primary importance[6].

14.39　　'Religious conviction' is not defined but is likely to be relatively uncontroversial. Certainly, a 'known religion' is included and would have the advantages flowing from that as regards observance under both Art 9 and Art 2 of the First Protocol[7]. Within the Commission and the Court, Scientology[8], the Krishna Consciousness movement[9] and Jehovah's Witnesses[10] have been accepted under Art 9 without argument, although Druidism[11] was left open.

14.40　　The duty of the State to 'respect' parents' religious and philosophical convictions entails more than simply acknowledging them or taking them into account and, indeed, 'respect' replaced the words 'have regard to' during the course of the drafting. The Court has held that 'although individual interests must

1　　4 EHRR 293, para 36 but cf *X, Y and Z* (1982) 31 DR 50 at 53 advice by parents to their child to 'refuse punishment if he thought it unjustified' implied that the parents were not in fact opposed to school corporal punishment and their views did not, therefore, attain 'a certain level of cogency seriousness, cohesion and importance'.

2　　Ibid, para 36.

3　　Ibid, para 36.

4　　*X, Y & Z v Federal Republic of Germany* (1982) 29 DR 224.

5　　*W & DM and M & HI v UK* 7 EHRR 135.

6　　*Family H v UK* (1984) 37 DR 105; *Ford v UK* (1996) EHRLR 534; *PD and LD v UK* (1989) 62 DR 292; *Simpson v UK* (1989) 64 DR 188.

7　　*Kokkinakis v Greece* 17 EHRR 397, para 32; *Valsamis v Greece* 24 EHRR 294, para 26.

8　　Application No 7805/77, *Sweden* (1979) 16 DR 68.

9　　*Ishkon v UK* Application No 20490/92, 76-A DR 90.

10　　*Kokkinakis v Greece* 17 EHRR 397.

11　　*Chappell v UK* 53 DR 241.

on occasion be subordinated to those of a group, democracy does not simply mean that the views of a majority must always prevail; a balance must be achieved which ensures the fair and proper treatment of minorities and avoids any abuse of a dominant position'[1]. The Court considered that it implied 'some positive obligation on the part of the State' which in the context of an application against corporal punishment within schools could not 'be overridden by the alleged necessity of striking a balance between the conflicting views involved' nor was the gradual move towards the abolition of corporal punishment 'in itself sufficient to comply with this duty'[2].

PARENTAL RIGHTS

14.41   It has been held that a mother, whose child has been adopted by a third person, no longer has the right to ensure the education of the child in accordance with her own religious and philosophical convictions[3], although the Commission left open the question as to whether Art 2 of the First Protocol could be considered to impose on the public authorities an obligation not to transfer parental authority over a child to persons who do not share the convictions of the natural parents in matters of education. This question was answered in *Olssen v Sweden (No 1)*[4] when the Commission stated that:

> 'a decision to take a child into care is of a different character from adoption or the removal of custody. A care order does not mean that the right to custody is removed from the parents. But it implies that the public authorities take over the responsibility for the actual care of the child for a period which is not normally fixed in advance. A care order is, however, of a temporary nature and the aim is that eventually the children should return to their parents ... the rights of the parents under Article 2 of Protocol No 1 are not removed as a result of a care order. However, since such an order temporarily transfers certain parental rights to the parental authorities, it is inevitable that the contents of the parents' rights in Art 2 of Protocol No 1 must be reduced accordingly. On the other hand, the responsible authorities must in the exercise of their rights under a care order have due regard to the parents' right under Art 2 of Protocol No 1.'[5]

14.42   In the above case, the parents had alleged a violation of Art 2 of the First Protocol, first, because one of their children had been placed in a family who belonged to a religious denomination and attended church with him whereas they did not wish their children to receive a religious upbringing and, secondly, because the placement of the children so far away from their parents and without consultation as to the choice of foster-home deprived the latter of the possibility of influencing the children's education. The Court agreed with the above view of the Commission although rejected the parents' application on the facts stating that the parents had given no serious indication of their being particularly concerned about giving their children a non-religious upbringing nor had the children's education whilst in care diverged from the parents' wishes.

---

1   *Young, James and Webster v UK* 4 EHRR 238, para 63 – applicants claiming that trade union closed shop violated Art 11.
2   *Campbell and Cosans v UK* 4 EHRR 293, para 37.
3   *X v UK* (1978) 11 DR 160.
4   11 EHRR 259.
5   Ibid, para 95 of the Commission report.

14.43   This decision sits easily within the concept of shared parental responsibility in care proceedings under the Children Act 1989, although, in reality, the shortage of suitable foster-carers often results in the parental view on their children's education whilst in care having a secondary importance.

Removal of rights

14.44   In *X v Sweden*[1], a father's claim that Art 2 of the First Protocol had been violated because he had been prevented from having his children educated in accordance with his cultural and religious background was declared inadmissible. The Commission stated that the right to determine the mode of a child's education is an integral part of the right of custody which in this case had been removed and, therefore, the father no longer had the right to determine the manner in which his child's education should be carried out.

14.45   In domestic private law proceedings, the concept of custody has given way to residence, contact and, significantly, parental responsibility. As such, the non-resident parent's rights are not extinguished and it is arguable, relying on *X v Sweden*, that if full 'rights of custody' have not been taken away, the right enshrined in Art 2 is preserved for that parent. In practice, this is unlikely to conflict with the domestic court's approach under the Children Act 1989 although the whole thrust of private law proceedings is based on the parent's responsibilities and obligations towards the child rather than the parent's rights in respect of the child.

THE RIGHTS OF ORGANISATIONS

14.46   Although nothing in the Convention prevents applications by groups of people, in the context of Art 2 of the First Protocol, complaints by organisations have been ruled inadmissible. In *Jordebo v Sweden*[2], it was held by the Commission that a school, 'The Foundation', could not claim to be a 'victim' of a breach of Art 2 of the First Protocol within the meaning of Art 25 of the Convention. However, the Commission has felt able to consider a complaint from the Church of Scientology (for a violation of Art 9) accepting that a Church body lodges an application on behalf of its members and the distinction between the Church and the members was artificial. The applications of the individuals were inadmissible because they were anonymous[3].

THE STATE'S DUTY

14.47   The extent of the State's responsibilities and the limitations of its power was examined in *Kjeldsen, Busk Madsen and Pedersen v Denmark*[4], a case where three couples, having children of school age, objected to integrated, and hence, compulsory sex education as introduced in State primary schools in Denmark.

---

1   Application No 7911/77, (1978) 12 DR 192.
2   (1987) 51 DR 125.
3   *Pastor X and the Church of Scientology v Sweden* (1979) 22 Yearbook 244 reversing the decision in *Church of X v UK* Application No 3798/68, (1969) 12 Yearbook 306.
4   1 EHRR 711.

Private schools were free to decide to what extent they wished to align their teaching in the field of sex education with the rules applicable to State schools. The parents had unsuccessfully asked the authorities to exempt their children from sex education. They argued before the Commission and the Court that compulsory sex education was contrary to the beliefs they held as Christian parents and constituted a violation of Arts 8, 9 and 14 and Art 2 of the First Protocol.

14.48   The Court unanimously held that there had been no violation of Arts 8 or 9 taken in conjunction with Art 2 of the First Protocol and held by a majority of 6 votes to 1 that there had been no breach of Art 14 in conjunction with Art 2 of the First Protocol.

14.49   The Court stated that the use of the words 'any functions' extended the State's responsibility in the sphere of education and teaching to include the organisation and *financing* of public education. The setting and the planning of the curriculum fall within the competence of the contracting States. In accordance with the doctrine of the margin of appreciation, the Court recognised that questions of expediency would be involved and solutions might legitimately vary from country to country and from era to era. The Court recognised the difficulty of preventing the State from imparting through teaching or education information or knowledge of a directly or indirectly religious or philosophical kind, not least because it was difficult for many of the subjects taught at school not to have some philosophical complexion or implications. This was also true of religious convictions bearing in mind that religions 'form a very broad dogmatic and moral entity which has or may have answers to every question of a philosophical, cosmological or moral nature'[1]. However, the State must not go over the boundary into indoctrination. Information or knowledge included in the curriculum has to be conveyed 'in an objective critical and pluralistic manner'[2].

14.50   From this, it might be thought that the information has to be imparted in a wholly neutral manner but the Court did not go that far. On the contrary, it appreciated that 'appraisals of fact easily lead on to value-judgments'[3] but considered the subject matter within the guide to the curriculum, for example excessive frequency of births outside wedlock, induced abortions and venereal diseases and felt that although these considerations were indeed of a moral order, they were very general in character and did not entail overstepping the bounds of what a democratic State may regard as the public interest[4].

14.51   On the specific facts, the Court emphasised that sex education integrated in the general teaching did not affect 'the right of parents to enlighten and advise their children ... or to guide their children on a path in line with the parents' own religious or philosophical convictions.'[5] Additionally, the parents' complaints failed because of the availability of private but heavily State subsidised education which did not have to conform to the rules on sex education to the same extent and the possibility of education at home. It appears that not only the manner of instruction but the existence of alternative forms of education, ie

---

1   1 EHRR 711, para 53.
2   Ibid, para 53.
3   Ibid, para 54.
4   Ibid.
5   Ibid.

private schools, allowing a variety and degree of teaching of sex education persuaded the Court that the State had not stepped over the line into indoctrination even if those alternatives required sacrifices and inconveniences by the parents. This has to be contrasted with the judgment in *Campbell and Cosans v UK*[1] which noted in the facts that the applicants had no realistic and acceptable alternative to sending their children to State schools for both practical and financial reasons. Although there is no further comment within the judgment, it is submitted that the lack of choice in the latter case was the distinguishing factor.

14.52   The Court did, however, distinguish between religious education from which the children could be exempted at the parents' request and sex education from which the children could not be exempted. 'The former of necessity disseminates tenets and not mere knowledge; the Court has already concluded that the same does not apply to the latter'[2].

14.53   It appears that the State can exercise its duty only if the parents have brought their views to the attention of the authority. An application failed because the parents had not objected to the imposition of corporal punishment on their child on 14 previous occasions nor had they made their views known to the headmaster when they were asked to persuade their son to accept the punishment on the final occasion[3].

DISCIPLINE

14.54   There have been a number of cases where parents have claimed that disciplinary measures, notably exclusion or suspension from school for a short period, has violated their child's right to education and/or breached the State's duty to respect parents' religious or philosophical convictions.

14.55   It has been argued that discipline was an ancillary function in the field of education but the Court has accepted that imposition of disciplinary penalties is an integral part of the process whereby a school seeks to achieve the object for which it was established, including the development and molding of the character and mental powers of its pupils[4]. Article 2 is binding in the exercise of 'each and every function' that they undertake in the field of education. So even if a function were considered ancillary, it would still fall within the ambit of Art 2.

Exclusion

14.56   In *Valsamis v Greece*[5], a child was suspended from school for one day because she refused and did not partake in a school parade on the day of a national holiday which commemorated the outbreak of war in 1940 between Greece and Italy. She and her parents were Jehovah's Witnesses. They stated that such a parade was contrary to their religious beliefs and in particular their belief in pacifism. They objected to what they regarded as the military overtones of the parade. The Greek Government contended that National Day commemorated

---

1   4 EHRR 293, para 8.
2   Ibid, paras 54 and 56.
3   *X,Y and Z v UK* (1982) 31 DR 50 at 53.
4   *Campbell and Cosans v UK* 4 EHRR 293, para 33.
5   24 EHRR 294.

Greece's attachment to the values of democracy, liberty and human rights. It argued that the communal celebration retained an idealistic and pacific character that was strengthened by the presence of the school parades. This view was supported by the Commission which felt that the school parade in question was not of a military character incompatible with pacifist convictions [1]. Although the Court expressed surprise that pupils could be required to parade, on pain of suspension, outside the school precincts on a holiday, it made clear that it was 'not for the Court to rule on the Greek State's decisions as regards the setting and planning of the school curriculum' [2] – an example of the margin of appreciation in action (or leading to inaction!). The Court also declined to rule on the parents' claims that history lessons were better suited to the provision of education rather than parades. The Court could not regard the penalty of suspension 'as an exclusively educational measure' and considered that it might 'have some psychological impact on the pupil on whom it is imposed'. However, it noted the limited duration of the penalty and the fact that a suspended pupil could remain at school and take part in various activities under the responsibility of the headmaster.

14.57 The tenor of the Court's judgment is consistent with that in *Kjeldsen, Busk Madsen and Pedersen v Denmark*[3] being one of consideration of the convictions of the parents in the context of the activity objected to and balancing them against the nature of the action taken or insisted upon or the severity of the punishment imposed. In this instance, the Court found there was no violation of Art 2 of the First Protocol but if the suspension had been for longer or had involved complete absence from school, the Court's decision may have been very different. Certainly, in *Campbell and Cosans v UK*[4], a suspension of nearly a whole school year was regarded as a violation of Art 2 albeit because access to the school was conditional on acceptance by the parents of a system which included corporal punishment and thus was in breach of the duty to respect the parents' philosophical convictions also enshrined in Art 2.

Corporal punishment and Article 2 of the First Protocol

14.58 By 1982, virtually all the contracting States had abolished or ceased to use corporal punishment within schools. The exception was the UK and, in particular, Scotland. At that stage, it was Government policy to end corporal punishment in schools and the view was taken that it was best done by consensus rather than by abolition under statute, not least because the form of discipline had the support not only of the teaching profession but also of a large number of Scottish parents and even, surprisingly, the pupils who even preferred it to some other forms of punishment. In those circumstances, it might be thought that a 'margin of appreciation' might be allowed. However, in a number of cases the right of the individual was held to be enshrined in the Article and overrode any alleged necessity to strike a balance between the conflicting views involved. Additionally, gradual movement by the Government to abolish corporal punishment in schools was insufficient to comply with the State's duty under the First Protocol.

---

1   24 EHRR 294, para 24.
2   Ibid, para 31.
3   1 EHRR 711.
4   4 EHRR 293.

14.59   In *Campbell and Cosans v UK*[1], the parents claimed that there was a violation of Art 2 of the First Protocol by virtue of the use of corporal punishment within their children's schools. Mrs Campbell had sought a guarantee that her son would not be subjected to this measure. This guarantee was refused although her son was never so punished whilst at the school. Mrs Cosans's child was caught trying to take a short cut through a cemetery which was prohibited by the school. He was told to report to the headmaster the next day to receive corporal punishment. On the advice of his father, the child duly reported but (supposedly respectfully) declined to accept the punishment. On that account, he was suspended from school until he was willing to accept the punishment. Some time later, the headmaster lifted the suspension on the basis that the long absence from school was punishment enough but when the parents, like Mrs Campbell, sought a guarantee that their child would not be subject to corporal punishment, no such guarantee was given and the child remained away from school until he ceased to be of compulsory school age. His suspension from school lasted for over 8 months.

14.60   The Court held that there was no violation of Art 3 because there had in fact been no application of corporal punishment, although even a mere threat, if sufficiently real and immediate, might in certain circumstances amount to at least 'inhuman treatment'. However, the situation of these two children did not amount to 'torture' or 'inhuman treatment' notwithstanding the fact that Mr and Mrs Cosans's child was faced with the prospect of corporal punishment. The Court did not consider whether corporal punishment would amount to a breach of Art 3, nor did it consider the reasonableness of the sanction in relation to the offence.

14.61   However, the Court held, by a majority of 6 to 1 (the UK judge dissenting) that Art 2 of the First Protocol had been violated because of the parents' views[2], which relate to a weighty and substantial aspect of human life and behaviour, namely:

–   the integrity of the person;
–   the propriety or otherwise of the infliction of corporal punishment;
–   the exclusion of the distress which the risk of such punishment entails.

Such views were held to satisfy the following criteria[3]:

–   that the 'philosophical convictions' were worthy of respect in a 'democratic society'[4];
–   that their convictions were not incompatible with human dignity;
–   that their convictions did not conflict with the child's right to education[5].

The Court clearly decided that the parents' views on corporal punishment of children fell into a wholly different category from opinions on other forms of discipline and, indeed, on discipline in general.

14.62   The UK Government had argued that gradual elimination of corporal punishment was the only way to strike a balance between the competing views and other possibilities such as separate schools for children whose parents objected to

---

1   4 EHRR 293.
2   Ibid, para 36.
3   Ibid.
4   *Young James and Webster v UK* 4 EHRR 38, para 63.
5   *Kjeldsen, Busk Madsen and Pedersen v Denmark* 1 EHRR 711, para 52.

this form of punishment would be 'incompatible with the provision of efficient instruction and training and the avoidance of unreasonable public expenditure'[1] and thus fell within the reservation made by the UK when the Protocol was signed by the United Kingdom in 1952. Whilst the Court accepted that a dual system would be incompatible, a system of exemption for individual pupils in a particular school would not and therefore the reservation did not apply.

14.63 Further, the very fact that Mr and Mrs Cosans' child could return to school only if the parents, contrary to their convictions, accepted the disciplinary regime, gave their child a conditional right of access alone which:

– conflicted with another right enshrined in Art 2 of the First Protocol;
– could not be described as reasonable;
– fell outside the State's power of regulation under Art 2[2];

and therefore deprived the child of a right of education under the first sentence in Art 2[3].

14.64 It is important to note that, under Scots law, the use of corporal punishment was controlled under the common law and the law of assault. The teacher's power to chastise derived, like that of the parent, from the relationship with the child under his care. Such power was not a creature of statute and, as such, was not in the nature of a power delegated by the State. Nevertheless, as the State had assumed responsibility for formulating general policy and because discipline was an integral and indispensable part of the educational system, the State could not abdicate responsibility to the individual by reference to the common law[4].

14.65 At first consideration, it is difficult to extract a common theme from a number of cases. It could be asked why corporal punishment violated 'philosophical convictions' when sexual education[5], and cultural and linguistic diversity[6] did not and, in fact, this was the substance of the UK judge's dissenting judgment. In *Kjeldsen*, the dominant idea was that children should be given information in a balanced and non-doctrinaire manner whilst in the *Belgian Linguistic Case (No 2)*, it was clear that cultural diversity could pose acute constitutional problems and was, therefore, best left to the State. However, corporal punishment was felt to go to the root of the dignity of the individual. It was clear that the Convention organs took a critical view of corporal punishment reflecting that the UK was virtually alone in considering that there may be legitimate physical punishment of children. The contemporaneous ideas and values held throughout the other contracting States gave the Court the moral authority to intervene. In any event, corporal punishment was considered to be conflicting with another right enshrined within the Convention (Art 3) whereas the other acts complained of did not.

---

1   See the UK reservation at **14.29**.
2   *Campbell and Cosans v UK* 4 EHRR 293, para 41.
3   Again a majority of 6 to 1, the British judge dissenting.
4   See also *Warwick v UK* (1986) 60 DR 5 infliction of one stroke of the cane on the palm of the hand of a 16-year-old girl by a man (the headmaster) in front of another man (the deputy headmaster) and another girl, leaving a bruise visible for several days after amounted to degrading treatment under Art 3.
5   *Kjeldsen, Busk Madsen and Pedersen* 1 EHRR 711.
6   *Belgian Linguistic Case (No 2)* 1 EHRR 252.

14.66   Ten years after *Campbell and Cosans v UK*, the Commission considered an application[1] under Art 3 by a 15-year-old schoolboy who was punished by his headmaster for bullying. He had been caned four times across his clothed buttocks leaving four weals across his buttocks. There had been a decision not to prosecute the headmaster for assault and a civil claim in the county court on behalf of the child had failed. The application was not considered by the Court because the parties had reached a 'friendly settlement' but it was noted that the Commission regretted that the application was not being proceeded with to judgment because of the 'strength of the claims under Articles 3 and 13' and the Commission's view 'that such injury to a teenage boy is unacceptable whoever were to inflict punishment, be it parent or teacher ... In particular, it can find no pedagogical reason for dealing with the applicant's bullying behaviour with a punishment on the same bullying level'[2]. This probably reflects the general public view, although the dissenting judgment pointed out that:

> 'As Article 2 of the 1st Protocol guarantees a right of parents to decide on the education of their children, one must respect the right of parents to use moderate corporal punishment against their children or to send their children to a school which uses such punishment. A total prohibition of all corporal punishment does not yet seem to be called for by present Western European standards.'[3]

The UK response

14.67   The *Campbell and Cosans* case resulted in a number of 'friendly settlements'[4] before the applications came before the Court but having been declared admissible by the Commission. It also resulted in the abolition by Statute of corporal punishment in State schools, in respect of 'assisted place' pupils in private schools and in certain other schools for which the State provided financial assistance[5]. In any event, this form of punishment disappeared quickly from both State and private schools with State funding because the schools could not have a two-tier system of discipline in the classroom differentiating between pupils of parents who objected to corporal punishment and of parents who did not.

Independent schools

14.68   Independent schools are not public authorities and it might be thought that the State would avoid any responsibility under the Convention for the content of the curriculum or administrative matters such as the disciplinary code. However, *Costello-Roberts v UK*[6] clarified that the State could not delegate such responsibility to the extent that it was extinguished.

14.69   The applicant, aged 7 years, was sent to an independent boarding preparatory school. No fees of the 180 pupils were paid out of public funds and there was no direct financial support from the Government. Following a series of demerit marks and warnings against poor conduct, the headmaster gave the child three 'whacks' on the bottom through his shorts with a rubber-soled gym shoe.

---

1   *Y v UK* 17 EHRR 238.
2   Ibid, para 44 and Commission report, para 36.
3   Ibid, p 247.
4   *Durairaj v UK* (1987) 52 DR 13; *Family A v UK* (1987) 52 DR 150.
5   Education (No 2) Act 1986, ss 47 and 48.
6   19 EHRR 112.

There was no visible bruising. Although the court had certain misgivings about the automatic nature of the punishment and the 3-day wait before its imposition, it did not consider that the minimum level of severity had been attained and thus the actions of the headmaster did not violate Art 3[1]. However, the Court dismissed the Government's submission that it was not directly responsible for every aspect of the way in which independent schools were run even if it did have a limited degree of control and supervision. In particular, the Government argued that it assumed no function in matters of discipline. Although the Government made no distinction between pupils in State and independent schools, it argued that their rights were guaranteed because English law prohibited the use of any corporal punishment which was not moderate or reasonable.

14.70   The Court emphasised that it had consistently held that the responsibility of a State is engaged if a violation of one of the rights and freedoms defined under the Convention is the result of non-observance by that State of its obligation under Art 1 to secure those rights and freedoms in its domestic law to everyone within its jurisdiction[2]. The Court noted that:

–   The State has an obligation to secure to children their right to education under Art 2 of the First Protocol.

–   Independent schools co-exist with a system of public education. The fundamental right of everyone to education is a right guaranteed equally to pupils in State and independent schools, no distinction being made between the two.

–   The State cannot absolve itself from responsibility by delegating its obligations to private bodies or individuals[3].

–   Nevertheless, there is no right to State subsidy for private education schools[4].

14.71   Primary education is compulsory in the UK and so the State must exercise some measure of control over private schools so as to safeguard the essence of Convention guarantees. One judge of the European Court has commented that the State cannot shift prison administration to the private sector and thereby make corporal punishment in prisons lawful and in the same way, it cannot permit the setting up of a system of private schools which are run irrespective of Convention guarantees[5]. Further, any privately run school must be subject to regulation in order to ensure the quality of education[6].

14.72   Furthermore, there is no right to State subsidy to set up or run schools which have a particular religious or philosophical character. The Commission has declared applications inadmissible on the grounds that:

–   these schools do receive assistance in the sense that they have charitable status[7];

PART B
IMPACT OF THE CONVENTION

---

1   19 EHRR 112, para 32.
2   Ibid, para 26.
3   Ibid, para 27.
4   *Verein Gemeinsam Lernen v Austria* 20 EHRR 78, CD.
5   *Costello-Roberts v UK* 19 EHRR 112; see the partly dissenting judgment.
6   *Jordebo v Sweden* (1987) 51 DR 125.
7   *X and Y v UK* (1982) 31 DR 210.

–   it was not unreasonable for a private body wishing to set up a school to bear 15
per cent of the capital costs even if, in the eyes of the applicants, such cost was
an insurmountable obstacle[1] or the failure to provide financial assistance
would result in the closure of the educational institution[2].

SPECIAL NEEDS

14.73   A system to provide education for children with special needs was
introduced by the Education Act 1944, albeit with many shortcomings. The real
foundation of the current system is found in the *Warnock Report* which was largely
adopted by the Government of the day and enacted in the Education Act 1981.
The legislation provided for a system of assessment of all children with special
educational needs following which those needs would be provided for. The
Education Act 1993 provided a system of statutory rights and procedures and
introduced a National Code of Practice. The Education Act 1996, although
making significant amendments, largely consolidates the legislation whilst the
Education Act 1998 extends the system to maintained schools.

14.74   The aim of the legislation is to make provision for the majority of the
children with special needs within ordinary schools and make provision for
specialist education where the work necessary was outside the capabilities of those
schools. As stated above, s 9 of the Education Act 1996 (replacing s 76 of the
Education Act 1944) requires that pupils are to be educated in accordance with
the wishes of their parents, so far as that is compatible with the provision of
efficient instruction and training and the avoidance of unreasonable public
expenditure.

14.75   This is echoed in s 316 of the Education Act 1996 whereby a child with
special needs has his education secured in a non-special school unless that is
incompatible with the wishes of his parents. This is subject to conditions that the
educational provision is compatible with:

–   the necessary special educational provision which the child's difficulties call
for;
–   the efficient education for the children with whom he will be educated;
–   the efficient use of resources.

14.76   The wish of the parents is a constant theme but, in reality, parental
choice is limited by resources. General choice of schools is already thus restricted
and the Convention has helped little on that aspect, for example parents'
complaints that their choice of a single sex school was not granted were declared
to be inadmissible and founding no violation of Art 2[3]. It is questionable whether
the introduction of the Convention into UK law will significantly alter this in the
field of special needs education where it appears to be subject to less rather than
more choice.

Many of the Convention cases involve applications where the local authority view
of the necessary education markedly differs from the view of the parents and the

---

1   *X v UK* (1978) 14 DR 179.
2   *40 Mothers v Sweden* (1978) 9 DR 27.
3   *W & DM and M & HI v UK* (1984) 37 DR 96.

parents have raised the complaint that their philosophical convictions have not been respected. On the whole, it appears that where there is such a clash, the State's view usually prevails either on the basis of the reasonable exercise of discretion in the efficient use of resources or on the child's right of access to education.

Family H v UK[1]

14.77 The four children of the applicants suffered from dyslexia. The parents tried different forms of education for them and resorted to educating the children at home, not least because they found the State system repugnant to them particularly as regards corporal punishment. Different methods such as boarding schools and home tutors were proposed and tried by the local authority but the parents considered the methods incompatible with their philosophical convictions and educational theories. Home education was allowed under the Education Act 1944 but only if the children were receiving efficient full-time education suitable for their age, ability and aptitude but the parents had refused permission to allow the local authority to assess the children.

14.78 The Commission made it clear that its role was not to consider whether one form of teaching was better than another but stated that it was implicit in Art 2 of the First Protocol that the State has a right to establish compulsory schooling, be it in State schools or in private tuition, of a satisfactory standard and that verification and enforcement of educational standards is an integral part of that right. Therefore, the requirement that the parents co-operate in an assessment of their children to ensure a certain level of numeracy and literacy was not unreasonable nor did it constitute a lack of respect for the parents' convictions.

Ford v UK[2]

14.79 The applicant was a child who was educated in a local State school until the age of 11. Following an assessment, the local education authority considered that he should be educated in a special needs school. This was against the wishes of the parents who educated him at home from that time. A further assessment at the age of 13 concluded again that this child should be educated in a special needs school. The application was based on a complaint that the local education authority had blocked the child's access to mainstream education. The Commission declared the complaint inadmissible having regard to the margin of appreciation accorded to national authorities in the efficient use of education resources[3].

PD and LD v UK[4]

14.80 The applicants were parents of a child who had suffered brain damage at birth. The parents wished her to be educated in an ordinary school and claimed that segregated education was inappropriate for their daughter and incompatible with their philosophical convictions. In fact, the local authority had offered the child attendance at an ordinary school for 2 days per week.

14.81 The Commission left open the question whether such views amounted to philosophical convictions or merely a disagreement with the authorities as to the best way of providing education for their child. The Commission stated that

---

1   (1984) 37 DR 105.
2   (1996) EHRLR 534.
3   Ibid.
4   (1989) 62 DR 292.

Art 2 of the First Protocol did not require the State to provide special facilities to accommodate particular convictions, although it may affect the use of existing facilities and referred to the Government's reservation to this provision, accepting Art 2: 'only insofar as it is compatible with the provision of efficient instruction and training and the avoidance of unreasonable public expenditure'. Whilst the authorities must place weight on the wishes of the parents, it cannot be said that Art 2 requires the placing of a child with severe developmental delay in a general school (with the expense of additional teaching staff which would be needed) rather than in an available place in a special school. Moreover, the very fact that the local authority had offered the compromise of two days in an ordinary school indicated that it was respecting the applicant's views 'as well as (the child's) right to have as effective an education as possible'.

Graeme v UK[1]

14.82   In a similar case to *PD and LD v UK* above, the applicants were the parents of a child who suffered from severe physical and developmental delay. The local authority took care proceedings, not so that the child would be taken away from the parents but so that an assessment could be undertaken. The parents responded by taking out wardship proceedings and the matter was eventually decided in the High Court where it was held that the child should go to a suitable residential boarding school where his needs would be catered for.

14.83   In deciding that the application was inadmissible, the Commission again left open whether the parents' deep-rooted views fell within the definition of 'philosophical convictions' but stated that 'even assuming that the applicants' philosophical convictions may be at issue in this part of the present case, the Commission refers to the dominant character of the child's right to education in Article 2 of the First Protocol'[2].

Cohen v UK[3]

14.84   The applicants were parents of a special needs child. The local authority had assessed his needs and considered a nearby school appropriate to provide for those needs. His parents wished him to go to a school which was further away and required him to be transported there. They asked for financial assistance for the transport but were refused. It was argued on behalf of the child that, as he had special needs, the need for this choice of school was at least as great in the case of children with special needs as in the case of other children. It was submitted that the local authority could not respect his parents' right to ensure he received the education of their choice if they permitted him to go there and then denied him free transport. Again, the Commission noted the reservation entered by the UK against Art 2 of the First Protocol and stated that such duties as were imposed on the State did not extend to providing free transport when there was a suitable school nearby to the child's home which would enable him to receive adequate education without the need for transport.

Simpson v UK[4]

14.85   The applicant was a child suffering from dyslexia. He was placed in a special school but, prior to that, he suffered behavioural problems because his

---

1   (1990) 64 DR 158.
2   Ibid, para 1.
3   21 EHRR 104.
4   (1989) 64 DR 188.

dyslexia had not been diagnosed. The local education authority paid his school fees. However, when the parents of the child moved areas, the competent local education authority were unwilling to continue to pay the school fees and proposed, under the statement, that he should attend an ordinary comprehensive school and that his 'needs' could be addressed through that school. The child complained that he was being denied the right to education in accordance with his educational needs.

14.86 The Commission declared that the application was inadmissible. It acknowledged that the authorities must place weight on parents' and pupils' views but concluded that Art 2 of the First Protocol fell short of the requirement to place a dyslexic child in a private specialised school, with the fees paid by the State, when a place is available in a ordinary State school which has special teaching facilities for disabled children. The Commission did not consider it was their task to assess the standard of the special facilities provided by the State school and relied on the fact that the applicant's progress at the school would be monitored and his needs kept under review by the education authorities[1].

As can be seen, parents of 'special needs' children have difficulty in showing a violation of Art 2 when they have not been granted education for their child at the school of their choice.

DISCRIMINATION

14.87 Article 14 of the Convention sets out the following:

'The enjoyment of the rights and freedoms set forth in this Convention shall be secured without discrimination on any ground such as sex, race, colour, language, religion, political or other opinion, national or social origin, association with a minority, property, birth or other status.'

14.88 Article 14 does not grant an independent right, that is a 'right to freedom from discrimination', but equally, it does not require a breach of another Convention right before it can be applied. If the latter were the case, the protection afforded by Art 14 would merely be accessory to the protection under the other Articles and would be limited to the 'aggravation of the violation of another provision of the Convention'[2]. The Commission places great importance in respect to those clauses in the Convention which 'do not precisely define the rights which they enshrine but leave states a certain margin of appreciation with regard to the fulfilment of their obligation'.

14.89 Article 14 has an autonomous existence and where a violation of an another Article has been found, the Court will frequently decide that it is unnecessary to decide whether there has been a violation of Art 14 as well. Conversely, if there is no breach of another Article, the court will go on to consider whether there has been a breach of that Article in conjunction with Art 14.

14.90 The *Belgian Linguistic Case (No 2)* was an early example of consideration of the question whether there had been any discrimination under Art 14 in conjunction with Art 2 of the First Protocol.

1   (1989) 64 DR 188, para 2.
2   *Belgian Linguistic Case (No 2)* 1 EHRR 252 at 277 quoting the Commission report.

14.91   For there to be a violation under Art 14, the Commission stated that it was enough for the discrimination to touch the enjoyment of a specific right or freedom already comprised within the right to education and that it was necessary for Art 2 to be read as though Art 14 were its third paragraph. In the sphere of education, the obligation not to discriminate is neither positive nor negative but conditional. If the State assumes, quite freely, functions in this sphere it must carry them out in a non-discriminatory manner[1].

14.92   However, the Court did not consider that Art 14 forbade every difference in treatment in the exercise of the rights and freedoms recognised, otherwise the many legal and administrative provisions which inevitably lead to a difference in treatment would amount to a violation of the Article resulting in unworkable legislation. The Court considered the criteria which enabled a determination to be made as to whether or not a given difference in treatment contravenes Art 14. It determined that the principle of equality of treatment is violated if 'the distinction has not objective and reasonable justification . . . when it is clearly established that there is no reasonable relationship of proportionality between the means employed and the aims sought to be recognised'[2].

14.93   In the *Belgian Linguistic Case (No 2)*, Art 14 did not guarantee the child or his parent the right to obtain instruction in the language of choice, but rather ensured that the right to education was secured by each contracting party to everyone within its jurisdiction without discrimination on the ground of language. The Court found that the purpose of the legislation complained against was to achieve linguistic unity within each of the two large regions of Belgium in which a large majority of the population speaks only one of the two national languages and such a purpose struck a fair balance between the protection of the interests of the Community and respect for the rights and freedoms safeguarded by the Convention. Thus, a failure to set up or subsidise French speaking schools in the Flemish speaking areas did not violate Art 14, whereas on the narrow issue of denying French speaking children access to certain schools on the grounds of where they lived where there was no similar restriction on Flemish speaking children, it was held that there was a violation of Art 14 because it was based on the consideration of language rather than for administrative or financial reasons[3].

14.94   In the light of the proportionality argument, the past refusal to fund Muslim schools could, if it had not already been reversed, amount to discrimination under Art 14 in conjunction with Art 2 of the First Protocol.

---

1   1 EHRR 252 at 279.
2   Ibid, para 10.
3   Ibid, para 32.

PART C

Case Summaries

INTRODUCTION

These case summaries are not intended as full reports of the judgments of the Court. Rather, they will add some flesh to the many cases that are frequently referred to throughout the text. Obviously, practitioners will have to get hold of the full reports in one form or another.

Citations are given, first, to the official reports of the Council of Europe, Series A and, secondly, to the European Human Rights Reports, published by Sweet & Maxwell. The reports can also be obtained by going to the web-site of the European Court of Human Rights at www.dhcour.coe.fr/hudoc and searching under the name of the applicant, or in many other ways.

Series A. These are generally cited by reference to the volume number and the page number. More recently, the system has changed to the Report of Judgments and Decisions, known as RJD. They are extremely slow in being published; RJD followed by a rule (RJD _____) indicates that the citation was not available at the time when these summaries were compiled. The reports often reprint the whole of the decision of the European Commission of Human Rights, and the judgments tend to be lengthy, with the ratio often tucked away where you do not expect it. The newer reports, particularly those produced on the internet, contain a helpful summary prepared by the Registry of the Court.

European Human Rights Reports. These reports cover all the significant judgments of the Court, and more recently, all the judgments. Cited by volume number and page number, there are currently 27 volumes. Some volumes also have references to other international jurisdictions. Under the old system, they would periodically produce a volume containing summaries of decisions of the Commission. The reports contain a very helpful summary of the decision at the front, and make it possible to ascertain the reasoning of the Court. They are published several times per year, and the reports appear far more quickly than the official series. It appears likely that they will become the reports of choice following incorporation. The only difficulty is that they are not used by any other countries of the Council of Europe. However, the paragraph numbers match those of Series A, and so it is possible to find any specific references quite easily.

A v UK

RJD _____, 27 EHRR 611

Beating with garden cane applied with considerable force on more than one occasion reaches level of severity prohibited by Art 3

Facts

A had previously been on the Child Protection Register due to known physical abuse by his step-father. In 1993, there was a further complaint through the school, and on examination by a paediatrician he found multiple red linear bruising to the child's right thigh, left thigh, bottom and left calf, administered over of period of one week, which in his opinion was consistent with being hit by a garden cane using considerable force. The step-father was tried with occasioning actual bodily harm, and relied on the defence of reasonable chastisement. In his summing up, the judge directed the jury in the following way:

> 'It is a perfectly good defence that the alleged assault was merely the correcting of a child by its parent, in this case the stepfather, provided that the correction be moderate in the manner, the instrument and the quantity of it. Or, put another way, reasonable.'

The defendant was acquitted by a majority verdict.

Complaint

The applicant complained that the State had failed to protect him from ill-treatment by his step-father, in violation of Arts 3 and/or 8 of the Convention; that he had been denied a remedy for these complaints in violation of Art 13; and that the domestic law on assault discriminated against children, in violation of Art 14 in conjunction with Arts 3 and 8.

Commission

The Commission unanimously found a violation of Art 3, and did not think it necessary to consider the complaint under Art 8.

Court

Before the Court the Government accepted that there was a violation, but asked the Court to limit its judgment to the facts of the case.

The Court in finding a violation of Art 3 held that:

(1) Ill-treatment must attain a minimum level of severity if it is to fall within the scope of Art 3. The assessment of this minimum is relative: it depends on all the circumstances of the case, such as the nature and context of the treatment, its duration, its physical and mental effects and, in some instances, the sex, age and state of health of the victim (see the *Costello-Roberts v UK* judgment of 25 March 1993, Series A, No 247-C, p 59, para 30).

(2) Treatment of this kind against a 9-year-old, on several occasions, reaches the level of severity prohibited by Art 3.

(3) Under Art 1 of the Convention, the UK has an obligation to take measures to ensure individuals are not subjected to inhuman or degrading treatment, including where administered by private individuals. Children and other vulnerable individuals, in particular, are entitled to State protection, in the form of effective deterrence, against such serious breaches of personal integrity (see, *mutatis mutandis*, the *X and Y v The Netherlands* judgment of 26 March 1985, Series A, No 91, pp 11–13, paras 21–27, the *Stubbings and Others v UK* judgment of 22 October 1996, Reports 1996-IV, p 1505, paras 62–64 and also the United Nations Convention on the Rights of the Child, Arts 19 and 37).

(4) With the defence of reasonable chastisement the law did not provide adequate protection to the applicant against treatment or punishment contrary to Art 3, and constitutes a violation of Art 3 of the Convention.

(5) It was not necessary to consider the issues under Art 8.

(6) Applicant awarded £10,000 in damages.

Airey v Ireland

(1979) Series A, No 32, 2 EHRR 305

Judicial separation as a civil right – need for effective access to a court – lack of legal aid – violation of Art 6

Facts

A wished to obtain a decree of judicial separation against her husband, who was an alcoholic and had been violent towards her. Irish law did not permit divorce proceedings but did provide for 'barring orders' excluding the spouse from the matrimonial home but such an order would not be permanent. Alternatively, a petition could be brought for judicial separation if adultery, cruelty or unnatural practices could be proved. Such a petition could be brought in the High Court only where the procedure was complex and costs would be in the region of £500 to £700 if the matter was uncontested and £800 to £1,200 if contested, the costs being recoverable from the unsuccessful respondent after taxation. Parties were entitled to conduct their case in person but, without exception, petitioners for judicial separation were legally represented by a lawyer. A had dependent children living with her and was in receipt of unemployment benefit and £20 per week maintenance from her husband under a court order. Legal aid was unavailable for any civil or matrimonial proceedings in Ireland. She consulted a number of solicitors about bringing a petition against her husband but, in the absence of legal aid or of the personal means to meet the costs, she could not find a solicitor who would act for her.

Complaint

She applied to the Commission in 1973 alleging breaches of, inter alia, Art 6(1) and Art 8 stating that the prohibitive cost of litigation prevented her from bringing proceedings, and that failing to ensure that there is an accessible legal procedure fails to respect her family life.

Court

The Court in finding a violation of Arts 6(1) and 8 held (by a majority) that:

(1) Judicial separation was a remedy provided for by Irish law which related to A's civil rights and obligations and so it was of no relevance that A stood to gain nothing from judicial separation.

(2) Although A had the right to conduct her case in person, her appearance before the court without the assistance of a lawyer would not have provided an effective right of access because of the complexity of the procedures and the necessity to call and examine witnesses, including the possibility of expert witnesses. Furthermore, marital disputes often entail an emotional involvement that is scarcely compatible with the degree of objectivity required by advocacy in court.

(3) The decision in respect of Art 6(1) did not have the consequence that legal aid or legal representation was required for all cases concerning civil rights and obligations, nor for all persons involved therein. Article 6 does not guarantee any general right to free legal aid. In certain eventualities, the possibility of appearing before a court in person will meet the requirements of Art 6(1), even on occasion in the High Court. The institution of legal aid is only one means by which an effective right of access to the courts can be guaranteed, there being others such as a simplification of procedure. Article 6 may sometimes compel the State to provide for the assistance of a lawyer when such assistance proves indispensable for an effective access to court, either because legal representation is rendered compulsory or by reason of the complexity of the procedure or of the case.

(4) Article 8 does not merely compel the State to abstain from interference in private and family life but may place positive obligations upon the State to ensure an effective respect for private and family life. Irish law recognised that the protection of a person's private or family life may sometimes necessitate their being relieved of the duty to live together by way of a decree of judicial separation, but Ireland had failed to make this means of protection effectively accessible to A, not having put her in a position to apply to the High Court.

Albert and Le Compte v Belgium

(1983) Series A, No 58, 5 EHRR 533

Disciplinary procedures – whether a contestation *over a civil right – Art 6 guarantees may apply*

Facts

The applicants were both doctors who were subjected to disciplinary proceedings by their professional body the *Ordre des Médecins* and both had been suspended from practice for a specified period. The disciplinary hearings were in camera, although Dr Le Compte requested that they be heard in public.

Complaint

The applicants alleged that the disciplinary proceedings breached their rights under the Convention in that the hearing had not been in public by a fair and impartial tribunal.

Court

In finding no violation of Art 3 and a violation of Art 6(1), the Court held that:

(1) The applicant's allegation that the punishment of suspension from practice constituted degrading or inhuman punishment was not well founded. The object of the punishment was to penalise serious professional misconduct and not to debase his personality.

(2) Article 6 applied as the effect of the proceedings was to deprive the applicants of a private and thus a civil right, namely to continue to pursue their profession of practising private medicine by entering into contractual relationships with their patients. Consequently, the hearing should satisfy the requirements of Art 6(1).

(4) The impartiality of the members of a disciplinary tribunal will be presumed until there is proof to the contrary.

(5) There was no justification for not holding the disciplinary hearings in public. The principles set out in Arts 6(2), (3)(a), (b) and (d) were *applicable* mutatis mutandis to disciplinary hearings subject to Art 6(1) in the same way as they applied to a criminal matter.

Andersson v Sweden

(1992) Series A, No 226, 14 EHRR 615

Child in care – no contact at all – disproportionate to aim – violation of Art 8

Facts

The applicant's son was taken into care when he was 11 years old after the authorities concluded that his health and behaviour were seriously disturbed due to his mother's behaviour. The courts prohibited access entirely, as it would be 'too dramatic' for the child, and later included a prohibition on telephone contact and correspondence.

Complaints

The applicant complained that such limits breached the right to family life.

Commission

The Commission expressed an opinion that there had been a violation of Art 8.

Court

In upholding the opinion of the Commission the Court held that:

(1) The mutual enjoyment by parent and child of each other's company constitutes a fundamental element of family life, and the natural family relationship is not terminated by reason of the fact that the child is taken into public care.

(2) To be 'in accordance with the law' the impugned measures should have a basis in domestic law, and the law must be accessible and formulated with sufficient precision to be able to foresee the consequences of a given action. A law which confers a discretion is not in itself inconsistent with this requirement, provided that the scope of the discretion and the manner of its exercise are indicated with sufficient clarity, having regard to the legitimate aim in question, to give the individual adequate protection against arbitrary interference.

(3) The relevant Swedish law was clearly aimed at protecting 'health or morals' and the rights and freedoms of the children.

(4) A parent's and child's right to respect for family life under Art 8 includes a right to the taking of measures with a view to their being reunited (*Olsson v Sweden* 11 EHRR 259; *Eriksson v Sweden* 12 EHRR 183).

(5) The restrictions on the meetings between mother and child and the prohibition of contact by mail or telephone were particularly far-reaching, and had to be supported by strong reasons to be consistent with the aim of re-unification of the family and justified under Art 8(2).

(6) The aggregate of the restrictions imposed on meetings and communications was disproportionate to the legitimate aims and was therefore not 'necessary in a democratic society' and therefore a breach of Art 8.

Ashingdane v UK

(1985) Series A, No 93, 7 EHRR 528

Detention of mentally ill – right of access to a court – that right not absolute

Facts

The applicant was a psychiatric patient. He had been committed to a secure psychiatric hospital after the commission of offences. After a number of years, in 1978, the Home Secretary authorised his release to his local psychiatric hospital. The health authority which governed that hospital refused to accept him as a patient as staff were unhappy with accepting offenders. The Secretary of State could have ordered the transfer to go ahead, but declined to do so. The applicant remained in the secure hospital for another 2 years at which point he was transferred to a local hospital. During those 2 years, he unsuccessfully brought legal proceedings to challenge the legality of his detention.

Complaint

The applicant complained that his detention between 1978 and 1980 and his inability to challenge the refusal of the decision not to transfer him breached the Convention, in that the difference in security levels and restriction of movement between the two hospitals amounted to the difference between detention and liberty, and that as he was certified fit for liberty such continued detention was unlawful. Furthermore, he was not able to challenge the decision of the Home Secretary in the courts.

Court

The Court in finding that there had been no breaches of Arts 5 and 6 held that:

(1) The detention of Mr Ashingdane was lawful for the purposes of Art 5(1)(e) as they had no reason to doubt the competence of the doctors who assessed him as a paranoid schizophrenic who might be dangerous if released into the community.

(2) The transfer involved moving from one regime of hospital detention to another, and that in law he remained in detention in both hospitals, regardless of the difference in freedom of movement.

(3) The right of access to a court is not absolute, and the legislative restrictions on recourse to the courts by mental patients was intended to protect those who deal with mental patients from harassment through the courts. The limitations applied must not restrict or reduce the access left to the individual in such a way or to such an extent that the very essence of the right is impaired (*Golder v UK* 1 EHRR 333). A limitation will not be compatible with Art 6(1) if it does not pursue a legitimate aim and if there is

not a reasonable relationship of proportionality between the means employed and the aim sought to be achieved. This was a legitimate aim, and a reasonable restriction of rights.

B v France

(1992) Series A, No 232-C, 16 EHRR 1

Transsexuals – inability to alter birth certificate or any other document – genuine effect on daily life – violation of right to respect for private life

Facts
The applicant is a male to female transsexual. She sought to alter her birth certificate to declare that she was of female sex for the purposes of marriage, but this was refused by the French courts, although such rectification was allowed in law.

Complaint
Miss B complained that the refusal of the French authorities to recognise her true sexual identity, in particular their refusal to allow her the change of civil status sought, was in breach of Arts 3, 8 and 12 of the Convention.

Commission
The Commission declared the complaint admissible and found a breach of Art 8 by 17 votes to one, and no breach of Art 3 by a majority.

Court
In finding a violation of Art 8, the Court held that:

(1)   The positive requirements of 'respect' for private and family life will vary from case to case balancing the interests of the individual and the general interest.

(2)   Although it is undeniable that attitudes have changed towards transsexualism, there are many complex issues remaining, and no sufficiently broad consensus between the Member States of the Council of Europe to persuade the Court to reach opposite conclusions to those in its *Rees* and *Cossey* judgments.

(3)   In France, birth certificates were intended to be updated throughout the person's life, and an amendment could be ordered, and a great many such amendments have been ordered by the courts. The applicant's manifest determination is a factor to be taken into account in the rectification of the civil status documents.

(4)   Under French law, which was not entirely settled, Miss B had to use her male name on all identity documents and quasi-official papers such as phone bills. This was a relevant factor for Art 8.

(5)   The inconveniences suffered by the applicant in having to disclose her original sex frequently in everyday life due to her description on official documents reaches a sufficient degree of seriousness to be taken into account for the purposes of Art 8.

(6)   These factors distinguish this case from *Rees* and *Cossey* in that she finds herself daily in a situation which, taken as a whole, is not compatible with the respect due to her private life, even having regard to the margin of appreciation. Violation of Art 8.

Belgian Linguistic Case (No 2)

(1968) Series A, No 6, 1 EHRR 252

Right to education – no right to linguistic requirements – must be treated equally or will be discriminatory

Facts
The applicants were French-speaking Belgians. Under the relevant Belgian law, the country was divided into regions and designated either a single language region or dual language region. Six areas had special status. In a single language area, the language of education was obviously that of the region. In a dual language area, it depended on the maternal language of the child. The law prevented the operation of the wrong type of school in a single language area, for example if you operated a French language school in an area that was designated Dutch-language only, the school could lose financial support and official recognition.

Complaints
The applicants argued that these measures breached the right to education guaranteed in Art 2 of the First Protocol, and the right to respect for private and family life contrary to Art 8 of the Convention, as well constituting discriminatory treatment contrary to Art 14.

Commission
The Commission held that the linguistic laws themselves did not breach any Articles of the Protocol, but that the penalties for breaching the legislation amounted to violations of the Convention. The Commission referred the case to the Court.

Court
In finding a breach of Art 2 the First Protocol in conjunction with Art 14 of different grounds, but no breach of the Convention in respect of the main complaint, the Court held that:

(1) There is a 'right' in the first sentence of Art 2 of the First Protocol, but the negative formulation of it indicates that it is not unlimited. It does imply the right to be educated in one of the national languages.
(2) There is not only a right of access to educational institutions existing at a given time, but also of drawing profit from the education received in the form of official recognition of the studies completed.
(3) There is no right to education in Art 8, although measure taken in the field of education may affect the right for private and family life.
(4) Article 14 is violated when it is clearly established that there is no reasonable relationship of proportionality between the means employed and the aim sought to be realised. National authorities are free to choose the measures they consider appropriate, if they conform with the Convention.
(5) Article 8 does not guarantee the right to be educated in the language of one's parent by the public authorities or with their aid.
(6) A difference in treatment was not per se discriminatory, provided that an objective and reasonable justification could be found. In this case, the court found that there was 'a fair balance between the protection of the interests of the community and respect for the rights and freedoms safeguarded by the Convention', and that there was therefore no breach of Art 14 in the general legislative provisions.
(7) As there was a difference in the treatment of French and Dutch speakers in the regions with special status, there was a breach of Art 2 of the First Protocol. It was not imposed in the interest of the schools, whether for administrative or financial reasons, but rather followed from considerations relating to language.

Benthem v The Netherlands

(1985) Series A, No 97, 8 EHRR 1

Decision by Minister on advice of tribunal – Art 6(1) applicable – not an impartial tribunal – violation

Facts
The applicant was granted a commercial gas supply licence by the municipal authorities, which was later revoked by the Minister concerned after receiving advice drafted by the Administrative Litigation Division of the Council of State, after a hearing. The practice was that the Minister would almost always follow the advice of the Litigation Division, which would in turn seek advice from the Minister's department. The applicant later went bankrupt as a result of the decision.

Complaint
The applicant complained that the tribunal was not fair and impartial in that the Litigation Division merely tendered an advice which had no binding force and the determination was made by the Minister; it was not impartial due to the fact that it consulted the department of the Minister, and there was no opportunity to challenge the evidence upon which the Minister decided because the text of the advice remained secret.

Commission
The Commission decided by 9 votes to 8 that Art 6(1) did not apply to this tribunal, and so did not make a decision as to whether there was a breach.

Court
In finding that Art 6(1) did apply and had been violated, the Court held as follows:

(1) The Court will look at the following principles:
   (a) The word *contestation* (dispute) should not be construed too technically, and given a substantive rather than a formal meaning.
   (b) The *contestation* may relate to the scope of a right as well as its existence.
   (c) It must be genuine and of a serious nature.
   (d) The result of the proceedings must be directly decisive for such a right.
(2) Here, the Court found that there was a genuine and serious dispute as to the actual existence of the right to a licence. The result of the proceedings could and did lead to a direct decision on that right.
(3) The licence was of a proprietary nature, to be used as part of his business, which had an effect on his customers and could be sold on. Therefore, it was a 'civil right' in terms of Art 6(1).
(4) The Litigation Division merely tenders an advice rather than makes a decision itself. Therefore, it does not provide the 'determination by a tribunal of the matters in dispute' as required by Art 6(1).
(5) The decision was actually rendered by Royal Decree, showing that the decision was an administrative act emanating from a Minister. Therefore, it was not the act of a 'tribunal', which it should have been, due to the lack of fundamental guarantees such as independence, impartiality and the guarantee of judicial procedure. Consequently, there was a violation.

Berrehab v The Netherlands

(1988) Series A, No 138, 11 EHRR 322

Expulsion of father after family ties established – breach of Art 8

Facts

The applicant was married in 1977 and was given permission to stay in the Netherlands 'for the sole purpose of enabling him to live with his Dutch wife'. They had a child in 1979, although the marriage had broken down before her birth, and the divorce was granted in August 1979. He was deported to Morocco in 1984. He was given a visa for the purposes of contact.

Complaint

The applicant complained that the refusal to grant him a new residence permit after the divorce and his resulting expulsion amounted to interferences with the right to respect for their family life, due to the distance to Morocco and the financial expense involved. He further complained that this amounted to inhuman treatment, particularly for the daughter.

Commission

The Commission found the complaints admissible on behalf of the father and the child but not for the mother. They concluded that there had been a violation of Art 8 by 11 votes to 2 but not of Art 3.

Court

In upholding the decision of the Commission, the Court held that:

(1) Failing to grant a residence permit and the expulsion prevented the applicants from maintaining regular contacts with each other, although such contacts were essential as the child was very young. Therefore they were interferences with the right to family life under Art 8(1).

(2) The interferences had the legitimate aim of the preservation of the country's economic well-being, specifically the regulation of the labour market; however, despite the margin of appreciation given to the State, it cannot be said that the interferences were 'necessary in a democratic society', weighing the legitimate aim pursued against the applicants' right to respect for family life. Mr Berrehab had lived in the Netherlands for several years, and already had a family there, rather than coming to the country for the first time so to do. He had developed close ties with his daughter. The interference was disproportionate.

(3) There was no suffering of a degree corresponding to the concepts of inhuman or degrading treatment.

Borgers v Belgium

(1991) Series A, No 214-B, 15 EHRR 92

Criminal proceedings – position of avocat général – equality of arms – breach of Art 6(1)

Facts

The applicant was convicted by the Antwerp Court of forgery and was given a 6-month suspended sentence. He appealed on a point of law to the Court of Cassation, on the basis that the lower court had not given sufficient reasons. The Court of Cassation heard submissions from the avocat général who was a member of the prosecutor's department although he did not appear as such on this occasion, but rather as an adviser to the court. He was then allowed to sit in on the judge's deliberations. The appeal was allowed. The case was remitted to the Ghent Court which imposed the same punishment. The applicant appealed on the same grounds as before, and the avocat général played the same role as in the previous appeal. This time the appeal was dismissed.

Complaints

The applicant complained that, in the Court of Cassation, he was not allowed to reply to the submissions of the avocat général, who could be seen as his opponent, which was in breach of the idea of equality of arms. Furthermore, the avocat général then participated in the judicial deliberations following the hearing, in breach of Art 6.

Commission

The Commission decided that there was a violation of Art 6(1).

Court

In finding a violation of Art 6(1) the Court held that:

(1) Their findings in *Delcourt* remained the same, that the impartiality and independence of the Court of Cassation and its procureur général's department were not in question. However, the law with regard to fair trial had developed in respect of the importance attached to appearances and the increased sensitivity of the public to the fair administration of justice.

(2) The official of the avocat général's department recommends that the appeal be allowed or dismissed, and therefore becomes his ally or opponent. In the view of the parties to the proceedings, he cannot be regarded as neutral.

(3) Furthermore, the applicant was not aware of the submissions to be made by the avocat général before they were made, and neither was he able to respond to them. There was no reason for the applicant not to be able to respond.

(4) The involvement of the avocat général in the deliberations of the court increased the view of inequality. Whilst he may be able to assist in drafting, that is really a job for the court, and it could reasonably be thought that the deliberations afforded him an opportunity to further promote his submissions.

Bouamar v Belgium

(1988) Series A, No 129, 11 EHRR 1

Detention of a juvenile – valid only in certain strict circumstances – need for review – breach of Art 5

Facts

The applicant was a minor who had been charged with criminal offences and on nine separate occasions placed in a remand prison as an interim measure until he could be committed to a suitable juvenile institution. Such remands were allowed for up to 15 days under Belgian law if it was 'materially impossible' to a find an institution able to accept the juvenile immediately. Although no one period of detention in prison exceeded 15 days, the applicant was deprived of his liberty for a total of 119 days in a period of 291 days. During that time, numerous other solutions were attempted such as placement in a reformatory and with members of the applicant's family but the applicant either absconded and/or persisted in his delinquent behaviour. The remand decisions in this case had been taken by a judge but were somewhat informal. The applicant's lawyers were not given notice of the hearings nor access to all the documentation relied on by the judge.

Complaint

The applicant contended that his treatment amounted to an deprivation of liberty in breach of Art 5(1) and that his detention had not been reviewed as required under Art 5(4). He further argued that he had been the subject of discrimination under Art 14.

Court

In finding a breach of Art 5 and no breach of Art 14 the Court held that:

(1) The list of circumstances set out in Art 5(1) in which detention is allowed is exhaustive and will be interpreted strictly (*Guzzardi v Italy* 3 EHRR 333). A juvenile may be detained only in those cases. The purpose of Art 5 is to protect the individual from arbitrariness. It is for the domestic courts to apply the laws of their State (*Bozano v France* 9 EHRR 297) but they must also comply with the Convention.

(2) Article 5(1)(d) does not preclude an interim custody measure being used as preliminary to a regime of supervised education even where it does not itself involve any supervised education. However, the imprisonment must be followed speedily by the implementation of such a regime with adequate resources.

(3) The Belgian State had chosen a system of educational supervision as a means to pursue its policy on juvenile delinquency. It was therefore under an obligation to establish appropriate institutions which met the objectives of security and education of juveniles as set out in its legislation and which satisfied Art 5(1) of the Convention.

(4) In fact, there were no secure institutions for highly disturbed juveniles like the applicant. He was detained in prison in virtual isolation. There were no staff with educational training in the prison and it was impossible to carry out any educational aim. Consequently, the nine placements were not compatible with Art 5(1)(d).

(5) The provisions in Art 5(1) and (4) were distinct and could be the subject of separate consideration.

(6) The scope of the obligation under Art 5(4) is not identical in all circumstances or in respect of every deprivation of liberty, but the individual should have the opportunity to be heard in person and the effective assistance of a lawyer. The mere presence in person at a hearing of a person as young as the applicant did not afford him the necessary safeguards under the Convention. Although there was an appeal procedure it was too slow to have any practical effect. There was therefore no review of detention as required by Art 5(4).

(7) The different treatment of the remand of juveniles and adults alleged to have committed criminal offences was not discrimination in contravention of the Convention. The differences were due to the protective rather than punitive nature of the proceeding relating to juveniles and there was, therefore, an objective and reasonable justification for the difference.

Boyle v UK

(1994) Series A, No 282-B, 19 EHRR 179

Pre-Children Act 1989 – right of access to child in care – breach of Art 8 accepted by Government

Facts

The applicant's nephew was removed into care following accusations of sexual abuse by his mother, who was arrested but not prosecuted. Although the Court found that the applicant had been a good father figure to the nephew, his repeated requests for access were refused as he denied the sexual abuse by his sister. He was not invited to attend any case conferences.

Complaints

The applicant contended that, prior to the entry into force of the Children Act 1989, there was no right of access for non-parental relatives which was a breach of Art 8.

Commission

The Commission in deciding by 14 votes to 4 that there was a breach of Art 8 stated that:

(1) Cohabitation is not a prerequisite for the maintenance of family ties which are to fall within the scope of the concept of 'family life'. It is, however, an important factor to be taken into account when considering the existence or otherwise of family ties.

(2) Where parents are denied access to a child there is, in general, an interference with family life. This is not necessarily the case with other close relatives, which is normally at the discretion of the parents or guardians. Here, where all contact was terminated, there was an interference.

(3) The interference was 'in accordance with the law'. The purpose was of safeguarding the child's health and rights within the meaning of Art 8(2).

(4) An uncle will not require as much involvement in the decision-making process as a parent (see *W v UK*). Here, there was no attempt to reach a compromise allowing meaningful dialogue between the local authority and the child's family. This amounted to a fundamental short-coming since the applicant as a result was not involved in the decision-making procedure to the degree sufficient to provide him with the requisite protection of his interest. Therefore, the interference was not 'necessary' in the sense of proportionate, and there was a breach.

Court

Following a friendly settlement, the Court struck out the application and accepted that:

(1) The Children Act 1989 remedied the situation to allow applications for contact for non-parental relatives for children in local authority care.

(2) The Government paid £15,000 to the applicant and his costs.

Brüggemann and Scheuten v Germany

2 EHRR 244

Abortion – restrictions – not just a matter for the mother – no violation of Art 8

Facts

This case concerned a German criminal law statute which came into force in 1976 after its provisions had been referred to the country's constitutional court. It provided that terminating a pregnancy, save in certain specified circumstances, was a criminal offence punishable by imprisonment. Broadly, a termination was expressed not to be punishable if it was carried out by a doctor within designated time-limits with the consent of the woman concerned and after she had been offered counselling *and* where either the child would be born seriously damaged, the pregnancy was the result of rape or sexual abuse of a child or other vulnerable person, or if the mother would suffer serious distress which it would not be reasonable to expect her to bear and which could not be otherwise averted than by an abortion.

Complaint

The applicants were two women who contended that the statute infringed Art 8 in that they were not free to have an abortion in the case of a pregnancy that was simply unwanted and were therefore forced either to abstain from sexual intercourse or use contraception or proceed unwillingly with a pregnancy.

Commission

In finding no violation of Art 8 the Commission decided that:

(1) The legislation regulating abortion concerned the sphere of private life. The question at issue therefore was whether the German statutory provisions constituted an 'interference' with private life.

(2) Article 8 secures an individual the right freely to develop and fulfil him or herself. This includes the ability to engage in sexual and other relationships with other people. In those circumstances, in principle any rule imposed by the State impinging on the individual's behaviour in this regard is an interference with private life and must be justified under Art 8(2).

(3) However, the right to individual development was restricted to the extent that it impacted upon public life and conflicted with other protected interests. In this case the exercise of the rights of the individual woman would impinge upon those of the developing foetus.

(4) The Commission expressly declined to decide whether the unborn child constituted a 'life' under Art 2 or whether it was an individual afforded protection under the 'protection of others' limb of Art 8(2).

(5) Questions relating to pregnancy and termination of pregnancy are not matters which relate solely to the private life of the mother. All Member States regulated the matter of abortion and, prior to the coming into force of the Convention all Member States had laws on abortion which were at least as restrictive as that now complained of, there was no evidence that the State parties had intended to bind themselves against such a solution as that adopted in Germany. There was therefore no breach of the Convention.

Campbell and Cosans v UK

(1982) Series A, No 48, 4 EHRR 293

Corporal punishment – no violation of Art 3 – violation of Art 2 of the First Protocol

Facts

Both applicants' children were at State schools in Scotland, and due to financial and practical considerations, there was no alternative to this. Both applicants complained of the use of corporal punishment in Scottish schools. Mrs Campbell asked for an assurance that her son would never be punished in such a way, which assurance was refused. In September 1976 Mrs Cosans's son Jeffrey was told to report to be punished for breaking school rules by taking a short-cut. On his father's advice, he reported but refused to accept the punishment. He was suspended. In January 1977 his parents were told he could return to school if he accepted the disciplinary requirements of the school. The parents said that they would not accept corporal punishment, which the school said amounted to a refusal. They were threatened with prosecution for failure to ensure Jeffrey's attendance at school. Jeffrey never returned to school.

Under s 29 of the Education (Scotland) Act 1962, subject to certain limitations, 'pupils are to be educated in accordance with the wishes of their parents'. Although the Home Secretary had responsibility for education he had issued no guidelines for the use of corporal punishment. In 1968 the local authority had issued such guidelines limiting the circumstances in which it could be used.

Complaint

Each applicant maintained that the use of corporal punishment as a disciplinary measure in the school attended by her child constituted treatment contrary to Art 3 and also failed to respect her right as a parent to ensure her son's education and teaching in conformity with her philosophical convictions, as guaranteed by the second sentence of Art 2 of the First Protocol. Mrs Cosans further contended that her son's suspension from school violated his right to education, protected by the first sentence of Art 2 of the First Protocol.

318 Family Law and the Human Rights Act 1998

Commission

The Commission found that there had been a violation of the second sentence of Art 2 of the First Protocol. They did not find it necessary to consider a separate violation of the first sentence. The found no violation of Art 3. The Government requested that the matter go to the Court.

Court

In finding no breach of Art 3 but a breach of Art 2 of the First Protocol, the Court held that:

(1) Although neither boy was actually strapped, the threat of such can amount to inhuman treatment. The circumstances did not amount to that in these cases.

(2) Discipline is included in the definition of 'education' and 'teaching' in Art 2 of the First Protocol. The education of children is the whole process whereby, in any society, adults endeavour to transmit their beliefs, culture and other values to the young, whereas teaching or instruction refers in particular to the transmission of knowledge and to intellectual development.

(3) The second sentence of Art 2 of the First Protocol is binding upon States in the exercise of 'each and every' function that they undertake in the sphere of education and training, so that the fact that a given function may be considered to be ancillary is irrelevant. Consequently, the State has assumed responsibility for all aspects of education.

(4) The term 'convictions' is not synonymous with the words 'opinions' and 'ideas', as used in Art 10; it is more akin to the word 'beliefs' in Art 9, and denotes views that attain a certain level of cogency, seriousness, cohesion and importance.

(5) The Government's submission that respect for the applicant's convictions was satisfied by the adoption of a policy of gradually eliminating corporal chastisement was rejected, as was their submission that the UK reservation applied, which states that the Protocol is accepted 'only so far as it is compatible with the provision of efficient instruction and training'. Consequently, there was a violation of the second paragraph of the Article.

(6) Article 2 of the First Protocol is dominated by the first sentence, with the second sentence an adjunct of the fundamental right to education. A condition of access to an educational establishment that conflicts with the parents' convictions cannot be described as reasonable, and falls outside the State's power of regulation within Art 2. Therefore, breach of the right to education in the case of *Cosans*.

(7) *Dissenting Judgment of Sir Vincent Evans*. The *travaux préparatoires* clearly show that the intention behind the phrase 'philosophical convictions' was to protect the rights of parents against the use of educational institutions by the State for the ideological indoctrination of children, the interpretation given by the Court in the *Kjeldsen, Madsen and Pedersen* judgment. Therefore, it is limited to the content of information and knowledge imparted to the child through education and teaching; the manner of imparting such information and knowledge and the views of parents on such matters as corporal punishment are outside the intended scope of the provision, as much as their linguistic preferences (see the *Belgian Linguistic Case (No 2)*). There may be very strongly held beliefs on such matters as the segregation of sexes, streaming and independent schools.

(8) There is not a practical system for exempting individual pupils from corporal punishment which would be compatible both with the provision of efficient instruction and training and with the avoidance of unreasonable public expenditure. Consequently, the UK reservation applies.

Cossey v UK

(1990) Series A, No 184, 13 EHRR 622, [1991] 2 FLR 492

Transsexual – unable to change birth certificate – whether breach of right to privacy – unable to legally marry – no violation

Facts

The applicant was born in 1954 as a male, but by the age of 15 realised that she was psychologically female. From the age of 18 she changed her name and lived her life as a woman. At the age of 20 she underwent gender reassignment surgery, to render the external anatomy nearer that of the female gender. She thereafter lived a full life as a woman. She was granted a passport as a woman, and pursued a successful career as a woman. In 1983 she attempted to marry Mr L, but was informed by the authorities that the marriage would be void as her birth certificate stated that she was male. She applied to be granted a new birth certificate, but that was refused. The engagement was broken off. In 1989 the applicant purported to marry Mr X. The marriage failed shortly afterwards, and in proceedings for ancillary relief the marriage was declared null and void on the basis that the parties were not respectively male and female.

Complaints

The applicant argued that her fundamental rights were breached in that the refusal to grant her a new birth certificate was an infringement of her right to privacy in Art 8, in that she had to reveal intimate personal details every time she produced her birth certificate, and the fact that she was consequently unable to marry constituted a breach of Art 12.

Commission

The Commission's opinion by 10 votes to 6 was that there had been a violation of Art 12, and that there had not been a violation of Art 8.

Court

In finding no violation of either Arts 8 or 12 the Court held that:

(1) There was no difference in circumstances than with the *Rees v UK* case; specifically, the fact that Ms Cossey had actually attempted to marry was not a relevant consideration.

(2) The Court is not bound by its previous findings, and the Court would depart from an earlier decision if there were cogent reasons for doing so, in order to ensure that the interpretation of the Convention reflects societal changes and remains in line with present-day conditions.

(3) It would follow the reasoning in *Rees*, in that the needs of the community had to be balanced with the needs of the individual, and in this case changing the entire system of registration would not be justified.

(4) There had not been sufficient scientific or societal changes to justify changing the previous view of the Court, despite the fact that some contracting States had made changes to their law.

(5) The purpose of Art 12 was to protect the traditional marriage as the basis of the family. Laws should not restrict or reduce the right in such as way that the very essence of the right was impaired.

Costello-Roberts v UK

(1993) Series A, No 247-C, 19 EHRR 112

Corporal punishment – private schools – not so severe as to breach Article 3 – no breach of Articles 8 or 13

Facts

The applicant was a 7-year-old boy at a Prep School in Barnstaple. Five weeks after starting school he was slippered by the headmaster after a series of minor breaches of school rules.

His parents were not informed. The slippering consisted of three 'whacks' on the bottom through his shorts with a rubber-soled gym shoe. His parents claimed that following the punishment he showed signs of considerable distress.

Complaint

The applicant complained that the punishment amounted to a breach of Art 3 and violated the right to respect for private and family life guaranteed by Art 8. The applicant complained of having no domestic remedy, in breach of Art 13.

Commission

The Commission held by 9 votes to 4 that there had been no breach of Art 3, as the punishment must 'attain a particular level of severity over and above the usual element of humiliation involved in any kind of punishment'. Although institutionalised violence could be a breach, the facts of this case did not compare with the thrashing administered in the case of *Tyrer v UK*. They further held by 9 votes to 4 that there was a breach of Art 8, in that it constituted an interference in his private life, though not family life, that had no social, educational, health or moral justification. They further found by 11 votes to 2 that there was a breach of Art 13 in that lawful chastisement was a defence to a charge of assault, which also prevented any civil action.

Court

The Court in finding no violation of any Article of the Convention held that:

(1)   The State has an obligation to secure the right to education under Art 2 of Protocol 1, of which discipline is an integral part. There is no distinction between State and private education in that respect. State responsibility cannot be delegated to individuals. Consequently, if the act of a headmaster is in breach of the Convention, the State has responsibility for it.

(2)   In order for punishment to be 'degrading' the humiliation involved must be other than the usual element of humiliation inherent in any punishment. Factors to take into account include the nature and context of the punishment, the manner and method of its execution, its duration, its physical and mental effects and the sex, age and health of the victim. Here, the lack of long-lasting effects indicated that the level of severity had not been reached.

(3)   Bearing in mind that sending a child to school necessarily involves an interference with private life, the punishment did not entail adverse effects for his physical or moral integrity sufficient to interfere with his private life in terms of Art 8.

(4)   The applicant did have an 'arguable' claim, and could have taken the matter to the civil courts; Art 13 does not depend on the certainty of a favourable outcome, nor does it guarantee the right to challenge domestic law on the ground of being contrary to the Convention.

Dombo Beheer v The Netherlands

(1993) Series A, No 274-A, 18 EHRR 213

Civil proceedings – one side barred from giving evidence – equality of arms – violation of Art 6

Facts

A commercial dispute arose between a bank and the applicant company in respect of an oral agreement allegedly made between the then managing director of the applicant company and a branch manager of the bank. No one else was present. By Netherlands law, a party to civil proceedings was, in general, precluded from giving evidence on his own behalf in those proceedings. This restriction applied also to a person who could be identified with the legal identity of a company. In this case at the time of the proceedings the managing director was no longer employed by the applicant company but he was nevertheless not allowed to testify as to the alleged oral agreement whereas the branch manager, not being in any sense a party to the proceedings, was so allowed.

Complaint

The applicant complained that there had been a breach of Art 6(1) in that there had not been a fair hearing as there was no equality of arms between the parties.

Court

In finding a breach of Art 6 the Court held that:

(1) The Court will not decide in general terms whether it is possible to exclude the evidence of one person in a civil proceedings, but rather whether those proceedings were fair in this case.
(2) The requirements for a 'fair hearing' are less severe in civil proceedings than in criminal proceedings, but it is clear that the requirement of 'equality of arms' in the sense of a 'fair balance' between the parties applies in principle to both forms of law.
(3) In circumstances where the whole case depended upon the evidence of two men as to the alleged oral agreement between them, to prevent the company relying on the only first-hand witness to fact at its disposal was to put it at a substantial disadvantage. The principle of equality of arms had been breached.

East African Asians v UK

78-A DR 5, 3 EHRR 76

Discriminatory legislation – degrading treatment – violation of Art 3 – treatment of husbands and wives differently – violation of Arts 8 and 14

Facts

The applicants were 25 Asians from East Africa who were UK citizens and a further six who were British protected persons. They had all unsuccessfully sought entry to the UK when they had effectively been forced to leave East Africa.

Complaint

The applicants stated that the UK's refusal to admit them to Britain or to allow them to stay permanently was racist and therefore degrading treatment under Art 3, and that there were also breaches of Arts 8 and 14.

Commission

In finding breaches of Arts 3, 8 and 14 and no breach of Art 5 the Commission decided that:

(1) The refusal of a right not itself protected by the Convention was capable of amounting to the violation of another right which was protected under the Convention. Thus although the right to enter one's country is not protected as such under the Convention, the refusal of this right may in appropriate circumstances itself violate a right under the Convention.
(2) 'Degrading treatment' in Art 3 is that which severely lowers a person in his or her rank, position, reputation or character in that person's own eyes or the eyes of other people; alternatively that which grossly humiliates a person before others or drives him or her to act against his or her will or conscience. The concept is not restricted only to physical treatment. The Convention will be interpreted objectively and not by reference to the understanding of one party at the time of ratification.
(3) Discrimination based on race or colour is capable of amounting to degrading treatment under Art 3 of the Convention. In this case, the question was whether British immigration legislation discriminated on the grounds of race or colour and, if so, whether in the particular cases before the Commission this constituted degrading

treatment. Here, the relevant legislation was discriminatory on the grounds of race or colour by subjecting to immigration control citizens of the UK and colonies in East Africa of Asian origin. The treatment of the applicants reduced them to the status of second-class citizens. The policies of governments in East Africa had the effect of depriving applicants of their homes and livelihoods, all of which had been foreseeable at the time the legislation was passed, and that they were now being refused entry by the only State to which they could make out any sort of claim for admission.

(4)   By a majority of 6 votes to 3, as regards the 25 British citizens, the racial discrimination and consequent interference with human dignity to which the applicants had been publicly subjected by the application of the immigration legislation was capable of constituting degrading treatment and in this case did constitute degrading treatment. As to the six protected citizens, their rights were not violated as they were not British subjects, their position had been unchanged by the 1968 legislation and they were not the subjects of discrimination on the grounds of race or colour.

(5)   The expressions 'liberty' and 'security of the person' were closely connected and that the latter was designed to protect the individual against arbitrary interference with his or her liberty by a public authority. Public authorities must therefore conform to the procedural and substantive requirements of an already existing law. By 8:1 they held that in this case there was no breach of Art 5 itself.

(6)   Article 14 has no autonomous role but that there could be a violation of that Article in conjunction with another Article notwithstanding that there was no breach of the latter Article per se. Here there was no breach.

(7)   The refusal to admit the husbands of Commonwealth citizens in circumstances where the wives of male Commonwealth citizens would have been admitted constituted an interference with family life under Art 8 by preventing the reunion of the applicants' families. In addition, this interference was contrary to Art 14 in conjunction with Art 8 in that it discriminated against male applicants.

The Committee of Ministers

The Committee noted that the majority of two-thirds of the members of the Commission entitled to sit, as required by Art 32(1), had not been attained, and decided to take no further action.

Engel and Others v The Netherlands (No 1)

(1976) Series A, No 22, 1 EHRR 647

Military discipline – whether criminal in nature – lack of fair hearing – breach of Art 6 – discrimination – no breach of Art 14

Facts

This case concerned a number of non-commissioned officers in the Netherlands armed forces who had committed and been punished for offences against military discipline. At the time, the nature of the penalties imposed differed according to the rank of the offender to the detriment of non-commissioned officers and ordinary servicemen. Disciplinary offences might affect a person's career in the forces but they did not appear on his or her criminal record. Hearings in respect of these offences were held in camera but judgment was pronounced in public.

Complaint

The applicants complained that the punishments imposed amounted to a deprivation of liberty contrary to Art 5 and that the military proceedings did not comply with Art 6 and that they were treated in a discriminatory manner contrary to Art 14 in conjunction with Art 6.

Two applicants in particular had been punished for distributing literature deemed to undermine military discipline. They complained that the proceedings against them breached Arts 10, 11, 14, 17 and 18.

Court
In finding a breach of Arts 5 and 6 and no breach of Art 14, the Court held that:

(1) The Convention does apply to members of the armed forces but that allowance would be made for the necessities of military life. Military discipline does fall within the ambit of Art 5. The list of exceptions in that Article whereby detention may be rendered lawful is exhaustive. The normal restrictions on members of the armed forces dictated by the requirements of military life are not within Art 5 and each State is entitled to organise its own system of military discipline in respect of which there will be a margin of appreciation. Therefore, the guarantees offered by Art 5 are not identical for military personnel and civilians. However, restrictions which are not within the range of those recognised as necessary for the proper conduct of military life may contravene Art 5. In considering whether there has been a breach, the Court will consider the nature, duration, effects and manner of execution of any measure or penalty imposed on the individual.

(2) The hierarchical structure in an armed force entails differentiation of rights and responsibilities according to rank. In this respect the individual States will be allowed a considerable margin of appreciation.

(3) In determining whether a charge counts as 'criminal' within the meaning of Art 6, the Court will consider:
   (a) the definition of the charge in the domestic legal system, in the light of the common denominator of the respective legislation of the contracting States;
   (b) more importantly, the nature of the offence; and
   (c) the degree of severity of the penalty that the person risks incurring. Deprivations of liberty are 'criminal' penalties, except where the nature, duration or manner of execution is not sufficiently detrimental.

(4) There was no breach of Art 6 in conjunction with Art 14 on the ground that members of the armed forces were treated less favourably than civilians charged with a criminal offence. While there were not the same guarantees as in the criminal courts, there were other substantial advantages to the individual being tried in the military court. The difference in treatment was explicable on the grounds of the differing conditions of civilian and army life and was not discriminatory.

(5) In respect of the distribution of undermining literature, although Art 10 does have application to service personnel it was held that it was legitimate for a Member State to restrict freedom of expression for the prevention not only of public disorder but also disorder within the confines of a specific social group such as the armed forces. There was no breach.

(6) Further there was no breach of Art 14 in conjunction with Art 10 as the differences in freedom of expression between civilians and military personnel are explicable on the grounds of the differences between civilian and military life.

Eriksson v Sweden

(1989) Series A, No 156, 12 EHRR 183

Prohibition of removal of child from care – restrictions to access – violation of right to family life and access to a court

Facts
The applicant's daughter was taken into care shortly after her birth on the ground that the conditions in the home were unsatisfactory. The applicant applied for contact and custody of the child. The courts decided that the child did not need to remain in care, but that she

could not be returned to the mother, due to the effect on the mental health of the child, who, now aged 5, had settled with her foster-parents. They granted contact, upon which restrictions were later imposed.

Complaints

The applicant complained on behalf of herself and her daughter that the prohibition for an indefinite period on the removal of the child from foster-care was a violation of the right to family life. She further complained that the inability to challenge the restrictions on access was a breach of Art 6(1).

Commission

The Commission found that there was a breach of the right to family life, and that the daughter's right of access to a court had been breached.

Court

The Court, in finding breaches of Arts 6(1) and 8 for both mother and daughter held that:

(1)   The mutual enjoyment by parent and child of each other's company constitutes a fundamental element of family life; furthermore, the natural family relationship is not terminated by reason of the fact that the child has been taken into public care (*Olsson v Sweden*). The order prohibiting the removal of the child from care was an interference with the right to respect for family life, and such an interference is not affected by the relationship between the child and the foster-parents. The restrictions on access were also an interference.

(2)   As to whether the interference was in accordance with the law, the prohibition against removal of the child from care was in accordance with Swedish law, but the restrictions on contact were not, as they had no legal basis.

(3)   Both decisions had the legitimate aims of protecting the child's health and rights.

(4)   To be 'necessary in a democratic society' the interference must be proportionate to the legitimate aim. Having regard to the margin of appreciation, the severe and lasting restrictions on access combined with the long duration of the prohibition on removal were not proportionate to the legitimate aims pursued. Specifically, the mother's right to respect for family life under Art 8 includes a right to take measures with a view to her being reunited with her child. Because of the restrictions on access, she was denied the opportunity to meet with her daughter to an extent and in circumstances likely to promote the aim of reuniting them or developing their relationship. This caused stress and anxiety, which continued for a period of 6 years.

(5)   The inability to challenge the restrictions on access was a violation of Art 6(1). The recourse available to challenge the prohibition on removal is distinct, as only with access is there any real possibility of challenging the prohibition.

F v Switzerland

(1987) Series A, No 128, 10 EHRR 411

Right to marry – restriction – breach of Art 12

Facts

The applicant was a Swiss national who had been married and divorced three times. On the occasion of the last divorce, the divorce court had prohibited him from marrying within three years of the divorce as it found him solely responsible for the breakdown of the marriage on the grounds of adultery.

Complaint

The applicant contended that the prohibition contravened his right to marry.

Court

In finding a violation of Art 12 by a majority the Court held that:

(1) Its role was not to review generally the domestic law complained of but to examine the way in which the law had been applied in the individual case.

(2) Article 12 secures the fundamental right of men and women to marry and found a family. Although marriage is the subject of domestic laws within the contracting States, those laws must not restrict or reduce this right in such a way that the essence of the right is impaired.

(3) Although the Court must apply the Convention in the light of present-day conditions, the fact that one country is out of step with the other States will not necessarily mean that there is a breach of the Convention especially in the case of matrimony which is so closely bound up with cultural and historical conditions in each society.

(4) The Court recognised that the stability of marriage is a legitimate aim in the public interest. In this case, however, the Court did not accept that the temporary prohibition on marriage was designed to preserve the rights of others, ie the future spouses of a divorced person. The Court was of the view that such persons and any child in utero pending the expiration of the waiting period might be disadvantaged.

(5) The Court distinguished the *Johnston* case (see below) in which a prohibition on divorce in a society adhering to the principle of monogamy was held not to be in conflict with Art 12. If national legislation allows divorce, which was not a requirement of the Convention, then Art 12 secures for the divorced person the right to marry without unreasonable restrictions. There was therefore a breach of Art 12. The disputed measure was disproportionate to the legitimate aim pursued.

Fayed v UK

(1994) Series A, No 294-B, 18 EHRR 393

Access to a court – determination of right to honour – Inspectors' report investigative not adjudicatory – legitimate aim of good practice in the City – not disproportionate interference

Facts

This case concerned the DTI report into the take-over by Mohammed Fayed and his brothers of the House of Fraser group in 1985. The report made provisional conclusions that were unfavourable to the applicants, suggesting that they had dishonestly misrepresented their origins, their wealth, their business interests and their resources to various government bodies and their own shareholders, and that they had produced evidence which they knew to be false in the course of the investigation. Extracts of the provisional report were leaked in *The Observer*, and the Secretary of State in a radio broadcast stated that the report 'clearly disclosed wrongdoing'. Public policy was that such reports were published, and the State considered that in this case there were specific grounds of general public interest justifying publication, and the final report was published, with wide publicity. The Minister of State for Trade and Industry stated in the House of Lords that it had been intended that publication of the report would allow people to judge for themselves whether they wished to do business with the Fayeds. A libel action against the Observer by the applicants was discontinued. A claim against the Inspectors was not possible due to the defence of privilege. Various official bodies in the City took action to censure and control the applicant's positions within their companies.

Complaints

The applicants complained that, in violation of Art 6(1) of the Convention, the Inspectors' report had determined their civil right to honour and reputation and denied them effective access to a court in determination of this civil right. They further alleged a denial of effective domestic remedies to challenge the findings of the Inspectors, contrary to both Art 6(1) and Art 13 of the Convention. They further complained that this was in breach of their right to respect for private life under Art 8.

Commission

The Commission declared admissible the complaints with regard to Art 6(1) and the lack of an effective domestic remedy contrary to Art 13. It expressed the opinion that there had been no violation of Art 6(1) as regards the actual making and publication of the Inspectors' report, nor as regards the applicants' access to court for proceedings against the Inspectors and the Secretary of State or any others. They also found no violation of Art 13.

Court

In finding no violation of the Convention the Court held that:

(1) In order for an individual to be entitled to a hearing before a tribunal, there must exist a 'dispute' ('*contestation*') over one of his civil rights or obligations. It follows that the proceedings in question must be directly decisive for such a right or obligation, mere tenuous connections or remote consequences not being sufficient to bring Art 6(1) into play.

(2) Although the Inspectors can only be appointed if it appears to the Secretary of State that there are circumstances suggesting one or more types of specified wrongdoing or unlawful action in the conduct of a company's affairs, the functions performed by the Inspectors were, in practice as well as in theory, essentially investigative. They did not adjudicate in form or in substance. They did not make a legal determination as to criminal or civil liability concerning the applicants or their civil right to honour and reputation. They established facts for other authorities to act upon. The disputes against Lonrho and *The Observer* took place in the libel courts. It cannot be said that the Inspectors' inquiry 'determined' the applicants' right to a good reputation for the purposes of Art 6(1) or that its result was directly decisive for that right.

(3) For a body carrying out preparatory investigations at the instance of regulatory or other authorities in accordance with Art 6(1) would in practice unduly hamper the effective regulation in the public interest of complex financial and commercial activities, and so such activities must fall outside the ambit of Art 6(1).

(4) As regards the proceedings to contest the Inspectors' findings, whether a person has an actionable domestic claim may depend not only on the substantive content or the relevant civil right under national law, but also on the existence of procedural bars. The Court may not create a substantive civil right which has no legal basis in the State concerned, but a State may not remove from the jurisdiction of the courts a whole range of civil claims or confer immunities from civil liability on large groups or categories of person.

(5) In balancing the competing interests of the community and the requirements of the protection of the individual's fundamental rights the Court will look at the issues of legitimate aim and proportionality. In conferring total or partial immunity from libel on the authors of the report, the legitimate aim is the proper conduct of the affairs of public companies whose owners benefit from limited liability, and the appointment of Inspectors and the publication or not of their report to that end, with courage and frankness.

(6) If the investigators are to have the necessary freedom to report without fear, there is a risk of some uncompensated damage to reputation. Not to publish the report would render the purpose of informing the public pointless. The State did not exceed their margin of appreciation, and a reasonable relationship of proportionality existed between the freedom of reporting given to the Inspectors and the legitimate aim pursued in the public interest.

Feldbrugge v The Netherlands

(1986) Series A, No 99, 8 EHRR 425

Social security appeals board – application of Art 6(1) to a tribunal – lack of proper participation – fair hearing guarantees apply – violation of Art 6(1)

Facts

The applicant was claiming a sickness benefit, which was stopped when the Occupation Association's doctor decided that she was fit for work. She appealed to the Appeals Board in Haarlem. The President sought the opinion of two experts, who each consulted the applicant's three medical practitioners. The experts reported her fit for work and the President ruled against her. She appealed on the basis that she had not had a fair hearing, but her appeal was rejected as not fulfilling the statutory criteria.

Complaint

The applicant claimed there was a breach of Art 6(1) in that she was not able to appear either in person or by a lawyer to argue her case. Also, the reports of the two experts had not been made available to her, so she was unable to comment on them or to call further experts if considered necessary.

Commission

The Commission reported that Art 6(1) did not apply to the facts of this case and so did not go on to consider the substantive issue of whether or not there was a breach.

Court

The Court, in finding that there was a breach of Art 6(1) held as follows:

(1) There was a *contestation* (dispute) which was genuine and serious, concerning the actual existence of the right asserted by the applicant to continue receiving a sickness allowance. The President of the Board had to determine that dispute.

(2) Article 6 does not cover just private-law disputes between individuals or between individuals and the State. It is the character of the right at issue which is relevant rather than the body which will hear it, be it administrative board or proper court.

(3) In this case, the fact that Dutch law classifies the right as a 'public-law right' is only a starting point. In *König v Germany* the Court stated that 'whether or not a right is to be regarded as civil ... must be determined by reference to the substantive content and effects of the right – and not its legal classification – under the domestic law of the State concerned'. The Court will take into account the law in other States. There exists no common standard, where the status of social security law as private or public law appears to have little effect on the application of Art 6(1) guarantees.

(4) There are factors which suggest that it is a public law right, such as the character of the legislation by which the State regulates the health insurance framework, the compulsory nature of the insurance and the assumption by the State of responsibility for social protection. However, there are also considerations which argue in favour of private law, such as the personal and economic nature of the asserted right, the connection with the contract of employment and the affinities with insurance under the ordinary law, all of which lead the Court to conclude that these features confer on the asserted entitlement the character of a civil right within the meaning of Art 6(1).

(5) Whilst it was accepted that there was equality of arms between the Occupational Association and the applicant, in that they were not able to present independent evidence, the procedure did not allow proper participation of the contending parties. The President did not hear the applicant or ask for written pleadings. He did not allow her or her representative to consult the evidence of the two reports in order to formulate objections. The proceedings were not attended, to a sufficient degree, by one of the principal guarantees of a judicial procedure.

(6)   The restrictive terms of the appeal process did not render the decision of the Appeal Board curable.

Gaskin v UK

(1989) Series A, No 160, 12 EHRR 36

Social Services file – refusal to give full access to subject – breach of Art 8 – no breach of Art 10

Facts
The applicant was in the care of Liverpool social services from 1959 to 1977. He alleged that he had been abused whilst in care. In order to overcome his problems and deal with his past, he asked to see his file. An individual social worker allowed him to look at it, and he removed it for some weeks. In 1979, he commenced an action for negligence against the local authority. He asked for disclosure of the file. The local authority successfully argued that public interest immunity meant that the documents should not be revealed, the judge balancing the public interest in the proper operation of the child care service if the writers of reports were reluctant to be frank, with the needs of the individual and the public interest in reviewing the standard of care of the local authority. The Court of Appeal supported the judge's ruling. Subsequently, the local authority agreed to disclose 65 out of a total of 352 documents where the author consented to the disclosure. The law was subsequently changed under the Access to Personal Files (Social Services) Regulations 1989, SI 1989/206 to impose a duty to disclose such documents to the individual concerned, save for exceptions from health professionals.

Complaint
The applicant complained that the refusal of access to all his case records held by Liverpool city council was in breach of his right to respect for his private and family life under Art 8 and his right to receive information under Art 10.

Commission
In the opinion of the Commission, by 6 votes to 6 with the casting vote of the President in favour, there was a violation of Art 8, and no violation of Art 10.

Court
In upholding the decision of the Commission the Court held as follows:

(1)   The file contained a substitute record for the memories and experience of the parents of the child who is not in care, and therefore contained information concerning highly personal aspects of the applicant's childhood, development and history and undoubtedly related to his private and family life in such a way that the question of his access thereto falls within the ambit of Art 8.

(2)   Although the essential object of Article 8 is to protect the individual against arbitrary interference by the public authorities, there may in addition be positive obligations inherent in an effective "respect" for family life', *Johnston v Ireland.*

(3)   As the file compiled and maintained by the local authority related to the basic identity of his formative years, refusal to allow access was an interference with his right to respect for private life to be justified under Art 8(2). There is a wide margin of appreciation to be applied in the balance between the competing interest of the child care system and the applicant's record of his personal history.

(4)   The confidentiality of the contents of the file contributed to the effective operation of the child care system and was a legitimate aim. It is a vital interest to know and understand one's childhood. A system of disclosure by consent could be proper, taking into account the margin of appreciation. However, it is only proportionate where an independent authority finally decides whether access has to be granted in

cases where a contributor fails to answer or withholds consent. There was no such procedure here and therefore a violation of Art 8.

(5) Following the *Leander v Sweden* judgment, 'the right to freedom to receive information basically prohibits a Government from restricting a person from receiving information that others wish or may be willing to impart to him'. There is no obligation to impart the information here and no breach.

Golder v UK

(1975) Series A, No 18, 1 EHRR 524

Serving prisoner – prevented from communicating with his solicitor – right of access to a court – interference with correspondence – breach of Arts 6 and 8

Facts

There was a serious disturbance at a prison where the applicant was imprisoned. The following day a prison warden tentatively identified the applicant as one of those involved. The applicant was put into segregation and given notice that disciplinary proceedings might be brought against him. The prison governor stopped letters which the applicant wrote to his MP, and to a chief constable. In the month following the incident, the prison warden withdrew the allegation, and the applicant was returned to his ordinary cell. The charges were not proceeded with, and a note to this effect was put in the applicant's prison record which contained notes about the incident. Five months after the incident the applicant sought, and was refused, access to a solicitor with a view to instituting libel proceedings against the prison warden.

Complaint

The applicant alleged breaches of Arts 6(1) and 8 on the grounds that his letters had been stopped, and that he had been prevented from consulting a solicitor.

Court

In finding breaches of Arts 6 and 8 the Court held that:

(1) Domestic remedies had not been exhausted in relation to the stopping of letters, which was not considered further.

(2) Refusing the applicant permission to consult a solicitor amounted to prevention of access to the court, which breached Art 6(1). The right of access to the courts was not absolute and there was room for implied limitations, although this case did not fall within those implied limitations.

(3) Refusing the applicant the right to write to his solicitor was interference with his right to respect for correspondence under Art 8(1). The court appreciated the necessity for interference with a prisoner's correspondence 'having regard to the ordinary and reasonable requirements of imprisonment'. Preventing the applicant from contacting a solicitor was not reasonable. It did not fall within the caveat of being 'necessary in a democratic society'.

H v Belgium

(1987) Series A, No 127, 10 EHRR 339

Legal disciplinary proceedings – civil right – Art 6 guarantees apply

Facts

H was struck off the roll of *avocats* in 1963 after disciplinary proceedings were taken against him. The decision to strike him off was affirmed on appeals to two superior courts. H was prosecuted in respect of a later alleged fraud but acquitted in 1968. In 1977, he was about to apply to have his name restored to the roll but was once again prosecuted for fresh offences. He was acquitted of those charges in 1979 and then applied to be readmitted to the roll. Belgian law permitted his readmission once 10 years had elapsed from his expulsion so long as exceptional circumstances could be shown. The Council of the *Ordre des avocats* had exclusive jurisdiction conferred upon it by the Belgian Judicial Code to decide on applications for restoration to the roll with no right of appeal from its decision. The Council's hearings were held in private and its previous decisions were unavailable to the public. H's application was made orally through his counsel at a hearing before the Council of the *Ordre des avocats* in 1980. The Council found there to be no exceptional circumstances justifying his readmission. No further reasons were given as to why the matters relied upon did not amount to exceptional circumstances. In 1981, H renewed his application, disclosing further grounds which he contended constituted exceptional circumstances. The Council rejected the application finding there to be no exceptional circumstances, again without giving reasons.

Complaint

The applicant applied to the Commission alleging that the Council's procedure when considering his applications for restoration to the roll infringed Art 6. The Commission declared the application admissible on 16 May 1984.

Court

In finding a breach of Art 6 the Court held by a majority that:

(1) There was a *contestation* (dispute) concerning the right to be readmitted to the roll which H asserted. H could arguably maintain that in Belgian law he had a right to be readmitted to the roll if the preconditions for readmission laid down by the Judicial Code could be met. The Court rejected the Belgian government's contention that H had no right to be readmitted to the roll because his striking off was a permanent sanction with no obligation upon the Council to readmit him.

(2) The right to be readmitted to the roll had the character of a civil right conferred upon it by the nature of the profession of an *avocat*. Whilst the Bar of Belgium had duties which gave *avocats* the character of 'officers of the court' and thus, in some respects, were part of the judicial system, *avocats* are part of an independent profession with many professional duties performed out of court which have no connection with judicial proceedings. The work of members of the Bar cannot be said to consist solely of the functioning of the country's courts.

(3) The Council was an independent and impartial tribunal but had failed to afford H a fair hearing by: (a) failing to make available to H the applicable provisions for deciding upon 'exceptional circumstances' nor its previous decisions thus preventing H from presenting his case with the requisite effectiveness; and (b) by failing to provide a right to challenge the Council's decision, to have any internal rules of procedure, or to give sufficient reasons for its decisions the Council gave H cause to fear he may be dealt with arbitrarily.

(4) H had been denied his right to a public hearing notwithstanding that he did not demand such a hearing and even though his applications to the Council may conceivably have raised questions coming within the exceptions allowed for in Art 6(1) there was no evidence in this case to show that the circumstances merited the hearings not being held in public.

Hadjianastassiou v Greece

(1992) Series A, No 252-A, 16 EHRR 219

Delay in communicating judgment – time-limits for appeal – inability to perfect appeal grounds – inadequate time and facilities for preparation of defence – violation of Art 6 – no violation of freedom of expression – justified by national security

Facts

The applicant was an aeronautical engineer and a captain in the air force. He was working on the design of military missiles. He communicated a separate report written by himself on the same subject to a private company. He was charged with disclosing military secrets. He was convicted and sentenced to 2½ years imprisonment. The appeal was heard on 21 and 22 November 1985 hearing 19 witnesses as to the similarity or otherwise of the two missile reports. The appeal court gave judgment against the applicant but altering his sentence so as to release him immediately. The President of the Court read out his judgment and indicated that a 'finalised version' would be made available subsequently. The applicant lodged his grounds of appeal within the 5-day time-limit, although he did not receive the final judgment until 10 January 1986. In the Court of Cassation he complained that the delay meant that he was not able to prepare his appeal properly. They declared his complaint inadmissible.

Complaints

The applicant complains that the court should have given full reasons for its judgment at the hearing itself, and that as he did not know the reasons for his conviction he could not prepare his appeal within the 5-day time-limit to comply with the Court of Cassation rules. He further complained that the information he imparted was generally known, even though classified as 'secret'. Therefore, to punish him for imparting that knowledge was an interference with his freedom of expression.

Commission

In the opinion of the Commission there was a violation of Art 6(1) together with Art 6(3)(b), and there was no violation of Art 10.

Court

In upholding the opinion of the Commission, the Court held as follows:

(1) The specific requirements in Art 6(3) form part of the general right to fair trial in Art 6(1).

(2) Individual countries may choose how to comply with Art 6, although they must indicate the grounds on which they base their decision so as to allow the accused to properly exercise any grounds of appeal available to him.

(3) In this case, the applicant was limited in preparing his appeal to those facts that he had heard in court. The judgment contained new reasons not previously mentioned, he was not allowed a copy of it until well after the time-limit for appealing, and he was not allowed to amend his grounds of appeal once he did receive it. These restrictions amounted to an interference with the right to fair trial.

(4) There was an interference with the applicant's Art 10 right, which applies to civilians and servicemen. The interference was prescribed by law. There was a legitimate aim under Art 10(2) in the interests of national security, as the prosecution was intended to punish such breach of confidentiality. The State had not overstepped the margin of appreciation.

Handyside v UK

(1976) Series A, No 24, 1 EHRR 737

Right to possessions – justified interference – no violation

Facts

The applicant, an English publisher, was charged and convicted under the Obscene Publications Acts 1959 and 1964 for 'having in his possession obscene books entitled *The Little Red Schoolbook* for publication for gain'. Copies of the book were seized and destroyed and the applicant was fined. The *Schoolbook* was then published elsewhere in Europe and circulated in the UK. The applicant subsequently published a revised edition. No renewed criminal proceedings were brought against him.

Complaint
The applicant alleged that the initial prosecution and seizure amounted to breach of Arts 1, 7, 9, 10, 13, 14 of the Convention and Art 1 of the First Protocol.

Commission
The Commission declared that the only admissible complaints were Art 10 of the Convention and Art 1 of the First Protocol.

Court
In finding that there was no breach of Art 1 of the First Protocol or of Art 10, the Court held that:

(1) There had been interference with the applicant's freedom of expression, but it was necessary in a democratic society, for the protection of morals. The word 'necessary' in this context does not mean 'indispensable', but implied the existence of a pressing social need. The Court recognised a significant margin of appreciation in this case, stating that State authorities were better placed than the international judge to assess the necessity for a restriction designed to protect.

(2) As the seizure and forfeiture was carried out with the aim of protecting morals, it was within the 'general interest' principle in the second paragraph of Art 1 of the First Protocol and did not amount to a breach.

Hoffman v Austria

(1993) Series A, No 255-C, 17 EHRR 293

Custody of children – choice of religion – Jehovah's Witness – disproportionate interference – breach of Arts 8 and 14

Facts
The applicant was an Austrian citizen. At the time of her marriage she was a Roman Catholic. She had two children. She then became a Jehovah's Witness. She left her husband taking her children with her and was subsequently divorced. There was a dispute as to custody of the children. The father alleged that if they remained with the applicant they would be brought up as Jehovah's Witnesses and would suffer harm thereby. The domestic law provided that the religious upbringing of a child should be the subject of agreement between the parents, and in the absence of such agreement the civil law would apply. No party could bring the child up in a religion different from those of the parties at the time of the marriage or in which the child had been hitherto brought up without the consent of the other.

On appeal to the Supreme Court, custody was awarded to the father on the grounds that the mother had breached the law in relation to religious upbringing and that if the children remained with her the consequences of her bringing them up as Jehovah's Witnesses would be to their detriment.

Complaint
The applicant contended that she had been denied custody due to her religion and that her right to respect to family life had been breached and she had been the subject of discrimination on religious grounds.

Court

(1) The children had been removed from the applicant's care although they had lived with her for 2 years after the separation of the parties. The transference of custody to the father was an interference with her right to respect for family life and thus fell within the ambit of Art 8.

(2) Article 14 ensures that people in similar situations should not be treated differently under the Convention unless there is some objective and reasonable justification for such treatment (eg *Sunday Times v UK (No 2)* (1991) Series A, No 217).

(3) The Court examined the reasoning of the Austrian Supreme Court and concluded that the applicant had been subjected to different treatment from others in similar situations. Such differences could be justified only by showing that they had a legitimate aim and that the means used to pursue it bore a reasonable relationship of proportionality to that aim. Although the court's aim of protecting the health and rights of the children was legitimate there was no reasonable relationship of proportionality between that and the means used to achieve it. In the circumstances, there was a breach of Art 8 in conjunction with Art 14.

Hokkanen v Finland

(1994) Series A, No 299-A, 19 EHRR 139

Contact and custody – failure to enforce court decisions – breach of right to family life

Facts

The applicant's wife died when their child was 2 years old. The child was sent to live with the maternal grandparents on a temporary basis. When the time came for the child to be returned, the grandparents refused, and legal proceedings were commenced. The Courts ordered interim contact, but the grandparents refused to comply. The applicant won custody of the child, but the grandparents again refused to comply and appealed, which took time. In the interim, the child remained with them. Requests were made by the applicant for coercive measures, but these were not acted upon. The proceedings went on until the child was 10 years old, by which time the courts decided that it would be better for her to stay with her grandparents, and custody was transferred to them. The applicant had only ever been allowed contact on a few occasions.

Complaint

The applicant complained that the refusal to enforce the court orders and the eventual transfer of the child to the grandparents was a violation of Art 8.

Commission

The Commission found a violation of Art 8.

Court

In finding a breach of Art 8 in respect of the non-enforcement of contact, but no breach with regard to the non-enforcement of custody, the Court held that:

(1) The object of Art 8 is to protect the individual from arbitrary interference by the public authorities, as well as additional positive obligations inherent in an effective 'respect' for family life. A balance has to be struck between the interests of the individual and the community as a whole. The Court will determine whether the domestic courts' reasons were relevant and sufficient under Art 8. The parent has a right to have measures taken with a view to his or her being reunited with the child and an obligation for the national authorities to take such action.

(2) The obligation for the national authorities to take measures to facilitate reunion is not absolute, since the reunion may not be able to take place immediately. The nature and extent of the preparation required will depend on each case. Any obligation to apply

coercion in this area must be limited since the interests as well as the rights and freedoms of all concerned must be taken into account, and more particularly the best interests of the child. What is decisive is whether the national authorities have taken all necessary steps to facilitate reunion as can reasonably be demanded in the circumstances.

(3)   With regard to contact, this failed mainly due to the animosity between the parties. However, the failure of the relevant decision or measure in actually bringing about contact cannot be attributed to the applicant. The applicant actively sought enforcement of the court orders. It cannot be said that the authorities made reasonable efforts to facilitate reunion, rather that their inaction placed the burden on the applicant to attempt time-consuming and ineffectual remedies.

(4)   With regard to custody, once the grandparents had made applications to challenge the applicant's custody, there were sufficient grounds to justify non-enforcement of his custody right pending the outcome of the proceedings.

(5)   The later transfer of custody from the father to the grandparents was 'in accordance with the law' and pursued the legitimate aim of protecting the right of the child, and was necessary in a democratic society. They did not overstep the margin of appreciation, and the measure was not disproportionate to the legitimate aim of protecting the child's interests.

Inze v Austria

(1987) Series A, No 126, 10 EHRR 394

Illegitimate children – property rights – no justification – breach of Convention

Facts
The applicant was an Austrian national living in Carinthia. He was born out of wedlock and had a younger legitimate half-brother. He sought to inherit his mother's farm. Carinthian law gave precedence in matters of inheritance to legitimate children.

Complaint
The applicant complained that he was the subject of discrimination due to his illegitimacy in respect of the enjoyment of property rights in his mother's farm.

Court
In finding that there was a breach of Art 1 of the First Protocol in conjunction with Art 14 the Court held that:

(1)   A 'victim' of a breach of the Convention is not in principle deprived of his locus to make complaint notwithstanding that he has entered into a judicial settlement which has mitigated the disadvantages suffered by him as a result of the breach.

(2)   The Court confirmed that a difference of treatment is discriminatory if it has no objective and reasonable justification, ie that it does not pursue a legitimate aim and if there is not a reasonable relationship of proportionality between the means employed and the aim sought to be realised. The Convention is a living instrument to be interpreted in the light of existing conditions.

(3)   The question of equality in civil rights as between legitimate and illegitimate children is now given importance by the Member States as evidenced by the 1975 European Convention on the Legal Status of children born out of wedlock which Austria had ratified. Therefore, very weighty reasons would be necessary before a difference in treatment on the ground of illegitimacy would be held compatible with the Convention. Arguments as to the wishes of the applicant's mother and the views of the rural population in Carinthia were not sufficient justification. In the circumstances, there was a breach of Art 1 of the First Protocol in conjunction with Art 14.

Ireland v UK

(1978) Series A, No 25, 2 EHRR 25

Emergency powers in Northern Ireland – distinction between torture and inhuman treatment – violation of Art 3 – breach of Art 5 justified under the UK reservation

Facts

This case concerned the special powers of arrest and detention without trial which the British Government introduced in an attempt to combat IRA and loyalist terrorism. Powers included initial arrest for interrogation, if required 'for the preservation of peace and maintenance of order', and unlimited detention (limited in practice to 28 days) if suspected of acting in a manner prejudicial to the preservation of peace and maintenance of order. The Government lodged notices of derogation under Art 15(1) with the Council of Europe, claiming that the special powers were a reaction to a 'public emergency threatening the life of the nation'.

Complaint

The Government of the Republic of Ireland brought an application before the Commission. They complained that various interrogation practices were in breach of Art 3, in particular the so-called 'five techniques', which included food and sleep deprivation and hooding. They further complained that extra-judicial detention infringed Art 5 (right to liberty) and was not saved by Art 15, and lastly that the special powers were used primarily against IRA members, which constituted discrimination contrary to Art 14.

Commission

The Commission decided that the five techniques did constitute torture, and that other practices amounted to inhuman and degrading treatment. However, the Commission found that there was no infringement of Art 14, and that the infringement of Art 5 was justified under Art 15. The applicant government referred the case to the Court.

Court

In finding a breach of Art 3, a breach of Art 5 allowed by the reservation and no breach of Art 14 the Court held that:

(1)   The 'five techniques' were applied in combination, with premeditation and for hours at a time, causing at least intense mental and physical suffering, and amounted to inhuman treatment. They were also degrading as they aroused fear, anguish and inferiority capable of humiliating and debasing the victims.

(2)   The five techniques did not, however, constitute torture. The distinction between torture and inhuman or degrading treatment was one of degree. The five techniques did not occasion suffering sufficient in intensity and cruelty to constitute torture.

(3)   The British Government were right in claiming that there was a public emergency.

(4)   The legislation providing for arrest and extra-judicial detention contravened, inter alia, Art 5(1)(c) in that detention was not 'effected for the purpose of bringing [the detainee] before the competent legal authority' and detainees were not entitled to 'trial within a reasonable time'. The Court found that the reason for the provisions was to seek information about offences and offenders from suspects against whom there was not enough evidence to proceed to trial.

(5)   Although Art 5 was breached, the breaches were within the measures 'strictly required by the exigencies' and therefore were justified under Art 15. States have a wide margin of appreciation, although not an unlimited power, when it comes to determining what is required in times of national emergency. In deciding that the arrest and detention provisions were 'strictly required', the Court noted that a nation would be rendered defenceless in times of public emergency if it were required to meticulously consider

every option available before acting. The Court had to take account of the prevailing
conditions, and not retrospectively assess the merits and efficacy of the provisions.
Accordingly, the British Government had acted within the requirements of Art 15 and
the derogations from Art 5 were not in breach of the Convention.

(6)   There was no breach of Art 14. Although the provisions were used far more against
      IRA members than against loyalists, this was explicable by other factors, particularly
      the higher frequency of attacks by the IRA as opposed to loyalist groups, and was not
      the result of discrimination.

James v UK

(1986) Series A, No 98, 8 EHRR 123

*The Duke of Westminster's case – legislation for compulsory purchase at less than market value –
no breach of the right to property*

Facts

The applicants are the Sixth Duke of Westminster, his accountant, banker and surveyor, all
trustees under the will of the Second Duke of Westminster. The case involves the Belgravia
estate owned by the trustees, who were deprived of their ownership of a number of
properties in this estate through the exercise by the occupants of rights of acquisition
conferred by the Leasehold Reform Act 1967, as amended. This legislation allows tenants of
long leases to acquire the freehold interest in the land at a preferential value. The case
concerned some 80 such acquisitions, some of whom had leased the land for a very long
time, and some for only a few years. The applicants claimed that due to having to sell the
freehold on the statutory terms rather than on the open market, they had lost over £2½
million.

Complaints

The applicants claimed that the compulsory transfer of their properties gave rise, ipso facto
and/or at the price paid, to a breach of Art 1 of the First Protocol. They also alleged that the
circumstances of the transfer involved discrimination contrary to Art 14, and the absence of
a system of appeal violated Art 13. Seventy further transactions were added as 'supplementary applications'.

Commission

The Commission declared the application admissible and in its Art 31 report unanimously
found no breach of any of the provisions of the Convention.

Court

In finding no breach of Art 1 of the First Protocol, the Court held that:

(1)   The Court would not look at individual transactions but only the legislation, as the
      Government was only responsible *qua legislator*. The decision was whether the State
      had breached the applicants' Convention rights by empowering tenants to acquire
      their properties under those terms. The individual cases are illustrations of that. The
      object complained of was the legislation itself, rather than how it was enacted; indeed,
      one of the complaints was that there was no discretion in its implementation.

(2)   A compulsory transfer of property from one individual to another may in principle be
      considered to be 'in the public interest' if the taking is effected in pursuance of
      legitimate social policies. In this case, there is no common principle identified in the
      law of the contracting States to warrant understanding the notion of public interest as
      outlawing compulsory transfer between private parties.

(3) The public does not have to benefit directly from the taking of the property; it may be in pursuance of a policy calculated to enhance social justice within the community.

(4) There is no difference between the concepts of 'public interest' and 'general interest' in Art 1.

(5) Although measures designed to ensure equitable distribution of economic advantages are mentioned only in the second paragraph of the Article, the Court sees no reason why a State should be prohibited from implementing such a policy by methods in the first paragraph, ie deprivation of property.

(6) National authorities are in principle better placed that the international judge to appreciate what is 'in the public interest'. For the implementation of social and economic policies, the margin of appreciation is a wide one. The Court will respect the national legislature's judgment unless it is manifestly without reasonable foundation. The margin of appreciation is wide enough to cover legislation aimed at securing greater social justice in the sphere of people's homes, even where such legislation interferes with existing contractual relations between private parties and confers no direct benefit on the State or the community at large.

(7) On the question as to whether there was a 'fair balance' struck between the demands of the general interest of the community and the requirements of the protection of the individual's fundamental rights, the requisite balance will not be found if the person concerned has had to bear 'an individual and excessive burden'. The measures must be both appropriate for achieving its aim and not disproportionate thereto.

(8) The taking of property without payment of an amount reasonably related to its value would normally constitute a disproportionate interference which could not be considered justifiable under Art 1 of the First Protocol. Legitimate objectives of 'public interest', such as pursued in measures of economic reform or measures designed to achieve greater social justice, may call for less than reimbursement of the full market value.

Johansen v Norway

(1996) RJD 1996-III, No 13, 23 EHRR 33

Child in care – lack of parental rights – denial of access – violation of Art 8

Facts

The applicant's child was taken into care in a home when he was 12 years old due to concerns as to his health and development. She gave birth to a daughter shortly afterwards, who, due to the state of health of the mother, was immediately taken into foster-care, the mother visiting. The situation was finalised after court proceedings, when the girl was taken into care with a view to adoption, access was terminated and the mother's parental rights were removed. Her 12-year-old son eventually came back to live with her. All appeals failed. She later had two further children who live with her.

Complaints

The applicant complains that there was a violation of her right to respect for family life on account of the care order, the termination of access, the deprivation of her parental rights and the length of proceedings.

Commission

The Commission declared the application admissible and expressed the opinion that there was a violation of Art 8 in respect of the removal of parental rights and the deprivation of access, no violation in respect of the care order, and no separate issue under Art 6 or Art 13.

Court

In upholding the decision of the Commission the Court held that:

(1) The mutual enjoyment by parent and child of each other's company constitutes a fundamental element of family life and that domestic measure hindering such enjoyment amount to an interference in Art 8, as in this case. Such interferences must be in accordance with the law and necessary in a democratic society.

(2) The interferences were in accordance with the law. The legitimate aim was to protect the interests of children. Children's measures vary throughout Europe, but consideration of what is in the best interest of the child is in any event of crucial importance. The national authorities have the benefit of direct contact with all the persons concerned, and the margin of appreciation will vary in the light of the nature of the issues and the seriousness of the interests at stake.

(3) There is a wide margin of appreciation in assessing the necessity of taking a child into care, but a stricter scrutiny is called for both of any further limitations, such as restrictions placed by those authorities on parental rights and access, and of any legal safeguards designed to secure an effective protection of the right of parents and children to respect for their family life. Such further limitations entail the danger that the family relations between the parents and a young child are effectively curtailed.

(4) The taking of the applicant's daughter into care and the maintenance in force of the care decision concerned were based on reasons which were not only relevant but also sufficient for the purposes of Art 8(2). The measures were supported by painstaking and detailed assessments by the experts, and the Court will not substitute its view for the national court's as to the relative weight to be given to that evidence. The State acted within the margin of appreciation. No violation.

(5) Taking a child into care should normally be regarded as a temporary measure to be discontinued as soon as circumstances permit and that any measures of implementation of temporary care should be consistent with the ultimate aim of reuniting the natural parent and the child. A fair balance has to be struck between the interests of the child in remaining in public care and those of the parent in being reunited with the child. Particular importance is attached to the best interests of the child. The parent cannot be entitled under Art 8 to have such measure taken as would harm the child's health and development.

(6) The deprivation of parental rights and access were far-reaching measures, totally depriving the applicant of her family life with the child, and inconsistent with the aim of reuniting them. Such measures should be applied only in exceptional circumstances and could be justified only if they were motivated by an overriding requirement pertaining to the child's best interests.

(7) It was in the child's interest to ensure that the process of establishing bonds with her foster-parents was not disrupted. There is no reason to doubt that the care in the foster home had better prospects of success if the placement was made with a view to adoption.

(8) Having regard to the earlier successful contact, the improvement in the applicant's lifestyle, and the fact that the difficulties experienced in implementing the care plan for her son did not affect the State's responsibilities under Art 8, the deprivation of access and parental rights was insufficiently justified in the child's best interests. Violation of Art 8.

(9) The court proceedings, at one year and 9 months, were not excessive in terms of Art 6(1), having regard to the complexity of the proceedings.

Johnston v Ireland

(1986) Series A, No 112, 9 EHRR 203

Constitutional bar on divorce – whether a breach of family life – whether breach of Art 12 – no violation – status of illegitimacy for child – violation of Art 8

Facts

The first applicant married in 1952 in the Church of Ireland, and had three children by that marriage, which subsequently broke down. In 1971 he started living with another woman, and they had a child in 1978. He concluded a financial settlement with his wife. However, under Irish law at the time there was an absolute prohibition on divorce. Furthermore, the father did not automatically receive parental responsibility. His daughter from the relationship was classified as illegitimate with different legal consequences to legitimate children.

Complaint

The applicant complained that the inability to divorce constituted a breach of the Art 12 right to marry, and that the status of himself and his partner constituted a breach of the right to family. It was claimed that the status of the daughter was also a breach of Art 8. There was a claim that this was discriminatory contrary to Art 14.

Commission

In the opinion of the Commission, there was no breach of Arts 8 or 12 in the lack of a guarantee of the right to divorce and remarry; there was no violation of the parents' family life in their lack of family status, but there was a breach in the way that the status of the daughter interfered with the family life of the whole unit.

Court

In upholding the opinion of the Commission the Court held that:

(1) A restriction on divorce does not injure the substance of Art 12. Such was not in the *travaux préparatoires* and cannot be derived by means of an evolutive interpretation.

(2) Article 8 applies to illegitimate as well as legitimate families. There are positive obligations arising out of the right to family life, for which there will be a wide margin of appreciation. In this case, the existence of a family does not mean that the Government has a positive obligation to permit divorce.

(3) The parents were able to live as a family, and take a number of steps towards that. Whilst it is accepted that there are certain legislative provisions not available to them, Art 8 does not impose on States a duty to establish a status analogous to married couples.

(4) The various legal limitations attaching to the daughter's situation amount to a breach of Art 8. Although her parents have managed to take a number of steps towards integrating her in the family, her status differs significantly from that of a legitimate child. Notwithstanding the wide margin of appreciation, the absence of an appropriate legal regime reflecting her natural family ties is a failure to respect her family life.

Kjeldsen, Busk Madsen and Pedersen v Denmark

(1976) Series A, No 23, 1 EHRR 711

Sex education – interference with parents' religious beliefs – no breach – scope of Art 2 of the First Protocol

Facts

The applicants were all the parents of children in the Danish education system in 1971 when the Government, due to concerns over teenage pregnancies, unmarried mothers, the high rate of abortions and venereal disease introduced new legislation with regard to sex education. This legislation made provision for there to be general teaching with regard to sex education throughout the school years, with specific classes in the sixth and ninth years. Under the new legislation, parents could exempt their children from the specific classes, and teachers could refuse to teach those classes. Private schools did not have to follow the new curriculum, and private school places were heavily subsidised (by about 90%) by the State at that time. Parents were also entitled to educate their children at home.

Complaints

The applicants complained that such sex education breached their right to have their children educated according to their Christian beliefs, contrary to Art 2 of the First Protocol. They complained about the textbooks that were used. They also complained that they were discriminated against on the grounds of religion, in that parents may exclude their children from religious education but not from sex education. The also complained that there were further breaches of Arts 8 and 9.

Commission

The Commission found that there was not a violation by 7 votes to 7, with the President of the Commission exercising his casting vote to find no violation.

Court

In finding that there was no violation of the Convention, the Court held that:

(1) It was only interested in whether or not primary and secondary legislation conformed with the Convention; they would not look into the methods of implementation of that legislation by the local authority.
(2) Onto the fundamental right to education is grafted the right of parents to respect for their religious and philosophical convictions, and the Article does not distinguish between State and private teaching. States assume functions in relation to education and teaching, and the grant of that assistance to private schools does not affect their duties in the State sector.
(3) The purpose of the second paragraph of the Article is to safeguard the possibility of pluralism in education which possibility is essential for the preservation of the 'democratic society' as conceived by the Convention.
(4) The Article does not permit a distinction to be drawn between religious instruction and other subjects. It enjoins the State to respect parents' convictions, be they religious or philosophical, throughout the entire State education programme.
(5) States are not prevented from imparting through teaching or education, information or knowledge of a directly or indirectly religious or philosophical kind. Article 2 does not even permit parents to object to the integration of such teaching or education in the school curriculum.
(6) The State, in fulfilling the functions assumed by it in regard to education and teaching, must take care that information or knowledge included in the curriculum is conveyed in an objective, critical and pluralistic manner. The State is forbidden to pursue an aim of indoctrination.
(7) Insofar as the applicants complained of discrimination on the grounds of religion, the Court makes a distinction between religious instruction and sex education; the former disseminates tenets and the latter mere knowledge. Article 14 requires discrimination based on a personal characteristic by which persons or groups are distinguishable. Therefore, there is no discriminatory treatment in the legislation.

Keegan v Ireland

(1994) Series A, No 290, 18 EHRR 342

Unmarried parents – adoption without consultation with father – interference with family life – not justified

Facts

The applicant and his girlfriend had been living together for a year when she became pregnant. The couple had planned to marry, but their relationship broke down before the child was born. The child was placed for adoption by the applicant's girlfriend without the applicant's knowledge. The relevant provision for the Adoption Act 1952 permitted adoption without the natural father's consent. The applicant successfully applied to the court under the Guardianship of Infants Act 1964, to be appointed as the child's guardian, which would have enabled him to challenge the proposed adoption. He was appointed guardian and awarded custody of the child. The High Court upheld the decision, but the Supreme Court ruled that the wishes of the natural father should not be considered if the prospective adopters could make significantly better provisions for the child's welfare. The case was remitted to the High Court, which found that if the placement with the prospective adopters, where the child had been for one year, was disrupted, the child was likely to suffer trauma and would have difficulties in forming relationships of trust. The High Court declined to appoint the applicant as guardian, and an adoption order was subsequently made.

Complaint

The applicant complained that there had been a violation of Art 8, a violation of the right of access to a court under Art 6 in that he had no *locus standi* in the proceedings before the Adoption Board, and discrimination as a married father would enjoy *locus standi* in adoption proceedings.

Commission

The Commission decided that there had been a violation of Art 8 and Art 6, and that it was not necessary to examine whether Art 14 had been breached.

Court

In finding a violation of Art 8 the Court held as follows:

(1)   The notion of the 'family' in Art 8 was not solely confined to marriage. A child born in a relationship where parents have lived together is part of that family from the moment of birth, even if the parents are no longer cohabiting or if their relationship has ended. In deciding that the child had been part of the applicant's family, the Court also noted that the conception of the child was the result of a deliberate decision, and that the couple had planned to get married.

(2)   The fact that Irish law permitted the secret placement of a child without the applicant's knowledge or consent, leading to the bonding of the child with the proposed adopters and therefore to the subsequent making of the adoption order, amounted to an interference with the applicant's right to respect for family life.

(3)   The interference was not justifiable as being necessary in a democratic society. The placement jeopardised the applicant's ties with the child. The placement also set in motion a process which was likely to prove to be irreversible, thereby putting the applicant at a significant disadvantage in the contest with the prospective adopters for the custody of the child. The Government had not shown that their permission of adoption without the natural father's consent was in any way in the interests of the child's welfare.

(4)   The Court held that the adoption process must be distinguished from the custody and guardianship process. The applicant had no right to directly challenge the placement of the child for adoption without his consent, either before the Adoption Board or before the courts. His only recourse was an indirect course of action, bringing guardianship and custody proceedings. By the time these proceedings had terminated, the scales concerning the child's welfare had tilted inevitably in favour of the prospective adopters. This was a breach of Art 8, and it was not necessary to decide whether the Adoption Board was a tribunal within the meaning of Art 6.

Kroon v The Netherlands

(1994) Series A, No 297-C, 19 EHRR 263

Inability to recognise paternity – breach of Art 8

Facts

The applicant had a child together with her partner of some years. She had been married 8 years earlier, although that relationship had broken down very quickly, and she had not seen her husband for 7 years. Under Dutch law, the applicant's husband was presumed to be the father of the child. All attempts to alter that failed, as such presumption of paternity could be rebutted only by the husband, not the wife, denying paternity. The father of the child did not wish to co-habit with the mother, nor to marry her.

Complaint

The applicant complained that she was unable to get the father's paternity recognised, and that the law discriminated in that only the husband could deny paternity, in breach of Arts 8 and 14.

Commission

The Commission declared the complaints admissible and found a violation of Art 8 by 12 votes to 6, although no violation of Art 14 in conjunction with Art 8.

Court

In finding a violation of Art 8 by 7 votes to 2 and no violation of Art 14, the Court held that:

(1)   'Family life' is not confined solely to marriage-based relationships and may encompass other *de facto* 'family ties' where parties are living together outside marriage. Co-habitation may be a requirement for such a relationship, but other factors may serve to demonstrate sufficient constancy to create 'family ties' sufficient for 'family life'. A child from such a relationship is part of that 'family unit' from the moment of its birth and by the very fact of it. The father has a bond amounting to family life, whatever his contribution to the child's care and upbringing.

(2)   The State enjoys a wide margin of appreciation in striking a fair balance between the interests of the individual and of the community as a whole. Once the family tie is established, the State must act to enable it to be developed and to integrate the child into the family.

(3)   Where the only way of creating a legal tie is for the parents to marry, such solution is not compatible with the notion of 'respect' for family life.

(4)   Respect for family life requires the biological and social reality to prevail over a legal presumption which flies in the fact of established fact and the wishes of those concerned, without actually benefiting anyone.

(5)   No separate issue arises under Art 14.

Marckx v Belgium

(1979) Series A, No 31, 2 EHRR 330

Illegitimate child – legal restrictions on rights of mother and child – not so restricted if legitimate – interference with family life – discrimination – interference with peaceful enjoyment of possessions – violations on all three

Facts

The applicant, Paula Marckx, was the mother of Alexandra, who was illegitimate. Under Belgian law, the applicant had restricted rights, viz: she had to apply for a formal act of recognition of maternal affiliation and there were limits on her right to give or bequeath property. Furthermore, the child was limited in her right to inherit property.

Complaints

The applicant made the following complaints:

(1) that she is only able to establish affiliation with her daughter by recognition through legal process, which does not amount to attribution;
(2) that there is no legal relationship between Alexandra and her wider family;
(3) that there is discrimination between legitimate and illegitimate families;
(4) that Alexandra's rights of inheritance and receiving dispositions ('patrimonial rights') are limited;
(5) that the applicant's rights of disposition and inter vivos gifts are also limited;
(6) that she is not allowed to use her property in an unlimited way;
(7) that such treatment was degrading in terms of Art 3;
(8) that it did not respect her right not to marry in not treating her the same as a married woman.

Commission

In the opinion of the Commission, there was a breach of Art 8 taken alone and in conjunction with Art 13.

Court

In finding a violation of Arts 8 and 14 in the requirement of establishing maternal affiliation; a violation of Arts 8 and 14 in the effect on Alexandra's family relationships; a violation of Art 14 but no breach of Art 8 or Art 1 of the First Protocol on the patrimonial rights relied on by Alexandra; a violation of Art 14 and Art 1 of the First Protocol but no breach of Art 8 on the patrimonial rights relied on by the applicant; no breach of Arts 3 or 12,

The Court held as follows:

(1) Article 8 applies to the 'family life' of legitimate and illegitimate families equally. Furthermore, it may go so far as to impose positive obligations on States rather than just preventing interferences. Therefore, such interferences to be legitimate must not prevent the child's integration into its family.
(2) A distinction is discriminatory if it has no objective and reasonable justification, that is, if it does not pursue a legitimate aim or if there is not a reasonable relationship of proportionality between the means employed and the aim sought to be realised. The State must avoid any discrimination grounded on birth.
(3) The fact that the applicant must apply for maternal affiliation and in so doing limits her child's patrimonial rights thwarts and impedes the normal development of family life, and is therefore in breach of Art 8.
(4) Whilst a State is allowed to encourage the traditional family, that may not be done by prejudicing the illegitimate family, which has the same rights. Distinctions between the two which may have been acceptable in 1948 were no longer so. Consequently, such distinctions have no justification or legitimate aim and are discriminatory.
(5) Family life includes connections with the wider family such as grandparents and grandchildren, and respect for this means that those ties must be allowed to develop normally. A failure to do so will be a violation of Art 8, and will also amount to discrimination in breach of Art 14.
(6) Matters of intestate succession – and disposition – between near relatives are intimately connected with family life, which includes material as well as social relations. There was no legitimate aim in restricting those rights, and consequently there was a breach of Art 14. However, the mother was not required by the law to give her property to the child, so Art 8 was not breached.

(7)   Article 1 of the First Protocol is concerned with existing possessions rather than the right to acquire them, and did not apply to the child's right to inherit. However, the mother did have such a right to dispose of her property, and therefore there was a violation in respect of her.

(8)   The treatment might be humiliating, but was not degrading in terms of Art 3.

(9)   Article 12 does not mean that all the legal effects attaching to marriage should apply equally to situations that are comparable to marriage. No breach.

McMichael v UK

(1995) Series A, No 308, 20 EHRR 205

Children's hearings – failure to disclose social services reports to parents – violation of Arts 6(1) and 8 – requirement for father to apply for parental rights – no discrimination

Facts

The first applicant, Anthony McMichael, was married to the second applicant, Margaret McMichael, in 1990. They had had a son, A, in 1987, at which time the mother denied that Mr McMichael was the father, and he was not identified on the birth certificate. The mother had suffered from psychiatric illness in 1986, and she was diagnosed as suffering from such on the birth of her son. Consequently, he was removed from her care under a place of safety order.

The local reporter for the children's panel stated that Mrs McMichael suffered from a major psychiatric illness and that she was unable to care for the child as she refused her medication. During 1988 there were a number of children's hearings and appeals to the Sheriff's Court, contesting the supervision order for A and, subsequently, a refusal of access. The procedure of those hearings meant that social services and medical reports were given to the Chairman or the Sheriff, but were not disclosed to the applicants, although the contents were made known to them. The supervision orders were maintained due to the mental health problems, their aggressive and hostile behaviour and Mrs McMichael's refusal to seek psychiatric help.

The Council applied to have the child adopted. The applicants were now married, and therefore Mr McMichael had parental responsibility for A. At a hearing in July 1990, they refused consent for the adoption. They were represented by solicitors, there was full disclosure and they were able to cross-examine witnesses. The Sheriff found that their consent was unreasonably withheld, and made the order freeing A for adoption.

Complaints

The applicants complained that they were not entitled to see the confidential reports and documents submitted at the children's hearings, and Mr McMichael complained that as the natural father he had no legal rights to the custody of A or to participate in the care proceedings and that he had been discriminated against.

Commission

In the opinion of the Commission: there was a violation of Art 8; there was a violation of Art 6(1) in respect of Mrs McMichael; and there was no violation of either Art 6 or Art 14 in respect of Mr McMichael.

Court

In upholding the opinion of the Commission the Court held that:

(1)   As Mr McMichael had not applied for an order for parental rights, the care proceedings did not involve the determination of civil rights in terms of Art 6(1), unlike the case of *Keegan v Ireland* (above). No breach.

(2) In the sensitive area of family law, it may be right to opt for an adjudicatory body rather than a classic court. However, the right to a fair – adversarial – trial 'means the opportunity to have knowledge of and comment on the observations filed or evidence adduced by the other party'. Here, the lack of disclosure of vital documents was capable of affecting the ability of the parents to influence the outcome of the children's hearing and any prospect of appeal.

(3) Similarly, the hearing in the Sheriff's Court did not satisfy the requirement of an adversarial trial due to the lack of disclosure, although it did satisfy the conditions of Art 6(1) as far as its composition and jurisdiction are concerned. Consequently, Mrs M did not receive a fair hearing either at first instance or on appeal and there has been a breach of Art 6(1).

(4) The mutual enjoyment by parent and child of each other's company constitutes a fundamental element of family life, and measures hindering such enjoyment amount to an interference with the right protected by Art 8 (*W v UK* 10 EHRR 29). Here, the care and custody procedures are obviously such an interference.

(5) The parents must be involved in the decision-making process to a degree sufficient to provide them with the requisite protection of their interests. If they are not, there will have been a failure to respect their family life and the interference resulting from the decision will not be capable of being regarded as 'necessary' within the meaning of Art 8 (*W v UK* 10 EHRR 29).

(6) Article 6(1) affords the procedural safeguard of access to a court. The procedural requirement of Art 8 covers administrative procedures and judicial proceedings, but is ancillary to the wider purpose of ensuring proper respect for family life. The failure of the procedures had a fundamental effect on the respect for family life, and therefore there has been a violation. The applicants were leading a joint 'family life' and so the violation is in respect of them both.

(7) A difference of treatment is discriminatory if it has no reasonable and objective justification, that is, if it does not pursue a legitimate aim or if there is not a reasonable relationship of proportionality between the means employed and the aim sought to be realised. Here, the aim of the legislation is to provide a mechanism for identifying 'meritorious' fathers who might be accorded parental rights, thus protecting the interest of the child and the mother. This is legitimate and proportionate. No violation of Art 14.

Nielsen v Denmark

(1988) Series A, No 144, 11 EHRR 175

Hospitalisation of 12-year-old against his wishes – with mother's consent – not a deprivation of liberty – proper reason for decision – no breach of Art 5

Facts

The applicant was a minor who was a Danish citizen born in 1971 to a single mother. Initially, by Danish law only she had parental rights over him and his father could not apply for custody. That had been the subject of complaint to the ECHR by the father but before the case was heard the relevant law was changed to allow the possibility of such an application. The father continued to have contact with the applicant until there came a time when the applicant went into hiding with his father so as to remain with him. Over a period of years, the father made two unsuccessful applications for custody. The father was ultimately arrested and imprisoned. The child did not want to live with the mother and was placed in the psychiatric ward of a State hospital upon the advice of the social services and a psychiatrist and with the mother's consent.

The applicant sought to challenge the lawfulness of his detention by way of judicial review in the domestic courts. The application was dismissed on the grounds that his placement in hospital was the result of an exercise of parental rights by his mother. (Ultimately the child was discharged into the care of a family other than his own.)

Complaint

The applicant contended that his committal to the child psychiatric ward constituted a deprivation of liberty contrary to Art 5(1) and (4).

Court

In finding no violation of Art 5 by a majority of 9 votes to 7 the Court held that:

(1)   Article 5 applies to minors but normally decisions about a child's care and upbringing are necessarily taken by his or her parents who will thereby impose restrictions on the child's liberty. Under Art 8, the exercise of parental rights is protected as a fundamental element in family life.

(2)   In this case the decision to place the child in hospital was taken by the mother in the exercise of her parental rights. Therefore, the question at issue was whether Art 5 was applicable to restrictions on the applicant's rights resulting from the exercise of the mother's rights.

(3)   The Court was satisfied that the mother took the decision on medical advice and that her objective was the protection of the applicant's health which was a proper purpose for the exercise of parental rights.

(4)   The rights of a holder of parental authority were not unlimited and the State must provide safeguards against abuse. In this case, the conditions under which the applicant was held did not differ greatly from those in many ordinary children's hospital wards and therefore the restrictions were not of a nature or degree similar to the cases of deprivation of liberty specified in Art 5(1). As to the applicant's views on hospitalisation, he was 12 years old at the relevant time and was therefore at an age where it was normal for such decisions to be made by a parent even against the wishes of the child.

(5)   The hospitalisation of the applicant was not a deprivation of liberty within Art 5 but a reasonable exercise of the mother's parental rights in the interests of the child.

Niemitz v Germany

(1992) Series A, No 251-B, 16 EHRR 97

Search of private offices – breach of respect for private life, home and correspondence – violation of Art 8 – no need to consider Art 1 of the First Protocol

Facts

The applicant, a lawyer, was suspected of knowing the identity of the writer of an anonymous letter to the local district court which was considered as amounting to the offence of insulting behaviour. In order to find that person, the local judge issued a warrant for the search of various addresses, including the applicant's office. Police officers conducted the search on 13 November 1986 in the presence of two office assistants, going through the filing cabinets although they did not find or seize any documents of interest. The criminal proceedings were later discontinued. An appeal against the warrant in the regional court was declared inadmissible as it had already been executed. The Federal Constitutional Court also declined to adjudicate the complaint.

Complaints

The applicant complained that the search of his office violated his right to respect for his home and correspondence as laid down in Art 8 of the Convention. He further complained that the search impaired his reputation as a lawyer, breaching Art 1 of the First Protocol.

Commission
The Commission unanimously decided that there had been a violation of Art 8, and that consequently no separate issue arises under Art 1 of the First Protocol.

Court
In upholding the opinion of the Commission, the Court held that:

(1) Unlike the jurisprudence of the ECJ which in *Hoechst v Commission* [1989] Case 227/88 decided that there was only a rule of law as to the inviolability of the home, respect for private life must also comprise to a certain degree the right to establish and develop relationships with other human beings, which includes in the course of their working lives. Furthermore, to deny Art 8 protection for professional activities could lead to an inequality of treatment. For example, telephone tapping is an interference for business and private calls.

(2) To interpret the words 'private life' and 'home' as including business premises is consonant with the essential object of Art 8. This would not unduly hamper the States, as they may still interfere in accordance with Art 8(2).

(3) Correspondence must also include professional correspondence.

(4) The interference was lawful under German law, and had legitimate aims under Art 8(2) to prevent crime. However, it was not proportionate to those aims and was therefore not necessary in a democratic society, due to the fact that it did not have proper procedural safeguards, and impinged on the professional privilege disproportionately.

Olsson v Sweden

(1988) Series A, No 130, 11 EHRR 259

Children taken into care – right to family life – breach only in manner in which decision implemented

Facts
The applicants are the parents of three children. There were mental health issues with one of the children, and parenting difficulties. Following a temporary separation and concerns over the care of the children, they were taken into care on a provisional basis after a hearing at which the applicants were present and made oral submissions. Six months later the children were taken into care permanently, following a hearing of the social district council. At that hearing, a written report was presented with medical and psychological evidence. As the applicants did not accept that the children should be taken into care, the matter was remitted to the county administrative court, where the applicants were represented by a lawyer and the children were also represented. The court found that the parents were incapable of looking after the children and they should go into care. The applicant appealed to the Administrative Court of Appeal, which, following a hearing, confirmed the judgment of the lower court, although not all of the judges concurred. Leave to appeal was refused by the Supreme Administrative Court.

Due to administrative difficulties, the three children were placed in care separately in homes and foster accommodation, which was at a long distance from the parents and each other. Contact was limited and varied on many occasions, normally at neutral places. Cooperation with the social workers broke down completely. Appeals against the contact decisions were made right through the courts, and the applicants were legally represented throughout.

Complaint
The applicants complained that the decision to take the children into care, the manner in which it had been implemented and the refusals to terminate the care had given rise to violations of Art 8.

Commission

The Commission expressed the opinion that the care decisions placing the children in separate foster-homes far from the applicants was a violation of Art 8, by eight votes to five. They rejected other complaints under Arts 3, 6, 13 and 14.

Court

In finding that there was a breach of Art 8 in the manner of the decision to place the children in care but not in the decision itself, and no breach of Arts 6 or 14, the Court held that:

(1) The mutual enjoyment by parent and child of each other's company constitutes a fundamental element of family life, and the natural family relationship is not terminated by reason of the fact that the child is taken into care (*W v UK*).

(2) Although the relevant legislation is rather general with a wide measure of discretion, circumstances where a child may be taken into care are very wide which makes a more exact formulation difficult. There is guidance as to the exercise of the discretion and safeguards against arbitrary interference together with review by several levels of administrative courts. Therefore, the discretion is reasonable and in accordance with the law. Furthermore, the purpose of the legislation is to protect children and is therefore a legitimate aim.

(3) As to whether the interference is proportionate to the aim and necessary in a democratic society, the Court will not just look to see if the State exercised its discretion reasonably, carefully and in good faith, but must determine whether the reasons adduced to justify the interferences at issue are 'relevant and sufficient'.

(4) The parents were sufficiently involved in the decision-making process, in that they attended the case conferences and meetings and the court hearings, where they were legally represented.

(5) Splitting up a family is a very serious interference which must be supported by sufficiently sound and weighty considerations in the interests of the child. It is not enough that the child would be better off if placed in care.

(6) The authorities had attempted to assist, with case conferences and a psychiatric team, and the intervention was with full knowledge of the background. They had a substantial report to go on, and there was full argument before the courts with the applicants present. Therefore, the authorities were reasonably entitled to think that it was necessary to take the children into care.

(7) As there was no adoption application, the care decision was temporary with the ultimate aim of reuniting the family. The distance of the placements and separation of the children was an impediment to that aim, compounded by the restrictions on parental access. This was not justified by any difficulties created by the parents.

(8) Good faith by the State is not enough. Administrative difficulties can never be allowed to play more than a secondary role. Therefore, the measures taken in implementation of the care decision were not supported by 'sufficient' reasons justifying them as proportionate to the legitimate aim pursued. They were, therefore, notwithstanding the domestic authorities' margin of appreciation, not 'necessary in a democratic society'.

(9) There was no violation of Art 6; the applicants were well able to cross-examine the State's expert and call their own evidence in rebuttal. Even though the children's education was not as the parents wished, it still existed, and there was no breach of the right to education. There was no issue under Art 3.

Osman v UK

RJD ____, [1999] 1 FLR 193

Inability to sue police – where harm of most serious type – no access to court – breach of Art 6

Facts

In 1986 a teacher, P, formed an attachment to his pupil, O. An investigation was commenced by the school which led to the police being contacted in 1987 but, as there was no apparent sexual element to P's relationship with O, no action was taken. A course of harassment of O's parents began in mid-1987, including vandalism at their home, which were denied by P. Further incidents occurred involving P in late 1987 and, in the light of further evidence, the police attempted to arrest him and charge him with the earlier criminal damage to O's home but P had left the area and could not be found.

In March 1988, P used a stolen shotgun to shoot and kill O's father, injuring O, and to shoot and kill the son of the deputy-headmaster of the school, injuring the deputy-headmaster. The family of O brought an action in negligence against the police. The Court of Appeal accepted that the family could show sufficient proximity to the police for the purpose of raising a duty of care but the action was struck out on the ground that public policy required police immunity from suit in relation to the investigation and suppression of crime.

Complaint

The family complained that, in breach of Art 2, the authorities had failed to protect the right to life of O's father against the threat posed by P; in breach of Art 6 O's family had been denied their right of access to the court to sue for damage caused by police negligence; and in breach of Art 8 the police had failed to secure O's personal safety by failing to protect him from harassment.

Court

In finding a breach of Art 6 but no breach of Arts 2 or 8, the Court held that:

(1) It could not be established that the police knew or should have known at the time that there was a real and immediate risk to the life of an identified individual or individuals from the criminal acts of a third party and that they failed to take measures within the scope of their powers which, judged reasonably, might have been expected to avoid that risk. Therefore, there was no breach of Art 2.

(2) Whilst the Government was entitled to a certain margin of appreciation in regulating the right to institute proceedings before a court in civil matters, any such limitations must not be such as to impair the Art 6(1) right to a court and must be proportionate to a legitimate aim which the limitation seeks to achieve. The public policy aim of the rule applied by the Court of Appeal was a legitimate aim to pursue but the effect of the Court of Appeal's decision was to confer a blanket immunity upon the police. The Court of Appeal had failed to balance other public policy considerations which pulled in the opposite direction to the immunity rule. The applicant's case involved the alleged failure to protect the life of a child by reason of a catalogue of acts and omissions amounting to grave negligence, they claimed that the police had given them assurances as to their safety, and the harm sustained was of the most serious nature. Accordingly, the application of the exclusionary rule in the applicants' case constituted a disproportionate restriction on their right of access to a court and violated Art 6(1).

(3) The Court's finding in relation to Art 2 also meant that there had been no breach of the applicant's Art 8 right to respect for their private and family life and their home by reason of the police's failure to investigate the harassment and vandalism by P, or to provide the applicants with evidence which might have supported proceedings for a civil injunction against P.

Rasmussen v Denmark

(1984) Series A, No 87, 7 EHRR 371

Paternity proceedings – father outside the time-limit for such an application – no such limit for mothers – whether discriminatory – no violation of Arts 6, 8 or 14

Facts

The applicant father was married in 1966 and there were two children of the marriage. Although he was always uncertain as to the parentage of the second child, he did not do anything about it until 1973 when he was divorced. Under the divorce settlement, the wife had custody of the children in return for maintenance. Eighteen months later, realising the marriage was over, the applicant took steps to challenge the paternity. However, his wife signed an agreement waiving claims for maintenance in return for his dropping the claim. They were divorced. The wife later rescinded the agreement, demanding maintenance, and he sought to challenge paternity again, although he was now out of time. The Court of Appeal (*Østre Landsret*) refused the application as the statutory criteria were not made out.

Complaints

The applicant complains that his right to challenge paternity was subject to time-limits, whereas that would not be the case for his wife, which was discriminatory contrary to Art 14, in conjunction with the right of access to a court (Art 6) and the right to respect for family life (Art 8).

Commission

The Commission expressed the opinion that there had been a breach of Art 14 taken in conjunction with Arts 6 and 8 (8 votes to 5).

Court

In finding that there was no violation the Court held that:

(1) Article 14 has no independent existence to the substantive provisions of the Convention, since it has effect solely in relation to the enjoyment of the rights and freedoms safeguarded by those provisions. It will be applied only where the facts fall within the ambit of one or more of those provisions.

(2) Although it is a matter of public interest, a paternity application is a matter of family law and is therefore 'civil' within the meaning of Art 6.

(3) Although the proceedings were designed to dissolve a 'family' relationship, such issues were undoubtedly 'private' in nature.

(4) There was a difference in treatment between mother and father. There was no need to decide if the mother and father were placed in analogous situations. The interference was for a justifiable aim of ensuring legal certainty and to protect the interests of the child, and did not differ much from other contracting States.

(5) The difference in treatment was on the basis that such time-limits were less necessary for mothers, as their interests closely coincided with the child's in that the mother was generally given custody. It was acceptable for the authorities to consider that the aim sought to be realised would be most satisfactorily achieved by the enactment of a statutory rule for the father and by the courts for the mother. Therefore, such interference was not disproportionate to the aim, and Art 14 was not breached.

Rees v UK

(1986) Series A, No 106, 9 EHRR 56

Transsexual – refusal to allow alteration of birth certificate – no violation of family life or of right to marriage

Facts

The applicant, registered at birth as a female, was transsexual. After medical treatment, he changed his name and began living as male. His birth certificate showed him to be female, and an application to alter this was refused, but other official documents showed him to be a male.

Complaint

The applicant alleged that the refusal to amend his birth certificate was a violation of Arts 8 and 12 of the Convention.

Commission

The Commission found that Art 8 but not Art 12 had been violated.

Court

In finding no violation of either Art 8 or Art 12 the Court held that:

(1) There are positive obligations inherent in an effective respect for private life but they did not extend to requiring a change in legislation to enable registration of a new sexual identity.

(2) In this area there is a wide margin of appreciation; a fair balance must be struck between the wishes of the individual and the interest of the community.

(3) The requirements of striking a fair balance did not justify imposing an obligation on the UK to create a system of registration of civil status, and a requirement to allow alteration of birth certificates would not constitute an effective safeguard for the integrity of private life as it would reveal a change of sexual identity.

(3) The right to marry guaranteed by Art 12 refers to people of the opposite biological sex. There is no violation of Art 12 in not permitting people of the same biological sex to marry.

Ringeisen v Austria (No 1)

(1971) Series A, No 13, 1 EHRR 455

Remand for 2½ years – length of proceedings – no violation of Art 6 – violation of Art 5

Facts

The applicant applied for approval by a regional commission of a contract for the sale of farmland, which was refused. Thereafter the applicant was charged with offences relating to fraudulent property dealing and fraudulent bankruptcy. Investigations commenced in February 1963. He was remanded in custody for a total period of 2 years and 5 months in respect of both cases. The fraud case was complex and the applicant made numerous applications and appeals on various points during the course of it. Ultimately, after the exhaustion of appeals procedures in the first case, when the applicant's conviction and sentence were confirmed, the fraudulent bankruptcy prosecution was discontinued.

Complaint

The applicant contended that there was a breach of Art 6(1) in that the regional commission which had refused approval for the contract of sale of farmland was biased. He further complained that the length of his detention in respect of the two sets of criminal charges was in breach of Art 5(3). He contended that the length of the criminal proceeding was in breach of Art 6(1).

Court

In finding a breach of Art 5 and no breach of Art 6 the Court held as follows:

(1) The proceedings relating to the sale of the farmland would determine civil rights as between the vendors and the applicant and Art 6(1) therefore applied. In fact, there was no evidence of bias by the commission which ruled on that matter and no

evidence that the proceedings were unfair. There was no rule that required a superior court which set aside a decision of a lower court or authority and remitted a matter for a fresh decision to remit the matter to a differently constituted lower court or authority.

(2) As regards the criminal bankruptcy proceedings, no investigation was undertaken on those for a period of 3 years. However, once there was a reasonable suspicion that the applicant had committed those further offences, his arrest was covered by Art 5(1)(c) and was not the subject of supervision by the Court.

(3) As to whether the length of detention was reasonable under Art 5(3), the Court examined the reasons relied on for that detention. It did not accept that there was any danger of the applicant colluding with others. As to the risk of further offending from the time the applicant was made bankrupt, he could not engage in financial dealings so further similar offences were precluded. From that date, his detention exceeded reasonable limits.

(4) The criminal proceedings themselves did not exceed the limits of reasonable time laid down. The proceedings were complex and the applicant contributed to their delay by his conduct in instituting numerous appeals and applications during their course. It was reasonable for the prosecution to wait until the final outcome of the appeals in the criminal proceedings on the fraudulent property dealing before discontinuing the fraudulent bankruptcy proceedings.

R v UK

(1987) Series A, No 121, 10 EHRR 74

Child in care – not able to challenge access decision – not involved in decision-making process – breaches of Arts 6 and 8

Facts

The applicant was a mother of two who was experiencing a difficult family situation caused by accommodation problems and her partner, Mr B's, drinking habits. On the advice of local social services, she placed both children into the voluntary care of the authority for certain periods between September 1980 and March 1981. The children were placed with short-term foster-parents. The applicant temporarily separated from Mr B. The applicant agreed with social services that she would seek an order banning her partner from contact with her and the children on the understanding that she would be provided with local authority housing for herself and her children. Before this took place, the applicant agreed with Mr B to try to resume their relationship. She was informed by a social worker that she could not have the children returned if she intended to resume the relationship. On 3 April 1981 the applicant was informed that her parental rights had been assumed by the local authority. At a case conference in August 1981, the authority took the contingent decision that if the parental rights resolution (which was under challenge by the applicant in the juvenile court) remained in force they would stop the applicant's access to her children and place them for adoption with long-term foster-parents. The applicant was not notified of this conference or its outcome, and in ignorance of it she withdrew her objection to the resolution. The applicant had access to the children until October 1981 when she was told that the children would be placed for adoption and she could no longer see them. The applicant unsuccessfully applied to the juvenile court for the discharge of the parental rights resolution, and the High Court upheld the decision. The applicant instituted wardship proceedings in January 1983 to obtain restoration of her access to the children; these proceedings were also unsuccessful. In October of that year, the authority rescinded the parental rights resolution. In November 1985 the High Court made the children wards of court and refused to dispense with the applicant's consent to the adoption and, in December, it ordered arrangements to be made for the applicant to have contact with her children three times per year.

Complaint

The applicant stated that her rights under Arts 6 and 8 had been violated, in that she was not able to challenge the arrangements and she had not been advised of the case conference which made fundamental decisions as to her family life.

Court

In finding a breach of Arts 6 and 8 the Court held as follows:

(1) Referring to *W v UK*, where the applicant had experienced similar inability to have the question of her access to her children determined in proceedings which complied with Art 6(1), there was in this case a breach.

(2) The applicant had been insufficiently involved in the authority's decision-making process. The decisions of April and August 1981 had altered the whole basis of the relationship between the mother and her children, and her views should patently have been considered. This was a breach of Art 8.

Saunders v UK

(1996) RJD, 1996-VI, No 24, 23 EHRR 313

Use of statement under compulsion – subsequent criminal proceedings – breach of right to silence

Facts

In the course of an investigation by the DTI into the takeover of Distillers PLC by Guinness PLC, the applicant was interviewed by inspectors of the DTI. By law, he was compelled to answer their questions, and his answers could be used in a criminal court, but he was not warned about self-incrimination. In the course of the subsequent criminal proceedings, prosecution counsel made substantial use of the DTI interviews to rebut statements made by the applicant in the witness box, and counsel for a co-defendant used them to show the applicant was not telling the truth. During the course of the trial, an application to exclude the evidence under ss 76 and 78 of PACE was rejected, the judge being satisfied that there was no oppression and nothing about the circumstances made the evidence unreliable. The Court of Appeal decided the same point in a linked case, finding that Parliament had expressly and unambiguously provided the DTI inspectors with those powers, even if it overrode the privilege against self-incrimination.

Complaint

The applicant complained that the use at his trial of statements made by him to the DTI inspectors under their compulsory powers deprived him of a fair hearing in violation of Art 6(1), which includes the requirement that a defendant is entitled to exercise the right not to incriminate himself. There is no justification in removing the protection against self-incrimination, only from the person in the position of the applicant.

Commission

The Commission found by 14 votes to 1 that there was a violation of Art 6(1).

Court

In following the opinion of the Commission the Court held as follows:

(1) The complaint was limited to the use of the interviews in the subsequent criminal trial. The DTI inspectors had an investigative function, which could be used for later

criminal proceedings. Article 6(1) does not apply to such investigations, as it would unduly hamper the effective regulation of the City.

(2) The right to silence and not to incriminate oneself lie at the heart of the notion of a fair procedure under Art 6. The right not to incriminate oneself presupposes that the prosecution in a criminal case seek to prove their case against the accused without resort to evidence obtained in defiance of the will of the accused.

(3) The right not to incriminate oneself is primarily concerned with respecting the will of an accused person to remain silent, but does not generally extend to material obtained from the accused with an existence separate from him, ie blood samples etc. Here, the question is whether the statements obtained were an unjustifiable interference with the right. Was he compelled to give evidence, and did the use of the evidence offend the basic principles of fair trial. He was compelled, under pain of contempt, and up to 2 years' imprisonment.

(4) Any answers containing admissions to knowledge of information which tended to incriminate him is incriminating, even if it may not appear so at the time; the later use of it is what matters. Here, the applicant was cross-examined on the statements over a 3-day period, clearly in a way which sought to incriminate the applicant.

(5) Any safeguards on the inspectors' powers, such as their independence, legal representation throughout etc, cannot provide a defence in the present case since they did not operate to prevent the use of the statements in the subsequent criminal proceedings.

Sheffield and Horsham v UK

RJD _____, 27 EHRR 163

Transsexuals – no development since Rees *and* Cossey *– no violation*

Facts

The applicants are both male to female transsexuals. They complained that the inability to get their status legally recognised in the UK had caused many problems, including an inability to marry, to have their birth certificates altered, and legal requirements to describe themselves as male in certain situations, such as court proceedings, police records and social security records.

Complaints

The applicants complained that the refusal of the State to give legal recognition to their status as women following gender reassignment surgery gave rise to violations of Arts 8, 12 and 14 of the Convention. Miss Horsham also complained of a violation of Art 3.

Commission

The Commission declared the applications admissible and concluded by 15 votes to 1 that there had been a failure to respect the private lives of the applicants, and that no separate issues arose under Arts 12 or 14. The Art 3 complaint was held to be inadmissible.

The Court

In finding no violation of Art 8 by 11 votes to 9, and no other violations of the Convention, the Court held that:

(1) At issue was whether the State had failed to take positive steps to modify a system which interfered with the applicants' rights.

(2) The notion of 'respect' has to have regard for the diversity of practices in the Contracting States, striking the balance between the individual and the general interest of the community.

(3) There had not been sufficient new findings in medical research to settle conclusively the doubts about transsexualism raised in the *Rees* and *Cossey* judgments. Nor had there been sufficient legal development to establish the existence of any common European approach.

(4) The personal histories did not demonstrate sufficient detriment so as to override the State's margin of appreciation. Certain requirements to disclose their original gender did not occur with a frequency which could be said to impinge to a disproportionate extent on their right to respect for their private lives.

(5) With regard to the right to marriage, the decision was the same as in the *Rees* and *Cossey* judgments, that any limitations must not restrict or reduce the right in such a way that the very essence of the right is impinged, and that the attachment to the traditional concept of marriage still provides sufficient reason for the law relying on the requirement for a biological distinction between partners.

(6) As the State has not overstepped the Margin of Appreciation in not according legal recognition to the applicants' new gender, that amounts to a 'reasonable and objective justification' so as to allow the difference in treatment suffered by the applicants, meaning there was no violation of Art 14.

Söderbäck v Sweden

[1999] 1 FLR 250

Child adopted by mother's husband – without natural father's permission – little previous contact – consideration of best interests of the child – not disproportionate interference – no breach of Art 8

Facts
The applicant was the father of a child after a relationship that was not particularly serious. He visited the child and mother in the maternity ward, attended the christening and visited twice in the first 6 months. Contact after that was difficult, due to concerns of the mother. Both mother and father ended up in different relationships. The mother married. When the child was 5 years old, the father asked for contact to be arranged. This did not happen, and he applied to the court. The court rejected his application, and recommended that the child be adopted by the mother's new husband, as they had been in a stable relationship for 6 years, and the husband was the child's psychological father.

Complaints
The applicant complained that the decision to grant, without his consent, permission to adopt his daughter had constituted a violation of his right to respect for family life as guarantees by Art 9 of the Convention.

Commission
The Commission declared the complaint admissible and expressed an opinion that there had been a violation of Art 8, by 10 votes to 5.

Court
The Court, in finding no violation of Art 8, held that:

(1) At the time of the adoption there were certain ties between the applicant and his daughter, and therefore Art 8 applies.

(2) The adoption is an interference with the right to respect for family life, but was in accordance with the law, and pursued the legitimate aim of being in the best interests of the child.

(3) With regard to whether the interference was necessary in a democratic society, this case was different from the *Johansen* judgment, where the mother had had regular contact for the first 6 months of her daughter's life, the care order was supposed to

be temporary, and the ultimate aim was to be reunification of mother and child; the deprivation of contact was inconsistent with that. In this case, the applicant never had custody of the child, who was not in temporary public care but in the permanent care of her mother, and his contact had, for various reasons, been infrequent.

(4) When the adoption was granted by the court, 'de facto' family ties had existed between the mother and the adoptive father for 5½ years. The adoption formalised those ties. The three domestic courts were in a better position than European judges in striking a fair balance between the competing interests involved. The decision fell within the margin of appreciation, and the adverse effects on the applicant's relations with the child were not disproportionate.

Stubbings and Others v UK

RJD, 1996-IV, No 18, 23 EHRR 213

Claims for damages for alleged childhood sexual abuse time-barred – whether denied access to a court – no violation of Arts 6, 8 or 14

Facts

The applicant alleged that she had suffered sexual abuse within her adoptive family during her childhood. She later developed severe psychological problems, which, following treatment by a psychiatrist, she connected to her earlier childhood abuse. She commenced proceedings against the adoptive family. The question arose as to whether or not the action was time-barred, on the basis of a 3-year limit from the date on which the plaintiff first knew the injury was significant and attributable to the defendants, and which could be extended if it was equitable to do so. The case went to the House of Lords, reported as *Stubbings v Webb* [1993] AC 498, which held that actions based on intentionally inflicted injuries such as indecent assault were subject to the 6-year limitation period which could not be disapplied. The applicant was out of time. Three other applications were joined, whose cases were also dismissed under the rule in *Stubbings v Webb*.

Complaints

The applicants complained that the time limitation effectively barred their access to court in the determination of their claims of psychological injury. In a case where the victim is rarely aware of the link between the damage suffered and the acts responsible, an inflexible time-limit is not appropriate. The limit did not pursue a legitimate aim or was not proportionate to such an aim. Furthermore, the recent understanding of the widespread nature of sexual abuse meant that the Government had a positive obligation to introduce new measures for the protection of minors in the respect of their private lives, which the Government had failed to do. The Limitation Act 1980 discriminated between victims of intentional and unintentional injury with no legitimate aim.

Commission

The Commission found a breach of Art 14 in conjunction with Art 6(1).

Court

The Court, in finding no breach of the Convention, held that:

(1) The right of access to a court is not absolute but may be subject to limitations, since the right calls for regulation by the State, who enjoy a margin of appreciation. The Court must be satisfied that the limitations to not restrict access so that the very essence of the right is impaired. Any limitation must have a legitimate aim and the means must be proportionate to the aim sought to be achieved.

(2) Many European countries have such limits. In the UK, there is a 6 year time-limit to bring a claim, so the very essence of the right of access was not impaired. The limit was not too short. International standards were less strict. If they had commenced an

action at the end of the limitation period, it would still have been 20 years after the events.

(3) The aim was to provide finality and legal certainty and to prevent stale claims from coming to court. This was a legitimate aim. As the very essence of the right was not impaired, there was a legitimate aim which was proportionate, no violation of Art 6(1).

(4) With regard to the failure to protect children from sexual abuse, although the object of Art 8 is to protect the individual against arbitrary interference by the State, it can create positive obligations. The State will have a large margin of appreciation to choose the means to comply with this obligation, which in the case of the UK was satisfied by the criminal law, with no limitation period and the severest penalties. There is no obligation to also provide unlimited civil remedies in those circumstances.

(5) As to the allegation of discrimination, not every difference in treatment will amount to a violation of Art 14. It must be established that other persons in an analogous or relevantly similar situation enjoy preferential treatment, and that there is no reasonable or objective justification for this distinction. There was no difference between the applicant and other victims of deliberate wrong-doing, and different considerations may apply to victims of deliberate and negligent wrong-doing.

Sunday Times v UK (No 1)

(1979) Series A, No 30, 2 EHRR 245

Freedom of expression – injunction – contempt of court – violation of Art 10

Facts
This case arose out of the publication by the *Sunday Times* of a series of articles with the aim of assisting the parents of children born deformed after their mothers had taken the drug Thalidomide. A number of parents issued writs against the manufacturer. The Attorney-General granted the drugs company an injunction restraining publication of one article, which was to deal with the testing, manufacture and marketing of the drug, on the grounds that publication would be contempt of court as it was a deliberate attempt to influence one of the parties in pending legal proceedings. The injunction was upheld by the House of Lords.

Complaint
The *Sunday Times* filed an application claiming that the injunction infringed their right to freedom of expression under Art 10.

Court
In finding a violation of Art 10 the Court held that:

(1) The interference with the applicant's freedom was 'prescribed by law' within the meaning of Art 10 as the principle on which the injunction was founded was formulated with sufficient precision in English law, and it was reasonably foreseeable to the *Sunday Times* that publication of the article might amount to contempt.

(2) It was necessary to decide whether the interference with the applicant's freedom corresponded to a pressing social need, and whether it was proportionate to the aim pursued.

(3) The court held that the thalidomide disaster was a matter of undisputed public concern, and that Art 10 governed not only the freedom of the press but also the right of the general public to be informed. It held that publication of the article was unlikely to have influenced the drug company to settle on better terms. The court concluded that the interference did not correspond with a social need sufficiently pressing to outweigh the public interest in freedom of expression. The court further held that the injunction was not a proportionate reaction.

Tyrer v UK

(1978) Series A, No 26, 2 EHRR 175

Corporal punishment – degrading punishment – violation of Art 3

Facts

The applicant, a 15-year-old boy, was convicted of ABH in the juvenile court at Castletown in the Isle of Man, and sentenced to three lashes of the birch. The sentence was carried out by a police officer some time later by striking his bare buttocks so as to cause the skin to rise, but not breaking the skin. His father was present during the infliction of the punishment.

Complaint

The applicant complained that such treatment was inhuman and degrading punishment in breach of Art 3.

Commission

The Commission decided in 1974 that there had been a breach of Art 3.

Court

In finding a violation of Art 3 the Court held that:

(1)   The applicant's treatment did not amount to 'torture', as it did not reveal the level of suffering inherent in this notion as interpreted in the *Ireland v UK* case (above). Furthermore, the Court did not consider that the punishment reached the level of 'degrading'. Punishment was by its very nature degrading, and therefore the Court had to find a further level of humiliation to find a breach. Such an assessment could be based only on the circumstances of the case, the nature and context of the punishment and the manner and method of its execution.

(2)   A physical assault on one person by another when ordered by the judicial authorities of a State constitutes an attack on that which it is one of the main purposes of Art 3 to protect, namely a person's dignity and physical integrity. The institutionalised nature of the violence is compounded by the procedural way in which it was carried out. In addition to the physical pain suffered, for several weeks the applicant had to suffer the mental anguish of anticipating the violence to be inflicted upon him.

(3)   The Court did not think it relevant that the applicant was being punished for an offence of violence. The fact that imprisonment was also an alternative was irrelevant. The indignity of having the punishment administered over the bare posterior aggravated to some extent the degrading character of the punishment.

W v UK

10 EHRR 29

B v UK

(1987) Series A, No 121

Children in care – denial of access – breach of right to family life – violation of Art 8 – no ability to challenge decision – violation of Art 6(1)

Facts

The applicant, W's son, had been placed in voluntary foster-care at the age of 12 months. Following this, the local authority made a parental rights resolution, which was agreed at that time by the parents as it was temporary. The local authority then decided that the child should be placed in long-term foster-care, with a view to adoption. The parents were informed of this decision. Following that, a decision was made that access to the child should be limited, and later terminated. Following a dramatic improvement in their home life, the parents managed to have the order discharged by the juvenile court. The local authority appealed, applying for wardship. Those proceedings were delayed by the local authority, and only fully concluded when the child was 2 years old, when it was held that the child should remain with the foster-parents and that access should be terminated.

The applicant, B's child, was assaulted by the applicant and taken into local authority care. The child was discharged into foster accommodation near the applicant's address. At a case conference of which the applicant was unaware, the local authority decided to move the child into foster accommodation further away from the applicant. At a case conference when the child was 20 months old the local authority decided to terminate all access. The applicant applied to the High Court for the child to be made a ward of court, but the summons was dismissed.

Complaint

The applicants complained that there was a breach of their right to family life in the decisions made by the Court to restrict and terminate access to the child, together with the length of time of the proceedings and the lack of remedies. They further complained that they were not able to have the issue of access determined in proceedings before a court, and in the case of W that the decision as to wardship took too long.

Commission

The Commission found a breach of Arts 8 and 6(1).

Court

In upholding the violations found by the Commission, the Court held that:

(1) The mutual enjoyment by parent and child of each other's company constitutes a fundamental element of family life and measures hindering such enjoyment amount to an interference with the right protected by Art 8.

(2) When a child is taken into care, the natural family relationship nevertheless remains, and so decisions as to parental access constitute interferences to be justified by the local authority under Art 8(2). As the decisions are often irreversible, there is a greater need for protection from arbitrary interferences, which allows the Court to look at the process itself.

(3) The parents must be involved in the decision-making process to a degree sufficient to provide them with the requisite protection of their interests. If they have not, there will have been a failure to respect their family life and the interference resulting form the decision will not be capable of being regarded as 'necessary' within the meaning of Art 8.

(4) The views of the parents must be taken into account, and they must be allowed to take advantage of any remedies available to them. In particular, mere delay must not be allowed to decide the outcome of the proceedings. In these cases, the parents were not sufficiently involved, and despite the broad margin of appreciation to be applied, there is a violation of Art 8.

(5) As it is not possible to extinguish parental rights entirely, the applicant should have been able to have access to a court, as there was clearly a 'dispute' in this case, and the scope of proceedings in judicial review is not wide enough. Consequently, there was also a breach of Art 6(1).

X and Y v The Netherlands

(1985) Series A, No 91, 8 EHRR 235

Sexual abuse – no ability to bring criminal proceedings – failure to respect family and private life

Facts

Y was sexually assaulted when just 16 years old whilst in a home for mentally handicapped children, causing her major mental disturbance. Her father, X, went to the police station to make a complaint on her behalf, due to her mental condition. The prosecutor did not bring proceedings against the assailant, on the condition that he did not re-offend within 2 years. X appealed this decision, but the Court of Appeal held that he was not entitled to bring the complaint on behalf of his daughter; in fact, there was a gap in the law, and no-one was entitled to bring a complaint.

Complaint

The applicants complained that the daughter had been subject to inhuman and degrading treatment and that their right to respect for private life had been violated. Further, the right to respect for family life meant that parents must be able to bring actions on behalf of children who are minors.

Commission

The Commission found the complaints admissible, and expressed the opinion that there had been a breach of Art 8 but not Art 3.

Court

The Court, in finding a breach of Art 8, held that:

(1) The positive obligations inherent in an effective respect for private or family life may involve the adoption of measures designed to secure respect for private life even in the sphere of the relations of individuals between themselves.
(2) The choice of the means calculated to comply with Art 8 in the sphere of the relations of individuals between themselves is in principle a matter that falls within the margin of appreciation. One of those methods is criminal law, but that is not the only answer.
(3) An action for damages is insufficient where fundamental values and essential aspects of private life are at stake. Effective deterrence is indispensable and can only be achieved by criminal provisions, as is the normal case.
(4) Whatever the reasons for the failing in the criminal law – and the Court will not interfere in the interpretation of domestic law by national courts – it failed to provide Y with practical and effective protection and therefore she was the victim of a violation of Art 8.
(5) No need to examine the case under Arts 13 and 14 as well.

X, Y and Z v UK

RJD, 1997-II, No 35, 24 EHRR 143

Artificial insemination – failure to recognise non-biological father of child where transsexual – existence of family ties – no violation of Art 8

Facts

X is a female to male transsexual, and from 1979 has lived in a permanent and stable relationship with Y. In 1992, Z was born to Y as a result of artificial insemination by donor. X was not entitled to be registered as the father of Z as only a biological man could be so registered, although the child took his surname.

Complaints

The applicants complained that they were denied respect for their family and private life as a result of the lack of recognition on the first applicant's role as father to the third applicant and that the resulting situation in which they are placed discloses discrimination.

Commission

The Commission declared the complaints admissible and concluded by 13 votes to 5 that there had been a violation of Art 8 and saw no further issues in Art 14.

Court

In finding no violation of Art 8 or Art 14, the Court held that:

(1)　The notion of 'family life' in Art 8 is not confined solely to families based on marriage and may encompass other *de facto* relationships. Relevant factors as to whether there is 'family life' include whether the couple live together, the length of their relationship and whether they have demonstrated their commitment to each other by having children together or by any other means. Here, there are family ties, and therefore Art 8 applies.

(2)　Article 8 protects individuals from arbitrary interferences and imposes positive obligations on the State. A fair balance must be struck between the competing interests of the individual and of the community as a whole, in which the State enjoys a certain margin of appreciation.

(3)　Here, the issue is one of family life rather than private life, as unlike the previous transsexual cases the complaint is not registering as a male, but as a father.

(4)　The Court has held in *Marckx v Belgium* amongst others that where a family tie with a child has been established, the State must act so as to enable that tie to be developed and legal safeguards must be established to integrate the child into the family. Here there are different issues as X is not the biological father of Z.

(5)　There is no consensus on this issue within the Member States of the Council of Europe, therefore the Court will afford the State a wide margin of appreciation.

(6)　In judging whether a fair balance has been struck, an amendment to the law might have undesirable or unforeseen ramifications for children in the same position; many children do not have the name of their parent on their birth certificates, which is not a cause of particular stigma; X is not prevented in any way from acting as Z's father in the social sense, and can apply for a joint residence order giving parental responsibility; it is not possible to predict how best to protect children in such a position.

(7)　In conclusion, given that transsexuality raises complex scientific, legal, moral and social issues, in respect of which there is no generally shared approach, Art 8 cannot be taken to imply an obligation to recognise as the father of a child a person who is not the biological father. The lack of legal recognition of that relationship is not a failure to respect family life.

Y v UK

(1992) Series A, No 247-A, 17 EHRR 233

Caning – breach of Art 3 – no interference with family life

Facts

The applicant was a 15-year-old schoolboy attending a private school who was caned by his headmaster. The punishment left four weals across his buttocks. The prosecuting authorities decided not to prosecute the headmaster for assault, and the applicant's claim for civil damages in the county court was rejected on the grounds that the applicant's parents had entered a contract with the school, and that the headmaster's behaviour did not go beyond the reasonable punishment permitted within the contract.

Complaint

The applicant claimed that corporal punishment amounted to degrading treatment within the meaning of Art 3 of the Convention, that it interfered with his family life contrary to Art 8, and that Art 13 had also been violated as he had no domestic remedy.

Commission

In finding a violation of Arts 3 and 13 and no violation of Art 8, the Commission held that:

(1) The Government had responsibility to ensure that all pupils, whether at State or private schools, were not subject to treatment which breached Arts 3 or 8.

(2) They would follow *Tyrer v UK* (1978) 2 EHRR 1 in holding that corporal punishment breached Art 3 where 'the humiliation and debasement involved must attain a particular level of severity over and above the usual element of humiliation involved in any kind of punishment'. The Commission found that in this case 'such injury to a teenage boy is unacceptable whoever were to inflict the punishment, be it parent or teacher'.

(3) The applicant's remedies in the English courts were not sufficient, and that Art 13 had therefore been breached. It was held that as what is considered to be moderate treatment in the UK could breach Art 3, a remedy in criminal or civil assault was inadequate. The Commission held that 'the applicant did not have an effective remedy before a national authority in respect of his claim that he suffered degrading treatment or punishment'.

(4) The Government reached a friendly settlement with the applicant and therefore the matter did not go on to the Court.

PART D

Appendices

APPENDIX 1

APPENDIX 2

APPENDIX 3

APPENDIX 4

PART D
APPENDICES

APPENDIX 1

Convention for the Protection of Human Rights and Fundamental Freedoms

Rome, 4.XI.1950

'The text of the Convention had been amended according to the provisions of Protocol No. 3 (ETS No. 45), which entered into force on 21 September 1970, of Protocol No. 5 (ETS No. 55), which entered into force on 20 December 1971 and of Protocol No. 8 (ETS No. 118), which entered into force 1 January 1990, and comprised also the text of Protocol No. 2 (ETS No. 44) which, in accordance with Article 5, paragraph 3 thereof, had been an integral part of the Convention since its entry into force on 21 September 1970. All provisions which had been amended or added by these Protocols are replaced by Protocol No. 11 (ETS No. 155), as from the date of its entry into force on 1 November 1998. As from that date, Protocol No. 9 (ETS No. 140), which entered into force on 1 October 1994, is repealed and Protocol No. 10 (ETS No. 146), which has not entered into force, has lost its purpose.'

The governments signatory hereto, being members of the Council of Europe,

Considering the Universal Declaration of Human Rights proclaimed by the General Assembly of the United Nations on 10th December 1948;

Considering that this Declaration aims at securing the universal and effective recognition and observance of the Rights therein declared;

Considering that the aim of the Council of Europe is the achievement of greater unity between its members and that one of the methods by which that aim is to be pursued is the maintenance and further realisation of human rights and fundamental freedoms;

Reaffirming their profound belief in those fundamental freedoms which are the foundation of justice and peace in the world and are best maintained on the one hand by an effective political democracy and on the other by a common understanding and observance of the human rights upon which they depend;

Being resolved, as the governments of European countries which are like-minded and have a common heritage of political traditions, ideals, freedom and the rule of law, to take the first steps for the collective enforcement of certain of the rights stated in the Universal Declaration,

Have agreed as follows:

Article 1[1]

Obligation to respect human rights

The High Contracting Parties shall secure to everyone within their jurisdiction the rights and freedoms defined in Section I of this Convention.

PART D
APPENDIX 1

SECTION I

RIGHTS AND FREEDOMS

Article 2[1]

Right to life

1. Everyone's right to life shall be protected by law. No one shall be deprived of his life intentionally save in the execution of a sentence of a court following his conviction of a crime for which this penalty is provided by law.

2. Deprivation of life shall not be regarded as inflicted in contravention of this Article when it results from the use of force which is no more than absolutely necessary:

    (a) in defence of any person from unlawful violence;
    (b) in order to effect a lawful arrest or to prevent the escape of a person lawfully detained;
    (c) in action lawfully taken for the purpose of quelling a riot or insurrection.

Article 3[1]

Prohibition of torture

No one shall be subjected to torture or to inhuman or degrading treatment or punishment.

Article 4[1]

Prohibition of slavery and forced labour

1. No one shall be held in slavery or servitude.

2. No one shall be required to perform forced or compulsory labour.

3. For the purpose of this Article the term 'forced or compulsory labour' shall not include:

    (a) any work required to be done in the ordinary course of detention imposed according to the provisions of Article 5 of this Convention or during conditional release from such detention;
    (b) any service of a military character or, in case of conscientious objectors, in countries where they are recognised, service exacted instead of compulsory military service;
    (c) any service exacted in case of an emergency or calamity threatening the life or well-being of the community;
    (d) any work or service which forms part of normal civic obligations.

Article 5[1]

Right to liberty and security

1. Everyone has the right to liberty and security of person. No one shall be deprived of his liberty save in the following cases and in accordance with a procedure prescribed by law:

    (a) the lawful detention of a person after conviction by a competent court;
    (b) the lawful arrest or detention of a person for non-compliance with the lawful order of a court or in order to secure the fulfilment of any obligation prescribed by law;

(c) the lawful arrest or detention of a person effected for the purpose of bringing him before the competent legal authority on reasonable suspicion of having committed an offence or when it is reasonably considered necessary to prevent his committing an offence or fleeing after having done so;

(d) the detention of a minor by lawful order for the purpose of educational supervision or his lawful detention for the purpose of bringing him before the competent legal authority;

(e) the lawful detention of persons for the prevention of the spreading of infectious diseases, of persons of unsound mind, alcoholics or drug addicts or vagrants;

(f) the lawful arrest or detention of a person to prevent his effecting an unauthorised entry into the country or of a person against whom action is being taken with a view to deportation or extradition.

2. Everyone who is arrested shall be informed promptly, in a language which he understands, of the reasons for his arrest and of any charge against him.

3. Everyone arrested or detained in accordance with the provisions of paragraph 1(c) of this Article shall be brought promptly before a judge or other officer authorised by law to exercise judicial power and shall be entitled to trial within a reasonable time or to release pending trial. Release may be conditioned by guarantees to appear for trial.

4. Everyone who is deprived of his liberty by arrest or detention shall be entitled to take proceedings by which the lawfulness of his detention shall be decided speedily by a court and his release ordered if the detention is not lawful.

5. Everyone who has been the victim of arrest or detention in contravention of the provisions of this Article shall have an enforceable right to compensation.

Article 6[1]

Right to a fair trail

1. In the determination of his civil rights and obligations or of any, criminal charge against him, everyone is entitled to a fair and public hearing within a reasonable time by an independent and impartial tribunal established by law. Judgment shall be pronounced publicly but the press and public may be excluded from all or part of the trial in the interests of morals, public order or national security in a democratic society, where the interests of juveniles or the protection of the private life of the parties so require, or to the extent strictly necessary in the opinion of the court in special circumstances where publicity would prejudice the interests of justice.

2. Everyone charged with a criminal offence shall be presumed innocent until proved guilty according to law.

3. Everyone charged with a criminal offence has the following minimum rights:

(a) to be informed promptly, in a language which he understands and in detail, of the nature and cause of the accusation against him;

(b) to have adequate time and facilities for the preparation of his defence;

(c) to defend himself in person or through legal assistance of his own choosing or, if he has not sufficient means to pay for legal assistance, to be given it free when the interests of justice so require;

(d) to examine or have examined witnesses against him and to obtain the attendance and examination of witnesses on his behalf under the same conditions as witnesses against him;

(e) to have the free assistance of an interpreter if he cannot understand or speak the language used in court.

Article 7[1]

No punishment without law

1. No one shall be held guilty of any criminal offence on account of any act or omission which did not constitute a criminal offence under national or international law at the time when it was committed. Nor shall a heavier penalty be imposed than the one that was applicable at the time the criminal offence was committed.

2. This Article shall not prejudice the trial and punishment of any person for any act or omission which, at the time when it was committed, was criminal according to the general principles of law recognised by civilised nations.

Article 8[1]

Right to respect for private and family life

1. Everyone has the right to respect for his private and family life, his home and his correspondence.

2. There shall be no interference by a public authority with the exercise of this right except such as is in accordance with the law and is necessary in a democratic society in the interests of national security, public safety or the economic well-being of the country, for the prevention of disorder or crime, for the protection of health or morals, or for the protection of the rights and freedoms of others.

Article 9[1]

Freedom of thought, conscience and religion

1. Everyone has the right to freedom of thought, conscience and religion; this right includes freedom to change his religion or belief and freedom, either alone or in community with others and in public or private, to manifest his religion or belief, in worship, teaching, practice and observance.

2. Freedom to manifest one's religion or beliefs shall be subject only to such limitations as are prescribed by law and are necessary in a democratic society in the interests of public safety, for the protection of public order, health or morals, or for the protection of the rights and freedoms of others.

Article 10[1]

Freedom of expression

1. Everyone has the right to freedom of expression. This right shall include freedom to hold opinions and to receive and impart information and ideas without interference by public authority and regardless of frontiers. This Article shall not prevent States from requiring the licensing of broadcasting, television or cinema enterprises.

2. The exercise of these freedoms, since it carries with it duties and responsibilities, may be subject to such formalities, conditions, restrictions or penalties as are prescribed by law and are necessary in a democratic society, in the interests of national security, territorial integrity or public safety, for the prevention of disorder or crime, for the protection of

health or morals, for the protection of the reputation or rights of others, for preventing the disclosure of information received in confidence, or for maintaining the authority and impartiality of the judiciary.

Article 11[1]

Freedom of assembly and association

1. Everyone has the right to freedom of peaceful assembly and to freedom of association with others, including the right to form and to join trade unions for the protection of his interests.

2. No restrictions shall be placed on the exercise of these rights other than such as are prescribed by law and are necessary in a democratic society in the interests of national security or public safety, for the prevention of disorder or crime, for the protection of health or morals or for the protection of the rights and freedoms of others. This Article shall not prevent the imposition of lawful restrictions on the exercise of these rights by members of the armed forces, of the police or of the administration of the State.

Article 12[1]

Right to marry

Men and women of marriageable age have the right to marry and to found a family, according to the national laws governing the exercise of this right.

Article 13[1]

Right to an effective remedy

Everyone whose rights and freedoms as set forth in this Convention are violated shall have an effective remedy before a national authority notwithstanding that the violation has been committed by persons acting in an official capacity.

Article 14[1]

Prohibition of discrimination

The enjoyment of the rights and freedoms set forth in this Convention shall be secured without discrimination on any ground such as sex, race, colour, language, religion, political or other opinion, national or social origin, association with a national minority, property, birth or other status.

Article 15[1] *Not in force.*

Derogation in time of emergency

1. In time of war or other public emergency threatening the life of the nation any High Contracting Party may take measures derogating from its obligations under this Convention to the extent strictly required by the exigencies of the situation, provided that such measures are not inconsistent with its other obligations under international law.

2. No derogation from Article 2, except in respect of deaths resulting from lawful acts of war, or from Articles 3, 4 (paragraph 1) and 7 shall be made under this provision.

3. Any High Contracting Party availing itself of this right of derogation shall keep the Secretary General of the Council of Europe fully informed of the measures which it has taken and the reasons therefor. It shall also inform the Secretary General of the Council of

Europe when such measures have ceased to operate and the provisions of the Convention are again being fully executed.

Article 16[1]

Restrictions on political activity of aliens

Nothing in Articles 10, 11 and 14 shall be regarded as preventing the High Contracting Parties from imposing restrictions on the political activity of aliens.

Article 17[1]

Prohibition of abuse of rights

Nothing in this Convention may be interpreted as implying for any State, group or person any right to engage in any activity or perform any act aimed at the destruction of any of the rights and freedoms set forth herein or at their limitation to a greater extent than is provided for in the Convention.

Article 18[1]

Limitation on use of restrictions on rights

The restrictions permitted under this Convention to the said rights and freedoms shall not be applied for any purpose other than those for which they have been prescribed.

SECTION II

EUROPEAN COURT OF HUMAN RIGHTS[2]

Article 19

Establishment of the Court

To ensure the observance of the engagements undertaken by the High Contracting Parties in the Convention and the Protocols thereto, there shall be set up a European Court of Human Rights, hereinafter referred to as 'the Court'. It shall function on a permanent basis.

Article 20

Number of judges

The Court shall consist of a number of judges equal to that of the High Contracting Parties.

Article 21

Criteria for office

1. The judges shall be of high moral character and must either possess the qualifications required for appointment to high judicial office or be jurisconsults of recognised competence.

2. The judges shall sit on the Court in their individual capacity.

3. During their term of office the judges shall not engage in any activity which is incompatible with their independence, impartiality or with the demands of a full-time

office; all questions arising from the application of this paragraph shall be decided by the Court.

Article 22

Election of judges

1. The judges shall be elected by the Parliamentary Assembly with respect to each High Contracting Party by a majority of votes cast from a list of three candidates nominated by the High Contracting Party.

2. The same procedure shall be followed to complete the Court in the event of the accession of new High Contracting Parties and in filling casual vacancies.

Article 23

Terms of office

1. The judges shall be elected for a period of six years. They may be re-elected. However, the terms of office of one-half of the judges elected at the first election shall expire at the end of three years.

2. The judges whose terms of office are to expire at the end of the initial period of three years shall be chosen by lot by the Secretary General of the Council of Europe immediately after their election.

3. In order to ensure that, as far as possible, the terms of office of one-half of the judges are renewed every three years, the Parliamentary Assembly may decide, before proceeding to any subsequent election, that the term or terms of office of one or more judges to be elected shall be for a period other than six years but not more than nine and not less than three years.

4. In cases where more than one term of office is involved and where the Parliamentary Assembly applies the preceding paragraph, the allocation of the terms of office shall be effected by a drawing of lots by the Secretary General of the Council of Europe immediately after the election.

5. A judge elected to replace a judge whose term of office has not expired shall hold office for the remainder of his predecessor's term.

6. The terms of office of judges shall expire when they reach the age of 70.

7. The judges shall hold office until replaced. They shall, however, continue to deal with such cases as they already have under consideration.

Article 24

Dismissal

No judge may be dismissed from his office unless the other judges decide by a majority of two-thirds that he has ceased to fulfil the required conditions.

Article 25

Registry and legal secretaries

The Court shall have a registry, the functions and organisation of which shall be laid down in the rules of the Court. The Court shall be assisted by legal secretaries.

Article 26

Plenary Court

The plenary Court shall

(a) elect its President and one or two Vice-Presidents for a period of three years; they may be re-elected;

(b) set up Chambers, constituted for a fixed period of time;

(c) elect the Presidents of the Chambers of the Court; they may be re-elected;

(d) adopt the rules of the Court, and

(e) elect the Registrar and one or more Deputy Registrars.

Article 27

Committees, Chambers and Grand Chamber

1. To consider cases brought before it, the Court shall sit in committees of three judges, in Chambers of seven judges and in a Grand Chamber of seventeen judges. The Court's Chambers shall set up committees for a fixed period of time.

2. There shall sit as an *ex officio* member of the Chamber and the Grand Chamber the judge elected in respect of the State Party concerned or, if there is none or if he is unable to sit, a person of its choice who shall sit in the capacity of judge.

3. The Grand Chamber shall also include the President of the Court, the Vice-Presidents, the Presidents of the Chambers and other judges chosen in accordance with the rules of the Court. When a case is referred to the Grand Chamber under Article 43, no judge from the Chamber which rendered the judgment shall sit in the Grand Chamber, with the exception of the President of the Chamber and the judge who sat in respect of the State Party concerned.

Article 28

Declarations of inadmissibility by committees

A committee may, by a unanimous vote, declare inadmissible or strike out of its list of cases an application submitted under Article 34 where such a decision can be taken without further examination. The decision shall be final.

Article 29

Decisions by Chambers on admissibility and merits

1. If no decision is taken under Article 28, a Chamber shall decide on the admissibility and merits of individual applications submitted under Article 34.

2. A Chamber shall decide on the admissibility and merits of inter-State applications submitted under Article 33.

3. The decision on admissibility shall be taken separately unless the Court, in exceptional cases, decides otherwise.

Article 30

Relinquishment of jurisdiction to the Grand Chamber

Where a case pending before a Chamber raises a serious question affecting the interpretation of the Convention or the protocols thereto, or where the resolution of a question before the Chamber might have a result inconsistent with a judgment previously delivered by the Court, the Chamber may, at any time before it has rendered its judgment, relinquish jurisdiction in favour of the Grand Chamber, unless one of the parties to the case objects.

Article 31

Powers of the Grand Chamber

The Grand Chamber shall

(a) determine applications submitted either under Article 33 or Article 34 when a Chamber has relinquished jurisdiction under Article 30 or when the case has been referred to it under Article 43; and
(b) consider requests for advisory opinions submitted under Article 47.

Article 32

Jurisdiction of the Court

1. The jurisdiction of the Court shall extend to all matters concerning the interpretation and application of the Convention and the protocols thereto which are referred to it as provided in Articles 33, 34 and 47.

2. In the event of dispute as to whether the Court has jurisdiction, the Court shall decide.

Article 33

Inter-State cases

Any High Contracting Party may refer to the Court any alleged breach of the provisions of the Convention and the protocols thereto by another High Contracting Party.

Article 34

Individual applications

The Court may receive applications from any person, non-governmental organisation or group of individuals claiming to be the victim of a violation by one of the High Contracting Parties of the rights set forth in the Convention or the protocols thereto. The High Contracting Parties undertake not to hinder in any way the effective exercise of this right.

Article 35

Admissibility criteria

1. The Court may only deal with the matter after all domestic remedies have been exhausted, according to the generally recognised rules of international law, and within a period of six months from the date on which the final decision was taken.

2. The Court shall not deal with any application submitted under Article 34 that

(a) is anonymous; or
(b) is substantially the same as a matter that has already been examined by the Court or has already been submitted to another procedure of international investigation or settlement and contains no relevant new information.

3. The Court shall declare inadmissible any individual application submitted under Article 34 which it considers incompatible with the provisions of the Convention or the protocols thereto, manifestly ill-founded, or an abuse of the right of application.

4. The Court shall reject any application which it considers inadmissible under this Article. It may do so at any stage of the proceedings.

Article 36

Third party intervention

1. In all cases before a Chamber of the Grand Chamber, a High Contracting Party one of whose nationals is an applicant shall have the right to submit written comments and to take part in hearings.

2. The President of the Court may, in the interest of the proper administration of justice, invite any High Contracting Party which is not a party to the proceedings or any person concerned who is not the applicant to submit written comments or take part in hearings.

Article 37

Striking out applications

1. The Court may at any stage of the proceedings decide to strike an application out of its list of cases where the circumstances lead to the conclusion that

   (a) the applicant does not intend to pursue his application; or
   (b) the matter has been resolved; or
   (c) for any other reason established by the Court, it is no longer justified to continue the examination of the application.

However, the Court shall continue the examination of the application if respect for human rights as defined in the Convention and the protocols thereto so requires.

2. The Court may decide to restore an application to its list of cases if it considers that the circumstances justify such a course.

Article 38

Examination of the case and friendly settlement proceedings

1. If the Court declares the application admissible, it shall

   (a) pursue the examination of the case, together with the representatives of the parties, and if need be, undertake an investigation, for the effective conduct of which the States concerned shall furnish all necessary facilities;
   (b) place itself at the disposal of the parties concerned with a view to securing a friendly settlement of the matter on the basis of respect for human rights as defined in the Convention and the protocols thereto.

2. Proceedings conducted under paragraph 1(b) shall be confidential.

Article 39

Finding of a friendly settlement

If a friendly settlement is effected, the Court shall strike the case out of its list by means of a decision which shall be confined to a brief statement of the facts and of the solution reached.

Article 40

Public hearings and access to documents

1. Hearings shall be in public unless the Court in exceptional circumstances decides otherwise.

2. Documents deposited with the Registrar shall be accessible to the public unless the President of the Court decides otherwise.

Article 41

Just satisfaction

If the Court finds that there has been a violation of the Convention or the protocols thereto, and if the internal law of the High Contracting Party concerned allows only partial reparation to be made, the Court shall, if necessary, afford just satisfaction to the injured party.

Article 42

Judgments of Chambers

Judgments of Chambers shall become final in accordance with the provisions of Article 44, paragraph 2.

Article 43

Referral to the Grand Chamber

1. Within a period of three months from the date of the judgment of the Chamber, any party to the case may, in exceptional cases, request that the case be referred to the Grand Chamber.

2. A panel of five judges of the Grand Chamber shall accept the request if the case raises a serious question affecting the interpretation or application of the Convention or the protocols thereto, or a serious issue of general importance.

3. If the panel accepts the request, the Grand Chamber shall decide the case by means of a judgment.

Article 44

Final judgments

1. The judgment of the Grand Chamber shall be final.

2. The judgment of a Chamber shall become final

   (a) when the parties declare that they will not request that the case be referred to the Grand Chamber; or
   (b) three months after the date of the judgment, if reference of the case to the Grand Chamber has not been requested; or
   (c) when the panel of the Grand Chamber rejects the request to refer under Article 43.

3. The final judgment shall be published.

Article 45

Reasons for judgments and decisions

1. Reasons shall be given for judgments as well as for decisions declaring applications admissible or inadmissible.

2. If a judgment does not represent, in whole or in part, the unanimous opinion of the judges, any judge shall be entitled to deliver a separate opinion.

Article 46

Binding force and execution of judgments

1. The High Contracting Parties undertake to abide by the final judgment of the Court in any case to which they are parties.

2. The final judgment of the Court shall be transmitted to the Committee of Ministers, which shall supervise its execution.

Article 47

Advisory opinions

1. The Court may, at the request of the Committee of Ministers, give advisory opinions on legal questions concerning the interpretation of the Convention and the protocols thereto.

2. Such opinions shall not deal with any question relating to the content or scope of the rights or freedoms defined in Section I of the Convention and the protocols thereto, or with any other question which the Court or the Committee of Ministers might have to consider in consequence of any such proceedings as could be instituted in accordance with the Convention.

3. Decisions of the Committee of Ministers to request an advisory opinion of the Court shall require a majority vote of the representatives entitled to sit on the Committee.

Article 48

Advisory jurisdiction of the Court

The Court shall decide whether a request for an advisory opinion submitted by the Committee of Ministers is within its competence as defined in Article 47.

Article 49

Reasons for advisory opinions

1. Reasons shall be given for advisory opinions of the Court.

2. If the advisory opinion does not represent, in whole or in part, the unanimous opinion of the judges, any judge shall be entitled to deliver a separate opinion.

3. Advisory opinions of the Court shall be communicated to the Committee of Ministers.

Article 50

Expenditure on the Court

The expenditure on the Court shall be borne by the Council of Europe.

Article 51

Privileges and immunities of judges

The judges shall be entitled, during the exercise of their functions, to the privileges and immunities provided for in Article 40 of the Statute of the Council of Europe and in the agreements made thereunder.

SECTION III

MISCELLANEOUS PROVISIONS[1, 3]

Article 52[1]

Inquiries by the Secretary General

On receipt of a request from the Secretary General of the Council of Europe any High Contracting Party shall furnish an explanation of the manner in which its internal law ensures the effective implementation of any of the provisions of the Convention.

Article 53[1]

Safeguard for existing human rights

Nothing in this Convention shall be construed as limiting or derogating from any of the human rights and fundamental freedoms which may be ensured under the laws of any High Contracting Party or under any other agreement to which it is a Party.

Article 54[1]

Powers of the Committee of Ministers

Nothing in this Convention shall prejudice the powers conferred on the Committee of Ministers by the Statute of the Council of Europe.

Article 55[1]

Exclusion of other means of dispute settlement

The High Contracting Parties agree that, except by special agreement, they will not avail themselves of treaties, conventions or declarations in force between them for the purpose of submitting, by way of petition, a dispute arising out of the interpretation or application of this Convention to a means of settlement other than those provided for in this Convention.

Article 56[1]

Territorial application

1. [4] Any State may at the time of its ratification or at any time thereafter declare by notification addressed to the Secretary General of the Council of Europe that the present Convention shall, subject to paragraph 4 of this Article, extend to all or any of the territories for whose international relations it is responsible.

2. The Convention shall extend to the territory or territories named in the notification as from the thirtieth day after the receipt of this notification by the Secretary General of the Council of Europe.

3. The provisions of this Convention shall be applied in such territories with due regard, however, to local requirements.

4. [4] Any State which has made a declaration in accordance with paragraph 1 of this Article may at any time thereafter declare on behalf of one or more of the territories to which the declaration relates that it accepts the competence of the Court to receive applications from individuals, non-governmental organisations or groups of individuals as provided by Article 34 of the Convention.

Article 57[1]

Reservations

1. Any State may, when signing this Convention or when depositing its instrument of ratification, make a reservation in respect of any particular provision of the Convention to the extent that any law then in force in its territory is not in conformity with the provision. Reservations of a general character shall not be permitted under this Article.

2. Any reservation made under this Article shall contain a brief statement of the law concerned.

Article 58[1]

Denunciation

1. A High Contracting Party may denounce the present Convention only after the expiry of five years from the date on which it became a party to it and after six months' notice contained in a notification addressed to the Secretary General of the Council of Europe, who shall inform the other High Contracting Parties.

2. Such a denunciation shall not have the effect of releasing the High Contracting Party concerned from its obligations under this Convention in respect of any act which, being capable of constituting a violation of such obligations, may have been performed by it before the date at which the denunciation became effective.

3. Any High Contracting Party which shall cease to be a member of the Council of Europe shall cease to be a Party to this Convention under the same conditions.

4. [4] The Convention may be denounced in accordance with the provisions of the preceding paragraphs in respect of any territory to which it has been declared to extend under the terms of Article 56.

Article 59[1]

Signature and ratification

1. This Convention shall be open to the signature of the members of the Council of Europe. It shall be ratified. Ratifications shall be deposited with the Secretary General of the Council of Europe.

2. The present Convention shall come into force after the deposit of ten instruments of ratification.

3. As regards any signatory ratifying subsequently, the Convention shall come into force at the date of the deposit of its instrument of ratification.

4. The Secretary General of the Council of Europe shall notify all the members of the Council of Europe of the entry into force of the Convention, the names of the High Contracting Parties who have ratified it, and the deposit of all instruments of ratification which may be effected subsequently.

Done at Rome this 4th day of November 1950, in English and French, both texts being equally authentic, in a single copy which shall remain deposited in the archives of the Council of Europe. The Secretary General shall transmit certified copies to each of the signatories.

Footnotes

1   Heading added according to the provisions of Protocol No. 11 (ETS No. 155).
2   New Section II according to the provisions of Protocol No. 11 (ETS No. 155).
3   The articles of this Section are renumbered according to the provisions of Protocol No. 11 (ETS No. 155).
4   Text amended according to the provisions of Protocol No. 11 (ETS No. 155).

Protocol to the Convention for the Protection of Human Rights and Fundamental Freedoms, as amended by Protocol No. 11

Paris, 20.III.1952

Headings of articles added and text amended according to the provisions of Protocol No. 11 (ETS No. 155) as of its entry into force on 1 November 1998.

The governments signatory hereto, being members of the Council of Europe,

Being resolved to take steps to ensure the collective enforcement of certain rights and freedoms other than those already included in Section I of the Convention for the Protection of Human Rights and Fundamental Freedoms signed at Rome on 4 November 1950 (hereinafter referred to as 'the Convention'),

Have agreed as follows:

Article 1

Protection of property

Every natural or legal person is entitled to the peaceful enjoyment of his possessions. No one shall be deprived of his possessions except in the public interest and subject to the conditions provided for by law and by the general principles of international law.

The preceding provisions shall not, however, in any way impair the right of a State to enforce such laws as it deems necessary to control the use of property in accordance with the general interest or to secure the payment of taxes or other contributions or penalties.

Article 2

Right to education

No person shall be denied the right to education. In the exercise of any functions which it assumes in relation to education and to teaching, the State shall respect the right of parents to ensure such education and teaching in conformity with their own religious and philosophical convictions.

Article 3

Right to free elections

The High Contracting Parties undertake to hold free elections at reasonable intervals by secret ballot, under conditions which will ensure the free expression of the opinion of the people in the choice of the legislature.

Article 4[1]

Territorial application

Any High Contracting Party may at the time of signature or ratification or at any time thereafter communicate to the Secretary General of the Council of Europe a declaration stating the extent to which it undertakes that the provisions of the present Protocol shall apply to such of the territories for the international relations of which it is responsible as are named therein.

Any High Contracting Party which has communicated a declaration in virtue of the preceding paragraph may from time to time communicate a further declaration modifying the terms of any former declaration or terminating the application of the provisions of this Protocol in respect of any territory.

A declaration made in accordance with this Article shall be deemed to have been made in accordance with paragraph 1 of Article 56 of the Convention.

Article 5

Relationship to the Convention

As between the High Contracting Parties the provisions of Articles 1, 2, 3 and 4 of this Protocol shall be regarded as additional Articles to the Convention and all the provisions of the Convention shall apply accordingly.

Article 6

Signature and ratification

This Protocol shall be open for signature by the members of the Council of Europe, who are the signatories of the Convention; it shall be ratified at the same time as or after the ratification of the Convention. It shall enter into force after the deposit of ten instruments of ratification. As regards any signatory ratifying subsequently, the Protocol shall enter into force at the date of the deposit of its instrument of ratification.

The instruments of ratification shall be deposited with the Secretary General of the Council of Europe, who will notify all members of the names of those who have ratified.

Done at Paris on the 20th day of March 1952, in English and *French*, both texts being equally authentic, in a single copy which shall remain deposited in the archives of the Council of Europe. The Secretary General shall transmit certified copies to each of the signatory governments.

Footnotes
1   Text amended according to the provisions of Protocol No. 11 (ETS No. 155).

Protocol No. 7 to the Convention for the Protection of Human Rights and Fundamental Freedoms, as amended by Protocol No. 11

Strasbourg, 22.XI.1984

Headings of articles added and text amended according to the provisions of Protocol No. 11 (ETS No. 155) as from its entry into force on 1 November 1998.

The member States of the Council of Europe signatory hereto,

Being resolved to take further steps to ensure the collective enforcement of certain rights and freedoms by means of the Convention for the Protection of Human Rights and Fundamental Freedoms signed at Rome on 4 November 1950 (hereinafter referred to as 'the Convention'),

Have agreed as follows:

Article 1

Procedural safeguards relating to expulsion of aliens

1. An alien lawfully resident in the territory of a State shall not be expelled therefrom except in pursuance of a decision reached in accordance with law and shall be allowed:

   (a) to submit reasons against his expulsion,
   (b) to have his case reviewed, and
   (c) to be represented for these purposes before the competent authority or a person or persons designated by that authority.

2. An alien may be expelled before the exercise of his rights under paragraph 1(a), (b) and (c) of this Article, when such expulsion is necessary in the interests of public order or is grounded on reasons of national security.

Article 2

Right of appeal in criminal matters

1. Everyone convicted of a criminal offence by a tribunal shall have the right to have his conviction or sentence reviewed by a higher tribunal. The exercise of this right, including the grounds on which it may be exercised, shall be governed by law.

2. This right may be subject to exceptions in regard to offences of a minor character, as prescribed by law, or in cases in which the person concerned was tried in the first instance by the highest tribunal or was convicted following an appeal against acquittal.

Article 3

Compensation for wrongful conviction

When a person has by a final decision been convicted of a criminal offence and when subsequently his conviction has been reversed, or he has been pardoned, on the ground that a new or newly discovered fact shows conclusively that there has been a miscarriage of justice, the person who has suffered punishment as a result of such conviction shall be compensated according to the law or the practice of the State concerned, unless it is proved that the non-disclosure of the unknown fact in time is wholly or partly attributable to him.

Article 4

Right not to be tried or punished twice

1. No one shall be liable to be tried or punished again in criminal proceedings under the jurisdiction of the same State for an offence for which he has already been finally acquitted or convicted in accordance with the law and penal procedure of that State.

2. The provisions of the preceding paragraph shall not prevent the reopening of the case in accordance with the law and penal procedure of the State concerned, if there is evidence of new or newly discovered facts, or if there has been a fundamental defect in the previous proceedings, which could affect the outcome of the case.

3. No derogation from this Article shall be made under Article 15 of the Convention.

Article 5

Equality between spouses

Spouses shall enjoy equality of rights and responsibilities of a private law character between them, and in their relations with their children, as to marriage, during marriage and in the event of its dissolution. This Article shall not prevent States from taking such measures as are necessary in the interests of the children.

Article 6

Territorial application

1. Any State may at the time of signature or when depositing its instrument of ratification, acceptance or approval, specify the territory or territories to which the Protocol shall apply and state the extent to which it undertakes that the provisions of this Protocol shall apply to such territory or territories.

2. Any State may at any later date, by a declaration addressed to the Secretary General of the Council of Europe, extend the application of this Protocol to any other territory specified in the declaration. In respect of such territory the Protocol shall enter into force on the first day of the month following the expiration of a period of two months after the date of receipt by the Secretary General of such declaration.

3. Any declaration made under the two preceding paragraphs may, in respect of any territory specified in such declaration, be withdrawn or modified by a notification addressed to the Secretary General. The withdrawal or modification shall become effective on the first day of the month following the expiration of a period of two months after the date of receipt of such notification by the Secretary General.

4.[1] A declaration made in accordance with this Article shall be deemed to have been made in accordance with paragraph 1 of Article 56 of the Convention.

5. The territory of any State to which this Protocol applies by virtue of ratification, acceptance or approval by that State, and each territory to which this Protocol is applied by virtue of a declaration by that State under this Article, may be treated as separate territories for the purpose of the reference in Article 1 to the territory of a State.

6.[2] Any State which has made a declaration in accordance with paragraph 1 or 2 of this Article may at any time thereafter declare on behalf of one or more of the territories to which the declaration relates that it accepts the competence of the Court to receive applications from individuals, non-governmental organisations or groups of individuals as provided in Article 34 of the Convention in respect of Articles 1 to 5 of this Protocol.

Article 7[1]

Relationship to the Convention

As between the States Parties, the provisions of Article 1 to 6 of this Protocol shall be regarded as additional Articles to the Convention, and all the provisions of the Convention shall apply accordingly.

Article 8

Signature and ratification

This Protocol shall be open for signature by member States of the Council of Europe which have signed the Convention. It is subject to ratification, acceptance or approval. A member

State of the Council of Europe may not ratify, accept or approve this Protocol without previously or simultaneously ratifying the Convention. Instruments of ratification, acceptance or approval shall be deposited with the Secretary General of the Council of Europe.

Article 9

Entry into force

1. This Protocol shall enter into force on the first day of the month following the expiration of a period of two months after the date on which seven member States of the Council of Europe have expressed their consent to be bound by the Protocol in accordance with the provisions of Article 8.

2. In respect of any member State which subsequently expresses its consent to be bound by it, the Protocol shall enter into force on the first day of the month following the expiration of a period of two months after the date of the deposit of the instrument of ratification, acceptance or approval.

Article 10

Depositary functions

The Secretary General of the Council of Europe shall notify all the member States of the Council of Europe of:

(a) any signature;
(b) the deposit of any instrument of ratification, acceptance or approval;
(c) any date of entry into force of this Protocol in accordance with Articles 6 and 9;
(d) any other act, notification or declaration relating to this Protocol.

In witness whereof the undersigned, being duly authorised thereto, have signed this Protocol.

Done at Strasbourg, this 22nd day of November 1984, in English and *French*, both texts being equally authentic, in a single copy which shall be deposited in the archives of the Council of Europe. The Secretary General of the Council of Europe shall transmit certified copies to each member State of the Council of Europe.

Footnotes

1   Text amended according to the provisions of Protocol No. 11 (ETS No. 155).
2   Text added according to the provisions of Protocol No. 11 (ETS No. 155).

APPENDIX 2

Rights Brought Home: The Human Rights Bill

PRESENTED TO PARLIAMENT BY THE SECRETARY OF STATE FOR THE HOME
DEPARTMENT

BY COMMAND OF HER MAJESTY

OCTOBER 1997

(CM 3782)

Contents

Preface by the Prime Minister

The Government is pledged to modernise British politics. We are committed to a comprehensive programme of constitutional reform. We believe it is right to increase individual rights, to decentralise power, to open up government and to reform Parliament.

The elements are well known:

- a Scottish Parliament and a Welsh Assembly giving the people of Scotland and Wales more control over their own affairs within the United Kingdom;
- new rights, based on bringing the European Convention on Human Rights into United Kingdom law;
- an elected Mayor and new strategic authority for London with more accountability in the regions of England;
- freedom of information:
- a referendum on the voting system for the House of Commons; and
- reform of the House of Lords.

This White Paper explains the proposals contained in the Human Rights Bill which we are introducing into Parliament. The Bill marks a major step forward in the achievement of our programme of reform. It will give people in the United Kingdom opportunities to enforce their rights under the European Convention in British courts rather than having to incur the cost and delay of taking a case to the European Human Rights Commission and Court in Strasbourg. It will enhance the awareness of human rights in our society. And it stands alongside our decision to put the promotion of human rights at the forefront of our foreign policy.

I warmly commend these proposals to Parliament and to the people of this country.

TONY BLAIR

Introduction and Summary

The Government has a Manifesto commitment to introduce legislation to incorporate the European Convention on Human Rights into United Kingdom law. The Queen's Speech at the opening of the new Parliament announced that the Government would bring forward a Bill for this purpose in the current Session. We are now introducing the Human Rights Bill into Parliament. This White Paper explains what the Bill does, and why.

Before the General Election the Labour Party published a consultation document, *Bringing Rights Home*, setting out in some detail the case for incorporation, and its preliminary proposals for the way this should be done. A number of individuals and organisations responded helpfully with a range of comments on the paper, and have continued to make their knowledge and advice available to the Government. The Government's proposals for the Bill take full account of the responses to *Bringing Rights Home*. Any further comments in response to this White Paper or on the Bill should be sent to:

Human Rights Unit
Home Office
50 Queen Anne's Gate
London SW1H 9AT.

We may make any comments we receive publicly available. Respondents who would prefer their comments to be treated in confidence are invited to indicate this expressly.

Chapter 1 of this White Paper explains the content and status of the European Convention on Human Rights and why the Government considers it desirable to give people in this country easier access to their Convention rights.

The United Kingdom is bound in international law to observe the Convention, which it ratified in 1951, and is answerable for any violation. In some limited circumstances, the United Kingdom courts can already take the Convention into account in domestic proceedings. But public authorities in the United Kingdom are not required as a matter of domestic law to comply with the Convention and, generally speaking, there is no means of having the application of the Convention rights tested in the United Kingdom courts. The Government believes that these arrangements are no longer adequate, given the importance which it attaches to the maintenance of basic human rights in this country, and that the time has come to 'bring rights home'.

Chapter 2 explains the Government's proposals to make the Convention rights enforceable directly in this country. The Bill makes it unlawful for public authorities to act in a way which is incompatible with the Convention rights. This will make it possible for people to invoke their rights in any proceedings' – criminal or civil – brought against them by a public authority, or in proceedings which they may bring against a public authority. The Government prefers a system in which Convention rights can be called upon as they arise, in normal court proceedings, rather than confining their consideration to some kind of constitutional court. Courts and tribunals will be able to award whatever remedy, within their normal powers, is appropriate in the circumstances.

Although the courts will not, under the proposals in the Bill, be able to set aside Acts of the United Kingdom Parliament, the Bill requires them to interpret legislation as far as possible in accordance with the Convention. If this is not possible, the higher courts will be able to issue a formal declaration to the effect that the legislative provisions in question are incompatible with the Convention rights. It will then be up to the Government and Parliament to put matters right. The Bill makes a 'fast-track' procedure available for the purpose of amending the law so as to bring it into conformity with the Convention.

Chapter 3 sets out the other measures which the Government intends to take to ensure that the Convention rights are taken more fully into account in the development of new policies and of legislation. It also suggests that Parliament should itself establish a new Human Rights Committee. Amongst the matters on which the Government would welcome advice from a Parliamentary Committee is the possible establishment of a Human Rights Commission, but for the time being the Government has concluded that a new Commission should not be set up by means of this Bill.

Chapter 4 reviews the position on the derogation and reservation which the United Kingdom currently has in place in respect of the Convention and its First Protocol. The Government has concluded that these must remain for the time being, but the Bill requires any derogation to be subject to periodic renewal by Parliament and reservations to be subject to periodic review.

Chapter 4 also reviews the position in respect of those Protocols to the Convention which guarantee other rights (Protocols 4, 6 and 7) and which the United Kingdom has not so far accepted. The Government does not propose that the United Kingdom should ratify at present Protocol 4 or Protocol 6, but it does propose to sign and ratify Protocol 7 once some existing legislation has been amended.

Chapter 1 – The Case for Change

The European Convention on Human Rights

1.1   The European Convention for the Protection of Human Rights and Fundamental Freedoms is a treaty of the Council of Europe. This institution was established at the end of the Second World War, as part of the Allies' programme to reconstruct durable civilisation on the mainland of Europe. The Council was established before the European Union and, although many nations are members of both, the two bodies are quite separate.

1.2   The United Kingdom played a major part in drafting the Convention, and there was a broad agreement between the major political parties about the need for it (one of its craftsmen later became, as Lord Kilmuir, Lord Chancellor in the Conservative Administration from 1954 to 1962). The United Kingdom was among the first group of countries to sign the Convention. It was the very first country to ratify it, in March 1951. In 1966 the United Kingdom accepted that an individual person, and not merely another State, could bring a case against the United Kingdom in Strasbourg (the home of the European Commission of Human Rights and Court of Human Rights, which were established by the Convention). Successive administrations in the United Kingdom have maintained these arrangements.

1.3   The European Convention is not the only international human rights agreement to which the United Kingdom and other like-minded countries are party, but over the years it has become one of the premier agreements defining standards of behaviour across Europe. It was also for many years unique because of the system which it put in place for people from signatory countries to take complaints to Strasbourg and for those complaints to be judicially determined. These arrangements are by now well tried and tested. The rights and freedoms which are guaranteed under the Convention are ones with which the people of this country are plainly comfortable. They therefore afford an excellent basis for the Human Rights Bill which we are now introducing.

1.4   The constitutional arrangements in most continental European countries have meant that their acceptance of the Convention went hand in hand with its incorporation into their domestic law. In this country it was long believed that the rights and freedoms guaranteed by the Convention could be delivered under our common law. In the last two decades, however, there has been a growing awareness that it is not sufficient to rely on the common law and that incorporation is necessary.

1.5   The Liberal Democrat Peer, Lord Lester of Herne Hill QC, recently introduced two Bills on incorporation into the House of Lords (in 1994 and 1996). Before that, the then Conservative MP Sir Edward Gardner QC introduced a Private Member's Bill on incorporation into the House of Commons in 1987. At the time of introducing his Bill he commented on the language of the Articles in the Convention, saying 'it is language which echoes right down the corridors of history. It goes deep into our history and as far back as Magna Carta.' (Hansard, 6 February 1987, col. 1224). In preparing this White Paper the Government has paid close attention to earlier debates and proposals for incorporation.

The Convention rights

1.6   The Convention contains Articles which guarantee a number of basic human rights. They deal with the right to life (Article 2); torture or inhuman or degrading treatment or punishment (Article 3); slavery and forced labour (Article 4); liberty and security of person (Article 5); fair trial (Article 6); retrospective criminal laws (Article 7); respect for private and family life, home and correspondence (Article 8); freedom of thought, conscience and religion (Article 9); freedom of expression (Article 10); freedom of peaceful assembly and freedom of association, including the right to join a trade union (Article 11); the right to marry and to found a family (Article 12); and discrimination in the enjoyment of these rights and freedoms (Article 14).

1.7   The United Kingdom is also a party to the First Protocol to the Convention, which guarantees the right to the peaceful enjoyment of possessions (Article 1), the right to education (Article 2) and the right to free elections (Article 3).

1.8   The rights in the Convention are set out in general terms, and they are subject in the Convention to a number of qualifications which are also of a general character. Some of these qualifications are set out in the substantive Articles themselves (see, for example, Article 10, concerning freedom of expression); others are set out in Articles 16 to 18 of the Convention. Sometimes too the rights guaranteed under the Convention need to be balanced against each other (for example, those guaranteed by Article 8 and Article 10).

Applications under the Convention

1.9   Anyone within the United Kingdom jurisdiction who is aggrieved by an action of the executive or by the effect of the existing law and who believes it is contrary to the European Convention can submit a petition to the European Commission of Human Rights. The Commission will first consider whether the petition is admissible. One of the conditions of admissibility is that the applicant must have gone through all the steps available to him or her at home for challenging the decision which he or she is complaining about. If the Commission decides that a complaint is admissible, and if a friendly settlement cannot be secured, it will send a confidential report to the Committee of Ministers of the Council of Europe, stating its opinion on whether there has been a violation. The matter may end there, with a decision by the Committee (which in practice always adopts the opinion of the Commission), or the case may be referred on to the European Court of Human Rights[1] for consideration. If the Court finds that there has been a violation it may itself 'afford just satisfaction' to the injured party by an award of damages or an award of costs and expenses.

The court may also find that a formal finding of a violation is sufficient. There is no appeal from the Court.

Effect of a Court judgment

1.10   A finding by the European Court of Human Rights of a violation of a Convention right does not have the effect of automatically changing United Kingdom law and practice: that is a matter for the United Kingdom Government and Parliament. But the United Kingdom, like all other States who are parties to the Convention, has agreed to abide by the decisions of the Court or (where the case has not been referred to the Court) the Committee of Ministers. It follows that, in cases where a violation has been found, the State concerned must ensure that any deficiency in its internal laws is rectified so as to bring them into line with the Convention. The State is responsible for deciding what changes are needed, but it must satisfy the Committee of Ministers that the steps taken are sufficient. Successive United Kingdom administrations have accepted these obligations in full.

Relationship to current law in the United Kingdom

1.11   When the United Kingdom ratified the Convention the view was taken that the rights and freedoms which the Convention guarantees were already, in substance, fully protected in British law. It was not considered necessary to write the Convention itself into British law, or to introduce any new laws in the United Kingdom in order to be sure of being able to comply with the Convention.

1.12   From the point of view of the **international** obligation which the United Kingdom was undertaking when it signed and ratified the Convention, this was understandable. Moreover, the European Court of Human Rights explicitly confirmed that it was not a necessary part of proper observance of the Convention that it should be incorporated into the laws of the States concerned.

1.13   However, since its drafting nearly 50 years ago, almost all the States which are party to the European Convention on Human Rights have gradually incorporated it into their domestic law in one way or another. Ireland and Norway have not done so, but Ireland has a Bill of Rights which guarantees rights similar to those guaranteed by the Convention and Norway is also in the process of incorporating the Convention. Several other countries with which we have close links and which share the common law tradition, such as Canada and New Zealand, have provided similar protection for human rights in their own legal systems.

The case for incorporation

1.14   The effect of non-incorporation on the British people is a very practical one. The rights, originally developed with major help from the United Kingdom Government, are no longer actually seen as British rights. And enforcing them takes too long and costs too much. It takes on average five years to get an action into the European Court of Human Rights once all domestic remedies have been exhausted; and it costs an average of £30,000. Bringing these rights home will mean that the British people will be able to argue for their rights in the British courts – without this inordinate delay and cost. It will also mean that the rights will be brought much more fully into the jurisprudence of the courts throughout the United Kingdom, and their interpretation will thus be far more subtly and powerfully woven into our law. And there will be another distinct benefit. British judges will be enabled to make a distinctively British contribution to the development of the jurisprudence of human rights in Europe.

1.15   Moreover, in the Government's view, the approach which the United Kingdom has so far adopted towards the Convention does not sufficiently reflect its importance and has not stood the test of time.

1.16   The most obvious proof of this lies in the number of cases in which the European Commission and Court have found that there have been violations of the Convention rights in the United Kingdom. The causes vary. The Government recognises that interpretations of the rights guaranteed under the Convention have developed over the years reflecting changes in society and attitudes. Sometimes United Kingdom laws have proved to be inherently at odds with the Convention rights. On other occasions, although the law has been satisfactory, something has been done which our courts have held to be lawful by United Kingdom standards but which breaches the Convention. In other cases again, there has simply been no framework within which the compatibility with the Convention rights of an executive act or decision can be tested in the British courts: these courts can of course review the exercise of executive discretion, but they can do so only on the basis of what is lawful or unlawful according to the law in the United Kingdom as it stands. It is plainly unsatisfactory that someone should be the victim of a breach of the Convention standards by the State yet cannot bring any case at all in the British courts, simply because British law does not recognise the right in the same terms as one contained in the Convention.

1.17   For individuals, and for those advising them, the road to Strasbourg is long and hard. Even when they get there, the Convention enforcement machinery is subject to long delays. This might be convenient for a government which was half-hearted about the Convention and the right of individuals to apply under it, since it postpones the moment at which changes in domestic law or practice must be made. But it is not in keeping with the importance which this Government attaches to the observance of basic human rights.

Bringing Rights Home

1.18   We therefore believe that the time has come to enable people to enforce their Convention rights against the State in the British courts, rather than having to incur the delays and expense which are involved in taking a case to the European Human Rights Commission and Court in Strasbourg and which may altogether deter some people from pursuing their rights. Enabling courts in the United Kingdom to rule on the application of the Convention will also help to influence the development of case law on the Convention by the European Court of Human Rights on the basis of familiarity with our laws and customs and of sensitivity to practices and procedures in the United Kingdom. Our courts' decisions will provide the European Court with a useful source of information and reasoning for its own decisions. United Kingdom judges have a very high reputation internationally, but the fact that they do not deal in the same concepts as the European Court of Human Rights limits the extent to which their judgments can be drawn upon and followed. Enabling the Convention rights to be judged by British courts will also lead to closer scrutiny of the human rights implications of new legislation and new policies. If legislation is enacted which is incompatible with the Convention, a ruling by the domestic courts to that effect will be much more direct and immediate than a ruling from the European Court of Human Rights. The Government of the day, and Parliament, will want to minimise the risk of that happening.

1.19   Our aim is a straightforward one. It is to make more directly accessible the rights which the British people already enjoy under the Convention. In other words, to bring those rights home.

---

1   Protocol 11 to the Convention, which will come into force on 1 November 1998, will replace the existing part-time European Commission and Court of Human Rights with a single full-time Court.

Chapter 2 – The Government's Proposals for Enforcing the Convention Rights

2.1   The essential feature of the Human Rights Bill is that the United Kingdom will not be bound to give effect to the Convention rights merely as a matter of international law, but will also give them further effect directly in our domestic law. But there is more than one way of achieving this. This Chapter explains the choices which the Government has made for the Bill.

A new requirement on public authorities

2.2   Although the United Kingdom has an international obligation to comply with the Convention, there at present is no requirement in our domestic law on central and local government, or others exercising similar executive powers, to exercise those powers in a way which is compatible with the Convention. This Bill will change that by making it unlawful for public authorities to act in a way which is incompatible with the Convention rights. The definition of what constitutes a public authority is in wide terms. Examples of persons or organisations whose acts or omissions it is intended should be able to be challenged include central government (including executive agencies); local government; the police; immigration officers; prisons; courts and tribunals themselves; and, to the extent that they are exercising public functions, companies responsible for areas of activity which were previously within the public sector, such as the privatised utilities. The actions of Parliament, however, are excluded.

2.3   A person who is aggrieved by an act or omission on the part of a public authority which is incompatible with the Convention rights will be able to challenge the act or omission in the courts. The effects will be wide-ranging. They will extend both to legal actions which a public authority pursues against individuals (for example, where a criminal prosecution is brought or where an administrative decision is being enforced through legal proceedings) and to cases which individuals pursue against a public authority (for example, for judicial review of an executive decision). Convention points will normally be taken in the context of proceedings instituted against individuals or already open to them, but, if none is available, it will be possible for people to bring cases on Convention grounds alone. Individuals or organisations seeking judicial review of decisions by public authorities on Convention grounds will need to show that they have been directly affected, as they must if they take a case to Strasbourg.

2.4   It is our intention that people or organisations should be able to argue that their Convention rights have been infringed by a public authority in our courts at any level. This will enable the Convention rights to be applied from the outset against the facts and background of a particular case, and the people concerned to obtain their remedy at the earliest possible moment. We think this is preferable to allowing cases to run their ordinary course but then referring them to some kind of separate constitutional court which, like the European Court of Human Rights, would simply review cases which had already passed through the regular legal machinery. In considering Convention points, our courts will be required to take account of relevant decisions of the European Commission and Court of Human Rights (although these will not be binding).

2.5   The Convention is often described as a 'living instrument' because it is interpreted by the European Court in the light of present day conditions and therefore reflects changing social attitudes and the changes in the circumstances of society. In future our judges will be able to contribute to this dynamic and evolving interpretation of the Convention. In particular, our courts will be required to balance the protection of individuals' fundamental rights against the demands of the general interest of the community, particularly in relation to Articles 8 – 11 where a State may restrict the protected right to the extent that this is 'necessary in a democratic society'.

Remedies for a failure to comply with the Convention

2.6   A public authority which is found to have acted unlawfully by failing to comply with the Convention will not be exposed to criminal penalties. But the court or tribunal will be able to grant the injured person any remedy which is within its normal powers to grant and which it considers appropriate and just in the circumstances. What remedy is appropriate will of course depend both on the facts of the case and on a proper balance between the rights of the individual and the public interest. In some cases, the right course may be for the decision of the public authority in the particular case to be quashed. In other cases, the only appropriate remedy may be an award of damages. The Bill provides that, in considering an award of damages on Convention grounds, the courts are to take into account the principles applied by the European Court of Human Rights in awarding compensation, so that people will be able to receive compensation from a domestic court equivalent to what they would have received in Strasbourg.

Interpretation of legislation

2.7   The Bill provides for legislation – both Acts of Parliament and secondary legislation – to be interpreted so far as possible so as to be compatible with the Convention. This goes far beyond the present rule which enables the courts to take the Convention into account in resolving any ambiguity in a legislative provision. The courts will be required to interpret legislation so as to uphold the Convention rights unless the legislation itself is so clearly incompatible with the Convention that it is impossible to do so.

2.8   This 'rule of construction' is to apply to past as well as to future legislation. To the extent that it affects the meaning of a legislative provision, the courts will not be bound by previous interpretations. They will be able to build a new body of case law, taking into account the Convention rights.

A declaration of incompatibility with the Convention rights

2.9   If the courts decide in any case that it is impossible to interpret an Act of Parliament in a way which is compatible with the Convention, the Bill enables a formal declaration to be made that its provisions are incompatible with the Convention. A declaration of incompatibility will be an important statement to make, and the power to make it will be reserved to the higher courts. They will be able to make a declaration in any proceedings before them, whether the case originated with them (as, in the High Court, on judicial review of an executive act) or in considering an appeal from a lower court or tribunal. The Government will have the right to intervene in any proceedings where such a declaration is a possible outcome. A decision by the High Court or Court of Appeal, determining whether or not such a declaration should be made, will itself be appealable.

Effect of court decisions on legislation

2.10   A declaration that legislation is incompatible with the Convention rights will not of itself have the effect of changing the law, which will continue to apply. But it will almost certainly prompt the Government and Parliament to change the law.

2.11   The Government has considered very carefully whether it would be right for the Bill to go further, and give to courts in the United Kingdom the power to set aside an Act of Parliament which they believe is incompatible with the Convention rights. In considering this question, we have looked at a number of models. The Canadian Charter of Rights and

Freedoms 1982 enables the courts to strike down any legislation which is inconsistent with the Charter, unless the legislation contains an explicit statement that it is to apply 'notwithstanding' the provisions of the Charter. But legislation which has been struck down may be re-enacted with a 'notwithstanding' clause. In New Zealand, on the other hand, although there was an earlier proposal for legislation on lines similar to the Canadian Charter, the human rights legislation which was eventually enacted after wide consultation took a different form. The New Zealand Bill of Rights Act 1990 is an 'interpretative' statute which requires past and future legislation to be interpreted consistently with the rights contained in the Act as far as possible but provides that legislation stands if that is impossible. In Hong Kong, a middle course was adopted. The Hong Kong Bill of Rights Ordinance 1991 distinguishes between legislation enacted before and after the Ordinance took effect: previous legislation is subordinated to the provisions of the Ordinance, but subsequent legislation takes precedence over it.

2.12   The Government has also considered the European Communities Act 1972 which provides for European law, in cases where that law has 'direct effect', to take precedence over domestic law. There is, however, an essential difference between European Community law and the European Convention on Human Rights, because it is a **requirement** of membership of the European Union that member States give priority to directly effective EC law in their own legal systems. There is no such requirement in the Convention.

2.13   The Government has reached the conclusion that courts should not have the power to set aside primary legislation, past or future, on the ground of incompatibility with the Convention. This conclusion arises from the importance which the Government attaches to Parliamentary sovereignty. In this context, Parliamentary sovereignty means that Parliament is competent to make any law on any matter of its choosing and no court may question the validity of any Act that it passes. In enacting legislation, Parliament is making decisions about important matters of public policy. The authority to make those decisions derives from a democratic mandate. Members of Parliament in the House of Commons possess such a mandate because they are elected, accountable and representative. To make provision in the Bill for the courts to set aside Acts of Parliament would confer on the judiciary a general power over the decisions of Parliament which under our present constitutional arrangements they do not possess, and would be likely on occasions to draw the judiciary into serious conflict with Parliament. There is no evidence to suggest that they desire this power, nor that the public wish them to have it. Certainly, this Government has no mandate for any such change.

2.14   It has been suggested that the courts should be able to uphold the rights in the Human Rights Bill in preference to any provisions of earlier legislation which are incompatible with those rights. This is on the basis that a later Act of Parliament takes precedence over an earlier Act if there is a conflict. But the Human Rights Bill is intended to provide a new basis for judicial interpretation of all legislation, not a basis for striking down any part of it.

2.15   The courts will, however, be able to strike down or set aside secondary legislation which is incompatible with the Convention, unless the terms of the parent statute make this impossible. The courts can already strike down or set aside secondary legislation when they consider it to be outside the powers conferred by the statute under which it is made, and it is right that they should be able to do so when it is incompatible with the Convention rights and could have been framed differently.

Entrenchment

2.16   On one view, human rights legislation is so important that it should be given added protection from subsequent amendment or repeal. The Constitution of the United States of America, for example, guarantees rights which can be amended or repealed only by securing qualified majorities in both the House of Representatives and the Senate, and among the States themselves. But an arrangement of this kind could not be reconciled with our own constitutional traditions, which allow any Act of Parliament to be amended or repealed by a subsequent Act of Parliament. We do not believe that it is necessary or would be desirable to attempt to devise such a special arrangement for this Bill.

Amending legislation

2.17   Although the Bill does not allow the courts to set aside Acts of Parliament, it will nevertheless have a profound impact on the way that legislation is interpreted and applied, and it will have the effect of putting the issues squarely to the Government and Parliament for further consideration. It is important to ensure that the Government and Parliament, for their part, can respond quickly. In the normal way, primary legislation can be amended only by further primary legislation, and this can take a long time. Given the volume of Government business, an early opportunity to legislate may not arise; and the process of legislating is itself protracted. Emergency legislation can be enacted very quickly indeed, but it is introduced only in the most exceptional circumstances.

2.18   The Bill provides for a fast-track procedure for changing legislation in response either to a declaration of incompatibility by our own higher courts or to a finding of a violation of the Convention in Strasbourg. The appropriate Government Minister will be able to amend the legislation by Order so as to make it compatible with the Convention. The Order will be subject to approval by both Houses of Parliament before taking effect, except where the need to amend the legislation is particularly urgent, when the Order will take effect immediately but will expire after a short period if not approved by Parliament.

2.19   There are already precedents for using secondary legislation to amend primary legislation in some circumstances, and we think the use of such a procedure is acceptable in this context and would be welcome as a means of improving the observance of human rights. Plainly the Minister would have to exercise this power only in relation to the provisions which contravene the Convention, together with any necessary consequential amendments. In other words, Ministers would not have carte blanche to amend unrelated parts of the Act in which the breach is discovered.

Scotland

2.20   In Scotland, the position with regard to Acts of the Westminster Parliament will be the same as in England and Wales. All courts will be required to interpret the legislation in a way which is compatible with the Convention so far as possible. If a provision is found to be incompatible with the Convention, the Court of Session or the High Court will be able to make a declarator to that effect, but this will not affect the validity or continuing operation of the provision.

2.21   The position will be different, however, in relation to Acts of the Scottish Parliament when it is established. The Government has decided that the Scottish Parliament will have no power to legislate in a way which is incompatible with the Convention; and similarly that the Scottish Executive will have no power to make subordinate legislation or to take executive action which is incompatible with the Convention. It will accordingly be possible to challenge such legislation and actions in the Scottish courts on the ground that the Scottish Parliament or Executive has incorrectly applied its powers. If the challenge is successful then the legislation or action would be held to be unlawful. As with other issues concerning the powers of the Scottish Parliament, there will be a procedure for inferior courts to refer such issues to the superior Scottish courts; and those courts in turn will be able to refer the matter to the Judicial Committee of the Privy Council. If such issues are decided by the superior Scottish courts, an appeal from their decision will be to the Judicial Committee. These arrangements are in line with the Government's general approach to devolution.

Wales

2.22 Similarly, the Welsh Assembly will not have power to make subordinate legislation or take executive action which is incompatible with the Convention. It will be possible to challenge such legislation and action in the courts, and for them to be quashed, on the ground that the Assembly has exceeded its powers.

Northern Ireland

2.23 Acts of the Westminster Parliament will be treated in the same way in Northern Ireland as in the rest of the United Kingdom. But Orders in Council and other related legislation will be treated as subordinate legislation. In other words, they will be struck down by the courts if they are incompatible with the Convention. Most such legislation is a temporary means of enacting legislation which would otherwise be done by measures of a devolved Northern Ireland legislature.

Chapter 3 – Improving Compliance with the Convention Rights

3.1 The enforcement of Convention rights will be a matter for the courts, whilst the Government and Parliament will have the different but equally important responsibility of revising legislation where necessary. But it is also highly desirable for the Government to ensure as far as possible that legislation which it places before Parliament in the normal way is compatible with the Convention rights, and for Parliament to ensure that the human rights implications of legislation are subject to proper consideration before the legislation is enacted.

Government legislation

3.2 The Human Rights Bill introduces a new procedure to make the human rights implications of proposed Government legislation more transparent. The responsible Minister will be required to provide a statement that in his or her view the proposed Bill is compatible with the Convention. The Government intends to include this statement alongside the Explanatory and Financial Memorandum which accompanies a Bill when it is introduced into each House of Parliament.

3.3 There may be occasions where such a statement cannot be provided, for example because it is essential to legislate on a particular issue but the policy in question requires a risk to be taken in relation to the Convention, or because the arguments in relation to the Convention issues raised are not clear-cut. In such cases, the Minister will indicate that he or she cannot provide a positive statement but that the Government nevertheless wishes Parliament to proceed to consider the Bill. Parliament would expect the Minister to explain his or her reasons during the normal course of the proceedings on the Bill. This will ensure that the human rights implications are debated at the earliest opportunity.

Consideration of draft legislation within Government

3.4   The new requirement to make a statement about the compliance of draft legislation with the Convention will have a significant and beneficial impact on the preparation of draft legislation within Government before its introduction into Parliament. It will ensure that all Ministers, their departments and officials are fully seized of the gravity of the Convention's obligations in respect of human rights. But we also intend to strengthen collective Government procedures so as to ensure that a proper assessment is made of the human rights implications when collective approval is sought for a new policy, as well as when any draft Bill is considered by Ministers. Revised guidance to Departments on these procedures will, like the existing guidance, be publicly available.

3.5   Some central co-ordination will also be extremely desirable in considering the approach to be taken to Convention points in criminal or civil proceedings, or in proceedings for judicial review, to which a Government department is a party. This is likely to require an inter-departmental group of lawyers and administrators meeting on a regular basis to ensure that a consistent approach is taken and to ensure that developments in case law are well understood by all those in Government who are involved in proceedings on Convention points. We do not, however, see any need to make a particular Minister responsible for promoting human rights across Government, or to set up a separate new Unit for this purpose. The responsibility for complying with human rights requirements rests on the Government as a whole.

A Parliamentary Committee on Human Rights

3.6   *Bringing Rights Home* suggested that 'Parliament itself should play a leading role in protecting the rights which are at the heart of a parliamentary democracy'. How this is achieved is a matter for Parliament to decide, but in the Government's view the best course would be to establish a new Parliamentary Committee with functions relating to human rights. This would not require legislation or any change in Parliamentary procedure. There could be a Joint Committee of both Houses of Parliament or each House could have its own Committee; or there could be a Committee which met jointly for some purposes and separately for others.

3.7   The new Committee might conduct enquiries on a range of human rights issues relating to the Convention, and produce reports so as to assist the Government and Parliament in deciding what action to take. It might also want to range more widely, and examine issues relating to the other international obligations of the United Kingdom such as proposals to accept new rights under other human rights treaties.

Should there be a Human Rights Commission?

3.8   *Bringing Rights Home* canvassed views on the establishment of a Human Rights Commission, and this possibility has received a good deal of attention. No commitment to establish a Commission was, however, made in the Manifesto on which the Government was elected. The Government's priority is implementation of its Manifesto commitment to give further effect to the Convention rights in domestic law so that people can enforce those rights in United Kingdom courts. Establishment of a new Human Rights Commission is not central to that objective and does not need to form part of the current Bill.

3.9   Moreover, the idea of setting up a new human rights body is not universally acclaimed. Some reservations have been expressed, particularly from the point of view of the impact on existing bodies concerned with particular aspects of human rights, such as the Commission for Racial Equality and the Equal Opportunities Commission, whose primary concern is to protect the rights for which they were established. A quinquennial review is currently being conducted of the Equal Opportunities Commission, and the Government has also decided to establish a new Disability Rights Commission.

3.10 The Government's conclusion is that, before a Human Rights Commission could be established by legislation, more consideration needs to be given to how it would work in relation to such bodies, and to the new arrangements to be established for Parliamentary and Government scrutiny of human rights issues. This is necessary not only for the purposes of framing the legislation but also to justify the additional public expenditure needed to establish and run a new Commission. A range of organisational issues need more detailed consideration before the legislative and financial case for a new Commission is made, and there needs to be a greater degree of consensus on an appropriate model among existing human rights bodies.

3.11 However, the Government has not closed its mind to the idea of a new Human Rights Commission at some stage in the future in the light of practical experience of the working of the new legislation. If Parliament establishes a Committee on Human Rights, one of its main tasks might be to conduct an inquiry into whether a Human Rights Commission is needed and how it should operate. The Government would want to give full weight to the Committee's report in considering whether to create a statutory Human Rights Commission in future.

3.12 It has been suggested that a new Commission might be funded from non-Government sources. The Government would not wish to deter a move towards a non-statutory, privately-financed body if its role was limited to functions such as public education and advice to individuals. However, a non-statutory body could not absorb any of the functions of the existing statutory bodies concerned with aspects of human rights.

Chapter 4 – Derogations, Reservations and other Protocols

Derogations

4.1 Article 15 of the Convention permits a State to derogate from certain Articles of the Convention in time of war or other public emergency threatening the life of the nation. The United Kingdom has one derogation in place, in respect of Article 5(3) of the Convention.

4.2 The derogation arose from a case in 1988 in which the European Court of Human Rights held that the detention of the applicants in the case before it under the Prevention of Terrorism (Temporary Provisions) Act 1984 for more than four days constituted a breach of Article 5(3) of the Convention, because they had not been brought promptly before a judicial authority. The Government of the day entered a derogation following the judgment in order to preserve the Secretary of State's power under the Act to extend the period of detention of persons suspected of terrorism connected with the affairs of Northern Ireland for a total of up to seven days. The validity of the derogation was subsequently upheld by the European Court of Human Rights in another case in 1993.

4.3 We are considering what change might be made to the arrangements under the prevention of terrorism legislation. Substituting judicial for executive authority for extensions, which would mean that the derogation could be withdrawn, would require primary legislation. In the meantime, however, the derogation remains necessary. The Bill sets out the text of the derogation, and Article 5(3) will have effect in domestic law for the time being subject to its terms.

4.4 Given our commitment to promoting human rights, however, we would not want the derogation to remain in place indefinitely without good reasons. Accordingly its effect in domestic law will be time-limited. If not withdrawn earlier, it will expire five years after the

Bill comes into force unless both Houses of Parliament agree that it should be renewed, and similarly thereafter. The Bill contains similar provision in respect of any new derogation which may be entered in future.

Reservations

4.5   Article 64 of the Convention allows a state to enter a reservation when a law in force is not in conformity with a Convention provision. The United Kingdom is a party to the First Protocol to the Convention, but has a reservation in place in respect of Article 2 of the Protocol. Article 2 sets out two principles. The first states that no person shall be denied the right to education. The second is that, in exercising any functions in relation to education and teaching, the State shall respect the right of parents to ensure that such education and teaching is in conformity with their own religious and philosophical convictions. The reservation makes it clear that the United Kingdom accepts this second principle only so far as it is compatible with the provision of efficient instruction and training, and the avoidance of unreasonable public expenditure.

4.6   The reservation reflects the fundamental principle originally enacted in the Education Act 1944, and now contained in section 9 of the Education Act 1996, 'that pupils are to be educated in accordance with the wishes of their parents so far as that is compatible with the provision of efficient instruction and training and the avoidance of unreasonable public expenditure'. There is similar provision in Scottish legislation. The reservation does not affect the right to education in Article 2. Nor does it deny parents the right to have account taken of their religious or philosophical convictions. Its purpose is to recognise that in the provision of State-funded education a balance must be struck in some cases between the convictions of parents and what is educationally sound and affordable.

4.7   Having carefully considered this, the Government has concluded that the reservation should be kept in place. Its text is included in the Bill, and Article 2 of the First Protocol will have effect in domestic law subject to its terms.

4.8   Whilst derogations are permitted under the Convention only in times of war or other public emergency, and so are clearly temporary, there is no such limitation in respect of reservations. We do not therefore propose to make the effect of the reservation in domestic law subject to periodic renewal by Parliament, but the Bill requires the Secretary of State (the Secretary of State for Education and Employment) to review the reservation every five years and to lay a report before Parliament.

Other Protocols

4.9   Protocols 4, 6 and 7 guarantee a number of rights additional to those in the original Convention itself and its First Protocol. These further rights have been added largely to reflect the wider range of rights subsequently included under the International Covenant on Civil and Political Rights. There is no obligation upon States who are party to the original Convention to accept these additional Protocols, but the Government has taken the opportunity to review the position of the United Kingdom on Protocols 4, 6 and 7.

4.10   **Protocol 4** contains a prohibition on the deprivation of liberty on grounds of inability to fulfil contractual obligations; a right to liberty of movement; a right to non-expulsion from the home State; a right of entry to the State of which a person is a national; and a prohibition on the collective expulsion of aliens. These provisions largely reflect similar (but not identical) rights provided under the International Covenant on Civil and Political Rights. Protocol 4 was signed by the United Kingdom in 1963 but not subsequently ratified because of concerns about what is the exact extent of the obligation regarding a right of entry.

4.11 These are important rights, and we would like to see them given formal recognition in our law. But we also believe that existing laws in relation to different categories of British nationals must be maintained. It will be possible to ratify Protocol 4 only if the potential conflicts with our domestic laws can be resolved. This remains under consideration but we do not propose to ratify Protocol 4 at present.

4.12 **Protocol 6** requires the complete abolition of the death penalty other than in time of war or imminent threat of war. It does not permit any derogation or reservation. The Protocol largely parallels the Second Optional Protocol to the International Covenant on Civil and Political Rights, which the United Kingdom has not accepted.

4.13 The death penalty was abolished as a sentence for murder in 1965 following a free vote in the House of Commons. It remains as a penalty for treason, piracy with violence, and certain armed forces offences. No execution for these offences has taken place since 1946, when the war-time Nazi propagandist William Joyce (known as Lord Haw-Haw) was hanged at Wandsworth prison. The last recorded execution for piracy was in 1830. Thus there might appear to be little difficulty in our ratifying Protocol 6. This would, however, make it impossible for a United Kingdom Parliament to re-introduce the death penalty for murder, short of denouncing the European Convention. The view taken so far is that the issue is not one of basic constitutional principle but is a matter of judgement and conscience to be decided by Members of Parliament as they see fit. For these reasons, we do not propose to ratify Protocol 6 at present.

4.14 **Protocol 7** contains a prohibition on the expulsion of aliens without a decision in accordance with the law or opportunities for review; a right to a review of conviction or sentence after criminal conviction; a right to compensation following a miscarriage of justice; a prohibition on double jeopardy in criminal cases; and a right to equality between spouses. These rights reflect similar rights protected under the International Covenant on Civil and Political Rights.

4.15 In general, the provisions of Protocol 7 reflect principles already inherent in our law. In view of concerns in some of these areas in recent years, the Government believes that it would be particularly helpful to give these important principles the same legal status as other rights in the Convention by ratifying and incorporating Protocol 7. There is, however, a difficulty with this because a few provisions of our domestic law, for example in relation to the property rights of spouses, could not be interpreted in a way which is compatible with Protocol 7. The Government intends to legislate to remove these inconsistencies, when a suitable opportunity occurs, and then to sign and ratify the Protocol.

4.16 The Secretary of State will be able to amend the Human Rights Act by Order so as to insert into it the rights contained in any Protocols to the Convention which the United Kingdom ratifies in future. The Order will be subject to approval by both Houses of Parliament. The Bill also enables any reservation to a Protocol to be added, but as with the existing reservation it will have to be reviewed every five years if not withdrawn earlier.

APPENDIX 3

Human Rights Act 1998

(1998 c 42)

ARRANGEMENT OF SECTIONS

Introduction

Legislation

Public authorities

Remedial action

Other rights and proceedings

Derogations and reservations

Judges of the European Court of Human Rights

Parliamentary procedure

Supplemental

SCHEDULES:

An Act to give further effect to rights and freedoms guaranteed under the European Convention on Human Rights; to make provision with respect to holders of certain judicial offices who become judges of the European Court of Human Rights; and for connected purposes.

[9th November 1998]

Introduction

1   The Convention Rights

(1)　In this Act, 'the Convention rights' means the rights and fundamental freedoms set out in—

(a)　Articles 2 to 12 and 14 of the Convention,
(b)　Articles 1 to 3 of the First Protocol, and
(c)　Articles 1 and 2 of the Sixth Protocol,

as read with Articles 16 to 18 of the Convention.

(2)　Those Articles are to have effect for the purposes of this Act subject to any designated derogation or reservation (as to which see sections 14 and 15).

(3)　The Articles are set out in Schedule 1.

(4)　The Secretary of State may by order make such amendments to this Act as he considers appropriate to reflect the effect, in relation to the United Kingdom, of a protocol.

(5)　In subsection (4) 'protocol' means a protocol to the Convention—

(a)　which the United Kingdom has ratified; or
(b)　which the United Kingdom has signed with a view to ratification.

(6)　No amendment may be made by an order under subsection (4) so as to come into force before the protocol concerned is in force in relation to the United Kingdom.

2   Interpretation of Convention rights

(1)　A court or tribunal determining a question which has arisen in connection with a Convention right must take into account any—

(a)　judgment, decision, declaration or advisory opinion of the European Court of Human Rights,
(b)　opinion of the Commission given in a report adopted under Article 31 of the Convention,
(c)　decision of the Commission in connection with Article 26 or 27(2) of the Convention, or
(d)　decision of the Committee of Ministers taken under Article 46 of the Convention,

whenever made or given, so far as, in the opinion of the court or tribunal, it is relevant to the proceedings in which that question has arisen.

(2)   Evidence of any judgment, decision, declaration or opinion of which account may have to be taken under this section is to be given in proceedings before any court or tribunal in such manner as may be provided by rules.

(3)   In this section 'rules' means rules of court or, in the case of proceedings before a tribunal, rules made for the purposes of this section—

   (a) by the Lord Chancellor or the Secretary of State, in relation to proceedings outside Scotland;
   (b) by the Secretary of State, in relation to proceedings in Scotland; or
   (c) by a Northern Ireland department, in relation to proceedings before a Tribunal in Northern Ireland—
      (i)   which deals with transferred matters; and
      (ii) for which no rules made under paragraph (a) are in force.

Legislation

3   Interpretation of legislation

(1)   So far as it is possible to do so, primary legislation and subordinate legislation must be read and given effect in a way which is compatible with the Convention rights.

(2)   This section—

   (a) applies to primary legislation and subordinate legislation whenever enacted;
   (b) does not affect the validity, continuing operation or enforcement of any incompatible primary legislation; and
   (c) does not affect the validity, continuing operation or enforcement of any incompatible subordinate legislation if (disregarding any possibility of revocation) primary legislation prevents removal of the incompatibility.

4   Declaration of incompatibility

(1)   Subsection (2) applies in any proceedings in which a court determines whether a provision of primary legislation is compatible with a Convention right.

(2)   If the court is satisfied that the provision is incompatible with a Convention right, it may make a declaration of that incompatibility.

(3)   Subsection (4) applies in any proceedings in which a court determines whether a provision of subordinate legislation, made in the exercise of a power conferred by primary legislation, is compatible with a Convention right.

(4)   If the court is satisfied—

   (a) that the provision is incompatible with a Convention right, and
   (b) that (disregarding any possibility of revocation) the primary legislation concerned prevents removal of the incompatibility,

it may make a declaration of that incompatibility.

(5)   In this section 'court' means—

   (a) the House of Lords;
   (b) the Judicial Committee of the Privy Council;
   (c) the Courts-Martial Appeal Court;
   (d) in Scotland, the High Court of Justiciary sitting otherwise than as a trial court or the Court of Session;
   (e) in England and Wales or Northern Ireland, the High Court or the Court of Appeal.

(6)   A declaration under this section ('a declaration of incompatibility')—

  (a) does not affect the validity, continuing operation or enforcement of the provision in respect of which it is given; and
  (b) is not binding on the parties to the proceedings in which it is made.

5   Right of Crown to intervene

(1)   Where a court is considering whether to make a declaration of incompatibility, the Crown is entitled to notice in accordance with rules of court.

(2)   In any case to which subsection (1) applies—

  (a) a Minister of the Crown (or a person nominated by him),
  (b) a member of the Scottish Executive,
  (c) a Northern Ireland Minister,
  (d) a Northern Ireland department,

is entitled, on giving notice in accordance with rules of court, to be joined as a party to the proceedings.

(3)   Notice under subsection (2) may be given at any time during the proceedings.

(4)   A person who has been made a party to criminal proceedings (other than in Scotland) as the result of a notice under subsection (2) may, with leave, appeal to the House of Lords against any declaration of incompatibility made in the proceedings.

(5)   In subsection (4)—

'criminal proceedings' includes all proceedings before the Courts-Martial Appeal Court; and
'leave' means leave granted by the court making the declaration of incompatibility or by the House of Lords.

Public authorities

6   Acts of public authorities

(1)   It is unlawful for a public authority to act in a way which is incompatible with a Convention right.

(2)   Subsection (1) does not apply to an act if—

  (a) as the result of one or more provisions of primary legislation, the authority could not have acted differently; or
  (b) in the case of one or more provisions of, or made under, primary legislation which cannot be read or given effect in a way which is compatible with the Convention rights, the authority was acting so as to give effect to or enforce those provisions.

(3)   In this section, 'public authority' includes—

  (a) a court or tribunal, and
  (b) any person certain of whose functions are functions of a public nature,

but does not include either House of Parliament or a person exercising functions in connection with proceedings in Parliament.

(4)   In subsection (3) 'Parliament' does not include the House of Lords in its judicial capacity.

(5)   In relation to a particular act, a person is not a public authority by virtue only of subsection (3)(b) if the nature of the act is private.

(6)   'An act' includes a failure to act but does not include a failure to—

(a) introduce in, or lay before, Parliament a proposal for legislation; or

(b) make any primary legislation or remedial order.

7 Proceedings

(1) A person who claims that a public authority has acted (or proposes to act) in a way which is made unlawful by section 6(1) may—

(a) bring proceedings against the authority under this Act in the appropriate court or tribunal, or

(b) rely on the Convention right or rights concerned in any legal proceedings,

but only if he is (or would be) a victim of the unlawful act.

(2) In subsection (1)(a) 'appropriate court or tribunal' means such court or tribunal as may be determined in accordance with rules; and proceedings against an authority include a counterclaim or similar proceeding.

(3) If the proceedings are brought on an application for judicial review, the applicant is to be taken to have a sufficient interest in relation to the unlawful act only if he is, or would be, a victim of that act.

(4) If the proceedings are made by way of a petition for judicial review in Scotland, the applicant shall be taken to have title and interest to sue in relation to the unlawful act only if he is, or would be, a victim of that act.

(5) Proceedings under subsection (1)(a) must be brought before the end of—

(a) the period of one year beginning with the date on which the act complained of took place; or

(b) such longer period as the court or tribunal considers equitable having regard to all the circumstances,

but that is subject to any rule imposing a stricter time limit in relation to the procedure in question.

(6) In subsection (1)(b) 'legal proceedings' includes—

(a) proceedings brought by or at the instigation of a public authority; and

(b) an appeal against the decision of a court or tribunal.

(7) For the purposes of this section, a person is a victim of an unlawful act only if he would be a victim for the purposes of Article 34 of the Convention if proceedings were brought in the European Court of Human Rights in respect of that act.

(8) Nothing in this Act creates a criminal offence.

(9) In this section 'rules' means—

(a) in relation to proceedings before a court or tribunal outside Scotland, rules made by the Lord Chancellor or the Secretary of State for the purposes of this section or rules of court,

(b) in relation to proceedings before a court or tribunal in Scotland, rules made by the Secretary of State for those purposes,

(c) in relation to proceedings before a tribunal in Northern Ireland—

(i) which deals with transferred matters; and

(ii) for which no rules made under paragraph (a) are in force,

rules made by a Northern Ireland department for those purposes,

and includes provision made by order under section 1 of the Courts and Legal Services Act 1990.

(10) In making rules regard must be had to section 9.

(11)   The Minister who has power to make rules in relation to a particular tribunal may, to the extent he considers it necessary to ensure that the tribunal can provide an appropriate remedy in relation to an act (or proposed act) of a public authority which is (or would be) unlawful as a result of section 6(1), by order add to—

(a) the relief or remedies which the tribunal may grant; or
(b) the grounds on which it may grant any of them.

(12)   An order made under subsection (13) may contain such incidental, supplemental, consequential or transitional provision as the Minister making it considers appropriate.

(13)   'The Minister' includes the Northern Ireland department concerned.

8 Judicial remedies

(1)   In relation to any act (or proposed act) of a public authority which the court finds is (or would be) unlawful, it may grant such relief or remedy, or make such order, within its powers as it considers just and appropriate.

(2)   But damages may be awarded only by a court which has power to award damages, or to order the payment of compensation, in civil proceedings.

(3)   No award of damages is to be made unless, taking account of all the circumstances of the case, including—

(a) any other relief or remedy granted, or order made, in relation to the act in question (by that or any other court), and
(b) the consequences of any decision (of that or any other court) in respect of that act,

the court is satisfied that the award is necessary to afford just satisfaction to the person in whose favour it is made.

(4)   In determining—

(a) whether to award damages, or
(b) the amount of an award,

the court must take into account the principles applied by the European Court of Human Rights in relation to the award of compensation under Article 41 of the Convention.

(5)   A public authority against which damages are awarded is to be treated—

(a) in Scotland, for the purposes of section 3 of the Law Reform (Miscellaneous Provisions) (Scotland) Act 1940 as if the award were made in an action of damages in which the authority has been found liable in respect of loss or damage to the person to whom the award is made;
(b) for the purposes of the Civil Liability (Contribution) Act 1978 as liable in respect of damage suffered by the person to whom the award is made.

(6)   In this section—

'court' includes a tribunal;
'damages' means damages for an unlawful act of a public authority; and
'unlawful' means unlawful under section 6(1).

9 Judicial acts

(1)   Proceedings under section 7(1)(a) in respect of a judicial act may be brought only—

(a) by exercising a right of appeal;
(b) on an application (in Scotland a petition) for judicial review; or

(c) in such other forum as may be prescribed by rules.

(2)   That does not affect any rule of law which prevents a court from being the subject of judicial review.

(3)   In proceedings under this Act in respect of a judicial act done in good faith, damages may not be awarded otherwise than to compensate a person to the extent required by Article 5(5) of the Convention.

(4)   An award of damages permitted by subsection (3) is to be made against the Crown; but no award may be made unless the appropriate person, if not a party to the proceedings, is joined.

(5)   In this section—

'appropriate person' means the Minister responsible for the court concerned, or a person or government department nominated by him;
'court' includes a tribunal;
'judge' includes a member of a tribunal, a justice of the peace and a clerk or other officer entitled to exercise the jurisdiction of a court;
'judicial act' means a judicial act of a court and includes an act done on the instructions, or on behalf, of a judge; and
'rules' has the same meaning as in section 7(11).

Remedial action

10   Power to take remedial action

(1)   This section applies if—

(a) a provision of legislation has been declared under section 4 to be incompatible with a Convention right and, if an appeal lies—
  (i) all persons who may appeal have stated in writing that they do not intend to do so;
  (ii) the time for bringing an appeal has expired and no appeal has been brought within that time; or
  (iii) an appeal brought within that time has been determined or abandoned; or
(b) it appears to a Minister of the Crown or Her Majesty in Council that, having regard to a finding of the European Court of Human Rights made after the coming into force of this section in proceedings against the United Kingdom, a provision of legislation is incompatible with an obligation of the United Kingdom arising from the Convention.

(2)   If a Minister of the Crown considers that there are compelling reasons for proceeding under this section, he may by order make such amendments to the legislation as he considers necessary to remove the incompatibility.

(3)   If, in the case of subordinate legislation, a Minister of the Crown considers—

(a) that it is necessary to amend the primary legislation under which the subordinate legislation in question was made, in order to enable the incompatibility to be removed, and
(b) that there are compelling reasons for proceeding under this section,

he may by order make such amendments to the primary legislation as he considers necessary.

(4)   This section also applies where the provision in question is in subordinate legislation and has been quashed, or declared invalid, by reason of incompatibility with a Convention right and the Minister proposes to proceed under paragraph 2(b) of Schedule 2.

(5)   If the legislation is an Order in Council, the power conferred by subsection (2) or (3) is exercisable by Her Majesty in Council.

(6)   In this section 'legislation' does not include a Measure of the Church Assembly or of the General Synod of the Church of England.

(7)   Schedule 2 makes further provision about remedial orders.

Other rights and proceedings

11   Safeguard for existing human rights

A person's reliance on a Convention right does not restrict—

    (a) any other right or freedom conferred on him by or under any law having effect in any part of the United Kingdom; or

    (b) his right to make any claim or bring any proceedings which he could make or bring apart from sections 7 to 9.

12   Freedom of expression

(1)   This section applies if a court is considering whether to grant any relief which, if granted, might affect the exercise of the Convention right to freedom of expression.

(2)   If the person against whom the application for relief is made ('the respondent') is neither present nor represented, no such relief is to be granted unless the court is satisfied—

    (a) that the applicant has taken all practicable steps to notify the respondent; or

    (b) that there are compelling reasons why the respondent should not be notified.

(3)   No such relief is to be granted so as to restrain publication before trial unless the court is satisfied that the applicant is likely to establish that publication should not be allowed.

(4)   The court must have particular regard to the importance of the Convention right to freedom of expression and, where the proceedings relate to material which the respondent claims, or which appears to the court, to be journalistic, literary or artistic material (or to conduct connected with such material), to—

    (a) the extent to which—

       (i)   the material has, or is about to, become available to the public; or

       (ii)   it is, or would be, in the public interest for the material to be published;

    (b) any relevant privacy code.

(5)   In this section—

'court' includes a tribunal; and

'relief' includes any remedy or order (other than in criminal proceedings).

13   Freedom of thought, conscience and religion

(1)   If a court's determination of any question arising under this Act might affect the exercise by a religious organisation (itself or its members collectively) of the Convention right to freedom of thought, conscience and religion, it must have particular regard to the importance of that right.

(2)   In this section 'court' includes a tribunal.

Derogations and reservations

14 Derogations

(1)   In this Act, 'designated derogation' means—

  (a) the United Kingdom's derogation from Article 5(3) of the Convention; and
  (b) any derogation by the United Kingdom from an Article of the Convention, or of any protocol to the Convention, which is designated for the purposes of this Act in an order made by the Secretary of State.

(2)   The derogation referred to in subsection (1)(a) is set out in Part I of Schedule 3.

(3)   If a designated derogation is amended or replaced it ceases to be a designated derogation.

(4)   But subsection (3) does not prevent the Secretary of State from exercising his power under subsection (1)(b) to make a fresh designation order in respect of the Article concerned.

(5)   The Secretary of State must by order make such amendments to Schedule 3 as he considers appropriate to reflect—

  (a) any designation order; or
  (b) the effect of subsection (3).

(6)   A designation order may be made in anticipation of the making by the United Kingdom of a proposed derogation.

15 Reservations

(1)   In this Act, 'designated reservation' means—

  (a) the United Kingdom's reservation to Article 2 of the First Protocol to the Convention; and
  (b) any other reservation by the United Kingdom to an Article of the Convention, or of any protocol to the Convention, which is designated for the purposes of this Act in an order made by the Secretary of State.

(2)   The text of the reservation referred to in subsection (1)(a) is set out in Part II of Schedule 3.

(3)   If a designated reservation is withdrawn wholly or in part it ceases to be a designated reservation.

(4)   But subsection (3) does not prevent the Secretary of State from exercising his power under subsection (1)(b) to make a fresh designation order in respect of the Article concerned.

(5)   The Secretary of State must by order make such amendments to this Act as he considers appropriate to reflect—

  (a) any designation order; or
  (b) the effect of subsection (3).

16 Period for which designated derogations have effect

(1)   If it has not already been withdrawn by the United Kingdom, a designated derogation ceases to have effect for the purposes of this Act—

  (a) in the case of the derogation referred to in section 14(1)(a), at the end of the period of five years beginning with the date on which section 1(2) came into force;

(b) in the case of any other derogation, at the end of the period of five years beginning with the date on which the order designating it was made.

(2)   At any time before the period—

(a) fixed by subsection (1)(a) or (b), or
(b) extended by an order under this subsection,

comes to an end, the Secretary of State may by order extend it by a further period of five years.

(3)   An order under section 14(1)(b) ceases to have effect at the end of the period for consideration, unless a resolution has been passed by each House approving the order.

(4)   Subsection (3) does not affect—

(a) anything done in reliance on the order; or
(b) the power to make a fresh order under section 14(1)(b).

(5)   In subsection (3) 'period for consideration' means the period of forty days beginning with the day on which the order was made.

(6)   In calculating the period for consideration, no account is to be taken of any time during which—

(a) Parliament is dissolved or prorogued; or
(b) both Houses are adjourned for more than four days.

(7)   If a designated derogation is withdrawn by the United Kingdom, the Secretary of State must by order make such amendments to this Act as he considers are required to reflect that withdrawal.

17   Periodic review of designated reservations

(1)   The appropriate Minister must review the designated reservation referred to in section 15(1)(a)—

(a) before the end of the period of five years beginning with the date on which section 1(2) came into force; and
(b) if that designation is still in force, before the end of the period of five years beginning with the date on which the last report relating to it was laid under subsection (3).

(2)   The appropriate Minister must review each of the other designated reservations (if any)—

(a) before the end of the period of five years beginning with the date on which the order designating the reservation first came into force; and
(b) if the designation is still in force, before the end of the period of five years beginning with the date on which the last report relating to it was laid under subsection (3).

(3)   The Minister conducting a review under this section must prepare a report on the result of the review and lay a copy of it before each House of Parliament.

Judges of the European Court of Human Rights

18   Appointment to European Court of Human Rights

(1)   In this section 'judicial office' means the office of—

(a) Lord Justice of Appeal, Justice of the High Court or Circuit judge, in England and Wales;

(b) judge of the Court of Session or sheriff, in Scotland;

(c) Lord Justice of Appeal, judge of the High Court or county court judge, in Northern Ireland.

(2)   The holder of a judicial office may become a judge of the European Court of Human Rights ('the Court') without being required to relinquish his office.

(3)   But he is not required to perform the duties of his judicial office while he is a judge of the Court.

(4)   In respect of any period during which he is a judge of the Court—

(a) a Lord Justice of Appeal or Justice of the High Court is not to count as a judge of the relevant court for the purposes of section 2(1) or 4(1) of the Supreme Court Act 1981 (maximum number of judges) nor as a judge of the Supreme Court for the purposes of section 12(1) to (6) of that Act (salaries etc);

(b) a judge of the Court of Session is not to count as a judge of that court for the purposes of section 1(1) of the Court of Session Act 1988 (maximum number of judges) or of section 9(1)(c) of the Administration of Justice Act 1973 ('the 1973 Act') (salaries etc);

(c) a Lord Justice of Appeal or a judge of the High Court in Northern Ireland is not to count as a judge of the relevant court for the purposes of section 2(1) or 3(1) of the Judicature (Northern Ireland) Act 1978 (maximum number of judges) nor as a judge of the Supreme Court of Northern Ireland for the purposes of section 9(1)(d) of the 1973 Act (salaries etc);

(d) a Circuit judge is not to count as such for the purposes of section 18 of the Courts Act 1971 (salaries etc);

(e) a sheriff is not to count as such for the purposes of section 14 of the Sheriff Courts (Scotland) Act 1907 (salaries etc);

(f) a county court judge of Northern Ireland is not to count as such for the purposes of section 106 of the County Courts Act (Northern Ireland) 1959 (salaries etc).

(5)   If a sheriff principal is appointed a judge of the Court, section 11(1) of the Sheriff Courts (Scotland) Act 1971 (temporary appointment of sheriff principal) applies, while he holds that appointment, as if his office is vacant.

(6)   Schedule 3 makes provision about judicial pensions in relation to the holder of a judicial office who serves as a judge of the Court.

(7)   The Lord Chancellor or the Secretary of State may by order make such transitional provision (including, in particular, provision for a temporary increase in the maximum number of judges) as he considers appropriate in relation to any holder of a judicial office who has completed his service as a judge of the Court.

Parliamentary procedure

19   Statements of compatibility

(1)   A Minister of the Crown in charge of a Bill in either House of Parliament must, before Second Reading of the Bill—

(a) make a statement to the effect that in his view the provisions of the Bill are compatible with the Convention rights ('a statement of compatibility'); or

(b) make a statement to the effect that although he is unable to make a statement of compatibility the government nevertheless wishes the House to proceed with the Bill.

(2)   The statement must be in writing and be published in such manner as the Minister making it considers appropriate.

Supplemental

20 Orders etc under this Act

(1)   Any power of a Minister of the Crown to make an order under this Act is exercisable by statutory instrument.

(2)   The power of the Lord Chancellor or the Secretary of State to make rules (other than rules of court) under section 2(3) or 7(9) is exercisable by statutory instrument.

(3)   Any statutory instrument made under section 14, 15 or 16(7) must be laid before Parliament.

(4)   No order may be made by the Lord Chancellor or the Secretary of State under section 1(4), 7(13) or 16(2) unless a draft of the order has been laid before, and approved by, each House of Parliament.

(5)   Any statutory instrument made under section 18(7) or Schedule 4, or to which subsection (2) applies, shall be subject to annulment in pursuance of a resolution of either House of Parliament.

(6)   The power of a Northern Ireland department to make—

   (a) rules under section 2(3)(c) or 7(9)(c), or
   (b) an order under section 7(11),

is exercisable by statutory rule for the purposes of the Statutory Rules (Northern Ireland) Order 1979.

(7)   Any rules made under section 2(3)(c) or 7(9)(c) shall be subject to negative resolution; and section 41(6) of the Interpretation Act (Northern Ireland) 1954 (meaning of 'subject to negative resolution') shall apply as if the power to make the rules were conferred by an Act of the Northern Ireland Assembly.

(8)   No order may be made by a Northern Ireland department under section 7(11) unless a draft of the order has been laid before, and approved by, the Northern Ireland Assembly.

21 Interpretation, etc

(1)   In this Act—

'amend' includes repeal and apply (with or without modifications);
'the appropriate Minister' means the Minister of the Crown having charge of the appropriate authorised government department (within the meaning of the Crown Proceedings Act 1947);
'the Commission' means the European Commission of Human Rights;
'the Convention' means the Convention for the Protection of Human Rights and Fundamental Freedoms, agreed by the Council of Europe at Rome on 4th November 1950 as it has effect for the time being in relation to the United Kingdom;
'declaration of incompatibility' means a declaration under section 4;
'Minister of the Crown' has the same meaning as in the Ministers of the Crown Act 1975;
'Northern Ireland Minister' includes the First Minister and the deputy First Minister in Northern Ireland;
'primary legislation' means any—

   (a) public general Act;
   (b) local and personal Act;
   (c) private Act;
   (d) Measure of the Church Assembly;
   (e) Measure of the General Synod of the Church of England;
   (f) Order in Council—

   (i) made in exercise of Her Majesty's Royal Prerogative;
   (ii) made under section 38(1)(a) of the Northern Ireland Constitution Act 1973 or the corresponding provision of the Northern Ireland Act 1998; or
   (iii) amending an Act of a kind mentioned in paragraph (a), (b) or (c);

and includes an order or other instrument made under primary legislation (otherwise than by the National Assembly for Wales, a member of the Scottish Executive, a Northern Ireland Minister or a Northern Ireland department) to the extent to which it operates to bring one or more provisions of that legislation into force or amends any primary legislation;

'the First Protocol' means the protocol to the Convention agreed at Paris on 20th March 1952;

'the Sixth Protocol' means the protocol to the Convention agreed at Strasbourg on 28th April 1983;

'the Eleventh Protocol' means the protocol to the Convention (restructuring the control machinery established by the Convention) agreed at Strasbourg on 11th May 1994;

'remedial order' means an order under section 10;

'subordinate legislation' means any—

   (a) Order in Council other than one—
      (i) made in exercise of Her Majesty's Royal Prerogative;
      (ii) made under section 38(1)(a) of the Northern Ireland Constitution Act 1973 or the corresponding provision of the Northern Ireland Act 1998; or
      (iii) amending an Act of a kind mentioned in the definition of primary legislation;
   (b) Act of the Scottish Parliament;
   (c) Act of the Parliament of Northern Ireland;
   (d) Measure of the Assembly established under section 1 of the Northern Ireland Assembly Act 1973;
   (e) Act of the Northern Ireland Assembly;
   (f) order, rules, regulations, scheme, warrant, byelaw or other instrument made under primary legislation (except to the extent to which it operates to bring one or more provisions of that legislation into force or amends any primary legislation);
   (g) order, rules, regulations, scheme, warrant, byelaw or other instrument made under legislation mentioned in paragraph (b), (c), (d) or (e) or made under an Order in Council applying only to Northern Ireland;
   (h) order, rules, regulations, scheme, warrant, byelaw or other instrument made by a member of the Scotish Executive, a Northern Ireland Minister or a Northern Ireland department in exercise of prerogative or other executive functions of Her Majesty which are exercisable by such a person on behalf of Her Majesty;

'transferred matters' has the same meaning as in the Northern Ireland Act 1998; and

'tribunal' means any tribunal in which legal proceedings may be brought.

(2)   The references in paragraphs (b) and (c) of section 2(1) to Articles are to Articles of the Convention as they had effect immediately before the coming into force of the Eleventh Protocol.

(3)   The reference in paragraph (d) of section 2(1) to Article 46 includes a reference to Articles 32 and 54 of the Convention as they had effect immediately before the coming into force of the Eleventh Protocol.

(4)   The references in section 2(1) to a report or decision of the Commission or a decision of the Committee of Ministers include references to a report or decision made as provided by paragraphs 3, 4 and 6 of Article 5 of the Eleventh Protocol (transitional provisions).

(5)   Any liability under the Army Act 1955, the Air Force Act 1955 or the Naval Discipline Act 1957 to suffer death for an offence is replaced by a liability to imprisonment for life or

any less punishment authorised by those Acts; and those Acts shall accordingly have effect with the necessary modifications.

22 Short title, commencement, application and extent

(1)   This Act may be cited as the Human Rights Act 1998.

(2)   Sections 18 and 20 and this section come into force on the passing of this Act.

(3)   The other provisions of this Act come into force on such day as the Secretary of State may by order appoint; and different days may be appointed for different purposes.

(4)   Paragraph (b) of subsection (1) of section 7 applies to proceedings brought by or at the instigation of a public authority whenever the act in question took place; but otherwise that subsection does not apply to an act taking place before the coming into force of that section.

(5)   This Act binds the Crown.

(6)   This Act extends to Northern Ireland.

(7)   Section 21(5), so far as it relates to any provision contained in the Army Act 1955, the Air Force Act 1955 or the Naval Discipline Act 1957, extends to any place to which that provision extends.

SCHEDULES

SCHEDULE 1

THE ARTICLES

PART I

THE CONVENTION

Rights and Freedoms

Article 2

Right to life

1.   Everyone's right to life shall be protected by law. No one shall be deprived of his life intentionally save in the execution of a sentence of a court following his conviction of a crime for which this penalty is provided by law.

2.   Deprivation of life shall not be regarded as inflicted in contravention of this Article when it results from the use of force which is no more than absolutely necessary:

   (a) in defence of any person from unlawful violence;
   (b) in order to effect a lawful arrest or to prevent the escape of a person lawfully detained;
   (c) in action lawfully taken for the purpose of quelling a riot or insurrection.

Article 3

Prohibition of torture

No one shall be subjected to torture or to inhuman or degrading treatment or punishment.

Article 4

Prohibition of slavery and forced labour

1. No one shall be held in slavery or servitude.

2. No one shall be required to perform forced or compulsory labour.

3. For the purpose of this Article the term 'forced or compulsory labour' shall not include:

(a) any work required to be done in the ordinary course of detention imposed according to the provisions of Article 5 of this Convention or during conditional release from such detention;

(b) any service of a military character or, in case of conscientious objectors in countries where they are recognised, service exacted instead of compulsory military service;

(c) any service exacted in case of an emergency or calamity threatening the life or well-being of the community;

(d) any work or service which forms part of normal civic obligations.

Article 5

Right to liberty and security

1. Everyone has the right to liberty and security of person. No one shall be deprived of his liberty save in the following cases and in accordance with a procedure prescribed by law:

(a) the lawful detention of a person after conviction by a competent court;

(b) the lawful arrest or detention of a person for non-compliance with the lawful order of a court or in order to secure the fulfilment of any obligation prescribed by law;

(c) the lawful arrest or detention of a person effected for the purpose of bringing him before the competent legal authority on reasonable suspicion of having committed an offence or when it is reasonably considered necessary to prevent his committing an offence or fleeing after having done so;

(d) the detention of a minor by lawful order for the purpose of educational supervision or his lawful detention for the purpose of bringing him before the competent legal authority;

(e) the lawful detention of persons for the prevention of the spreading of infectious diseases, of persons of unsound mind, alcoholics or drug addicts or vagrants;

(f) the lawful arrest or detention of a person to prevent his effecting an unauthorised entry into the country or of a person against whom action is being taken with a view to deportation or extradition.

2. Everyone who is arrested shall be informed promptly, in a language which he understands, of the reasons for his arrest and of any charge against him.

3. Everyone arrested or detained in accordance with the provisions of paragraph 1(c) of this Article shall be brought promptly before a judge or other officer authorised by law to exercise judicial power and shall be entitled to trial within a reasonable time or to release pending trial. Release may be conditioned by guarantees to appear for trial.

4. Everyone who is deprived of his liberty by arrest or detention shall be entitled to take proceedings by which the lawfulness of his detention shall be decided speedily by a court and his release ordered if the detention is not lawful.

5. Everyone who has been the victim of arrest or detention in contravention of the provisions of this Article shall have an enforceable right to compensation.

Article 6

Right to a fair trial

1.   In the determination of his civil rights and obligations or of any criminal charge against him, everyone is entitled to a fair and public hearing within a reasonable time by an independent and impartial tribunal established by law. Judgment shall be pronounced publicly but the press and public may be excluded from all or part of the trial in the interest of morals, public order or national security in a democratic society, where the interests of juveniles or the protection of the private life of the parties so require, or to the extent strictly necessary in the opinion of the court in special circumstances where publicity would prejudice the interests of justice.

2.   Everyone charged with a criminal offence shall be presumed innocent until proved guilty according to law.

3.   Everyone charged with a criminal offence has the following minimum rights:

(a) to be informed promptly, in a language which he understands and in detail, of the nature and cause of the accusation against him;
(b) to have adequate time and facilities for the preparation of his defence;
(c) to defend himself in person or through legal assistance of his own choosing or, if he has not sufficient means to pay for legal assistance, to be given it free when the interests of justice so require;
(d) to examine or have examined witnesses against him and to obtain the attendance and examination of witnesses on his behalf under the same conditions as witnesses against him;
(e) to have the free assistance of an interpreter if he cannot understand or speak the language used in court.

Article 7

No punishment without law

1.   No one shall be held guilty of any criminal offence on account of any act or omission which did not constitute a criminal offence under national or international law at the time when it was committed. Nor shall a heavier penalty be imposed than the one that was applicable at the time the criminal offence was committed.

2.   This Article shall not prejudice the trial and punishment of any person for any act or omission which, at the time when it was committed, was criminal according to the general principles of law recognised by civilised nations.

Article 8

Right to respect for private and family life

1.   Everyone has the right to respect for his private and family life, his home and his correspondence.

2.   There shall be no interference by a public authority with the exercise of this right except such as is in accordance with the law and is necessary in a democratic society in the interests of national security, public safety or the economic well-being of the country, for the prevention of disorder or crime, for the protection of health or morals, or for the protection of the rights and freedoms of others.

Article 9

Freedom of thought, conscience and religion

1. Everyone has the right to freedom of thought, conscience and religion; this right includes freedom to change his religion or belief and freedom, either alone or in community with others and in public or private, to manifest his religion or belief, in worship, teaching, practice and observance.

2. Freedom to manifest one's religion or beliefs shall be subject only to such limitations as are prescribed by law and are necessary in a democratic society in the interests of public safety, for the protection of public order, health or morals, or for the protection of the rights and freedoms of others.

Article 10

Freedom of expression

1. Everyone has the right to freedom of expression. This right shall include freedom to hold opinions and to receive and impart information and ideas without interference by public authority and regardless of frontiers. This Article shall not prevent States from requiring the licensing of broadcasting, television or cinema enterprises.

2. The exercise of these freedoms, since it carries with it duties and responsibilities, may be subject to such formalities, conditions, restrictions or penalties as are prescribed by law and are necessary in a democratic society, in the interests of national security, territorial integrity or public safety, for the prevention of disorder or crime, for the protection of health or morals, for the protection of the reputation or rights of others, for preventing the disclosure of information received in confidence, or for maintaining the authority and impartiality of the judiciary.

Article 11

Freedom of assembly and association

1. Everyone has the right to freedom of peaceful assembly and to freedom of association with others, including the right to form and to join trade unions for the protection of his interests.

2. No restrictions shall be placed on the exercise of these rights other than such as are prescribed by law and are necessary in a democratic society in the interests of national security or public safety, for the prevention of disorder or crime, for the protection of health or morals or for the protection of the rights and freedoms of others. This Article shall not prevent the imposition of lawful restrictions on the exercise of these rights by members of the armed forces, of the police or of the administration of the State.

Article 12

Right to marry

Men and women of marriageable age have the right to marry and to found a family, according to the national laws governing the exercise of this right.

Article 14

Prohibition of discrimination

The enjoyment of the rights and freedoms set forth in this Convention shall be secured without discrimination on any ground such as sex, race, colour, language, religion, political or other opinion, national or social origin, association with a national minority, property, birth or other status.

Article 16

Restrictions on political activity of aliens

Nothing in Articles 10, 11 and 14 shall be regarded as preventing the High Contracting Parties from imposing restrictions on the political activity of aliens.

Article 17

Prohibition of abuse of rights

Nothing in this Convention may be interpreted as implying for any State, group or person any right to engage in any activity or perform any act aimed at the destruction of any of the rights and freedoms set forth herein or at their limitation to a greater extent than is provided for in the Convention.

Article 18

Limitation on use of restrictions on rights

The restrictions permitted under this Convention to the said rights and freedoms shall not be applied for any purpose other than those for which they have been prescribed.

PART II

THE FIRST PROTOCOL

Article 1

Protection of property

Every natural or legal person is entitled to the peaceful enjoyment of his possessions. No one shall be deprived of his possessions except in the public interest and subject to the conditions provided for by law and by the general principles of international law.

The preceding provisions shall not, however, in any way impair the right of a State to enforce such laws as it deems necessary to control the use of property in accordance with the general interest or to secure the payment of taxes or other contributions or penalties.

Article 2

Right to education

No person shall be denied the right to education. In the exercise of any functions which it assumes in relation to education and to teaching, the State shall respect the right of parents to ensure such education and teaching in conformity with their own religious and philosophical convictions.

Article 3

Right to free elections

The High Contracting Parties undertake to hold free elections at reasonable intervals by secret ballot, under conditions which will ensure the free expression of the opinion of the people in the choice of the legislature.

PART III

THE SIXTH PROTOCOL

Article 1

Abolition of the death penalty

The death penalty shall be abolished. No one shall be condemned to such penalty or executed.

Article 2

Death penalty in time of war

A State may make provisions in its law for the death penalty in respect of acts committed in time of war or of imminent threat of war; such penalty shall be applied only in the instances laid down in the law and in accordance with its provisions. The State shall communicate to the Secretary of the Council of Europe the relevant provisions of that law.

SCHEDULE 2

REMEDIAL ORDERS

Orders

1.—(1)   A remedial order may—

   (a) contain such incidental, supplemental, consequential or transitional provision as the person making it considers appropriate;
   (b) be made so as to have effect from a date earlier than that on which it is made;
   (c) make provision for the delegation of specific functions;
   (d) make different provision for different cases.

(2)   The power conferred by sub-paragraph (1)(a) includes—

   (a) power to amend primary legislation (including primary legislation other than that which contains the incompatible provision); and
   (b) power to amend or revoke subordinate legislation (including subordinate legislation other than that which contains the incompatible provision).

(3)   A remedial order may be made so as to have the same extent as the legislation which it affects.

(4)   No person is to be guilty of an offence solely as a result of the retrospective effect of a remedial order.

Procedure

2.   No remedial order may be made unless—

   (a) a draft of the order has been approved by a resolution of each House of Parliament made after the end of the period of 60 days beginning with the day on which the draft was laid; or
   (b) it is declared in the order that it appears to the person making it that, because of the urgency of the matter, it is necessary to make the order without a draft being so approved.

Orders laid in draft

3.—(1)   No draft may be laid under paragraph 2(a) unless—

(a) the person proposing to make the order has laid before Parliament a document which contains a draft of the proposed order and the required information; and

(b) the period of 60 days, beginning with the day on which the document required by this sub-paragraph was laid, has ended.

(2)   If representations have been made during that period, the draft laid under paragraph 2(a) must be accompanied by a statement containing—

(a) a summary of the representations; and

(b) if, as a result of the representations, the proposed order has been changed, details of the changes.

Urgent cases

4.—(1)   If a remedial order ('the original order') is made without being approved in draft, the person making it must lay it before Parliament, accompanied by the required information, after it is made.

(2) If representations have been made during the period of 60 days beginning with the day on which the original order was made, the person making it must (after the end of that period) lay before Parliament a statement containing—

(a) a summary of the representations; and

(b) if, as a result of the representations, he considers it appropriate to make changes to the original order, details of the changes.

(3)   If sub-paragraph (2)(b) applies, the person making the statement must—

(a) make a further remedial order replacing the original order; and

(b) lay the replacement order before Parliament.

(4)   If, at the end of the period of 120 days beginning with the day on which the original order was made, a resolution has not been passed by each House approving the original or replacement order, the order ceases to have effect (but without that affecting anything previously done under either order or the power to make a fresh remedial order).

Definitions

5.   In this Schedule—

'representations' means representations about a remedial order (or proposed remedial order) made to the person making (or proposing to make) it and includes any relevant Parliamentary report or resolution; and
'required information' means—

(a) an explanation of the incompatibility which the order (or proposed order) seeks to remove, including particulars of the relevant declaration, finding or order; and

(b) a statement of the reasons for proceeding under section 10 and for making an order in those terms.

Calculating periods

6.   In calculating any period for the purposes of this Schedule, no account is to be taken of any time during which—

(a) Parliament is dissolved or prorogued; or

(b) both Houses are adjourned for more than four days.

SCHEDULE 3

DEROGATION AND RESERVATION

PART I

DEROGATION

The 1988 notification

The United Kingdom Permanent Representative to the Council of Europe presents his compliments to the Secretary General of the Council, and has the honour to convey the following information in order to ensure compliance with the obligations of Her Majesty's Government in the United Kingdom under Article 15(3) of the Convention for the Protection of Human Rights and Fundamental Freedoms signed at Rome on 4 November 1950.

There have been in the United Kingdom in recent years campaigns of organised terrorism connected with the affairs of Northern Ireland which have manifested themselves in activities which have included repeated murder, attempted murder, maiming, intimidation and violent civil disturbance and in bombing and fire raising which have resulted in death, injury and widespread destruction of property. As a result, a public emergency within the meaning of Article 15(1) of the Convention exists in the United Kingdom.

The Government found it necessary in 1974 to introduce and since then, in cases concerning persons reasonably suspected of involvement in terrorism connected with the affairs of Northern Ireland, or of certain offences under the legislation, who have been detained for 48 hours, to exercise powers enabling further detention without charge, for periods of up to five days, on the authority of the Secretary of State. These powers are at present to be found in Section 12 of the Prevention of Terrorism (Temporary Provisions) Act 1984, Article 9 of the Prevention of Terrorism (Supplemental Temporary Provisions) Order 1984 and Article 10 of the Prevention of Terrorism (Supplemental Temporary Provisions) (Northern Ireland) Order 1984.

Section 12 of the Prevention of Terrorism (Temporary Provisions) Act 1984 provides for a person whom a constable has arrested on reasonable grounds of suspecting him to be guilty of an offence under Section 1, 9 or 10 of the Act, or to be or to have been involved in terrorism connected with the affairs of Northern Ireland, to be detained in right of the arrest for up to 48 hours and thereafter, where the Secretary of State extends the detention period, for up to a further five days. Section 12 substantially re-enacted Section 12 of the Prevention of Terrorism (Temporary Provisions) Act 1976 which, in turn, substantially re-enacted Section 7 of the Prevention of Terrorism (Temporary Provisions) Act 1974.

Article 10 of the Prevention of Terrorism (Supplemental Temporary Provisions) (Northern Ireland) Order 1984 (SI 1984/417) and Article 9 of the Prevention of Terrorism (Supplemental Temporary Provisions) Order 1984 (SI 1984/418) were both made under Sections 13 and 14 of and Schedule 3 to the 1984 Act and substantially re-enacted powers of detention in Orders made under the 1974 and 1976 Acts. A person who is being examined under Article 4 of either Order on his arrival in, or on seeking to leave, Northern Ireland or Great Britain for the purpose of determining whether he is or has been involved in terrorism connected with the affairs of Northern Ireland, or whether there are grounds for suspecting that he has committed an offence under Section 9 of the 1984 Act, may be detained under Article 4 or 10, as appropriate, pending the conclusion of his examination. The period of this examination may exceed 12 hours if an examining officer has reasonable grounds for suspecting him to be or to have been involved in acts of terrorism connected with the affairs of Northern Ireland.

Where such a person is detained under the said Article 9 or 10 he may be detained for up to 48 hours on the authority of an examining officer and thereafter, where the Secretary of State extends the detention period, for up to a further five days.

In its judgment of 29 November 1988 in the Case of *Brogan and Others*, the European Court of Human Rights held that there had been a violation of Article 5(3) in respect of each of the applicants, all of whom had been detained under Section 12 of the 1984 Act. The Court held that even the shortest of the four periods of detention concerned, namely four days and six hours, fell outside the constraints as to time permitted by the first part of Article 5(3). In addition, the Court held that there had been a violation of Article 5(3) in the case of each applicant.

Following this judgment, the Secretary of State for the Home Department informed Parliament on 6 December 1988 that, against the background of the terrorist campaign, and the over-riding need to bring terrorists to justice, the Government did not believe that the maximum period of detention should be reduced. He informed Parliament that the Government were examining the matter with a view to responding to the judgment. On 22 December 1988, the Secretary of State further informed Parliament that it remained the Government's wish, if it could be achieved, to find a judicial process under which extended detention might be reviewed and where appropriate authorised by a judge or other judicial officer. But a further period of reflection and consultation was necessary before the Government could bring forward a firm and final view.

Since the judgment of 29 November as well as previously, the Government have found it necessary to continue to exercise, in relation to terrorism connected with the affairs of Northern Ireland, the powers described above enabling further detention without charge for periods of up to 5 days, on the authority of the Secretary of State, to the extent strictly required by the exigencies of the situation to enable necessary enquiries and investigations properly to be completed in order to decide whether criminal proceedings should be instituted. To the extent that the exercise of these powers may be inconsistent with the obligations imposed by the Convention the Government has availed itself of the right of derogation conferred by Article 15(1) of the Convention and will continue to do so until further notice.

Dated 23 December 1988.

The 1989 notification

The United Kingdom Permanent Representative to the Council of Europe presents his compliments to the Secretary General of the Council, and has the honour to convey the following information.

In his communication to the Secretary General of 23 December 1988, reference was made to the introduction and exercise of certain powers under section 12 of the Prevention of Terrorism (Temporary Provisions) Act 1984, Article 9 of the Prevention of Terrorism (Supplemental Temporary Provisions) Order 1984 and Article 10 of the Prevention of Terrorism (Supplemental Temporary Provisions) (Northern Ireland) Order 1984.

These provisions have been replaced by section 14 of and paragraph 6 of Schedule 5 to the Prevention of Terrorism (Temporary Provisions) Act 1989, which make comparable provision. They came into force on 22 March 1989. A copy of these provisions is enclosed.

The United Kingdom Permanent Representative avails himself of this opportunity to renew to the Secretary General the assurance of his highest consideration.

23 March 1989.

PART II

RESERVATION

At the time of signing the present (First) Protocol, I declare that, in view of certain provisions of the Education Acts in the United Kingdom, the principle affirmed in the second sentence of Article 2 is accepted by the United Kingdom only so far as it is compatible with the provision of efficient instruction and training, and the avoidance of unreasonable public expenditure.

Dated 20 March 1952. Made by the United Kingdom Permanent Representative to the Council of Europe.

SCHEDULE 4

JUDICIAL PENSIONS

Duty to make orders about pensions

1.—(1)   The appropriate Minister must by order make provision with respect to pensions payable to or in respect of any holder of a judicial office who serves as an ECHR judge.

(2)   A pensions order must include such provision as the Minister making it considers is necessary to secure that—

  (a) an ECHR judge who was, immediately before his appointment as an ECHR judge, a member of a judicial pension scheme is entitled to remain as a member of that scheme;
  (b) the terms on which he remains a member of the scheme are those which would have been applicable had he not been appointed as an ECHR judge; and
  (c) entitlement to benefits payable in accordance with the scheme continues to be determined as if, while serving as an ECHR judge, his salary was that which would (but for section 18(4)) have been payable to him in respect of his continuing service as the holder of his judicial office.

Contributions

2.   A pensions order may, in particular, make provision—

  (a) for any contributions which are payable by a person who remains a member of a scheme as a result of the order, and which would otherwise be payable by deduction from his salary, to be made otherwise than by deduction from his salary as an ECHR judge; and
  (b) for such contributions to be collected in such manner as may be determined by the administrators of the scheme.

Amendments of other enactments

3.   A pensions order may amend any provision of, or made under, a pensions Act in such manner and to such extent as the Minister making the order considers necessary or expedient to ensure the proper administration of any scheme to which it relates.

Definitions

4.   In this Schedule—

'appropriate Minister' means—

  (a) in relation to any judicial office whose jurisdiction is exercisable exclusively in relation to Scotland, the Secretary of State; and

(b) otherwise, the Lord Chancellor;

'ECHR judge' means the holder of a judicial office who is serving as a judge of the Court;

'judicial pension scheme' means a scheme established by and in accordance with a pensions Act;

'pensions Act' means—

(a) the County Courts Act (Northern Ireland) 1959;
(b) the Sheriffs' Pensions (Scotland) Act 1961;
(c) the Judicial Pensions Act 1981; or
(d) the Judicial Pensions and Retirement Act 1993; and

'pensions order' means an order made under paragraph 1.

APPENDIX 4

European Court of Human Rights

Rules of Court

(4 November 1998)

REGISTRY OF THE COURT

STRASBOURG

CONTENTS

TITLE I – Organisation and Working of the Court

Chapter I – Judges

Chapter II – Presidency of the Court

Chapter III – The Registry

Chapter IV – The Working of the Court

Chapter V – The Chambers

TITLE II – Procedure

Chapter I – General Rules

Chapter II – Institution of Proceedings

Chapter III – Judge Rapporteurs

Chapter IV – Proceedings on Admissibility

Inter-State applications

Individual applications

Inter-State and individual applications

TITLE III – Transitional Rules

TITLE IV – Final Clauses

The European Court of Human Rights,

Having regard to the Convention for the Protection of Human Rights and Fundamental Freedoms and the Protocols thereto,

Makes the present Rules:

Rule 1

Definitions

For the purposes of these Rules unless the context otherwise requires:

(a) the term 'Convention' means the Convention for the Protection of Human Rights and Fundamental Freedoms and the Protocols thereto;

(b) the expression 'plenary Court' means the European Court of Human Rights sitting in plenary session;

(c) the term 'Grand Chamber' means the Grand Chamber of seventeen judges constituted in pursuance of Article 27, para 1 of the Convention;

(d) the term 'Section' means a Chamber set up by the plenary Court for a fixed period in pursuance of Article 26(b) of the Convention and the expression 'President of the Section' means the judge elected by the plenary Court in pursuance of Article 26(c) of the Convention as President of such a Section;

(e) the term 'Chamber' means any Chamber of seven judges constituted in pursuance of Article 27, para 1 of the Convention and the expression 'President of the Chamber' means the judge presiding over such a 'Chamber';

(f) the term 'Committee' means a Committee of three judges set up in pursuance of Article 27, para 1 of the Convention;

(g) the term 'Court' means either the plenary Court, the Grand Chamber, a Section, a Chamber, a Committee or the panel of five judges referred to in Article 43, para 2 of the Convention;

(h) the expression '*ad hoc* judge' means any person, other than an elected judge, chosen by a Contracting Party in pursuance of Article 27, para 2 of the Convention to sit as a member of the Grand Chamber or as a member of a Chamber;

(i) the terms 'judge' and 'judges' mean the judges elected by the Parliamentary Assembly of the Council of Europe or *ad hoc* judges;

(j) the term 'Judge Rapporteur' means a judge appointed to carry out the tasks provided for in Rules 48 and 49;

(k) the term 'Registrar' denotes the Registrar of the Court or the Registrar of a Section according to the context;

(l) the terms 'party' and 'parties' mean

- the applicant or respondent Contracting Parties;
- the applicant (the person, non-governmental organisation or group of individuals) that lodged a complaint under Article 34 of the Convention;

(m) the expression 'third party' means any Contracting State or any person concerned who, as provided for in Article 36, paras 1 and 2 of the Convention, has exercised its right or been invited to submit written comments or take part in a hearing;

(n) the expression 'Committee of Ministers' means the Committee of Ministers of the Council of Europe;

(o) the terms 'former Court' and 'Commission' mean respectively the European Court and European Commission of Human Rights set up under former Article 19 of the Convention.

TITLE I

ORGANISATION AND WORKING OF THE COURT

Chapter I

Judges

Rule 2

Calculation of term of office

(1) The duration of the term of office of an elected judge shall be calculated as from the date of election. However, when a judge is re-elected on the expiry of the term of office or is elected to replace a judge whose term of office has expired or is about to expire, the duration of the term of office shall, in either case, be calculated as from the date of such expiry.

(2) In accordance with Article 23, para 5 of the Convention, a judge elected to replace a judge whose term of office has not expired shall hold office for the remainder of the predecessor's term.

(3) In accordance with Article 23, para 7 of the Convention, an elected judge shall hold office until a successor has taken the oath or made the declaration provided for in Rule 3.

Rule 3

Oath or solemn declaration

(1) Before taking up office, each elected judge shall, at the first sitting of the plenary Court at which the judge is present or, in case of need, before the President of the Court, take the following oath or make the following solemn declaration:

'I swear' – or 'I solemnly declare' – 'that I will exercise my functions as a judge honourably, independently and impartially and that I will keep secret all deliberations.'

(2) This act shall be recorded in minutes.

Rule 4

Incompatible activities

In accordance with Article 21, para 3 of the Convention, the judges shall not during their term of office engage in any political or administrative activity or any professional activity which is incompatible with their independence or impartiality or with the demands of a full-time office. Each judge shall declare to the President of the Court any additional activity. In the event of a disagreement between the President and the judge concerned, any question arising shall be decided by the plenary Court.

Rule 5

Precedence

(1) Elected judges shall take precedence after the President and Vice-Presidents of the Court and the Presidents of the Sections, according to the date of their election; in the event of re-election, even if it is not an immediate re-election, the length of time during which the judge concerned previously held office as a judge shall be taken into account.

(2) Vice-Presidents of the Court elected to office on the same date shall take precedence according to the length of time they have served as judges. If the length of time they have served as judges is the same, they shall take precedence according to age. The same Rule shall apply to Presidents of Sections.

(3) Judges who have served the same length of time as judges shall take precedence according to age.

(4) *Ad hoc* judges shall take precedence after the elected judges according to age.

Rule 6

Resignation

Resignation of a judge shall be notified to the President of the Court, who shall transmit it to the Secretary General of the Council of Europe. Subject to the provisions of Rules 24, para 3 *in fine* and 26, para 2, resignation shall constitute vacation of office.

Rule 7

Dismissal from office

No judge may be dismissed from his or her office unless the other judges, meeting in plenary session, decide by a majority of two-thirds of the elected judges in office that he or she has ceased to fulfil the required conditions. He or she must first be heard by the plenary Court. Any judge may set in motion the procedure for dismissal from office.

Chapter II

Presidency of the Court

Rule 8

Election of the President and Vice-Presidents of the Court and the Presidents and Vice-Presidents of the Sections

(1) The plenary Court shall elect its President, two Vice-Presidents and the Presidents of the Sections for a period of three years, provided that such period shall not exceed the duration of their terms of office as judges. They may be re-elected.

(2) Each Section shall likewise elect for a renewable period of three years a Vice-President, who shall replace the President of the Section if the latter is unable to carry out his or her duties.

(3) The Presidents and Vice-Presidents shall continue to hold office until the election of their successors.

(4) If a President or a Vice-President ceases to be a member of the Court or resigns from office before its normal expiry, the plenary Court or the relevant Section, as the case may be, shall elect a successor for the remainder of the term of that office.

(5) The elections referred to in this Rule shall be by secret ballot; only the elected judges who are present shall take part. If no judge receives an absolute majority of the elected judges present, a ballot shall take place between the two judges who have received most votes. In the event of a tie, preference shall be given to the judge having precedence in accordance with Rule 5.

Rule 9

Functions of the President of the Court

(1) The President of the Court shall direct the work and administration of the Court. The President shall represent the Court and, in particular, be responsible for its relations with the authorities of the Council of Europe.

(2) The President shall preside at plenary meetings of the Court, meetings of the Grand Chamber and meetings of the panel of five judges.

(3) The President shall not take part in the consideration of cases being heard by Chambers except where he or she is the judge elected in respect of a Contracting Party concerned.

Rule 10

Functions of the Vice-Presidents of the Court

The Vice-Presidents of the Court shall assist the President of the Court. They shall take the place of the President if the latter is unable to carry out his or her duties or the office of President is vacant, or at the request of the President. They shall also act as Presidents of Sections.

Rule 11

Replacement of the President and the Vice-Presidents

If the President and the Vice-Presidents of the Court are at the same time unable to carry out their duties or if their offices are at the same time vacant, the office of President of the Court shall be assumed by a President of a Section or, if none is available, by another elected judge, in accordance with the order of precedence provided for in Rule 5.

Rule 12

Presidency of Sections and Chambers

The Presidents of the Sections shall preside at the sittings of the Section and Chambers of which they are members. The Vice-Presidents of the Sections shall take their place if they are unable to carry out their duties or if the office of President of the Section concerned is vacant, or at the request of the President of the Section. Failing that, the judges of the Section and the Chambers shall take their place, in the order of precedence provided for in Rule 5.

Rule 13

Inability to preside

Judges of the Court may not preside in cases in which the Contracting Party of which they are nationals or in respect of which they were elected is a party.

Rule 14

Balanced representation of the sexes

In relation to the making of appointments governed by this and the following chapter of the present Rules, the Court shall pursue a policy aimed at securing a balanced representation of the sexes.

Chapter III

The Registry

Rule 15

Election of the Registrar

(1) The plenary Court shall elect its Registrar. The candidates shall be of high moral character and must possess the legal, managerial and linguistic knowledge and experience necessary to carry out the functions attaching to the post.

(2) The Registrar shall be elected for a term of five years and may be re-elected. The Registrar may not be dismissed from office, unless the judges, meeting in plenary session, decide by a majority of two-thirds of the elected judges in office that the person concerned has ceased to fulfil the required conditions. He or she must first be heard by the plenary Court. Any judge may set in motion the procedure for dismissal from office.

(3) The elections referred to in this Rule shall be by secret ballot; only the elected judges who are present shall take part. If no candidate receives an absolute majority of the elected judges present, a ballot shall take place between the two candidates who have received most

votes. In the event of a tie, preference shall be given, firstly, to the female candidate, if any, and, secondly, to the older candidate.

(4) Before taking up office, the Registrar shall take the following oath or make the following solemn declaration before the plenary Court or, if need be, before the President of the Court:

'I swear' – or 'I solemnly declare' – 'that I will exercise loyally, discreetly and conscientiously the functions conferred upon me as Registrar of the European Court of Human Rights.'

This act shall be recorded in minutes.

Rule 16

Election of the Deputy Registrars

(1) The plenary Court shall also elect two Deputy Registrars on the conditions and in the manner and for the term prescribed in the preceding Rule. The procedure for dismissal from office provided for in respect of the Registrar shall likewise apply. The Court shall first consult the Registrar in both these matters.

(2) Before taking up office, a Deputy Registrar shall take an oath or make a solemn declaration before the plenary Court or, if need be, before the President of the Court, in terms similar to those prescribed in respect of the Registrar. This act shall be recorded in minutes.

Rule 17

Functions of the Registrar

(1) The Registrar shall assist the Court in the performance of its functions and shall be responsible for the organisation and activities of the Registry under the authority of the President of the Court.

(2) The Registrar shall have the custody of the archives of the Court and shall be the channel for all communications and notifications made by, or addressed to, the Court in connection with the cases brought or to be brought before it.

(3) The Registrar shall, subject to the duty of discretion attaching to this office, reply to requests for information concerning the work of the Court, in particular to enquiries from the press.

(4) General instructions drawn up by the Registrar, and approved by the President of the Court, shall regulate the working of the Registry.

Rule 18

Organisation of the Registry

(1) The Registry shall consist of Section Registries equal to the number of Sections set up by the Court and of the departments necessary to provide the legal and administrative services required by the Court.

(2) The Section Registrar shall assist the Section in the performance of its functions and may be assisted by a Deputy Section Registrar.

(3) The officials of the Registry, including the legal secretaries but not the Registrar and the Deputy Registrars, shall be appointed by the Secretary General of the Council of

Europe with the agreement of the President of the Court or of the Registrar acting on the President's instructions.

Chapter IV

The Working of the Court

Rule 19

Seat of the Court

(1) The seat of the Court shall be at the seat of the Council of Europe at Strasbourg. The Court may, however, if it considers it expedient, perform its functions elsewhere in the territories of the member States of the Council of Europe.

(2) The Court may decide, at any stage of the examination of an application, that it is necessary that an investigation or any other function be carried out elsewhere by it or one or more of its members.

Rule 20

Sessions of the plenary Court

(1) The plenary sessions of the Court shall be convened by the President of the Court whenever the performance of its functions under the Convention and under these Rules so requires. The President of the Court shall convene a plenary session if at least one-third of the members of the Court so request, and in any event once a year to consider administrative matters.

(2) The quorum of the plenary Court shall be two-thirds of the elected judges in office.

(3) If there is no quorum, the President shall adjourn the sitting.

Rule 21

Other sessions of the Court

(1) The Grand Chamber, the Chambers and the Committees shall sit full time. On a proposal by the President, however, the Court shall fix session periods each year.

(2) Outside those periods the Grand Chamber and the Chambers shall be convened by their Presidents in cases of urgency.

Rule 22

Deliberations

(1) The Court shall deliberate in private. Its deliberations shall remain secret.

(2) Only the judges shall take part in the deliberations. The Registrar or the designated substitute, as well as such other officials of the Registry and interpreters whose assistance is deemed necessary, shall be present. No other person may be admitted except by special decision of the Court.

(3) Before a vote is taken on any matter in the Court, the President may request the judges to state their opinions on it.

Rule 23

Votes

(1) The decisions of the Court shall be taken by a majority of the judges present. In the event of a tie, a fresh vote shall be taken and, if there is still a tie, the President shall have a casting vote. This paragraph shall apply unless otherwise provided for in these Rules.

(2) The decisions and judgments of the Grand Chamber and the Chambers shall be adopted by a majority of the sitting judges. Abstentions shall not be allowed in final votes on the admissibility and merits of cases.

(3) As a general rule, votes shall be taken by a show of hands. The President may take a roll-call vote, in reverse order of precedence.

(4) Any matter that is to be voted upon shall be formulated in precise terms.

Chapter V

The Chambers

Rule 24

Composition of the Grand Chamber

(1) The Grand Chamber shall be composed of seventeen judges and three substitute judges.

(2) The Grand Chamber shall be constituted for three years with effect from the election of the presidential office-holders referred to in Rule 8.

(3) The Grand Chamber shall include the President and Vice-Presidents of the Court and the Presidents of the Sections. In order to complete the Grand Chamber, the plenary Court shall, on a proposal by its President, divide all the other judges into two groups which shall alternate every nine months and whose membership shall be geographically as balanced as possible and reflect the different legal systems among the Contracting Parties. The judges and substitute judges who are to hear each case referred to the Grand Chamber during each nine-month period shall be designated in rotation within each group; they shall remain members of the Grand Chamber until the proceedings have been completed, even after their terms of office as judges have expired.

(4) If he or she does not sit as a member of the Grand Chamber by virtue of paragraph 3 of the present Rule, the judge elected in respect of any Contracting Party concerned shall sit as an *ex officio* member of the Grand Chamber in accordance with Article 27, paras 2 and 3 of the Convention.

(5)(a) Where any President of a Section is unable to sit as a member of the Grand Chamber, he or she shall be replaced by the Vice-President of the Section.

(b) If other judges are prevented from sitting, they shall be replaced by the substitute judges in the order in which the latter were selected under paragraph 3 of the present Rule.

(c) If there are not enough substitute judges in the group concerned to complete the Grand Chamber, the substitute judges lacking shall be designated by a drawing of lots amongst the members of the other group.

(6)(a) The panel of five judges of the Grand Chamber called upon to consider requests submitted under Article 43 of the Convention shall be composed of

- the President of the Court,

- the Presidents or, if they are prevented from sitting, the vice-Presidents of the Sections other than the Section from which was constituted the Chamber that dealt with the case whose referral to the Grand Chamber is being sought,

- one further judge designated in rotation from among the judges other than those who dealt with the case in the Chamber.

(b) No judge elected in respect of, or who is a national of, a Contracting Party concerned may be a member of the panel.

(c) Any member of the panel unable to sit shall be replaced by another judge who did not deal with the case in the Chamber, who shall be designated in rotation.

Rule 25

Setting up of Sections

(1) The Chambers provided for in Article 26(b) of the Convention (referred to in these Rules as 'Sections') shall be set up by the plenary Court, on a proposal by its President, for a period of three years with effect from the election of the presidential office-holders of the Court under Rule 8. There shall be at least four Sections.

(2) Each judge shall be a member of a Section. The composition of the Sections shall be geographically and gender balanced and shall reflect the different legal systems among the Contracting Parties.

(3) Where a judge ceases to be a member of the Court before the expiry of the period for which the Section has been constituted, the judge's place in the Section shall be taken by his or her successor as a member of the Court.

(4) The President of the Court may exceptionally make modifications to the composition of the Sections if circumstances so require.

(5) On a proposal by the President, the plenary. Court may constitute an additional Section.

Rule 26

Constitution of Chambers

(1) The Chambers of seven judges provided for in Article 27, para 1 of the Convention for the consideration of cases brought before the Court shall be constituted from the Sections as follows.

(a) The Chamber shall in each case include the President of the Section and the judge elected in respect of any Contracting Party concerned. If the latter judge is not a member of the Section to which the application has been assigned under Rule 51 or 52, he or she shall sit as an *ex officio* member of the Chamber in accordance with Article 27, para 2 of the Convention. Rule 29 shall apply if that judge is unable to sit or withdraws.

(b) The other members of the Chamber shall be designated by the President of the Section in ,rotation from among the members of the relevant Section.

(c) The members of the Section who are not so designated shall sit in the case as substitute judges.

(2) Even after the end of their terms of office judges shall continue to deal with cases in which they have participated in the consideration of the merits.

Rule 27

Committees

(1) Committees composed of three judges belonging to the same Section shall be set up under Article 27, para 1 of the Convention. After consulting the Presidents of the Sections, the President of the Court shall decide on the number of Committees to be set up.

(2) The Committees shall be constituted for a period of twelve months by rotation among the members of each Section, excepting the President of the Section.

(3) The judges of the Section who are not members of a Committee may be called upon to take the place of members who are unable to sit.

(4) Each Committee shall be chaired by the member having precedence in the Section.

Rule 28

Inability to sit, withdrawal or exemption

(1) Any judge who is prevented from taking part in sittings shall, as soon as possible, give notice to the President of the Chamber.

(2) A judge may not take part in the consideration of any case in which he or she has a personal interest or has previously acted either as the Agent, advocate or adviser of a party or of a person having an interest in the case, or as a member of a tribunal or commission of inquiry, or in any other capacity.

(3) If a judge withdraws for one of the said reasons, or for some special reason, he or she shall inform the President of the Chamber, who shall exempt the judge from sitting.

(4) If the President of the Chamber considers that a reason exists for a judge to withdraw, he or she shall consult with the judge concerned; in the event of disagreement, the Chamber shall decide.

Rule 29

Ad hoc judges

(1) If the judge elected in respect of a Contracting Party concerned is unable to sit in the Chamber or withdraws, the President of the Chamber shall invite that Party to indicate within thirty days whether it wishes to appoint to sit as judge either another elected judge or, as an *ad hoc* judge, any other person possessing the qualifications required by Article 21, para 1 of the Convention and, if so, to state at the same time the name of the person appointed. The same rule shall apply if the person so appointed is unable to sit or withdraws.

(2) The Contracting Party concerned shall be presumed to have waived its right of appointment if it does not reply within thirty days.

(3) An *ad hoc* judge shall, at the opening of the first sitting fixed for the consideration of the case after the judge has been appointed, take the oath or make the solemn declaration provided for in Rule 3. This act shall be recorded in minutes.

Rule 30

Common interest

1. If several applicant or respondent Contracting Parties have a common interest, the President of the Court may invite them to agree to appoint a single elected judge or *ad hoc*

judge in accordance with Article 27, para 2 of the Convention. If the Parties are unable to agree, the President shall choose by lot, from among the persons proposed as judges by these Parties, the judge called upon to sit *ex officio*.

(2) In the event of a dispute as to the existence of a common interest, the plenary Court shall decide.

TITLE II

PROCEDURE

Chapter I

General Rules

Rule 31

Possibility of particular derogations

The provisions of this Title shall not prevent the Court from derogating from them for the consideration of a particular case after having consulted the parties where appropriate.

Rule 32

Practice directions

The President of the Court may issue practice directions, notably in relation to such matters as appearance at hearings and the filing of pleadings and other documents.

Rule 33

Public character of proceedings

(1) Hearings shall be public unless, in accordance with paragraph 2 of this Rule, the Chamber in exceptional circumstances decides otherwise, either of its own motion or at the request of a party or any other person concerned.

(2) The press and the public may be excluded from all or part of a hearing in the interest of morals, public order or national security in a democratic society, where the interests of juveniles or the protection of the private life of the parties so require, or to the extent strictly necessary in the opinion of the Chamber in special circumstances where publicity would prejudice the interests of justice.

(3) Following registration of an application, all documents deposited with the Registry, with the exception of those deposited within the framework of friendly-settlement negotiations as provided for in Rule 62, shall be accessible to the public unless the President of the Chamber, for the reasons set out in paragraph 2 of this Rule, decides otherwise, either of his or her own motion or at the request of a party or any other person concerned.

(4) Any request for confidentiality made under paragraphs 1 or 3 above must give reasons and specify whether the hearing or the documents, as the case may be, should be inaccessible to the public in whole or in part.

Rule 34

Use of languages

(1) The official languages of the Court shall be English and French.

(2) Before the decision on the admissibility of an application is taken, all communications with and pleadings by applicants under Article 34 of the Convention or their representatives, if not in one of the Court's official languages, shall be in one of the official languages of the Contracting Parties.

(3)(a) All communications with and pleadings by such applicants or their representatives in respect of a hearing, or after a case has been declared admissible, shall be in one of the Court's official languages, unless the President of the Chamber authorises the continued use of the official language of a Contracting Party.

  (b) If such leave is granted, the Registrar shall make the necessary arrangements for the oral or written translation of the applicant's observations or statements.

(4)(a) All communications with and pleadings by Contracting Parties or third parties shall be in one of the Court's official languages. The President of the Chamber may authorise the use of a non-official language.

  (b) If such leave is granted, it shall be the responsibility of the requesting party to provide for and bear the costs of interpreting or translation into English or French of the oral arguments or written statements made.

(5) The President of the Chamber may invite the respondent Contracting Party to provide a translation of its written submissions in the or an official language of that Party in order to facilitate the applicant's understanding of those submissions.

(6) Any witness, expert or other person appearing before the Court may use his or her own language if he or she does not have sufficient knowledge of either of the two official languages. In that event the Registrar shall make the necessary arrangements for interpreting or translation.

Rule 35

Representation of Contracting Parties

The Contracting Parties shall be represented by Agents, who may have the assistance of advocates or advisers.

Rule 36

Representation of applicants

(1) Persons, non-governmental organisations or groups of individuals may initially present applications under Article 34 of the Convention themselves or through a representative appointed under paragraph 4 of this Rule.

(2) Following notification of the application to the respondent Contracting Party under Rule 54, para 3(b), the President of the Chamber may direct that the applicant should be represented in accordance with paragraph 4 of this Rule.

(3) The applicant must be so represented at any hearing decided on by the Chamber or for the purposes of the proceedings following a decision to declare the application admissible, unless the President of the Chamber decides otherwise.

(4)(a) The representative of the applicant shall be an advocate authorised to practise in any of the Contracting Parties and resident in the territory of one of them, or any other person approved by the President of the Chamber.

(b) The President of the Chamber may, where representation would otherwise be obligatory, grant leave to the applicant to present his or her own case, subject, if necessary, to being assisted by an advocate or other approved representative.

(c) In exceptional circumstances and at any stage of the procedure, the President of the Chamber may, where he or she considers that the circumstances or the conduct of the advocate or other person appointed under the preceding sub-paragraphs so warrant, direct that the latter may no longer represent or assist the applicant and that the applicant should seek alternative representation.

(5) The advocate or other approved representative, or the applicant in person if he or she seeks leave to present his or her own case, must have an adequate knowledge of one of the Court's official languages. However, leave to use a non-official language may be given by the President of the Chamber under Rule 34, para 3.

Rule 37

Communications, notifications and summonses

(1) Communications or notifications addressed to the Agents or advocates of the parties shall be deemed to have been addressed to the parties.

(2) If, for any communication, notification or summons addressed to persons other than the Agents or advocates of the parties, the Court considers it necessary to have the assistance of the Government of the State on whose territory such communication, notification or summons is to have effect, the President of the Court shall apply directly to that Government in order to obtain the necessary facilities.

(3) The same rule shall apply when the Court desires to make or arrange for the making of an investigation on the spot in order to establish the facts or to procure evidence or when it orders the appearance of a person who is resident in, or will have to cross, that territory.

Rule 38

Written pleadings

(1) No written observations or other documents may be filed after the time-limit set by the President of the Chamber or the Judge Rapporteur, as the case may be, in accordance with these Rules. No written observations or other documents filed outside that time-limit or contrary to any practice direction issued under Rule 32 shall be included in the case file unless the President of the Chamber decides otherwise.

(2) For the purposes of observing the time-limit referred to in paragraph 1, the material date is the certified date of dispatch of the document or, if there is none, the actual date of receipt at the Registry.

Rule 39

Interim measures

(1) The Chamber or, where appropriate, its President may, at the request of a party or of any other person concerned, or of its own motion, indicate to the parties any interim measure which it considers should be adopted in the interests of the parties or of the proper conduct of the proceedings before it.

(2) Notice of these measures shall be given to the Committee of Ministers.

(3) The Chamber may request information from the parties on any matter connected with the implementation of any interim measure it has indicated.

Rule 40

Urgent notification of an application

In any case of urgency the Registrar, with the authorisation of the President of the Chamber, may, without prejudice to the taking of any other procedural steps and by any available means, inform a Contracting Party concerned in an application of the introduction of the application and of a summary of its objects.

Rule 41

Case priority

The Chamber shall deal with applications in the order in which they become ready for examination. It may, however, decide to give priority to a particular application.

Rule 42

Measures for taking evidence

(1) The Chamber may, at the request of a party or a third party, or of its own motion, obtain any evidence which it considers capable of providing clarification of the facts of the case. The Chamber may, *inter alia*, request the parties to produce documentary evidence and decide to hear as a witness or expert or in any other capacity any person whose evidence or statements seem likely to assist it in the carrying out of its tasks.

(2) The Chamber may, at any time during the proceedings, depute one or more of its members or of the other judges of the Court to conduct an inquiry, carry out an investigation on the spot or take evidence in some other manner. It may appoint independent external experts to assist such a delegation.

(3) The Chamber may ask any person or institution of its choice to obtain information, express an opinion or make a report on any specific point.

(4) The parties shall assist the Chamber, or its delegation, in implementing any measures for taking evidence.

(5) Where a report has been drawn up or some other measure taken in accordance with the preceding paragraphs at the request of an applicant or respondent Contracting Party, the costs entailed shall be borne by that Party unless the Chamber decides otherwise. In other cases the Chamber shall decide whether such costs are to be borne by the Council of Europe or awarded against the applicant or third party at whose request the report was drawn up or the other measure was taken. In all cases the costs shall be taxed by the President of the Chamber.

Rule 43

Joinder and simultaneous examination of applications

(1) The Chamber may, either at the request of the parties or of its own motion, order the joinder of two or more applications.

(2) The President of the Chamber may, after consulting the parties, order that the proceedings in applications assigned to the same Chamber be conducted simultaneously, without prejudice to the decision of the Chamber on the joinder of the applications.

Rule 44

Striking out and restoration to the list

(1) When an applicant Contracting Party notifies the Registrar of its intention not to proceed with the case, the Chamber may strike the application out of the Court's list under Article 37 of the Convention if the other Contracting Party or Parties concerned in the case agree to such discontinuance.

(2) The decision to strike out an application which has been declared admissible shall be given in the form of a judgment. The President of the Chamber shall forward that judgment, once it has become final, to the Committee of Ministers in order to allow the latter to supervise, in accordance with Article 46, para 2 of the Convention, the execution of any undertakings which may have been attached to the discontinuance, friendly settlement or solution of the matter.

(3) When an application has been struck out, the costs shall be at the discretion of the Court. If an award of costs is made in a decision striking out an application which has not been declared admissible, the President of the Chamber shall forward the decision to the Committee of Ministers.

(4) The Court may restore an application to its list if it concludes that exceptional circumstances justify such a course.

Chapter II

Institution of Proceedings

Rule 45

Signatures

(1) Any application made under Articles 33 or 34 of the Convention shall be submitted in writing and shall be signed by the applicant or by the applicant's representative.

(2) Where an application is made by a non-governmental organisation or by a group of individuals, it shall be signed by those persons competent to represent that organisation or group. The Chamber or Committee concerned shall determine any question as to whether the persons who have signed an application are competent to do so.

(3) Where applicants are represented in accordance with Rule 36, a power of attorney or written authority to act shall be supplied by their representative or representatives.

Rule 46

Contents of an inter-State application

Any Contracting Party or Parties intending to bring a case before the Court under Article 33 of the Convention shall file with the registry an application setting out

   (a) the name of the Contracting Party against which the application is made;

(b) a statement of the facts;

(c) a statement of the alleged violation(s) of the Convention and the relevant arguments;

(d) a statement on compliance with the admissibility criteria (exhaustion of domestic remedies and the six-month rule) laid down in Article 35, para 1 of the Convention;

(e) the object of the application and a general indication of any claims for just satisfaction made under Article 41 of the Convention on behalf of the alleged injured party or parties; and

(f) the name and address of the person(s) appointed as Agent; and accompanied by

(g) copies of any relevant documents and in particular the decisions, whether judicial or not, relating to the object of the application.

Rule 47

Contents of an individual application

(1) Any application under Article 34 of the Convention shall be made on the application form provided by the registry, unless the President of the Section concerned decides otherwise. It shall set out

(a) the name, date of birth, nationality, sex, occupation and address of the applicant;

(b) the name, occupation and address of the representative, if any;

(c) the name of the Contracting Party or Parties against which the application is made;

(d) a succinct statement of the facts;

(e) a succinct statement of the alleged violation(s) of the Convention and the relevant arguments;

(f) a succinct statement on the applicant's compliance with the admissibility criteria (exhaustion of domestic remedies and the six-month rule) laid down in Article 35, para 1 of the Convention; and

(g) the object of the application as well as a general indication of any claims for just satisfaction which the applicant may wish to make under Article 41 of the Convention; and be accompanied by

(h) copies of any relevant documents and in particular the decisions, whether judicial or not, relating to the object of the application.

(2) Applicants shall furthermore

(a) provide information, notably the documents and decisions referred to in paragraph 1(h) above, enabling it to be shown that the admissibility criteria (exhaustion of domestic remedies and the six-month rule) laid down in Article 35, para 1 of the Convention have been satisfied; and

(b) indicate whether they have submitted their complaints to any other procedure of international investigation or settlement.

(3) Applicants who do not wish their identity to be disclosed to the public shall so indicate and shall submit a statement of the reasons justifying such a departure from the normal rule of public access to information in proceedings before the Court. The President of the Chamber may authorise anonymity in exceptional and duly justified cases.

(4) Failure to comply with the requirements set out in paragraphs 1 and 2 above may result in the application not being registered and examined by the Court.

(5) The date of introduction of the application shall as a general rule be considered to be the date of the first communication from the applicant setting out, even summarily, the object of the application. The Court may for good cause nevertheless decide that a different date shall be considered to be the date of introduction.

(6) Applicants shall keep the Court informed of any change of address and of all circumstances relevant to the application.

Chapter III

Judge Rapporteurs

Rule 48

Inter-State applications

(1) Where an application is made under Article 33 of the Convention, the Chamber constituted to consider the case shall designate one or more of its judges as Judge Rapporteur(s), who shall submit a report on admissibility when the written observations of the Contracting Parties concerned have been received, Rule 49, para 4 shall, in so far as appropriate, be applicable to this report.

(2) After an application made under Article 33 of the Convention has been declared admissible, the Judge Rapporteur(s) shall submit such reports, drafts and other documents as may assist the Chamber in the carrying out of its functions.

Rule 49

Individual applications

(1) Where an application is made under Article 34 of the Convention, the President of the Section to which the case has been assigned shall designate a judge as Judge Rapporteur, who shall examine the application.

(2) In their examination of applications Judge Rapporteurs

    (a) may request the parties to submit, within a specified time, any factual information, documents or other material which they consider to be relevant;

    (b) shall, subject to the President of the Section directing that the case be considered by a Chamber, decide whether the application is to be considered by a Committee or by a Chamber.

(3) Where a case is considered by a Committee in accordance with Article 28 of the Convention, the report of the Judge Rapporteur shall contain

    (a) a brief statement of the relevant facts;

    (b) a brief statement of the reasons underlying the proposal to declare the application inadmissible or to strike it out of the list.

(4) Where a case is considered by a Chamber pursuant to Article 29, para 1 of the Convention, the report of the Judge Rapporteur shall contain

    (a) a statement of the relevant facts, including any information obtained under paragraph 2 of this Rule;

    (b) an indication of the issues arising under the Convention in the application;

    (c) a proposal on admissibility and on any other action to be taken, together, if need be, with a provisional opinion on the merits.

(5) After an application made under Article 34 of the Convention has been declared admissible, the Judge Rapporteur shall submit such reports, drafts and other documents as may assist the Chamber in the carrying out of its functions.

Rule 50

Grand Chamber proceedings

Where a case has been submitted to the Grand Chamber either under Article 30 or under Article 43 of the Convention, the President of the Grand Chamber shall designate as Judge Rapporteur(s) one or, in the case of an inter-State application, one or more of its members.

Chapter IV

Proceedings on Admissibility

Inter-State applications

Rule 51

(1) When an application is made under Article 33 of the Convention, the President of the Court shall immediately give notice of the application to the respondent Contracting Party and shall assign the application to one of the Sections.

(2) In accordance with Rule 26, para 1(a), the judges elected in respect of the applicant and respondent Contracting Parties shall sit as *ex officio* members of the Chamber constituted to consider the case. Rule 30 shall apply if the application has been brought by several Contracting Parties or if applications with the same object brought by several Contracting Parties are being examined jointly under Rule 43, para 2.

(3) On assignment of the case to a Section, the President of the Section shall constitute the Chamber in accordance with Rule 26, para 1 and shall invite the respondent Contracting Party to submit its observations in writing on the admissibility of the application. The observations so obtained shall be communicated by the Registrar to the applicant Contracting Party, which may submit written observations in reply.

(4) Before ruling on the admissibility of the application, the Chamber may decide to invite the parties to submit further observations in writing.

(5) A hearing on the admissibility shall be held if one or more of the Contracting Parties concerned so requests or if the Chamber so decides of its own motion.

(6) After consulting the Parties, the President of the Chamber shall fix the written and, where appropriate, oral procedure and for that purpose shall lay down the time-limit within which any written observations are to be filed.

(7) In its deliberations the Chamber shall take into consideration the report submitted by the Judge Rapporteur(s) under Rule 48, para 1.

Individual applications

Rule 52

Assignment of applications to the Sections

(1) Any application made under Article 34 of the Convention shall be assigned to a Section by the President of the Court, who in so doing shall endeavour to ensure a fair distribution of cases between the Sections.

(2) The Chamber of seven judges provided for in Article 27, para 1 of the Convention shall be constituted by the President of the Section concerned in accordance with Rule 26, para 1 once it has been decided that the application is to be considered by a Chamber.

(3) Pending the constitution of a Chamber in accordance with the preceding paragraph, the President of the Section shall exercise any powers conferred on the President of the Chamber by these Rules.

Rule 53

Procedure before a Committee

(1) In its deliberations the Committee shall take into consideration the report submitted by the Judge Rapporteur under Rule 49, para 3.

(2) The Judge Rapporteur, if he or she is not a member of the Committee, may be invited to attend the deliberations of the Committee.

(3) In accordance with Article 28 of the Convention, the Committee may, by a unanimous vote, declare inadmissible or strike out of the Court's list of cases an application where such a decision can be taken without further examination. This decision shall be final.

(4) If no decision pursuant to paragraph 3 of the present Rule is taken, the application shall be forwarded to the Chamber constituted under Rule 52, para 2 to examine the case.

Rule 54

Procedure before a Chamber

(1) In its deliberations the Chamber shall take into consideration the report submitted by the Judge Rapporteur under Rule 49, para 4.

(2) The Chamber may at once declare the application inadmissible or strike it out of the Court's list of cases.

(3) Alternatively, the Chamber may decide to

(a) request the parties to submit any factual information, documents or other material which it considers to be relevant;
(b) give notice of the application to the respondent Contracting Party and invite that Party to submit written observations on the application;
(c) invite the parties to submit further observations in writing.

(4) Before taking its decision on admissibility, the Chamber may decide, either at the request of the parties or of its own motion, to hold a hearing. In that event, unless the Chamber shall exceptionally decide otherwise, the parties shall be invited also to address the issues arising in relation to the merits of the application.

(5) The President of the Chamber shall fix the procedure, including time-limits, in relation to any decisions taken by the Chamber under paragraphs 3 and 4 of this Rule.

Inter-State and individual applications

Rule 55

Pleas of inadmissibility

Any plea of inadmissibility must, in so far as its character and the circumstances permit, be raised by the respondent Contracting Party in its written or oral observations on the admissibility of the application submitted as provided in Rule 51 or 54, as the case may be.

Rule 56

Decision of a Chamber

(1) The decision of the Chamber shall state whether it was taken unanimously or by a majority and shall be accompanied or followed by reasons.

(2) The decision of the Chamber shall be communicated by the Registrar to the applicant and to the Contracting Party or Parties concerned.

Rule 57

Language of the decision

(1) Unless the Court decides that a decision shall be given in both official languages, all decisions shall be given either in English or in French. Decisions given shall be accessible to the public.

(2) Publication of such decisions in the official reports of the Court, as provided for in Rule 78, shall be in both official languages of the Court.

Chapter V

Proceedings after the Admission of an Application

Rule 58

Inter-State applications

(1) Once the Chamber has decided to admit an application made under Article 33 of the Convention, the President of the Chamber shall, after consulting the Contracting Parties concerned, lay down the time-limits for the filing of written observations on the merits and for the production of any further evidence. The President may however, with the agreement of the Contracting Parties concerned, direct that a written procedure is to be dispensed with.

(2) A hearing on the merits shall be held if one or more of the Contracting Parties concerned so requests or if the Chamber so decides of its own motion. The President of the Chamber shall fix the oral procedure.

(3) In its deliberations the Chamber shall take into consideration any reports, drafts and other documents submitted by the Judge Rapporteur(s) under Rule 48, para 2.

Rule 59

Individual applications

(1) Once the Chamber has decided to admit an application made under Article 34 of the Convention, it may invite the parties to submit further evidence and written observations.

(2) A hearing on the merits shall be held if the Chamber so decides of its own motion or, provided that no hearing also addressing the merits has been held at the admissibility stage under Rule 54, para 4, if one of the parties so requests. However, the Chamber may exceptionally decide that the discharging of its functions under Article 38, para 1(a) of the Convention does not require a hearing to be held.

(3) The President of the Chamber shall, where appropriate, fix the written and oral procedure.

(4) In its deliberations the Chamber shall take into consideration any reports, drafts and other documents submitted by the Judge Rapporteur under Rule 49, para 5.

Rule 60

Claims for just satisfaction

(1) Any claim which the applicant Contracting Party or the applicant may wish to make for just satisfaction under Article 41 of the Convention shall, unless the President of the Chamber directs otherwise, be set out in the written observations on the merits or, if no such written observations are filed, in a special document filed no later than two months after the decision declaring the application admissible.

(2) Itemised particulars of all claims made, together with the relevant supporting documents or vouchers, shall be submitted, failing which the Chamber may reject the claim in whole or in part.

(3) The Chamber may, at any time during the proceedings, invite any party to submit comments on the claim for just satisfaction.

Rule 61

Third-party intervention

(1) The decision declaring an application admissible shall be notified by the Registrar to any Contracting Party one of whose nationals is an applicant in the case, as well as to the respondent Contracting Party under Rule 56, para 2.

(2) Where a Contracting Party seeks to exercise its right to submit written comments or to take part in an oral hearing, pursuant to Article 36, para 1 of the Convention, the President of the Chamber shall fix the procedure to be followed.

(3) In accordance with Article 36, para 2 of the Convention, the President of the Chamber may, in the interests of the proper administration of justice, invite or grant leave to any Contracting State which is not a party to the proceedings, or any person concerned who is not the applicant, to submit written comments or, in exceptional cases, to take part in an oral hearing. Requests for leave for this purpose must be duly reasoned and submitted in one of the official languages, within a reasonable time after the fixing of the written procedure.

(4) Any invitation or grant of leave referred to in paragraph 3 of this Rule shall be subject to any conditions, including time-limits, set by the President of the Chamber. Where such conditions are not complied with, the President may decide not to include the comments in the case file.

(5) Written comments submitted in accordance with this Rule shall be submitted in one of the official languages, save where leave to use another language has been granted under Rule 34, para 4. They shall be transmitted by the Registrar to the parties to the case, who shall be entitled, subject to any conditions, including time-limits, set by the President of the Chamber, to file written observations in reply.

Rule 62

Friendly settlement

(1) Once an application has been declared admissible, the Registrar, acting on the instructions of the Chamber or its President, shall enter into contact with the parties with a view to securing a friendly settlement of the matter in accordance with Article 38, para 1 (b)

of the Convention. The Chamber shall take any steps that appear appropriate to facilitate such a settlement.

(2) In accordance with Article 38, para 2 of the Convention, the friendly settlement negotiations shall be confidential and without prejudice to the parties' arguments in the contentious proceedings. No written or oral communication and no offer or concession made in the framework of the attempt to secure a friendly settlement may be referred to or relied on in the contentious proceedings.

(3) If the Chamber is informed by the Registrar that the parties have agreed to a friendly settlement, it shall, after verifying that the settlement has been reached on the basis of respect for human rights as defined in the Convention and the protocols thereto, strike the case out of the Court's list in accordance with Rule 44, para 2.

Chapter VI

Hearings

Rule 63

Conduct of hearings

(1) The President of the Chamber shall direct hearings and shall prescribe the order in which Agents and advocates or advisers of the parties shall be called upon to speak.

(2) Where a fact-finding hearing is being carried out by a delegation of the Chamber under Rule 42, the head of the delegation shall conduct the hearing and the delegation shall exercise any relevant power conferred on the Chamber by the Convention or these Rules.

Rule 64

Failure to appear at a hearing

Where, without showing sufficient cause, a party fails to appear, the Chamber may, provided that it is satisfied that such a course is consistent with the proper administration of justice, nonetheless proceed with the hearing.

Rule 65

Convocation of witnesses, experts and other persons; costs of their appearance

(1) Witnesses, experts and other persons whom the Chamber or the President of the Chamber decides to hear shall be summoned by the Registrar.

(2) The summons shall indicate

    (a) the case in connection with which it has been issued;
    (b) the object of the inquiry, expert opinion or other measure ordered by the Chamber or the President of the Chamber;
    (c) any provisions for the payment of the sum due to the person summoned.

(3) If the persons concerned appear at the request or on behalf of an applicant or respondent Contracting Party, the costs of their appearance shall be borne by that Party unless the Chamber decides otherwise. In other cases, the Chamber shall decide whether such costs are to be borne by the Council of Europe or awarded against the applicant or third party at whose request the person summoned appeared. In all cases the costs shall be taxed by the President of the Chamber.

Rule 66

Oath or solemn declaration by witnesses and experts

(1) After the establishment of the identity of the witness and before testifying, every witness shall take the following oath or make the following solemn declaration:

'I swear' – or 'I solemnly declare upon my honour and conscience' – 'that I shall speak the truth, the whole truth and nothing but the truth.'

This act shall be recorded in minutes.

(2) After the establishment of the identity of the expert and before carrying out his or her task, every expert shall take the following oath or make the following solemn declaration:

'I swear' – or 'I solemnly declare' – 'that I will discharge my duty as an expert honourably and conscientiously.'

This act shall be recorded in minutes.

(3) This oath may be taken or this declaration made before the President of the Chamber, or before a judge or any public authority nominated by the President.

Rule 67

Objection to a witness or expert; hearing of a person for information purposes

The Chamber shall decide in the event of any dispute arising from an objection to a witness or expert. It may hear for information purposes a person who cannot be heard as a witness.

Rule 68

Questions put during hearings

(1) Any judge may put questions to the Agents, advocates or advisers of the parties, to the applicant, witnesses and experts, and to any other persons appearing before the Chamber.

(2) The witnesses, experts and other persons referred to in Rule 42, para 1 may, subject to the control of the President of the Chamber, be examined by the Agents and advocates or advisers of the parties. In the event of an objection as to the relevance of a question put, the President of the Chamber shall decide.

Rule 69

Failure to appear, refusal to give evidence or false evidence

If, without good reason, a witness or any other person who has been duly summoned fails to appear or refuses to give evidence, the Registrar shall, on being so required by the President of the Chamber, inform the Contracting Party to whose jurisdiction the witness or other person is subject. The same provisions shall apply if a witness or expert has, in the opinion of the Chamber, violated the oath or solemn declaration provided for in Rule 66.

Rule 70

Verbatim record of hearings

(1) The Registrar shall, if the Chamber so directs, be responsible for the making of a verbatim record of a hearing. The verbatim record shall include

(a) the composition of the Chamber at the hearing;

(b) a list of those appearing before the Court, that is to say Agents, advocates and advisers of the parties and any third party taking part;

(c) the surnames, forenames, description and address of each witness, expert or other person heard;

(d) the text of statements made, questions put and replies given;

(e) the text of any decision delivered during the hearing by the Chamber or the President of the Chamber.

(2) If all or part of the verbatim record is in a non-official language, the Registrar shall, if the Chamber so directs, arrange for its translation into one of the official languages.

(3) The representatives of the parties shall receive a copy of the verbatim record in order that they may, subject to the control of the Registrar or the President of the Chamber, make corrections, but in no case may such corrections affect the sense and bearing of what was said. The Registrar shall lay down, in accordance with the instructions of the President of the Chamber, the time-limits granted for this purpose.

(4) The verbatim record, once so corrected, shall be signed by the President and the Registrar and shall then constitute certified matters of record.

Chapter VII

Proceedings before the Grand Chamber

Rule 71

Applicability of procedural provisions

Any provisions governing proceedings before the Chambers shall apply, *mutatis mutandis*, to proceedings before the Grand Chamber.

Rule 72

Relinquishment of jurisdiction by a Chamber in favour of the Grand Chamber

(1) In accordance with Article 30 of the Convention, where a case pending before a Chamber raises a serious question affecting the interpretation of the Convention or the protocols thereto or where the resolution of a question before it might have a result inconsistent with a judgment previously delivered by the Court, the Chamber may, at any time before it has rendered its judgment, relinquish jurisdiction in favour of the Grand Chamber, unless one of the parties to the case has objected in accordance with paragraph 2 of this Rule. Reasons need not be given for the decision to relinquish.

(2) The Registrar shall notify the parties of the Chamber's intention to relinquish jurisdiction. The parties shall have one month from the date of that notification within which to file at the Registry a duly reasoned objection. An objection which does not fulfil these conditions shall be considered invalid by the Chamber.

Rule 73

Request by a party for referral of a case to the Grand Chamber

(1) In accordance with Article 43 of the Convention, any party to a case may exceptionally, within a period of three months from the date of delivery of the judgment of a Chamber, file in writing at the Registry a request that the case be referred to the Grand Chamber. The party shall specify in its request the serious question affecting the interpretation or

application of the Convention or the protocols thereto, or the serious issue of general importance, which in its view warrants consideration by the Grand Chamber.

(2) A panel of five judges of the Grand Chamber constituted in accordance with Rule 24, para 6 shall examine the request solely on the basis of the existing case file. It shall accept the request only if it considers that the case does raise such a question or issue. Reasons need not be given for a refusal of the request.

(3) If the panel accepts the request, the Grand Chamber shall decide the case by means of a judgment.

Chapter VIII

Judgments

Rule 74

Contents of the judgment

(1) A judgment as referred to in Articles 42 and 44 of the Convention shall contain

- (a) the names of the President and the other judges constituting the Chamber concerned, and the name of the Registrar or the Deputy Registrar;
- (b) the dates on which it was adopted and delivered;
- (c) a description of the parties;
- (d) the names of the Agents, advocates or advisers of the parties;
- (e) an account of the procedure followed;
- (f) the facts of the case;
- (g) a summary of the submissions of the parties;
- (h) the reasons in point of law;
- (i) the operative provisions;
- (j) the decision, if any, in respect of costs;
- (k) the number of judges constituting the majority;
- (l) where appropriate, a statement as to which text is authentic.

(2) Any judge who has taken part in the consideration of the case shall be entitled to annex to the judgment either a separate opinion, concurring with or dissenting from that judgment, or a bare statement of dissent.

Rule 75

Ruling on just satisfaction

(1) Where the Chamber finds that there has been a violation of the Convention, it shall give in the same judgment a ruling on the application of Article 41 of the Convention if that question, after being raised in accordance with Rule 60, is ready for decision; if the question is not ready for decision, the Chamber shall reserve it in whole or in part and shall fix the further procedure.

(2) For the purposes of ruling on the application of Article 41 of the Convention, the Chamber shall, as far as possible, be composed of those judges who sat to consider the merits of the case. Where it is not possible to constitute the original Chamber, the President of the Court shall complete or compose the Chamber by drawing lots.

(3) The Chamber may, when affording just satisfaction under Article 41 of the Convention, direct that if settlement is not made within a specified time, interest is to be payable on any sums awarded.

(4) If the Court is informed that an agreement has been reached between the injured party and the Contracting Party liable, it shall verify the equitable nature of the agreement and, where it finds the agreement to be equitable, strike the case out of the list in accordance with Rule 44, para 2.

Rule 76

Language of the judgment

(1) Unless the Court decides that a judgment shall be given in both official languages, all judgments shall be given either in English or in French. Judgments given shall be accessible to the public.

(2) Publication of such judgments in the official reports of the Court, as provided for in Rule 78, shall be in both official languages of the Court.

Rule 77

Signature, delivery and notification of the judgment

(1) Judgments shall be signed by the President of the Chamber and the Registrar.

(2) The judgment may be read out at a public hearing by the President of the Chamber or by another judge delegated by him or her. The Agents and representatives of the parties shall be informed in due time of the date of the hearing. Otherwise the notification provided for in paragraph 3 of this Rule shall constitute delivery of the judgment.

(3) The judgment shall be transmitted to the Committee of Ministers. The Registrar shall send certified copies to the parties, to the Secretary General of the Council of Europe, to any third party and to any other person directly concerned. The original copy, duly signed and sealed, shall be placed in the archives of the Court.

Rule 78

Publication of judgments and other documents

In accordance with Article 44, para 3 of the Convention, final judgments of the Court shall be published, under the responsibility of the Registrar, in an appropriate form. The Registrar shall in addition be responsible for the publication of official reports of selected judgments and decisions and of any document which the President of the Court considers it useful to publish.

Rule 79

Request for interpretation of a judgment

(1) A party may request the interpretation of a judgment within a period of one year following the delivery of that judgment.

(2) The request shall be filed with the Registry. It shall state precisely the point or points in the operative provisions of the judgment on which interpretation is required.

(3) The original Chamber may decide of its own motion to refuse the request on the ground that there is no reason to warrant considering it. Where it is not possible to constitute the original Chamber, the President of the Court shall complete or compose the Chamber by drawing lots.

(4) If the Chamber does not refuse the request, the Registrar shall communicate it to the other party or parties and shall invite them to submit any written comments within a

time-limit laid down by the President of the Chamber. The President of the Chamber shall also fix the date of the hearing should the Chamber decide to hold one. The Chamber shall decide by means of a judgment.

Rule 80

Request for revision of a judgment

(1) A party may, in the event of the discovery of a fact which might by its nature have a decisive influence and which, when a judgment was delivered, was unknown to the Court and could not reasonably have been known to that party, request the Court, within a period of six months after that party acquired knowledge of the fact, to revise that judgment.

(2) The request shall mention the judgment of which revision is requested and shall contain the information necessary to show that the conditions laid down in paragraph 1 have been complied with. It shall be accompanied by a copy of all supporting documents. The request and supporting documents shall be filed with the Registry.

(3) The original Chamber may decide of its own motion to refuse the request on the ground that there is no reason to warrant considering it. Where it is not possible to constitute the original Chamber, the President of the Court shall complete or compose the Chamber by drawing lots.

(4) If the Chamber does not refuse the request, the Registrar shall communicate it to the other party or parties and shall invite them to submit any written comments within a time-limit laid down by the President of the Chamber. The President of the Chamber shall also fix the date of the hearing should the Chamber decide to hold one. The Chamber shall decide by means of a judgment.

Rule 81

Rectification of errors in decisions and judgments

Without prejudice to the provisions on revision of judgments and on restoration to the list of applications, the Court may, of its own motion or at the request of a party made within one month of the delivery of a decision or a judgment, rectify clerical errors, errors in calculation or obvious mistakes.

Chapter IX

Advisory Opinions

Rule 82

In proceedings relating to advisory opinions the Court shall apply, in addition to the provisions of Articles 47, 48 and 49 of the Convention, the provisions which follow. It shall also apply the other provisions of these Rules to the extent to which it considers this to be appropriate.

Rule 83

The request for an advisory opinion shall be filed with the Registry. It shall state fully and precisely the question on which the opinion of the Court is sought, and also

   (a) the date on which the Committee of Ministers adopted the decision referred to in Article 47, para 3 of the Convention;

(b) the names and addresses of the person or persons appointed by the Committee of Ministers to give the Court any explanations which it may require.

The request shall be accompanied by all documents likely to elucidate the question.

Rule 84

(1) On receipt of a request, the Registrar shall transmit a copy of it to all members of the Court.

(2) The Registrar shall inform the Contracting Parties that the Court is prepared to receive their written comments.

Rule 85

(1) The President of the Court shall lay down the time-limits for filing written comments or other documents.

(2) Written comments or other documents shall be filed with the Registry. The Registrar shall transmit copies of them to all the members of the Court, to the Committee of Ministers and to each of the Contracting Parties.

Rule 86

After the close of the written procedure, the President of the Court shall decide whether the Contracting Parties which have submitted written comments are to be given an opportunity to develop them at an oral hearing held for the purpose.

Rule 87

If the Court considers that the request for an advisory opinion is not within its consultative competence as defined in Article 47 of the Convention, it shall so declare in a reasoned decision.

Rule 88

(1) Advisory opinions shall be given by a majority vote of the Grand Chamber. They shall mention the number of judges constituting the majority.

(2) Any judge may, if he or she so desires, attach to the opinion of the Court either a separate opinion, concurring with or dissenting from the advisory opinion, or a bare statement of dissent.

Rule 89

The advisory opinion shall be read out in one of the two official languages by the President of the Court, or by another judge delegated by the President, at a public hearing, prior notice having been given to the Committee of Ministers and to each of the Contracting Parties.

Rule 90

The opinion, or any decision given under Rule 87, shall be signed by the President of the Court and by the Registrar. The original copy, duly signed and sealed, shall be placed in the archives of the Court. The Registrar shall send certified copies to the Committee of Ministers, to the Contracting Parties and to the Secretary General of the Council of Europe.

Chapter X

Legal Aid

Rule 91

(1) The President of the Chamber may, either at the request of an applicant lodging an application under Article 34 of the Convention or of his or her own motion, grant free legal aid to the applicant in connection with the presentation of the case from the moment when observations in writing on the admissibility of that application are received from the respondent Contracting Party in accordance with Rule 54, para 3(b), or where the time-limit for their submission has expired.

(2) Subject to Rule 96, where the applicant has been granted legal aid in connection with the presentation of his or her case before the Chamber, that grant shall continue in force for purposes of his or her representation before the Grand Chamber.

Rule 92

Legal aid shall be granted only where the President of the Chamber is satisfied

    (a) that it is necessary for the proper conduct of the case before the Chamber;
    (b) that the applicant has insufficient means to meet all or part of the costs entailed.

Rule 93

(1) In order to determine whether or not applicants have sufficient means to meet all or part of the costs entailed, they shall be required to complete a form of declaration stating their income, capital assets and any financial commitments in respect of dependants, or any other financial obligations. The declaration shall be certified by the appropriate domestic authority or authorities.

(2) The Contracting Party concerned shall be requested to submit its comments in writing.

(3) After receiving the information mentioned in paragraphs 1 and 2 above, the President of the Chamber shall decide whether or not to grant legal aid. The Registrar shall inform the parties accordingly.

Rule 94

(1) Fees shall be payable to the advocates or other persons appointed in accordance with Rule 36, para 4. Fees may, where appropriate, be paid to more than one such representative.

(2) Legal aid may be granted to cover not only representatives' fees but also travelling and subsistence expenses and other necessary expenses incurred by the applicant or appointed representative.

Rule 95

On a decision to grant legal aid, the Registrar shall

    (a) fix the rate of fees to be paid in accordance with the legal-aid scales in force;
    (b) the level of expenses to be paid.

Rule 96

The President of the Chamber may, if satisfied that the conditions stated in Rule 92 are no longer fulfilled, revoke or vary a grant of legal aid at any time.

TITLE III

TRANSITIONAL RULES

Rule 97

Judges' terms of office

The duration of the terms of office of the judges who were members of the Court at the date of the entry into force of Protocol No. 11 to the Convention shall be calculated as from that date.

Rule 98

Presidency of the Sections

For a period of three years from the entry into force of Protocol No. 11 to the Convention,

   (a) the two Presidents of Sections who are not simultaneously Vice-Presidents of the Court and the Vice-Presidents of the Sections shall be elected for a term of office of eighteen months;
   (b) the Vice-Presidents of the Sections may not be immediately re-elected.

Rule 99

Relations between the Court and Commission

(1) In cases brought before the Court under Article 5, paras 4 and 5 of Protocol No. 11 to the Convention the Court may invite the Commission to delegate one or more of its members to take part in the consideration of the case before the Court.

(2) In cases referred to in the preceding paragraph the Court shall take into consideration the report of the Commission adopted pursuant to former Article 31 of the Convention.

(3) Unless the President of the Chamber decides otherwise, the said report shall be made available to the public through the Registrar as soon as possible after the case has been brought before the Court.

(4) The remainder of the case file of the Commission, including all pleadings, in cases brought before the Court under Article 5, paras 2 to 5 of Protocol No. 11 shall remain confidential unless the President of the Chamber decides otherwise.

(5) In cases where the Commission has taken evidence but has been unable to adopt a report in accordance with former Article 31 of the Convention, the Court shall take into consideration the verbatim records, documentation and opinion of the Commission's delegations arising from such investigations.

Rule 100

Chamber and Grand Chamber proceedings

(1) In cases referred to the Court under Article 5, para 4 of Protocol No. 11 to the Convention, a panel of the Grand Chamber constituted in accordance with Rule 24, para 6 shall determine, solely on the basis of the existing case file, whether a Chamber or the Grand Chamber is to decide the case.

(2) If the case is decided by a Chamber, the judgment of the Chamber shall, in accordance with Article 5, para 4 of Protocol No. 11, be final and Rule 73 shall be inapplicable.

(3) Cases transmitted to the Court under Article 5, para 5 of Protocol No. 11 shall be forwarded by the President of the Court to the Grand Chamber.

(4) For each case transmitted to the Grand Chamber under Article 5, para 5 of the Protocol No. 11, the Grand Chamber shall be completed by judges designated by rotation within one of the groups mentioned in Rule 24, para 3, the cases being allocated to the groups on an alternate basis.

Rule 101

Grand of legal aid

Subject to Rule 96, in cases brought before the Court under Article 5, paras 2 to 5 of Protocol No. 11 to the Convention, a grant of legal aid made to an applicant in the proceedings before the Commission or the former Court shall continue in force for the purposes of his or her representation before the Court.

Rule 102

Request for interpretation or revision of a judgment

(1) Where a party requests interpretation or revision of a judgment delivered by the former Court, the President of the Court shall assign the request to one of the Sections in accordance with the conditions laid down in Rule 51 or 52, as the case may be.

(2) The President of the relevant Section shall, notwithstanding Rules 79, para 3 and 80, para 3, constitute a new Chamber to consider the request

(3) The Chamber to be constituted shall include as *ex officio* members

    (a) the President of the Section; and, whether or not they are members of the relevant Section,
    (b) the judge elected in respect of any Contracting Party concerned or, if he or she is unable to sit, any judge appointed under Rule 29;
    (c) any judge of the Court who was a member of the original Chamber that delivered the judgment in the former Court.

(4)(a) The other members of the Chamber shall be designated by the President of the Section by means of a drawing of lots from among the members of the relevant Section.
  (b) The members of the Section who are not so designated shall sit in the case as substitute judges.

TITLE IV

FINAL CLAUSES

Rule 103

Amendment or suspension of a Rule

(1) Any Rule may be amended upon a motion made after notice where such a motion is carried at the next session of the plenary Court by a majority of all the members of the Court. Notice of such a motion shall be delivered in writing to the Registrar at least one month before the session at which it is to be discussed. On receipt of such a notice of motion, the Registrar shall inform all members of the Court at the earliest possible moment.

(2) A Rule relating to the internal working of the Court may be suspended upon a motion made without notice, provided that this decision is taken unanimously by the Chamber concerned. The suspension of a Rule shall in this case be limited in its operation to the particular purpose for which it was sought.

Rule 104

Entry into force of the Rules

The present Rules shall enter into force on 1 November 1998.

INDEX

References are to paragraph numbers. References in *italics* are to page numbers.